8e

REAL ESTATE
PRINCIPLES & PRACTICES

Arlyne Geschwender

D1363787

CENGAGE
Learning™

Australia • Brazil • Japan • Korea • Mexico • Singapore • Spain • United Kingdom • United States

Real Estate Principles and Practices, 8e

Arlyne Geschwender

Vice President/Editor-in-Chief: Dave Shaut

Executive Editor: Scott Person

Acquisitions Editor: Sara Glassmeyer

Senior Marketing Manager: Mark Linton

Frontlist Buyer, Manufacturing: Charlene Taylor

Art Director: Jennifer Wahi

Content Project Manager: Corey Geissler

Production Service: S4Carlisle

Internal Designer: Beckmeyer Design

Cover Designer: Beckmeyer Design

Cover Images from top left/clockwise:

©GettyImages, Inc./Digital Vision Collection/ Mark Segal

©GettyImages, Inc./Stockbyte Collection/ George Doyle

©iStockphoto.com

©iStockphoto.com/Kevin Russ Photography Manager

For product information and technology assistance, contact us at
Cengage Learning Customer & Sales Support, 1-800-354-9706

For permission to use material from this text or product, submit all requests online at **www.cengage.com/permissions**

Further permissions questions can be emailed to **permissionrequest@cengage.com**

© 2008 Cengage Learning. All Rights Reserved.

Library of Congress Control Number: 2008944380
ISBN-13: 978-0-324-78455-8
ISBN-10: 0-324-78455-4

Cengage Learning
5191 Natorp Boulevard
Mason, OH 45040
USA

Cengage Learning products are represented in Canada by Nelson Education, Ltd.

For your course and learning solutions, visit **www.cengage.com**
Purchase any of our products at your local college store or at our preferred online store **www.ichapters.com**

Printed in the United States of America
1 2 3 4 5 6 7 12 11 10 09 08

Brief Contents

Contents

Preface

At some point in life every person is involved with real estate. Since the time when early beings sought refuge in caves, the need for shelter has been a fact of life. With the great housing boom of the late 1970s and early 1980s, people began to realize that real property ownership could be a hedge against rising inflation. Today, real estate is still considered a solid investment and is rising in importance with interest rates at their lowest point since the late 1950s. Buyers are refinancing their existing mortgages or purchasing homes, enjoying home-ownership in the 21st century.

After many years of teaching real estate classes, I felt strongly that there was a need for a principles and practices textbook written in a clear and concise manner—one that would be understandable to the novice entering the world of real estate. Furthermore, it seemed only logical to organize the textbook around the natural sequence of events in a real estate transaction. This text is divided into three parts: basic real estate concepts, the process of a sale, and other aspects of real estate.

Part 1 begins by giving the reader a brief overview of real estate in Chapter 1, and Chapter 2 discusses property rights and ownership interests and introduces readers to the concepts of real estate ownership. Chapter 3 covers land descriptions and survey systems, acquainting the reader with legal descriptions. Chapter 4 covers land use controls and regulations. Chapter 5 explains estates, deeds, and the various methods by which title to real property can be taken.

Part 2 follows the process of a real estate transaction. In Chapter 6, readers are introduced to the important role that contracts play in the process of listing, selling, leasing, and optioning real property. Chapter 7 covers the timely issue of agency representation, explaining the varied relationships the agent may have with buyers and sellers. Using the sale of a single property as an example, Chapters 8 through 12 illustrate the natural sequence of the process, beginning with the listing contract and concluding with the closing of the sale. Chapter 8 explains the listing contract. The offer to purchase the property is discussed in Chapter 9. Finding a lending source (Chapter 10) and financing the purchase (Chapter 11) are the next steps in the process. Chapter 12 discusses closing procedures from both the lender's and the broker's viewpoint and includes settlement statements for the seller and the buyer.

Part 3 deals with other aspects of real estate ownership. Other forms of residence, such as condominiums, cooperatives, and time-sharing units, are covered in Chapter 13; leases are explained in Chapter 14; and a discussion of property management is offered in Chapter 15. Investments and tax aspects of real estate ownership are covered in Chapter 16. A discussion of appraisals (Chapter 17) is followed by material on environmental issues and real estate (Chapter 18).

Federal fair housing laws as they apply to sales and rentals of real property are covered in Chapter 19. A brief overview of the license laws act, which mandates the licensing of persons engaging in the real estate business, is offered in Chapter 20.

Finally, Chapter 21 considers the various math applications encountered in real estate transactions. Problems on computing interest, profit and loss, taxes and commission, ratio and proportion, and loan amortization are provided as examples of basic real estate arithmetic. A practice examination consisting of 100 multiple-choice questions covers material presented in the 21 chapters. An in-depth glossary of real estate terms and answer keys to the chapter review questions and the practice exam conclude the text.

Never before has real estate been so complex or challenging. It is my hope that this textbook will provide students with the foundation of knowledge they need to enter the field of real estate.

To the Student

This text has been written especially for the person who is taking a first course in real estate. It provides an easily understood introduction to this many-faceted subject. Whether the reader plans to pursue a career in real estate or is interested in learning for the purpose of buying, selling, leasing, or managing real estate, the text covers the fundamentals of real estate principles and practices.

To assist you in using this text, I recommend the following.

1. Review the key words that begin each chapter, watch for **boldfaced** key words as they are used within the chapter, and review the glossary when necessary. Once you have learned the vocabulary of real estate, you will be surprised at how quickly the concepts become clear.

2. Read the chapters in sequence. It may help you to better understand the strange new language of real estate if you also reread portions of some chapters. The wide margins are for your use in making notes and jotting down any questions you have. By placing your questions in these margins, you will have them available to ask in class.

3. Answer the discussion questions at the end of each chapter. These questions will help you consider what you have learned and put ideas into your own words. Your instructor may use these questions to stimulate class discussions.

4. Answer the review questions at the end of each chapter and check your answers with the answer key at the end of the book. If you miss a question, reread the pages on which the material appears.

5. When you finish the text, take the practice examination offered at the end of the book and then review your answers. Use your score on this test to evaluate your progress and indicate problem areas that will need review.

6. Purchase the workbook for this text. The purpose of the workbook is to help students grasp the information and put the material into perspective. Four types of questions are covered in each chapter. Matching terms and concepts, Concept and term review, Points to remember, Multiple choice. An answer key at the back of the book not only provides the correct answers, but also includes brief explanations for questions that you may have regarding an answer. When you complete the tests you will have approached the

subject matter from various points of view thus enhancing your learning and retention ability.

While text headings outline the contents of the book, the special phrases placed in the margins bring out important topics and ideas. As you review the material, these marginal notes will help you identify and locate the main concepts in each chapter.

Since Part 2 of the text follows the natural sequence of events in a real estate transaction, it will help you put the process in perspective. Legal documents are introduced as they are used in the listing and sale of real estate, and each instrument is explained in detail. Understanding these documents and the part they play in a real estate transaction will enhance your ability to become a true professional in the field.

**There will always be more people,
but there will never be more land.**

(continued)

BASIC CONCEPTS OF REAL ESTATE

PART 1

5 Estates, Interests, Deeds, and Title

Chapter 5 introduces how title to real property is held, explaining estates, the various types of deeds, and methods of holding title.

Real Estate and the Economy

KEY TERMS

business cycles

economic base

free enterprise

gross national product (GNP)

open market system

ownership cycle

OVERVIEW

Each of us at some time in our lives becomes involved with real estate. Since we all need shelter, we either rent or purchase a place in which to live. Moreover, as one of the largest industries in the United States, real estate has a direct impact on our economy, community, and society. Thus, it seems appropriate to begin this text by exploring the role and contribution of real estate.

As homeownership became available to the average man and woman at affordable prices, real estate became a vehicle by which individuals could prosper and the nation could grow. Often, the largest portion of the estate the average person accumulates in a lifetime is the equity built up through homeownership. Thus, homeownership can serve as a forced savings plan.

More immediately, real estate provides us with a sense of belonging to a community in an otherwise very mobile society. With advanced modes of transportation to facilitate our mobility, Americans have been on the move throughout this country's history. To own a home signifies establishing roots. Better housed than people in any other nation, Americans in all age groups and economic levels take pride in their homes. Homeownership in the United States is the underpinning of the ideal of the American way of life and assists in promoting pride in citizenship.

This chapter explains how real estate helps to support a community and, conversely, how the **economic base** of a community impacts the value of real estate. In addition, the chapter discusses how housing changes to meet public needs as demographics change in a region. A look to the future concludes the chapter.

Housing Needs

In 1990 the Census Bureau counted 249.5 million people in the United States. As we entered the 21st century the 2000 census report swelled that number to 281.4 million people. In the coming years increasing immigration numbers may push that figure even higher. This anticipated growth in population accentuates the importance of land and housing as a marketable commodity. The largest increase in population occurred in the state of Nevada with a percentage growth of 66.3 followed by Arizona with a 40.0 increase.

Housing for the senior citizen

The population increase can in part be contributed to the "graying" of America—citizens are living longer and more productive lives. Some indicators estimate this increase will rise by 20 percent. In the last 25 years, the age 65 and older population has been escalating at a rate double that of the rest of the population, and for the first time in our country's history, we have more senior citizens than teenagers. We see an increase in housing built strictly for the retiree and the elderly. Housing provisions for this aging segment of the population have been springing up in all parts of the country, with special emphasis in the sunbelt areas of Arizona, Texas, Florida, California, and Nevada. Currently, the population growth in these sunbelt states is triple the rate of the rest of the country. However, much of this active, older generation will elect to remain near family or where their working lives were spent. Realizing this, communities all over America are gearing up to meet this trend and to produce housing for this segment of the population.

Population characteristics

Changes in population distribution patterns are continually monitored by real estate analysts. Population demographics change slowly. Consequently, this change needs to be analyzed over a period of decades. Any rapid growth in a particular area of the country will require additional housing units. Conversely, if statistics reveal a decline in population, housing needs will be lessened. Tracking these changes includes determining the population's characteristics, since this will affect not only the number but also the type of housing units needed. For example, provisions for the single student in college cities are evidenced by dormitories and apartments surrounding the campuses.

Changing family definition

The greatest apparent sociological change relevant to real estate in the last decade has appeared in the composition of the family structure. Single parent status has increased, as has the number of singles living alone, resulting in a trend toward single households. Many unmarried young people are opting for ownership rather than renting. Young adults are beginning to accumulate equity through homeownership at an early age, and condominiums are now popular since they provide ownership without the care and maintenance required by a single-family home. (See Chapter 13 on condominiums.)

An increase in "mingles" (unrelated singles) purchasing real estate together is also prevalent among young adults. Another market is first-time buyers who later decide to upgrade their investment and move into a larger home. For many of these individuals, the size, location, and luxury features of the home are important aspects of social status; thus, an increase in family income often creates a desire for a more prestigious home.

We have determined that age, population, and changing family structure are factors in the distribution of housing needs. Also of importance is inflation. In the 1970s and 1980s inflated values made housing increasingly unaffordable to much of the population. Housing costs escalated the highest in the northeast and western sections of the United States. In some areas of the country the entry-level buyer was virtually priced out of the market. Two major contributing factors were *rising land costs* and *financing rates*. Land costs increase when the supply becomes scarce in areas where housing is needed. Naturally this need is greater near employment centers. Financing rates fluctuate according to the availability of funds to the housing market and play a major role in determining who can afford housing. In addition to these factors, as our country grows and prospers, the cost of all commodities increases. Housing is no exception. Vast changes have occurred as the simple shelter which afforded few amenities has been transformed into the home with many creature comforts we enjoy today. A community must offer sufficient and desirable living accommodations, since housing is essential to any society.

Impact of inflation on housing

Contribution to the Economy

We have established that everyone needs housing. Therefore, it is not surprising to learn that nearly three-fourths of the nation's wealth is directly related to real estate, and that residential real estate contributes the largest number of units. In addition, commercial and industrial buildings, factories, and agricultural land contribute to this figure.

The rights and benefits inherent in real property ownership contribute to the economy of our country. Through taxation, real estate provides the monetary basis upon which schools, parks, recreation areas, public transportation, utility services, and roads are built and maintained. Large corporations establish factories and businesses in areas where employees can live well. The community that can offer a favorable and attractive economic environment will prosper and grow.

In some communities, blighted areas are reclaimed and restored or redeveloped by concerned community members, ultimately adding to the tax rolls of the area. Buildings with historic significance are renovated and become prized landmarks. The social impact that real estate has upon the economy of an area is immense.

Real Estate Creates Employment

On the national level, real estate accounts for a substantial share of the **gross national product (GNP)**. The gross national product is the sum (value) of all goods and services produced and used in the country. Dividing the GNP by

Contribution of real estate to GNP

the total population gives us a means of measuring the flow of income for that particular year, indicating our standard of living (although inflation changes the impact of these figures to a degree).

Through the study of economics, which is the production, circulation, and use of income, wealth, and goods, we become aware of the resources people use to produce goods to satisfy the needs and desires of purchasers. Our natural resources are used in developing the products that are produced by the labor of our people. The buyers ultimately dictate how much of any given product will be produced. If the supply is greater than the demand, the supplier is left with inventory that may need to be reduced in price or withheld from the market until the present supply is consumed.

Our economic system has changed greatly since the first settlers came to these shores. Each settler filled many roles, since it was necessary to produce everything they needed. The pioneers made their own soap and candles, wove their own cloth, cut trees and built their log cabins, tilled the soil, and hunted wild game for food. Today a great many people produce these goods in an assortment of factories and production centers, resulting in specialization. As an example, electrical power dispelled the need for candles, so today we find specialty shops selling candles for aesthetic reasons. Commercial farmers produce our food, and it is packaged in a variety of ways: fresh, canned, dried, and frozen, in an attempt to meet everyone's desires.

Consider the tremendous number of people who are either directly or indirectly involved with housing. Begin with the plotting of a subdivision, which requires the services of engineers and surveyors. Operators of heavy equipment construct the roads, and workers install public utilities in preparation for the homes. The construction of the house itself requires a general contractor, subcontractors, and builders and suppliers of all the materials that compose the structure, from the foundation, siding, drywall, windows, doors, and cabinetry to the plumbing, electrical, and gas connections. Appliances and furnishings that ultimately go into the house must be supplied and installed.

The services performed include the savings and loan institutions' financing the sale, the title companies' insuring the title, the insurance companies' insuring the premises, and the appraisers' placing a value on the property. Attorneys oversee the closing, city offices record the documents, and nurseries provide the lawn and plantings. Local, state, and federal governments have departments devoted entirely to real estate issues.

Local government interests include land use planning and zoning laws. The U.S. Department of Housing and Urban Development (HUD) was established solely to monitor and administrate housing needs. Finally, approximately 2.1 million licensed real estate professionals service the public in the listing, selling, renting, and management of real property.

As we can see, the numbers of people added to the employment rolls through transactions in real estate are indeed large, adding to the prosperity of the community. Clearly, real estate is big business.

Purchasing a Home

At an individual level, the decision to purchase a home is one of the most important decisions made by the average person. That first home is a most meaningful step and is looked upon by the owner as much more than mere shelter. It represents pride, accomplishment, and security. In making a selection, the considerations faced by the purchaser include deciding upon the location, the style, the condition, and the size of the home and its proximity to public transportation, schools, shopping, and employment. Buyers' needs vary; what is perfect for the young family with school-age children may not meet the needs of the childless couple.

New homeowners become involved in their new neighborhood and contribute to the socioeconomic qualities of the community, participating in the school system, churches, and neighborhood associations. Some become involved in the local political arena, taking an active part not only with their votes, but also by campaigning for their choice of candidate or becoming candidates themselves. They make purchases at the nearby shopping centers, contributing to the success of the business community.

The Ownership Cycle

The **ownership cycle** of real estate in an average person's experience in real estate usually begins with renting, which creates a need for apartment units. The first move into a home allows the individual to begin building an equity that will supply the basis for the next move into a larger home. Often moves are necessitated by employment transfers to other parts of the country. As an owner's equity builds and salary increases, a place must be sought to put the savings to work. For many, investment takes the form of the purchase of additional real estate. Whether the purchase is residential income property or an office building or a commercial structure, the investor adds to the prosperity of the area, since each individual property affects the community. After the family is raised and people grow older and retire, their needs change, and they choose smaller homes with less maintenance. Some of this senior citizen group may return to renting. (See Figure 1.1.)

How Economic Conditions Affect Real Estate

Our **free enterprise** system is based on the premise that the more you produce, the more you receive. The **open market system** allows consumers to decide what they want and the producers to compete to supply those needs. Extremely successful in encouraging economic progress, the open market system forces suppliers to be competitive in offering goods for consumption, giving both buyers and sellers choices. When a product is in great demand, more people become involved in its production in the hopes of making money to have the purchasing

Figure 1.1	The Ownership Cycle

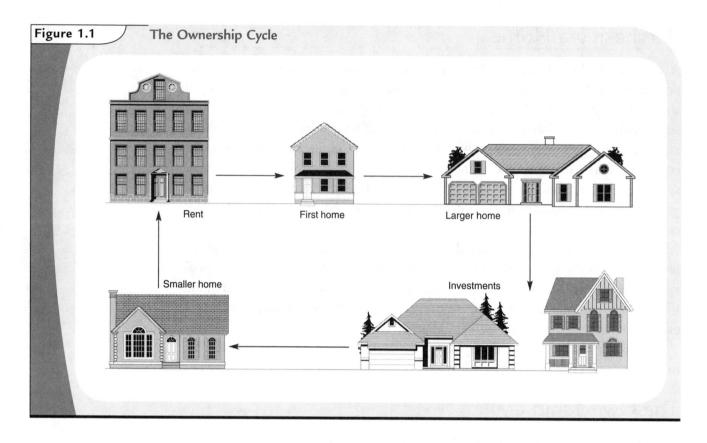

Rent   First home   Larger home

Smaller home   Investments

Effect of business cycles on real estate

power to buy other commodities. Competition results in improved products, thus elevating our standard of living. Currently, great competition in the field of electronics and especially in the advancement of the computer has benefited the consumer in the form of better equipment at lower prices. Buyers are the decision makers and have many choices in today's market, whether it is food, electronics, automobiles, or housing.

Business cycles create problems for the economy in general and especially for the real estate industry. The economic conditions of the country play a great part in the real estate cycle. We can track the fluctuations of real estate values to the conditions in the marketplace. When interest rates rose to an all-time high of 17.5 percent in 1982, sales of housing slowed dramatically in most areas of the country. As interest rates fell, buyers once again began the home search, and the marketplace hummed with sales.

However, each region experiences "buyer's" and "seller's" markets, depending on what is happening locally. In 1985–1986 a sluggish land market was in effect in the farm belt. When farmers with overextended credit failed to meet their loan obligations, the farms were foreclosed and auctioned off to the highest bidder. During this same time, astronomical prices were being paid for homes in the northeastern section of the country. A reversal of these conditions occurred in the late 1980s when a drastic slowdown occurred in the northeast and values in the farm belt began rising. Unlike most other commodities, real estate relates to the economy of the particular area in which it is located, with supply and demand a strong force in the market value of the property. In 2006 some areas of the country experienced a rash of foreclosures on mortgage loans. Interest rates had been lowered and lending institutions offered loans with little down payment. However, many of these loans were with adjustable rates, so as the payments increased the buyers could not meet the higher rates. The housing market began to slow as a glut of homes came onto the market. The media described it as a "correction" in the market. After years of a booming industry some lenders who sold their loans on the secondary market found those sources closed, and as a result their businesses faltered.

Real estate is exciting, not only because it is a needed commodity, but also because "owning a piece of the earth" has long been a dream of the American people. Many early immigrants came to our land for personal freedom, including the right to own real property. Today, the desire to own our own piece of land and the promise that it is possible to do so are a large part of our American dream. Thus, real estate has implications far beyond the exchange of money and land.

Real estate is the center of everything that we produce and use. Because we need it, a demand is created and real estate becomes a valuable asset. When demand and need are carefully anticipated and balanced with supply, a favorable real estate environment will exist. The value of real estate is also determined by a number of other issues.

1. The federal, state, and local governments enact laws and rules that govern the legal rights we have in our real estate and thus determine how we may use it.
2. Location affects value, which we will study in our appraisal chapter.
3. The productivity of the land also determines its value. Agricultural land produces our food. Construction of homes, offices, and commercial and industrial sites create the housing and buildings we need. All land is productive in some manner.

Economic Base

To the economist, land is the supreme substance from which all our nation's goods are produced. The farmers use land to produce crops, the lumber mills cut trees to supply wood for houses and furniture and to provide the pulp for the paper upon which this book is printed, and so on. To have a sound economic base, each community must produce commodities (goods or services) that it can sell and in turn use the funds earned to purchase what the community does not produce. The areas that do not produce goods for export may provide services. Resort towns offer their services as a commodity, relying upon vacationers who come to enjoy the ocean beaches, the ski resorts, or a favorable climate. Also in the category of services are hospitals, schools, and restaurants.

A community offers goods or services

Cities like to maintain a broad economic base rather than relying on one industry, because if that industry should collapse and the city's residents are without jobs, it could mean the decline of property values and tax bases. The ghost towns near the abandoned mines that ran out of ore are examples of communities that died out because they were dependent solely upon one commodity. In modern times, similar problems arose in Detroit when the automobile industry encountered financial difficulties. It is not unusual for a city to offer concessions to large business enterprises that are planning to relocate or expand. In an attempt to entice industry to their area, concessions may be in the form of tax incentives or a gift of land on which to erect the buildings a business will need. With the prospect of employment for people of the community, the industry will bring greater prosperity to the area.

The 1980s, the 1990s, and into the 21st Century

Market conditions of a decade

Sharp changes in market conditions influence the eventual success of a real estate project, so investors and real estate salespersons must be aware of the trends that produce these cycles. If we review the status of the economy in the 1980s, we see that it fluctuated up and down, having a seesaw effect upon the national and local real estate markets. The crisis during the decade of the 1980s, which began in mild recession, included the unequaled deficit of the federal government and the collapse of savings and loans nationwide. We witnessed bankruptcies in the farm communities and a halt to inflation. The Tax Reform Act of 1986 greatly affected real estate investments, we experienced a shocking stock market plunge in 1987, and fluctuating interest rates prevailed. While other factors played a role in the condition of the economy, the volatile factors listed above can be justifiably blamed for the up and down swings the real estate market endured. We eased out of the 1980s intact, with a slowed growth in some parts of the country that began to climb as we entered the 1990s. When buyers spend, the GNP experiences growth.

In the early 1990s, lower interest rates spurred a recessionary economy. As inflated property values recorrected due to market pressures, mortgage interest rates fell to 7 percent and even lower, a rate unheard of for decades. Real estate practitioners and the rest of the country waited to see if the United States would climb out of its ongoing recession. By the mid 1990s the Federal Reserve began raising interest rates to ward off an increase in inflation. We saw unprecedented economic growth in the late 1900s, and interest rates lowered as we left the 1990s and the economy stabilized. However, interest rates remained low, 7 percent being the norm in most parts of the country. The economy balanced, unemployment rates were low, and consumer optimism propelled new home sales to record levels.

With the year 2000 we entered the 21st century and witnessed changes in the economic stability of our nation. The stock market plummeted and large corporations filed bankruptcy, leaving many investors witnessing their savings vanish. Interest rates were lowered to the 5 and 6 percent range, a rate not seen since the late 1950s. People scurried to refinance existing home mortgages and many buyers saw it as a time when they could afford to become home owners. By the mid 2000s a brisk sales market was prevalent, especially for entry-level buyers who were able to purchase due to lower interest rates and small down payments. However, beginning in 2006 as the adjustable rate loans meant increased monthly payments, foreclosures began to occur. Sales slowed and prices were lowered as the market began to correct itself.

Summary of Important Points

Some of the factors that determine the market demand for real estate are as follows:

1. Relocation of families. Our mobile society has families on the move, largely because of employment opportunities and a desire for environmental change.
2. Formation of nontraditional households. Young singles have become more interested in owning property and, in addition to married couples, create a demand for a first home.
3. Cost of housing. High prices can eliminate the first-time buyer.
4. Financing. When interest rates rise, the demand for loans declines, causing many buyers to be priced out of the market.
5. Changing lifestyles. Our cycle of ownership illustrated that as individuals age, they tend to downsize their housing needs. Also to be considered are the new innovations in appliances and labor-saving devices and the house styles themselves that prompt people to move up as their income increases.
6. Real estate creates wealth. Real estate is the largest contributor to the wealth of the nation. A strong and varied economic base ensures continued prosperity for a city.

Discussion Points

1. Why can we say that real estate creates employment?
2. Are housing needs constant in a given area? Explain.
3. Explain business cycles as they relate to real estate.
4. How do economic conditions affect the real estate market?
5. What is the most prominent economic base in your area? Has it changed over the past few decades?

Review Questions

Answers to these questions are found in the Answer Key section at the back of the book.

1. The sum of all goods and services produced and used in the country is referred to as:
   a. the residual
   b. gross national product
   c. economic indicators
   d. contributions

2. The theory that the more you produce, the more you receive is the system known as:
   a. free enterprise system
   b. welfare system
   c. economic survival
   d. gross national product

3. Population growth can in part be attributed to:
   a. migration
   b. people living longer
   c. economic conditions
   d. increased housing units

4. All of the following statements are true EXCEPT:
   a. to be economically sound, a community must produce goods or provide services
   b. changes in market conditions have an influence on real estate values
   c. the high cost of housing can eliminate the first-time buyer
   d. in the past decade there has been no apparent change in the composition of the family structure

5. Through taxation, real estate contributes to the monetary basis for all of the following EXCEPT:
   a. schools
   b. public transportation
   c. churches
   d. utility services

6. Three-fourths of the nation's wealth is directly related to:
   a. gross national product
   b. economic conditions
   c. real estate
   d. inflation

7. The open market system can best be described as:
   a. producers of goods decide what consumers will buy
   b. allowing consumers to decide what they want and producers to supply their needs
   c. suppliers need not be competitive as buyers will purchase that which is available
   d. encouraging economic progress

Land: Its Characteristics and Acquisition

KEY TERMS

accretion	intestate
ad valorem tax	involuntary alienation
adverse possession	land
allodial system	land patent
avulsion	littoral rights
bundle of rights	mill
chattel	nonhomogeneous
codicil	personal property
color of title	police power
descent	probate
devise	profit a prendre
doctrine of prior appropriation	quiet title action
durability	real estate
easement by prescription	real property
eminent domain	riparian rights
escheat	scarcity
feudal system	situs
fixtures	tenements
hereditaments	testate
immobility	voluntary alienation
indestructible	

OVERVIEW

Historically, land acquisition has been the crux of major battles throughout the world. Landownership has played a part in everything from the rise of great political powers to the development of individual self-worth. We have learned a great deal from the past. Many of today's fundamental ideas concerning ownership and transfer of real property have been handed down relatively unchanged from medieval times.

This chapter defines the feudal and allodial systems of landownership and covers the physical and economic characteristics of land and how they affect the value of land. It also defines and differentiates between real and personal property, explains real property rights, and discusses government rights and/ or powers regarding private property. The chapter concludes with explanations of how one acquires real property and how one can lose ownership.

Evolution of Landownership

The evolution of landownership began when tribes of nomads stopped roaming to settle and form communities. Staying in one area, they began to cultivate crops and build shelters. Tribal chiefs controlled the village, allocating areas of land to individual families to use. The tribe often found it necessary to fight off aggressors who sought to infringe on their possessory rights. As time passed, the feudal concept developed.

Feudal System

The **feudal system** prevailed in Europe during the Middle Ages and gave the king control of all the land. Feudalism formed the political, economic, and social organization of medieval Europe. Under the feudal system, social position was determined by the amount of land held. The king maintained ownership of the land, distributing it among lords and nobles who in return pledged to support the king with taxes and their allegiance. The lords supervised serfs who worked the land. In the early Middle Ages the lords did not own property as we do today; they merely had the right to use or administer the land.

Our nation was developed from a vast wilderness just a few hundred years ago by the British, the first to colonize North America in large numbers. The king of England granted charters to private enterprises as joint stock companies, vesting them with authority to found and govern chartered colonies. The governors appointed by the king were to rule these colonies. Many people coming to our shores were seeking religious freedom and an opportunity to prosper. Independent-thinking colonists united against Britain when they felt that trade and taxes were unfair—declaring their independence July 4, 1776. The doors to this new world, with opportunity of private ownership of land, were then opened to all people.

Allodial System

Freedom to own land

Our system of landownership is the **allodial system**, which gives individuals the right to own land. We can acquire real estate without government interference and then buy, sell, exchange, option, lease, or will the real estate we own.

Perhaps the most dramatic chapter in the history of land acquisition occurred during America's westward expansion. Pioneers explored and settled a wilderness, carving out homesites for their families and for generations to come.

To encourage the settlement of public lands, as early as the 1770s the federal government granted land to land companies, mining claims, individuals, and, later, railroads. Thus, early in our country's history promises of individual ownership through public grants by the United States government prompted thousands of Americans to forsake the comforts of established cities for the spartan life of the western frontier.

In 1862 Congress enacted the Homestead Act. To stimulate the settlement of public lands, Congress gave land to all settlers who complied with the homestead laws. These laws stipulated that those who submitted a nominal fee and actually lived on the land and tilled the soil for a period of five years would be granted a deed by the government. The document that transferred the land was referred to as a **land patent**. Veterans of the War of 1812 also received land patents to land in settlement of claims due the war veterans.

There was little exchange of properties in those early days, but as the territories and states became more settled, the need for land to supply food and shelter for new arrivals became more apparent, and people began to sell off portions of their holdings.

Land continues to be the most prized possession of the average individual in the United States. The pioneers of a century ago would view with amazement the concrete empires that have replaced their sod houses. As the U.S. population continues to grow and shift, so do land development and use.

Characteristics of Land

The distinct characteristics of land can be classified into two general categories: physical and economic (see Figure 2.1). These characteristics determine its utility and value.

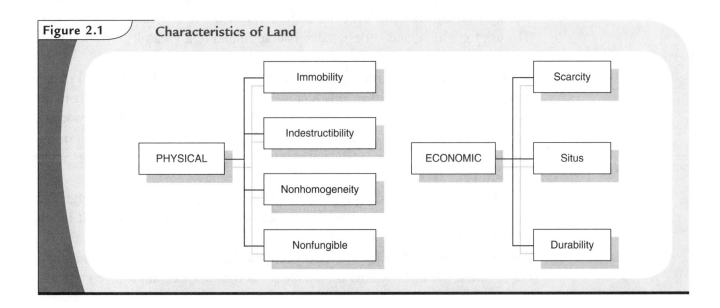

Figure 2.1   Characteristics of Land

Physical Characteristics

The physical characteristics of land are its immobility, its indestructibility, and its nonhomogeneity.

Immobility

Land consists of various types of soil, rocks, and minerals. It contains valleys and plains, lakes and rivers, mountains and canyons. Whatever the makeup of the land, it is fixed; that is, it is not movable. It remains permanently in a fixed geographical location. This **immobility** of land determines its value. That a parcel of land will always be exactly where it lies does not, however, guarantee that its value will remain constant.

Indestructibility

Since land remains in a permanent location, except for erosion and depletion, it never wears out. Hills have been leveled in the construction of highways and building sites, rivers have changed channels, minerals have been taken from the soil, but the land is still there; it is literally **indestructible**. We are living on the same land as our ancestors and the natives before them. When improvements (buildings, utilities, and so on) are added to the land, they too are of a permanent nature, though unlike the land they will depreciate and need to be replaced over a period of time. Land's durability makes it an ideal commodity for investors, though the economic climate of an area can have an impact on its value.

Nonhomogeneity

Since there are no two identical parcels of land, land is unique. Its uniqueness is also referred to as **nonhomogeneous**. Unlike manufactured goods that are duplicated many times, any two parcels of land will vary. The fact that the location of each parcel is different creates a variance in itself.

Recognizing that land is nonhomogeneous has resulted in its being legally referred to as *nonfungible* (not substitutable). One property cannot be substituted for another. While the same house plan may be followed on several sites, differences in materials and craftsmanship will occur in the construction. The parcels of land, though similar to the eye, will also vary.

Because of the differences in the physical characteristics of land, it is divided into agricultural, residential, commercial, industrial, and special purpose uses. The use for which land is designated is determined to a great degree by what it is best suited for.

Agricultural

Agriculture began with the early settlers who farmed the valleys and plains and cleared forestlands that lent themselves to cultivation. Some agricultural land is best suited for raising wheat, as in the central plains states. In warmer climates, the temperature and soil are ideal for orange groves. Irrigation can supplement the lack of rainfall, but northern temperatures would freeze many fruit crops.

Residential

As cities develop and their populations grow, they encroach onto neighboring farmland. Although the land is physically suited to raising crops, it is put to a new use. Desire by workers to live near employment creates a demand for housing in close proximity to the job centers. Homesites must be adaptable to construction. While hilly land is suitable for homesites, extremely steep hills are undesirable, particularly in areas of the country where snow and rain could create travel problems. Known flood zones and areas with the possibility of mud slides are also to be avoided as possible homesites.

Commercial

The commercial property category covers a broad mix of users. Office space is used by professional and business enterprises. Insurance companies, real estate firms, accountants, attorneys, doctors, and corporate offices constitute some of the users of commercial space. Larger commercial space is needed for nurseries, feed and grain stores, and other agricultural sales and services. Automobile dealerships, service stations, grocery stores, hotels, banks, restaurants, and other sales and service businesses need higher visibility than most office users to generate business. These businesses usually locate along busy streets, where their properties are easily accessible to the consumer.

Industrial

Industrial land is generally located near transportation facilities, such as railways, trucking, airlines, and waterways. In order to attract industrial users, tracts are developed around these services.

Special purposes

Land unsuitable for other uses may be perfect for special purposes. The mountains of Colorado abound with ski lodges and nature trails. Rivers and lakes are used for boating, fishing, and water sports. Resort areas are developed near ocean beaches, especially in warmer climates. Stated briefly, the physical characteristics of land determine to a great extent its use. Churches, schools, parks, hotels, and nursing homes are other examples of special purpose uses.

Economic Characteristics

While its physical and economic characteristics overlap to some degree, land has some distinct economic characteristics, including *scarcity, situs* (location), and *durability* (permanence). To determine value, think of the acronym DUST (demand, utility, scarcity, and transferability).

Economic conditions in an area dictate if its worth will rise or fall. Demand and scarcity are the greatest influences on its value. Land's fixity makes it vulnerable for the collection of debt. Liens may be placed against the property and a sale ordered so that payment to the creditor is made.

To Determine Value
Demand
Utility
Scarcity
Transferability

Land acquires value when it is desired. Since we cannot develop or manufacture more land, the supply is *fixed*. If there is a **scarcity** of usable land for homesites in a given area, the value of the land tends to rise. Creativity has resulted in more high-rise construction in congested areas where the supply of open land is limited. The air about us is absolutely essential to us, but because of its abundance, we do not have to purchase it; it is free. Likewise, when too many homes in a similar price range are placed on the market in a given area, the abundance may cause a decrease in value and a buyer's market will occur. That is, a large selection may lead the prospective buyer to offer less than the asking price. If, on the other hand, few homes are available, the buyer who needs housing may be willing to pay more. Demand for a commodity is created in part by its scarcity. The law of supply and demand dictates that scarcity influences supply, and desire influences demand.

Situs
Greatest effect on value

The **situs**, or location, of the land also determines its value. You may have heard the phrase, "location, location, location," a prime factor in establishing value. Travel 20 miles out of the city, and the land is not as costly because it is farther from the center of employment. We are not in short supply of land across the United States, but the available sites near heavily populated areas are limited. In large part, the availability of utilities determines the direction of growth. Near large metropolitan cities such as Chicago and New York, many workers spend hours commuting daily to and from their employment. Homes by the sea command a higher price than similar homes situated two blocks from the shore. Lots with views or with trees are considered more valuable than those without these amenities, and weather is still another important factor to some. Location has the greatest effect on property value.

Value is further determined by what the soil contains. Land rich in oil and gold will be far more valuable than arid desert void of minerals. Fertile agricultural land will be more productive, and hence more valuable, than dry, rocky grazing land.

Durability

While land is considered indestructible, the **durability** of the improvements that have been made to it must be considered. Although, unlike land, such improvements are vulnerable to natural disasters, such as earthquakes, tornadoes, or fire, with proper maintenance they can have an indefinite economic life. However, the use for which a structure may have originally been intended may change. For example, obsolete warehouses in downtown areas of large cities are being renovated and converted into residential apartments, condominiums, and specialty shops. Houses more than 100 years old have been updated and modernized and continue to be used as residences. Many cities have historic preservation committees that bestow landmark designations on old, architecturally significant buildings to preserve our heritage. A move back to urban areas, especially by young professionals, has been due in part to the aesthetic value of these older homes.

Land is indeed where it all begins: it produces food for animals and humans, it provides water and minerals, and it provides for recreation.

Real Property Rights

The largest classification of property is referred to as **hereditaments**. This includes lands, tenements, and incorporeal rights. We think of *land, real estate,* and *real property* as one and the same. However, there are understated differences between these terms. To distinguish between them:

Distinguish Between
· Land
· Real estate
· Real property

Land is the earth's surface, including the soil that goes down to the earth's core. It further includes all that is affixed by nature; such as trees, grasses, and shrubs. Land may be farmed, mined, or built upon.

Real estate includes not only the land but also the *improvements* that are added to the land, such as buildings and fences.

Real property includes the land and the real estate.

Tenements refers to all the rights of a permanent nature that can be seen or felt and accompany ownership, including the corporeal and incorporeal rights. Corporeal is derived from the Latin word *corpus*, meaning "body"; *corporeal rights* are tangible and refer to things such as trees and buildings. *Incorporeal rights* are intangible rights, objects that cannot be seen, and refer to things such as a right of way or encroachment. These appurtenances are all the rights that pass with the title to real estate.

Private ownership of real property gives the owner the right to possess and use the land to the exclusion of all others. All legal rights attached to the property are the owner's, including the right to possess, exclude, sell, lease, mortgage, give away, exchange, and will (Figure 2.2). This combination of privileges is often referred to as a **bundle of rights**. It gives the owner the *surface rights,* the *subsurface rights,* and the *air rights* above the land as well. An owner may diminish his bundle of rights by selling or leasing these privileges to another. For example, the owner may lease the subsurface rights to one party, lease the air rights to a second person, and retain the surface rights for his use. A landowner may lease or sell the surface rights to farm the land to one party and the subsurface rights to explore for oil to another. When real property is sold, a purchaser receives no more rights than the seller's real property interest.

Bundle of rights

Surface rights are the most readily visible. These rights include buildings erected on the land or fences of various materials and heights built to designate boundaries and provide security and privacy. The land itself may be cultivated to produce crops or planted in trees. The *subsurface rights* give the holder the right to drill for oil or gas, to dig for gravel and sand, and to extract other minerals. While the owner may own either specific or unlimited minerals, the right of exploration for or removal of minerals may be severely restricted due to deed restrictions or environmental laws.

Surface and subsurface rights

Figure 2.2	Bundle of Rights

The right to extract minerals such as oil and gas may be sold by one land-owner to another. Commonly referred to as oil and gas leases with the right to capture, it permits the holder to drill beneath the surface and to remove the mineral. This is a **profit a prendre**, which is the right to use and extract from the land of another. There will be a royalty clause which gives the lessor (land-owner) a percentage of the proceeds. It may also include a statement that allows the owner to collect rent if there is no production activity. (See Figure 2.3.)

Air rights

The owner of land also possesses the air rights over the property (see Figure 2.4). *Air rights* may be leased or sold and allow the holder to occupy the open space above the designated space of another. This can be in the form of a walk-way over a busy street or between buildings. A restaurant may be built over a freeway, or a building may be erected over railroad tracks. The original concept of landownership was that not only did one own the surface rights, but also the rights from the core of the earth to the heavens above. With the emergence of air travel, the courts decreed that it is reasonable that air flights over one's property are not considered trespassing.

One's air rights may also be converged upon by factory smoke and fumes from automobiles. When this becomes hazardous to health, environmental laws are passed, such as the emission controls placed on automobiles.

Water Rights
- Riparian rights—moving body of water
- Littoral rights—nonmoving body of water
- Doctrine of prior appropriation—first owner has first claim to water

Water is one of our most valuable natural resources, essential to our very existence. Since rainfall is distributed unevenly across the United States, most areas have a water problem of some kind. Considering this, the appropriation of water rights is of prime importance in some states. *Water rights* are established by either the doctrine of **riparian** and **littoral rights** or by the **doctrine of prior appropriation**. The lakes and flowing streams are surface waters available for use under these doctrines.

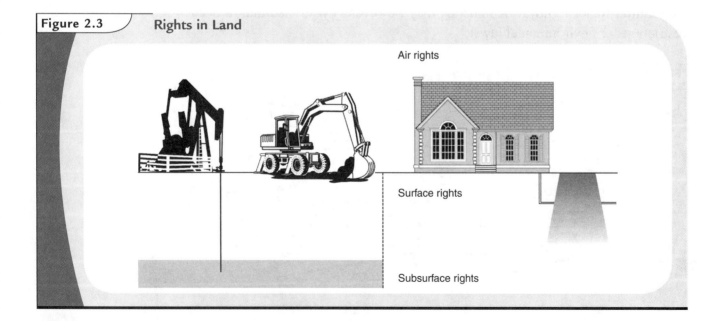

Figure 2.3 **Rights in Land**

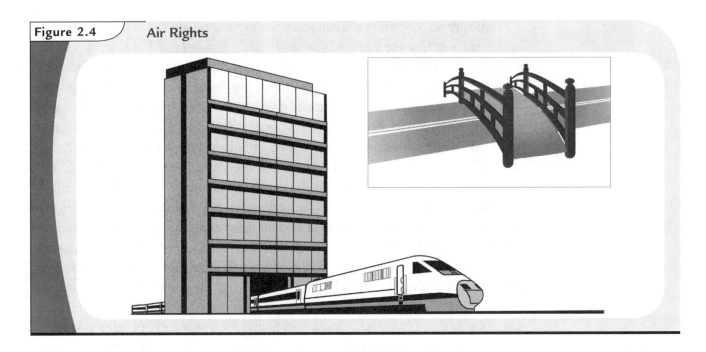

Figure 2.4   Air Rights

If an owner's land borders a *moving body of water,* such as a stream or a waterway, under *riparian rights* the landowner is entitled to share in the use of the water. These rights do not extend to damming the water and depriving a neighbor downstream of the use of the water, nor do they extend to actual ownership of the water, but merely to the main characteristics of riparian rights, equality of rights, and reasonable use. If the water is nonnavigable, the landowner has rights out to the middle of the stream (see Figure 2.5). However, if the sides of the lot have designated lengths, the designated length prevails over the wording that indicates ownership to the middle of the stream. Under riparian rights, if a shortage of water develops, first priority is given to necessary household use. When that need is filled, agricultural use will be served, followed by commercial and industrial uses. Most states east of the Mississippi employ this method of water rights.

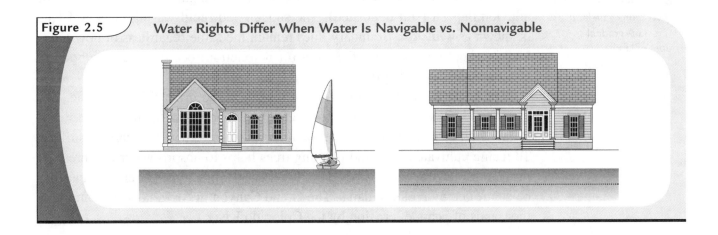

Figure 2.5   Water Rights Differ When Water Is Navigable vs. Nonnavigable

If the property borders a *nonmoving body of water,* such as a lake or ocean, the landowner abutting the water has *littoral rights. Littoral* is a Latin word referring to shore; this water does not have the characteristics of a watercourse. Ordinarily holding title only to the high-water mark, the owners may use and enjoy the water bordering their land but cannot divert the water. In some states, however, this right has been reduced by the *doctrine of prior appropriation.* Adopted in the arid western states, this principle was originally based upon custom and necessity, and finally established in law. Colorado adheres strictly to this doctrine. Simply said, the first owner is privileged with the first claim on the water. This law allows the first user to channel the water for use, depriving other landowners along the watercourse of their equal share. This right established by the appropriator stays with the landowner. The prior appropriator must have an intent to use the water and actually divert the water from the source of supply. However, this use must be of benefit to the owner and not diverted by the owner for another's use, and the water must actually be diverted by an artificial structure. At least 10 states subscribe to a combination of the riparian and the prior appropriation doctrine.

- Groundwater—water in the earth
- Percolating water—underground water
- Floodwaters—overflows
- Tidelands—shorelines

Groundwater refers to that water in the earth beneath the saturation point. The water passes beneath the land's surface and does not flow in an underground stream, nor is it supplied by streams flowing on the earth's surface. Ownership of land includes the right to drill below the surface, whether near the surface or hundreds of feet below. *Percolating water* is the water found underground and is that tapped by the farmer for a well. The farmer may not drill an excessive number of wells and sell the water, thus draining this percolating water from the adjoining landowner. In agricultural areas, heavy irrigation uses could create a water shortage.

Floodwaters are the waters that overflow the channels of a stream or body of water. In such instances the abutting landowner can erect a dike to guard against this overflow. *Tidelands* refers to the shorelines that are affected by the tides. The landowner that adjoins these shores owns land to the high-water mark.

Gaining and Losing Land
- Accretion—gain land
- Erosion—gradual loss of land
- Avulsion—rapid loss of land

An owner whose land borders a body of water may actually gain land due to the slow build-up of soil caused by natural forces such as wind and waves. This process is referred to as **accretion**, and the land gained by accretion is the alluvion deposit (soil deposited). The sudden and rapid washing away of land is known as **avulsion**. Boundary lines remain the same regardless of how much land is swept downstream. *Reliction* (or dereliction) occurs when the body of water recedes, exposing dry land.

The opposite of accretion, *erosion* results in the gradual loss of land. The erosion of soil is a gradual process created by the action of the natural elements. Rain, wind, water, and extreme weather changes erode the earth's surface. Terracing cultivated land and planting trees helps to absorb water and preserve fertile topsoil from being washed or blown away. Some types of erosion can also be controlled by building dams. The Grand Canyon in Arizona is an example of thousands of years of erosion by the Colorado River.

Rights of Government

The rights of the government over an individual's real estate include the right of taxation, special assessments, eminent domain, escheat, and police power. A memory tool for recalling these rights is PETE:

The right to **P**olice powers

The right to **E**minent domain

The right to **T**ax

The right to **E**scheat

Taxation

Private ownership of land is subject to government rule, "for the common good." Thus, laws controlling the land are among the government's basic functions. Ever since feudal times when land was controlled by the king, it has been necessary for governments to protect their citizens in time of war. In the Middle Ages, taxes were collected and allegiance was pledged to the king in return for this protection. So it is today. The Constitution of the United States provides for the collection of taxes for the general welfare and common defense of the nation. Consequently, taxes are collected on all real property according to its value. On new property, the cost of construction determines to a great extent the real value of the property. In many cities buyers are required by law to disclose the purchase price on a tax assessment form that must accompany the deed when it is recorded. The property is then placed on the tax rolls at the new sale price. To unify taxes on property in the area, the assessor's office may periodically call for a reappraisal of all property values. This enables the assessor to adjust tax values to keep them consistent with market values.

Property taxes vary greatly between cities because of the different needs and services a community may offer. If a city offers schools, libraries, public transportation, parks and community centers, public utilities, trash hauling, and well-maintained streets and parks, the cost of these services must be borne in part by property taxes. On the other hand, the property's value is indirectly enhanced by these services. The more properties on the tax roll, the greater the number of people there are to contribute to the cost of the services.

Location will also determine the cost of property taxes. The costs of road maintenance will be higher in areas of the country where snow removal and subsequent additional street repairs are necessary. If a community is basically a retirement city, services such as schools and playgrounds may not be in the tax budget.

Other revenue generated by the city from sources, such as taxes placed on gambling casinos and lotteries or oil royalties received from property owned by the city, will assist in offsetting high property taxes.

An equal charge of taxes is made on all real property according to value and is known as an **ad valorem tax**. The assessor appraises the property for taxation

Ad valorem tax

purposes, and the assessed value is provided by the law of the municipality. Some municipalities assess real estate at a percentage of its appraised value, and others assess at the full appraised value. The city, county, or state then sets the *rate* or *levy* (the mill, or the tax expressed in dollars) according to the amount of money needed to meet the budget and expenses of the government. The amount needed is divided by the total assessed value of a property in the taxing body to determine the rate. One mill equals one-tenth of one cent.

To determine the amount of taxes on a property, the assessed value is multiplied by the rate:

$80,000	appraised value
× .35	percentage of taxation
$28,000	assessed value
× .080	mill levy
$ 2,240	taxes

Taxes are sometimes expressed in dollars, for example, $2.75 per $100 of appraised value:

$80,000	appraised value
× .0275	per $100 of value
$ 2,200	taxes

Special Assessments

To pay for the cost of improvements, such as pavement, sidewalks, curbs, streetlights, and public utilities, an assessment is levied against property adjacent to the improvements. For example, if a street is paved, each of the abutting homeowners will pay a proportionate share, which is usually based on the front footage of each property. If a sewer line is being extended into a specific neighborhood, ordinarily each of the property owners in that area will be equally assessed since it will benefit the entire area.

Eminent Domain

Eminent domain:
www.realtor.org

Government's right to condemn property

The right of **eminent domain** permits the government to take private property for public use with "just compensation" to the owners. The act of taking the property is accomplished through *condemnation proceedings*. The U.S. Constitution prohibits the confiscation of private property without just compensation.

A series of events takes place when a unit of government finds it necessary to take private property. The condemnor (city, county, state, or federal agency) negotiates with the condemnee (the owner) as to the purchase price. If an agreement can be reached, the condemnor purchases the property for the agreed-upon price, and no condemnation action is necessary. However, if an agreement cannot be reached, legal proceedings are in order. A petition is filed in the county court to condemn the property. Appraisers (usually three) are appointed by the judge of the county court to appraise the property. Market value is established by these fee appraisers, who may be called upon as witnesses to validate their appraisal. After a hearing is held, during which evidence from both the condemnee and the condemnor is given, a determination of price is made. If either of the parties feels the award is not just, an appeal may be made to the district court, and a trial by jury will be held.

Many times only a partial segment of a property is taken, and the appraisers must determine what the value of the portion taken was and what the remaining value is. This is referred to as the *before and after value.*

Examples of eminent domain proceedings can include the need for public recreation areas, the widening of streets or installing of sidewalks, a water company needing to lay a water line, or the expansion needs of a university.

Escheat

The term **escheat** means reverting or lapsing of property back to the sovereign state through legal procedures. The doctrine of escheat dates from feudal days when all land was ultimately owned by the king.

Today, the state (or in some cases the county) acquires the property of an **intestate** person (one who dies without leaving a will) who has no heirs.

Each state's statutes set the parameters and the judicial process for establishing the right to acquire the property. Many states cannot claim the property until the court so orders; others acquire title immediately upon the death of an intestate. In the latter situation, the state must go to probate court to establish ownership. If no heirs come forth, the sovereign state succeeds to the property according to statute (law). In some states, this means that property goes to the county where the parcel is located. The majority of decedents have either made wills or have heirs, so escheat is not an ordinary means for the state to acquire property.

The right of escheat also extends to abandoned property. If property owners desert and abandon their property, the law of escheat allows the government to acquire ownership.

Police Power

Through enabling acts passed by a state's legislature, the local government may be given the power to impose additional restrictions and controls upon land. This power of state and local governments to regulate land use is referred to as **police power** and must be in the interest of the public welfare, safety, and health.

Using police power, a local government can place restrictions on real property through zoning ordinances, building codes, subdivision restrictions, traffic regulations, and environmental protection laws. These imposed limitations on the private use of land are necessary for an orderly growth pattern within the community. Generally, no compensation is given to the land holder when restrictions are placed on the property through the exercise of police power.

Personal Property vs. Real Property

If something can be owned, it is property, either real or personal. Ownership of land gives us the right to use and possess it to the exclusion of all others. As defined earlier, *real estate* refers to the land and anything that is permanently affixed to the land by nature or by humans, such as a house. *Real property* is the interest held in the real estate. **Personal property** is referred to as **chattel**, or *personalty,* and is any kind of property that is movable in nature, such as a chair or a table, and is therefore not *real property* (see Figure 2.6). A tree is real property until you fell it, and then it becomes personal in nature. Build a bookcase from this wood, and it would be considered personal property; but attach it to the wall in the library of the house, and it becomes real property once again. If there is a question as to whether a particular piece of property is real or personal, intention of the owners is considered. If the owners intended to take the object in question with them when they conveyed the property, then it is considered personal property.

A memory device for whether an object should be considered real or personal is MARIA:

Manner of attachment

Appropriateness to use intended

Relationship of parties

Intent of parties

Agreement to the contrary

The manner in which the item was attached to the real property determines if it should remain real property. The drapery rods are nailed to the wall and are considered real property, but the draperies that hang on the rods are easily slipped off and are therefore personal property. A mailbox is permanently affixed to the house or to a post beside the driveway and thus becomes real property. The gas line that is run to the pole on which the gas grill sits is for the sole purpose of supplying gas to the grill. While the grill could be easily removed, the "appropriateness to use intended" dictates that the grill is real property. The water heater, a necessary item in any dwelling, is installed with piping in a very permanent manner. While it could be removed, it is essential to the property and therefore considered a part of the real property. Clearly the intention of the parties who had the water heater installed was that it remain with the property.

To be positive that no unpleasant circumstances arise from a misunderstanding on the part of either party upon the transfer of real property, it is prudent to list articles that are to be included with the sale in the purchase contract. Certain questionable items that are to be considered real property should be clearly stated as being transferred in the sale. Built-in bookcases, mail boxes, gas grills, and built-in appliances are a few examples of articles that could

---

Margin notes:

· Real property is permanently affixed to land
· Personal property is movable

Manner of attachment

Appropriateness to use intended

Relationship and intent of parties

Agreement to the contrary

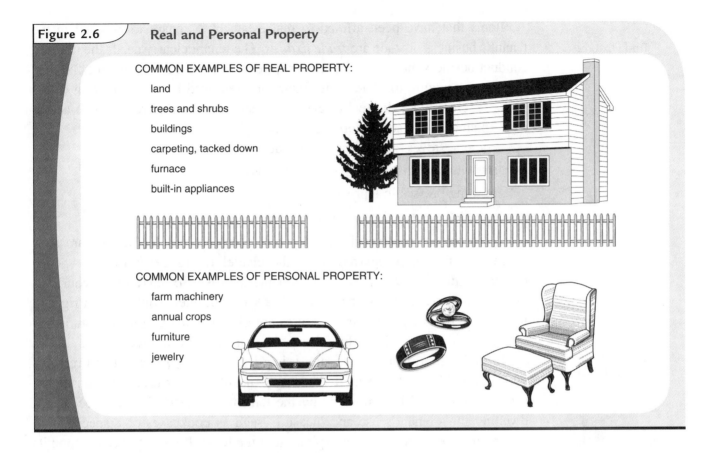

Figure 2.6   **Real and Personal Property**

COMMON EXAMPLES OF REAL PROPERTY:

    land

    trees and shrubs

    buildings

    carpeting, tacked down

    furnace

    built-in appliances

COMMON EXAMPLES OF PERSONAL PROPERTY:

    farm machinery

    annual crops

    furniture

    jewelry

trigger misunderstanding. If the sellers state that they are taking the gas grill or the mailbox, this should be stipulated in the contract.

Things attached to real estate by roots, such as trees and produce growing on the land, are classified in two groups.

1. *Fructus naturales,* or fruits of nature, that grow continuously and do not need annual cultivation are considered by law to be real estate. Examples of this permanent growth include trees, perennial bushes, shrubs, and grasses.

2. *Fructus industriales,* or *emblements,* are annual crops, including vegetables, fruits, and grains (corn, wheat, and oats), and are not referred to as real property. When selling farmland, the crops are normally considered personal property since they are replanted annually. This allows the tenant farmer the right to harvest the crops since they are considered personal property of the tenant. Provisions should be made in the sales contract stating whether the crops will be transferred to the purchaser or be harvested by the seller or tenant.

Fixtures are items of personal property that become real once they are affixed to real estate; for example, light fixtures, cabinets, bookcases, plumbing fixtures, carpeting, and shrubbery. Once attached, they are considered a part of the real estate.

Trade fixtures

Items that have been affixed to real estate by a tenant to be used in the tenant's business or trade are *trade fixtures.* The tenant clearly needs the items to conduct business, but when the lease expires will expect to remove the fixtures. Most states require that the trade fixtures be removed before expiration of the lease. If left behind, the real estate owner acquires the fixtures through accession. Examples of trade fixtures include:

- coolers, stoves, and ovens in a restaurant
- shelving and display cases in a retail store
- printing presses in a print shop
- a dentist chair and equipment

If fixtures are purchased on a payment plan, the suppliers can secure their interest by fixture filing (recording the chattel mortgage) before the goods become fixtures or within 10 days after the item is affixed. Refer to your particular state law. If the business should fail, the supplier would have a right to remove the fixture. Many times fixtures are used as collateral for a loan, and if it is recorded prior to the fixture filing, the loan would take precedence.

Leasehold fixtures vs. trade fixtures

If the landlord installs a fixture, it is a *leasehold improvement* and remains with the building. However, if the tenant installs the fixture, it is considered a *trade fixture* and is removable by the tenant. Domestic fixtures placed in a dwelling for a tenant's use and pleasure, such as bookcases or a special light fixture, may be removed upon expiration of the lease. If damage occurs upon its removal, any repairs would be the responsibility of the tenant.

Interests in
real estate:
www
.law.cornell.edu/
topics/
realproperty.html

Acquiring Ownership: Voluntary Alienation

While the government can acquire property through its right of eminent domain and by escheat, there are many avenues by which an individual may assume title to real estate. Real estate can be obtained by *purchase.* The owner sells it voluntarily **(voluntary alienation)** to the purchaser.

Acquire Ownership
· By purchase
· By will
· By descent

Ownership of real estate also can be obtained through a *will,* a formal written document that permits the distribution of an owner's property after death. To be legal, a will must be in writing, signed, witnessed, and attested. The maker of a will has died **testate** and is said to have left a last will and testament. The person who made the will is the *testator* (masculine) or *testatrix* (feminine). The will states who is to inherit the property. Willed real estate is known as a **devise**, and the receiver is the devisee. An *executor* (masculine) or *executrix* (feminine) should be named in the will to carry out the terms of the will. If no executor is named, an *administrator* (personal representative) is appointed by the court. If personal property is being willed, it is referred to as a *legacy* or *bequest,* and the receiver is the *legatee.*

The parties named in the will have no rights until the death of the owner. Most state laws mandate that the will be filed for probate with the court prior to distribution to the devisee. **Probate** is a legal process that determines the exact assets of the deceased person. Any debts must be satisfied before the proceeds are distributed to the heirs. The will is filed at the court by the person named as executor. The validity of the will is determined at a hearing held by the court, and the terms of the will are carried out by the executor or the administrator.

Probate

The laws of each state must be adhered to for the will to be legal. If the will provides for less than this statutory right, the surviving spouse can renounce the will and request the minimum rights as stated under the law. The right to renounce a will is usually reserved by law to only the spouse and not to any other heir.

The person who dies without leaving a will has died **intestate**, and this property passes to heirs by **descent**. The laws of inheritance are statutory and vary from state to state. The premise of these laws is that intestate decedents would undoubtedly desire their property to succeed to their heirs. In the majority of the states, the surviving spouse receives one-half or one-third of the estate. The children receive the estate if there is no surviving spouse. Any claims and debts against the estate will be satisfied first.

Twenty-seven states* recognize the holographic will, which is a handwritten will, dated, written, and signed entirely in the maker's handwriting. It is important not to have any printed words in or on the holographic will, or it becomes invalid.

A written amendment to an existing will is a **codicil**. The codicil changes some conditions of the will without the need for rewriting the entire document. Just as with the original will, the codicil must be signed, dated, and witnessed. The amendment by a codicil to a will is the only way to change the terms of the will since to alter the will by penciling in notations or deletions is not acceptable under the law.

Codicil to will

Losing Ownership Rights: Involuntary Alienation

Under certain conditions property may be taken from the rightful owner and title transferred by involuntary alienation. A true owner may lose ownership if another person occupies the property for a prescribed statutory period in a hostile, continuous, distinct, visible, and actual way. This is known as **adverse possession**. Do not confuse adverse possession with squatter's rights. The latter pertains to the right to occupy land by undisturbed and lengthy use but not with legal title. In acquiring land by adverse possession, the adverse claimant must make an actual claim of ownership to the occupied property. This claimant brings a **quiet title action** suit in a local court against anyone who may have

Adverse possession

---

* *The following states recognize holographic wills: Alaska, Arizona, Arkansas, California, Colorado, Idaho, Kentucky, Louisiana, Maryland, Mississippi, Montana, Nebraska, Nevada, New Jersey, New York, North Carolina, North Dakota, Oklahoma, Pennsylvania, Rhode Island, South Dakota, Tennessee, Texas, Utah, Virginia, West Virginia, and Wyoming.*

any claim to the property. If the claim is valid, the court will award title to the claimant. If the adverse claimant has been paying taxes on the land, it reveals some appearance of ownership and is referred to as **color of title**. Many states will permit one adverse claimant to tack his possession onto a previous adverse occupant if the first occupant is a relative or if the *tacking is done by contract*. For example, a mother may occupy a property for three years, after which her son takes possession of the premises and tacks on to the previous possession of his mother. An example of taking property by contract would be "A" sells his rights to "B," and "B" could take possession, continue to occupy the property, and file claim to the property when the statutory term has been met. The adverse claimant must follow the procedure in filing the claim as outlined in the state's statutes. States vary in the occupancy requirements of an adverse claimant from 5 years to 25 years. The adverse possession law encourages true owners not to abandon their property.

Adverse possession by tacking

Adverse possession by contract

A Case in Point

In Boulder, Colorado, a judge and his attorney-wife were awarded one-third of a neighbor's million-dollar property. They stated they regularly walked the land and under adverse possession they laid claim to it. The owners bought the land two decades ago with plans to build on it. They lived down the block and maintained the property and paid the taxes. The owners are left with mounting legal fees, with land now too small to build on. The legal process drags on.

The statute of limitations determines the adverse claimant's rights. Possession must be open and notorious, exclusive, and uninterrupted. The owner must commence legal action from the wrongful occupant within the period of time stated in the state's statutes or is subject to losing the property. Most states with Torrens registration recognize that those registered cannot be lost through adverse possession (see Chapter 12 for further discussion of Torrens registration).

Another example of the loss of land **involuntarily** is the foreclosure on a debt that was secured by real estate, such as a mortgage. Condemnation of the land under the right of eminent domain is also an involuntary act.

Prescription is an easement one acquires in the land of another through continuous use for a statutory period. It is sometimes referred to as an **easement by prescription**. An example would be a privately owned road used continuously by the public. The owner should permanently post a sign stating that the road is private property or barricade the road once a year, indicating it is indeed privately owned, to avoid losing rights of ownership through prescription. The owner does not lose title; the trespasser has acquired only the right to go over the land. See Figure 2.7 for a summary of involuntary alienation.

Easement by prescription

Figure 2.7 / Involuntary Alienation

Process	Act	Real Estate Acquired By
Eminent domain	Land taken for public use	Government or public agency
Adverse possession	Adverse use of another's land for statutory period	Adverse claimant
Foreclosure	Overdue debt secured by realty	Creditor
Escheat	Owner dies intestate and has no heirs	State or county

Public Acquisition of Property

Title to property may be obtained by private grant, such as a gift by dedication in which real estate is transferred by an individual to the public and accepted by someone on behalf of the public. An example of a gift by dedication would be a street dedicated to the city when a new subdivision is formed. The developer must lay the streets in the subdivision, but by dedicating them to the city, any maintenance responsibility would be transferred to the city. The developer also may dedicate common areas and parks in the subdivision. Acceptance must be made by a public official.

Ownership by dedication

Summary of Important Points

1. Under the feudal system, landownership was by the ruling monarch. The *allodial system* of today permits individuals to own land.
2. The *physical* characteristics of land include its *immobility* (it cannot be moved), its *indestructibility* (it cannot be destroyed), and its *nonhomogeneity* (no two parcels of land are identical).
3. The *economic* characteristics of land include *scarcity, situs*, and *durability*.
4. The combination of privileges in real property are referred to as a *bundle of rights*. These give the owner the right to possess, sell, lease, exclude, mortgage, will, or give away real property.
5. *Water rights* are established by riparian and littoral rights or by the doctrine of prior appropriation.
6. The government has rights over private ownership, including the rights to tax, levy special assessments, and condemn land under the right of eminent domain. The government may obtain land by escheat if a person dies without leaving a will and has no heirs.

7. Through enabling acts and the use of police power, a local government can impose controls and restrictions on land.

8. *Real property* is an interest held in *real estate*; *personal property* is *chattel,* or any property movable in nature.

9. Voluntary alienation occurs when an owner divests of property voluntarily. Involuntary alienation occurs when someone takes a property against the owner's wishes.

10. Adverse possession is an involuntary taking of property when another person occupies the owner's land for the statutory period in a hostile, continuous, distinct, visible, and actual manner.

Discussion Points

1. How can property owners provide for the disposition of their property after death?

2. Under what circumstances can personal property become real property?

3. What rights, if any, does the government have over privately owned property?

4. What are the two methods of acquiring ownership of land by adverse possession?

5. Explain why police power is advantageous to the property owner.

6. When is real property considered abandoned?

7. An individual can acquire title to real property by several methods. By which means would you prefer to obtain title? Give reasons for your answer.

8. Can you think of a business or industry that is not connected in some capacity to real estate?

Review Questions

Answers to these questions are found in the Answer Key section at the back of the book.

1. Possession of property through the removal of the true owner's rights is called:
   a. adverse possession
   b. codicil
   c. dedication
   d. reliction

2. Title to real property may be obtained by means of:
   a. adverse possession
   b. inheritance
   c. devise
   d. all of the above

3. When a person dies intestate and no heirs can be located for intestate succession, the real property of the deceased will revert to the state through a process known as:
   a. reconveyance
   b. escheat
   c. reversion
   d. condemnation

4. Land can be taken by adverse possession:
   a. if adverse claimant cultivates crops
   b. if it is possessed in a manner hostile to owner
   c. if possessed with owner's knowledge and consent
   d. if owner receives rent

5. When property is transferred by adverse possession:
   a. it is involuntary
   b. it is governed by statute
   c. both of the above
   d. neither of the above

6. Abandoned private property redeemed by local government is an example of:
   a. police power
   b. eminent domain
   c. taxation
   d. escheat

7. If a person dies testate, any real estate owned by the deceased will:
   a. come under the laws of escheat
   b. go into a life estate
   c. pass to the heirs
   d. be titled to the devisee

8. The act of the state exercising its right of eminent domain is:
   a. escheat
   b. police power
   c. adverse possession
   d. condemnation

9. All of the following are governmental rights EXCEPT:
   a. taxation
   b. police power
   c. eminent domain
   d. adverse possession

10. The physical characteristics of land include all of the following EXCEPT:
    a. scarcity
    b. fixity
    c. permanence
    d. nonhomogeneity

11. The legal rights attached to real estate are referred to as:
    a. situs
    b. bundle of rights
    c. severance rights
    d. reliction rights

12. Which of the following does not include a right in real property?
    a. surface rights
    b. subsurface rights
    c. water rights
    d. avulsion rights

13. Which of the following is NOT real property?
    a. garage
    b. mail boxes
    c. tractor
    d. trees

14. The doctrine of prior appropriation of water rights provides for:
    a. the first owner to have first claim on water
    b. the water rights to be held by the state
    c. water rights to be leased from the local government
    d. the prevention of erosion

15. A tax levied against a property because it will benefit from the improvement is a(n):
    a. escheat
    b. special assessment
    c. ad valorem tax
    d. percentage tax

16. The most prominent economic characteristics of land include:
    a. scarcity, durability, nonhomogeneity
    b. scarcity, situs, durability
    c. situs, permanence, immobility
    d. permanence, immobility, indestructibility

17. Because no two parcels of land are identical, land is referred to as:
    a. permanent
    b. durable
    c. quaint
    d. nonhomogeneous

18. Common examples of personal property include all of the following, EXCEPT:
    a. farm machinery
    b. trade fixtures
    c. a furnace
    d. annual crops

19. A right acquired in another's real property through continuous use is:
    a. eminent domain
    b. descent
    c. easement by prescription
    d. easement by color of title

20. Taxation of real property provides in part for all of the following services EXCEPT:
    a. schools
    b. street maintenance
    c. libraries
    d. airline transportation

Land Descriptions

KEY TERMS

acre	lot and block number system
base line	meridian
bench marks	metes and bounds
check	monument
correction lines	plat
datum	rectangular survey system
fractional sections	section
government lots	surveys
landmark	township

OVERVIEW

The surveying of land dates from early times. No one knows for certain when the surveying of land first began but historians believe that it was practiced by the Chinese and Egyptians thousands of years ago. All legal descriptions are founded upon **surveys**, so some historical background in the development of land surveying may be of interest to the novice in real estate. Surveying is important because it is necessary to have a sufficient description of the property to correctly identify and locate it. Every parcel of land that is sold or mortgaged must have a legal description. While a street address is the commonly used means of identifying the location of a property, legal documents require the legal description since street addresses may be changed. For example, when a city annexes a nearby subdivision or village, it is not unusual to extend the streets of that city into the newly annexed area.

To arrive at an accurate description of a particular parcel of land, several methods are followed. This chapter explains how a survey is conducted and discusses the metes and bounds system of measurement, the government rectangular survey system, and the final platting of a subdivision using the lot and block system.

The Art of Surveying

Surveying is the technique of measuring the size and shape of a parcel of land and thus fixing its boundaries. The surveyor uses a transit, which is a telescope set on a tripod. Attached are a compass and horizontal and vertical arcs used to measure angles. The surveyor adjusts the lens to meet the marks on a sight pole held by another surveyor (the rodman), thus measuring distances. For precise measurements, a surveyor may use an invar tape made of nickel and steel. Unlike a steel tape, it is less affected by temperature changes. The surveyor will use iron pins and concrete stakes to mark the area's boundaries. Since monuments may be moved, the surveyor will state references to the bearings and distances from the point of beginning.

Surveying is based on geometry, so surveyors must know mathematics and must also be capable of using the sensitive instruments that are the tools of the surveyor's trade.

Metes and Bounds

The **metes and bounds** method of measuring land is the oldest known method used in the United States. The original 13 colonies were surveyed by this method, but precise directions and measurements were not used. A selected **monument** served as the reference point, or point of beginning (POB), and the particular piece of land was described in terms of other natural and artificial monuments. Natural boundaries are those created by nature, such as trees, rivers, and lakes. Artificial monuments are highways, section corners, and roads. Because of the vagueness involved, descriptions using monuments usually are concluded by referring to the area as being "xx acres, more or less." A typical description is shown in Figure 3.1.

Monument

WEB SITE

www.outfitters
.com/genealogy/
land/land.html

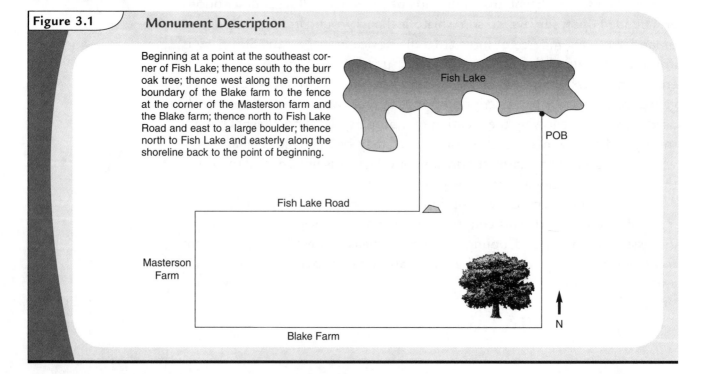

Figure 3.1   **Monument Description**

Beginning at a point at the southeast corner of Fish Lake; thence south to the burr oak tree; thence west along the northern boundary of the Blake farm to the fence at the corner of the Masterson farm and the Blake farm; thence north to Fish Lake Road and east to a large boulder; thence north to Fish Lake and easterly along the shoreline back to the point of beginning.

Because of the possible destruction of natural boundaries, the description lacks the permanence needed to correctly identify the property in later years. The old oak tree died, rivers changed channels, and artificial monuments were removed. Surveyors did not always record their surveys, causing disputes and subsequent legal complications. Today metes and bounds descriptions usually make reference to government survey lines as the place of beginning. If an owner sells off a portion of land that is irregular in shape or if it cannot be identified except by using courses and distances, the surveyor will elect to use the metes and bounds in combination with the **rectangular survey system**, the government method of surveying.

Metes refers to the measurement of length or distance from one point to another. *Bounds* pertains to the direction of the course. In the metes and bounds description in Figure 3.2, the metes (distance) are shown in feet, and the bounds (direction) are in degrees, minutes, and seconds. Two important factors must be present in this survey.

1. The description must begin at some known point, which is referred to as the point of beginning, usually a monument.

2. The description must close, that is, the survey needs to come back to the point of beginning.

In Figure 3.2, note that the description begins with a permanent marker called a monument. This monument is used as the reference point, and the surveyor will go to the nearest corner of the property being surveyed. In Figure 3.2 the surveyor traveled 80 feet south and 40 feet west to the point of beginning. Reading through the legal description and traveling clockwise, we come back to the true point of beginning. The surveyors place iron pins or stakes into the land at the corners of the boundaries.

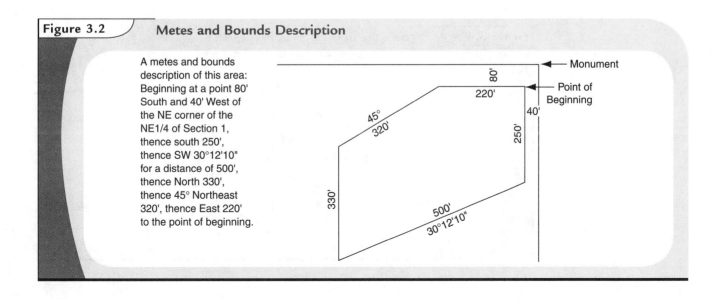

Figure 3.2   **Metes and Bounds Description**

A metes and bounds description of this area: Beginning at a point 80' South and 40' West of the NE corner of the NE1/4 of Section 1, thence south 250', thence SW 30°12'10" for a distance of 500', thence North 330', thence 45° Northeast 320', thence East 220' to the point of beginning.

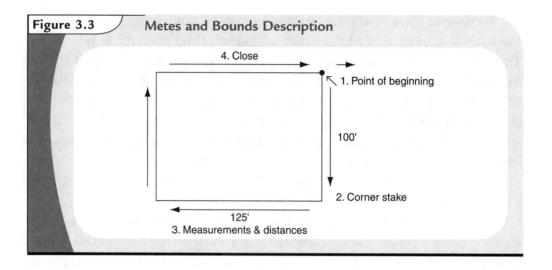

Figure 3.3   Metes and Bounds Description

The metes and bounds land description (see Figure 3.3) contains:

1. a point of beginning
2. the corners, usually defined by the placement of iron pins
3. definite measurements and distances
4. a close, or return to the point of beginning

In the metes and bounds description, the course will usually not run due east and west or due north and south, but will be angular, such as south 40 degrees east. In this instance, it is necessary to measure the angles by the units of degrees, minutes, and seconds. A degree is 1/360 of a circle and is divided into 60 minutes; each minute has 60 seconds (see Figure 3.4). Measuring angles in a **plat** (detailed plan) is done by using an instrument called a protractor.

Bench marks are permanent reference marks placed by U.S. government surveyors to designate locations and elevations. Surveyors use them as references when locating boundaries of a particular parcel of land. Bench marks may

Bench marks

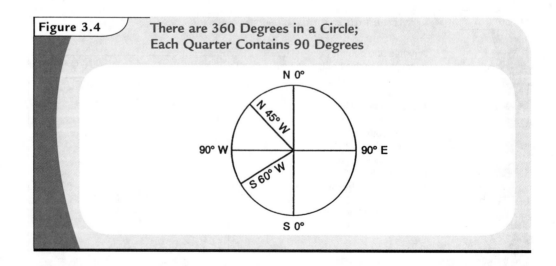

Figure 3.4   There are 360 Degrees in a Circle; Each Quarter Contains 90 Degrees

also be the brass markers surveyors place into a concrete drive or sidewalk. The bench mark is more permanent than a natural monument, such as a tree or a large rock, and if it is destroyed, its position is easier to relocate, since it is mutually dependent with other reference points of the survey.

As time passed, problems arose with the metes and bounds system because the natural boundaries would disappear. This resulted in a lack of permanence. With the rapid expansion toward the western part of the United States, it soon became apparent that a system with more uniformity needed to be adopted.

The Government Rectangular System

The rectangular survey system of land description was adopted by the federal government in 1787. It was used by most of the United States except for the original 13 colonies and the Atlantic Coast states, with the exception of Florida. Upon admission to the Union, the states of West Virginia, Tennessee, Texas, Kentucky, and Hawaii retained regulation over surveys of land within their borders, and they have not conformed to the rectangular system. A total of 30 of the 50 states use the rectangular system of survey.

When traveling by air over the country, it is interesting to note that the land far below appears as an orderly series of squares and rectangles, a result of the rectangular survey system.

www.nationalatlas
.gov/index.html

Meridians and Base Lines

In the rectangular system of survey there are 36 principal meridians and 32 base lines in the country. Latitude and longitude lines provide these base lines and meridians. A **meridian** is a line that runs directly north and south, and a **base line** is a line that runs east and west. These imaginary lines grid the surface of the earth. Starting from some tangible **landmark**, the surveyors ran a line due north through the area to be surveyed. This line running north and south was designated as the meridian for that particular state or area. In some states, these lines were called the first or second meridian. In others, they were actually given names, such as the Indian Meridian in Oklahoma. A base line was fixed at right angles to the meridian, to run due east and west, and this line was designated as the base line for that area. The surveyors would use the point where the meridian and base line intersected as their point of beginning (see Figure 3.5).

Surveying by latitude
and longitude

U.S. Geological Survey:
www.usgs.gov

Correction Lines

Because of the curvature of the earth, it was necessary to place **correction lines** at 24-mile intervals along the meridians to the north and south of the base lines. While the eye cannot see this curvature, it is very real. The north line of a township is many feet shorter than its south line. At every fourth township north of the base line, the difference could be 200 feet.

Figure 3.5

The Meridian and Base Line System of Surveying

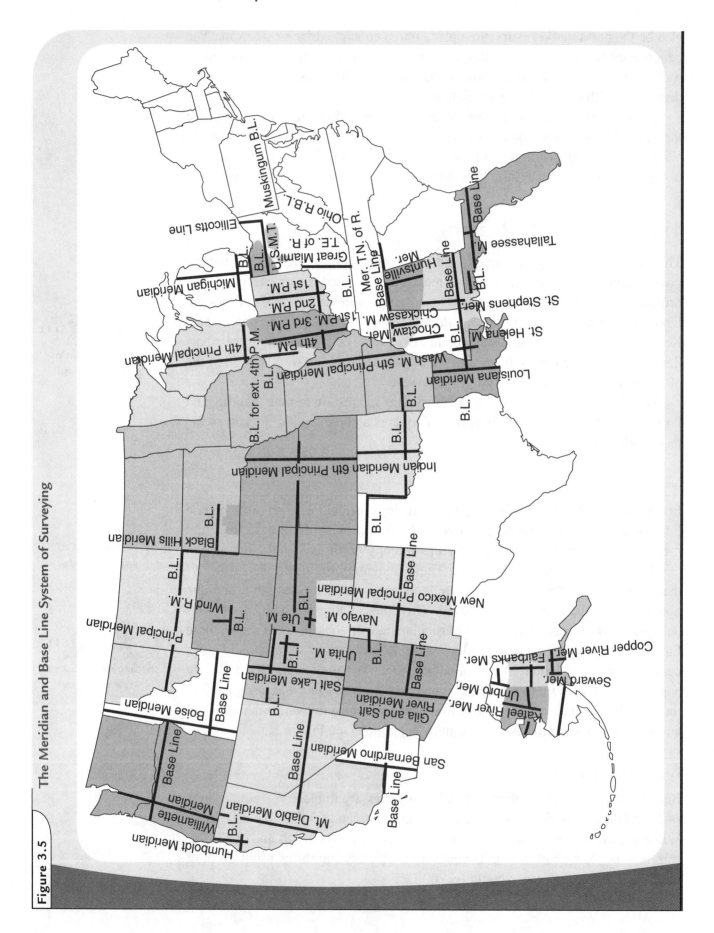

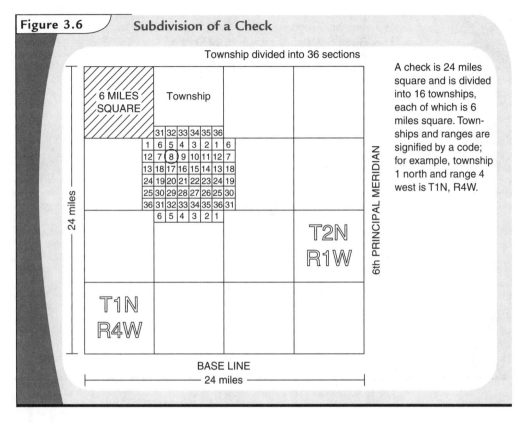

Figure 3.6   Subdivision of a Check

Township divided into 36 sections

6 MILES SQUARE   Township

| 31 | 32 | 33 | 34 | 35 | 36 |

1	6	5	4	3	2	1	6
12	7	8	9	10	11	12	7
13	18	17	16	15	14	13	18
24	19	20	21	22	23	24	19
25	30	29	28	27	26	25	30
36	31	32	33	34	35	36	31
	6	5	4	3	2	1	

24 miles

T2N R1W

6th PRINCIPAL MERIDIAN

T1N R4W

BASE LINE
24 miles

A check is 24 miles square and is divided into 16 townships, each of which is 6 miles square. Townships and ranges are signified by a code; for example, township 1 north and range 4 west is T1N, R4W.

The correction lines, combined with guide meridians, enabled the surveyors to divide the territory into squares approximately 24 miles on each side, which are known as **checks** (see Figure 3.6).

Checks

Townships

The check was divided by **township** lines into smaller tracts of land. These lines run parallel to the base lines at six-mile intervals, resulting in a grid of squares of approximately six miles on each side. These grids and ranges are thus described as being east and west of the principal meridians.

A township contains 36 sections.

To facilitate locating a township in the grid, the townships have both a township number and a range number. The first townships adjacent to and parallel to the base line are numbered one north or south, the next is numbered two north or south, proceeding on until reaching the next base line.

Likewise, a range number was given to each township running parallel to the principal meridian, commencing with number one east if it were directly east of the meridian or range one west if it were west (see Figure 3.6).

Range

Sections

The townships were further subdivided into 36 sections of one square mile each, with a **section** containing 640 **acres**. These sections were numbered 1 to 36, beginning with 1 in the northeast corner of the township and proceeding west and east alternately, ending in the southeast corner with section 36 (see Figure 3.7).

640 acres in a section

Figure 3.7   A Township Containing 36 Sections. Section 16 Has Been Set Aside as a School Section

6	5	4	3	2	1
7	8	9	10	11	12
18	17	16	15	14	13
19	20	21	22	23	24
30	29	28	27	26	25
31	32	33	34	35	36

By using the section number, the township number north or south of the base line, and the range number east or west of the controlling principal meridian, a parcel of land can be easily identified. The description may read: Section 8 of Township 3 North, Range 3 West of the 6th Principal Meridian. By looking at Figure 3.6, we can locate the section.

Let us take it a step further. A legal description reads: The NE¼ of the SE¼ of Section 5 in T5N, R11W of the 6th PM. Legal descriptions are always read starting backward; thus we would locate the range and township and then the section. The SE¼ would be identified and then we would proceed on to locate the NE¼ of said SE¼, which contains 40 acres (see Figure 3.8).

WEB SITE

www.outfitters
.com/twprange.html

Fractional Sections and Government Lots

Not all sections form an exact square because of the convergence of the meridians or due to bordering areas of water. To make allowances for this, the government added or deducted from one row of sections—from sections 1 through 6 (the north row) of the township if the difference occurred when measuring from south to north, and from the west row (sections 6, 7, 18, 19, 30, and 31) if the excess or deficiency occurred in the east or west measurements. These sections bordering on the north and west sides of a township are referred to as **fractional sections** (see Figure 3.9).

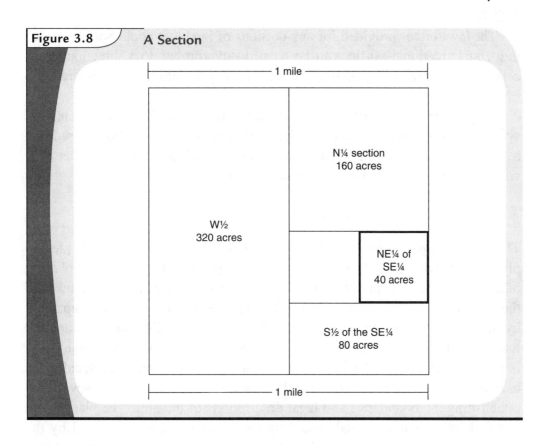

Figure 3.8 A Section

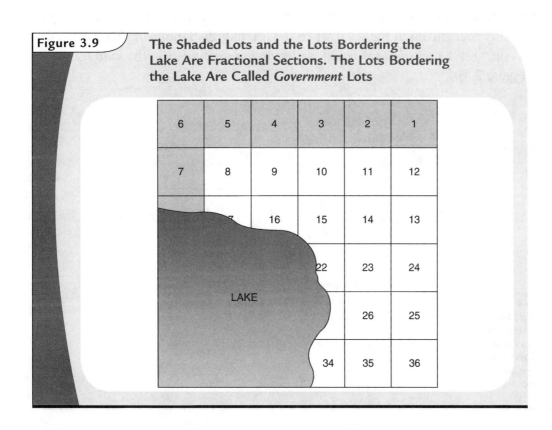

Figure 3.9 The Shaded Lots and the Lots Bordering the Lake Are Fractional Sections. The Lots Bordering the Lake Are Called *Government* Lots

The law further provided for any portions of land that could not be divided into equal fractional portions to be termed **government lots**. Fractional parcels were also created by bodies of water converging into a particular area (see Figure 3.9).

Existing Indian reservations were excluded by law from the rectangular system, as were military posts and land privately owned. As time passed and reservations were abandoned, the surveyors were unable to establish exact lines with the original survey, thus fractional sections resulted.

The Lot and Block System

The plat

The **lot and block number system** of land description is used by subdividers in platting subdivisions of land. This can usually be considered the final platting of an area. A careful survey is made by a surveyor before any development of the land can begin. The tract of land is divided into blocks, which are separated by streets. The blocks are platted into lots for single-family dwellings, and the lots are numbered in sequence for easy identification. Usually the subdivision is given a name to further identify the area. Once the subdivider decides the manner in which the area is to be laid out, a surveyor prepares a survey sketch establishing the boundaries and legal descriptions of the area. The plat will be certified by the surveyor and signed by the developer. Upon approval by the planning board of the local municipality, the plat is recorded and placed in a map book, which contains plats of all the subdivisions in the county. The book is indexed and may be inspected by anyone. The lots in the subdivision may be readily recognized in the deed when the lot and block number, the subdivision name, and the section, township, and range are recorded in the *map book* (see Figure 3.10).

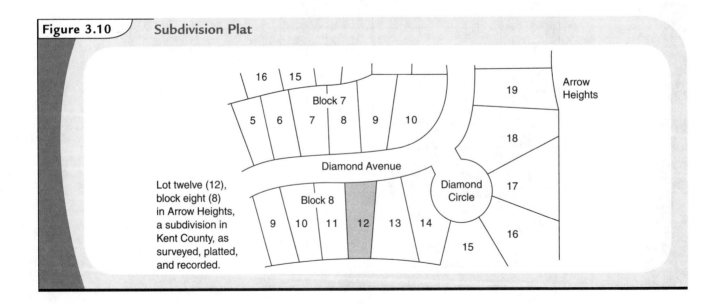

Figure 3.10   Subdivision Plat

Lot twelve (12), block eight (8) in Arrow Heights, a subdivision in Kent County, as surveyed, platted, and recorded.

Assessor's Map Book

In many areas of the country assessors attach a number to every registered parcel of land in their county. This method assists the assessor in preparing the tax roll. The *assessor's map book* is prepared from the plats submitted by the developer of the subdivision. Each page has the assigned parcel number, book and page, and the lot and block number of the parcel. The book is generally available for purchase, and many real estate offices find it convenient to have a copy for reference.

Vertical Land Descriptions

Chapter 13 relates how condominium and townhouse ownership divides the single lot even further. In a high-rise condominium, the owner owns an *air lot* plus an interest in the common elements of the property. The master deed permits individual fee simple ownership within a larger estate. This horizontal property law has permitted owners of apartment houses to sell individual units and give fee simple ownership to the purchasers.

    In preparing a survey of an air lot, a surveyor describes each unit by reference to the elevation above the lot and the land beneath it. The point from which the lot is measured is referred to as a datum. The **datum** is a level surface from which heights are measured. It may be mean sea level (zero feet), or the city may have established its own datum. The surveyor will start from this datum when measuring air lots.

Air lot

Datum

Land Measurements and Conversions

Measurements used in land surveying include:

1. *Rod:* 16.5 feet, or 5.029 meters.
2. *Chain:* 4 rods, 100 links, 66 feet, or 20.117 meters. Chain measurements were made by actual metallic chain constructed in early days of iron and later of heavy steel links. Accuracy was difficult because the links tended to stretch and the chain would twist and knot. In the 1900s surveyors started using steel ribbon tapes.
3. *Link:* 7.92 inches. A link originally referred to one loop of the chain that surveyors formerly used.
4. *Mile:* 5,280 feet, 1,760 yards, 320 rods, 80 chains, or 1.609 kilometers.
5. *Acre:* 43,560 square feet, 4,840 square yards, 160 square rods, or 4,047 square meters.
6. *Section:* 640 acres, or 1 square mile.
7. *Township:* 36 sections, or 6 miles square (36 square miles).
8. *Check:* 24 miles square (576 square miles), or 16 townships.

Summary of Important Points

1. Surveying is the method of measuring the size and shape of a parcel of land to identify its boundaries.

2. The metes and bounds system of measuring land uses a point of beginning, describing the area by applying natural and artificial boundaries and using the metes and bounds.

3. The government rectangular system employs the use of latitude and longitude lines that provide base lines and meridians.

4. Correction lines compensate for the earth's curvature and are placed at 24-mile intervals along the meridian.

5. A check comprises a 24-mile-square area.

6. A township within the check is 6 miles square and contains 36 sections, each of which is 640 acres in area.

7. The lot and block system is used by subdividers in platting a subdivision.

8. The map book of an area contains all the recorded platted subdivisions in a county.

Discussion Points

1. Does your state use the rectangular survey system of land description? If so, what principal meridian and base line is used? Refer to Figure 3.5 in this chapter.

2. Explain why surveyors rely on the use of bench marks.

3. Give the legal description of your school location.

4. Explain how surveyors compensate for the curvature of the earth.

5. Why isn't a street address a sufficient means of identifying a property?

Review Questions

Answers to these questions are found in the Answer Key section at the back of the book.

1. To simplify and improve the system of determining individual parcels of land, the federal government adopted which type of land description?

   a. metes and bounds
   b. lot and block number
   c. monuments
   d. rectangular survey

2. Section 36 of a township can be found at the:

   a. northeast corner of the township
   b. northwest corner of the township
   c. southeast corner of the township
   d. southwest corner of the township

3. An acre contains:
   a. 3,840 square feet
   b. 6,490 square feet
   c. 4,356 square feet
   d. 43,560 square feet

4. Which of the following is true of a section of land?
   a. it contains 640 acres
   b. a half section is a quarter-mile square
   c. it contains 320 acres
   d. it contains 3,860 square feet

5. The NW¼ of the SE¼ of the SW¼ of section 9 contains:
   a. 160 acres
   b. 80 acres
   c. 40 acres
   d. 10 acres

6. Section 9 of a township is directly below:
   a. section 5
   b. section 3
   c. section 4
   d. section 16

7. The length of the north side of the NE¼ of the SE¼ of a section is how many feet?
   a. 660 feet
   b. 2,640 feet
   c. 1,320 feet
   d. 5,280 feet

8. Because of the curvature of the earth, it is necessary to compensate for shortages in the rectangular survey system through:
   a. correction lines
   b. fractional lots
   c. bench marks
   d. principal meridians

9. The legal description of the shaded area in the diagram is: 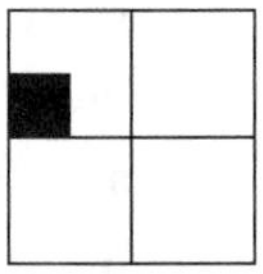
   a. NW¼ of the SW¼
   b. SW¼ of the NE¼
   c. SW¼ of the NW¼
   d. SW¼ of the SW¼ of the NW¼

10. Give the township and range for the four areas surrounding township 9 north and range 1 west of the 6th principal meridian:
    a.
    b.
    c.
    d.

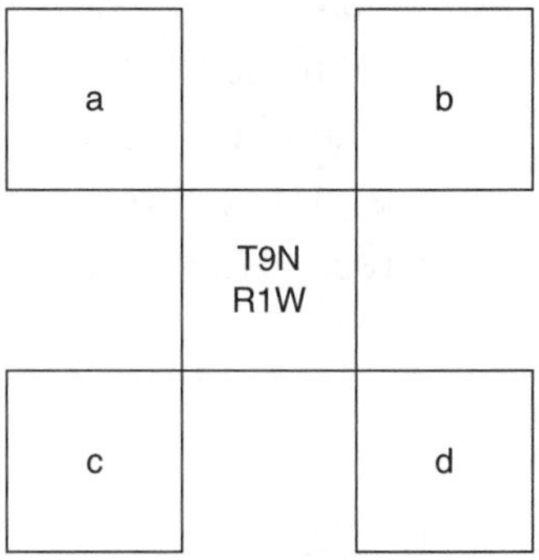

11. Establish the number of acres in the following description of a section of land: Beginning at the NE corner of the N½, thence in a diagonal line to the SW corner of the NE¼, thence in a diagonal line to the SE corner of the SE¼, thence north to the point of beginning:
    a. 40 acres
    b. 80 acres
    c. 160 acres
    d. 320 acres

12. Special provisions in the rectangular survey system were made for all of the following EXCEPT:
    a. Indian reservations
    b. fractional lots
    c. schools
    d. churches

13. Below is a diagram of a section of land. Establish the following parcels and give the number of acres in each:
    a. SE¼ of the SW¼
    b. SE¼ of the SE¼ of the NW¼
    c. S½ of the SW¼ of the NE¼
    d. W½ of the SE¼

14. A land developer is going to subdivide the N½ of the SW¼ of the NW¼ of a section of land into residential lots 70 feet × 110 feet. He is allowing 420,450 square feet for streets. How many lots will be realized?
    a. 5
    b. 58
    c. 59
    d. 100

15. Identification objects used by surveyors to establish description points are referred to as:
    a. metes and bounds
    b. correction lines
    c. monuments
    d. meridians

16. Which surveying method uses boundaries and measurements of length in distances from one point to another?
    a. monuments
    b. metes and bounds
    c. rectangular survey
    d. lot and block

17. Fractional sections that contain more or less than 640 acres are referred to as:
    a. government lots
    b. irregular plots
    c. lots and blocks
    d. school sections

18. Which of the following would not be included as part of the legal description of a parcel of land?
    a. metes and bounds
    b. street address
    c. lot and block
    d. rectangular survey

19. If a parcel of land is priced at $1,350 an acre, what is the cost of the N½ of the SW¼?
    a. $10,800
    b. $27,000
    c. $54,000
    d. $60,000

20. Vertical land descriptions are used in:
    a. developing a housing subdivision
    b. the metes and bounds land description
    c. the division of a single building into multiple units
    d. measuring the area of a parcel of land

Land Use Controls

KEY TERMS

assemblage

buffer zone

building codes

cluster lots

covenants

deed restrictions

dominant tenant

down zoning

easement

easement appurtenant

easement in gross

encroachment

homogeneous

Interstate Land Sales Full
   Disclosure Act

license

master plan

nonconforming use

planned unit development (PUD)

plat

police power

servient tenant

setback

spot zoning

variance

zero lot lines

zoning

OVERVIEW

The importance of the wise utilization of our land dates from the beginning of this country's history when the authors of the Constitution determined that the government would need to exercise some control over the use of the land. Title to land was granted by the federal government to individuals, and most titles can be traced back to the original land grant or patent. To encourage settlement, especially of the western territories, land was sold at auction and offered as a bonus to soldiers who served in the Continental Army. Title provided for allodial ownership in fee simple interest, but controls were placed over the use of the land, and today these use restrictions include the addition of private controls. This chapter will cover these controls and restrictions along with the development of a subdivision.

Federal Controls on Land Use

From the start, some land was set aside for park areas. In 1872, Congress created the first national park preserve in the world. Yellowstone National Park was followed by 29 other preserves containing mountains, volcanoes, glaciers, and spacious virgin forests. Today all 50 states have established parks within their boundaries as recreational areas for picnicking, hiking, camping, and enjoying nature. With the increased attention to tourism, expanded park facilities welcome and encourage out-of-state visitors. City parks, often with playgrounds and recreational facilities, have been developed for the enjoyment of the residents.

Regulating interstate land sales

With the growth of our country, many additional federal laws covering the disposition and use of real estate have been enacted. In 1969, the federal government enacted the Interstate Land Sales Full Disclosure Act, which regulates subdivided land. HUD requires developers to register interstate land sales with the Office of Interstate Land Sales Registration (OILSR) if the development contains 25 or more units.

Controls include the Real Estate Settlement Procedures Act (RESPA), which covers conditions that must be addressed when transferring real estate (see Chapter 10).

In July 1982, Congress passed a law stating that savings and loan institutions do not have to allow mortgages to be assumed upon transfer of title. This superseded law to the contrary that had been mandated in some states. Finally, the Civil Rights Act of 1968 and its amendments in 1989 provide for fair housing throughout the United States (see Chapter 19).

Although all 50 states have control over land within their boundaries, the federal interstate highways, parks, and schools are examples of land under the jurisdiction of the U.S. government.

Interstate Land Sales Full Disclosure Act

WEB SITE

U.S. Department of Housing and Urban Development: Office of housing: www.hud.gov/offices/hsg/index.cfm

The **Interstate Land Sales Full Disclosure Act** was passed by Congress in 1969 and amended in 1980. The act provides protection to consumers who purchase, sight unseen, unimproved lots in another state. This act is administered by HUD and strict regulations must be adhered to.

Before a subdivision that contains 25 or more lots can be offered for sale across state lines (referred to as *interstate sales*), the subdivider must register with the Interstate Land Sales Agency. The statement filed will include disclosure of precise information regarding the land and the plans for its sale. A developer cannot offer a portion of a tract and limit the subdivison to less than 25 lots in an effort to bypass the Interstate Land Sales Full Disclosure Act. A common plan to develop the land must include all of the subdivision.

A property report that reveals zoning and other regulations for the use of the land must be given to all prospective purchasers. The report includes information about the type of title the buyer will receive, the number of homes that are presently occupied, utility services and charges, any liens against the property, the distance to the nearest community, whether roads are paved, soil conditions that may affect foundations, and available recreation facilities. This report must be given to the prospective purchaser a minimum of three days before the signing of a contract. After signing a contract, the buyer has a "cooling off" period until midnight of the seventh day after entering into the contract. If a purchaser does not receive a report prior to signing the contract, the purchaser has two years to bring action to revoke the contract. This "cooling off" period allows the buyer to analyze the wisdom of the decision. This law was implemented to prevent people from purchasing land presented as a great opportunity that may in truth be greatly misrepresented.

Exceptions to this law include the following.

- It does not apply to a subdivision containing less than 25 lots.
- Tracts of 20 acres or more are also exempt.
- Lots sold to developers are exempt.
- Lots with existing buildings or lots that require construction of a building within 2 years are exempt.

State and Local Controls on Land Use

States exercise control over their highways, parks, lakes, water use, and government buildings. Some states have comprehensive plans for orderly development, with special emphasis placed on their natural resources. Through enabling acts passed by many states, chartered cities are given the power to regulate land use within their jurisdiction with zoning laws. Zoning regulations give local governments the power to impose controls and restrictions over the private use of land. This power of the government to regulate land use is referred to as **police power** and must be used in the interest of the public. These controls ensure that the growth of a city, whether a large metropolis or an incorporated village, proceeds in a coordinated and harmonious manner. Public land use controls may include the development of a **master plan** for the city, zoning laws, **building codes**, and subdivision regulations.

Regulating land use in communities

In establishing a comprehensive master plan for land use, a careful study and analysis of existing physical, economic, and social conditions in the community is made. Master planning is needed to meet the ever-changing social and economic requirements of a community. The master plan considers housing, schools, health care, transportation, and public utilities as the present conditions and projects future needs. This plan serves as a guide so that growth will proceed in the manner that best promotes the general welfare of citizens and protects their real estate investments. Decisions are reached and expenditures are decided upon when capital improvements are required. Often changes are unforeseen, so proper adjustments must be made. For instance, as our mode of

Creating a master plan

Planning for growth

transportation changed, the one-lane dirt road was exchanged for paved streets to accommodate the transition from the horse and carriage to the automobile. Moving traffic to avoid congestion remains one of the most crucial responsibilities of the cities.

The land use planners will survey present land uses and consider the vacant land that lies in the path of possible future development. Projections of future use are analyzed in considering the hierarchy of rights in real estate. The laws must not only be concerned with the present owner, but with the rights of the community and future generations. Thus, land use laws proposed by a municipality safeguard and protect the rights of all parties. A county's laws must not be inconsistent with the city government so that an orderly pattern of development may ensue. If the properties in a given area are **homogeneous**, or compatible, values will be stable.

Since the desire for land is concentrated around employment areas, land is more in demand in and near large cities. City planning, with a broader outlook to the future, is under constant study by urban governmental agencies, with zoning regulations of extreme importance.

Changing Property Uses

Revitalizing
downtown areas

Originally the downtown area of a city represented the primary retail and office center. Significant changes have developed in the past 30 years as neighborhood shopping centers and industrial and office parks began to emerge. New emphasis was focused on a changing downtown economy as large retailers abandoned the area for the suburbs, and citizens gravitated to neighborhood shopping centers where parking was adequate and free.

Planning boards across the nation have proposed a variety of land uses to revitalize downtown areas into mixed-use districts. To attract visitors, many cities have established "old town" atmospheres in what were old brick warehouses and industrial plants. New uses have been created with sleek, updated interiors converted into apartments, condominiums, specialty shops, eateries, and entertainment to appeal to downtown employees and visitors. To accommodate the automobile, parking garages have expanded in space and number. Many of these downtown areas have riverfronts that attract the tourist trade. Marketing this revitalization has been a major focus of local chambers of commerce.

The preservation of historic buildings has added to the interesting mix of old and new as the character of the area changed. Tax credits are available to owners for rehabilitating buildings that qualify under the historic guidelines.

The forces of change are ever present. As time passes, neighborhoods change. Property values will decline in some areas and rise in others. As new home styles are introduced, an area may become outdated and value will recede. When economic decadence occurs in an area new uses may replace the old.

Transfer Development Rights (TDRs)

Transfer development rights (TDRs) permit the transfer of a building right to another piece of land. Based on the premise that rights of land use should be equal, it allows the owner of a property, such as a historic landmark, to sell her TDR to an owner down the street and therefore preserve the historic building from demolition. Likewise, an owner of farmland adjacent to the city could sell the TDR to a person located in a district more suitable for construction. It promotes the fill-in of urban areas without jeopardizing the right to make a profit for the person owning the farmland. For the most part, TDRs have been used in Chicago and New York in an effort to save historic buildings. TDRs allow a parcel of land to be developed to greater use if another parcel is developed for a lesser use.

Zoning

Zoning limits the rights of property owners, specifying allowable and prohibited uses. Zoning restrictions can be traced to early colonial days when the residential areas were separated from industries, with saloons, blacksmith shops, stables, and tanneries placed on the opposite side of the village.

Protection of property rights

The fundamental reasons to have zoning laws are apparent: to protect the interests of the property owner and to achieve an aesthetically pleasing environment in the community. Limiting uses within a zone provides that protection. Imagine how difficult it would be to retain value in your home if an automobile dealership or a saloon could operate next door. Zones place each type of residence, business, and industry in compatible areas.

Today a zoning board or planning commission is appointed to pass and regulate restrictions on land use. A city development plan reviews the physical development patterns and establishes policies to direct and finance the growth and improvement of the urban environment. It is not unusual for a city to have a strategic plan in place that establishes the general goals for land use, including economic development, parks and recreation, and transportation. In exercising its police power, the planning board of the local government establishes the zoning ordinances that regulate and control land use.

Zoning falls into four general categories: residential, commercial, industrial, and agricultural. Since it is wise to have homogeneous divisions, each of these four categories is further divided into more specific areas. A typical key to zoning follows, but keep in mind this varies from city to city.

Zoning categories

1. Residential is represented by R-1 through R-7. R-1 may be the most restrictive, requiring larger lots. Within these classifications the regulations are set as to minimum requirements for the square footage of the lot; minimum lot width; and minimum front, side, and rear **setbacks** from the perimeter of the property boundaries. Maximum building height and coverage of the lot are other stipulations found in these categories.

2. O-1 is for office uses.

3. C-1 might permit a neighborhood business with C-2 used for community business, C-3 for general business, and C-4 for central business. Again, the size and use will be dictated by the zoning in each of the business categories.

4. I-1 may be used for light industrial, I-2 for heavy industrial, and I-M for manufacturing use.

5. A represents agricultural.

In each of these areas the zoning laws of the municipality govern the type of structure one can erect and the uses to which the property can be adapted. The residential areas are usually buffered from busy streets by multifamily units with office space following and commercial uses abutting the main streets. The strip of land that separates the areas is referred to as a **buffer zone**.

Buffer zones

Most cities need the land use to be regulated within a one- to three-mile radius of the city. This right to control is acquired by legislative enactment. As the community spreads, it merges into the rural agricultural areas, and the need for converting the farmland into other uses arises. City dwellers desiring to move into the country may force the conversion of agricultural land into 5- and 10-acre plots.

Changes in Zoning

Change of use

Requests for zoning changes from an existing use to another purpose are generally made with the intention of bringing a higher return to the property. For example, a property in an older residential area now lies in the path of commercial use but, with minor remodeling, can be converted to office or business space. No longer desirable for a residence because of the outside influences, it will lend itself nicely to a new use if the zoning can be changed.

Special use permits are available in some states and allow the conversion of a property to another use. Generally, the person is requesting a use that does not conform to the current zoning of the area. For example, a homeowner requests permission to operate a beauty salon from her home. A special use permit is usually quite restrictive and can be only for the purpose requested. If the owner later decides to open a tailor shop and close the beauty salon, she will have to go through the same procedure of applying for the new use.

A *conditional use* permit would grant a use that would be beneficial to the public, such as a sandwich shop in an industrial tract. Convenience for the employees in the area creates an inducement to permit the use.

Exclusionary zoning requires larger lots, thus excluding people who cannot afford the extra land costs. Restrictions are often placed on agricultural land adjacent to cities requiring the purchase of 5- to 10-acre sites, thus placing it beyond the reach of many people who want the flavor of uncongested country living.

Inclusionary zoning is the exact opposite as it requires that lower income properties must be included in new housing developments. This eliminates discrimination in zoning of properties that tends to limit purchase to the higher income brackets.

Occasionally a community will place a *moratorium* on building, halting the construction of new houses. This has been practiced in areas that want to preserve the mountainsides and natural surroundings and retain the aesthetic beauty that accounts for the popularity of the community. This *zoning freeze* may place a hardship on the person who has purchased a lot with the intention of building at a later date only to discover a building permit is unobtainable.

Moratorium

Zoning ordinances can be changed and rezoning permitted by *amendment.* If it appears another use of the property would be appropriate for the area as it now exists, a zoning amendment allowing the use may be instituted. A residential area may have been infringed upon by commercial use, and changing the ordinance to accommodate the uses now developing in the area might be prudent.

A **nonconforming use** of property is a use in violation of present zoning laws but lawful at the time the use was begun. "Grandfather" rights exist since zoning regulations cannot be retroactive. For example, consider a grocery store built in 1975 on the edge of an undeveloped area. In 1991 a developer plats out the remaining land into large single-family lots. The grocery store is not compatible, so it is now considered a nonconforming use. The grocer is not required to close his business, but another merchant would be prohibited from starting a new store.

Spot zoning is zoning of isolated properties for activities other than those called for in existing regulations. The law generally does not favor spot zoning since it is inconsistent with the present zoning of the area. A vacant lot zoned for commercial use in an area zoned residential would be an example of spot zoning. A change to allow construction of a multiunit building in a neighborhood of single-family residences is another example of spot zoning.

Spot zoning

If an individual owner needs an exception to the zoning ordinance and if the use is not detrimental to the public, a **variance** can be requested. For example, an owner may wish to build a garage but is unable to adhere to the zoning laws because the structure will be 5 feet from the lot line and the regulations in the subdivision call for setbacks of 10 feet from lot lines. In such a case, a variance would probably be granted if the surrounding neighbors have no negative complaint to the variance. The zoning board of appeals can approve variances and grant a waiver when strict adherence to the ordinance produces a hardship to the owner in need of the exception.

An exception to present zoning

Down zoning occurs when a property is rezoned to a lower use. For example, a property zoned for an apartment building is down zoned to permit only single-family homes. The new uses for these properties do not use the land to its highest and best use for which it was originally zoned. If the down zoning is executed by ordinance, the property owner may be awarded compensation for the loss in property value caused by the new restriction.

Rezoning for a lower use

Procedure for Rezoning or Variance

In most cities zoning can be changed only by ordinance. Usually a two-tier system exists: the planning board recommends action to the city council, and the city council acts on the ordinance. The planning board members are mayoral-appointed positions, generally selected from a broad employment base. The process will follow a sequence of steps similar to the following.

Changing property use

1. The applicant contacts the planning department for a zoning change.
2. The planning department inspects the site and makes a recommendation.
3. Announcement of a pending hearing is made in the newspaper.
4. Notification of the petition is sent to surrounding property owners.
5. A public hearing is held, and the applicant presents the request with valid substantiation for the zoning change. Evidence is presented as to why the change is necessary, a beneficial use of the property, and not harmful to the surrounding properties.
6. The general public may speak for or against the approval of rezoning.
7. An administration meeting is held, and the request is denied or approved. If denied, the applicant can request an appeal of the denial.
8. If approved, the planning board prepares the ordinance.
9. The city council generally holds three meetings (one is a public hearing), and the request is voted upon at the final hearing. If the request is denied and the city council members concur with the planning board, the applicant may appeal the decision to the district court.
10. If approved, the rezoning becomes effective.

Private Control of Land Use

As mentioned at the beginning of this chapter, private individuals also have control over real property. It is understood that the property owner must abide by the restrictions placed on the property through the zoning laws and the covenants established when the property was platted.

Grantor may restrict future use

Deed restrictions can determine how a property may be used. You can sell your property "subject to" and place a restriction that prohibits or permits a use, providing it is not inconsistent with the zoning and covenants of the area. **Covenants** are restrictions or agreements that regulate use of property (as discussed later in this chapter). The deed restriction may state that a fence will never be allowed around the property, or a farmer may sell his 80 acres and stipulate that its use always remain agricultural. If the covenants of an area are not adhered to by your neighbor, you may bring suit for loss of value to your property. The covenants may state that no wooden fences can be installed that obscure the view of another owner so a neighbor cannot install a six-foot fence that blocks your view of the lake.

Zoning protects property owners from nonconforming uses affecting value, and covenants protect each subdivision, but this does not ensure compatibility of neighbors. If covenants are violated, the surrounding neighbors need to band together to ensure conformance and resort to filing suit if the problem is not abated. A *nuisance* complaint would involve loud noises, barking dogs that interrupt sleep, or a lack of property maintenance.

Subdivision Development

Site Selection

When a subdivider wishes to divide raw land into housing sites, the site should be in a location that follows the growth of the area. The location can make the difference between the success or failure of the subdivision. It should be convenient to utilities and employment centers. The general plan should be consistent and competitive with surrounding developments.

Subdividing raw land

Before the purchase is made, it is critical that the subdivider determines that there is a sufficient demand for new housing in the area. A decision is then made concerning the market that will be targeted. Once the site is selected, the subdivider usually hires an experienced subdivision planner to develop layout concepts in conformance with current styles and trends. Environmental concerns should be considered, along with lot views and street placement.

Sometimes a subdivider will gather together two or more parcels of land to make the whole more valuable. This practice is known as **assemblage**. The value achieved by joining the parcels is referred to as *plottage* value.

The Plat

The preparation of the **plat** will include anticipating any problems and endeavoring to solve them before presenting the plat for approval to the planning board. If it is a large plat, the site will be developed in phases, and the developer may be required to dedicate land for future school or park use. The availability of public utilities will be of prime importance to the subdivider, as well as whether there is easy access to sewers, water, electricity, and gas. Since people automatically resist change, the applicant expects neighborhood opposition to the plan, so the developer should be ready with alternatives and concessions.

The subdivider must submit the proposed plat and the development plans to the city planning department. Subdivision regulations are laws enacted by a local governing body to control the conversion of bare land into building sites. This places legal control over the community's design, thus eliminating the misuse of property and protecting community values, health, and safety. The plat is reviewed by various professionals and city officials, including the planning department, city engineer, health department, utility officials, and the parks and recreation department.

Plat approval

The preliminary plat usually has areas designated for schools and parks and the required number of streets laid out. When the subdivider files the plan, he also files a declaration of covenants and restrictions for the subdivision. In the covenants, the subdivider dedicates these streets to the city (or county, if the area is outside the city limits). In addition, areas must be reserved or dedicated for public use, public utilities must be installed, and lots and blocks must be clearly specified as to size and length. Once approval of the plat is obtained, the subdivider begins construction of the subdivision improvements.

The Engineer's Role

Engineers provide professional services that assist with the development and offer constructive criticism of ideas that may not be fully formed. The engineer may point out a site's physical limitations or such limitations as imposed by governmental regulations. It is the engineer's responsibility to evaluate the proposed development, giving consideration to the atmosphere the developer wants to achieve, the type and styles of buffers from existing or future development, lot sizes, and lot spacing. The cost of public improvements, or infrastructure, is usually a major cost of the site. Reasonably detailed estimates of the cost of streets, sidewalks, utilities, sewers, and streetlights are assembled by the engineer, and any other site-related expenses, such as platting, zoning, subdividing, and grading, are also estimated for the developer. A detailed topographic study is done to determine grading and in-fill needs, boundaries are surveyed, and soil test borings may be made.

Plat certification

The final plat is certified by the engineer and the subdivider and is then recorded. The last task of the engineer is overseeing the final grading and seeding and installation and maintenance of erosion controls.

Covenants

Covenants concerning building lines, setbacks, and side yards must be stipulated in the subdivider's plan. Use restrictions are for the public good and generally relate to how the land can be best utilized and the sort of construction permissible. These covenants and restrictions will protect the purchaser's investment. The square footage required in a dwelling, the architectural design, whether outbuildings may be constructed, or whether one- or two-car garages are required are examples of restrictions placed in covenants. Restrictive covenants remain in effect for specific time periods—for example, for 10 years, 20 years, or in perpetuity. Local zoning regulations and restrictive covenants filed with the plat plan for a particular subdivision regulate the distance from the perimeter of the property that a building may be erected. Referred to as a *setback,* this applies to front, side, and rear yards.

Protection for property owners

The Builder's Role

Building permits

The builder reviews three basic documents: the plans and specifications, the site plan, and the elevations and plan views. Upon approval of the plans by the city, a building permit is granted. A survey of the lot is made by a surveyor, and iron stakes are imbedded in the ground at each corner of the lot since it is vital that the boundary lines are accurate before construction commences. The builder will use a transit to stake out the exact location of the house on the lot. Consideration is given to surface drainage, the required slope of the sewer line, and if a view is preferable in one direction as opposed to another. Each phase of the construction, from the initial digging of the foundation to the exterior paint, is carefully monitored by the general contractor.

Building Codes

Building permits are required each time a contractor starts to construct a building, thus ensuring compliance with the zoning ordinances and building codes. The city is most concerned that code requirements are met for electrical and sanitary systems and fire and safety standards. As phases of the building are completed, inspectors will check to be certain that code standards are being followed. Upon completion, a final inspection is made and a certificate of occupancy is issued prior to the dwelling being occupied. If the inspection reveals any flaws in the construction, the contractor must bring the building up to code.

Permits are also required to remodel an existing structure or even to erect a fence. The building must not violate a covenant or deed restriction of the area, or the contractor will be stopped in midconstruction. It is the responsibility of neighboring homeowners to enforce their covenants.

Lot Variations

New lot variations have become popular in some areas of the country. Greater density can be achieved by clustering homes. **Cluster lots** are usually only half the size of conventional house lots; however, they can provide as much privacy and green space as the normal lots. Instead of breaking up the areas into front, side, and rear yards, the aggregate of all the yards is molded into one open space around the homes, preserving natural features and thus providing less environmental disturbance. With proper design and variance in roof and window placements, visual and noise barriers will exist between the homes, maintaining residential character and privacy. Because the structures are clustered, the developer can pass the savings of fewer sidewalks and utility connections on to the purchasers. There is a perception of safety since through traffic is lessened.

Zero lot line is another concept in lot use whereby single-family homes are built on the lot line, with the owner having an easement, usually five feet, on the neighbor's lot so that access for painting or repairs is available. This saves land since the owner has just one side yard, which is more usable than two small side yards (see Figure 4.1).

Figure 4.1   Normal and Zero Lot Lines

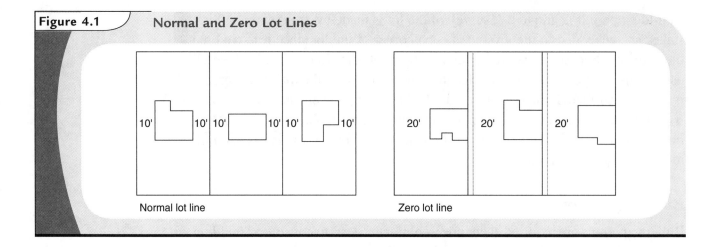

Normal lot line

Zero lot line

Planned Unit Developments

A **planned unit development (PUD)** shares many of the same characteristics as a cluster housing development. PUDs can be small developments planned to accommodate the clustering of houses on smaller lots, or they can be large platted areas that set aside sites for retail shops, parks, and hiking trails for a total planned community that includes single-family homes, apartments, and condominiums or cooperatives. A PUD offers a compact community extending many conveniences to its residents.

The development plan must be platted, detailing the various uses the site will have and the acres involved in each use. A timetable for construction completion of each phase will be stated, and if the development will cause traffic congestion, the applicant may be required to share in the cost of expanding the streets. Design considerations should include adequate parking and landscaping to create privacy.

Easements

An **easement** is the right-of-way through the land of another, referred to as the right of ingress and egress (entering and leaving) over another's land.

Creation of an Easement

An easement may be created by law, by people, or by use. Because an easement represents an interest in another's land, the grant must be in writing to conform with the statute of frauds. Easements may be found on almost all subdivided land, and a deed states whether property is subject to "easements of record." The covenants outline the easements that go with the property.

An easement is classified as either an **easement appurtenant** or an **easement in gross**.

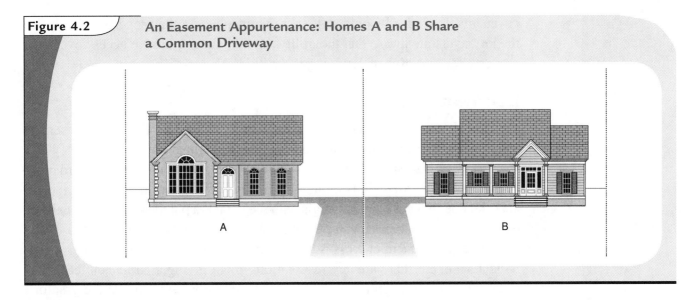

Figure 4.2 An Easement Appurtenance: Homes A and B Share a Common Driveway

Easement Appurtenant

An easement appurtenant, which accompanies a piece of land, is the right one party has to the use of the adjacent owners' land. Two parties are always involved and the two pieces of land must be adjacent and owned by separate individuals for an appurtenant easement to exist. If one party buys the property adjoining their property, the easement is automatically canceled as the need for it no longer exists. Examples of an easement appurtenant include shared driveways, party walls, or the right of passage through an adjoining property. In Figure 4.2, A and B share a common driveway; thus, each has the right to use the adjoining land of the other.

The party who receives the easement acquires a benefit or gain over the other and is referred to as the **dominant tenant**. The **servient tenant** gives the easement, thus is "serving" the other party and the easement is an *encumbrance* on the servient tenant's property. Most easements appurtenant are specifically written in the deed or by express written contract. If the servient tenant (giver of the easement) sells the property, the easement transfers with the property unless the dominant tenant (receiver of the easement) agrees to cancel the easement.

Owner A has a large section of land and splits the property, selling a portion to B. Owner A may reserve the right to use part of the property sold as another means of access to the remaining property. This is an example of an *easement by reservation.* Owner A has *reserved or retained this right of access.* It is written, permitting owner A to trespass over owner B's land. The easement created will transfer with the land in the event that owner A decides to sell the balance of the land. It is not necessary to be landlocked to have such an easement.

When owner A above granted the parcel of land to owner B the reverse could have occurred. If owner A gave owner B an easement over owner A's land it would be an example of an *easement by grant.* A developer of a subdivision gives an easement by grant to utilities, and this easement is stipulated in the covenants. Each deed would state that easements over the property exist so that the lot buyers are aware that the utility would have reasonable access over their property for purposes of servicing the utilities.

Easement in Gross

An easement in gross may be personal or commercial. Unlike an easement appurtenant, there is a servient tenant but not a dominant tenant.

A *personal easement* in gross cannot be mortgaged or assigned to a third party. The individual's easement is limited to the holders' lifetime, thus it is not inheritable and does not automatically pass with the land. If a purchaser wants an existing easement in gross to pass with title, it is necessary to state this in the deed.

Since an easement in gross is for an individual's lifetime, a landowner should issue a **license** if there are any reservations about giving a permanent easement to the other person. Unlike an easement, a license is revocable at the grantor's option, is not transferable to another, and is not assigned upon sale of the property. Generally a license is not issued in writing but is simply an oral agreement between the parties.

A *commercial easement* usually is held by a utility company or an agency of the government. Examples include gas, water, sewer, power lines, pipelines, and telephone lines. The holder of the easement has no interest in the land except the right of use. A utility company's right allows the utility access to its lines for purpose of repair. The utility holds the right to assign the use to another, such as a cable television company to place cable TV lines in telephone easements. See Figure 4.3.

Easements of Necessity and Other Easements

Dominant and servient tenants

An *easement of necessity* arises when there is a special need, as in the case of a landlocked owner. For example, in Figure 4.4, X sold the back portion of her land to Y, and an easement was necessary for Y to get to his land. The *dominant*

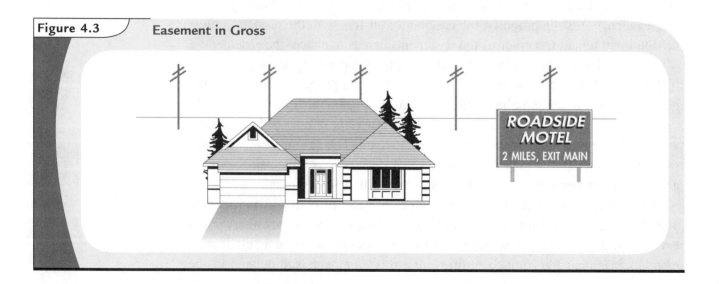

Figure 4.3   **Easement in Gross**

ROADSIDE MOTEL
2 MILES, EXIT MAIN

Figure 4.4   Easement of Necessity: Owner X Sold the Back Part of Her Land to Y, Making an Easement Necessary for Y to Get to His Land

tenant (Y) receives the easement, and the *servient tenant* (X) gives the easement. Easements granted by one party to another cannot be rescinded by the owner of the land. The land in this example has no other access, and since a purchaser cannot be landlocked, the easement was mandatory.

If a servient tenant allows the dominant tenant to remove minerals or soils from the land, it is called *profit a prendre*. These rights may be extended to just the one dominant tenant, or they may be assignable to a future owner of the land.

An *easement by prescription* is the right acquired through long-term, continuous use of another's property. This use must be in an adverse manner, that is, without the consent of the owner.

Party wall easements exist between two owners when a common wall built on the lot line separates two structures, as in row houses or condominiums. Each owner has the responsibility to maintain his side of the wall, which cannot be removed or changed without approval of both, and each has an easement on the other owner's side. Party wall easements may also exist when a fence separates the boundaries of two properties.

Termination of an Easement

An easement may be terminated when the reason for the easement no longer exists. The following examples generate the termination of an easement.

1. If an easement by prescription is abandoned by the easement owner, the easement will expire.
2. An appurtenant easement will cease to exist if the property of the dominant and servient tenant is merged.

3. If the dominant tenant releases the easement right back to the servient owner, it ceases.

4. Upon the filing of a suit to quiet title opposing a person with a claim to an easement, the easement may be rescinded.

5. If a public road is built to a property that needed an easement of necessity, the easement will no longer be necessary.

Encroachment

An **encroachment** exists when one owner's property infringes onto another's land. Examples of common encroachments include fences carelessly erected on neighboring land or driveways and patios extending onto the adjoining property. Tree branches or shrubbery hanging over the property line can create an encroachment.

Since encroachments are generally not covered by title insurance, it is important for a purchaser to have a survey if there is any doubt concerning the accuracy of the boundaries. If the encroachment has existed long enough, an easement by prescription may be in effect or even a claim to the title by adverse possession.

Summary of Important Points

1. While ownership of real estate legally gives one a bundle of rights that extends below the earth's surface and into the sky, the use of land is controlled by various units of government.

2. A broad outlook to future development must be considered, and a general master plan laid out for streets, public transportation, park areas, and utility services. Keeping controls over land within a one- to three-mile radius of the city further assists in regulating land use.

3. The zoning ordinances established by local governments also regulate land use.

4. Plans and specifications must be presented to the planning board before a building permit is issued so that enforcement of the ordinances is ensured.

5. Private control over land is exercised by subdividers, who establish the covenants and restrictions for their developments. The surrounding owners may enforce these restrictions if a violation occurs.

6. An easement is a right-of-way or interest in the land of another. Common easements include shared driveways and party walls.

7. Any protrusion over a property line is an encroachment and can be discovered by survey. Encroachments are not covered by title insurance and should thus be carefully checked by a prospective purchaser.

Discussion Points

1. Why is a master plan for a city necessary?
2. Differentiate between platting a subdivision into conventional lots, cluster lots, and zero lot lines.
3. Explain the difference between a nonconforming use and a variance.
4. What is the purpose of a planned unit development? Do you have any in your city?
5. How does an easement in gross differ from an easement appurtenant?

Review Questions

Answers to these questions are found in the Answer Key section at the back of the book.

1. To the owner of the land it runs across, an easement is:
   a. an appurtenance
   b. an encumbrance
   c. a common interest
   d. an attachment

2. Zoning laws are the utilization of a governing body's:
   a. police power
   b. power of eminent domain
   c. escheat
   d. license laws

3. A use not in compliance with present zoning, but legal when it was enacted is called a(n):
   a. variance
   b. spot zoning use
   c. nonconforming use
   d. encroachment

4. The gathering together of two or more parcels to make the whole more valuable is a(n):
   a. easement
   b. appurtenance
   c. subdivision
   d. assemblage

5. If there is a party wall between two lots, which of the following is NOT true?
   a. each person must be responsible for its maintenance
   b. each person owns a common interest in the wall
   c. the neighborhood association will be responsible for any repairs
   d. it is placed on the lot line

6. Ingress and egress make reference to:
   a. appurtenance
   b. an easement
   c. subservience
   d. police power

7. Which of the following restricts the use of land?
   a. townships
   b. monuments
   c. surveys
   d. covenants

8. Communities regulate the use of land by means of:
   a. controlling the population
   b. exercising zoning laws
   c. buying and selling land themselves
   d. annexing nearby towns

9. Mr. Jones's good friend, Charlie Smith, lives next door and uses a portion of Jones's land as a driveway. As much as Jones likes his friend, he does not want to grant him the use of the land in perpetuity. Since he wants to retain the privilege of reviewing the situation on a regular basis, Jones should grant his friend:
   a. a license
   b. an easement
   c. an easement appurtenance
   d. a permit

10. All of the following are established by the private sector EXCEPT:
    a. building styles
    b. restrictive covenants
    c. subdivision plats
    d. building codes

11. The governmental regulations that most affect the value of real property are:
    a. zoning ordinances
    b. covenants of deed restrictions
    c. laws of escheat
    d. Federal Housing Administration regulations

12. The police power of a city is used to enforce all of the following EXCEPT:
    a. building codes
    b. zoning restrictions
    c. deed restrictions
    d. subdivision regulations

13. The government of a municipality holds control over real property through all of the following EXCEPT:
    a. taxation
    b. assessments
    c. encumbrance
    d. eminent domain

14. Which of the following is an example of an easement appurtenance?
    a. a shared driveway
    b. a power line
    c. sewer system
    d. view

15. A gas station was built in 1980 in an area that was rezoned to residential in 2008. The gas station constitutes:
    a. a variance
    b. a nonconforming use
    c. spot zoning
    d. a violation

16. The separating of two incompatible zoning districts from each other is referred to as:
    a. a variance
    b. a buffer zone
    c. a nonconforming use
    d. a zero lot line concept

17. A building complied with the zoning laws except for the setback. The owners need to request:
    a. spot zoning
    b. a variance
    c. a nonconforming use
    d. a compliance

18. To increase open space and conserve land, a developer will group lots together by:
    a. deed restrictions
    b. placing cul de sacs in the plat
    c. clustering
    d. building apartments

19. The Interstate Land Sales Full Disclosure Act protects the public by all of the following EXCEPT:
    a. the out-of-state subdivision containing 25 or more lots must be registered
    b. a report is given to the customer three days prior to the signing of the contract
    c. lots cannot be sold to a developer
    d. disclosure of the land and plans for its sale must be presented to a buyer

20. The planned unit development (PUD) provides all of the following EXCEPT:
    a. permitting mixed uses and density
    b. requiring single-family housing lots
    c. allowing for open spaces
    d. offering residents a variety of nearby shops and recreational facilities

21. The party who receives an easement acquires a benefit and is referred to as:
    a. the servient tenant
    b. the dominant tenant
    c. an encumbrance to the dominant tenant
    d. holder of a license

22. The roof of a building protrudes over a public alley. This is an example of:
    a. an easement
    b. an encroachment
    c. escheat
    d. adverse possession

Estates, Interests, Deeds, and Title

KEY TERMS

acknowledgment	grantor
community property	habendum clause
consideration	homestead
co-ownership	joint tenancy
curtesy	legal life estate
deed	life estate
dower	nonfreehold estate
estate	recordation
fee simple	remainderman
fee simple absolute	reversion
fee simple defeasible	severalty ownership
fee simple determinable	tenancy by the entireties
fee simple to a condition subsequent	tenancy in common
	title
freehold estate	warranty deed
grantee	

OVERVIEW

An **estate** in land determines the legally recognized interest the person has in the real property. There are two main types of estates in real estate: freehold and nonfreehold, also referred to as less than freehold.

This chapter covers the quantity and the quality of estates the holder may possess. The contents of a deed and conveying of title by various types of deeds are explained. Alternate means of holding title and legal life estates complete the chapter.

Freehold Estates

A **freehold estate** is ownership for an indefinite duration. The term *freehold*, passed down from English common law, means that any interest held in land is uncertain; thus, the length of time a freehold estate will exist cannot be predetermined. Freehold estates include *fee simple, fee simple defeasible,* and *life estates.* The freehold estates may be an *estate of inheritance,* giving the holder the right to pass the real property on to the owner's heirs; or a *not of inheritance freehold estate,* which does not carry the right to will property but is only for the duration of the owner's life.

Fee simple absolute

Fee simple absolute is the most complete type of estate, giving the estate holder complete rights to the land with absolute ownership. The owner of an estate in **fee simple** title can sell it, will it, give it away, or retain possession for as long as the person desires. While the estate is subject to governmental and land use restrictions, the owner has the most power over the land that may be acquired in real estate.

Fee simple defeasible

There are two types of **fee simple defeasible** (qualified fee) estates. The **fee simple determinable**, or conditional, limits the estate holder to the terms set forth by the grantor. A parent may deed property to a child with the stipulation that it can never be sold, but must be passed down to the next generation (a fee tail). Land may be given to the city for a park on the condition that it never be used for any other purpose. The deed will specifically make reference to the fact that the estate is conditional "as long as" the land is used for the purpose stated and the grantor has "qualified" the estate being granted. If the city vacates the property as a park, deciding instead to use it for a parking lot, the land will revert to the original grantor, the grantor's heirs, or a **reversioner** named by the grantor. That person holds a future or contingent interest in the property. While the holder of a fee simple determinable has fee simple title, the holder is limited by the conditions set forth by the grantor.

Fee simple to a condition subsequent

The **fee simple to a condition subsequent** gives the same possession and use rights as the fee simple determinable. However, when the fee simple is subject to a condition subsequent, the original grantor must take action to reenter the property and gain possession if the condition has been broken, as in the city abandoning the property as a park. If the grantor does not take action to regain the property, the fee simple subject to a condition subsequent will continue even though the terms have been broken.

To summarize, the basic variance of the condition subsequent is that the violation of the conveyance must have occurred, and the original owners must go to court and demand return of the property, whereas the fee simple determinable terminates ownership, and the property automatically reverts to the remainderman (see below).

WEB SITE

www.law.cornell.edu/
topics/
realproperty.html

Life Estates

A **life estate** is granted by an owner through a will or deed or by operation of law without the owner's consent. A **legal life estate** that is created by law, such as dower, curtesy, or homestead (see later), is not recognized in all states. Two conventional forms of a life estate may be granted by the holder of the estate: (1) an ordinary life estate measured by the life of the recipient (life tenant) or (2) a life estate measured by the life of another *(pur autre vie)*. In the latter type of life estate, the estate held by A would be determined by the life of B.

The estate holder, referred to as a life tenant, loses all rights to the estate upon death. During his life, while the estate is in effect, the life tenant has the right of use, possession, enjoyment, and income. The life tenant is responsible to maintain the property in reasonable repair and to pay property taxes. The life tenant can do nothing to diminish the value of the real estate, which is referred to as laying waste to the property. Nor can the life tenant change the use of the property; a farm could not be subdivided into housing lots or dug up for a gravel pit. While the life tenant may lease the property, all leases will automatically be canceled upon the death of the life tenant. Similarly, while the property may be mortgaged, the mortgage would terminate upon the life tenant's death. The mortgagee would thus want the protection of being named beneficiary of a term life insurance policy on the property or the cosignature of the remainderman on the mortgage note. The life tenant may sell the property, the grantee receiving only the rights of the holder. The remainderman could also sell his interest, which would be subject to the life tenant's interest. The purchaser would not come into possession until the life tenant's death. If the remainderman and the life tenant both convey their interests, the grantee would receive fee simple title. Since the life estate ceases to exist upon the death of a named party or parties, it cannot be bequeathed. (See Figure 5.1.)

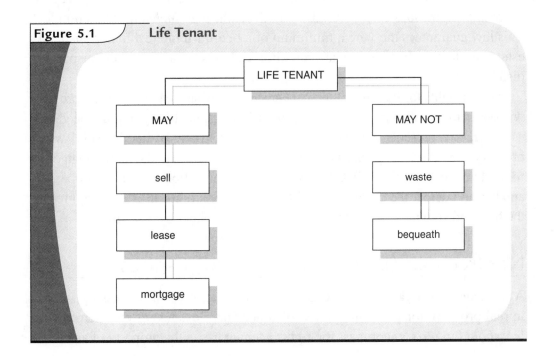

Figure 5.1   Life Tenant

Future Interests in Life Estates

Remainderman

Future interest consists of two basic types: **remainderman** and **reversion**. The grantor of the life estate makes provisions for the property upon the life tenant's death by either naming a remainderman or creating a reversionary interest. The remainderman is the person named in the establishment of the life estate to succeed to the property. For example, Jones gives an estate to his wife for her life; upon her death, the remainder estate goes to his brother. Jones has given a life estate to his wife and to his brother a future interest, a remainder or nonpossessory estate. These ordinary life estates are conventional, unlike the legal estates of dower, curtesy, and homestead rights, which are created by statute.

Reversionary interest

A reversionary interest would revert at some future time to the grantor or the grantor's heirs. If Jones does not name his brother (or anyone else) as remainderman, upon the death of his wife, the estate will revert to Jones. If Jones is not living, it will pass to his devisee as stated in his will or to his heirs if no will is left. This is referred to as a reversionary interest.

Legal Life Estates

As stated earlier, legal life estates are established by statute and include dower, curtesy, and homestead as a result of marriage. While many states have abolished dower and curtesy rights and have initiated statutory laws as substitutions, other states still maintain many features of old English common law. The underlying reason for curtesy and dower rights is to legally protect property rights of a surviving spouse. There is an old expression, "one to buy, two to sell," meaning both parties must release their rights.

Inchoate rights

Dower is the right a wife has to her husband's estate at the time of his death. Since this right does not materialize until death, it is *inchoate* or incomplete. This law guarantees the wife a minimum of a one-third interest in her husband's estate, protecting her against any creditor's claims or acts by her husband to disinherit her.

Dower rights further protect the wife since the husband cannot sell real property without her consent. The wife must relinquish her rights by signing the deed.

Curtesy represents the husband's life interest in any of his deceased wife's property. However, many states require that a child be born to the marriage in order for curtesy rights to take effect. The wife also has the option to will her property to another and defeat the curtesy rights. As with dower rights, all states require that the husband sign any deed affecting title to property held by the wife.

Nonfreehold (Less Than Freehold) Estates

Leasehold interests

A **nonfreehold estate**, or less than freehold estate, gives a possessory interest in real property for a definite period of time. These estates, often referred to as *leasehold interests*, encompass the rights a tenant has in the property of an owner.

Generally conveyed by contract, they include an *estate for years, periodic estate, estate at will,* and a *tenancy at sufferance.* A leased fee estate gives the rights of occupancy to the lessee (tenant) with the lessor (landlord) retaining title. At the expiration of the lease, the lessor regains possession. Less than freehold estates will be covered in detail in Chapter 14.

The Deed

After becoming aware of the estate that is granted in real property, it is important to understand the document that transfers title to that estate.

Title (evidence of ownership) is acquired by transferring the property to the new owner with a written instrument known as a **deed**. The deed conveys the grantor's interest in the real property to the grantee. Thus:

Conveying title

1. The deed gives tangible proof of title conveying the property from the grantor to the grantee.
2. Title declares the quality of the estate as defined in the deed. Title is actually an intangible thing.
3. Estate defines the quantity and refers to the amount the grantor is deeding to the grantee.

The DEED is proof that the person has TITLE, and the title defines the quality (value) of the ESTATE.

DEED gives proof of TITLE which represents quality of the ESTATE.

This means of conveying ownership of land has been in existence for many years. Prior to this, it was customary to merely go out on the land and pass a handful of soil or break a twig and shake hands. By this basic ritualistic action the land was transferred. This act was referred to as *livery of seizin,* which simply means "transfer of possession." Today, the **grantor**, *the seller* of real property, conveys title to the **grantee**, the *purchaser,* by means of a written document that is the deed.

Livery of seizin

A deed must be properly executed, delivered, and accepted for title to pass. According to statutes in most states, the deed must be in writing. The deed is *executed* (signed) only by the grantor(s).

A *corporation* may hold title to real property. When it sells the property, the deed will contain the name of the designated officer who signs on behalf of the corporation. In many states, the corporate seal is required on the deed. A partnership may also hold title to real property. The title is in the name of one of the general partners, or a trustee.

Corporations and partnerships often have a fictitious name, but this does not preclude them from holding title in the name of their enterprise. Title can be held in an assumed name, provided that the person or enterprise is truly in existence.

Acknowledgment

Signatures are notarized

Most states require that the grantor's signature be **acknowledged** (sworn to under oath) for it to be recorded. In many states the grantor is required to sign the deed in the presence of a witness and a notary public, agreeing that this is a voluntary act and deed. The notary public attests to the fact that the signatures are genuine by placing his seal and signature on the deed. Note that the notary is attesting to the *validity* of the signatures, not the document, and should request identification from the person signing the document. The notary public has been appointed by the secretary of state to administer oaths and witness signatures. Others authorized to validate signatures may include judges, justices of the peace, and all officers in the military service. Many real estate brokers and salespersons obtain a notary commission so that they can witness documents as a service to their clients and customers.

Delivery and Acceptance

It is necessary to establish that the deed has been *delivered and accepted* for title to pass. This delivery must be made by the grantor. For an owner to place a deed in a safety deposit box with the intention that title pass after the owner's death is not allowable; the deed must be delivered within the grantor's lifetime. A third party, such as a real estate agent, an escrow agent, or an attorney who represents the grantee, may accept the deed, and delivery is presumed. In most states, delivery to a third party must be acceptable to the grantee.

Recordation

Constructive notice

The purpose of recording any instrument is to give constructive notice to the world of the transaction. State laws require mandatory **recordation** of liens against a property and assessments against real property for public improvements, divorce decrees, and unpaid taxes. However, recording a deed or any document that affects ownership in land is not compulsory in most states, but is a right of the holder. If such documents are recorded, the "chain of title" continues on record. Normally, purchasers will want the deed recorded to protect their interests in the event the deed is misplaced. Prompt recording protects the owner if someone later tries to claim title.

Chain of title

Recording is usually performed at the county office in which the property is located. A fee based upon the nature of the document and the number of pages is collected on every instrument recorded. The document must be the original. The recorder will endorse in the instrument the correct filing number and the exact time at which the document was filed, including the year, month, day, hour, and minute that it was received. The contents of the document are then transferred in writing to the appropriate book of records, and the original instrument is returned to the person who left it to be recorded. Thus, anyone desiring to look up information regarding a particular piece of property may do so by visiting the county courthouse where the document was recorded. If the deed is lost or burned in a fire, its destruction will not affect the owner's title since it is now recorded in the public records.

Actual notice refers to having actual knowledge of who holds ownership of a property. If a deed was not recorded but a second buyer had knowledge that a sale took place, the party would not have a valid claim to the property. While possession of the property gives actual notice, a prudent buyer will give constructive notice by recording the deed, since it affords the owner absolute protection from anyone else claiming ownership.

Actual notice

Contents

A deed must contain certain elements, including the following:

1. competent parties, usually identified with names and addresses
2. consideration (something of value)
3. words of conveyance (granting clause)
4. description of the real estate
5. restrictions
6. the quantities or quality of the interest being conveyed (**habendum clause**)
7. signatures of the grantors

The parties to the deed consist of the **grantor**, who is conveying title to the real property (Figure 5.2, number 1) and the **grantee**, the person who is receiving title to the real property (Figure 5.2, number 4). As in any legal contract, the parties involved must be *competent* and capable of entering into a contract. Minors or persons adjudged insane are considered legally incompetent, and the deed could be voided by the incompetent. If a grantee is determined to be mentally incapable of decision making, the deed may be revoked by the grantee. If it appears that a grantor is under undue influence of another, the courts will request the grantee to correct the situation as it exists. Such a situation may occur between a child and an elderly parent. However, legal capacity can exist regardless of age or eccentric behavior. With court consent, a minor or a person judged incompetent can receive and/or transfer real estate by the appointment of a guardian or trustee who executes the document for the minor or incompetent.

Competent parties

The **consideration**, or the price paid for the property, must be recited on all deeds (see Figure 5.2, number 2). Even a token amount may be stated, such as, "One dollar ($1.00) and other valuable consideration." If the property is being conveyed as a gift, the simple phrase, "for love and affection," may be used in some states. The full consideration must be stated if the transfer is by order of the court or if the deed is from a trustee or a corporation.

Consideration

The *words of conveyance* are the words that expressly grant the title to the grantee, and are contained in the granting clause. Various kinds of deeds will state the granting clause differently, but all must express the grantor's intention to convey the property

Words of conveyance

Figure 5.2   General Warranty Deed

WARRANTY DEED, VESTING ENTIRE TITLE IN SURVIVOR

KNOW ALL MEN BY THESE PRESENTS, That   OMAHA PRINTING COMPANY

       Harvey J. Wender and Della J. Wender, husband and wife, **1**

in consideration of One Hundred Eighty Four Thousand and no/100 ($184,000.00)-----**2**-----
DOLLARS in hand paid, do hereby grant, bargain, sell, convey and confirm unto **3**

       Kyle A. Albright and Judy A. Albright, husband and wife **4**

as **JOINT TENANTS,** and not as tenants in common; the following described real estate, situate in the County of
      Kent   and State of   to-wit:

      Lot Eight (8), Block One (1), in Confusion Hill
      subdivision, an Addition to Any City, Kent   **5**
      County, USA, as surveyed, platted and recorded.

      STATE
      DOCUMENTARY **6**
      STAMPS
      $276.00

together with all the tenements, hereditaments, and appurtenances to the same belonging, and all the estate, title, dower, right of homestead, claim or demand whatsoever of the said grantors   , of, in or to the same, or any part thereof, subject to covenants, restrictions and easements of record, all regular taxes and subsequent taxes and assessments. **7**

     IT BEING THE INTENTION OF ALL PARTIES HERETO, THAT IN THE EVENT OF THE DEATH OF EITHER OF SAID GRANTEES, THE ENTIRE FEE SIMPLE TITLE TO THE REAL ESTATE DESCRIBED HEREIN SHALL VEST IN THE SURVIVING GRANTEE. 8

     TO HAVE AND TO HOLD the above described premises, with the appurtenances, unto the said grantees as **JOINT TENANTS,** and not as tenants in common, and to their assigns, or to the heirs and assigns of the survivor of them, forever, and we the grantors named herein for ourselves **9** and our heirs, executors, and administrators, do covenant with the grantees named herein and with their assigns and with the heirs and assigns of the survivor of them, that we are lawfully seized of said premises; that they are free from incumbrance except as stated herein, and that we the said grantors have good right and lawful authority to sell the same, and that we will and our heirs, executors and administrators shall warrant and defend the same unto the grantees named herein and unto their assigns and unto the heirs and assigns of the survivor of them, forever, against the lawful claims of all persons whomsoever, excluding the exceptions named herein.

     IN WITNESS WHEREOF we have hereunto set our hands this 14th day of
     May   A. D., **2008**   _Harvey J. Wender_
      In presence of   (Harvey J. Wender)
     Judy M. Selling   **11**   _Della J. Wender_   **10**
                           (Della J. Wender)

STATE OF
County of Kent   } ss.   On this 14th day of May
A. D. 2008 , before me, a Notary Public in and for said County, personally came the above named
     Harvey I. Wender and Della I. Wender, husband and wife

12 who are personally known to me to be the identical persons whose names affixed to the above instrument as grantors , and they have acknowledged said instrument to be their voluntary act and deed.
     WITNESS my hand and Notarial Seal the date last aforesaid.

   SEAL   _Judy M. Selling_ Notary Public.
My commission expires on the 8th day of July A. D., 2011

(see Figure 5.2, number 3). The grantee(s) name(s) will follow the granting clause and will spell out their relationship. In the **warranty deed** (see Figure 5.2, number 4) Kyle A. and Judy A. Albright, husband and wife, are taking title. If Kyle Albright was taking title by himself, the deed would state: Kyle Albright, a married man.

The specific rights of the grantees are recited after their names. In the example shown, the Albrights are taking title as joint tenants, vesting their entire rights in the survivor. This is a very important phrase in any deed since it determines the rights of the survivor should one of the parties die.

The *description* of the property must be sufficient to identify the real estate. In most states the legal description, citing the lot, block, and subdivision, is preferred (see Figure 5.2, number 5).

Description

Restrictions may be written into the deed such as, "subject to real estate taxes and subsequent assessments" (see Figure 5.2, number 7). If the grantee is assuming an existing mortgage, it would also be recited in the "subject to" section of the deed. Generally, the phrase "subject to easements and restrictions of record" does not recite what these easements and restrictions may be. The subdivider filed the covenants and restrictions that relate to the subdivision, and so the deed merely refers to this fact. The grantor may place further restrictions in the deed limiting the use of the property.

Restrictions

The *qualities and quantity of the interest* being conveyed by the grantor will be shown in the deed. In the warranty deed, the grantors warrant the title through themselves, their heirs, and even their predecessors. The clause specifies that there are no liens on the property except as shown in section 7 and that upon signing the deed the grantors give up any present or future claim to the property (see Figure 5.2, number 9). However, when a grantor conveys title with a quitclaim deed, no warranties are given.

Quality and quantity of interest

The *signatures of the grantors* (see Figure 5.2, number 10) must also appear on all deeds. All the owners of the property must execute the instrument. In most states, if a married person holds title alone, the spouse must still sign the deed to extinguish any rights to the property. If a grantor cannot write, the grantor must place an "X" for his mark in the presence of witnesses. If the property is owned by a corporation, the deed is signed by its authorized officer(s), and the corporate seal is placed on the deed.

Signatures

The deed illustrated in Figure 5.2 is a warranty deed, vesting entire title to the grantee. This deed is for joint tenancy ownership, which will be explained under "Types of deeds" in this chapter. The numbers on the deed designate the following.

1. The sellers' names appear conveying the property. Their names must be exactly as they appeared when they took title. The marital status of the grantors is stated as well.

2. The amount the real estate is selling for. While we have used the actual amount, in some states it is legal to merely put a token amount such as, "$1.00 and other valuable consideration."

3. The clause of conveyance must be present in all deeds. This deed states that the seller will "grant, bargain, sell, convey and confirm" the property to the buyer.

4. The buyers' names, along with their marital status.

5. The complete legal description of the property.

6. Tax stamps affixed or evidence of payment made (in states where a transfer fee is required).

7. This paragraph enumerates any limitations that exist in the conveyance of the property and includes the loan assumption clause if a loan is being assumed.

8. This is the joint tenancy clause, vesting entire rights in the survivor.

9. The **habendum clause** defines the quantity of the estate being granted to the grantees and is referred to as the "to have and to hold" clause.

10. Signatures of the grantors—exactly as shown at number 1.

11. Signature of witness (not needed in all states).

12. The acknowledgment of the document by the notary public. In this instance, the real estate agent was a notary public, and so she witnessed the owners' signatures to the deed. Some people feel that it is best to have some other disinterested party do this.

Conveyance Fee (Real Estate Transfer Tax)

Title transfer tax

When title to real property is transferred, the state may collect a sales tax on the transfer of the property. The cost of this transfer tax varies from state to state, with some states charging no revenue upon the sale of real estate. Generally, this transfer fee is paid by the grantor, and the amount is stamped on the deed by the registrar of deeds at the time the instrument is recorded. For example, if the tax is based on the rate of $1.50 per $1,000 or any part thereof and a property sells for $100,000, the state would collect $150. If a property sold for $105,000, it would be necessary to add another $7.50 to the $150.00. In the deed shown in Figure 5.2, the purchase price of the property was $184,000. At the rate of $1.50 per $1,000, the grantors would pay a sales tax of $276.00 (see number 6).

Types of Deeds

The following deeds are the most commonly used:

General Warranty Deed

Guarantees title

The *general warranty deed* conveys the highest and most complete ownership in real estate. The grantors of a general warranty deed guarantee the title against the whole world. They are telling the grantee that it is free and clear of all liens and that they are relinquishing all rights through themselves, their heirs, and even their predecessors. A sample of a warranty deed is shown in Figure 5.2. The warranties that a grantor conveys in a general warranty deed include the following.

1. *Covenant of seizin:* The grantors declare they are in full possession of the interests granted.

2. *Quiet enjoyment:* No one with a prior title will evict the grantee.

3. *Freedom from encumbrances:* There will be no liens, physical encumbrances, or unpaid taxes on the interest deeded unless specifically noted in the deed. (For example, a grantee might agree to assume an existing mortgage.) Title defects warranted against in addition to liens and unpaid taxes include mortgages, assessments, dower rights, and leases. Physical defects would include easements, building restrictions, fences, and encroachments.

4. *Further assurances:* Insures good title and, should any faults be found in the deed, the grantor will correct them.

5. *Right to convey:* Guarantees possession and title; states the grantor has the authority to pass title.

6. *Covenant of warranty:* The grantor will indemnify the grantee for any loss that may occur due to a defect in the title.

Special Warranty Deed

In the *special warranty deed* the grantors guarantee the title through themselves and their heirs, but not their predecessors. Basically, the grantors are giving the same guarantee as in a general warranty deed, but they are covering only the time they owned interest in the property. The grantors further warrant that they have not encumbered the property. The period of time covered represents the only difference from a general warranty deed. This form is most used by corporations because of limitations that are placed on them. Some states use the special warranty deed in lieu of a general warranty.

Guarantees title since owners held title

Grant Deed

A *grant deed* contains warranties as in a warranty deed, but they are created by the grantors themselves. The grantors imply that they own title and that they have not previously conveyed the real property to another. The warranty includes encumbrances made while the grantors owned it, but not those made during another's ownership. As in the special warranty deed, the grantors warrant only for their time of ownership.

Implies warranty

Bargain and Sale Deed

A *bargain and sale deed* is similar to the quitclaim deed in that it contains no warranties. However, in this deed the grantors do acknowledge that they have an interest in the real property. The grantees must have the title searched to be absolutely certain that they are receiving a good and marketable title.

Contains no warranties— implies grantor holds title and is in possession

The words of conveyance usually will state "grant, bargain, and sell" or "grant and release," implying that the grantor holds title to the property. If the deed contains covenants against the grantor's acts (which can be added to the deed), it has the same validity as a special warranty deed.

Quitclaim Deed

No warranties given by grantor

The *quitclaim deed* gives no warranties to the grantee. The grantors may not have clear title and may be conveying only the interest they have in the property. The grantors "quit their claim," and the grantee receives whatever interest the grantors have. This deed is often used to remove a *cloud on the title,* which is a partial interest in real property. It is also used to correct defects in a title, such as an incorrect description or an error in the spelling of a grantor's name.

Deed of Trust

Deed of trust secures payment of a debt

A *deed of trust* is not merely a deed but is a deed to secure payment of a debt. Not only does it convey title, but it is held in trust by a third disinterested party for the benefit of the lender and is sometimes referred to as a *trust deed.* When the terms of this deed are satisfied by the repayment of the debt, title is conveyed to the borrower by a deed of reconveyance. Further explanation of this type of deed can be found in Chapter 11 on financing, since the main function of a deed of trust is to secure a note.

Gift Deed

A *gift deed* is used to donate real property. Since all deeds must state a valuable consideration, a gift deed may simply state "for $1.00 and other valuable consideration" or the donor may substitute the words "for love and affection." Any type of deed may be used, but a deed such as a quitclaim deed would not bind the grantor to any warranties.

Deed of Surrender

A *deed of surrender* is sometimes used in place of a quitclaim deed to convey the interest of a life tenant or remainderman.

Deed of Release

A *deed of release* is issued when a mortgage is paid in full, thus clearing the title from the debt.

Correction Deed

A *correction deed* (sometimes referred to as a reformation deed or a deed of confirmation) is used to correct an error, such as a mistake in the spelling of a name, an inaccuracy in the legal description of a property, or some omission. The grantors must correct the mistake if they gave a covenant of further assurances (as with a warranty deed). The correction deed must conform to the requirements of a legal document; usually a quitclaim deed is used.

Cession Deed

A *cession deed* is given by the subdivider when dedicating the streets in the subdivision to the county or city. All street rights (and the obligation of maintenance) are transferred to the appropriate unit of government.

Special Purpose Deeds

Special purpose deeds are used to comply with certain legal purposes. These judicial deeds are court-ordered and direct the official named to execute the deed. They include:

Sheriff's Deed

The *sheriff's deed,* also referred to as referee's deed, transfers real estate sold at a public sale, usually the result of foreclosure on a judgment or mortgage. Because the sheriff is acting on behalf of the public, there are no warranties or representations with this deed. The deed will recite the sale price, and the court will issue the order that permits the sheriff to dispense the deed.

Administrator's Deed

The *administrator's deed* is used by the administrator of an estate in selling property as ordered by the court. A referee's deed in partition is used when the court appoints a referee to partition or liquidate a property.

Tax Deed

A *tax deed* transfers real estate that has been sold by the government because taxes have not been paid. As with the sheriff's deed, there are no warranties.

Executor's Deed

The *executor's deed* is issued by an executor of an estate upon the sale of the deceased person's real property. This is a judicial deed and is executed under court approval and carries no warranty other than against the executor's acts. Unlike other deeds, the executor's deed must state the full purchase price.

Guardian's Deed

The *guardian's deed,* issued to convey a minor's interest in real property, passes title carrying the covenant that neither the guardian nor the minor have encumbered the property.

Director's Deed

A *director's deed* is used when a public agency sells surplus land.

Taking Title to Real Property

When taking title to real property, ownership may be described as joint tenancy, tenancy in common, concurrent ownership, tenancy by the entirety, severalty ownership, or multiple ownership. (See Figure 5.3 for a diagram of different types of ownership and Figure 5.4 for a list of the form of ownership allowed in each state.)

Joint Tenancy

Rights of survivorship

Joint tenancy is ownership by two or more persons with the right of survivorship. This must be clearly stated in the deed, otherwise tenancy in common may be assumed in most states. Joint tenancy means that when one of the owners dies, the surviving joint tenant(s) obtain the property. The following must all be the same for joint tenants.

1. *Time*: Their interests must be acquired at the same time.
2. *Title*: All joint tenants must receive their interest through a single deed.
3. *Interest*: The rights of the owners must be equal.
4. *Possession*: All owners must have equal rights of possession and may share in the occupancy, use, and profits, and each have equal responsibility for maintenance and costs of the property ownership.

Joint tenancy is generally used only by family members because of the right of survivorship, but may be used by others. If parties own property under joint tenancy, when one dies, the survivor receives the property. However, the value of the entire property would be subject to estate taxes twice. Because of possible tax consequences such as these, it has become increasingly important for people to seek counsel when taking title. In joint tenancy ownership, if one of the parties

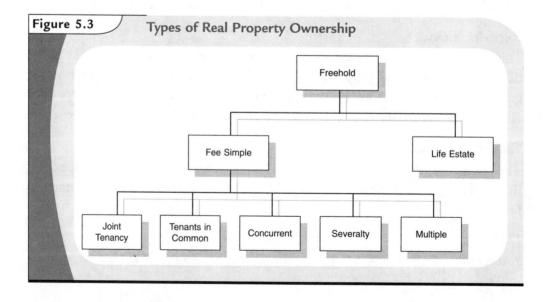

Figure 5.3   **Types of Real Property Ownership**

| Figure 5.4 | Forms of Ownership Allowed in Each State | | | |

	Tenancy in Common	Joint Tenancy	Tenancy by the Entirety	Community Property
Alabama	X	X		
Alaska	X	X	X	
Arizona	X	X		X
Arkansas	X	X	X	
California	X	X		X
Colorado	X	X		
Connecticut	X	X		
Delaware	X	X	X	
District of Columbia	X	X	X	
Florida	X	X	X	
Georgia	X	X		
Hawaii	X	X	X	
Idaho	X	X		X
Illinois	X	X	X	
Indiana	X	X	X	
Iowa	X	X		
Kansas	X	X		
Kentucky	X	X	X	
Louisiana*				
Maine	X	X	X	
Maryland	X	X	X	
Massachusetts	X	X	X	
Michigan	X	X	X	
Minnesota	X	X		
Mississippi	X	X	X	
Missouri	X	X	X	
Montana	X	X		
Nebraska	X	X		
Nevada	X	X		X
New Hampshire	X	X		
New Jersey	X	X	X	
New Mexico	X	X		X
New York	X	X	X	
North Carolina	X	X	X	
North Dakota	X	X		
Ohio	X		X	
Oklahoma	X	X	X	
Oregon	X		X	
Pennsylvania	X	X	X	
Rhode Island	X	X	X	
South Carolina	X	X		
South Dakota	X	X		
Tennessee	X	X	X	
Texas	X	X		X
Utah	X	X	X	
Vermont	X	X	X	
Virginia	X	X	X	
Washington	X	X		X
West Virginia	X	X		
Wisconsin	X	X		
Wyoming	X	X	X	

*Louisiana's state statutes create ownership interests that differ from joint tenancy, tenancy by the entireties, or community property.

dies, the unity of ownership continues. For example, if three individuals own a property in joint tenancy and one of the parties dies, the remaining two parties still own the property in joint tenancy, receiving the deceased person's share under the right of survivorship. The decedent's share is not passed to the heirs, nor does it pass by will.

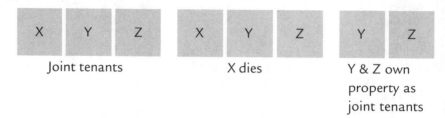

Joint tenants   X dies   Y & Z own property as joint tenants

Conversely, if one of the three parties sold her share to another, the joint tenancy would cease to exist between the three parties. The remaining two owners would be joint tenants, but the new owner would be a tenant in common since there is no unity of time.

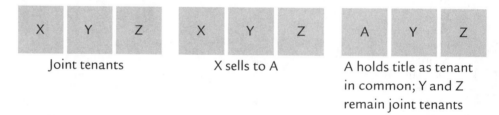

Joint tenants   X sells to A   A holds title as tenant in common; Y and Z remain joint tenants

Advantages of Joint Tenancy Ownership

1. Probate expenses may be eliminated.
2. The surviving joint tenant automatically succeeds to the title immediately.
3. Estate held in joint tenancy would not be subject to debts incurred by the decedent.

Disadvantages of Joint Tenancy Ownership

1. Other than the decedent's spouse (if the spouse is a joint tenant), the decedent's heirs will not inherit the property.
2. Joint tenants relinquish the right to will their share of the property.
3. It may create tax problems.
4. It does not replace the need for a will.

Tenancy in Common

Without survivorship

Tenancy in common is ownership by two or more persons without the right of survivorship. If one of the owners dies, that owner's interest passes to heirs or to a devisee and not to the surviving tenant in common. Each owner has an undivided interest in the whole. That is, one person cannot designate ownership of the south side of the lot and the other owner the north side; they own the whole with an *undivided interest*. This is true in all types of ownership. However, each person's share need not be equal; one tenant-in-common owner could own two-thirds of the value of the whole while the other owns one-third. In addition, one owner may sell her interest without the consent of the other owner so that, unlike joint tenancy, title may be taken at different times.

Tenancy by the Entirety

Tenancy by the entirety can only be held by husband and wife. As with joint tenancy, it vests entire rights in the surviving spouse. Neither the husband nor wife can convey the property without the consent of the other. Not all states recognize tenancy by the entirety. While it provides for automatic survivorship, it can establish inheritance tax problems and should not be used as a replacement for a will. In states that recognize tenancy by the entirety, the deed generally will need to specifically state this fact.

Historically, under English common law, the wife was considered a "part" of her husband with no separate rights in property. Thus, as a "single unit" the tenancy by the entireties gave him absolute control. However, the laws today recognize a wife's rights and benefits as equal to a husband's and states that use tenancy by the entireties acknowledge this. Should the couple divorce, tenancy by the entireties automatically ceases to exist, and the parties become tenants in common.

Concurrent ownership is held by two or more persons in **co-ownership**, as in joint tenants, tenants in common, partnership, or corporations. This multiple ownership can include any number of persons.

Ownership by husband and wife

Severalty Ownership

Severalty ownership is the sole ownership of a property by one person. Do not think of the term as implying several, but look at the first five letters, *sever;* the person's ownership is "severed" from all others.

While a married person may own property in severalty, most states will require the spouse to sign away any marital rights upon the sale of the property.

In law, a corporation is a legal person and as such takes title to property in severalty.

There are advantages in sole ownership of real property. The individual makes the decision when to buy or sell and on what terms. Unlike concurrent ownership, the owner has total control. Needless to say, with that control comes all responsibility of maintenance and care.

Sole ownership

Community Property

In the seven states* that recognize community property laws, ownership of property acquired by either husband or wife during the marriage is considered **community property**. They are considered to have contributed equally to the

---

* *Arizona, California, Idaho, Nevada, New Mexico, Texas, and Washington.*

marriage, and thus any property they purchase will be equally shared, giving each spouse a one-half interest in any property acquired since the marriage. This is true even if one of the spouses does not work outside the home.

Property held prior to the marriage does not apply and is considered separate property. Property that is acquired *after* marriage by inheritance or gift is also excluded from community property. If one of the parties purchased property with separate funds, this too would be excluded.

Community property states differ in the rules covering real and personal property. They allow the spouse to devise by will that spouse's portion of the estate to anyone. In the states of California, Idaho, Nevada, New Mexico, and Washington, if no will is left, the deceased person's estate reverts to the surviving spouse. However, in Arizona and Texas, the heirs of the deceased would be the beneficiaries, although Texas permits the right of survivorship of community property. Community property states do not recognize dower and curtesy rights.

Partition

A co-owner of real property may petition a court of law to terminate the shared ownership. If the co-owners have not voluntarily agreed to dissolving the estate, one co-owner can sue for *partition,* and the courts will conduct a compulsory division of the land. If it is not feasible to actually divide the land, a sale will be ordered, and the proceeds will be split in accordance with each owner's share. For example, A, B, and C own an apartment building and A wants to sell his share. If B and C do not agree to buy A's share or to sell the building, A can demand through court action to partition the ownership and the whole property will be sold because it cannot be divided. A co-owner may demand partition regardless of the amount of the co-owner's share.

In addition to the individual and concurrent forms of ownership, group ownership is held by business enterprises. Partnerships, corporations, syndications, and trusts hold real estate for business purposes.

Partnership

A *partnership* is formed when two or more people join together in a business venture for the purpose of making a profit. The partnership will operate under its own name or in the name of the owners. If operating under a trade name— for example, XYZ Partnership—the property will be held in severalty since a partnership is considered by law as a single entity. If held in the names of the individual owners, title would be held as tenants in common or joint tenancy.

Homestead Laws

Homestead rights

The family's place of residence is classified as their **homestead**. Most states have enacted homestead laws to exempt the home from a forced sale due to liens and judgments by creditors. It is protection for the family in the event of a financial disaster, conceived primarily to benefit dependents.

States that have established homestead laws require that the real estate is the family's permanent residence. Additionally, the property may have to be filed as a homestead at the county courthouse. States vary in the requirements of establishing a homestead. Some states will designate a single person as fulfilling the term *family.* Each state determines the amount to be exempt. For example, if the law exempts $10,000 from debts, upon the sale and satisfaction of any taxes due, mortgages, and mechanic's liens, the owner would receive the first $10,000 with the remainder applied toward other outstanding debts.

Most homestead laws were legislated when much of the country was rural and the laws served as protection for the farmer and his family. Some states exempt a certain amount of farmland, such as 160 acres. Today the amount is often less than the farmer's debts.

While the homestead exemption benefits the owner to a degree, there are some claims that are not exempt. They include:

1. real estate taxes
2. real estate special assessments
3. real estate mortgages
4. mechanic's liens

Summary of Important Points

1. A freehold estate is ownership of real estate in fee simple title or for life and conveys the maximum interest available.
2. A life estate gives the holder the right of possession and use of the property for that person's lifetime.
3. A deed establishes title to real estate. To be valid, the deed must contain the property description, a conveyance clause, consideration, the names of the grantee and grantor, and the grantor's signature.
4. A warranty deed conveys the greatest quality of interest.
5. In a special warranty deed, the grantor warrants the title only since the grantor took possession.
6. A bargain and sale deed confirms that an interest is held by the grantor, but the grantor is not warranting that interest.
7. In a quitclaim deed no warranties are given, as signers give only whatever interest they hold. If I gave you a quitclaim deed to the Brooklyn Bridge, you would receive exactly the interest I have, which is zero.
8. When taking title to real property, the grantee may hold interest by means of:
   a. joint tenancy, which gives the right of survivorship
   b. tenancy in common, which is shared ownership without right of survivorship

      c. severalty, which is sole ownership by one person

      d. tenancy by the entireties, which is a form of joint ownership by married persons that carries the right of survivorship

9. Community property is ownership with spouses each owning half of whatever they acquire since their marriage.

10. If a party wants to terminate shared ownership and the co-owners do not agree, they can petition the court to have the property sold.

Discussion Points

1. How would you prefer to hold title to real property? Give reasons for your answer.

2. Explain why a buyer would prefer to receive a warranty rather than a quit-claim deed.

3. If a married couple takes title as tenants in common, what consequences may arise if one person dies?

4. When property in your city is sold, is a tax levied upon the transfer of title? If so, compute the tax on the property in Figure 5.2 using your tax levy.

5. What would be the preferred way for two business partners to take title to a building they purchased to accommodate their business? Explain pros and cons of joint tenancy and tenancy in common ownership in this instance.

6. Explain the difference among title, deed, and estate.

7. If you were selling property you owned, what type of deed would you give the purchaser? Explain.

Review Questions

Answers to these questions are found in the Answer Key section at the back of the book.

1. The essential ingredients of a deed include:
   a. the signatures of the grantees and grantors
   b. words of conveyance
   c. recordation
   d. date of birth

2. If Charlie Brown purchases a property and receives title from the grantor by a quitclaim deed:
   a. Brown does not receive clear title
   b. Brown receives whatever title the grantor had
   c. Brown can force the grantor to correct any title defects
   d. Brown receives no title

3. The responsibility of recording a deed lies with:
   a. the state
   b. the county
   c. the grantor
   d. the grantee

4. Deed restrictions are considered:
   a. general liens
   b. escheat
   c. an encumbrance
   d. enforceable only by the property owner

5. Property held in joint tenancy, upon the death of one of the tenants, would pass to:
   a. the state
   b. the owner's heirs
   c. the spouse
   d. the surviving joint tenant

6. A life tenant can do all of the following with her interest EXCEPT:
   a. sell
   b. lease
   c. bequeath
   d. mortgage

7. A warranty deed guarantees against all EXCEPT:
   a. the grantor's heirs
   b. easements of record
   c. a mortgage
   d. a judgment creating a lien

8. Susan Jones lists her home with Sam Suresell and indicates that she wishes to deliver the deed that best protects her when she passes title. Ms. Jones will convey title by means of:
   a. a quitclaim deed
   b. a warranty deed
   c. a special warranty deed
   d. a grant deed

9. Henry Dudd subsequently views the Jones home and decides to make an offer to purchase the property. He informs the sales agent, Diane Dealquick, that he wants the deed that will give him the most assurance of receiving a clear title. Ms. Dealquick suggests:
   a. a quitclaim deed
   b. a warranty deed
   c. a special warranty deed
   d. a grant deed

10. After much negotiation, Jones and Dudd agree that Jones will deliver a deed that ensures good title through her time of ownership only. The deed agreed upon was:
    a. a quitclaim deed
    b. a warranty deed
    c. a special warranty deed
    d. a grant deed

11. A deed that is executed by the grantor several days before it is delivered is:
    a. invalid and not enforceable
    b. valid as long as it is recorded
    c. valid upon delivery
    d. invalid if not recorded within 10 days

12. For a deed to be recorded, it must contain:
    a. the signatures of the grantors and grantees
    b. consideration
    c. the grantee's signature
    d. the grantor's social security number

13. For a deed to be conveyed, it must be:
    a. signed
    b. accepted
    c. acknowledged
    d. recorded

14. One deed of conveyance an owner of real estate may use to voluntarily transfer right, title, or interest in real estate is a:
    a. warranty deed
    b. sheriff's deed
    c. foreclosure deed
    d. deed of trust

15. Two friends jointly purchase a property. To protect their heirs, they should take title in:
    a. joint tenancy
    b. severalty
    c. life estate
    d. tenancy in common

16. The "to have and to hold" clause in a deed is represented by the:
    a. consideration
    b. acknowledgment
    c. words of conveyance
    d. habendum clause

17. Tenancy by the entirety may exist between:
    a. family members only
    b. any two parties of legal age
    c. siblings
    d. persons married to each other

18. Joel Smith and Mark Jones lived together in a home they purchased. Joel dies in an automobile accident. Mark now owns the property in severalty. Joel and Mark had title to the property as:
    a. tenants by the entirety
    b. joint tenants
    c. tenants in common
    d. owners in severalty

19. What is the primary purpose of a deed?
    a. transfer of title
    b. quantity of ownership
    c. recordation
    d. legal evidence

20. For a deed to be considered valid, it must:
    a. contain an adequate description of the property
    b. be acknowledged
    c. be recorded
    d. be drawn on any day but Sunday

21. The covenant of quiet enjoyment refers to:
    a. occupancy
    b. ownership
    c. the prevention of interference by other parties
    d. the absence of liens on the property

22. Marcia Moore had a life estate to which her daughter was named remainderman. Ms. Moore leased the property for five years. Three years later, she passed away, and the daughter decided to cancel the lease. Which of the following is true?
    a. the lease was totally void from the beginning
    b. the terms of the lease prevailed
    c. the lease was void upon the death of the life tenant
    d. the lessee can sue for damages if evicted

23. Ownership of real property in fee simple title gives the title holder:
    a. a nonfreehold estate
    b. a freehold estate
    c. a less than freehold estate
    d. an estate in remainder

24. A fee simple determinable estate can best be described as:
    a. an unqualified estate
    b. an estate of inheritance
    c. a fee simple absolute estate
    d. limiting the estate holder to the terms set forth by the grantor

25. If a state transfer tax upon the sale of a property is $2.50 per $1,000 or any part thereof, the tax on a sale of $92,500 would be:
    a. $92.50
    b. $230.00
    c. $231.25
    d. $235.50

6 Contracts and Business Law

This section begins the explanation of the process of the sale. Chapter 6 introduces contracts and business law so the reader can develop an understanding of the various contracts used in real estate transactions.

7 Agency Law and Representation

Chapter 7 covers agency law and focuses on the many changes taking place in defining who the agent represents. The chapter explains the agent's fiduciary obligations when representing the principal and the agent's duties to the customer. Once this foundation has been laid, the rest of the chapters in this section follow the natural sequence of events in listing and selling a property. Throughout this section, a single property is used as an example to give continuity to the procedures involved in a transaction.

8 Listing the Property

Chapter 8 explains the role of the real estate brokerage firm and its relationship

(continued)

THE ORDERLY PROCESS OF A SALE

PART 2

to the seller when listing a property for sale. The listing contract is explained and the various types of listings are described.

9 Marketing and Selling Real Estate

Chapter 9 builds upon Chapter 8, dealing with locating the buyer to purchase the property. The offer to purchase is written after the buyers are given an estimate of the costs involved. A step-by-step analysis of the agreement is covered with an explanation of rejections and counteroffers.

10 Lending Institutions and Loans

Chapter 10 covers the role of financial institutions, since most real estate sales are financed, and gives a background of the lending institutions and the loans they issue.

11 Financing

Chapter 11 further develops an understanding of finance by explaining the mortgage and deed of trust—the financing instruments used by the lending institutions. A description of the many types of mortgages available completes the chapter.

12 Closing Statements

Chapter 12 completes this section with the closing of the transaction. The responsibilities of the real estate firm (or the escrow company), the lender, and the title company are all covered. The many forms used in closing a sale are shown, concluding with the buyer's and seller's closing statements and the broker's trust account balance sheet.

Contracts and Business Law

KEY TERMS

bilateral contract

consideration

contract

dual contract

duress

executed contract

executory contract

express contract

fraud

implied contract

latent defect

misrepresentation

novation

offer and acceptance

option

parol evidence rule

patent defect

rescind

specific performance

statute of frauds

undue influence

unenforceable contract

Uniform Commercial Code (UCC)

unilateral contract

valid contract

voidable contract

void contract

OVERVIEW

Since contracts are an essential part of real estate transactions and we could not do business without them, it is necessary to fully understand contract law. This chapter will take you through the "making of a contract," explaining all the elements and legal requirements of a valid and binding contract.

The contracts most frequently used in real estate are the listing and purchase agreements, leases, installment contracts, options, escrow agreements, and mortgages. Their use is an everyday occurrence for real estate professionals, and subsequent chapters will cover each in detail.

Definition and Types of Contracts

WEB SITE

Contract law:
www.findlaw.com/
01topics/
07contracts

A **contract** is a voluntary agreement between two or more parties to perform (or abstain from performing) a legal act on which they have had a "meeting of the minds." In other words, they agreed on the subject matter of the contract. In this legally enforceable agreement, the parties are bound to the conditions of the contract. Contracts may be implied or expressed, oral or written.

Implied Contract

Created by an act

An **implied contract** is neither written nor explicitly stated orally, but is *created by an act* of the party. Most people enter into implied business contracts every day when they ask for a cup of coffee at a restaurant, take public transportation to work, make a purchase at a store, or have the dentist fill a cavity. No promise was exchanged, but the implication is that they will pay for these services and goods. Also referred to as an *ostensible contract*, an implied contract is not enforceable and is rarely used in real estate transactions. Real estate salespeople want to be sure that they are paid for their services and want protection against being sued if one of the parties fails to fulfill a contractual obligation. An express written contract helps to guard against these problems, as the law provides protection on express contracts.

Express Contract

Parties declare their intentions

An **express contract** may be written or oral, but all written contracts are express. A purchase agreement will be in writing and specifically spell out the intentions of the parties. A lease may be oral or written. However, tenants taking possession of the premises show their express consent to occupy and pay rent. The landlord expresses consent by permitting the party to move into the premises.

Bilateral Contract

Promise on part of two parties

A **bilateral contract** embodies the promise on the part of both parties to the contract. In a purchase contract, the offeror (buyer) promises to buy, and the offeree (seller) promises to sell. A lease is another example of a bilateral contract; the lessee (tenant) agrees to pay rent and the lessor (landlord) to give possession. Mortgages and land contracts are other examples of bilateral contracts.

Unilateral Contract

Promise by one party

A **unilateral contract** is the promise on the part of one party to complete an act. In a listing contract the owner lists the property and agrees to pay the agent a commission upon the sale. The agent naturally hopes to sell the property and earn a commission, but the contract does not bind the salesperson to perform. Likewise, in an option contract the optionor agrees to sell the property to the optionee, but the optionee is not bound to purchase. The listing agreement and option become bilateral only if performance occurs through the sale of the property.

Executory Contract

A contract that has not been completed is an **executory contract**; complete performance has not taken place. A purchase agreement in which the seller has not yet transferred title is an example of an executory contract. A lease is also considered an executory contract as it requires monthly rent payments over a period of time. Upon expiration of the lease, the contract will be completed. This is also true of a mortgage as payments continue until the debt is paid off.

An incomplete contract

Executed Contract

The contract becomes **executed** when performance has completely taken place. Once the purchase agreement has been signed, the sale has been closed, and title is passed to the purchaser, the contract has been executed. When the mortgage debt is paid in full, the contract between the debtor and the mortgage company will be fully executed.

Contract is completed

Dual Contracts

When real estate is sold or purchased, it is illegal to have **dual contracts** between buyer and seller, with each contract containing a different price so that the buyer can obtain a larger loan from a lender. Such a dual contract, written for the purpose of obtaining a larger loan from the lender, would subject a sales agent to a fine or revocation of their license. Nor could the sales agent declare to the lender that the earnest-money deposit was greater than it truly was or delay in depositing the earnest money so it appears that the purchaser has more assets than actually is the case.

Elements of a Contract

A valid, legally binding contract requires certain basic elements and qualities.

1. *Offer and acceptance:* A meeting of the minds on the subject matter.
2. *Consideration:* Good or valuable exchange, something of value.
3. *Capacity of the parties:* Capable of entering into a contract.
4. *Legality of the object:* For a legal purpose.
5. *Written and signed contract:* When required by law.

Upon fulfillment of these five conditions, a valid and binding agreement is "contracted" and becomes legally enforceable. These contract conditions are expanded upon below.

Offer and Acceptance

Parties agree to terms
of the contract

The concept of **offer and acceptance** means that the parties have agreed by mutual consent to the terms of a contract. For example, in the purchase agreement the buyer (offeror) agrees to purchase the property on the terms stated. If the sellers (offerees) sign the contract, they agree to the terms offered, and both parties are obligated to abide by the contract. The terms of the contract must be precise and clearly defined. If they are not specified in detail so that each party understands the terms, mutual agreement does not exist.

Consideration

The **consideration** must be evident in all contracts, indicating a mutual exchange of promises, for the contract to be legally binding. This consideration must offer a benefit or a detriment, with one party giving and the other receiving. In the example of a purchase agreement, the buyer agrees to purchase the property for a stated price, and upon acceptance by the seller, a transaction is agreed to. The earnest-money deposit the buyer places with the broker shows the purchaser's good faith in wanting to perform according to the terms of the contract, and while it is "consideration," it does not represent the consideration that makes a valid contract. In real estate the word *consideration* means something of value, such as money, and something that is also necessary for the contract to be legally valid. In the event the buyer should decide not to perform, the earnest money may be dispersed to the seller as liquidated damages, which will be covered later in Chapter 9.

Good consideration

A promise must be accompanied by consideration from one party to another to be enforceable. You may have heard the term *good or valuable consideration.* Good consideration is recognized by law when an act is given for consideration. You hire a nursery to trim your trees on the promise that upon completion of the act you will pay the agreed-upon fee. Another example: "A" promises to sell his condominium to "B" for one-half its market value if "B" marries "A's" daughter. If "B" marries the daughter, "A" must fulfill his promise since the act was carried out. In this situation, "A's" daughter had other plans for her life so the transfer did not take place. Nevertheless, "A" wanted his daughter to have the property, so he deeded it to her for "love and affection," which meets the legal requirement of consideration in some states.

Valuable consideration

The vast majority of contracts carry valuable consideration in the form of money. The deed used in Chapter 5 carries the phrase, "in consideration of Eighty Four Thousand and no/100 ($84,000)—DOLLARS in hand paid," representing the valuable consideration the buyers are giving to the sellers. One party agrees to sell property to another for a stated price; in other words, one gives money, and the other relinquishes property for the monetary consideration.

Capacity of the Parties

The law is emphatic in stating who is able and who is not able to enter into a contract. To be capable of entering into a contract, one must be able to understand what the contract contains and to carry out its terms.

Minors

In many states the age of majority is 18 years, while in other states it may be up to the age of 21 years. A person not of legal age may rescind a contract; however, the person who accepts the minor's contract is still bound to the terms of the contract. This law provides protection for minors since they may not be able to understand contract terms. The minor must request release from the contract while still a minor or within a reasonable time period after reaching majority. Failure to rescind the contract makes it valid. Since few minors would have the funds to purchase real estate, the problem is not prevalent. A guardian or trustee may act for a minor in the event the minor had received property (as through inheritance) and it was deemed in the best interest of the minor that the property be sold.

Must be of legal age to contract

Mental Incompetency

A mentally incompetent person cannot enter into a contract since the person is not responsible for his actions. Mental instability is sometimes difficult to prove. An insane or mentally handicapped person must have someone appointed by law as a guardian or conservator to act on the person's behalf. An elderly person may feel competent but not possess the ability to deal with the complex involvement of selling a home. The real estate salesperson should inquire if the person has a family member to assist in the decision-making process. Careful consideration must be given to anyone the salesperson feels is borderline incompetent.

Some states have extended the law to include intoxicated persons or persons high on drugs and chemically dependent. If property was sold to a person, knowing the party was intoxicated and unable to make a sound judgment, the party to the contract may ask the courts to annul the contract. This would need to be done within a reasonable time after the party becomes sober and realizes what has transpired. In West Virginia, someone entering into a contract while drunk is considered insane, and therefore the contract is void. Court action is necessary.

Legality of the Object

The purpose of the promise in a contract must be a lawful one. One could not enter into a legal contract with someone to burn down a house, irrespective of the consequences, as it could not be legally completed or enforced.

Lawful object

If one party to a contract is not at fault, the courts will intervene to avenge the injured party. As an example, Evans purchases a property and opens a delicatessen only to be closed down because zoning laws did not permit the space to be used for a commercial purpose. Evans can **rescind** (cancel) the purchase contract upon proof that the property was sold under false pretense.

Written and Signed Contract

All states have enacted a statute of frauds requiring that certain contracts be in writing in order to be enforceable. These statutes of frauds protect against fraud and perjury. The document must be signed by the party or parties against whom enforcement would be sought. In lieu of a legal document, a written memorandum, such as a series of letters and telegrams, would suffice. The memorandum must describe the property and contain the names of the parties, conditions, terms of the sale, and signatures of the party (or parties) against whom compliance is sought.

While some state statutes do not require a lease of less than a year to be in writing, it is far wiser to have it written than to rely on oral evidence. If the oral lease were for two years, it would be unenforceable at the very beginning.

Statute of Frauds

All real estate transactions are subject to the **statute of frauds** law. The law was first established in England in 1677, and has been adopted by all 50 states. It requires that *all real estate transfers be in writing* and signed by the parties in order to avoid fraudulent practices and to be enforceable in a court of law. This includes offers to purchase, acceptance of an offer, land contracts, contracts for the exchange of real estate, options to purchase, and deeds.

The law does not preclude an oral contract to buy or sell, but if a dispute arises between the parties, the contract would not be upheld in the courts. Written contracts are less disputable and clearly state the intent of the parties. Preprinted contracts approved and provided by your state real estate association or the licensee's broker are recommended.

All real estate transfers must be in writing

Parol Evidence Rule

The **parol evidence rule** forbids the admittance of any prior verbal or written evidence to vary or add to the terms of a written instrument. If the contract has been properly written, there is no valid reason to introduce such evidence. One particular point to remember is that the execution of a written contract, whether the law requires it to be written or not, supersedes all the negotiations and stipulations that preceded or accompanied the execution of the instrument. For example, if a buyer informed a broker that she wants the drapes to remain with the house, but this was not put into the purchase agreement nor transmitted to the seller, and the seller signed and accepted the contract as written expecting to remove the drapes, the buyer could not bring in the oral statement that preceded the written document. In this instance, the broker was remiss in not placing it in the contract, and the buyer was negligent in not reading the contract carefully before signing it.

Uniform Commercial Code

The **Uniform Commercial Code (UCC)** has been mandated in varying degrees in all 50 states in an effort to make laws covering chattel (personal property) sales uniform. The law covers any conditional sales contracts and chattel mortgages, including stocks and commercial paper. It covers the sale of personal property (transferred by a bill of sale) and relates to real estate only when fixtures are involved. If a chattel is purchased and financed, the financial statement can be filed at the recorder's office. If the chattel is not subsequently paid for, the creditor can repossess it from the property.

Chattel sales

Bulk transfers are also regulated by the UCC. This act covers the transfer of a large amount of inventory or material. The merchant cannot sell out stock and keep the money, leaving creditors unpaid. Any buyer of the merchandise is required by the UCC to receive an inventory of the goods from the seller along with a list of creditors. The buyer must then give notice to any creditor that a sale is pending. The induction of bulk transfers takes place if a business is sold or if it is liquidated.

Validity of Contracts

A contract may be valid, void, voidable, or unenforceable.

Valid Contract

The **valid contract** complies with all the requirements of contract law. It exists when all parties agree to the terms of an enforceable contract. It has been contracted with all the essential elements previously discussed in this chapter and is legally binding and enforceable on all parties. If one of the parties defaults on the contract, it is enforceable in a court of law.

Void Contract

A **void contract** has no legal force even if it contains all the essential elements of a contract. A void contract results when: (1) the contract was entered into for an illegal purpose, (2) the contract cannot be completed due to an operation of law, or (3) an act of nature prevents the contract from being completed. Therefore, a contract to burn down a house is illegal and thus void. Conversely, if the home is struck by lightning and burns down, the purpose of the contract no longer exists and is void. A void contract is, in effect, no contract.

Voidable Contract

A contract is **voidable** when one person may cancel the promise, for example, if the party is a minor. The contract is a valid act but may be rescinded by the minor. This is also true of parties who acted under duress or undue influence.

Unenforceable Contract

An **unenforceable contract** appears to be valid but cannot be enforced. It may not be in writing in accordance with the statute of frauds and consequently cannot be enforced by court action. For example, a property owner may orally state to a salesperson that he may sell his property, but without a written contract, the salesperson may have trouble proving the oral agreement.

Misrepresentation

False information given unintentionally

Misrepresentation can result in an unenforceable contract. Misrepresentation is an erroneous statement made without the intention to deceive, but with an effect on the finalization of the contract. This does not include expressions of opinion. For example, if an agent tells a prospective buyer that "in my opinion, this is the best view in the city," this statement merely reveals how the agent feels about the property.

Misrepresentation can result from an unintentional error in facts given to the other party. For example, prospects ask the seller's agent if their children may attend the school located two blocks away. The agent responds that the home is in that school district. After the purchase contract has been accepted by the sellers, the purchasers learn that the school will close at the end of the current school term. The buyers relied on the agent's statement, and even though the agent was unaware of the scheduled closing of the school and did not make the statement with the intent to induce the party to the contract, the buyers may have cause to rescind their contract.

In the past, courts have ruled against agents who knew or should have known about a material defect or a fact regarding the property that may affect its value.

In the case of a sale, if a seller withholds a pertinent fact that has an effect on the property value, the buyer may retain the property but sue the seller for any difference between the actual value and the purchase value.

Fraud

Contract is voidable

Fraud is an outright attempt to cheat someone. If a false statement is knowingly made regarding a material fact, and if the other party relies upon that statement and suffers damages, fraud has been committed. For example, a seller shows her property, and when asked if the home is on public sewer responds affirmatively, even though this is a deliberate misstatement of fact. After the sale is consummated, the purchaser learns that the house has a septic system. The actions of the seller constitute fraud. Had the seller honestly believed the property was on sewer, it would be a mistake but the contract would still be voidable. The defrauded party may rescind the contract or collect money damages.

Mistake

If a buyer has a "change of heart" and regrets entering into the purchase contract, the law will not protect the buyer from poor judgment. If the sellers change their minds after signing the contract, no relief will be given them for their desire not to sell. However, if both parties agree that a mutual mistake was made, they can mutually agree to rescind the contract.

Duress

A contract must be entered into by the free will of all parties; that is, an offer and acceptance must be freely given on the part of all parties to a contract. **Duress** occurs when coercion, threat, or force overcomes a person's will. To force persons to perform against their will is unlawful constraint. A contract entered into when a person is placed in a position of physical fear or threat is voidable by the threatened person.

Undue Influence

A party cannot take unfair advantage of another by exercising **undue influence** to the extent that the second party cannot use his own judgment. All parties must act of their own free will and not be coerced due to their lack of understanding or ability to comprehend the contract. A person may be intimidated by another who is believed to be more knowledgeable. Contracts initiated under such circumstances are voidable.

Carrying Out Terms of a Contract

Performance of a Contract

The contract terms should state when the performance of the contract is to transpire. Purchase contracts call for a set date upon which the closing of the sale will take place; leases state the length of the lease and the date of termination. If a contract does not contain a date, the act should be performed within a reasonable time. The type of contract will determine the definition of reasonable time.

Assignment of a Contract

Since all contracts are assignable, unless they specifically state to the contrary, the *assignor* (holder of the contract) may assign all rights to the *assignee* (receiver of the contract). If a purchaser assigns all rights in a purchase agreement to a third party, the assignee has all the rights, privileges, and obligations that the buyer had under the contract terms. The terms of the contract must be fulfilled as they were stated. If a contract requires an obligation that is personal (as with a listing contract), it is not assignable without the consent of the seller. If a renowned artist is contracted to paint a portrait, he cannot assign another artist to complete the painting.

Assigning holders' rights to another

The terms of a contract may also be completed by **novation**. Novation requires the substitution of a new contract for the existing contract. For example, John Blair contracts with Joe Bright for the removal of snow from Blair's

Novation

property for the winter months of November through March for a certain amount of money. In December, Joe Bright moves to another state, but Jim Jones is willing to carry out the contract as written. This substitution of names is novation.

Discharging of a Contract

When terms of a contract have been fulfilled, the contract is completed or discharged. If performance has not taken place, the contract has been breached unless the parties have agreed to cancel. Under the following conditions, complete performance has failed to take place.

1. *Damage to the property:* If the property is destroyed (as by fire, tornado, or hurricane) prior to performance, the contract may be canceled. The contract will generally state who bears the loss if the property is damaged or destroyed.

2. *Death:* If the contract cannot be completed by someone else equally capable of performing the act, it will be discharged. For example, a renowned portrait artist with a unique painting style dies; the party who employed the artist justifiably may cancel the contract. However, in the situation of a purchase agreement, if the buyer dies, the estate can be held responsible to complete the terms of the contract. Death of the seller may prevent completion unless the deed has been delivered into escrow.

3. *Rescission of the contract by mutual agreement:* All parties involved decide to rescind the contract. For example, the parties who contract to purchase the property learn that they are to be transferred to another city and inform the salesperson that they wish to cancel the contract. With the seller's agreement the cancellation is agreed upon. This agreement to cancel the contract should be in writing and signed by the purchasers and the seller so that the rights of both parties are protected. Any commission earned by the listing broker should be taken into account.

4. *Partial performance:* The parties agree to terminate the contract before completion. For example, a designer is contracted to redecorate a house, but after a portion is completed, decides to cancel the contract because the homeowner is displeased.

Statute of Limitations

The statute of limitations sets a time limit within which one party may claim a legal right. This time limit varies greatly among states. If the party does not exercise this right within that time, the claim is waived. For example, a house constructed on a vacant lot does not have a wood roof as was stipulated in the covenants of the subdivision. The neighbors must bring action within the required time or lose their legal right to insist upon compliance.

Laches

Laches is delay or negligence in asserting one's legal rights; the party has waited too long to complain. A contract must be acted upon by the date set forth in the agreement. If no time limit has been stated, the offer will lapse after a reasonable time period. Because what constitutes a "reasonable time period" can vary depending upon the situation, it is wise to avoid such complications by always including a set time for performance of the contract.

If one of the parties to the contract has failed to carry out conditions of the agreement, a breach is committed. For example, a tenant decides to move but has six months remaining on the lease. If the tenant defaults on paying the remainder due, the contract has been breached.

Latent and Hidden Defects

A defect hidden from the view of the purchaser (for example, defective plumbing) is known as a **latent defect** and must be revealed to the intended purchaser. However, if a defect can be seen, it is a **patent defect**, and the buyer must observe it personally. A large crack on a dining room wall can be seen, and the purchaser can examine the defect. If the sales agent has any thought that the buyer would not notice the defect, it should be pointed out to the buyer. If a seller neglects to reveal the defect, the buyer may rescind the contract or receive damages.

Defects
· Latent—hidden from view
· Patent—visible

Breach of Contract

Specific performance is a remedy in a court of equity compelling the defendant to carry out the terms of the contract. A decree of specific performance may be brought by the injured party, demanding that the defendant perform the promise made or pay damages for losses suffered. When a party brings such a suit, the party agrees to abide by the decree of the court. The general belief of the court is that the injured party should be compensated to the extent of the party's position prior to the breach of the contract. In real estate transactions these actual damages could include a seller's loss upon failure of the buyer to fulfill the contract, a buyer's loss if a seller defaults, a real estate agent's commission, a change in interest rates or closing costs, or the expense of making a double move.

In the purchase of a property, if the buyer does not go through with the purchase, the seller may take recourse in one of the following actions.

Seller's recourse

1. The seller may rescind the contract and release the buyer from any obligation.
2. The seller may retain the earnest money and declare it forfeited as liquidated damages.
3. The seller may resell the property and sue the buyer for the difference if a loss occurs on the second sale.
4. The seller may sue for the balance of the purchase price.

The usual procedure is to retain the earnest money, dividing it equally between the brokerage firm and the seller (if this is written in the listing agreement). The mechanics of a legal suit are involved and lengthy, and the seller usually favors placing the property on the open market again for a sale.

Buyer's recourse

If the seller refuses to transfer the property to the buyer in accordance with the contract, the buyer has a choice of the following remedies.

1. The buyer may agree to rescind the contract and receive the return of any earnest deposit that was placed with the broker.

2. The buyer may sue for specific performance in an effort to force the seller to perform.

3. The buyer may bring action for money damages against the seller. For example, if the buyers purchase property with the expectation of moving into the new premises and suddenly find they will not be able to take possession, this could result in the cost of two moves if they are forced to seek temporary housing until they locate and close on the purchase of a substitute house.

Option to Purchase

Option offers "right to buy"

An **option** is a contract granting the exclusive right to buy for a limited time. In an option, time is of the essence. The optionee (prospective purchaser) takes the option, and the optionor (owner) gives the option. Again, this contract must be in writing to be enforceable and must contain a consideration (dollar value) to be valid. If the optionee does not wish to carry out the option, the consideration is forfeited. The optionor retains all the rights of ownership during the term of the option. The optionee is not entitled to any rents or benefits, having only the exclusive right to buy. If the option expires and the parties choose to renew the option, an additional consideration is necessary. The optionee may also assign the option to another. An option is a unilateral contract since it embodies a promise on the part of only one person, the optionor. There are two differences between an option and a purchase contract.

1. An option gives the right to buy to the purchaser, who may or may not choose to exercise that right.

2. A purchase contract is an offer to purchase real estate; if accepted by the seller, it becomes a binding contract.

Commonly Used Contracts

The contracts used most frequently in real estate transactions are the following.

1. *Listing contract:* The employment contract between the seller and the brokerage firm (Chapter 8).

2. *Purchase agreement:* The contract between the buyer and the seller (Chapter 9).

3. *The option contract:* Used to reserve the right to purchase a property.

4. *Lease:* Between the tenant and the landlord (Chapter 14).

5. *Property management contract:* Between the property manager and the owner (Chapter 15).

6. *Mortgage:* Between the owner (mortgagor) and the lender (mortgagee) (Chapter 11).

7. *Deed of trust:* A mortgage lien in which a borrower conveys title to a trustee who acts as security for the lender (Chapter 11).

8. *Land contract:* An installment sale contract between the vendee (buyer) and vendor (seller) (Chapter 10).

Although other contracts are used, the above will be covered in depth in the chapters mentioned. The columns below explain the position of the parties involved in contracts.

Contract	Buyer	Owner/ Seller	Lender	Third Party	Tenant
purchase agreement	grantee	grantor			
land contract	vendee	vendor	owner		
option	optionee	optionor			
assignment	assignee	assignor			
offer to purchase	offeror	offeree			
mortgage	mortgagor		mortgagee		
deed of trust	trustor		beneficiary	trustee	
lease		lessor			lessee

The listing contract is not included in the above since the seller (grantor to be) is only granting permission to the real estate firm to sell the property. The firm is not taking title; it has merely received an employment contract to offer the property for sale.

Summary of Important Points

1. A contract is an agreement between two or more parties to perform a legal act.

2. The essential elements in the making of a contract include the offer and acceptance, consideration, capacity of the parties, and legality of the object.

3. A contract is either implied by an act or expressed, orally or in writing.

4. The statute of frauds requires that contracts must be in writing to be enforceable. The written contract leaves no doubt as to the intention of the parties. A written contract must be signed by the parties to the contract.

5. The unilateral contract obligates only one of the parties, whereas in the bilateral contract both parties must perform according to the terms of the contract.

6. A contract in which performance has not taken place is an executory contract, such as a purchase agreement. The contract is binding when the seller accepts the buyer's offer, but completion does not occur until later. Upon finalization of a contract, it is said to be executed; the terms have been carried out.

7. A valid contract meets all the requirements of law, whereas a void contract has no legal force. A contract is voidable if one of the parties can cancel, such as a minor. A contract may have the appearance of being valid but may be unenforceable.

8. When misrepresentation or fraud is involved, the contract may be set aside. Misrepresentation is the act of giving misinformation with no intent to commit fraud. However, the person giving the incorrect information is responsible and, if the person is a licensed sales agent, may be subject to losing his license. Fraud is done deliberately in an effort to obtain someone's consent to enter into the contract.

9. Any defect that cannot be seen by a prospective purchaser is a latent defect and must be revealed to the buyer if it is known. A patent defect is in plain view and need not be pointed out.

10. Contracts are assignable unless they specifically state otherwise. All obligations pass to the assignee, and the contract must be performed as it was written. Assumable mortgages are transferred to the purchaser by novation, the new owner taking over the responsibility of paying the loan.

11. Sometimes contracts are not completed, either due to destruction of the property, death, or partial performance. If one of the parties defaults, there are remedies for the injured party.

Discussion Points

1. Give an example of a void, a voidable, and an unenforceable contract.

2. Why is a consideration necessary in a contract?

3. Alice Dunbar signed a contract to purchase a larger home so that she would have more storage space for the computer equipment she sells as a representative for a computer company. Before the sale closed, she received complaints from several neighbors stating that they heard she was going to run a business from the home and felt that trucks making deliveries several times weekly would be a danger to their small children. Ms. Dunbar informed the salesperson that she wanted to cancel the contract because of unpleasant confrontations she foresaw. Can she legally rescind the contract? If so, why?

4. Explain a situation in which a contract may be discharged without fulfilling the terms of a written agreement.

5. Give examples of a situation in which an option would be used.

Review Questions

Answers to these questions are found in the Answer Key section at the back of the book.

1. A contract based upon which of the following would NOT be capable of being voided by the injured party?
   a. error
   b. undue influence
   c. fraud
   d. change of heart

2. A latent defect is best described as:
   a. a defect that the prudent buyer can see
   b. an old defect
   c. a defect that is hidden from view
   d. a breach of contract by the seller

3. Which of the following persons cannot be held to a contract?
   a. a minor
   b. an unmarried woman
   c. an elderly person
   d. a widow or widower

4. The difference between an option and a purchase agreement is:
   a. the option gives the right to buy; the purchase contract, if accepted by the seller, is a binding contract to buy
   b. the option need not be in writing, but the purchase contract must be in writing
   c. the option is always in favor of the optionee, while the purchase contract favors the grantee
   d. the option is a bilateral contract, while the purchase agreement is a unilateral contract

5. If an optionee fails to exercise his option within the stated time:
   a. he may sue the optionor for the consideration
   b. he may automatically renew the option if he puts down another consideration
   c. he forfeits the consideration
   d. the purchase is automatically confirmed

6. The important object in the offer and acceptance of a contract is:
   a. the good intent of both grantee and grantor in fulfilling the contract
   b. "meeting of the minds" on the subject matter of the contract
   c. the capability of each party entering into the contract
   d. the legality of the contract

7. Rescission of a contract most nearly means:
   a. all goes back to the way it was before the contract
   b. ratification of the contract
   c. affirmation of the contract
   d. execution of the contract

8. "Meeting of the minds" refers to:
   a. the consummation of the contract
   b. the consideration
   c. the offer and acceptance
   d. the closing of the transaction

9. The term contractual ability refers to:
   a. the contract containing all of the covenants needed to make it legal
   b. the attorney having the ability to draw the contract
   c. the capability of two people to enter into a written agreement
   d. the legality of the contract

10. All of the following are essential to a valid contract EXCEPT:
    a. consideration
    b. duress
    c. offer and acceptance
    d. legality of object

11. If the purchaser assigns her interest in the property while the contract is still pending, realizing a profit:
    a. the seller receives the profit
    b. it cancels the contract
    c. the broker receives the profit
    d. the original purchaser receives the profit

12. A contract between a competent and an incompetent party can be voided by:
    a. the incompetent
    b. the competent
    c. no one; can't be voided
    d. agreement of the parties only

13. A unilateral contract:
    a. embodies a promise on the part of both parties
    b. binds only one party to the contract terms
    c. is voidable by the maker
    d. has been executed by all parties

14. The substitution of a new contract for an existing contract is:
    a. execution
    b. breach of contract
    c. specific performance
    d. novation

15. Upon the default of a contract, all of the following are remedies to the injured party EXCEPT:
    a. specific performance
    b. retention of the earnest deposit as liquidated damages
    c. execution of the contract
    d. rescission of the contract

16. A purchase contract has been accepted by the property owner, but the sale will not close for 60 days. This is an example of:
    a. an executory contract
    b. an executed contract
    c. a bilateral contract
    d. a land contract

17. A listing contract can best be defined as:
    a. a unilateral contract
    b. a bilateral contract
    c. an executed contract
    d. a dual contract

18. Tom Smith sold his home but did not reveal to the agent or the buyer that the air conditioner has not worked for two years. This is an example of:
    a. misrepresentation
    b. a mistake
    c. a patent defect
    d. fraud

19. A real estate agent shows prospective buyers a cabin on Elk Lake. When the prospective buyers ask if they can fish on the lake, the agent responds by pointing to a boat on the lake in which a person is casting a fishing line. After the sale closes, the buyers learned that the lake is contaminated and fishing is not permitted. The agent:
    a. is not guilty of misrepresentation
    b. is guilty of misrepresentation
    c. used undue influence by pointing out the boat
    d. used duress

20. The homeowner paid off a 30-year mortgage in 15 years. The mortgage contract is:
    a. a dual contract
    b. an executory contract
    c. an executed contract
    d. a unilateral contract

Agency Law and Representation

KEY TERMS

agency

agency by estoppel

agency by ratification

agency law

agent

buyer agency

client

common law

consensual dual agency

customer

dual agency

facilitator

fiduciary

general agency

limited agent

ostensible agency

principal

seller agency

special agency

statutory law

subagency

transactional agent

universal agency

OVERVIEW

"Whom do I represent?" is an important question for all licensees. In the great majority of real estate transactions in the past, the traditional philosophy was that both the listing agent and the selling agent (through subagency with the listing brokerage) represented the seller. Another common presumption was that the agent represented the party who paid the compensation. However, in such traditional transactions, many buyers mistakenly thought the selling agent was working for them instead of with them. Real estate licensees themselves were often caught in the quandary, wondering "Whom do I represent?"

Common laws are the rules that have evolved from customary practice and decisions of the courts. **Statutory laws** are the laws and rules and regulations that have been enacted by legislation. The laws of agency have become more demanding in respect to who the licensee represents. Higher standards of accountability have been established for the real estate licensee. Clear definitions of who the licensee works for must be established prior to entering into a contract with a buyer or seller.

Over the past decade new concepts have evolved regarding agency representation. A licensee may represent the buyer, the seller, or, in some states, both buyer and seller via dual agency. Subagency is no longer automatically pre-sumed, and other new representation arrangements continue to evolve, such as limited agency, facilitation, and transactional agency. Many states have enacted legislation to clarify the duties and legality of agency representation.

This chapter covers the various types of agency and how agency rela-tionships are created. It explores agency issues and the different representa-tion choices that are available to practitioners and explains the obligations imposed upon licensees by the law of agency through listing contracts, buyer agency agreements, sales contracts, and multiple listing agreements.

The Agency Relationship

The creation of an **agency** occurs when one party appoints another to act on his or her behalf in transacting business with a third party. **Agency law** has evolved from common practices (common law) and from legislated law. A real estate agency relationship implies a **fiduciary** responsibility in which one person (the fiduciary) is entrusted to exercise skill and knowledge in the negotiation of a transaction for the client. It is a situation of trust on the part of the clients, whether buyers or sellers, and agency laws are directed at protecting these clients.

Parties to an agency   Three parties are generally involved in a transaction regarding the sale or leas-ing of real estate. The parties directly involved in the agency relationship are the **principal** (or **client**), the party who hires an agent to act on his behalf; the **agent**, the licensee who represents the principal; and the **customer**, the party (also referred to as the third party) with whom the licensee *does not* have an agency relationship.

The Evolution of the Real Estate Business

Although at one time a broker sold only those properties the brokerage firm listed, today the Multiple Listing Service (MLS) provides a cooperative service that permits all subscribing members to sell each other's listings. With the MLS, *Subagency through MLS*   it is possible for a licensee to sell a property and *never* actually *meet* the seller. Originally, the MLS of the National Association of REALTORS® (NAR) stated that every licensee involved in the transaction was an automatic subagent of the listing broker unless that subagency was declined. Thus, the selling agent that showed and/or sold the property of the listing agent was a subagent. But the dis-tance between the seller and the many potential subagents had a tendency to dilute the fiduciary relationship that the law specified. Today the MLS requires the listing broker to indicate whether subagency is being offered. If it is not, an alternative relationship must be established for a possible transaction to move forward.

Classification of Agencies

There are specific agencies into which the parties to a contract may enter. A description of each follows.

Special Agency

The agency created between a principal and the agent that authorizes the agent to perform *one specific act* is a **special agency**. Whether working for buyer or seller, the real estate agent is generally a special agent, meaning that the agent's responsibility and authority are limited to producing a buyer for the seller as stated under the terms of the listing contract or to help the buyer purchase a home as agreed under the terms of the buyer brokerage contract.

Real estate agent acts as a special agent

There are three components involved in a special agency.

1. *Limited time:* Listing contracts with sellers and buyer agency agreements with buyers are limited to a specific time period; they are not ongoing, long-term relationships. As Chapter 8 explains, listings must specify a termination date.

2. *Limited purpose:* Agency is for a specific purpose. The seller or landlord wants the agent to find a ready, willing, and able buyer or tenant. When working for a buyer or tenant, the agent is hired to find a property that meets the desires and ability to pay of the buyer or tenant.

3. *Limited authority:* The principal gives the agent limited authority and responsibility. Basically, the agent is hired to sell or lease the property as directed in the contract between the principal and the agent. The power of attorney can create a special agency if it is for a limited time, purpose, and responsibility.

General Agency

In **general agency** agents have more latitude and can literally "speak" for the principal. The general agent might be given power of attorney to represent the principal, who would outline the framework under which the principal wants the agent to act, as in buying and selling investment properties. Other examples of a general agent would be the general manager of a business who has been given a great amount of decision-making authority in operating the business or the property manager who manages business properties for an absentee owner.

Agent given greater authority

WEB SITE

Real Estate Buyers Agent Council: www.rebac.net

Another example of a general agency is the salesperson-broker relationship that permits the salesperson to represent the broker and perform all the duties relevant to working for that broker, such as listing and selling property.

Universal Agency

A **universal agency** is generally created by power of attorney, since the principals are delegating the agent to act in their behalf for an unlimited range of legal matters, not just for a specific purpose such as a real estate transaction.

Power of attorney

Creation of an Agency

An **ostensible agency** or *implied agency* or **agency by estoppel** occurs when third parties are led to believe that someone is their agent. For example: Agent

Agency created by implication

Lucy Brown of A-1 Realty tells John Windsor of Landmark Realty that she has a listing on her neighbor's house. Windsor shows the property while the neighbor is home and writes a contract with the prospect. The neighbor later refuses to pay compensation, stating that no listing was entered into with Lucy Brown. An *ostensible* agency would exist in such a case since the neighbor never denied that Lucy Brown had the listing when Windsor showed the property and thus John Windsor had no reason to disbelieve Lucy Brown. Another example would be a customer (the third party in a transaction) who believes the selling agent is their agent when, in fact, the agent is a subagent to the seller.

An **agency by ratification** occurs when an event takes place and is "ratified" and agreed to after the event. In the above example, if Lucy Brown's neighbor had agreed to pay the commission, he would be ratifying the sale and agreeing that Lucy is his agent.

The Need for Agency Disclosure

In the past, agents represented sellers in the vast majority of real estate transactions. Although today many buyers enter into an agency relationship with brokers, many buyers still in fact work with the seller's agent (or a subagent of the seller) when shopping for a home. As a result of this interaction between the buyer and the seller's agent, the question of agent loyalty needs to be addressed.

A recent Federal Trade Commission survey revealed that more than 70 percent of buyers in real estate transactions thought that when two agents were involved, the selling agent was representing them; 82 percent believed that whatever they told the selling agent was confidential. Clearly the majority of buyers believe that real estate agents are acting on their behalf when the sales agent is showing them properties that seem to best suit their needs and writing and presenting offers on their behalf. Because of the rapport that develops naturally between home buyers and the selling agent, the buyers come to believe that the selling agent represents them. Hence, they may confide to the selling agent that the price offered is not their final bid for the property, not realizing that the selling agent is obligated to work in the best interest of the principal, in this case the seller.

This common misinterpretation of the standard seller agency relationship has led to stricter legislation regarding disclosure of agency status. Currently, 44 states and the District of Columbia have passed laws or regulations requiring agency disclosure by real estate agents. A few states do not require disclosure in writing, but *oral notice should be given at the first meeting* because early disclosure minimizes the chances of misunderstanding. Written disclosure benefits licensees since both buyer and seller then understand whether their interests are being advanced in an agency relationship.

Disclosure of agency states

Each state sets forth its laws and rules to regulate its real estate industry. Further, each brokerage develops its own policies and procedures for conducting business based on state requirements. One company may choose to list and sell, working with both clients and customers. Another may decide to represent only buyers, and still another may only list property and work for sellers.

To give you an idea of how states are addressing the issue of agency disclosures, here are a few examples.

- The state of Colorado has modified an earlier requirement for verbal disclosure. Effective July 1, 1993, Colorado requires written disclosure on a form adopted by the state real estate commission. The form, "Working with a Real Estate Broker," is intended to ensure that those involved in a transaction understand from the outset whom each licensee in a transaction is working for and that each participant receives adequate, uniform information concerning current agency law and practice. Although no time is set for giving the disclosure, it must be made prior to providing specific assistance.

- Nebraska law, effective July 1, 1995, states that all selling agents represent the buyer (no written agreement is necessary) unless they have written evidence to the contrary or they are acting as a subagent of another broker who has an agency relationship with the client. The rationale is that this is consistent with the public perception that the selling agent represented the buyer.

- As of January 1995, Illinois prohibits automatic subagency and requires written agency disclosure, including definitions and information regarding alternate forms of agency to be offered prior to providing specific assistance or creating an agency relationship.

- West Virginia law states that the buyer must sign a Notice of Agency Disclosure form prior to signing a purchase agreement.

- In some states, the agency statement can appear in the offer-to-purchase contract. For example, the statement in bold type above the blank for the buyer's signature might read "All parties signing the document acknowledge that they have been informed that all real estate agents involved in this transaction are agents of and are representing the seller." If a buyer agent is involved, the wording would reflect that fact. When written disclosure is used, the form can be very simple since the object is to have *written* acknowledgment that buyers and sellers realize who the agent is representing. Many other states are passing legislation to clarify the agent's position in listing and selling property and working with clients and customers.

Possible Agency Relationships

Today, consumers may choose from a variety of possible agency alternatives. Following is a brief outline of basic agency relationships.

Seller Agency

Representing the seller

When a property is listed, the seller is known as the principal and an agency relationship is created between the broker and the seller. The real estate firm represents the seller and a **seller agency** has been formed that establishes a *fiduciary* relationship between the broker and the seller. The seller has faith, trust, and confidence in the broker who represents him and derives authority for the specific purpose of securing a buyer. The principal is bound by his agent's acts, within the scope of authority granted the broker. The listing contract is a special agency; that is, a specific broker is employed for a particular purpose. When the broker accomplishes that purpose, the broker's authority ends. In many states verbal listings are not enforceable.

Buyer Agency

Representing the buyer

Buyers also may enter into a legally binding agency relationship by hiring a *real estate agent* to represent them in the transaction. In **buyer agency** relationships the buyer becomes the principal in the fiduciary relationship, and the broker's loyalty is owed to the buyer. The broker will give the buyer complete loyalty and work strictly for the buyer's best interest.

In the buyer agency arrangement, compensation must be addressed early in the contract process. *Compensation does not necessarily determine agency.* Several options are available.

1. The buyer may agree to pay a flat fee or a percentage of the purchase price.
2. The buyer may have the agent ask the seller to pay the fee, with the buyer agent and the seller agent splitting the fee. The idea here is that the efforts of both agents bring about the sale.
3. The parties may pay their agents as per their respective contracts. This can result in a higher total percentage being paid, depending on the amount being paid by each party. However, if a buyer and seller each hire an attorney to represent them, they both pay separately.

In the past, a buyer agency was generally used for the purchase of commercial rather than residential real estate. However, the use of buyer agency for residential transactions is becoming more widespread across the country. In some parts of the United States, buyers of residential properties are being exposed to advertising by real estate practitioners who wish to represent them. In such cases, the buyer and the buyer's agent have a very clear understanding that the agent is solely responsible to the buyer and has no other loyalties.

When the buyer's agent makes the first contact with the listing agent, it is important that the listing agent is immediately informed that either:

1. the buyer's agent is declining the usual subagency arrangement and is operating strictly as a buyer's agent, and as such will be paid by the buyer, or
2. the agent is acting as a buyer's agent and expects the normal commission split.

Buyer Agency Agreement

An employment contract is entered into when the buyer wishes to be represented in his search for a home. The agreement states that the broker is being employed by the buyer; thus the buyer is the *principal.*

The buyer agency agreement (See Figure 7.1) follows the lines of the listing agreement in that it may be:

- An exclusive right to represent. The agreement will stipulate that the broker will receive compensation when the buyer purchases a property as described in the agreement. This is true even if the buyer locates the property on his own.

- An exclusive buyer agency agreement will state that the broker receives compensation only if he finds the property that the buyer purchases. If the buyer locates the property she is under no obligation to the broker.

- An open agency agreement is not exclusive. The buyer can enter into agreements with any number of brokers, and is only obligated to the broker who finds the property the buyer purchases.

As in any agency agreement, the broker will explain to the buyer what services he will provide. The compensation should be set forth in the agreement as negotiated.

Buyer Self-Representation

Another option available to buyers is to represent themselves. Buyers who do not work with a buyer agent are *customers* and as such have no representation. The selling agent who shows the property will be representing the seller, but will be honest and fair with the buyer. The buyers may call upon the services of various professionals to assist them in the successful completion of the purchase. They may employ an attorney or other specialists, such as mechanical inspectors, to represent them. These specialists are usually paid by and work for the buyer.

Buyer represents self

Subagency

As stated earlier, **subagency** was spawned through use of MLS, the computerized information network for real estate firms who subscribe to the service. MLS listings are available to all subscribing firms. The NAR's MLS listing agreement lets firms designate whether they are offering subagency when they list a property.

Subagency must be authorized by *both the client and the designated broker.* The offer of subagency may be made through an MLS or be negotiated by the brokers involved. If the principal (seller) offers subagency to cooperating brokers, she has the same obligations to the subagent who accepts subagency as she does to her listing agent. The subagent, who represents the listing agency when showing the listing, is bound by the same fiduciary duties to the seller as the listing agent. Figure 7.2 illustrates the subagency concept.

Representing another agent's client

Figure 7.1 / Exclusive Buyer Agency Agreement

EXCLUSIVE BUYER AGENCY AGREEMENT
This is a legally binding agreement. If not understood, seek legal advice.
Professional Service Fees and Agreement Terms are not regulated by law.

_____ (Buyer), contracts exclusively with_____ (REALTOR®) for the purposes and under the terms set forth below, with the name of my specified limited Buyer's Agent to be _____. All responsibilities and duties of REALTOR® shall also be the Responsibilities and duties of the Buyer's Agents.

1. Exclusive Right to Conduct Negotiations. In consideration of REALTOR®'s agreement to use REALTOR®'s best efforts to locate a property for Buyer to purchase at a price and upon terms acceptable to Buyer, the Buyer, whether one or more, grants to REALTOR® the sole and exclusive right to conduct all negotiations for Buyer's purchase of real property described in general terms as follows:
_____

2. Term of Agreement. The term of this Agreement shall begin _____, and end
                                                                    date
_____. Any renewal or extension of this Agreement shall be in writing and shall bear the
          date
signature(s) of all parties to the original agreement. Buyer represents and covenants that Buyer has not engaged any other brokers or agents to represent Buyer.

3. Compensation of REALTOR® Buyer agrees to pay fees to REALTOR® for professional services rendered as shown in paragraph(s) # _____ following:

    a.   **Property Subject to Listing Agreement with REALTOR®.** If the property is subject to a Listing Agreement with REALTOR®, all fees paid to REALTOR® shall be paid by Seller.

    b.   **Property Subject to Listing Agreement with Another Company.** If Buyer enters into an agreement to buy a property subject to a Listing Agreement with any party other than REALTOR®, a fee of _____;

    c.   **For Sale by Owner.** If Buyer enters into an agreement to buy a property not subject to a Listing Agreement, a fee of _____;

    d.   **Retainer.** A retainer fee of $_____ due upon signing of this Agreement, which shall be deposited in REALTOR®'s trust account and held until the earlier of closing or the expiration of this Agreement. REALTOR® shall keep this fee even if Buyer does not acquire a property. However, this amount shall be applied as a credit to any other fees due from Buyer.

    e.   **Hourly Rate.** Buyer will pay REALTOR® at the rate of $_____ per hour for time spent by REALTOR® pursuant to this Agreement, to be paid when billed whether or not Buyer acquires a property. REALTOR® shall keep this fee even if Buyer does not acquire a property. However, this amount shall be applied as a credit to any other fees due from Buyer.

The fee stated in paragraphs (b) and (c) above is due and payable upon closing of the transaction even if Buyer does not use REALTOR®'s services. The fee shall apply to any transaction(s) made within _____ days after this Agreement expires or is terminated, unless Buyer enters into an Exclusive Buyer Agency Agreement with another real estate broker.

4. REALTOR® Compensation Disclosure. Buyer agrees that REALTOR® may accept a fee from the Seller or the Seller's Agent as a result of Buyer's purchase of a property. Any fee received from the Seller or Seller's Agent shall be disclosed to Buyer and applied as a credit to the fee due from the Buyer as shown above. Buyer agrees that any fee paid by Seller or Seller's Agent may exceed the fee due by this Agreement.

5. Failure to Close. If the Seller of a transaction made with Buyer fails to close the agreement through no fault of the Buyer, the fee owed to Buyer's Agent shall be waived. If Buyer refuses to close the transaction for any reason other than as agreed with the Seller in the original agreement, the fee shown above shall be due and payable immediately.

6. Dual Agency Disclosure. Buyer understands that REALTOR® currently serves as the agent for both Sellers and Buyers for the purpose of sale of real property, and Buyer is aware that REALTOR® may be the agent for a Seller of property that Buyer becomes interested in acquiring. If Buyer becomes interested in a property listed with REALTOR®, REALTOR® shall immediately notify Buyer that REALTOR® is serving as the agent of the Seller of the property. Buyer consents that REALTOR® may act as a Dual Agent in the sale of the listed property. If REALTOR® serves as a Dual Agent, REALTOR® shall make no representations to Seller of the price Buyer is willing to pay for the property except as set forth in the Purchase Agreement submitted by Buyer, nor any representation to Buyer of the price Seller is willing to accept for the property except as set forth in the Listing Agreement. REALTOR® shall not make any other representations to Seller that would violate REALTOR®'s agency relationship with Buyer, nor any representations to Buyer that would violate REALTOR®'s agency relationship with Seller. Buyer acknowledges that if a Dual Agency exists, the ability of REALTOR® to represent either party fully and exclusively is limited. If a Dual Agency situation develops, Buyer agrees to sign a Consent to Dual Agency. Except for limitations on disclosure of confidential information discussed in paragraph 9, a dual agent has the same duties and responsibilities of a limited agent to a buyer as stated in paragraph 7 and to a seller as stated in paragraph 8.

Figure 7.1 continued

Exclusive Buyer - cont.

7. Duties and Obligations of Buyer's Agent. A REALTOR® representing a Buyer as Buyer's Agent shall be a limited agent with the following duties and obligations:

- (a)   To perform the terms of any written agreement made with the client;
- (b)   To exercise reasonable skill and care for the client;
- (c)   To promote the interests of the client with the utmost good faith, loyalty, and fidelity, including:
  - (i)   Seeking a price and terms which are acceptable to the client, except that the REALTOR® shall not be obligated to seek other properties while the client is a party to a contract to purchase property or to a lease or letter of intent to lease;
  - (ii)   Presenting all written offers to and from the client in a timely manner regardless of whether the client is already a party to a contract to purchase property or is already a party to a contract or a letter of intent lease;
  - (iii)   Disclosing in writing to the client adverse material facts actually known by the REALTOR®; and
  - (iv)   Advising the client to obtain expert advice as to material matters about which the REALTOR® knows but the specifics of which are beyond the expertise of the REALTOR®;
- (d)   To account in a timely manner for all money and property received;
- (e)   To comply with all requirements of Neb. Rev. Stat. Sections 76-2401 to 76-2430, the Nebraska Real Estate License Act, and any rules and regulations promulgated pursuant to such sections or act; and
- (f)   To comply with any applicable federal, state, and local laws, rules, regulations, and ordinances, including fair housing and civil rights statutes or regulations.

8. Duties and Obligations of Seller's Agent. A REALTOR® representing a Seller as a Seller's Agent shall be a limited agent with the following duties and obligations:

- (a)   To perform the terms of any written agreement made with the client;
- (b)   To exercise reasonable skill and care for the client;
- (c)   To promote the interest of Seller with the utmost good faith, loyalty and fidelity including:
  - (i)   Seeking the price and terms which are acceptable to Seller except that REALTOR® shall not be obligated to seek additional offers to purchase the Property while the Property is subject to a contract for sale or to seek additional offers to lease the Property while the Property is subject to a lease or letter of intent to lease.
  - (ii)   Presenting all written offers to and from Seller in a timely manner regardless of whether the Property is subject to a contract for sale or lease or letter of intent to lease;
  - (iii)   Disclosing in writing to Seller all adverse material facts actually known by REALTOR®; and
  - (iv)   Advising Seller to obtain expert advice as to material matters of that which REALTOR® knows but the specifics of which are beyond the expertise of REALTOR®;
- (d)   To account in a timely manner for all money and property received.
- (e)   To comply with all requirements of Neb. Rev. Stat. Sections 76-2401 to 76-2430, the Nebraska Real Estate License Act, and any rules and regulations promulgated pursuant to such sections or act; and
- (f)   To comply with any applicable federal, state, and local laws, rules, regulations, and ordinances, including fair housing and civil rights statutes or regulations.

9. Confidential Information. A REALTOR®, acting as a Buyer's Agent or a Seller's Agent, shall not disclose any confidential information about the Client without the Client's written permission, unless disclosure is required by statute, rule, or regulation, or failure to disclose the information would constitute fraudulent misrepresentation. No cause of action shall arise against a REALTOR® acting as a Buyer's agent or a Seller's Agent for making any required or permitted disclosure.

10. Nondiscrimination Buyer and REALTOR® agree not to discriminate against any prospective Seller because of Seller's race, color, sex, religion, familial status, handicap, or national origin.

11. Copy of Agreement. Receipt of a copy of this Agreement is acknowledged.

_____
Agent's Signature   date

_____
Agent's Telephone (Business)

_____
Telephone (Residence/Cellular)

_____
Buyer's Signature   date

_____
Buyer's Address

_____
Buyer's Telephone (Residence)

_____
Buyer's Telephone (Business)

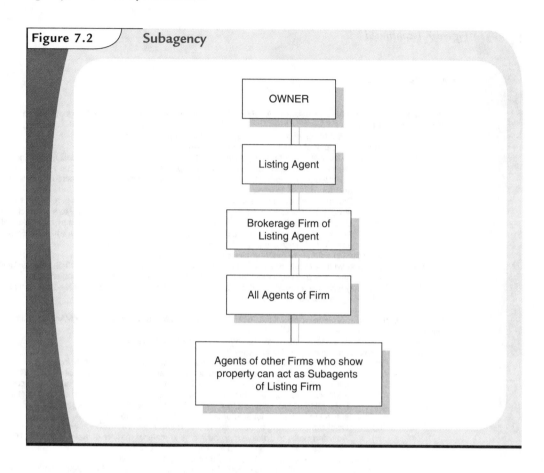

Figure 7.2 / Subagency

OWNER

Listing Agent

Brokerage Firm of Listing Agent

All Agents of Firm

Agents of other Firms who show property can act as Subagents of Listing Firm

Dual Agency

In a **dual agency** situation, a broker represents both parties to the contract. Thus, if the broker is acting in a dual capacity and representing both parties in a transaction, disclosure must be made early to both buyer and seller. Many states require this **consensual dual agency** disclosure to be made in writing and signed by both buyer and seller. Referred to as *informed consent,* both parties are aware that the broker is working in a dual capacity for both buyer and seller.

Representing both parties to a contract

Since the buyers and sellers have adverse interests, the broker who represents both may have a difficult time representing both effectively and fairly. The broker must be equally fair to both parties.

When the broker has written consent of all parties to the transaction to represent both the buyer and the seller, the broker may disclose any information to one client that is gained from the other, except that he cannot under the fiduciary obligation of *confidentiality* disclose:

1. that the buyer is willing to pay more than the purchase price offered
2. that the seller is willing to accept less than the asking price
3. the motivating factors of the buyer and seller
4. that the seller or buyer will agree to financing terms other than those offered

Dual agency may occur unintentionally. For instance, if licensee A is acting as a subagent of the seller and shows property to a buyer, it is possible that subagent A has never even met the seller since the licensee is not the original listing licensee. Therefore, even though subagent A owes loyalty to the seller by virtue of the listing contract, he may in fact feel more loyalty to the buyer, with whom he has established rapport. Real estate practitioners must be wary of such situations, since they are legally obligated to represent the seller's best interests in such cases, regardless of their relationship with the buyer. *Undisclosed dual agency,* even though unintentional, is usually a violation of state licensing law.

Exploring the Role of the Facilitator

Although it would mean abandoning the legal basis on which real estate practitioners have conducted business since the early 1900s, some states are investigating the alternative of changing the licensee's role from "agent" to **facilitator** or **transactional agent** of the sale. As a facilitator, the licensee acts as an intermediator in the transaction, working for the mutual interest of all parties to the transaction. The licensee has no fiduciary responsibility to buyer or seller because *no agency relationship has been formed.*

No representation by agent

When problems result in lawsuits, the broker is usually brought into the suit because the broker represents the principal. If the licensee were a facilitator, the risk would be considerably diminished.

The role of the "nonagent facilitator" is recognized in several states, including Colorado, Florida, Michigan, Minnesota, Oregon, and Wisconsin. Proponents of the concept feel that the real estate practitioner is the middleperson who conducts negotiations between buyer and seller and as such should have no legal liability. Advocates of the facilitator concept believe rules could be established to see that the practitioner acts in a fair, honest, and ethical manner. In states offering the facilitator option, the concept is based on the premise that a practitioner's responsibility is simply to produce a sale between buyer and seller.

Opponents of the facilitator concept argue that to change the existing law would diminish the practitioners' accountability to consumers by removing their fiduciary duties. Most state license laws are structured to support an agency affiliation that conveys fiduciary duties, so the laws would have to be rewritten or expanded to accommodate the nonagency facilitator relationship.

Limited Agency

If state law permits, a broker may appoint a specific licensee within her firm to act for a particular buyer or seller. For example, a licensee lists a property for the company the licensee is associated with. The company has an agency policy that the licensee who "takes" the listing will be the **limited agent** (or designated agent) of that seller. It further states that the designated broker can appoint additional licensees in the firm to be limited agents of the seller. Assuming the broker

Designated agent

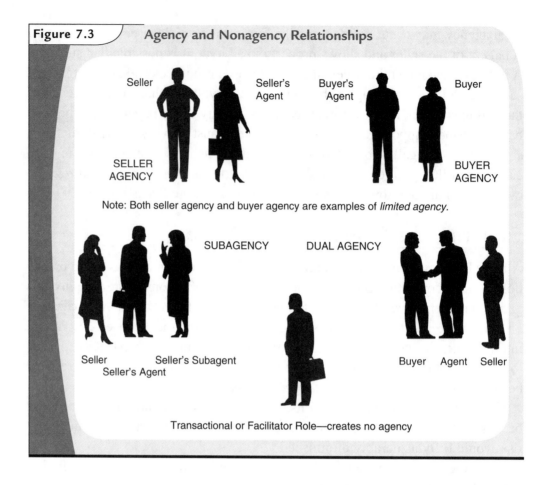

Figure 7.3   Agency and Nonagency Relationships

Seller   Seller's
Agent

Buyer's
Agent   Buyer

SELLER
AGENCY

BUYER
AGENCY

Note: Both seller agency and buyer agency are examples of *limited agency*.

SUBAGENCY   DUAL AGENCY

Seller   Seller's Subagent
Seller's Agent

Buyer   Agent   Seller

Transactional or Facilitator Role—creates no agency

appoints two other agents to represent the seller, now three agents are limited agents of the seller. All the remaining agents with the firm could represent prospective buyers. The states that offer this option do not consider it a dual agency unless the limited agent of the seller sells the property to a buyer with whom the agent has established a buyer agency. Please note that some states consider any "in-house" sale in which a property is listed and sold by the same firm to be dual agency. Figure 7.3 illustrates various agency and nonagency relationships.

Agents' Duties to the Client and the Customer

Although an agent owes absolute allegiance to the principal (the *client*), the agent must be fair and honest to the third party involved in the transaction (the *customer*).

The fiduciary obligations of the agent to the client and the customer are as follows:

Client/Principal	Customer
1. loyalty and honesty	1. disclose agency
2. obedience	2. avoid misrepresentation
3. full disclosure	3. present offers in a timely manner

4. skill

5. confidentiality

6. accounting

4. provide good service

5. provide information

When the Seller Is the Principal

The agent's obligations to the *principal/seller* when the buyer is the customer, as required by agency law, include the following.

1. *Loyalty and honesty:* The agent must always act solely in the best interests of the principal to the exclusion of all other interests, including the agent's own self-interest. The agent must protect the client's position in the marketing and sale of the client's property.

2. *Obedience:* The agent is obligated to obey promptly and efficiently all lawful instructions of the principal.

3. *Disclosure:* Although the agent must reveal any latent defects, no information may be disclosed to the customer (buyer) that would jeopardize the seller's bargaining position. All facts relevant to the transaction, such as a property appraisal for less than the sale price, must be revealed to the buyer.

4. *Skill:* The seller enters into the listing contract expecting competence and skill from every agent involved in the transaction. The terms of the listing agreement require that these services be provided with skill and knowledge. Anything less would violate that agreement and could be the basis of litigation. All reasonable efforts should be expended to sell the property.

5. *Confidentiality:* The agent must not reveal whether the seller is willing to take less than the asking price or will agree to finance terms other than those offered. Information concerning the seller's finances or personal life is confidential, as are his motivation and reasons for selling the property, which could convey a sense of urgency and thus lower the buyer's offer. However, *with the seller's permission,* disclosures can be made. In some situations, to know why the seller is moving could satisfy concerns of the buyer.

6. *Accounting:* Any money entrusted to the agent must be accounted for. This includes earnest money deposits and money advanced by the principal for expenditures on behalf of the principal.

When the Buyer Is the Customer

Responsibilities to the *buyer/customer* include the following.

1. *Disclosure:* At the first practical opportunity when meeting with the buyer, the agent must disclose that she does not represent the buyer (except in a buyer agency situation). As discussed earlier, states differ on exactly when disclosure should be made and if it needs to be in writing.

2. *Misrepresentation:* The agent must relay information in a fair and honest manner. For example, the seller's agent must disclose any environmental hazards, pending zoning changes, flood zone status, or any hidden defects.

3. *Presentation of offers:* The agent must write all offers when requested to do so and present them promptly to the sellers.

4. *Good service:* The customer is entitled to good service and the agent's skill and care in locating the home that best suits the buyers' needs at the price they can afford.

5. *Information:* The agent's duties include providing information about the transaction in a true and honest manner.

When the Buyer Is the Client

Agent's duties to buyer/client

When working with the buyer as the client, the agent will provide *more counseling and less selling.* Fiduciary duties include the following.

1. *Loyalty and honesty:* The agent must assist the buyer in negotiating the lowest price and the most favorable terms that meet their needs. The agent will advise the client on how to craft their offers to their own benefit. If the agent feels that the property is overpriced or the terms offered by the seller are not realistic, the information should be shared with the buyers.

2. *Obedience:* The agent must follow all lawful instructions of the buyer regarding the offering price and terms and arranging for inspections and repairs.

3. *Disclosure:* The agent owes to the buyer full, fair, and timely disclosure of all known facts relevant to the transaction, such as
   a. the agent's relationship with the seller, such as the seller being a good friend
   b. the agent's true opinion of the property
   c. any information the agent is aware of concerning the seller's reason for selling or that the seller is agreeable to negotiate the sale terms. (Please note: if this information was learned by the agent while representing this seller—perhaps the agent had this property listed previously—the agent would not be able to disclose this information, since the duty of confidentiality persists even after the termination of the agency.)
   d. any provision for a commission split with the listing broker

4. *Reasonable skill and care:* The agent must explain the purchase contract, endeavor to find the property that best suits the buyer's needs, and assist the buyer in drawing up offers.

5. *Confidentiality:* The agent must not disclose any of the following except with the informed written consent of the buyer or when required by law or judicial proceedings:

   a. the buyer's motivation for buying

   b. the buyer's willingness to offer a higher price

   c. the buyer's willingness to accept finance terms other than those offered

   d. the buyer's identity if he wishes to remain anonymous

   e. the buyer's future plans for the property, such as reselling it or the acquisition of surrounding properties

   Once an offer is accepted, confidentiality does not require the agent to conceal material facts, such as the buyer's inability to perform.

6. *Accounting:* The agent is responsible for all funds deposited in the agent's care, such as earnest-money deposits or money advanced by the buyer or seller for expenditures on their behalf.

Real Estate Practice Today

Agents, customers, and clients all must be familiar with the laws of agency. Misunderstanding and poor communication between the parties can result in conflict and lawsuits. While the basics of agency law are covered in this chapter, *readers must check with their states to clarify which methods of doing business are legal where they practice.* Across the nation, real estate and agency laws, rules, and regulations are constantly changing and often confusing, even to experienced practitioners.

With the many new concepts being used today, the agent can be protected by the use of a written disclosure form, regardless of whether it is a state license law requirement.

Chapter 20 covers license law that all states require the licensee to adhere to.

Summary of Important Points

1. An agency is created when one party appoints another to act on her behalf.

2. The principal, or client, hires the agent to act for him; the agent represents the principal; and the customer has no representation unless a separate agency relationship is created.

3. There are several classifications of agencies: the special agent, general agent, and universal agent. The real estate agent is generally a special agent, whose authority is to produce a buyer for the seller or, if representing a buyer, to find a suitable property for the buyer.

4. The agent owes the client complete allegiance, but must be fair and honest with the customer.

5. Seller agency is created between the seller and the broker; buyer agency is between the buyer and the broker.

6. In a dual agency, the broker represents both the buyer and the seller.

7. Subagency typically occurs when an agent shows another agent's listing and thus becomes an agent of the seller through the subagency.

8. The facilitator concept imposes no fiduciary responsibility since no agency has been formed. The facilitator is a negotiator who puts the sale together.

9. A limited agent acts for one party in a transaction.

10. Disclosure of whom an agent represents must be made to all parties in the transaction.

Discussion Points

1. Would you prefer to represent the buyer or the seller in a transaction? Give reasons for your preference.

2. If a broker does not offer subagency, would a seller who wishes to offer subagency have to seek a broker who does?

3. Why is having a written disclosure from all parties regarding agency a good idea?

4. You represent the sellers in a transaction, so the buyers are your customers. If the buyers inform you that they will raise their offered price if the sellers do not accept the contract, can you relay this information to the seller?

5. In your state, is agency disclosure necessary? If so, must it be written and when must the disclosure be made?

6. What are the responsibilities of the agent to the client? To the customer?

7. In a dual agency, the broker represents both parties in the same transaction. When could a potential dual agency occur?

Review Questions

Answers to these questions are found in the Answer Key section at the back of the book.

1. These three parties are typically involved in a real estate transaction:
   a. principal, client, and agent
   b. customer, client, and agent
   c. customer, client, and seller
   d. principal, client, and buyer

2. The three components of a special agency include:
   a. limited time, limited purpose, and limited authority
   b. limited time, general authority, and limited purpose
   c. agent representation, limited purpose, and ratification
   d. limited purpose, limited authority, and power of attorney

3. Most states require the real estate licensee to disclose the type of relationship they have with buyers and sellers. Disclosure should be made:
   a. before the sale is finalized
   b. prior to writing a contract
   c. by written notice sent to the party by registered mail
   d. at the earliest practicable opportunity during or following the first substantial contact with the party involved

4. The agent owes the customer all of the following EXCEPT:
   a. disclosure of the agency with the principal
   b. the reason the seller is moving
   c. good service
   d. providing information

5. An agent who acts for two principals with adverse interests in the same transaction is referred to as a:
   a. double agent
   b. subagent
   c. single agent
   d. dual agent

6. The purchaser who has no representation is known as the:
   a. principal
   b. customer
   c. client
   d. subagent

7. This party hires an agent to act on his or her behalf:
   a. customer
   b. subagent
   c. principal
   d. dual agent

8. Under this agency, the agent showing the property represents the listing agent:
   a. dual agent
   b. special agent
   c. subagent
   d. broker's agent

9. A broker meets a prospect and before showing a property explains that she is an agent of the seller. The agent's obligations to the buyer include all of the following EXCEPT:
   a. full disclosure of the property condition
   b. presentation of a contract in a fair and timely manner
   c. disclosure of any previous offers and the amount offered
   d. showing various properties that fit the buyer's needs

10. A broker has been given written consent by the buyer and seller to represent them both in a transaction. Under the law of confidentiality the broker cannot disclose certain facts. However, the broker must disclose:
    a. that the buyer is willing to pay more than the purchase price offered
    b. the motivating factors of the buyer and seller
    c. that the property is scheduled to be rezoned
    d. that the seller is willing to accept less than the asking price

11. Any offer of subagency must be given by:
    a. client and broker
    b. customer and broker
    c. client and customer
    d. subagent and broker

12. In a dual agency, the agent's responsibilities, along with confidentiality, include all of the following EXCEPT:
    a. the agent will not work to the advantage of one client and the detriment of the other
    b. the agent will use diligence and care in performing her duties
    c. the agent will consider the best interests of the clients
    d. the agent must consider the seller's interests first

13. All of the following are true of the facilitator concept EXCEPT:
    a. no agency relationship has been formed
    b. the practitioner acts as an intermediator
    c. the practitioner is responsible to the seller
    d. the practitioner has no fiduciary responsibility to buyer or seller

14. All of the following are true EXCEPT:
    a. a buyer agent can be compensated by the seller
    b. compensation does not necessarily determine agency
    c. a subagent can represent only the buyer
    d. broker represents both buyer and seller in a dual agency

15. The real estate agent is generally hired to perform one act, such as selling the principal's home. This agency is referred to as:
    a. a special agency
    b. a universal agency
    c. a general agency
    d. an implied agency

Listing the Property

KEY TERMS

Antitrust Act

broker

comparable market analysis (CMA)

discount broker

employee

exclusive agency

exclusive right to sell

flat fee listing

independent contractor

license

listing contract

multiple listing service (MLS)

National Association of REALTORS® (NAR)

net listing

open listing

REALTOR®

salesperson

OVERVIEW

A real estate brokerage firm lists property by entering into a listing contract with the seller. When a prospective buyer signs an offer to purchase and it is accepted by the seller, a sale has been made. Once the financing has been secured, the closing of the transaction takes place.

This chapter covers the obligations of both the seller and the brokerage firm by following a hypothetical property listing. The various types of listings, the commission structure between the seller and brokerage firm, and the difference between an employee and an independent contractor are explained.

The Brokerage Firm

License

As in most industries and professions, specialization has emerged in the field of real estate. The most familiar of these specialized services is provided by the real estate brokerage firm. The complexity of the laws dealing with the sale and transfer of land makes it difficult for the average citizen to handle the entire operation without assistance. Real estate brokerage firms serve the public by listing and selling the property of others. To provide this service, it is necessary to have a **license** to sell real estate—a privilege granted by the real estate commission or regulatory agency of each state. All 50 states have statutes governing real estate brokerage; therefore, to maintain a license, a high degree of professionalism is required.

Salesperson and Broker

Licensing the agent

Generally a state issues two types of real estate licenses: the salesperson's and the broker's. A **salesperson** is a licensed individual who has complied with the regulations set forth by the state real estate commission or regulatory agency and has subsequently become licensed to sell the property of others. The salesperson must always operate under the jurisdiction and supervision of a **broker**. A broker must fulfill additional qualifications before being issued a broker's license. Brokers may conduct real estate business under their own name or under a trade name, they may form a partnership with another broker, or they may be part of a corporation. In some states a broker working under the employ of another broker is referred to as an associate broker. Chapter 20 covers license law in greater detail.

Generally speaking, privately owned real estate brokerage firms may be involved in the listing, selling, exchanging, optioning, leasing, managing, building, appraising, or buying of real estate (see Figure 8.1). They may sell new and existing residential properties, raw land, farms, and commercial or industrial properties. Many firms have a separate department to handle the leasing and management of clients' income property. Others subdivide and develop land to erect homes, apartments, shopping centers, and office buildings.

Some real estate agents also obtain an appraiser license and appraise properties on a fee basis. In August 1989, Congress adopted the Financial Institutions Reform, Recovery and Enforcement Act (FIRREA). Title XI of the act provides for the regulation of real estate appraisers when they appraise real estate in "federally related transactions" as defined in Title XI. As a consequence, states have legislated the licensing of appraisers. This is discussed more fully in Chapter 17. Insurance is sold in connection with some real estate offices, supplying buyers with protection on their newly purchased properties. A separate insurance license is needed.

| Figure 8.1 | Possible Departments in a Real Estate Firm |

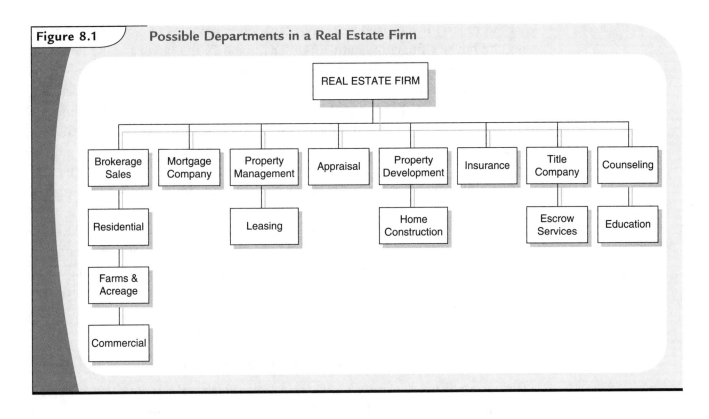

Persons deciding to make real estate their profession can look forward to interesting and varied experiences. The large sums of money involved in the purchasing of real estate demand close supervision of each licensee by state real estate commissions. However, professionalism, experience, and knowledge are just as important as state licensing requirements. For the prospective sales representative, expertise and professionalism are essential ingredients for a successful career in real estate.

Need for a Professional

While the law permits property owners to sell their own homes, the owners quickly become aware of the many complex details that are involved in the marketing of real estate. To begin with, they must determine the value of the property. The owner's concept of the worth of the property may be influenced by sentimental attachments and by the costs of maintenance and additions made over the years, but for an accurate valuation the owners need to be familiar with the current real estate market and the trends of the buying public.

Complex real estate procedures

The owner must next attract the right sales prospects—people who are ready, willing, and able to buy, not just those who are curious to see what the interior of the home looks like. The real estate salesperson will qualify customers in advance, ensuring that only those who are definitely prospective buyers will be shown the house.

WEB SITE

National Association of REALTORS®:
www.realtor.org

A property owner is at a disadvantage when it comes to tactfully questioning the buyer's financial status in order to qualify the buyer for the purchase of the property. Hours may be spent showing the home to prospects who cannot afford to purchase it. A vital cog in almost every real estate transaction is the financing. What types of loans are available to the buyer? What are the current interest rates? Should the purchaser buy under FHA? Can the prospect qualify for VA financing? Would a conventional loan, a fixed or an adjustable rate mortgage, or a land contract better suit the buyer's needs? The real estate agent qualifies the prospect or has a mortgage loan officer prequalify the buyer.

The owner must also know how to prorate such items as property taxes, the insurance (if the policy is to be assumed by the purchaser), and the interest on the existing loan if it is to be assumed. Real estate salespersons are specialists in their field since they deal in such transactions every day. Sales ability is learned and perfected through specialized practice and training.

Contract Between Broker and Salesperson

Independent contractor

Real estate firms generally do not hire their salespeople as **employees** or pay them a salary. Instead, salespeople typically work as **independent contractors** and are paid strictly on the basis of production; when a sale is finalized, they receive a percentage of the total commission earned. Unlike the requirements in paying salaried employees, the broker does not need to withhold social security and income taxes on commissions paid to independent contractors; the responsibility for paying these taxes belongs to the salesperson. A written contractual agreement should be entered into between the broker and the salesperson to safeguard the broker in the event of an Internal Revenue Service (IRS) investigation.

Unless salespeople are employees, the broker cannot pay any of the associated expenses, such as entertainment costs, license and trade membership fees, or automobile expenses. And since these salespeople are not employees, the broker cannot make it mandatory that they attend sales meetings or require office hours. To summarize the differences, see below:

Employee	Independent Contractor
1. receives a salary	1. receives no minimum salary
2. broker must withhold social security, income tax, and unemployment tax from salary	2. salesperson pays taxes
3. broker can require set hours for agent	3. sets own hours
4. broker can pay extras (as fees for agents)	4. pays for all expenses—receives no extra compensation

Hiring a Personal Assistant

Some licensees hire a *personal assistant* to perform specified duties for the agent. A number of states require the personal assistant to be licensed. It is preferable that the person have a basic knowledge of real estate procedures. The assistant will help with bookkeeping and clerical duties, scheduling of appointments, and telemarketing. A licensed assistant may hold open houses and meet with clients and customers. Having help with the volumes of paperwork involved in a real estate transaction frees the licensee to concentrate on listing property and making sales.

Using Technology

As the practice of real estate has evolved, so too the use of the *computer,* which gives the licensee instant updated information. Licensees have access to not only the MLS data but local property tax information, mortgage rates, and even aerial maps showing the location of a property. This information can be transmitted to clients and customers across the country, so if they are moving into a new area they have a basic knowledge of what is available to purchase. The personal *laptop* computer gives the licensee instant access wherever he may be to information the consumer requests on a given property.

There is software that a licensee can purchase for designing promotional advertising and business cards or for help in creating a Web site. A real estate company with a Web site offers the viewer a preview of a property, including photographs, the number of rooms, and other data on the property.

E-mail has proven to be a quick and effective means of getting information to the customer. Once communication has begun it is imperative that the licensee respond to all inquirers promptly.

Cell phones keep the agent in constant touch with buyers, sellers, mortgage companies, and closing offices. The licensee may be on the way to an appointment but is never out of touch with the office. Today's cell phone allows for high-speed communication services, such as accessing e-mail and relaying text messages, and includes the use of a digital camera.

Voice mail allows the caller to leave a message at the licensee's office, and the agent can call into the office and be connected to the voice mail and retrieve the message.

A *personal digital assistant (PDA)* organizes the licensee's appointments and stores other data. The licensee can input information on a consumer's needs or any comments made about a property. Typical PDA capabilities include access to calendars, calculations, and e-mail.

Obtaining the Listing

It is important for the real estate firm to secure listings because listings represent the merchandise the company has to offer for sale. Salespeople will seek these listings through relatives, friends, neighbors, business associates, and acquaintances. Salespeople may also develop a "listing farm," that is, they will select a certain neighborhood of homes where a reasonable turnover in ownership is expected and actively "farm" the area. Many salespeople prepare newsletters with information on household tips, recipes, financing trends, current interest rates, and data on recent sales in the area and deliver them to homeowners in the selected neighborhood. By calling on the homeowners in person, by telephone, and by mail the salesperson will become known to the owners.

When property owners call brokerage firms to list their houses, they are naturally anxious to obtain top dollar for the property. Pricing the property at its fair market value will result in the best price in the quickest period of time and at the least inconvenience to the seller. The agent will determine the property value by comparing it to similar properties that have recently sold, which is referred to as a **comparable market analysis (CMA)**. The salesperson follows a series of steps in the preparation of the market analysis, which typically include:

Comparable market analysis

1. measuring the house for square footage
2. comparing the subject property with recent sales and with competition on the market similar in square footage and style. (The **multiple listing service [MLS]** is of great value in easily locating the sold properties. If the MLS is computerized and the firm has a computer, the salesperson can pull up comparable sold listings.)
3. completing a proceeds to seller form to inform the seller what the proceeds will be from the sale (see Figure 8.2).
4. completing a listing contract as shown in Figure 8.3.
5. preparing several well-written ads to show the seller how the property would be marketed.

This packet of information is presented to the sellers in the expectation of obtaining the listing. A professional approach such as this lends credence to the salesperson's ability to successfully market the home.

The Listing Contract

The **listing contract** defines the relationship between the real estate firm and the seller: it specifies the price and terms the seller agrees to, the services provided by the brokerage firm, and the amount of commission that will be paid upon closing the sale.

Signed by all owners

The listing contract must be *signed by all the owners of the property,* as it constitutes employment of the agent. If the property is held by a partnership or by a corporation, the agent should verify that the partner or officer signing the listing agreement has the capacity to authorize the sale. Any *restrictions* on the sale should be noted in the listing agreement. Once the salesperson's broker has accepted the listing, the broker is responsible to the principal and cannot delegate this authority to another. This does not necessarily mean that the agent will not

Figure 8.2 / **Proceeds to Seller Form**

Estimate of Proceeds to Seller

Date _____ Property _____ Settlement

	Debit	Credit
Sale Price		$_____
Loan discount points	$_____	$_____
Property tax proration from ____ to ____		
days at $_____ per day	$_____	$_____
Title insurance	$_____	
State revenue stamps @ $1.00 per 1000	$_____	
Infestation report	$_____	
Loan pay-off / assumption	$_____	
Interest per diem ____ x ____	$_____	
Professional services fee	$_____	$_____
Buyer concessions	$_____	
Record release of mortgage(s) liens(s)	$_____	
Escrows reserve account (*)	$_____	$_____
Association dues	$_____	
Escrow closing fee	$_____	
Other	$_____	
Total Debits and Credits	$_____	$_____
Estimates net to seller		$_____

(*) Depending on your lender, your escrow account may be refunded directly to you after your loan has been paid off, or your escrow reserves may be credited toward your principal balance and reflected in your loan payoff.
The above information is merely an estimate of projected costs with regard to the sale of your property. You are advised that the actual charges and costs at close of escrow may vary from the above estimated figures.

Seller _____   A-One Realty

Seller _____   By _____

Date _____   Date _____

cooperate with other brokers, but the responsibility for making appointments for showing of the property, for negotiating agreements of sale with the owners, and for closing the transaction generally rests with the listing broker and salesperson.

The listing broker must ask the principal what personal property, if any, will remain with the property. These items will then be included on the listing contract. An example might be draperies custom-made for a particular room; the owners may decide it will facilitate a sale to leave them.

If the owners have an attached fixture, which is rightly real estate, that they do not want to leave, they should indicate it is to be shown as excluded from the listing and sales agreement, or it should be removed and replaced prior to any showings of the property. For example, Aunt Harriet may have given the owners the crystal chandelier in the dining room as a wedding gift. Removing it will prevent the problem of a buyer seeing the chandelier and insisting it must stay if he purchases the home.

Figure 8.3   Exclusive Right to Sell Listing Contract

EXCLUSIVE RIGHT TO SELL LISTING CONTRACT

1 In consideration of your agreement to list and offer for sale the property hereafter described, and to use your efforts to find a purchaser therefore, I hereby give you the sole and exclusive right to and including 6-10-08 to sell _1040 Clear St._ Legal _Lot 8 Block 1 Confusion Hill Subdivision_ together with attached fixtures, including shades, rods, blinds, storm sash & screens, for the sum of $ _$184,000.00_ upon the following terms: _Cash, Conventional_
I agree to pay you a cash commission of _7_ % of the gross sale price.

2 If a sale is made, or a purchaser found, who is ready, willing, and able to purchase the property before the expiration of this listing, by you, myself, or any other person, at the above price and terms or for any other price and terms I may agree to accept, or if this agreement is revoked or violated by me, or if you are prevented in closing the sale by existing liens, judgments, or suits pending against this property, or the owners thereof, or if you are unfairly hindered by me in the showing of or attempting to sell said premises, within said period, or if within _90_ days after the expiration of this listing I make a sale of said premises to any one due to your efforts or advertising, done under this listing. This property is offered without respect to race, color, national origin, or religion.

I hereby represent that to the best of my knowledge, information and belief the following describes the true condition of the hereinbefore described real estate and premises, to wit: a) there are no termites in the buildings; and b) the lower level or basement level under such residence is free from leakage or seepage of water. However, if termites or leakage or seepage are found in said building and it is known or discovered that any such condition existed prior to closing, I shall indemnify you for any loss or expense incurred by you as a result.

I agree to pay any assessment for paving, curb, sidewalk or utilities previously constructed or now under construction, but not yet assessed.

3 In case of the forfeiture, by a prospective purchaser, of any earnest money, said earnest money, after expenses by you has been deducted, shall be divided one-half to the owners and one-half to the agent

4 I agree to furnish a complete abstract certified to date showing marketable title, or a Title Insurance Policy to complete said sale and to pay any expense incurred in perfecting the title in case the same is found defective, and convey within _30_ days from date of sale, the property by warranty deed., or _none other_ Executed by all persons having any interest therein, and clear of all encumbrances except _no exceptions_

Possession to be given _30 days after closing_

5 I agree to maintain until delivery of possession, the heating, air conditioning, water heater, sewer, plumbing and electrical systems and any built-in appliances in good and reasonable working condition. I further agree to hold you harmless from any and all causes of action, loss, damage or expense you may be subjected to arising in connection therewith.

For sale sign and lock box permitted. Permission is given you to process, advertise and distribute this listing through the Multiple Listing Service to its participants.
Further, I authorize my mortgage lender to release all pertinent information relative to the status of my mortgage loan # _____ on subject property, to my agent.

I hereby agree the above listing and agree to the terms thereon this day and date above written. Receipt of a copy of this agreement is hereby acknowledged.

6 Owners' Name (printed)_____ Owner _Harvey J. Wender_
A-1 Real Estate Realtor Owner _Della J. Wender_
Address_____ Address _1040 Clear St._
By _Judy M. Selling_ Telephone Res. _313-0234_ Bus. _313-0003_

In addition, it is important that at the time the property is listed the salesperson clearly explain to the sellers all costs involved in the sale of the real property. The salesperson should never assume that the sellers understand their obligations and costs concerning the sale, but should always enumerate them clearly. The "Proceeds to Seller" form (see Figure 8.2) should be completed by the salesperson at the time of listing, giving the sellers an estimate of what they will net after all costs. Some states have enacted a law that requires the broker to submit a proceeds to seller form before signing a purchase agreement.

The listing contract itself allows the real estate firm to review listed properties at a glance. If a purchaser calls on a particular property, all the pertinent and accurate data are readily accessible on the contract. This eliminates errors that could arise if this information were not readily available. Listing contracts vary in different areas of the country. Some states allow verbal listings, but in many states the law requires listing contracts to be in writing to be enforceable. In these states, the contract must also be signed by the parties to be charged or held to the agreement in order to be legally enforceable.

The listing contract should contain the following basic information:

1. a description of the property
2. the amount of commission to be paid and when it will be paid
3. the expiration date
4. the signature of the party or parties to be charged

There are four types of listing contracts. Each differs in the degree of responsibility and the legal rights assigned to the broker.

Exclusive Right to Sell

The **exclusive-right-to-sell** contract gives the real estate firm the sole right to act as agent for the sellers. Should the principals find a purchaser during the term of the listing, they are obligated by the employment contract to pay a commission to the brokerage firm. Appointments for showings of the property by other firms generally are made through the listing firm, as they are responsible to the seller. The exclusive right to sell listing is the most popular listing, since the firm that lists the property receives a commission regardless of who sells the property.

In the exclusive-right-to-sell contract (shown in Figure 8.3), the numbered sections outline the contract terms as follows:

Section 1 states the expiration date of the listing and the street address and legal description of the property. It also states the offering price and the terms of sale.

Section 2 states the commission to be paid and the terms under which the sellers agree to pay the broker. These conditions include the following:

a. if an offer is made by a bona fide purchaser during the term of the listing for the listed price or any other price or terms the sellers agreed would be acceptable

b. if the sellers unfairly hinder showings of the property

c. if the sale cannot close due to liens, judgments, or suits pending against the property

d. if a sale is made due to the salesperson's efforts or advertising during the listing or within a specified number of days of the expiration date

Section 3 states that if the purchaser forfeits the earnest-money deposit, it will be divided equally between owner and broker after the broker's expenses have been deducted.

Section 4 states that the owners agree to provide either an abstract of title that has been brought to date or a title insurance policy and that the owners agree to correct any defects in the title. On this contract, the owners will give a warranty deed. The possession date is stated.

Section 5 states that the owners promise to maintain the property and permit a lock box and MLS coverage.

Section 6 lists the owners' signatures and the sales agent's signature.

Exclusive Agency

Exclusive Agency
· Seller retains right to sell
· List with one agent
· Commission paid to agent only if a sale is produced

Under the terms of the **exclusive agency** contract only one firm is hired to sell the property, but the owners retain the right to sell the property themselves without paying a commission to the firm. If the broker is the procuring cause in the transaction, the owner would be liable for the commission, that is, if the brokerage firm caused the sale to happen, as by introducing the buyers to the property.

With this type of contract, problems may arise as to whether the listing broker actually was instrumental in introducing the purchaser to the property. A buyer may see the sign in the yard, stop and visit with the owner, and subsequently purchase the home directly from the owner. In this case, the broker's "For Sale" sign was the procuring cause, and the owner would be responsible for paying the broker's fee. Under the exclusive agency listing the broker may be reluctant to spend money on advertising and promoting the property knowing that if the owner finds a buyer before the broker, the broker will not receive a commission.

If another broker sells the property as a subagent of the listing broker, the seller is committed to pay a commission.

Open Listing

Open Listing
· Hires more than one firm
· Only selling agent receives a commission
· Seller retains right to sell without obligation

An **open listing** is open to any number of brokers the sellers wish to employ. The sellers are obligated to pay a commission only to that broker who successfully produces a buyer ready, willing, and able to purchase the home. If the owners sell it themselves, they need not pay anyone a fee. Generally under an open listing the owners will not allow signs on the property, and salespeople will be less enthusiastic in trying to find a buyer. An agent will be reluctant to advertise a property on which there is no protection should a sale result.

Open listings are not always in writing, and while the owner may feel "everyone will be working to sell it," the opposite is usually true. The brokers are more inclined to spend their time and money on properties for which they will be ensured a return on their investment when a sale occurs.

Net Listing

In a **net listing** a property is listed at an agreed-upon net price, and the broker receives the excess over and above the net listing as the earned commission. Net listings are illegal in some states and frowned on by other real estate regulatory agencies, as they can easily lead to disputes and misunderstandings.

California real estate law requires that the broker give to the seller in writing before the seller signs the contract (1) the exact sale price and (2) broker's total earnings.

A net listing may be an exclusive right to sell, an exclusive agency, or an open listing. A net listing is not a type of listing but a way of calculating the commission.

Net Listing
Seller receives net amount agreed upon. Broker receives balance

$$100\%$$
$$- 7\%$$
$$93\% = .93$$
$$\$150,000 \div .93 = \$161,300 \text{ (rounded up)}$$

The property will need to sell for $161,300 if the listing broker wishes to net a 7 percent commission.

Flat Fee Listing

Brokers who take **flat fee listings** offer a range of services according to the fee charged. The broker's duties typically include listing the property, furnishing the sign, composing the advertising, writing the purchase contract, and guiding the sellers in negotiating the sale. The seller will generally pay the advertising costs, set up appointments for showings, show the property, and hold open houses.

The homeowner who opts for performing some of the functions normally taken care of by the brokerage firm pays a lower commission fee. However, the fee is collected up front and is retained by the broker regardless of whether the property sells. If the seller wants the listing broker to cooperate with other brokers and the property is sold by another firm, the seller will be charged an additional sum. It may be the rate the selling broker usually receives, or it may be a smaller sum, whatever the brokers agree upon.

Discount Broker

In an attempt to create listings, a **discount broker** will charge a fee that is less than the prevailing rate in the area. For example, the broker may charge as little as 3 percent or 4 percent, even if most brokers are charging 5 percent to 7 percent.

The discount broker usually offers all the services that other brokers do. Therefore, discount brokers must keep costs at a minimum to survive financially. Properties have to be priced competitively so they sell swiftly and, thus, keep the broker's advertising costs down.

Agent Compensation

Fee is negotiable

The rate of the professional service fee depends upon the contract, as there is no set commission. To set commission rates would be a violation of federal and state antitrust laws. The fee is negotiable between the seller and the real estate firm. The commission is payable under the following terms.

1. The broker must produce a buyer who is ready to buy now, willing (has not been forced), and financially able to buy. The exception would be a flat fee listing.
2. The broker must be able to prove performance (with a signed listing).
3. The sale must be consummated.
4. If the sale is terminated by the seller's refusal to close after accepting the offer, the fee must still be paid to the broker.

Terminating the Listing

By mutual consent

The listing will prevail until the property is sold or the listing expires, whichever occurs first. However, a listing may be terminated by mutual consent of the principal and the brokerage firm. Upon entering into the listing contract, the seller agrees not to hinder the brokerage firm and its agents in their endeavors to show the property. If the principal simply decides to break the contract for no valid reason, the brokerage firm, under the terms of the contract, has a right to sue for damages. Conversely, the real estate firm must spend time on marketing the property and make an earnest effort to locate prospective purchasers. If no such effort is made, ample reason to terminate the listing would exist. Should either of the parties die, the listing would be canceled. If there are any economic changes in the property that would affect the property's value, such as a zoning change, the listing contract can be terminated. Certain acts over which the principal and the broker have no control will nullify the listing. If the property is destroyed by fire, tornado, hurricane, earthquake, or other act of nature, cancellation of the listing would become effective since the property listed no longer exists.

Expiration of time

At the end of the listing term, the listing expires unless the parties agree to extend the employment contract. Most states require that written listings state a specific termination date. Automatic extensions, which state that the contract will continue until either party gives written notice to terminate the listing, are generally not recognized and are illegal in some states. However, many times owners will relist the property with the same broker if they are satisfied with the servicing of the listing. Market conditions may have prevented a sale within the listed time frame.

Multiple Listing Services

A **multiple listing service (MLS)** does not offer a different type of listing, but an organized exchange of real estate listings conducted by a group of brokers, usually members of a real estate board. A standard multiple listing form is used by the members, who turn all their listings in to a central service bureau that distributes them to all members.

On July 1, 1992, the **National Association of REALTORS® (NAR)** initiated a policy change in its multiple listing service. Offer of subagency through the MLS PLUS, a new feature, is now optional rather than mandatory. When submitting listings, MLS participants are now required to offer cooperation either in the form of subagency or to buyers' agents or both. All offers must include an offer of compensation. This rule is a result of the emergence of buyer agencies in many parts of the country and allows buyer brokers to participate in a commission split while retaining a fiduciary relationship to the buyer and not to the seller.

With an MLS, brokerage firms cooperate on the sale of the properties; a single dwelling has not only the members of one agency working on its sale, but the majority of the firms belonging to the MLS exchange, thus exposing the property to more customers. If for any reason the owner does not want her property in the MLS exchange, a signed waiver will protect the listing broker.

If a salesperson does not have a property among his own company's listing that meets the requirements of a prospect, the MLS broadens the chances for making a sale. Many large services publish the listings in book form, distributing them to the members on a weekly or other regular basis.

Computer terminals are another service made available by MLS. Salespeople can search the computer for new listings on a daily basis and thus enhance their ability to locate properties for their prospects. Not only may the sales office have a terminal, but personal computers in small carrying cases may be available to the individual, providing instant access wherever the salesperson may be. The MLS has become very sophisticated in recent years, with some services offering not only the data on the property but also a photo of the property so a prospect can "see" the property via the broker's computer.

Some services have a broker load system where the listing is loaded into the computer from the broker's office, thus shortening the time to make the listing available to all members.

Most MLS services will require that new listings be turned in for processing within a limited time frame, such as 48 hours. A penalty may be imposed upon members who fail to comply with the time requirement for processing the listing.

Antitrust Law

The Sherman **Antitrust Act** was enacted to maintain fair trade among competitors. Price fixing is contrary to the open market system as we know it. Real estate   *Price fixing is illegal* firms must be certain to make it clear that the commission payable is negotiated between the real estate firm and the client, not predetermined by the MLS or any real estate association or group of brokers. Although it is common for rates to be uniform in a given area, brokers can charge any fee that is agreed upon between the firm and the principal. Discussion regarding commissions should never involve anyone but the broker and the principal.

Often the market dictates the fee. If sales are brisk, the fee may be negotiated for less. If sales are slow, the property owner may offer a higher commission rate in hopes of a quicker sale. Expensive properties are frequently listed at a commission rate several percent lower than normal.

Restraint of trade and denial of multilisting services are other areas that have challenged real estate brokers. A case in point involves seven brokers in the Sunrise Community who met together and decided to charge 6.5 percent for listing properties. This was in violation of the anti-trust law. They also decided not to show the listings of two other brokers, creating a form of boycotting in an attempt to hinder competition; also illegal under the antitrust law.

Real Estate Associations

Trade organizations

A real estate board is a voluntary organization whose membership comprises persons engaged in some phase of the real estate business or who are directly or indirectly interested in real estate. Most boards maintain an affiliate classification of membership that is open to lending institutions, appraisers, title and abstracting companies, and others whose duties or interests are related to real estate.

The purpose of a real estate board is to promote good ethics among its members, promote the enactment of legislation for the protection of property rights and interests, and secure the benefits of united efforts for its members. The board upholds fair practices and generally endeavors to professionalize the industry.

Members of the local real estate board also belong to the state association. The salesperson or broker who resides in areas where no local board exists is a member-at-large of the state association. Yearly conventions are held by the members where ideas are exchanged and new concepts within the industry are discussed. Educational seminars are always an important part of the conventions.

The NAR is the parent organization of the state boards and is headquartered in Chicago, Illinois. Its membership is composed of members of local boards and state associations. All members that belong to the organization can refer to

The REALTOR®

themselves as **REALTORS**®, a registered trademark that can be used only by NAR members. The NAR has set forth a strict code of ethics to which all members must adhere.

Under the umbrella of NAR are numerous affiliate organizations that offer a wide range of educational opportunities. Some of the institutes offer designations upon completion of courses and successfully passing their examinations. For example, the Institute for Real Estate Management (IREM) has specialized property management courses, and the Women's Council of REALTORS® (WCR) has developed leadership training courses and relocation courses. With specialization becoming more prevalent in real estate, the availability of these courses is an important reason to belong to NAR.

A *Realtist* is a member of a group of brokers known as the National Association of Real Estate Brokers. The association began in 1947 and is composed of minority brokers who promote improved housing in the areas they serve.

Summary of Important Points

1. There are four types of listings a broker may have with a property owner:
   a. The exclusive right to sell gives the real estate firm the right to act as the sole agent of the owner.
   b. The exclusive agency listing allows the owners the right and opportunity to sell their own property.
   c. The open listing is used by owners who desire to list a property with more than one agent.
   d. The net listing sets the dollar amount that the seller wants to net from the sale, with the agency receiving the excess.
2. A personal assistant performs tasks for the licensee, thus freeing the agent to pursue listings and sales.
3. New technology such as computers, e-mail, cell phones, and personal digital assistant (PDA) enable the licensee to be more efficient.
4. Most real estate agents insist upon the exclusive-right-to-sell contract because they spend time and money obtaining a buyer for the property owner.
5. The multiple listing service is the vehicle used by real estate companies to make known to other firms the data on their listings. This method encourages cooperation among companies because all salespeople are aware of a property's availability.
6. The National Association of REALTORS® is the parent organization to state and local real estate boards. These voluntary trade associations help promote good ethics among their members and generally endeavor to professionalize the industry.

Discussion Points

1. What are the possible consequences of overpricing a property?
2. As a real estate salesperson, what type of listing would you prefer? Give reasons for your answer.
3. In what circumstances can a listing be canceled?

4. Give reasons that property owners would list their property with a real estate firm in lieu of selling it "by owner."

5. If you worked for a brokerage firm, would you prefer to be an employee or an independent contractor? Give reasons for your answer.

6. What are the advantages of a flat fee listing for the seller?

7. Explain the advantages of listing with a real estate firm that belongs to a multiple listing service.

Review Questions

Answers to these questions are found in the Answer Key section at the back of the book.

1. A real estate salesperson must:
   a. always be under the employ of a broker
   b. never refuse to accept a listing
   c. hold a national real estate license
   d. belong to a multiple listing service

2. An exclusive-right-to-sell listing contract:
   a. gives the broker a commission based on an agreed price the seller wishes to net, with the broker receiving the excess over the agreed amount
   b. makes the brokerage firm the exclusive agent for a stipulated period of time
   c. allows the owner the right to sell the property without paying a commission to the listing broker
   d. will automatically be renewed if it expires before the property is sold

3. Under the terms and conditions of an open listing:
   a. the owner may sell the property but must pay a commission to the listing broker
   b. the listing is given to any number of brokers the seller wishes to hire, with a commission going only to the selling firm
   c. one broker is given the listing, but it is "open" for other brokers to sell
   d. upon the sale, the commission is split between all the brokers who were given the listing

4. It is mandatory that a listing contract:
   a. have a termination date
   b. be signed by the purchasers
   c. have an automatic renewal clause
   d. be processed through a multiple listing service

5. Under the rules of a multiple listing service:
   a. only the firm that has the listing may show the property
   b. all members of the MLS cooperate in selling the property
   c. all the firms belonging to the MLS may place their signs on the property
   d. properties are advertised only in the MLS book

6. The term REALTOR® is a coined word:
   a. available for use only by members of the multiple listing service
   b. used only by members of the National Association of REALTORS®
   c. used by all licensed real estate agents
   d. issued for the use of real estate brokers, but not salespersons

7. A real estate broker is:
   a. appointed by the property owner to act for and in his stead in the sale of the owner's property
   b. not responsible for the salesperson's actions
   c. responsible to sell the property within the listed time frame
   d. always employed as a general agent to the property owner

8. The most desirable type of listing for a real estate broker is a(n):
   a. open listing
   b. net listing
   c. exclusive-right-to-sell listing
   d. exclusive listing

9. An owner gives an open listing to firms X and Y. Firm X sells the property to a buyer to whom firm Y had previously shown the property. The commission was:
   a. earned by firm X
   b. earned by firm Y
   c. split evenly between X and Y
   d. arbitrated by the Board of REALTORS®

10. If an owner sells her own home on which you have an exclusive agency:
    a. you receive no commission
    b. you receive a full commission
    c. you receive half commission
    d. you receive 40 percent

11. Which is the closest to a multiple listing?
    a. cooperative
    b. net listing
    c. exclusive agency
    d. exclusive right to sell

12. Mr. Jennings lists his house with Ms. Walls, a real estate salesperson employed by the A-1 Real Estate Company. The agency exists:
    a. between Jennings and Walls
    b. between Jennings and the A-1 Real Estate Company
    c. between A-1 Realty, the multiple listing service, and Jennings
    d. for the duration of the listing time between the salesperson and the principal

13. The least protection a broker has is with a(n):
    a. exclusive agency
    b. open listing
    c. exclusive right to sell
    d. multiple listing

14. The brokerage firm receives the excess over and above a specified sales price in a(n):
    a. net listing
    b. gross listing
    c. open listing
    d. exclusive listing

15. Broker X has an exclusive agency on a property that she learns has been sold by broker Y. Broker Y receives a full commission. Broker X should:
    a. request half commission from broker Y
    b. request full commission from broker Y
    c. request full commission from the owner
    d. realize that no commission is due her

16. A listing may be canceled for all of the following reasons EXCEPT:
    a. the owner of the property dies
    b. the broker files bankruptcy
    c. the property is destroyed by fire
    d. the owner changes his mind

17. Sally Wells obtains two listings: one is an open listing from owner A, and the other is an exclusive agency listing from owner B. After one week A and B, who had previously visited about their properties, decide to exchange their real estate. Sally Wells will obtain the following:
    a. a commission from A and B
    b. a commission from A
    c. a commission from B
    d. no commission since the owners exchanged their properties

18. What happens when a principal sells his home under an exclusive-right-to-sell listing?
    a. the broker receives no commission
    b. the broker receives a commission on the gross sales price
    c. the broker receives half the commission ordinarily due him
    d. legal action will need to be instigated if the broker is to receive a commission

19. The only way a seller could terminate an exclusive agency is if:
    a. a buyer is introduced by a broker from another real estate firm
    b. a buyer is introduced by the seller
    c. the seller decides the broker is not advertising the property often enough
    d. the seller writes a contract with a buyer who was shown the property by the listing agent

20. Which of the following listings is least likely to be defined as a percentage of the sale price?
    a. open listing
    b. net listing
    c. exclusive agency
    d. exclusive right to sell

21. A licensed broker brings a buyer and seller together. The buyer later finds out he is being transferred. The buyer goes to the seller, and they agree to rescind the contract. The broker involved:
    a. gets to keep the earnest deposit as liquidation damage
    b. gets a full commission from the seller
    c. gets no monetary compensation
    d. keeps half the commission

Marketing and Selling Real Estate

KEY TERMS

auction

bill of sale

counteroffer

disclosure statement

earnest money

equitable interest

errors and omissions insurance

home buyer's insurance

home warranty insurance

lease option

marketable title

purchase agreement

right of first refusal

straw man

trust account

OVERVIEW

Once a property has been listed for sale, the real estate firm proceeds to perform the function for which it was employed—finding a buyer. Usually the broker advertises the property in the newspaper and places a "For Sale" sign on the premises to elicit responses from prospective purchasers. In addition, the sales representatives check their lists of prospects to see if the new listing will meet anyone's requirements. If the firm belongs to a multiple listing service, it immediately sends the listing information to the service for processing. Open houses (holding the house open for inspection) are another means of attracting would-be buyers.

This chapter covers the elements of a purchase agreement, presenting and handling a counteroffer, and obtaining the earnest-money deposit and placing it in a trust account. The importance of the seller disclosure statement is also covered.

The Purchase Agreement

The salesperson prequalifies buyers prior to showing them properties to determine the price range they will qualify to purchase. When a prospective buyer makes the decision to purchase a particular property, the salesperson completes an estimated buyer's figures form. These costs will vary across the country and among lenders. The form gives the buyer a clear picture of how much money will be needed to close the loan and what the monthly payments will be. With the buyer's approval of the estimated costs, a **purchase agreement** is then written. In some parts of the country this document is referred to as an offer and acceptance or a deposit receipt.

Upon acceptance, the agreement is a contract and, according to the statute of frauds in most states, must be in writing to be enforceable. While the writing of the contract is generally done by the selling agent, some states require that since a contract is a legal document, the actual writing of the offer to purchase must be done by an attorney. In this instance, after the buyers have selected the property they desire to purchase, the licensee directs them to an attorney. Other states have the view that the completion of a printed purchase agreement (see Figure 9.1) does not constitute the practice of law. If the printed document contains all the essential elements and provisions for contingencies, protection for both parties is provided. Regardless of the laws of your state, the presentation of the offer to the seller will in most communities still be the listing agent's responsibility.

Offer to Purchase

The offer-to-purchase contract shown in Figure 9.1 contains the following information:

Elements of a purchase contract

Section A states the date the offer to purchase was signed, along with the street and legal address of the property. Any personal property included in the sale is written in this section of the agreement.

Section B stipulates that the owners will convey good title, free of all liens (unless the buyers are assuming an existing mortgage). The sellers further agree that any existing indebtedness against the property will be paid.

Section C sets forth the purchase price and the amount of the earnest deposit. The balance of the purchase price will be paid according to the type of financing checked in Section D.

Section D contains four choices: the buyers may either (1) pay cash, (2) assume the existing mortgage, (3) obtain a new loan, or (4) request a land contract (owner financing).

Section E contains any additional conditions of the agreement that need to be clarified.

Section F provides for proration of taxes.

Section G states that the buyers have inspected the premises and agree to accept the property in its present condition. The sellers agree to maintain all

Figure 9.1	Offer-to-Purchase Contract

PURCHASE AGREEMENT

<u>April 8, 2008</u>

A I, the undersigned purchaser, hereby agree to purchase the property described as follows:
Address _____<u>1040 Clear Street</u>_____
Legal description ____<u>Lot 8, Block 1 Confusion Hill Subdivision</u>_____ -__
Including all fixtures and equipment permanently attached to said premises. The only
personal property included is as follows: ____<u>living room drapes</u>_____

B Subject, however, and on condition that the owner thereof has good, valid, and marketable
Title In fee simple, and said owner and said owner agrees to convey title to said property to
me or my nominees by warranty deed or _____<u>none other</u>_free and clear of all liens,
encumbrances, or special taxes levied or assessed, except ____<u>no exceptions</u>_____

C This offer subject to all building and use restrictions, utility easements not exceeding 10 feet in
width abutting the boundary of said property, and covenants now of record. Seller agrees to
pay any assessments for paving, curb, sidewalk or utilities previously constructed or now
under construction but not yet assessed.

I agree to pay for same <u>One hundred eighty four thousand and no cents ($)184,000.00 dollars,</u>
on the following terms: <u>$4,000</u> deposited herewith as evidenced by your receipt
attached below. Balance to be paid only as shown in following paragraphs: <u>3, 5 and 6</u> .

D # 1 CASH
Balance of $_____to be paid in cash or by certified check at time of delivery of deed, no
financing being required.

#2 LOAN ASSUMPTION
I agree to assume and pay existing mortgage balance in favor of _____in the
approximate amount of $_____and pay the balance in cash or by certified check at
the time of delivery of deed; it being understood the present mortgage terms call for stated
interest rate of _____% per annum and payments of $_____per ___. Said payment
includes _____. Stated interest on existing loan to be prorated to date of
closing.
I agree to reimburse the seller for the amount in the escrow account which is to be assigned
to me.

#3 CONDITIONAL UPON LOAN
Balance of _____ to be paid in cash or by certified check at time of delivery of deed,
conditional however, upon my ability to obtain a loan, to be secured by first mortgage, or
deed of trust, on above described property in the amount of $_____. Said loan to be
VA____FHA_____Conventional____X___PMI_____or VA/FHA_____, with terms providing
for stated interest not exceeding _____% per annum, and monthly payments of
approximately $_____plus taxes and insurance. Loan origination fee/service to be paid
by purchaser. I agree to make application for said loan within 10 days of acceptance of this
offer. I hereby authorize you to negotiate for a loan on the above basis and I agree to sign all
papers and pay all costs in connection therewith.

4 LAND CONTRACT
Balance to be evidenced by land contract with present owner, providing for additional cash
payment or certified check of $_____at time of execution of the contract, and remainder
$_____to be paid in monthly payments of $_____ , or more, which monthly payments
shall include interest at the rate of____% per annum computed monthly on the unpaid portion
of the principal. All other terms and conditions of the land contract shall be mutually agreed.

E #5 <u>Possession no later than May 14, 2008.</u>

(continued)

Figure 9.1 continued

F ⌐ 6 TAXES
└ All real estate taxes shall be pro-rated as of date of possession May 14, 2008

G ⌐ This offer is based upon my personal inspection or investigation of the premises and not
   upon any representation or warranties of condition by the seller or his agent. Seller agrees
   to maintain, until delivery of possession, the heating, air conditioning, water heater, sewer,
   plumbing and electrical systems and any built-in appliances in working condition.
   Any risk of loss to the property shall be borne by the Seller until title has been conveyed to
   the Purchaser. In the event prior to closing, the structure on said property are materially
   damaged by fire, explosion or any other cause, Purchaser shall have the right to rescind this
   agreement, whereupon Seller shall then refund to Purchaser the deposit made hereunder.
   Purchaser, except for VA loan, agrees to pay the cost of a termite inspection of the house
   and attached structures, and Seller agrees to pay for any treatment or repair work found
   necessary. If repairs are found to be needed for issuance of termite warranty, upon
   └ completion of repairs, Purchaser agrees to accept said treated real estate.

H ⌐ This offer is binding upon both parties and the heirs and assigns of said parties.

   _____   _____Purchaser
   └   _____Purchaser
                                     Address 328 Harbor Lane

I ⌐ Received from _____the sum of four thousand dollars
   ($4,000) Dollars (by check) to apply on the purchase price of the above described property.
   In the event the above offer is not accepted by the owner of said property within the time
   hereinafter specified, or in the event there are any defects in the title which cannot be cured
   as specified above, the money hereby paid is to be refunded. If purchaser fails to consumate
   the purchase, the owner may, at his option, retain said money herein paid as liquidated
   damages for such failure to carry out said agreement of sale, subject to the terms of the
   listing agreement.
   This receipt is not an acceptance of the above offer, it being understood that the above
   proposition is taken subject to the written approval and acceptance by the owner on or
   before _____.

   445 Homestead Avenue 303-3030_____ A-1 Real Estate Company
   └ Office address   phone #

J ⌐ ACCEPTANCE

   We agree to the above stated terms and will deliver possession and title and perform
   according to this contract. We agree to pay A-1 Real Estate a cash fee of 7% of the sale.

   _____   _____
   └ Witness   Seller

                                    _____
                                    Seller

K ⌐ We are in receipt of the seller's acceptance of our contract

   _____   _____
   └ Witness   Buyer

                               _____
                               Buyer

the component parts in working order. The sellers further state they will be responsible for any loss to the property until title is conveyed. If any termite damage is found, they promise to pay for repairs.

Section H states the contract is binding upon the parties and their heirs and assigns. The purchasers sign the agreement.

Section I is the statement of receipt for the earnest deposit and the time allowed for the owners to accept the offer. The real estate company's name and address are also stated.

Section J shows the date of acceptance and the signatures of the accepting owners and of the witness.

Section K is signed by the buyers to show that they received a copy of the accepted contract.

Presenting the Offer

When the offer to purchase is written, a copy is given to the offeror (purchaser) as a receipt. The selling agent then takes the offer to the offeree (seller) for formal acceptance. Generally it is the listing agent who contacts the sellers to present the offer. If the sellers agree to all the conditions of the offer, they sign the acceptance. In Figure 9.1 at Section J, the sellers accepted the offer as written.

When the terms of the contract are agreed upon, a copy is left with the seller, and the agent notifies the buyer that the offer was accepted and gives the buyer a copy of the signed contract. In our sample purchase agreement at Section K, the buyers sign that they have received a copy of the seller's acceptance.

An offer may be rescinded at any time prior to the seller's acceptance, so it behooves the sales agent to deliver the contract promptly.

Counteroffers

To alter any portion of the offer nullifies the entire agreement. If the seller does not accept the terms, the seller may elect to make a **counteroffer.** Any counteroffer revokes the previous offer and is replaced with a new contract. A counteroffer is not a partial acceptance since an acceptance cannot be conditional. However, the counteroffer can be dated and signed by the owner and the time limit for acceptance of this new offer be stated. The buyer can now agree to the new terms or decide against purchasing the property.

When an offer is countered, the property is available for another offer, whether from the original offeror or from another party. If the seller counters an offer and meanwhile another offer from a second party is presented to the seller, the seller may accept the second party's offer after withdrawing the counteroffer to the first party (assuming the first party did not act upon and accept the counter). Time is of the essence, and a would-be buyer may lose the property he is attempting to purchase by negotiating terms and price. Conversely, the buyer may save money in such negotiating tactics. (See Figure 9.2.)

Countering the Offer
- Accept terms of seller's offer
- Write a new offer
- Ask selling agent to return earnest deposit

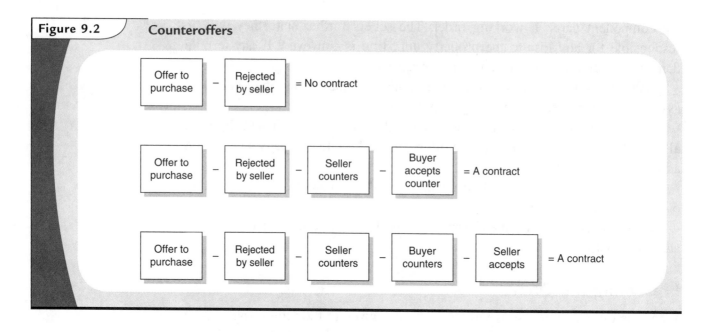

Figure 9.2   Counteroffers

Earnest-Money Deposits

The **earnest money** is the deposit that the purchaser gives to the broker at the time the written contract to purchase is offered. It binds the contract and demonstrates the good intent of the purchaser. In some states the earnest deposit is referred to as hand money or a binder. This earnest money deposit must be placed in the broker's **trust account** upon acceptance of the offer. It is credited to the buyer's total payment at the time of closing. If the offer is not accepted, the earnest money is returned to the would-be purchaser.

The amount of the earnest money is negotiable and not set by law, though in some areas it is common practice to ask for 5 or 10 percent of the purchase price as a deposit. The size of the deposit should be sufficient to show the seller that the buyer's offer is sincere. However, in the final analysis the sellers determine what they will accept. The earnest money will be forfeited if the buyer defaults on the contract because the seller took the property off the market and may have missed an opportunity to sell it to someone else.

Many states require the broker to obtain a release in writing covering the forfeiture of the funds if the buyer decides not to complete the contract. This penalty must be disclosed in writing at time of acceptance by the broker and before presentation of the contract to the seller. Although the funds are entrusted to the broker's care, the broker must not make decisions as to their dispersal without written permission. In the case of the buyer defaulting, not only would the buyer agree in writing to relinquish the earnest deposit, but the seller would agree in writing to accept the deposit as liquidated damages. If the property later sells for less, the seller has been compensated, at least in part, for the difference.

Some brokers have a statement in their listing contract that in case of the forfeiture by a prospective purchaser of any earnest-money deposit, after expenses

Seller determines amount of deposit

Earnest Deposits
· Encourage buyers not to default
· Seller is compensated for buyer's lack of performance

incurred by the broker are deducted, the money is divided one-half to the owners and one-half to the broker. Some also have a statement that if there is a dispute as to what and who caused the breach, the funds will be turned over to a third or disinterested party called an interpleader, which is usually the circuit court.

Trust Accounts

In most states a broker must maintain a trust account in the firm's name in a depository in the state where the broker is doing business. All customer or client money coming into the possession of the broker must be kept in that trust account, unless there is written agreement to the contrary, or until the transaction is consummated or terminated. Ledgers and journals showing all entries must be kept by the broker. This includes earnest-money deposits, down payments, and security deposits on leased property. Many states require separate trust accounts for processing sales and for rents received from managing rental properties. Each deposit must be separately identified in the trust account records, and the broker is not entitled to any part of the money as a commission until the sale is final. Most states require the trust account to be a non-interest-bearing checking account; however, if a substantial earnest-money deposit is given and the closing is scheduled for a time months later, the buyer may desire his deposit to be earning interest. In such a situation, with written approval of both buyer and seller, the broker may place the deposit in an interest-bearing account.

Earnest-money deposit is safeguarded

The trust accounts are audited in most states, generally on an annual basis. If the books reveal any discrepancies, the broker's license could be in jeopardy. It is the broker's duty to safeguard the funds of others in all transactions.

Lease Options

Another means of purchasing property is the **lease option**, that is, leasing with an option to buy. The option permits the lessee to purchase the property within a set period of time at the price and terms defined in the lease option agreement. The lessee must execute the right to buy within the time frame stated in the lease option or the right is forfeited. If the lessee elects to perform on the option agreement, a purchase agreement will be completed as in a regular sale. If the lessee chooses not to exercise the option, either the lease will expire or be renewed or the property owner can place the property on the open market for sale.

Option gives right to buy

The use of the lease option generally occurs when financing terms are not advantageous to the purchaser or when the seller is having difficulty finding a buyer for a particular property. It permits someone to lease the property and later make the decision to buy or not. In some instances the property owner may allow a portion of the rent to apply toward the down payment. If the property has not appreciated in value, the seller may be eager to apply the rent toward the purchase price. Conversely, the lessee may not be as eager to purchase it if similar properties can be bought for less.

Right of First Refusal

A tenant may wish to rent a property with the **right of first refusal** to purchase. This allows the tenant the right to match any offer that the property owner may receive. It *does not obligate the renter to perform,* but gives the tenant an advantage in having the first right to buy. This could prove to be a disadvantage to the owner as prospective purchasers may shy away from offering to buy when aware that the tenant holds a previous right to meet any offer presented to the owner.

Lease Purchase

Unlike an option to buy, a *lease purchase binds the lessee to the terms of the lease purchase agreement.* It is generally used if the lessee wants to purchase the property but does not have the funds, if financing is difficult to obtain, or if the title needs to be cleared. Usually a portion of the rent is applied toward the purchase price. This method of buying allows the lessee to obtain possession, with title transferred to the lessee at a later date as stated in the lease purchase agreement.

Equitable Interest

Once an offer is accepted by the owner, the buyer has an **equitable interest** in the real estate. The seller is still the title holder of record until the closing of the transaction and delivery of the deed, but the buyer has what is known as *equitable title.* The seller must perform in accordance with the signed contract and now holds title in name only.

Assignment of contract   The question may arise: Can the buyer assign the contract to another? As stated in the chapter on contracts, unless it specifically states to the contrary, the buyer has the right to transfer the equitable interest. However, the assignee must perform according to the terms of the contract. In some instances the buyer may have been acting as a **straw man**—that is, the offer was made with the intent of transferring the contract prior to the closing. In this case, the true buyer may have wanted to remain anonymous until the seller accepted the terms of the offer.

Most contracts, including options, leases, mortgages, and land contracts, are assignable unless they specifically state to the contrary. However, if the contract is for a personal right, as in a listing contract, the assignor would need the consent of the seller.

Bill of Sale

Occasionally a purchase offer for real property will include personal property. Although a deed is used to transfer the real property, a **bill of sale** is used when chattel (personal property) is sold. The bill of sale transfers the goods.

Marketable Title

The owner is responsible to deliver good and **marketable title** to the buyer. It must be free of any defects, liens, and encumbrances. The only time an existing mortgage remains against the property would be when the purchaser is assuming the loan.

Sale by Auction

Auction sales are a more recent method of selling real estate. A *licensed auctioneer* is hired as the agent of the property owner. The auctioneer is responsible for advertising the property in the newspaper and printing notices to be sent to prospective buyers or posted in public places. The notices will describe the property and any personal property that may also be offered with the sale.

An auction may be *absolute* or *with reserve.* An *absolute* auction means that the property will be sold to the highest bidder, no matter how low the bid is. No property may be removed once the bidding begins, and the seller (offeror) is bound to accept the high bid, which creates a contract.

An auction *with reserve* permits the owner to reject bids and the auctioneer or the owner to remove the property from the sale. In this type of auction, the bidder is the offeror.

No warranties are given by the auctioneer or the owner in an auction sale *except* that they warrant that the property is being sold and that they have the legal right to sell the property and transfer title to the bidder.

Auction sales are sometimes the result of a foreclosure on a defaulted mortgage. The courts have the property sold at a public auction with the real estate passing to the highest bidder. This would be an absolute auction with the proceeds applied against the debt and any excess going to the debtor.

> **Auction**
> · Absolute sale—sold to highest bidder
> · Sale with reserve—owner may reject bid

Representing the Seller

While the selling agent represents the seller, the agent nonetheless owes the buyer fair treatment. While confidentiality is owed to the principal, the buyer is entitled to true disclosure of all the facts concerning the property. In fact, new accountability for real estate agents was raised when suit was brought by the Eastons over structural problems of a home they purchased 25 miles east of San Francisco. Two months after the Eastons bought their $250,000 hillside ranch home, the land began to buckle and creep. Years of litigation followed that broadened to include not only the previous owner but also three real estate companies and two contractors. The lawsuit raised the question of whether the real estate brokers are financially liable if they sell a defective property, even if they were unaware of the problem at the time of the sale. Both the trial court and the California Supreme Court decided the selling broker was negligent and had been obligated to investigate the property. Previously it was considered sufficient that the selling agent disclose facts that the agent knew about the property. The landmark Easton case reached beyond this and stated it was the selling broker's responsibility to discover and disclose that there may be a problem on a property.

> Agent owes buyer true disclosure

The courts awarded the Eastons in excess of $200,000 in damages, which was largely covered by insurance held by one of the real estate firms.

Disclosure Statement from Seller

Seller disclosure
statement

The case resulted in California legislation that requires a seller to complete a standardized **disclosure statement**. The form has a checklist of inspections of potential problem areas, such as settling, landfill areas, septic tanks, room additions that were noncode, and appliances (see Figure 9.3). The California law states that a broker's responsibility is limited to areas that are accessible for visual inspection. A real estate broker is not expected to be a specialist in areas such as engineering and architecture or land faults and soil compaction. It is the responsibility of the seller to disclose *all* defects, hidden (latent) or visible (patent).

Other states have followed California's action and are mandating that the seller complete a disclosure statement form. In states without such legislation, many brokers are requesting that the sellers sign a disclosure form. Some forms merely ask the seller to respond to the questions by checking the appropriate box—yes, no, or I don't know.

Errors and Omissions Insurance

Insurance protection
for agents

Because of the Easton case, other lawsuits followed, and brokers are concerned that it may result in frivolous claims. Many have purchased malpractice insurance, commonly referred to as **errors and omissions insurance**. For an annual premium the broker is defended against a claim. Kentucky was the first state to enact legislation mandating such insurance. Some real estate companies are being denied errors and omissions insurance if they are involved in more than listing and selling real property, since additional risks are incurred if the company is in property management, construction, or land development. While the insurance rates are high, the trend toward consumerism has propelled brokers to insure against unhappy buyers. A case in point was a problem that resulted when the purchaser of an acreage was alarmed several months after the sale by the sight of a backhoe digging a trench across his property. He learned the adjoining property owners had been given an easement by the past owner to tap into his well. The easement was never recorded, so the buyer had no knowledge of its existence. The seller declared he had told the sales agent about the easement, but the sales agent had no recollection of the conversation. Fortunately, attorneys for the errors and omissions insurance company defended the broker and his sales agent.

Subscription to errors and omissions insurance has increased as more states are mandating that all licensees carry the insurance. The states that legislate the requirement also offer the insurance through a selected provider that must insure every licensee. The annual fee is nominal, usually anywhere from $65 to $100.

| Figure 9.3 | Seller Disclosure Statement Form |

Seller Property Condition Disclosure Statement
Residential Real Property

THIS DISCLOSURE STATEMENT IS BEING COMPLETED AND DELIVERED IN ACCORDANCE WITH STATE LAW. STATE LAW REQUIRES THE SELLER TO COMPLETE THIS STATEMENT (REV. STAT. §76-2,120).

Seller _____ is _____ is not occupying the real property.

How long has Seller owned the real property? _____ year(s)

This Disclosure Statement concerns the real property located at _____

_____

in the City of _____, County of _____ State of _____ legally described as

_____

_____

_____

_____

THIS STATEMENT IS A DISCLOSURE OF THE CONDITION OF THE REAL PROPERTY KNOWN BY THE SELLER ON THE DATE ON WHICH THIS STATEMENT IS SIGNED. THIS STATEMENT IS NOT A WARRANTY OF ANY KIND BY THE SELLER OR ANY AGENT REPRESENTING A PRINCIPAL IN THE TRANSACTION, AND SHOULD NOT BE ACCEPTED AS A SUBSTITUTE FOR ANY INSPECTION OR WARRANTY THAT THE PURCHASER MAY WISH TO OBTAIN. EVEN THOUGH THE INFORMATION PROVIDED IN THIS STATEMENT IS NOT A WARRANTY, THE PURCHASER MAY RELY ON THE INFORMATION CONTAINED HEREIN IN DECIDING WHETHER AND ON WHAT TERMS TO PURCHASE THE REAL PROPERTY. ANY AGENT REPRESENTING A PRINCIPAL IN THE TRANSACTION MAY PROVIDE A COPY OF THIS STATEMENT TO ANY OTHER PERSON IN CONNECTION WITH ANY ACTUAL OR POSSIBLE SALE OF THE REAL PROPERTY. THE INFORMATION PROVIDED IN THIS STATEMENT IS THE REPRESENTATION OF THE SELLER AND NOT THE REPRESENTATION OF ANY AGENT, AND IS NOT INTENDED TO BE PART OF ANY CONTRACT BETWEEN THE SELLER AND PURCHASER.

Seller please note: You are required to complete this Disclosure Statement in full. If any particular item or matter does not apply and there is no provision or space for so indicating, insert "N/A".

SELLER STATES THAT, TO THE BEST OF SELLER'S BELIEF AND KNOWLEDGE AS OF THE DATE THIS DISCLOSURE STATEMENT IS COMPLETED AND SIGNED BY THE SELLER, THE CONDITION OF THE REAL PROPERTY IS:

PART I - If there is more than one of each item listed in this Part, the statement made applies to each and all of such items unless otherwise noted in the Comments section, PART III of this Disclosure Statement. If an item in this Part is not on the property or will not be included in the sale, check only the "None/Not Included" column for that item.

SECTION A. Appliances.

	WORKING	NOT WORKING	DO NOT KNOW IF WORKING	NONE/NOT INCLUDED		WORKING	NOT WORKING	DO NOT KNOW IF WORKING	NONE/NOT INCLUDED
1. Built-in vacuum system and equipment	☐	☐	☐	☐	9. Microwave oven	☐	☐	☐	☐
2. Clothes dryer	☐	☐	☐	☐	10. Oven	☐	☐	☐	☐
3. Clothes washer	☐	☐	☐	☐	11. Range	☐	☐	☐	☐
4. Dishwasher	☐	☐	☐	☐	12. Refrigerator	☐	☐	☐	☐
5. Disposal	☐	☐	☐	☐	13. Room air conditioner	☐	☐	☐	☐
6. Freezer	☐	☐	☐	☐	14. TV antenna/satellite dish	☐	☐	☐	☐
7. Gas grill	☐	☐	☐	☐	15. Trash compactor	☐	☐	☐	☐
8. Range ventilation systems	☐	☐	☐	☐	16. Other (Specify) _____	☐	☐	☐	☐

SECTION B. Electrical Systems.

	WORKING	NOT WORKING	DO NOT KNOW IF WORKING	NONE/NOT INCLUDED		WORKING	NOT WORKING	DO NOT KNOW IF WORKING	NONE/NOT INCLUDED
1. Electrical service panel (Capacity _____ amp, if known) _____ Fuse _____ Circuit Breakers	☐	☐	☐	☐	7. Smoke/fire alarm	☐	☐	☐	☐
					8. Room vent fan	☐	☐	☐	☐
					9. 220 volt service	☐	☐	☐	☐
2. Ceiling fan(s)	☐	☐	☐	☐	10. Security system ___ owned ___ leased ___ Central station monitoring	☐	☐	☐	☐
3. Garage door opener/remote controller(s) (number of controllers, if included ___)	☐	☐	☐	☐	11. Other (Specify) _____	☐	☐	☐	☐
4. Telephone wiring and jacks	☐	☐	☐	☐	12. Have you experienced any problems with the electrical system or its components? ___ no ___ yes				
5. Cable TV wiring and jacks	☐	☐	☐	☐					
6. Intercom or sound system wiring and built-in speakers	☐	☐	☐	☐	If yes, explain the condition in the Comments section, PART III of this Disclosure Statement.				

SECTION C. Heating and Cooling Systems

	WORKING	NOT WORKING	DO NOT KNOW IF WORKING	NONE/NOT INCLUDED		WORKING	NOT WORKING	DO NOT KNOW IF WORKING	NONE/NOT INCLUDED
1. Air purifier	☐	☐	☐	☐	7. Gas log	☐	☐	☐	☐
2. Attic fan	☐	☐	☐	☐	8. Gas starter (fireplace)	☐	☐	☐	☐
3. Whole house fan	☐	☐	☐	☐	9. Heat pump	☐	☐	☐	☐
4. Central air conditioning	☐	☐	☐	☐	10. Humidifier	☐	☐	☐	☐
5. Fireplace/fireplace insert	☐	☐	☐	☐	11. Propane tank (___ rent ___ own).	☐	☐	☐	☐
6. Heating system (__ gas __ electric ___ other, specify)	☐	☐	☐	☐	12. Woodburning stove	☐	☐	☐	☐
					13. Other (Specify) _____	☐	☐	☐	☐

(continued)

Figure 9.3 continued

SECTION D. Water Systems.	WORKING	NOT WORKING	DO NOT KNOW IF WORKING	NONE/NOT INCLUDED		WORKING	NOT WORKING	DO NOT KNOW IF WORKING	NONE/NOT INCLUDED
1. Hot tub/whirlpool	☐	☐	☐	☐	5. Water heater	☐	☐	☐	☐
2. Plumbing	☐	☐	☐	☐	6. Water purifier	☐	☐	☐	☐
3. Swimming pool	☐	☐	☐	☐	7. Water softener (___Rent ___Own)	☐	☐	☐	☐
4. Underground sprinkler	☐	☐	☐	☐	8. Well system	☐	☐	☐	☐
___ backflow preventer	☐	☐	☐	☐	9. Other (Specify) _____	☐	☐	☐	☐

SECTION E. Sewer Systems.	WORKING	NOT WORKING	DO NOT KNOW IF WORKING	NONE/NOT INCLUDED		WORKING	NOT WORKING	DO NOT KNOW IF WORKING	NONE/NOT INCLUDED
1. Plumbing	☐	☐	☐	☐	3. Septic System	☐	☐	☐	☐
2. Sump pump	☐	☐	☐	☐	4. Other (Specify) _____	☐	☐	☐	☐
(Discharges to _____)					5. Other (Specify) _____	☐	☐	☐	☐

PART II - In this part, in Sections A, B, and C, if the answer to any item is "Yes", explain the condition in the Comments section, PART III of this Disclosure Statement.

Section A. Structural Conditions. If there is more than one of any item listed in this Section, the statement made applies to each and all of such items unless otherwise noted in the Comments section, PART III of this Disclosure Statement.

	YES	NO	DO NOT KNOW		YES	NO	DO NOT KNOW
1. Age of Roof (if known) _____ years				8. Is there presently damage to the chimney?	☐	☐	☐
2. Does the roof leak?	☐	☐	☐	9. Are there any windows which presently leak, or do any insulated windows have broken seals?	☐	☐	☐
3. Has the roof leaked?	☐	☐	☐	10. Have you experienced any moving or settling of the following:			
4. Is there presently damage to the roof?	☐	☐	☐	foundation?	☐	☐	☐
5. Has there been leakage/seepage in the basement or crawl space?	☐	☐	☐	floor?	☐	☐	☐
6. Has there been any damage to the real property or any of the structures thereon due to the following occurrences including, but not limited to, wind, hail, fire, flood, wood-destroying insects, or rodents?	☐	☐	☐	wall?	☐	☐	☐
				sidewalk?	☐	☐	☐
				patio?	☐	☐	☐
7. Are there any structural problems with the structures on the real property?	☐	☐	☐	driveway?	☐	☐	☐
				retaining wall?	☐	☐	☐

SECTION B. Environmental Conditions. Have any of the following substances, materials, or products been on the real property? If tests have been conducted for any of the following, provide a copy of all test results, if available.

	YES	NO	DO NOT KNOW		YES	NO	DO NOT KNOW
1. Asbestos	☐	☐	☐	7. Underground fuel, chemical or other type of storage tank	☐	☐	☐
2. Contaminated soil or water (including drinking water)	☐	☐	☐	8. Have any other hazardous substances, materials, or products identified by the Environmental Protection Agency or its authorized Nebraska designee been on the real property?	☐	☐	☐
3. Landfill or buried materials	☐	☐	☐				
4. Lead-based paint	☐	☐	☐				
5. Radon gas	☐	☐	☐				
6. Toxic materials	☐	☐	☐				

SECTION C. Title Conditions. - Do any of the following conditions exist with regard to the real property?

	YES	NO	DO NOT KNOW		YES	NO	DO NOT KNOW
1. Any features, such as walls, fences and driveways, which are shared?	☐	☐	☐	9. Any lawsuits regarding this property during the ownership of the seller?	☐	☐	☐
2. Any easements, other than normal utility easements?	☐	☐	☐	10. Any notices from any governmental or quasi-governmental agency affecting the real property?	☐	☐	☐
3. Any encroachments?	☐	☐	☐	11. Any planned road or street expansions, improvements or widenings adjacent to the real property?	☐	☐	☐
4. Any zoning violations, nonconforming uses, or violations of "setback" requirements?	☐	☐	☐	12. Any unpaid bills or claims of others for labor and/or materials furnished to or for the real property?	☐	☐	☐
5. Any lot-line disputes?	☐	☐	☐	13. Any deed restrictions or other restrictions of recording affecting the real property?	☐	☐	☐
6. Have you been notified, or are you aware, of any work planned or to be performed by a utility or municipality close to the real property including but not limited to sidewalks, streets, sewers, water, power, or gas lines?	☐	☐	☐	14. Any unsatisfied judgments against Seller?	☐	☐	☐
				15. Any dispute regarding a right of access to the real property?	☐	☐	☐
7. Any condominium, homeowners', or other type of association which has any authority over the real property?	☐	☐	☐	16. Any other title conditions which might affect the real property?	☐	☐	☐
8. Does ownership of the property entitle the owner to use any "common area" facilities such as pools, tennis courts, walkways, or other common use areas?	☐	☐	☐				

SECTION D. Other Conditions.

	YES	NO	DO NOT KNOW		YES	NO	DO NOT KNOW
1. Are the dwelling and the improvements connected to a public water system?	☐	☐	☐	7. Is trash removal service provided to the real property? If so, the trash service is public ____ private ____	☐	☐	☐
Is the system operational?	☐	☐	☐	8. Have the structures been mitigated for radon? If yes, when? _____	☐	☐	☐
2. Are the dwelling and the improvements connected to a public sewer system?	☐	☐	☐	9. Is the property connected to a natural gas system?	☐	☐	☐
Is the system operational?	☐	☐	☐	10. Has a pet been domiciled in the dwelling?	☐	☐	☐
3. Are the dwelling and the improvements connected to a private or community (non-public) water system?	☐	☐	☐	type(s) _____			
Is the system operational?	☐	☐	☐	**If the answer to any of the following items is "Yes", explain in the Comment section, PART III of this Disclosure Statement.**	YES	NO	DO NOT KNOW
Year last tested _____				11. Are any trees or shrubs on the real property diseased or dead?	☐	☐	☐
4. Are the dwelling and the improvements connected to a private or community (non-public) sewer system?	☐	☐	☐	Are any trees or shrubs scheduled to be removed?	☐	☐	☐
Is the system operational?	☐	☐	☐	12. Are there any flooding, drainage, or grading problems in connection with the real property?	☐	☐	☐
5. Are the dwelling and the improvements connected to a septic system?	☐	☐	☐	13. Have you made any insurance or manufacturer claims with regard to the property?	☐	☐	☐
Is the system operational?	☐	☐	☐	14. Are you aware of any problems to the exterior wallcovering of the structure including, but not limited to, siding, synthetic stucco, masonry, or other materials?	☐	☐	☐
6. Is the real property in a: ____ flood plain? ____ floodway?	☐	☐	☐				

_____
Property Address

Figure 9.3 continued

SECTION E. Cleaning/Service Conditions. Have you ever performed or had performed the following? State the most recent year:

	YEAR	YES	NO	DO NOT KNOW	NONE/NOT INCLUDED
1. Servicing of air conditioner	_____	☐	☐	☐	☐
2. Cleaning of fireplace, including chimney	_____	☐	☐	☐	☐
3. Servicing of furnace	_____	☐	☐	☐	☐
4. Servicing of septic system	_____	☐	☐	☐	☐
5. Cleaning of woodburning stove, including chimney	_____	☐	☐	☐	☐

	YEAR	YES	NO	DO NOT KNOW	NONE/NOT INCLUDED
6. Treatment for wood-destroying insects or rodents	_____	☐	☐	☐	☐
7. Tested well water	_____	☐	☐	☐	☐
8. Serviced/treated well water	_____	☐	☐	☐	☐

PART III - Comments. Please reference comments on items responded to above by PART I or II, Section letter and item number. Use additional pages if necessary.

_____

_____

_____

_____

_____

_____

_____

_____

_____

_____

If checked here _____, PART III is continued on a separate page(s).

SELLER'S CERTIFICATION

Seller hereby certifies that this Disclosure Statement, which consists of _____ pages, has been completed by Seller; that Seller has completed this Disclosure Statement to the best of Seller's belief and knowledge as of the date hereof, which is the date this Disclosure Statement is completed and signed by Seller.

Seller_____   Date_____

Seller_____   Date_____

ACKNOWLEDGMENT OF RECEIPT OF DISCLOSURE STATEMENT, UNDERSTANDING AND CERTIFICATION

I/We: acknowledge receipt of a photocopy of the above Seller Property Condition Disclosure Statement; understand that such Disclosure Statement is not a warranty of any kind by the Seller or any agent representing any principal in the transaction; understand that such Disclosure Statement should not be accepted as a substitute for any inspection or warranty that I/we may wish to obtain; understand the information provided in this Disclosure Statement is the representation of the Seller and not the representation of any agent, and is not intended to be part of any contract between the Seller and Purchaser; and certify that such Disclosure Statement was delivered to me/us or my/our agent on or before the effective date of any contract entered into by me/us relating to the real property described in such Disclosure Statement.

Purchaser_____   Receipt Date _____

Purchaser _____   Receipt Date _____

ENVIRONMENTAL CONDITIONS
02/02

Lead in Soil

Seller's Disclosure (initial)

_____ The housing is located in an area which EPA tests have shown may contain concentrations of lead in the soil that may pose a unacceptable risk to human health and the environment. The Lead Site may or may not be included on EPA's Superfund National Priorities List.

Purchaser's Acknowledgment (initial)

_____

Property Address: _____

Counseling the Seller

Because of the increased use of buyer agents, a discussion with the sellers should ensue at the time the sales agent takes the listing regarding the possibility that a buyer's agent may sell the property. The listing agent should explain to the seller that if this occurs the seller has a couple of avenues to pursue:

1. pay only the listing broker's commission and request the selling (buyer) broker to obtain his commission from the buyer
2. pay the full commission to the listing broker with the understanding that the listing broker will give the buyer broker the same share as the firm usually splits with a cooperating broker

It is important to inform the seller that a buyer's agent will not be representing the seller's interest. The deciding factor for the seller, however, should be that he has listed the property to get it sold, and that should remain his primary concern.

A listing agent can share a commission with a buyer broker only when he has the *express consent* of the principal. Informing the seller when the listing is signed permits the seller to make an informed decision so that no problems occur when it is time to close the sale.

Remember, the commission is paid when the transaction is consummated. Some agents feel that the agent should be paid only by whom he represents: the listing broker by the seller and the buyer broker by the buyer. This has little to do with negotiating and finalizing a sale, however.

Buyer's Warranties

Home Buyer's Insurance

New construction

Home buyer's insurance is available in many areas of the country for the purchaser's protection. If it is a newly constructed home, the builder may insure the house under the Home Owners Warranty Corporation, referred to as the HOW program. A 10-year warranty plan, the insurance covers defects in material, faulty workmanship, and structural problems. If a major defect should arise, the buyer is protected against costly repairs.

Home Warranty Insurance

Existing property

Home warranty insurance is also available on existing homes. The policy may be purchased by the buyer or seller and covers such items as heating, air conditioning, electrical, plumbing, and appliances. These policies generally carry a deductible amount, and coverage on some items may be excluded.

If insurance is not available, some buyers may request an inspection on such major items as heating and air conditioning as a contingency of the purchase agreement. Preinspections by qualified service representatives or home inspection agencies assure the buyer that the items in question are in workable order.

Property Insurance

Property owners will also want to protect against financial loss in the event their investment is damaged by fire, tornado, flood, or other perils. While fire is the most common cause for concern, extended coverage is available to insure against other catastrophes. The property owner (insured) makes payments (referred to as an insurance premium) to the insurance company (insurer), and if a loss does occur, the insurance company indemnifies (pays) the insured for the loss. Insurance companies invest the premiums received from the insured, building up reserves to cover losses of their policy holders, to pay dividends to their stockholders, and to meet operating expenses. A property owner could self-insure by setting aside funds to cover a loss, but most homeowners feel that the gamble is too great. If they borrowed funds to purchase the property, they have little choice since the mortgagee will want protection for the funds advanced on the loan. Insurance is based on a large number of risks, and insurance companies are able to spread their risk by serving a large clientele over a broad section of the country. Many companies also diversify into other types of insurance, such as life, automobile, and annuities.

Any addition to the basic insurance contract (called the insurance policy) is an endorsement or rider, and it covers losses beyond those ordinarily covered. For example, if a property is located in an area where earthquakes may occur, a rider could protect the owner from such an event.

There are five different policies written to cover the owner of a single-family home. The basic policy is the Homeowner 1 (HO-1). Homeowner 2 (HO-2) is broader in scope, and Homeowner 5 (HO-5) covers all risks except those perils listed as exclusions.

Types of policies

Basic Homeowner 1 (HO-1) covers the following losses:

1. fire
2. lightning
3. windstorm or hail
4. explosion
5. loss sustained upon removal of property from an endangered premises
6. riot or civil commotion
7. aircraft
8. vehicles
9. smoke
10. theft
11. vandalism and malicious mischief
12. breaking of glass (that is part of the building)

Broad Homeowner 2 (HO-2) covers all of the above 12 perils, plus the following:

13. collapse of all or a part of building(s)
14. falling objects

15. weight of ice, snow, or sleet

16. sudden and accidental tearing asunder, cracking, burning, or bulging of a steam or hot water heating system or of appliances for heating water

17. freezing of plumbing, heating, and air conditioning systems

18. sudden and accidental damages to electrical appliances

19. sudden and accidental injury from artificially generated currents to electrical appliances, devices, fixtures, and wiring

Comprehensive Homeowner 3 (HO-3) covers all the above 19 items plus risks of physical loss to buildings.

Comprehensive Homeowner 4 (HO-4) is a tenant's policy used by renters that covers household goods and personal belongings from loss that may occur under the broad form HO-2.

Comprehensive Homeowner 5 (HO-5), in addition to the above coverage in Homeowner 1, 2, and 3, covers all perils *except* flood, landslide, mudflow, tidal wave, earthquakes, underground water, settling, cracking, war, and nuclear accident. Also excluded are mortgages and debts, currency, money, bonds, and manuscripts.

Tenants should carry insurance on their personal belongings so that they are protected from loss in the event of fire. Commercial tenants need to obtain insurance to cover their business equipment and any interruption of their business due to a catastrophe.

If a property is in a known flood zone, the mortgage company will insist on the owner having flood insurance. It is a separate policy that can be purchased from the National Flood Insurance Program. It covers floods caused by broken dams and levees, heavy rains, and blocked drainage systems.

Insurance companies also offer optional coverages that may be added to a policy. They include jewelry and furs, silverware, firearms, backup from sewer or drains, home computers, and earthquakes. Due to a rash of lawsuits over fungus and molds, they are excluded from most insurance policies.

Policies have deductible amount clauses; if the deductible is $100, the first $100 of loss would be paid by the homeowner. Since the basic purpose is to protect owners from losses they cannot cover, the deductible prevents nuisance claims and saves the expense of having a claim adjustor investigate these small items.

To collect under an insurance policy the person must have an insurable interest such as a property owner or mortgagee holds. The insurance rates are in direct proportion to the risk involved. Brick buildings have lower rates than frame, tile roofs are rated lower than wood shingles, and the proximity to fire hydrants is considered. Insurance companies will have standard rates set so each property does not have to be analyzed and rated on an individual basis. If the insured pays a premium of $210 a year for $60,000 coverage, the annual rate is figured as:

$$\text{Rate} = \frac{210}{\$60,000} = .0035 \text{ or } \$3.50 \text{ per } \$1,000 \text{ of coverage}$$

Coinsurance

When loss to property occurs, it generally is not a total and complete loss. If the property was insured for less than its market value, without the coinsurance clause the owner would be entitled to collect the full amount without paying a premium that justifies the coverage. Typically the homeowner carries a policy that covers to 80 percent of the property improvement value. The formula used is:

$$\text{amount recovered} = \frac{\text{amount carried}}{\text{amt. should be carried}} \times \text{loss}$$

Thus, if the property improvements are valued at $70,000, and the owner carries insurance with an 80 percent coinsurance clause, the owner must carry $56,000 of insurance to collect 100 percent of the losses. If a $10,000 loss occurs:

$56,000 = 100\%$ so $10,000 loss $\times 100\% = \$10,000$ amount covered

If the insured carried more insurance than was needed, no additional amount could be received. Since more was not lost, the insured would receive only the $10,000, so it would prove foolish to insure for more than one could recover. Using the $70,000 value again, assume the owner insured the property for only $49,000 (70 percent of value).

$$\frac{\text{amount carried}}{\text{amount required}} \quad \frac{\$49,000}{\$56,000} \times \$10,000 \text{ loss} = \$8,750$$

In this situation $1,250 of the owner's loss will need to be paid by the owner.

Liability

The homeowner's policy will cover personal liability in the event someone slips on an icy driveway, falls off a porch, or is otherwise injured. A tree limb falling on a visitor's automobile causing damage could result in a lawsuit, and the insurance protects against such events. This also protects the family if they are injured or cause injury to another even if they are off the premises. Any legal costs for defending the insured is also covered up to the amount stated on the policy.

The price of an insurance policy is a small annual fee to pay when one analyzes the broad coverage and protection it offers. Not only does it insure the real estate, but additionally any personal liability that would rise from injury to oneself or others.

Summary of Important Points

1. A purchase agreement is an offer to buy, and when it is accepted by the seller, it becomes a binding contract.
2. An offer may be rescinded at any time prior to acceptance.
3. If the seller does not accept the buyer's offer, the seller may counteroffer in response to the buyer's offer.
4. An earnest-money deposit accompanies the offer to purchase and indicates the buyer's good faith.
5. To safeguard the purchaser's deposit, the real estate firm is required by law to place the earnest-money deposit in a trust account after the offer is accepted.
6. A lease option gives the option holder the right to buy for a stated period of time.
7. The right of first refusal gives the holder the first right to purchase.
8. A lease purchase binds the lessee to purchase a property under the terms of the lease purchase agreement.
9. Equitable interest refers to the buyer's interest in the seller's property once the offer is accepted.
10. A purchase agreement is used to buy real property, and a bill of sale is used to purchase personal property.
11. Errors and omissions insurance protects the policyholder in the event an error is made.
12. A homeowner insurance policy protects both the owner and the lender who finances the sale.

Discussion Points

1. Why would a broker carry errors and omissions insurance?
2. What is the purpose of a trust account?
3. Who benefits from the property disclosure statement?
4. What insurance protection is available to the purchaser before the sale is finalized? After the sale is closed?
5. If a seller counteroffers the buyer's offer, what are the buyer's alternatives?
6. Explain how the coinsurance clause in an insurance policy benefits the policyholder.

Review Questions

Answers to these questions are found in the Answer Key section at the back of the book.

1. A broker's trust account is used:
   a. for the deposit of earnest money only
   b. in lieu of a general account
   c. for the deposit of money belonging to others that comes into the broker's possession
   d. to compensate the broker for expenditures

2. Which of the following statements concerning a counteroffer is true?
   a. if the counteroffer is rejected, the original offer to purchase can be accepted
   b. counteroffers are rarely accepted
   c. the offeree and the offeror have reversed their positions
   d. the counteroffer will remain open for acceptance for 10 days

3. If a purchaser assigns her interest in the property while the contract is still pending, realizing a profit:
   a. the seller receives the profit
   b. it cancels the contract
   c. the broker receives the profit
   d. the original purchaser receives the profit

4. Ms. Jones hires A-1 Realty to sell her house and explains to agent Judy Jewel the reason she wants to sell is that the house has a faulty sewer system. Jewel does not include this information on the listing agreement. The property is sold by salesperson Paul Parker of another real estate firm, who looked only at the listing agreement. Whose license is in jeopardy?
   a. Judy Jewel's
   b. Paul Parker's
   c. both Judy's and Paul's
   d. neither Judy's nor Paul's

5. To whom must a copy of the accepted purchase agreement be delivered?
   a. buyer
   b. seller
   c. buyer and seller
   d. real estate commissioner

6. Funds deposited in a trust account that will ultimately belong to the broker:
   a. cannot be used by the broker until the sale is consummated or terminated
   b. may be transferred to the broker's business account if one of the parties to the contract has agreed in writing
   c. are advanced to the seller as part of the proceeds
   d. are kept in the account until the monthly audit

7. A lessee may have the right as specified in the lease contract to purchase the property because of:
   a. a lease clause
   b. the right of first refusal
   c. a reversionary clause
   d. a transfer clause

8. This type of auction results in a sale to the highest bidder:
   a. an absolute auction
   b. with reserve auction
   c. guaranteed by bidder
   d. warranted sale auction

9. An offeror may withdraw an offer until:
   a. the closing date
   b. the deed is recorded
   c. the contract is signed
   d. the offeror is notified that the offer has been accepted

10. When a contract for the sale of real estate is signed by the purchaser and the seller, the purchaser acquires:
    a. equitable title to the property
    b. legal title to the property
    c. immediate possession
    d. a nonfreehold interest

11. The amount and type of earnest deposit required is determined by the:
    a. seller
    b. buyer
    c. law
    d. broker

12. A salesperson should prepare all of the following for the purchaser who wants to make an offer on a property EXCEPT:
    a. an estimate of the buyer's closing costs
    b. an estimate of the monthly principal, interest, taxes, and insurance payment
    c. an offer to purchase agreement
    d. a right of first refusal document

13. If personal property is included in the sale of real property, the following document is used:
    a. purchase agreement
    b. bill of sale
    c. lease option
    d. list contract

14. All of the following are essential to an agreement to purchase contract EXCEPT:
    a. purchase price
    b. description of the property
    c. buyer's and seller's signatures
    d. mortgage assumption

15. The sale price of a property and the amount of the earnest deposit are all determined by:
    a. state law
    b. negotiation
    c. the real estate board
    d. the broker who has the property listed

16. Coinsurance can best be described as:
    a. an insurance policy that is held jointly by the mortgage company and the property owner
    b. insurance that partially covers a loss
    c. insurance that entitles the homeowner to collect the full amount without paying a premium that justifies the coverage
    d. an insurance policy with an 80 percent coinsurance clause

Lending Institutions and Loans

KEY TERMS

annual percentage rate (APR)

automated underwriting

conventional loan

disintermediation

Equal Credit Opportunity Act (ECOA)

Federal Home Loan Mortgage Corporation (FHLMC)

Federal Housing Administration (FHA)

Federal National Mortgage Association (FNMA)

Federal Reserve (FED)

FHA loan

Government National Mortgage Association (GNMA)

land contract

mortgage-backed security (MBS)

mortgage banker

mortgage broker

mortgage insurance premium (MIP)

novation

primary mortgage market

private mortgage insurance (PMI)

Real Estate Settlement Procedures Act (RESPA)

Regulation Z

Resolution Trust Corporation (RTC)

Savings Association Insurance Fund (SAIF)

secondary mortgage market

truth-in-lending law

underwriter

upfront mortgage insurance premium (UFMIP)

VA loans

OVERVIEW

We refer to the business enterprise whose purpose it is to make available various kinds of financing as the *money market*. Most of the funds used for financing real estate are savings from firms and individuals who deposit their money in return for interest earned on their savings. The lending institutions are called *financial fiduciaries,* and as such they are responsible for safeguarding the funds entrusted to them by their depositors. These lending institutions and the loans they originate are covered in this chapter.

Until recently, bankers did not search for customers but waited for business to come to them. The borrower felt lucky to get a loan. Not so today. In today's competitive world of real estate finance it takes more than low rates and discount points to obtain business. When the real estate agent sells a property, the sales agent generally guides the borrower to a loan officer whose service and knowledge assist in providing a smooth closing for the customer.

Up until the 1970s most buyers took their business to the savings and loan institutions where interest rates were relatively constant from month to month and discount points were almost nonexistent. Then, in the mid to late 1970s, deposits left the savings and loans for the higher interest rates provided by the money market funds. The process whereby funds left the savings and loans to go to the higher paying money markets is called **disintermediation**. This left savings and loan institutions with insufficient reserves to make real estate loans, and the home borrower was forced to seek funds on Wall Street and compete with industry and government for the limited savings available for lending. Interest rates were now determined by the marketplace, and loans had to be sold on a **secondary mortgage market** to investors at a discount from face value. The situation led to the birth of a new multimillion dollar industry called mortgage banking. **Mortgage bankers** originate new loans and package them in million dollar pools. These pools form collateral for **mortgage-backed securities (MBS)**, which are sold to investors through an auction process. Following the creation of the Real Estate Mortgage Investment Conduit (REMIC) in 1986, this auction process for MBS's grew dramatically to where by 2000, these massive pools of mortgages contained various risk factors including high risk "sub-prime" loans. This large expansion in the supply of money created a real estate housing "bubble." By the summer of 2007, this real estate bubble started to collapse. This collapse, combined with higher than expected default on the risky loans, caused extensive lender and Wall Street investor failure and consolidation. This resulted in unprecedented involvement in this process that vastly changed the landscape for real estate finance. In this chapter you will learn where the money for home mortgages comes from, why we sometimes pay discount points, and the roles played by various financial institutions, along with Fannie Mae, Ginnie Mae, and Freddie Mac, to provide a source of mortgage money for home buyers. We will begin by taking a glance at how the supply of money is manipulated by the Federal Reserve.

The Federal Reserve (FED)

Monetary policy control

We often hear about the **Federal Reserve (FED)** manipulating the supply of money. How is this accomplished and how can the economy be regulated? The Federal Reserve or FED was established in 1913 and is referred to as the nation's "monetary manager" because it manages the money supply using "instruments of Credit Policy" which include three major tools.

1. Discount Rate (the rate banks pay to borrow money from the FED).
2. Reserve Requirements (requirements stipulating how much banks must keep in reserve, thereby influencing the amount of deposits banks can make available for loans).

3. Open Market Operations (discounting government securities, thereby making them more or less attractive for purchase or sale).

The FED comprises 12 districts with leadership totaling 5 presidents and 7 governors. These 12 individuals make up the Federal Reserve Board who utilize the aforementioned instruments of Credit Policy to control the actual amount of money in circulation, which further determines the level of money available to our economy, including available funds for real estate finance. The crucial decisions made by this board directly influence how much capital will be added to or withdrawn from circulation. In addition to setting monetary policy, the FED is also charged with regulating member banks. Any bank can be a member, however, federally chartered banks must be members. The FED is "owned" by the member banks and is not a division of the federal government.

The board meets on the third Thursday of each month to analyze reports and make decisions that are reported to the New York Federal Reserve Bank, and that staff carries out the decisions rendered by these 12 people. The nation's monetary policy is based on money supply and prevailing interest rates and controls the direction of the economy: whether it grows or withdraws.

In formulating policy, consideration is given to what the supply of money is, what spendable funds are available to the nation's consumers, the rate of inflation, and economic growth. Too much money causes inflation, which, as it eases off, results in recession. A balance must be adhered to and the right formula achieved for the situation at any given period. To accomplish this, the Federal Reserve looks at the future to determine where the economy is headed. Thus, the amount of money available at any one time for use in mortgage lending is dependent on the competition for these same funds and the money that is pumped into the system by the Federal Reserve.

The **primary mortgage market** consists of the institutions where the borrower has personal contact to obtain financing to enable the purchase of real estate, often the local bank or savings and loan. This is the source that takes the loan application and where the borrower sends his monthly payments. The primary lender often does not have sufficient funds from depositors, so the loan is sold on the secondary market. These loans are purchased by the following sources.

Federal Reserve Board
· Regulates flow of money
· Sets monetary policy

Federal Reserve Board:
www.federalreserve.gov

Sources of Finance

Savings and Loans: A Glance Back

The history of the savings and loan associations dates from January 1, 1831. In Frankford, Pennsylvania, a borough of 2,000 near Philadelphia, six men met to discuss forming a "building club." Modeled after a building society formed 50 years earlier in Birmington, England, the organization was named the Oxford Providence Building Association. Thirty-seven members made regular deposits into a common fund, and when each contributor had purchased a home, the Oxford Providence Building Association was dissolved. Five months after the association was formed, in May 1831, they had collected sufficient funds to grant their first loan. Comly Rich was the highest bidder, paying $10 for a $375 loan. The two-story, 450-square-foot frame home that he purchased with the loan still stands in Philadelphia.

In the years to follow many such organizations were patterned after the club. Groups of people purchased shares of stock from which they would later be able to borrow. It was necessary that each association collect enough money to have the funds available to make these loans. The borrower not only pledged his home, but also his shares as collateral. Today, the borrower at a savings and loan association does not have to be a depositor.

As housing needs increased, the expansion of savings and loans grew. By the time of the 1929 stock market crash, there were more than 12,000 savings and loan associations in the United States. The Great Depression caused many savings and loans to collapse due to runs on deposits combined with excessive foreclosures.

Following the Great Depression years, legislation was enacted to provide protection to depositors. The Federal Home Loan Act of 1932 required reserve funds from which the savings and loans could draw. The Homeowners Act of 1933 established a system for federal chartering of savings and loan associations. In 1934, the National Housing Act created the **Federal Housing Administration (FHA)**, which provides federal insurance on home mortgages. The Federal Savings and Loan Insurance Corporation (FSLIC) insured the savings of depositors in savings and loans for up to $100,000. Today, the FSLIC no longer exists. It has been replaced by the Savings Association Insurance Fund (SAIF). A savings and loan association must be state or federally chartered to operate.

Savings and Loans Today

The years following World War II up to the early 1970s were considered "the best of times" for the mortgage finance and the housing industries. We enjoyed a thriving economy that offered low interest rates that, coupled with inflation, created housing appreciation and income growth. Bankers and borrowers were stimulated by government policies that made housing a top priority, and business enjoyed one of the most productive periods in our history. For an entertaining illustration of the role savings and loans (or "thrifts" as they are often called) played during this time in history, watch the movie *It's a Wonderful Life* starring Jimmy Stewart. In this time-honored holiday classic, Mr. Stewart's character is an owner of a small-town S&L. The movie accurately depicts the various dynamics of the industry while offering a great message as well.

Disintermediation   Savings and loans originated loans locally, kept them in their own portfolio, and serviced the loans. However, government regulations restricted rates to their depositors, the S&Ls began to see money flow to higher yielding sources, and disintermediation began to occur.

Today the savings and loans are no longer the primary source of home financing. Their role has changed greatly since the 1980s. During the early 1980s they were caught with long-term mortgages at 7 percent to 8 percent while current market rates were running 12 percent to 16 percent. They needed to replace these loans with adjustable rate loans where the rate would move up or down with current market conditions. This type of loan places the burden of future interest rate increases squarely on the shoulders of the borrower. Consequently, savings and loans began to lend short-term mortgages, three to five years, or use adjustable rate mortgage (ARM) loans from their own portfolios.

In the mid 1980s we saw a trend wherein large savings and loans bought or formed their own mortgage banking operations that originated long-term, fixed-rate real estate loans and sold these loans on the secondary market to investors, such as insurance companies, pension and trust funds, and large corporations. Deregulation of the savings and loans in the 1970s changed their approach away from the primary market of home loans into diversified markets, resulting in less money for home financing. Savings and loans began to test areas outside their realm of expertise as they moved into riskier investments and placed more assets into commercial properties. The loans, coupled with poor regulatory supervision, led to losses among many S&Ls. Investments rose, but local markets began to crumble, and troubles began to mount. Failing thrifts offering higher depositor rates only put other thrifts at a disadvantage to attract capital. Blame was placed in part on poor appraisals, causing Congress to pass into law the requirement that all appraisers, when appraising real estate involved in a federally related transaction, must be licensed or registered. Today massive restructuring has occurred among savings and loan institutions. The **Resolution Trust Corporation (RTC)** was formed to liquidate the insolvent thrifts, which placed the FSLIC fund more than $95 billion in the red. With more than 500 failed savings and loans and the bailout cost estimated at $100 to $130 billion, the entire industry has been jeopardized. The FSLIC was disbanded, and thrifts have become subject to more stringent banking regulations. Fortunately, through federal legislation such as FIRREA and strong economic growth through the 1980s, these problems with the savings and loans were largely dissipated.

Resolution Trust Corporation

The Financial Institutions Reform, Recovery and Enforcement Act (FIRREA) of 1989, which brought these changes about, benefits customers in three primary ways.

1. FSLIC insurance fund was replaced by the **Savings Association Insurance Fund (SAIF)**, managed under the Federal Deposit Insurance Corporation (FDIC).

Formation of SAIF

2. Disbandment of the Federal Home Bank Boards separated district banks from the role of regulator.

3. New regulations on investment and lending practices were designed to limit the risks that institutions take in the future.

Today the savings and loans (or thrifts) operate similar to the commercial banks by offering consumer lending, charge cards, checking accounts, and business loans. While their charter still requires them to keep the majority of their deposits invested in real estate loans, most of these institutions operate much like mortgage bankers by pooling and selling the real estate loans they originate to Wall Street investors while servicing these loans on behalf of the investors. The credit crisis of 2008 resulted in the failure of the largest thrift in the United States; Washington Mutual. Other thrift failures and acquisitions by banks left the future of the thrift industry in question. Once again, we see history repeating itself.

Insurance Companies

Other loan sources

Life insurance companies have funds available to invest in real estate and are heavy investors in mortgage-backed securities sold on the secondary mortgage market. Their large amounts of cash available from insurance premiums need to be invested to provide for future cash needs.

Insurance firms usually favor commercial loans greater than $1 million and are the biggest suppliers of funds for large mortgages on apartment complexes, commercial buildings, and shopping centers. Since they are not concerned with quick liquidity, they often enter into an equity position in the projects they finance. Referred to as *participation financing,* it affords them greater returns on the investment.

All insurance companies are state chartered, which means less regulation than savings and loans, and thus they have greater latitude in their investment approaches.

Commercial Banks

Commercial banks are either federally or state chartered. Originally they served the community with short-term (3- to 5-year), high-yield loans, such as automobile, mobile home, and household loans. Today, however, they also offer 15- and 30-year fixed-rate loans and balloon loans, although many of the 15- and 30-year loans are sold on the secondary market.

These banks also make short-term construction and home improvement loans. They may also grant interim financing, called a bridge loan, to fill the gap if a purchaser buys a home prior to selling an existing one. Today commercial banks have begun to play a larger role in residential financing, especially FHA and VA loans. At the end of 1989, commercial banks' share of home loan originations surpassed S&Ls for the first time in 19 years, with a 38 percent share to the S&Ls' 35 percent, and with mortgage bankers accounting for 19 percent of all originations. Commercial banks continue to widen this margin.

Trust Funds

Commercial banks and some title companies have trust departments that manage and supervise real estate holdings and properties of clients. The money held in trust funds is placed there for the benefit of a third party. Their fiduciary position includes acting as executor for estates, guardians for the estates of minors, and serving as trustees for individuals and corporations. They are known for their conservative approach since their responsibility is to safeguard the property entrusted to them. Little of this money is used for residential loans. It is usually placed in large commercial investments, or some of it may be used to purchase mortgage-backed securities.

Mutual Savings Banks

Primarily located in the northeastern United States, mutual savings banks are all state chartered. They favor long-term investments since they are basically savings institutions owned by their depositors, and they prefer a low-risk position. They are also quite diversified in their investment approach; they buy blue chip stocks, bonds, and government securities. Mutual savings banks have no stockholders, so all earnings after operational costs are met are returned to depositors as interest earned. The majority of mutual banks holds membership in FDIC, with the balance state insured. However, some state-chartered mutual savings banks failed to protect depositors by not keeping sufficient funds in reserve. In such instances, the depositors lost their savings.

Credit Unions

Credit unions were founded by individual firms as savings programs for their employees, with regular payroll deductions taken from participating employees' checks. Many people feel this is a painless way to save, since most people don't miss money they never receive. Credit unions usually pay a higher rate of interest and offer lower interest rates to employees wishing to borrow money. Credit unions generally do not make many long-term real estate loans, but normally limit their funds to home improvement and personal property loans. Some credit unions are providing long-term, fixed-rate loans for their members and selling them to the Credit Union National Association (CUNA), much like mortgage bankers sell to the secondary market.

Pension Funds

The purpose of a pension fund is much like that of the social security program—it offers a forced savings program for its contributors. Pension funds are deducted from employees' salaries and held in trust until retirement, when they are paid out in monthly sums. This cash requirement dovetails nicely with the home buyer's need for money. Most pension funds are invested in corporate and government stocks and bonds or mortgage-backed securities (MBS) purchased from the secondary market. Dividends are passed on to the subscribers to increase their retirement savings as inflation continues to climb.

Real Estate Investment Trusts (REIT)

The Real Estate Investment Trust Act, passed by Congress in 1960, offered tax exemptions to qualifying REITs. Among other requirements, a minimum of 90 percent of the profits must be distributed annually to the investors. Income is passed to the investors without the trust paying taxes as a corporation does. REITs do not issue stock to their investors, but "certificates of beneficial ownership." These certificates represent the shares owned in a pool of mortgages.

There are two basic types of REITs.

Buys real estate investments

1. The equity REIT uses its capital to purchase real estate. Secured by long-term mortgages, the income received from the investments makes the loan payments and pays a profit to the investors.

Finances real estate investments

2. The mortgage REIT finances real estate developments. Generally the funds finance large commercial properties, such as shopping malls, large office buildings, and apartment complexes. Mortgage REITs also purchase and sell real estate mortgages. For the most part, income received is from interest and origination fees.

REITs have evolved to be the favored structure for the holding of mortgage backed certificates for which the favored investment instrument became the Real Estate Investment Conduit (REMIC). The credit crisis of 2008 which resulted in the closure of some investment firms such as Lehman Brother and Bear Stearns, largely destroyed the private issued MBSs to where only Fannie Mae, Freddie Mac, and Ginnie Mae securities remained viable.

State Housing Bond Market

A state issues bonds and sells them to investors in the bond market for the purpose of providing funds for housing. The proceeds received from the investors are used to provide mortgage financing to borrowers. Certain provisions must be met to qualify for the financing. These provisos include the following.

1. The property must be the borrower's principal residence.
2. The borrower must not have owned a home in the past three years.
3. There is a purchase price limit.
4. The borrower's income must not exceed certain levels.
5. Borrowers are prohibited from refinancing.

The issuance of municipal obligation bonds is generally held to be a matter of local concern.

One of the most important characteristics of these bonds is that the interest received by the investor is exempt from federal tax. To meet this standard and qualify under the Internal Revenue Code 57-187, a constituted authority must be organized under a state statute that sets forth the specific public purpose for which the authority can be created and issue obligations in furtherance of this purpose. The entity must be approved and controlled by a political subdivision, may not be organized for profit, and no part of the entity's net earnings may inure to the benefit of any private person. The "yield" on the bonds is determined by the issue price (original offering price to the public) and on the term length of the bonds. The practice among bond counsel is to obtain certification from the underwriters or placement agents of a bond issue to determine the initial price of the issue and the net benefit of the fees for insurance or other credit enhancement.

The mortgagor may be subject to a special "recapture tax" for federal income tax purposes, which would be imposed at the time of the sale of the residence financed by the mortgage loan. This tax is not imposed unless the property is sold. The tax is based on the concept that because the bonds are tax exempt, the federal government has enabled the borrower to take advantage of this tax exemption through a lower interest rate on the mortgage loan. The amount of the tax increases for the first five years and reduces thereafter. In no event will the recapture amount on the indebtedness exceed 50 percent of any gain. No tax is imposed if the borrower retains the property for nine years or more.

Recapture tax upon sale

Mortgage Correspondents

Acting as the middleman, the loan correspondent is generally a mortgage broker or mortgage banker acting in the capacity of an agent for the lender, placing the loan for the borrower. With the expansion of the national and international markets, financing boundaries have widened, and the lenders require a network of knowledgeable correspondents to keep them informed on local economic markets in any given area.

Financial middleman

Mortgage Brokers

The primary purpose of the **mortgage broker** is to locate lenders and borrowers and bring them together, much as the real estate broker brings together buyers and sellers of property. These financial middlemen do not lend their own money nor do they normally service the loan (collect payments or handle foreclosures). For his effort, the mortgage broker earns a placement or finder's fee, usually a percentage of the loan. The mortgage broker ordinarily specializes in commercial loans, locating sources for loans as he finds borrowers for them. Care must be taken in placing the loans so that no high-risk loans affect the mortgage broker's credibility. Large investors, such as insurance companies, often prefer working through a mortgage broker rather than directly with the people seeking capital.

Because of the expansion of Mortgage Backed Securities (MBS) from 1986 to 2007, mortgage brokers expanded geometrically and included vast amounts of brokers dealing in residential mortgages. With the collapse of this MBS market in 2008, we again experienced a consolidation of these mortgage brokers for residential real estate. The future of this sector of real estate finance providers is unknown.

Mortgage Bankers

The services of mortgage bankers extend beyond just bringing the borrower and lender together. They originate mortgages, then sell the loans to investors through the secondary mortgage market or to private investors. They assume the risk of underwriting the loans and may have to buy the loan back if it does not meet the **Federal National Mortgage Association** (FNMA or Fannie Mae), **Federal Home Loan Mortgage Corporation** (FHLMC), and the **Government National Mortgage Association** (GNMA or Ginnie Mae) standards. Funds are sometimes committed by the investors prior to the mortgage banker's original loan. Serving as an intermediary, mortgage bankers earn their income from origination fees and service fees for collecting monthly payments and handling foreclosures. The origination fee generally is 1 percent of the loan amount, with the servicing fee generating an income of ½ percent to 1 percent of the monthly payment. Most mortgage bankers started in business in the 1930s after the Federal Housing Administration created FHA loans, which they originated and serviced, selling them to life insurance companies and other investors.

Mortgage bankers play a significant role in residential loan placement. Home loans are originated in what is referred to as the primary mortgage market. The borrower visits the mortgage banker and requests a loan on the property being purchased. The originator of the loan packages the loans and sells them on the secondary market to investors in million-dollar blocks. GNMA, FNMA, and FHLMC are the primary source of these pools. Today the mortgage bankers lead in originating mortgages, operating with little of their own funds.

Government Regulations on Loans

The federal government requires credit arrangers to comply with certain laws to protect the consumer. These federal lending laws include the following:

Truth-in-Lending Act

Real Estate Settlement Procedures Act (RESPA)

Equal Credit Opportunity Act (ECOA)

Fair Credit Reporting Act

National Flood Insurance Act

Community Reinvestment Act

Americans with Disabilities Act (ADA)

Home Mortgage Disclosure Act (HMDA)

Home Ownership and Equity Protection Act (HOEPA)

Housing and Economic Recovery Act of 2008

The Truth-in-Lending Law

Truth-in-lending is a federal law enforced and administered by the Federal Reserve. **Regulation Z**, as published by the Board of Governors of the Federal Reserve System, implements the act. As part of the Consumer Protection Act, truth-in-lending became effective July 19, 1969. However, the act was simplified and refined, and in October 1982 the Truth-in-Lending Simplification and Reform Act (TILSRA) became law.

The law requires that disclosure of the true **annual percentage rate (APR)** be made to the borrower within three days of the loan application. The APR shows the result of upfront finance charges made by the lender on the note rate. A disclosure statement form discloses hidden finance charges to the borrower and allows the borrower to compare one lender's loan with a competitor's. In the past, lenders may have advertised low rates and then charged the borrower large fees up front on the day of closing, increasing the lender's yield on the loan. Now lenders must calculate the APR utilizing the net loan proceeds and disclose this to the borrower. The finance charges include all costs the consumer must pay either directly or indirectly over the life of the loan, such as discount points, private mortgage insurance, loan fees, and interest paid in advance. Designed to protect the consumer, Regulation Z requires the lender to reveal in writing where the borrower's money is going through a good faith estimate. This disclosure must be given at the time of the loan application and must include the following:

Disclosure of loan costs

1. the date the finance charge commences
2. the annual percentage rate
3. the number of monthly payments
4. the date payments are due
5. any pay-off penalties
6. charges made in case of late payment or default
7. sufficient description of the property
8. the total finance charges

Disclosure to the borrower

The discount points and loan origination fees are added to the interest paid over the life of the loan to calculate the APR. The interest rate the lender quotes is known as the note rate, which does not include the discount points or the loan origination fee.

This law applies to all extenders of credit on a regular basis, including savings and loan associations, commercial banks, mortgage brokers, and finance companies. It does *not* apply to arrangers of credit but only to lenders who actually extend credit. Assumptions of existing mortgages and contracts from creditors must also adhere to the law if any terms are changed or the lender charges in excess of $50 for the assumption fee. While the real estate agent and mortgage

Creditors covered

broker bring the consumer and the lender together, they are not considered arrangers of credit since they do not finance the sale themselves.

Exemptions to the Truth-in-Lending Act include:

Exempt from truth-in-lending

1. business loans
2. commercial loans
3. loans to corporations and partnerships
4. installment loans with four or fewer installments
5. loans on which no finance charges are made
6. assumptions of a loan by a new borrower

Three-day right of rescission

For some types of loans, such as refinancing of a residence or home improvement, the borrower may cancel the loan up until midnight of the third working day after signing the loan note. The buyer does not have this three-day "cooling off" period, however, with the loans that real estate salespeople help secure for their customers, such as a first mortgage or a deed of trust.

Advertising guidelines

Regulation Z of the act further determines how credit terms are advertised, a condition with which the real estate industry must comply. Advertising the annual percentage rate (APR) and the price of the property is permissible; however, if credit terms are further mentioned, all terms must be disclosed. No advertisement may say simply "7 percent mortgage" or "no down payment" unless all terms are disclosed.

In a mortgage assumption, the advertiser can state the rate of finance charge without any other disclosure, but the finance charge must be stated as an annual percentage rate; that is, "assume 10 percent mortgage" is wrong, but "assume 10 percent annual percentage rate mortgage" or "assumable loan" is right. However, you cannot advertise "assume 10 percent annual percentage rate mortgage" if the note rate is 10 percent. Remember, the note rate and the annual percentage rate are not the same thing.

If any credit terms are stated, the price, down payment, and the amount of the mortgage must be stated, together with the due date, the number of payments, and the annual percentage rate. An advertisement that mentions price alone is beyond suspicion.

Truth-in-lending penalties

The penalties for not complying with the Truth-in-Lending Act when advertising are administered by the Federal Trade Commission and include criminal liability of a fine of up to $4,000 and one year in jail or both and civil liability to the mortgagor, who must file a complaint within one year of the closing. The mortgagee's liability shall not exceed $1,000 and costs. The arranger of credit may eliminate any fines by complying with the law within 15 days after notification.

WEB SITE

U.S. Department of Housing and Urban Development: www.hud.gov

RESPA

On June 20, 1975, the **Real Estate Settlement Procedures Act (RESPA)** became effective. This act, administered by HUD, was intended to provide the purchaser and seller with regulated and standardized procedures in closing a federally related mortgage loan sale. Because of the many complaints from lenders and real estate brokers concerning the involved implementation of the act, it was modified in June 1976. In 1983 it was amended to address the emergence of "one-stop shopping," so financial institutions with service subsidiaries could offer their customers a variety of services. The controlled business amendment, while supported by the thrift industry, was opposed by traditional suppliers of services such as title insurance companies. The position of Congress was that consumers would benefit from the bundling of services provided that safeguards were put in place.

RESPA applies only to *first mortgages* and covers:

1. savings and loan institutions insured by the FDIC
2. banks
3. FHA-insured loans
4. VA-guaranteed loans
5. HUD-administered loans
6. any loan that the lender sells to Fannie Mae, Ginnie Mae, or Freddie Mac

HUD issued a new rule, effective December 2, 1992, permitting a real estate broker to collect a fair fee for actual services in conjunction with a home sale transaction. A broker may use a computerized loan originator (CLO) system to assist a homebuyer in selecting a mortgage for a fee, provided the fee is disclosed in writing to the home buyer.

On a CLO system, a real estate broker can call up a menu of mortgage products and start the loan application and approval process. The broker may offer products of a single lender or multiple lenders.

If a controlled business arrangement exists in which the broker has an affiliate firm, such as a title company, escrow service, or mortgage brokerage, the broker may provide these services to the customer if the broker discloses the relationship in writing. The customer is free to obtain these services elsewhere. Fees are not exchanged between affiliated companies merely for the referral of business.

RESPA's main thrust is to eliminate any kickbacks that might occur through referrals by closing agents or attorneys for particular title companies. It also prevents the seller of the property from insisting that the purchaser buy title insurance from a specific title company.

Prevents kickbacks

Some of the provisions of RESPA, namely the specific layout of the good faith estimate (GFE) and HUD-1 closing statement has changed in a 2008 law change. These new forms go into effect in 2009.

The act further limits the amount of tax and insurance escrow funds that the lender can require the borrower to pay in advance. Only one-sixth of the amount due in a one-year period, commencing at the settlement date, may be collected. This amount will adequately cover the lender by the taxes and insurance due

Limits escrow account

date, but will not leave more than necessary (one-sixth of the amount due in a one-year period) in the reserve account.

When applying for a loan, the mortgagor can expect the following:

1. an information booklet from HUD explaining RESPA
2. the lender's use of the Uniform Settlement Statement as required by HUD (see Chapter 11)
3. the receipt of a good faith estimate of closing costs at loan application
4. the right to inspect the Uniform Settlement Statement one day prior to settlement

Disclosure of closing costs

A good faith estimate of closing costs has been substituted for the repealed 12-day advance disclosure of settlement costs. The good faith estimate must be supplied by the lender within 3 days of the time of the loan application. When a good faith estimate cannot be provided, a range of charges must be supplied. HUD encourages but does not require estimates of loan-related fees. The booklet "Settlement Cost and You" is an information guide for borrowers that must also be given to the borrower applicant within 3 days.

The settlement statement must be made available to the borrower at or prior to the settlement except when:

1. the secretary of HUD exempts the above requirements in a particular locality, or
2. the borrower has waived the requirement, in which case the statement shall be mailed or delivered at the earliest practical date.

The Uniform Settlement Statement is virtually unchanged from the original RESPA Disclosure Statement. The new statement, however, has been revised to eliminate references to advance disclosure and truth-in-lending.

In early 2008, the *Federal Register* published HUD's long-awaited proposed regulation on the Real Estate Settlement Procedure Act. The 94-page proposed regulation included, among other things, a mandatory four-page good faith estimate (GFE) and a modified HUD-1/1A, a required "closing script" that must be read orally at settlement, enhanced disclosures and new rules concerning volume discounts, average cost pricing, and "required use." The new form has three columns, which are (1) the original estimate, (2) HUD-1/1A, and (3) any dollar increase.

WEB SITE

www.realtor.org

The Equal Credit Opportunity Act (ECOA)

In 1974 the **Equal Credit Opportunity Act (ECOA)** was passed to prohibit lenders from discrimination on the basis of sex or marital status. It has since

Lenders must not discriminate

been amended to prohibit discrimination on the basis of race, color, religion, national origin, age, or receipt of public assistance. The goal is to ensure that lenders do not give favorable treatment to one group of people over another.

Discrimination cannot occur because all or a portion of a borrower's income may stem from public assistance programs, alimony, separate maintenance, or child support. Exceptions to the law are individuals who are not citizens, since their status could affect a creditor's rights and remedies in the event of default. Also excluded are minors, since they do not possess contractual power.

Discounting a woman's income because she is of child-bearing age or has part-time employment is no longer permissible, nor can young adults and singles be refused a loan just because they may be considered likely to move more readily. The senior citizen is another category that cannot be ignored. Under the ECOA the focus is on job stability, net worth, credit rating, and sufficient income. If a loan is denied, the rejected applicant must receive notice within 30 days, stating reasons for the refusal.

Fair Credit Reporting Act

In April 1971 the Fair Credit Reporting Act was passed by the federal government, entitling borrowers to see a summary of the report and examine information regarding their credit. If errors are found, such as may occur with common names, the borrower has a right to correct them. The act restricts access to the consumer's credit record to people who evaluate an applicant for credit, employment, or insurance and to those who secure consumer permission or court permission.

Borrowers may see credit report

National Flood Insurance

The National Flood Insurance Program was passed by Congress in 1968 and implemented in 1973. It requires flood insurance or a certificate stating whether the property is in a flood zone on all government-insured mortgages or mortgages written by federally insured or regulated lending institutions. The objectives of the federal government and the insurance companies are to encourage cities to regulate and control development in flood zone areas and to provide flood insurance at reasonable rates. The policy is administered by HUD. Maps that recognize definite areas prone to flooding have been prepared by the Army Corps of Engineers.

Flood zone property must be insured

Community Reinvestment Act

To prevent lenders from refusing to make loans or impose stricter terms in certain neighborhoods that may be higher economic risk areas, Congress passed the Community Reinvestment Act. The practice of *redlining* by lenders literally cut off funds in certain neighborhoods. One can equate it to encircling the area in red because of its income level, racial, cultural, or religious composition. Lenders must now comply with the act by taking care not to exclude homes in these areas. This does not imply that the lender has to loan on a property that does not meet city safety and building codes or a residence in an area that is primarily commercial in use.

Redlining prohibited

Americans with Disabilities Act (ADA)

The Americans with Disabilities Act (ADA) was passed into law July 26, 1990. The four sections are as follows.

1. Title I—Employment: Employers with 15 or more employees cannot discriminate against qualified individuals with disabilities.

2. Title II—Public Services: State and local government must modify all government buildings and public transportation facilities to meet the accessibility needs of individuals in wheelchairs and others who are disabled. Regardless of the size of the building or the number of employees, all owners of commercial space must comply.

3. Title III—Public Accommodations: All business establishments were given 18 months to comply with the act. By January 26, 1992, all private businesses were to have been made accessible to persons with disabilities.

4. Title IV—Public Communications: Telephone companies must provide telecommunications relay services for hearing-impaired and speech-impaired individuals 24 hours a day.

This civil rights legislation has had a significant impact on the sale and lease of buildings. Real estate salespersons and property owners must be versed on the requirements of Title III. Buyers and sellers will want assurances that the buildings they are going to purchase, sell, or lease are in full compliance with ADA standards for architectural accessibility.

Home Mortgage Disclosure Act (HMDA)

WEB SITE

http://www.ffiec.gov/
hmda/glossary.htm

The Home Mortgage Disclosure Act (HMDA) requires lenders to supply information and or disclosures for a number of different events including, but not limited to, HOEPA (see below). Predominately, HMDA requires lenders to supply to the government the race, sex, and income data on all mortgage applications and their outcome in an effort to police lenders for compliance to ECOA. For additional information on HMDA and a complete glossary of HMDA terms and definitions, visit the HMDA Web site.

Home Ownership and Equity Protection Act (HOEPA)

Lenders are required to report whether a loan is subject to the provisions of the Home Ownership and Equity Protection Act (HOEPA). Enacted as part of the Truth-in-Lending Act, HOEPA imposes substantive limitations and additions disclosures on certain types of home mortgage loans with rates or fees above a certain percentage or amount. For more information about HOEPA, see the Board of Governors' Regulation Z, 12 CFR part 226, sections 31, 32, and 34.

Loans

The Federal Housing Administration (FHA)

The Federal Housing Administration (FHA) has been in existence since 1934. Prior to that time, most borrowers in need of home financing were dependent upon banks to renew short-term (generally five-year) loans. During the Great Depression of the 1930s, many banks closed or could not renew loans, resulting in the debtor losing the property and any equity acquired.

The FHA was created during the depression to create construction jobs, stimulate the housing industry, and help Americans obtain good quality, affordable housing. FHA has been a boon to housing financing for the following reasons.

1. It established a set of standards concerning the construction and appraisal of property to qualify for FHA insurance.
2. It set up new standards for qualifying buyers for mortgage insurance.
3. It initiated the long-term amortized mortgage loan, thereby providing lower monthly house payments so that more Americans could own their own homes.
4. The above innovations made it possible to sell mortgages through a national clearinghouse, later to be called the secondary mortgage market.

FHA-Insured Loans

The FHA does not make loans, plan housing, or do any actual construction; it *insures loans made by approved lenders.* The FHA offers protection to the lender in the event of a foreclosure. If the borrower defaults on the loan, the lender may foreclose, and the FHA will repay the lender's loss, if any. If the homeowner misses two payments, FHA requires that the lender notify the local credit bureau and the local HUD office. The lender attempts to contact the borrower to establish an alternative to foreclosure. Prior to starting the foreclosure process, the lender must work with the borrower by providing a counseling agency, recasting the mortgage, or offering a long-term repayment plan. The borrower must provide a complete financial history, and the lender must try to determine the reason for default and assist the borrower with a solution. These steps reduce the losses paid out of the insurance fund from HUD to the lenders.

Because borrowers are required to show good employment patterns and reasonable credit control, the risk to the FHA or the lender has been minimal. To eliminate fraud and the misuse of FHA financing, guidelines have been tightened.

The credit crisis of 2008 led to significantly greater than expected defaults and foreclosures. Many were due to high risk real estate loans made with adjustable rate features unfavorable to many borrowers. As a result, the Federal government through the FHA, created a program called FHA Secure. This program, now used to refer to all non-streamline FHA refinances, allows homeowners who are delinquent on their mortgage payments to refinance their home loans with FHA.

FHA Mortgage Insurance Premium (MIP)

The FHA protects itself from risk of loss by charging every FHA borrower a **mortgage insurance premium (MIP)**. Most FHA-insured loans carry this MIP. While the formula has changed through the years, currently, the FHA borrower will pay both an **upfront mortgage insurance premium (UFMIP)** and a monthly MIP premium. The UFMIP is calculated on the base principal amount of the loan and equals 1.75 percent of the base loan amount. The monthly premium is also based upon the unpaid principal balance and equals .55 percent per year divided by 12 to derive the monthly amount added to the monthly payment. The monthly amount will reduce each year based upon the reduced principal amount of the loan. In the event the loan is paid off prior to maturity, upon request, the unused portion of the UFMIP is refunded to the borrower based upon a formula given by HUD.

EXAMPLE Let's assume on a $150,000 purchase with UFMIP added to a 30-year loan

Down payment: 3.5 percent of $150,000 = $5,250 down payment
(See discussion below of FHA down payment)

Loan amount: $150,000 − $5,250 = $144,750
Calc. UFMIP: $144,750 × 1.75% = 2,533.13
Add UFMIP: $144,750 + $2,533.13 = $147,283.13/MIP

Calc. monthly MIP: $144,740 (base loan) × .55% = $796.13
$796.13 divided by 12 = $66.34

FHA loans are based on the borrower investing a minimum of 3.5 percent of the purchase price. The borrower's funds may be a gift.

Adding the UFMIP has increased loan amounts, but it provided the purchaser the opportunity to obtain housing with a minimum down payment. A problem that surfaces is that adding the UFMIP and closing costs to FHA loans can result in a loan greater than the value of the property.

FHA loans are based either on the purchase price or on the FHA-appraised value, whichever is lower. To figure this on FHA loans the lender compares the purchase price with the appraised value, using the lower of the two amounts. Once this amount is derived, the lender figures the maximum allowable closing cost on the good faith estimate to arrive at the acquisition cost.

Discount points

The Federal Housing Administration requires the loan to be paid back in periodic payments of both principal and interest. The loans are generally issued for 15 or 30 years, with insurance and taxes included in the monthly payment. There is no prepayment penalty if the loan is repaid before maturity. Lenders may vary as to their requirements in making an FHA loan. Discount points are charged if the borrower wants a below-current-market interest rate. It is permissible to charge either the seller or the buyer for points if it is disclosed in the purchase agreement.

FHA 203B Loan

FHA insures loans only for one- to four-family housing. The FHA section 203B program under Title II requires a minimum down payment with the maximum loan based on local market conditions, which vary across the nation. The purchaser must make a 3.5 percent down payment (96.50%) plus pay applicable closing costs and prepaid expenses. One positive aspect of FHA financing is that the seller can pay up to 6 percent of the purchase price toward buyer's closing cost and prepaid expenses. Minimum buyer requirement is 3.5 percent for down payment.

FHA standards have established that the mortgage limits in high-cost areas ("the ceiling") may increase up to 87 percent of the dollar amount limitations set by the FHLM Corporation Act. In these high-cost areas the loan limit will be equal to the lesser of 95 percent of the area median house price or the statutory ceiling for the high cost areas. FHA does not permit investor financing on a new loan, and effective December 15, 1989, the home must be purchased as the buyer's principal residence or, under certain conditions, a secondary residence. Borrowers must have down payment from their own funds with the following exceptions.

1. The down payment may be a "gift" from a blood relative or non-profit organization (church, for example).
2. The money may be borrowed against collateral to secure the cash needed for down payment and closing costs (understandably, the borrower must qualify for the added debt).
3. The seller may pay all of the closing costs and prepaid expenses.

The maximum seller contribution for an FHA loan is 6 percent of the sales price. If the contribution exceeds 6 percent, the FHA mortgage is reduced dollar for dollar of excess contribution.

FHA Interest Rates

Until November 1983, the government controlled the amount of interest the lender could charge on FHA loans. However, because of spiraling interest rates in the late 1970s and early 1980s, lenders were reluctant to loan out money at lower rates than they could receive on conventional loans. The alternative was to charge enormous discount points, which meant the seller was generally asked to pay them. This in effect meant sellers were taking less for their homes after deducting the cost of paying the points.

Eliminating the controlled ceiling on the FHA interest rates allows the borrowers to "shop" rates for their loans. The rate will adjust or float with the market, and any party may pay the points. The rate will be determined by discount points paid; the formula is complex and has many variables. Rate and points may be locked in for a set period of time from the date of the loan application, or they may float and lock in at a time prior to the closing. The longer a lock, the more points a borrower will pay. For example: if the current rate is 10.5 percent with 2 points for a 60-day lock, then for every additional 30 days it could cost anywhere from .25 percent to .75 percent more (depending on the lender). So, using .50 percent for every 30 days, a 10.5 percent rate with 3 points would be good for a 120-day lock. When shopping for an FHA loan, not only should the rate and points be "shopped," but the length of the lock and the cost of extending it another 30 days should be considered.

The FHA buydown program offers the buyer a lower rate for the first two or three years, depending on the program, thus allowing the borrower to qualify for a higher loan amount. The buydown is a seller-subsidized loan with the funds placed in an escrow account by the seller.

FHA Loan Assumptions

Congress passed the HUD Reform legislation bill in November 1989, creating new rules on FHA-insured mortgages.

FHA loan assumption

1. Increased requirements on loan assumptions state that any subsequent purchaser must pass a credit check and qualify for the payment prior to title passing or the acceleration (due-on-sale) clause will be invoked. This substitution of liability to a new debtor is termed **novation**.
2. New loans issued after December 14, 1989, can be assumed only by a buyer who will occupy the property, thus eliminating the investor–purchaser.
3. No new loans will be issued to investors after December 14, 1989.
4. The new guidelines recommend that borrowers use no more than 29 percent of their monthly gross income to make the mortgage payment and no more than 41 percent of their gross income for monthly payment of all debts.

FHA loan assumptions become extremely popular when interest rates are high. Not only is the interest usually lower, but the cost of originating a new loan is bypassed. Since the loans have generally been in force for a number of years and the owner's equity has built up, a larger down payment is necessary. However, since it is not a new loan the purchaser can borrow some of the down payment from the seller. Purchasers must be realistic in what amount they can allot for a monthly house payment. The guidelines set down by lenders are a wise plan for any buyer assuming an existing loan. Conversely, the larger down payment lessens the risk the seller has of foreclosure. With the new rulings from FHA, the loan assumptions will be cut considerably.

Other FHA Loans

While most FHA loans are under the 203B program, variations from the original FHA plan have developed to fill the needs of buyers. Some FHA programs have been discontinued. Those still in existence in addition to the 203B program include

The FHA 234. The FHA 234 program covers loans for condominiums, a plan equivalent to the 203B program.

Subsidized FHA plan

The FHA 245. The FHA 245 program requires a somewhat larger down payment than a 203B but offers a graduated payment plan which permits the borrower to begin payments at a substantially lower interest rate with a gradual increase the first four to five years of the loan. The 245 program is designed to assist buyers who initially need low monthly payments to qualify and whose income is expected to grow in the next four to five years. When the adjustable rate rises and the payment remains fixed, the shortage is added to the principal. Thus, if the interest that occurred in the first year equals more than the payments, the outstanding principal balance increases, resulting in what is called *negative amortization.* That is, the debt increases over time instead of decreasing. At the end of five years the maximum mortgage is reached, and the debt will begin to decline just as a regularly amortized real estate loan. Negative amortization may be up to 97 percent of appraised value or acquisition cost.

FHA 203K Plan. The FHA 203K plan is an ideal means of rehabilitating the existing housing inventory in the United States. A fully disbursed loan, the 203K allows a borrower to purchase or refinance a property plus finance the cost of rehabilitation with one closing. The mortgage amount of these loans is based on the projected value of the property with the rehabilitation completed, taking into consideration the cost of the rehabilitation. The 203K's advantages include the following.

1. There is no upfront mortgage insurance premium.
2. Up to the first six months' mortgage payment can be financed.
3. Regular FHA down payment and special HUD down payment programs are available.
4. Any one- to four-family dwelling is eligible, excluding condominiums.
5. The loan can be used to finance necessary repairs.
6. The loan has no income limits.
7. The down payment can be only 3 percent, all of which can be a gift.

FHA Adjustable Rate Mortgage (ARM)

In an unstable market, the FHA ARM program proves to be an excellent product. Down payment and qualifying guidelines do not vary from FHA standards; this buydown program allows the borrower to qualify at the first year rate. Some local HUD offices require the borrower to qualify at 1 percent above the first year rate. Two key words used in implementing this program are the *margin,* which adds 2 to 3 percent to the *index,* which is the weekly average of one-year Treasury bills (T-bills). The maximum the rate can increase is 1 percent per year, and the highest rate the ARM can increase is 5 percent above the first year rate. For example:

FHA buydown program

Year	Rate	Index
1st year	5%	N/A for 1st year
2nd year	6%	1 yr T/Bill 4%
3rd year	7%	1 yr T/Bill 5%
4th year	8%	1 yr T/Bill 6%
5th year	9%	1 yr T/Bill 7%
6th year	10%	1 yr T/Bill 8%

This example shows the worst-case scenario if T-bills were to go up every year after you obtained an FHA ARM loan.

FHA Title I

FHA home improvement loans

The FHA Title I Act authorized the FHA to insure lending institutions against losses on loans made to finance repairs and improvements to existing structures and to build new structures for nonresidential use. FHA liability is limited to 90 percent of the loss on individual loans and to 10 percent of all such loans made by the institutions. Borrowers must have a satisfactory income and credit record. They must own the property or have a lease expiring not less than six months beyond the maturity of the loan. The loan may not exceed $5,000 or have a maturity greater than 7 years and 32 days. The lender pays an insurance charge on each loan made. This revenue, plus recoveries on defaulted notes, is sufficient to make the program self-supporting and establish a substantial reserve for paying off losses.

Department of Veteran Affairs (VA) Loans

U.S. Department of Veteran Affairs: www.va.gov

The Department of Veteran Affairs (VA) designed the **VA loans** for veterans who qualify under the law. A minimum of 90 or 181 days active service with an honorable discharge is required, depending on when the individual served. The eligibility entitlement covers World War II, the Korean Conflict, the Vietnam War, and the Persian Gulf War. This eligibility is valid until used and extends to widows and widowers of veterans who died on active duty if they have not remarried. In October 1992 the law was expanded to include members of the National Guard and military reserves who have served a minimum of six years.

No down payment for VA loans

Unlike FHA loans, there is no down payment with VA loans. VA loan terms can be for 15 or 30 years. These loans are guaranteed by the VA, with maximum guarantees to eligible veterans as follows.

1. For loans of $45,000 or less, 50 percent of the loan is guaranteed.
2. For loans above $45,000, 40 percent of the loan is guaranteed, up to $36,000, whichever is less, but not less than $22,500. For loans from $45,000 to $56,250, the minimum guarantee will result in a percentage of guarantee over 40 percent.
3. For home purchases, construction, or condominium loans that are for an amount in excess of $203,000, 25 percent of the loan is guaranteed up to $50,750, whichever is less. These guarantees may not exceed the veteran's remaining entitlement.

The above assumes the veteran has *full* entitlements and includes the funding fee.

VA loans guaranteed

If there is a default on a guaranteed loan, the government reimburses the lender for loss up to the amount of the VA guarantee (veteran's eligibility). The maximum loan depends upon the lending institution, with most lenders stopping at four times the veteran's entitlement with no down payment. In order to sell a VA loan on the secondary market, it cannot exceed a 75 percent loan-to-value ratio.

The veteran must secure a *certificate of eligibility* and sign a statement that the veteran intends to occupy the home, as the VA loan cannot be used solely for income property. Loans can be made on one- to four-family housing units. When the loan is paid off, the veteran's eligibility will be fully restored. If a VA loan is assumed and if the assumption is with substitution of eligibility along with release of liability, the veteran will be given entitlement again. If the loan is paid off before maturity, there is no prepayment penalty. A buyer does not need to be a veteran to assume an existing VA loan. After March 1, 1988, all assumptions require release of liability and qualifications.

As of October 1992, the government ceased fixing the interest rate on VA loans. Veterans and lenders may negotiate the interest rate. The seller no longer is required to pay the veteran buyer's discount points.

The VA funding fee is figured on the amount of the down payment in four different levels:

Item	No Down Payment	5% to 10% Down	10% or More
Veteran	2.15% funding fee	1.5% funding fee	1.25%
National Guard and Reservist	2.40% funding fee	1.75% funding fee	1.50%
2nd use of benefit	3.3% funding fee	1.5% funding fee	1.25%

Refinancing or no down payment requires 2.15 percent for veterans and 2.40 percent for others using the benefits. The funding fee may be paid in cash or financed; there is no preference for either. However, if no new money is involved and the rate requested is lower, then the funding fee is .5 percent.

With both FHA and VA loans, an escape clause is a mandatory part of the purchase agreement and is signed by both seller and buyer. If the lender does not appraise the property for the purchase price, the purchaser need not carry through with the purchase. If the purchaser agrees to buy the property, the difference between the purchase price and the appraisal will be renegotiated between the buyer and the seller or paid in cash.

The Rural Economic and Community Development (RECD)

The Rural Economic and Community Development, formerly known as *Farmers Home Administration (FmHA),* became effective October 1, 1995. RECD is a federal lender with the U.S. Department of Agriculture that makes loans for home purchases or construction in rural areas and small communities outside

Certificate of eligibility

metropolitan areas. These areas are defined as having a population of 20,000 or less. In addition to the property location, RECD requires that borrowers demonstrate a limited income record and a need for housing. The loans are reviewed periodically, and payments are increased as the borrower's income rises. The loans are either: (1) made directly by RECD or (2) made by a private lender, with RECD guaranteeing a certain percentage.

Private Mortgage Insurance (PMI)

PMI insurance covers conventional loans

A great boost to the housing industry came in the early 1960s, when the Mortgage Guarantee Insurance Corporation (MGIC) of Milwaukee, Wisconsin, introduced a mortgage that allowed borrowers to obtain homes with a minimal down payment. New houses not built under FHA and VA requirements could now be purchased with a minimum 10 percent down payment. Discount points were charged but could be paid by either the buyer or the seller. A .50 percent insurance premium was paid by the borrower for the first year and .25 percent from then on, on the mortgage amount. Other private mortgage insurance companies followed, and in 1971, they were approved by the Federal Home Loan Bank. **Private mortgage insurance (PMI)** accounts for a large percentage of loans, requiring only 5 percent to 15 percent as a down payment. The insurance expense will vary depending on the depth of exposure to the insuring company.

Similar to FHA, PMI insures its lenders, but only for the top 20 or 25 percent of the loan. After the loan is paid down to the insured amount, the insurance premium can usually be eliminated, at the discretion of the agency in the secondary market that purchased the loan from the local lender. However, a controversial issue has arisen alleging that lenders were taking advantage of mortgagors by not informing them that they could stop making PMI payments. Legislation was passed in 1998, becoming effective in the summer of 1999, requiring that most private mortgage insurance be automatically terminated when the loan balance declines to 78% of the original property value of the home. If the loan is considered high risk, borrowers may need to continue the PMI payment until the halfway point of the mortgage term, regardless of how promptly they pay.

The credit crisis of 2008 with its extensive defaults and foreclosures put undo pressure on the mortgage insurance industry. As a result, significant tightening of the approval standards occurred especially as it applied to mortgage broker originated transactions. This tightening of standards reduced the amount of qualified home buyers thereby further exasperating the already challenged real estate market.

Conventional Loans

The lender of a **conventional loan** is not insured, nor is the loan guaranteed by the federal government. The lending institution sets its own requirements and policies. If a borrower requests a shorter term loan with a larger down payment, the lender may decrease the interest rate, depending on the availability of funds. Conventional loans ordinarily require a minimum of 20 percent down except when private mortgage insurance is used. This type of loan will be discussed in greater detail in Chapter 11.

Private Loans

Private loans are often used when the credit of the borrower is not extremely good. Usually a private loan has a higher interest rate since there is greater risk involved and requires a larger down payment. A buyer may not have a sufficient down payment or income to qualify for a loan, so a private lender is needed. When home mortgage interest rates are high, the position of lender has become attractive to individuals with sufficient capital.

Land Contracts

Variously referred to as **land contracts**, land sales contracts, installment sales contracts, or contracts for deed, these financing arrangements are contracts to buy wherein the seller finances the purchaser. In this type of contract, the seller takes the role of lender. Historically, land contracts are used in the sale of vacant land, since lenders do not categorize bare land as property that is eligible for loans. Land contracts are also used if the property is not readily salable and would not qualify for a long-term loan, if the purchaser has insufficient funds for a minimum down payment or an unstable income, or if the seller does not want all the equity immediately but prefers to receive a regular monthly income from the land contract. In the tight-money period of the late 1970s and the early 1980s, land contracts were often the only means of obtaining financing.

Vendor retains title

In a land contract sale, the vendor (seller) retains legal title to the real property with the vendee (buyer) receiving the equitable title. While the vendee does not become the owner of record, he has the right to use, possess, and transfer the property and should record that right. Customarily, the purchaser pays the insurance and maintenance expenses. Upon fulfillment of the terms of the contract, the deed is delivered to the vendee. For the benefit of both vendee and vendor, the deed should be placed in escrow. If the vendor dies, the vendee then is certain to receive the deed upon meeting the contract terms. If the vendee fails to live up to the terms of the contract, the vendor may terminate the contract and recapture the property. Many purchasers are concerned about the risks involved in land contracts since title is retained by the seller. However, the seller would have to go through the normal foreclosure procedures of her particular state if the vendee defaulted. The greatest potential risk of a land contract would be claims brought against the vendor during the term of the contract that could prohibit the vendee from obtaining clear title.

Vendee receives equitable interest

The Loan Process

A series of steps takes place before a mortgage lender will finance a purchase. The lender's main concern is that payment will be received as agreed upon in the mortgage contract. A detailed sequence of events that the mortgagee follows in placing a loan is outlined in Figure 10.1.

Making Application

The first step involves the borrower's loan application. The loan officer verifies the information and qualifies the applicant. If the borrower passes the preliminary step, the loan processor orders all credit documentation, a credit report, and an appraisal.

Property Appraisal

An appraisal of the property is made by a licensed or certified appraiser in conformance with the laws of each state. The appraiser will use a Uniform Appraisal Report and include all the data pertinent to determining the property value.

Qualifying the Buyer

Underwriter's duties

An **underwriter**, employed by a lending institution or mortgage banking company, reviews the borrower's loan application and makes a recommendation to the loan committee on the advisability of making the loan. The underwriter's opinion is largely based on the applicant's ability to repay the loan, credit history, and the property value. This is a vital part of the lending process. Some of the factors underwriters consider when qualifying the borrower include the following:

Income qualification

1. credit report
2. job stability and ability to meet future debt retirement
3. cash equity invested
4. bonus (must be verified)
5. second job (these are usually short term, so lenders are strict; they want a minimum two-year work record)
6. child support payments (lender takes into account that it may not be received; the borrower must have a one-year record of payment and must be entitled to receive payments for five more years)
7. overtime pay (it must be consistent, substantiated, and guaranteed by employer; a two-year history is necessary)
8. bankruptcy (lenders consider whether action was made to repay creditors, if two or three years have passed, and if applicant has a good credit history since the bankruptcy; they also consider whether there was a valid reason for bankruptcy)

Figure 10.1 The Cycle of a Loan, from Application to Sale of the Loan to the Secondary Market

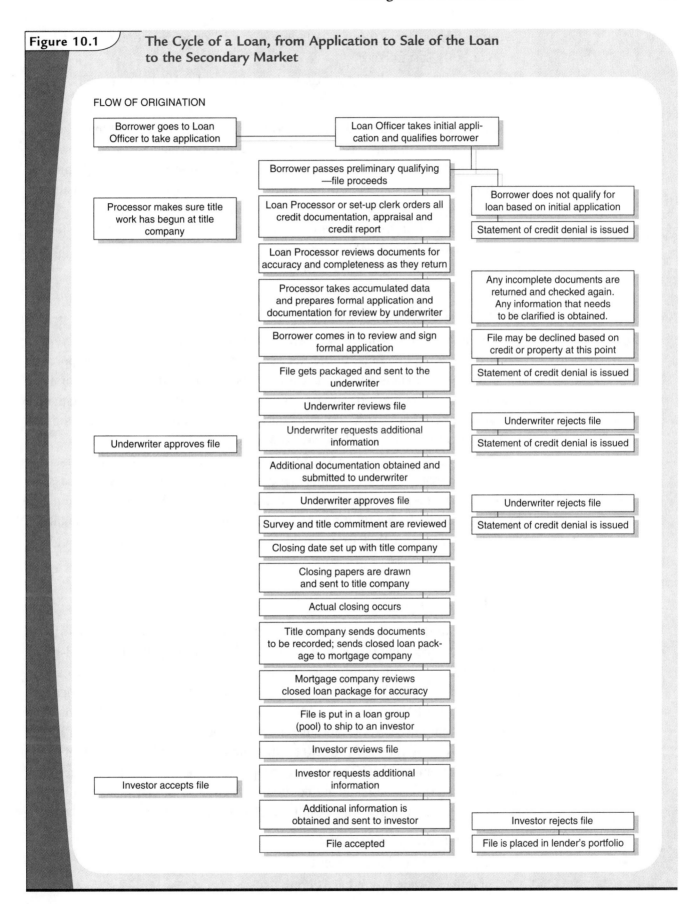

FLOW OF ORIGINATION

Borrower goes to Loan Officer to take application

Loan Officer takes initial application and qualifies borrower

Borrower passes preliminary qualifying —file proceeds

Borrower does not qualify for loan based on initial application

Statement of credit denial is issued

Processor makes sure title work has begun at title company

Loan Processor or set-up clerk orders all credit documentation, appraisal and credit report

Loan Processor reviews documents for accuracy and completeness as they return

Processor takes accumulated data and prepares formal application and documentation for review by underwriter

Any incomplete documents are returned and checked again. Any information that needs to be clarified is obtained.

Borrower comes in to review and sign formal application

File may be declined based on credit or property at this point

Statement of credit denial is issued

File gets packaged and sent to the underwriter

Underwriter reviews file

Underwriter requests additional information

Underwriter rejects file

Statement of credit denial is issued

Underwriter approves file

Additional documentation obtained and submitted to underwriter

Underwriter approves file

Underwriter rejects file

Survey and title commitment are reviewed

Statement of credit denial is issued

Closing date set up with title company

Closing papers are drawn and sent to title company

Actual closing occurs

Title company sends documents to be recorded; sends closed loan package to mortgage company

Mortgage company reviews closed loan package for accuracy

File is put in a loan group (pool) to ship to an investor

Investor reviews file

Investor requests additional information

Investor accepts file

Additional information is obtained and sent to investor

Investor rejects file

File accepted

File is placed in lender's portfolio

9. installment debts (usually a factor if for 10 or more months; credit cards carefully scrutinized)

10. total debt ratio (should not exceed 41 percent for VA loans and FHA loans and 43 percent for conventional loans)

When the lender is satisfied that the borrower has the ability to repay the debt and the property appraisal is satisfactory, the loan is issued.

Today most lenders utilize automated underwriting (see below). While the traditional buyer qualification measures described above are still considered, the **automated underwriting** programs use a form of artificial intelligence that allows for deviation from standard guidelines when strong compensating factors exist. For example, the debt ratios indicated above may be exceeded if the borrower displays significant cash assets.

Automated Underwriting

Electronic loan processing is the newest technology available today. The emergence of the computer and Internet services permits almost instant loan approval, although the applicants' credit must still be approved and the property appraised. The property is not viewed as to its condition or location, but rather by statistical analysis that compares it with recent sales of similar properties. This is a break with what conventional lenders have done.

Both FHLMC and FNMA offer automated underwriting to lenders. The desktop originator software enables lenders and mortgage brokers to access the system and receive loan approval in a matter of minutes. Pertinent data required by the automated underwriting system may include alternate documentation, such as two years of W-2 forms, bank statements, pay stubs, and the source of funds needed to close.

Credit Scoring

Just a few short years ago, credit scoring was not even a factor in the mortgage industry, but electronic processing has now made that possible. The broad-based deterioration of credit quality forced the industry to seek new means to assess loan risk. Credit scoring is now used to determine mortgage performance and is endorsed by FNMA and FHLMC in underwriting conventional loans. The most commonly used credit score is Fair, Isaac and Company, creators of FICO. The FICO scoring ranges from 350 to 900; the lower the number, the higher the likelihood of default. FICO's model is proprietary, meaning that the exact variables that determine the result are not common knowledge. The 33 variables that are used to determine the final result are grouped into five areas:

1. previous credit performance

2. current level of indebtedness

3. amount of time credit has been in use

4. pursuit of new credit

5. types of credit available

The industry is using credit scoring primarily to try to predict the future performance of mortgage loans. Credit scores are objective, consistent, predictive of mortgage default, and more easily incorporated into automated underwriting (AU) systems than rule-based measures of borrower credit risk.

FNMA released an industry letter disclosing that 50 percent of its eventual defaults (of loans reviewed) were loans with scores below 620. Compensating factors when faced with a score under 620 include:

1. a strong equity position

2. debt ratios below the agency's 33/38 percent housing debt and total debt-to-income ratios

3. more cash in reserve than typically required to meet agency guidelines

4. a successful history of paying housing expenses equivalent to the monthly housing obligation if credit is granted

The introduction of electronic loan processing and credit scoring eliminates subjective judgments made by lenders and underwriters, hence resulting in greater impartiality and additional loan possibilities. On the flip side, some observers feel that FICO scores are too rigid and impersonal, thus discounting uncharacteristic situations.

The Internet is also available to individuals, enabling them to search for a home and mortgage rates and compare values. The future is evolving toward a credit scoring system that will allow good credit scores to receive better pricing from the secondary market.

The Secondary Mortgage Market

As discussed earlier, the primary mortgage market consists of the lenders who originate loans and finance them with their funds. These are the S&Ls, commercial banks, mutual savings banks, and mortgage companies. The borrower makes application and the loan is processed and formulated at that institution. However, these primary lenders do not have sufficient funds for all the loans they make, so they sell them to the secondary market. This secondary market is available through funds deposited by savers and funds that are pooled.

The secondary mortgage market refers to the sale of mortgages by the primary lender to investors (see Figure 10.2). The choice of resale affords lenders an opportunity to dispose of their inventory, enabling them to obtain new funds and make new mortgages. The original lender continues to service the loan and receives a fee for this service if the loan is sold to Fannie Mae, Freddie Mac, or Ginnie Mae. If a lender prefers not to continue servicing the loan, the lender may opt to sell the Service Release Premium (SRP) to another lender. When the

Resale of mortgages

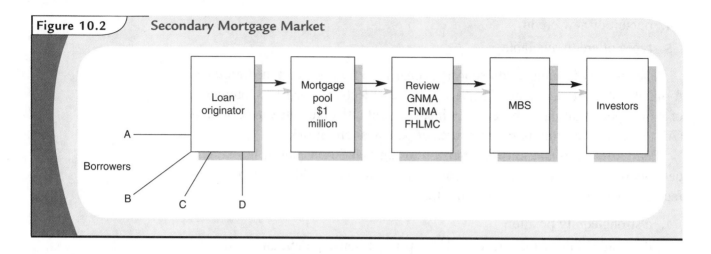

Figure 10.2   Secondary Mortgage Market

loan is sold to another lending institution, the new lender will generally service the loan.

When a mortgage is sold, it is *assigned* to the new mortgage holder. A borrower has no authority over the sale and makes the monthly mortgage and interest payments to the new holder of the mortgage.

FNMA

The Federal National Mortgage Association (FNMA), dubbed Fannie Mae, was created by the government to stimulate the housing market. Originally chartered in 1938 as a government agency, it was primed with $10 million, especially to purchase FHA loans from that recently created program. FNMA purchased loans from commercial banks and savings and loans, providing the institutions with new funds to lend. Revised as a federal agency in 1954, FNMA was acquired from the Department of Housing and Urban Development by the private sector in 1968 and is now owned by stockholders, with the stock traded on the New York Stock Exchange. It is called a quasi-government enterprise because the board of directors must get government approval before issuing bonds and making other financial decisions. Fulfilling its role as a "warehouse" for loans, FNMA buys, sells, and services loans. FNMA, along with Freddie Mac, are now the mortgage industry leaders in defining standards in underwriting loans and appraising property for one- to four-family dwellings.

In 1999, in an effort to expand housing to those of low-moderate income, Fannie Mae and Freddie Mac with strong encouragement and support of government leaders, vastly expanded the risk profile of the loans they would purchase. These high risk loans, often referred to as "sub-prime" loans, were made to borrowers with weak credit, less down payment, and questionable income verification. When housing prices started to drop in 2006 and 2007 (referred to as a collapse of the real estate bubble), combined with the risky nature of these sub-prime loans, home loan defaults skyrocketed nationally. As a result, both Fannie Mae and Freddie Mac nearly collapsed as did many large banks and thrifts and Wall Street Investment firms. For example, the stock in Fannie Mae and Freddie Mac dropped from highs of nearly $90.00 per share to a low of $30.00 per share in 2008. This all resulted in the federal government stepping in by putting Fannie Mae and Freddie Mac into conservatorship which is much akin to bankruptcy. In effect, Fannie Mae and Freddie Mac went back under the control of the federal government.

GNMA

Government National Mortgage Association (GNMA), called Ginnie Mae, was established in 1968 and is operated by HUD. GNMA receives the funds to purchase loans from the sale of long-term bonds on Wall Street. These bonds are often purchased by insurance companies, pension and trust funds, and mutual funds or money market funds. GNMA's purpose is to provide housing and to stabilize mortgage money. GNMA provides reduced interest rates to lower income home purchasers. Ginnie Mae is involved in the tandem plan, which allows FNMA to buy high-risk, low-yielding mortgages at full market price; GNMA guarantees the payment, absorbing the difference between the market rate and the low yield expected. In recent years its largest focus has been on the purchase and sale of these mortgage-backed securities.

FHLMC

The **Federal Home Loan Mortgage Corporation (FHLMC)**, called Freddie Mac, was under the control of the Federal Home Loan Bank Board. It was created in 1970 to buy conventional loans from banks and S&Ls, much the same as FNMA initially bought FHA and VA loans from commercial banks and S&Ls. Originally owned by lending institutions, shares were sold to the public in 1988. Freddie Mac buys mortgages and pools them to sell in the marketplace, but does not guarantee them.

Mortgage-Backed Securities (MBS)

The secondary mortgage market affects everyone involved in real estate financing—builder, seller, borrower, lender, sales agent, broker, and investor—particularly in residential transactions.

Figure 10.2 explains where the money for home mortgages comes from and why we now have to pay discount points to obtain the funds for our mortgages.

The *loan originator* is the institution that takes the loan application and gets the loan approved and closed. It can be a bank, savings and loan, mortgage broker, or mortgage banker. After the loans are closed, they are placed in a mortgage pool with an aggregate amount of $1 million or more. All the loans in the mortgage pool must be homogeneous; that is, they must fall within a restrictive range of rates and the same term.

Loan originator

The mortgage pools are reviewed for compliance with applicable regulations and approved by Fannie Mae, Ginnie Mae, or Freddie Mac. A *mortgage-backed security* (MBS) is then issued and auctioned to investors, such as insurance

Mortgage "pools"

companies, pension and trust funds, or money market funds. The proceeds from the sale, after commissions and discount points are subtracted, are then sent to the originator (primary lender) to be lent out again for new mortgages. The average life of an MBS is 12 years; by then most of the loans have been paid off when the property was sold or refinanced.

The lower the interest rate of the MBS relative to the current money market, the higher the discount. For example, if an MBS containing 32 mortgages with an average rate of 9 percent is being auctioned when the current market rate (as determined by long-term Treasury bills and bonds) is 10 percent, investors will pay only 94 cents on the dollar because they could buy T-bills with no risk for 10 percent. This discount of 6 cents on the dollar, or 6 points, is collected from the borrower or the seller at closing.

As many as three months may elapse between the time the borrower signs the note at closing and the time the MBS is sold on the secondary market. Mortgage bankers and brokers often play the market, betting that they can sell the mortgage three months later at a profit. This is a high-risk game, and millions of dollars are at stake.

Most mortgage-backed securities issued today are in the form of Real Estate Mortgage Investment Conduits (REMIC). Because of changes in the 1986 Tax Reform Act, most collateralized mortgage obligations (CMOs) are now issued in REMIC form to create certain advantages for the issuer. The terms REMIC and CMO are now used interchangeably. It is a corporation, partnership, or trust that holds a fixed pool of mortgages.

Summary of Important Points

1. The backbone of the housing industry, savings and loan institutions, have historically provided the bulk of the funds for financing one- to four-family homes. Dating from the original building club of the early 19th century, the idea of saving money in savings and loan institutions spread tremendously. Today the borrower does not need to be a depositor in a savings and loan to obtain a loan. Along with savings and loans, mortgage bankers now provide a large percentage of home loans on their own or through various brokers.

2. Great changes in the savings and loan industry have occurred. In the late 1980s many insolvent savings and loans were closed down by the federal government, causing chaos in the housing industry.

3. The great "bail out" began and the Resolution Trust Corporation (RTC) was formed to begin the liquidation and sale of the failed institutions.

4. The bankrupt FSLIC was dissolved and replaced by the Savings Association Insurance Fund (SAIF). Chapter 11 will further explain the changes that have taken place in the mortgage market.

5. Mortgage brokers help join lenders and borrowers, but do not service the loans.

6. Government regulations on lending are outlined by Regulation Z and the Real Estate Settlement Procedures Act.

7. The government is also active in insuring FHA loans and guaranteeing VA loans. Conventional loans, private loans, and land contracts may also be obtained to finance mortgages.

8. The secondary mortgage market involves the resale of mortgages. The FNMA, GNMA, and FHLMC all serve to provide a stable market for mortgages.

Discussion Points

1. Why is the Federal Reserve organized to control fiscal policy?

2. Explain how the FHA has changed its program since its inception in 1934. Why were these changes necessary?

3. Explain the purpose of mortgage-backed securities.

4. Why is there a need for the secondary mortgage market?

5. What causes disintermediation?

6. What effect, if any, have the failed savings and loans had on financing for housing?

7. Explain the reasons a purchaser would prefer to use FHA financing.

8. When would it be advisable to use a land contract as a means of financing?

Review Questions

Answers to these questions are found in the Answer Key section at the back of the book.

1. Money for FHA financing is provided by:
   a. any governmental agency
   b. the FDIC
   c. any qualified lending institution
   d. the Federal Housing Administration

2. The Federal Housing Administration:
   a. makes loans
   b. builds houses
   c. purchases land
   d. insures loans

3. In order to make financing for homes available, the most common source of secondary mortgage money is:
   a. the seller taking a second mortgage
   b. the Federal National Mortgage Association
   c. insurance companies
   d. the Federal Housing Administration

4. Which of the following is NOT true regarding a federally chartered savings and loan?
   a. it must be a member of the Federal Home Loan Bank system
   b. it needs to be federally insured
   c. deposits are insured up to $100,000
   d. deposits of any amount are insured

5. In securing a residential loan:
   a. no down payment is required on conventional loans
   b. no down payment can be made on a VA loan unless the selling price of the home is greater than the appraised value
   c. a down payment is made when obtaining an FHA loan
   d. there always must be a 10% (or greater) down payment

6. Which of the following statements is true concerning VA loans?
   a. a VA loan on a fourplex cannot exceed 15 years
   b. a buyer must pay the difference between the amount at which the VA appraises the home and the purchase price
   c. a VA loan can be assumed by a nonveteran
   d. a VA loan can only be issued to a veteran of a foreign war

7. Which of the following is true regarding a property that has been financed with a VA loan?
   a. the loan may be assumed by a person who is not a veteran
   b. the present owner can transfer the loan to a new home she is purchasing
   c. the loan is not assumable
   d. only another veteran that uses his eligibility can assume the loan

8. In securing a loan on a home:
   a. escrow accounts are mandatory
   b. through FHA, the buyer must have a below average income
   c. through VA, the buyer must occupy the home as a residence
   d. the VA loan has no guarantee limit

9. Which of the following is NOT exempt from Regulation Z of the Truth-in-Lending Act?
   a. commercial and business loans
   b. loans of four or fewer installments
   c. loans to corporations or partnerships
   d. loans of five or fewer installments

10. The maximum amount guaranteed by the government on any VA loan is:
    a. the same as on an FHA loan
    b. $50,750
    c. 50% of the purchase price
    d. $60,000

11. The Department of Veterans Affairs:
    a. insures loans
    b. guarantees loans
    c. sells loans
    d. originates loans

12. The private corporation that buys federally insured or guaranteed mortgages for resale is:
    a. FNMA
    b. PMI
    c. MGIC
    d. FDIC

13. When a purchaser of real estate assumes the seller's existing loan:
    a. she buys out the lender's equity
    b. she becomes responsible for the repayment of the debt along with the original borrower
    c. the original borrower is always relieved of responsibility for repayment of the debt
    d. the new owner is always solely responsible for the debt

14. Conventional loans are:
    a. never insured
    b. insured by FHA
    c. not insured by the federal government
    d. guaranteed

15. The substitution of a new contract for an existing agreement is known as:
    a. novation
    b. satisfaction
    c. release
    d. reversion

16. In an FHA loan, discount points are paid by:
    a. the buyer
    b. the seller
    c. buyer and seller
    d. buyer or seller

17. A young couple wants to buy a home. Their income is low, but should increase greatly in the next few years. They will apply for:
    a. an FHA 203
    b. a conventional, insured loan
    c. an FHA 245
    d. an FNMA

18. The mortgage broker who brings the lender and borrower together receives a fee for this service, which is referred to as:
    a. a finder's fee
    b. a service fee
    c. an insured fee
    d. a participation fee

19. Which of the following government regulations entitles borrowers to review their credit report?
    a. Truth-in-Lending
    b. Fair Credit Reporting
    c. Equal Credit Opportunity
    d. Real Estate Settlement Procedures

20. The Mortgage Guarantee Insurance Corporation insures which of the following types of loans?
    a. FHA
    b. VA
    c. conventional
    d. land contract

21. The Community Reinvestment Act was passed to:
    a. prevent lenders from discriminating because of sex or age
    b. permit borrowers to view their credit report to be certain there are no errors
    c. assure all low-income borrowers that they can receive loans
    d. prevent redlining

22. The primary lender may sell the mortgage to the secondary mortgage market. These transactions result in the issuance of certificates that are secured by a pool of mortgages. The certificates are referred to as:
    a. mortgage-backed securities
    b. second mortgages
    c. purchase money mortgages
    d. stock options

23. The secondary mortgage market can best be described as:
    a. lenders of FHA loans carry back second mortgages
    b. primary lenders retain the mortgages in their portfolio
    c. the property owner carries back a second mortgage
    d. after loans are originated, they are purchased and sold

24. The primary purpose of the Federal Home Loan Mortgage Corporation (FHLMC), called Freddie Mac, is to:
    a. buy mortgages and pool them to sell in the marketplace
    b. originate loans
    c. service loans
    d. insure loans made by qualified lenders

25. A purchaser buys a home for $48,000. What amount will the lender finance in a standard FHA 203B loan?
    a. $1,200.00
    b. $1,440.00
    c. $46,920.00
    d. $47,400.00

26. If the buyer of an $83,000 home wants to finance the UFMIP, the maximum 30-year loan would be:
    a. $1,785.38
    b. $79,350.00
    c. $81,000.00
    d. $82,924.00

27. This loan allows for financing both the purchase and the cost of rehabilitating the property:
    a. FHA 234 loan
    b. FHA 203B loan
    c. FHA 203K plan
    d. VA loan

Financing

KEY TERMS

adjustable rate mortgage (ARM)	lien
amortization	lien theory
balloon payment	moratorium
blanket mortgage	mortgage
deed of trust	mortgagee
discount points	mortgagor
equity	open-end mortgage
escrow agreement	PITI
estoppel certificate	short-sale
foreclosure	specific liens
general liens	straight loan
hypothecation	tax lien
interest	title theory
involuntary lien	voluntary lien

OVERVIEW

One of the most important components of any real estate transaction is the financing. Since the purchase of a home is the largest investment the average person enters into, almost everyone needs to finance at least a portion of the purchase price. Without adequate financing the sale can be lost.

When interest rates for real estate mortgages escalated to all-time highs in the late 1970s and early 1980s, financiers developed many creative financing techniques. The traditional financing practices gave way to innovative methods. Many of these practices remain with us today even though interest rates are lower.

This chapter explains interest rates, the various clauses found in notes and mortgages, and the different types of mortgages available to the borrower. Descriptions of the foreclosure procedure on a defaulted mortgage and the numerous specific and general liens complete this chapter.

Interest Rates

Renting money

Interest is rent for the use of money. Interest rates depend upon many complex economic factors, including:

1. the risk involved in making the loan
2. the business outlook for the future
3. the market rate for alternate investments such as Treasury bonds (If there are fewer buyers for bonds, then bond prices fall, which results in a corresponding increase in rates. This is a simple application of the law of supply and demand.)
4. the outlook for inflation in the future

Since investors are in business to make a profit, they require a certain rate of return on their investments. Under the free market system in the United States, the market rates of interest are not set by the government, but by auction process.

Mortgage Payment Methods

Term Loans

Interest and principal repaid separately

Under a term loan, also referred to as a **straight loan**, the borrower pays only the interest due for each period, with the sum borrowed repaid on the due date of the loan. Prevalent before the depression of the 1930s, they resulted in many people losing their homes because the banks were unable to negotiate a new loan when the principal became due. The borrower had no resources from which to repay the loan and foreclosures resulted. As mentioned in Chapter 10, the government intervened by creating the Federal Housing Administration to make amortized FHA loans. Today term loans are used by builders and land developers who need short-term financing.

Fully Amortized Mortgages

ray.met.fsu.edu/
-bret/amortize.html

The most common means of repaying a mortgage is by making equal payments that gradually reduce the balance of the loan within a stated period of time. The equal payments include a portion for interest and a portion for principal, which reduces the unpaid balance. Basically, **amortization** is the liquidation of a financial obligation on the installment basis. For example, on a $90,000 loan at 7 percent interest for 30 years, the interest and principal payment would be

$599.40 monthly. After the first payment, the balance due would be figured as follows:

$90,000.00	loan amount
$\times$ .07	interest rate
$ 6,300.00	yearly interest

$6,300 ÷ 12 months = $525 monthly interest

$ 599.40	principal and interest payment
− 525.00	first month's interest
$ 74.40	toward principal
$90,000.00	
− 74.40	
$89,925.60	balance due after first payment

As this example shows, the debt is reduced by $74.40 the first month. Since the borrower pays each month on the unpaid balance due, a larger amount is attributed to the principal reduction each month. Some lending institutions require that monthly mortgage payments include not only the principal and interest (known as P and I) payment, but one-twelfth of the yearly taxes and insurance. This amount is kept in an escrow or reserve account from which the lender pays the taxes and insurance as they become due. The lender is then assured protection on the investment; for example, if the dwelling burns down, it is covered by insurance. Similarly, the taxes are paid, so there will be no tax foreclosure sale.

The following equation demonstrates the calculation of a **PITI** (principal, interest, taxes, and insurance) payment. To the $599.40 payment on a $90,000 loan at 7 percent interest, add one-twelfth of the $2,200 yearly tax and one-twelfth of the $360 yearly insurance premium.

$ 599.40	P&I
183.33	taxes
30.00	insurance
$ 812.73	total PITI monthly payment

A departure from the traditional 30-year mortgage is the 15- or 20-year fixed-rate loan. One advantage is that it is often available at a lower interest rate and with reduced discount points. The following examples illustrate the difference in interest paid on 15-, 20-, and 30-year mortgages. Check the amortization chart to determine the P and I payment (see Figure 11.1).

A. $50,000 loan for 30 years at 8% interest
$367.00 P&I × 360 payments = $132,120
$132,120 − $50,000 loan = $82,120 interest paid

Figure 11.1   Amortization Chart

EQUAL MONTHLY PAYMENTS TO AMORTIZE A LOAN OF $1000

Years	6.00%	7.00%	8.00%	8.50%	9.00%	9.50%	10.00%	10.50%	11.00%	11.50%	12.00%
1	86.07	86.53	86.99	87.22	87.46	87.69	87.92	88.15	88.39	88.62	88.85
2	44.33	44.78	45.23	45.46	45.69	45.92	46.15	46.38	46.61	46.85	47.08
3	30.43	30.88	31.34	31.57	31.80	32.04	32.27	32.51	32.74	32.98	33.22
4	23.49	23.95	24.42	24.65	24.89	25.13	25.37	25.61	25.85	26.09	26.34
5	19.34	19.81	20.28	20.52	20.76	21.01	21.25	21.50	21.75	22.00	22.25
6	16.58	17.05	17.54	17.78	18.03	18.28	18.53	18.78	19.04	19.30	19.56
7	14.71	15.10	15.59	15.84	16.09	16.35	16.61	16.87	17.13	17.39	17.66
8	13.15	13.64	14.14	14.40	14.66	14.92	15.18	15.45	15.71	15.98	16.26
9	12.01	12.51	13.02	13.28	13.55	13.81	14.08	14.36	14.63	14.91	15.19
10	11.11	11.62	12.14	12.40	12.67	12.94	13.22	13.50	13.78	14.06	14.35
11	10.37	10.89	11.42	11.69	11.97	12.24	12.52	12.81	13.10	13.39	13.68
12	9.76	10.29	10.83	11.11	11.39	11.67	11.96	12.25	12.54	12.84	13.14
13	9.25	9.79	10.34	10.62	10.90	11.19	11.48	11.78	12.08	12.38	12.69
14	8.82	9.36	9.92	10.20	10.49	10.79	11.09	11.39	11.70	12.01	12.32
15	8.44	8.99	9.56	9.85	10.15	10.45	10.75	11.06	11.37	11.69	12.01
16	8.12	8.68	9.25	9.55	9.85	10.15	10.46	10.78	11.10	11.42	11.74
17	7.84	8.40	8.99	9.29	9.59	9.90	10.22	10.54	10.86	11.19	11.52
18	7.59	8.16	8.75	9.06	9.37	9.68	10.00	10.33	10.66	10.99	11.32
19	7.37	7.95	8.55	8.86	9.17	9.49	9.82	10.15	10.48	10.82	11.16
20	7.17	7.76	8.37	8.68	9.00	9.33	9.66	9.99	10.33	10.67	11.02
21	6.99	7.59	8.21	8.53	8.85	9.18	9.51	9.85	10.19	10.54	10.89
22	6.84	7.44	8.07	8.39	8.72	9.05	9.39	9.73	10.08	10.43	10.78
23	6.69	7.30	7.94	8.27	8.60	8.93	9.28	9.62	9.98	10.33	10.69
24	6.56	7.18	7.83	8.16	8.49	8.83	9.18	9.53	9.89	10.25	10.61
25	6.45	7.07	7.72	8.06	8.40	8.74	9.09	9.45	9.81	10.17	10.54
26	6.34	6.97	7.63	7.97	8.31	8.66	9.01	9.37	9.74	10.10	10.47
27	6.24	6.88	7.55	7.89	8.24	8.59	8.95	9.31	9.67	10.05	10.42
28	6.16	6.80	7.47	7.82	8.17	8.52	8.88	9.25	9.62	9.99	10.37
29	6.08	6.73	7.40	7.75	8.11	8.47	8.83	9.20	9.57	9.95	10.33
30	6.00	6.66	7.34	7.69	8.05	8.41	8.78	9.15	9.52	9.91	10.29

B. $50,000 loan for 20 years at 8% interest
$418.50 × 240 payments = $100,440
$100,440 − $50,000 loan = $50,440 interest paid

C. $50,000 loan for 15 years at 8% interest
$478.00 × 180 payments = $86,040
$86,040 − $50,000 loan = $36,040 interest paid

Partially Amortized Mortgages

The partially amortized mortgage requires periodic payments on the principal, but at the due date a balance remains because the principal has been only partially reduced. If a loan does not amortize out at the due date, the total unpaid sum is much larger than the regular monthly payment. In some situations the mortgagor may only make interest payments, with the full amount of the principal due at an agreed-upon time. This results in a **balloon payment**.

Balloons are used when the lender prefers not to lend money for a long period of time. The mortgage is generally a 3- to 5-year fixed loan with an amortization schedule of 15 to 30 years. The mortgage holder is under no obligation to refinance the loan, so the borrower must find other means of financing when the balloon payment is due.

Interest-Only (I/O) and Option ARMs

As previously mentioned, some loans allow for payment of interest-only for a period of time. Due to rising property values over the past five to seven years, these I/O loans became very popular because they allowed the borrower to qualify for higher loan amounts and therefore higher sale prices. The problem, of course, is that when one only pays interest, the principal amount borrowed does not reduce. When property values continue to rise, the concern is mitigated by the continued increase in equity. Unfortunately, with property values in many parts of the country leveling or declining, the use of I/O loans has caused greater concern with both lenders and borrowers. Caution should be the guide when considering use of interest-only-type loans.

An alternative payment plan has been used fairly extensively over the past few years as an offset to the I/O plan and offers more flexibility. The "option ARM" is an adjustable rate mortgage that allows the borrower the added flexibility of paying one of several different options per month. These option ARMs are essentially interest-only at their onset but, with each month's mortgage statement, the borrower is given the option to pay either the low, interest-only amount or a 15-year, 20-year, or 30-year amortized payment.

The credit crisis of 2008 resulted in most of the "exotic" payment plans to all but disappear. The future of these payment plans is unclear.

Budget Mortgage

A *budget mortgage* requires the borrower to repay not only the principal and interest in set monthly payments, but also one-twelfth of the annual taxes and insurance. This frees the borrower from the expense of paying taxes and insurance in a lump sum when they become due, thus the term *budget* is often applied to this mortgage. Budget mortgages are synonymous with direct-reduction mortgages, as used in FHA, VA, and some conventional loans.

Equity

The **equity** an owner has in property represents the difference between the value of the property and what is owed. A $60,000 property with a $50,000 mortgage represents equity of $10,000 for the owner. As the principal is paid off through the monthly amortized payments, equity increases. In the early years of the mortgage, equity build-up is slow because most of the payment is for interest. If there is more than one loan, equity is the difference between the total owed and the market value.

Usury

Illegal interests

Interest charged or accepted by a money lender in excess of the amount allowed by law is considered usury and is illegal. Usury laws are not federal laws, but are set by state statutes. With the unprecedented rise of interest rates during the early 1980s, many states placed a **moratorium** on their usury laws, since many were originally lower than the national market for mortgage money. During the first three months of 1980, Congress placed a suspension order on all state usury laws. Designed to protect the borrower from paying excessive interest rates, the usury laws may indeed be a symbol of the past. Some states change the legally allowed rate as interest rates fluctuate.

Discount Points

Percentage charges
made on new loans

Discount points are charged by money lenders to increase the yield on money lent to the borrower. Originally, discount amounts were based on the quality of the property, market conditions, and the ability of the purchaser to borrow and repay. Today the amount is determined by market conditions.

If yields on mortgage loans are lower than yields on other investments, funds will be drawn away from the home mortgage market, and money for home mortgages will become scarce and more expensive. The fixed-rate mortgage lender has to determine the cost of doing business and allow for a reasonable profit to arrive at the yield needed to make the sale of a mortgage at a given discount economically sound.

One discount point is equal to 1 percent of the loan amount. Thus, if a lender charges two discount points on a $30,000 loan, the lender will be receiving 2 percent of $30,000, or $600. This will be paid to the lender at the time the loan closes. While most loans are paid off before the 30-year maturity, a general rule is that each discount point lowers the note rate by one-eighth of 1 percent. So the two discount points in the example would lower the interest rate by .25 percent. As the interest rate increases, the discount points are lower until you reach the market or "par" rate at which no points are charged.

Origination fee

Do not confuse discount points with the *origination fee.* The origination fee is paid by the borrower to the lender for the originating and processing of the new loan and is generally an additional 1 percent of the loan. Both the discount points and loan origination fee are considered prepaid interest and can be deducted on your income tax form.

Loan-to-Value Ratio (LTV)

The lender makes a loan on the property for a proportionate value of the real estate. If the property appraises for $40,000 and the purchaser is putting 20 percent down, the loan-to-value ratio will be 80 percent of the $40,000, or $32,000. Needless to say, the greater the loan-to-value ratio, the greater the risk involved for the lending institution, since the down payment represents the borrower's equity. Mortgages are made as high as 95 percent of LTV; however, the borrower must have excellent credit to qualify. The property must appraise at the purchase price. If not, the lender will only loan on 80 percent of the appraised value, and the buyer will need to pay the balance at closing if a PMI loan is used. However, if the property appraises higher than the purchase price, the lender will loan on the basis of the purchase price. The lender loans on whichever is lower, purchase price or appraised value.

Percentage loaned by lender

The Promissory Note

In real estate financing the borrower signs a promissory note in which the promise is made to pay the specified debt at a rate and time specified in the note. The note is backed by a mortgage that pledges the property as security for the loan.

Promise to repay debt

The note and mortgage may be incorporated into a single document, but technically they are two legal instruments. The note must state the terms of payment, the due date, and interest rate and sometimes will include a prepayment penalty. Since lenders often sell their loans to the secondary mortgage market, a standardized form is used in all states.

The promissory note shown in Figure 11.2 has no prepayment penalty. A prepayment penalty would require the mortgagor to pay a penalty for repaying the amount borrowed before the due date. If the mortgagor pays the note off before its due date, no charge is made for prepaying the amount borrowed. This may be important to the borrower since the average person changes residence every seven years due to employment transfers, changes in family size, or other personal reasons. The descriptions following Figure 11.2 match the corresponding numbers on Figure 11.2.

1. Shows the amount borrowed and the name of the lender and permits the lender to transfer the note.
2. Indicates the amount of interest to be charged to the borrower.

Elements of a note

3. Provides for the time, place, and monthly amount to be paid.
4. States that the borrower has the option to prepay all or a portion of the note without penalty. This note carries no prepayment penalty.
5. Explains that if a law should be established that causes the interest rate to exceed the amount that is lawful, the lending institution will reduce the loan charges (interest) to the amount necessary to meet the new requirement and refund to the borrower any excess collected.

Figure 11.2   Promissory Note

NOTE

May 14, 2008   Any City   Any State
                                    City   State
1040 Clear Street
                              Property Address

1. BORROWER'S PROMISE TO PAY

In return for a loan that I have received, I promise to pay U.S. $ 147, 200.00   (this amount is called "principal"), plus interest, to the order of the Lender. The Lender is   Ready Savings and Loan

I understand that the Lender may transfer this Note. The Lender or anyone who takes this Note by transfer and who is entitled to receive payments under this Note is called the "Note Holder."

2. INTEREST

Interest will be charged on unpaid principal until the full amount of principal has been paid. I will pay interest at a yearly rate of   6   %

The interest rate required by this Section 2 is the rate I will pay both before and after any default described in Section 6(B) of the Note.

3. PAYMENTS

(A) TIME AND PLACE OF PAYMENTS

I will pay principal and interest by making payments every month.

I will make my monthly payments on the   1st   day of each month beginning on   July 1, 2008   . I will make these payments every month until I have paid all of the principal and interest and any other charges described below that I may owe under this Note. My monthly payments will be applied to interest before principal. If, on   July 1, 2038   , I still owe amounts under this Note, I will pay those amounts in full on that date, which is called the "maturity date."

I will make my monthly payments at   Ready Savings and Loan, 8250 Alert Dr., Any City, USA

or at a different place if required by the Note Holder.

(B) AMOUNT OF MONTHLY PAYMENTS

My monthly payment will be in the amount of U.S. $ $1224.20   .

4. BORROWER'S RIGHT TO PREPAY

I have the right to make payments of principal at any time before they are due. A payment of principal only is known as a "prepayment." When I make a prepayment, I will tell the Note Holder in writing that I am doing so.

I may make a full prepayment or partial prepayments without paying any prepayment charge. The Note Holder will use all of my prepayments to reduce the amount of principal that I owe under this Note. If I make a partial prepayment, there will be no changes in the due date or in the amount of my monthly payment unless the Note Holder agrees in writing to those changes.

5. LOAN CHARGES

If a law, which applies to this loan and which sets maximum loan charges, is finally interpreted so that the interest or other loan charges collected or to be collected in connection with this loan exceed the permitted limits, then: (i) any such loan charge will be reduced by the amount necessary to reduce the charge to the permitted limit; and (ii) any sums already collected from me which exceeded permitted limits will be refunded to me. The Note Holder may choose to make this refund by reducing the principal I owe under this Note or by making a direct payment to me. If a refund reduces principal, the reduction will be treated as a partial prepayment.

6. BORROWER'S FAILURE TO PAY AS REQUIRED

(A) LATE CHARGE FOR OVERDUE PAYMENTS

If the Note Holder has not received the full amount of any monthly payment by the end of   10   calendar days after the date it is due, I will pay a late charge to the Note Holder. The amount of the charge will be   4   % of my overdue payment of principal and interest. I will pay this late charge promptly but only once on each late payment.

(B) DEFAULT

If I do not pay the full amount of each monthly payment on the date it is due, I will be in default.

(C) NOTICE OF DEFAULT

If I am in default, the Note Holder may send me a written notice telling me that if I do not pay the overdue amount by a certain date, the Note Holder may require me to pay immediately the full amount of principal which has not been paid and all the interest that I owe on that amount. That date must be at least 30 days after the date on which the notice is delivered or mailed to me.

(D) NO WAIVER BY NOTE HOLDER

Even if, at a time when I am in default, the Note Holder does not require me to pay immediately in full as described above, the Note Holder will still have the right to do so if I am in default at a later time.

(E) PAYMENT OF NOTE HOLDER'S COSTS AND EXPENSES

If the Note Holder has required me to pay immediately in full as described above, the Note Holder will have the right to be paid back by me for all of its costs and expenses in enforcing this Note to the extent not prohibited by applicable law. Those expenses include, for example, reasonable attorney's fees.

7. GIVING OF NOTICES

Unless applicable law requires a different method, any notice that must be given to me under this Note will be given by delivering it or by mailing it by first class mail to me at the Property address above or at a different address if I give the Note Holder a notice of my different address.

Any notice that must be given to the Note Holder under this Note will be given by mailing it by first class mail to the Note Holder at the address stated in Section 3(A) above or at a different address if I am given a notice of that different address.

MULTISTATE FIXED RATE NOTE-Single Family-FNMA/FHLMC UNIFORM INSTRUMENT   Form 3200 12/83

Figure 11.2 continued

8. OBLIGATIONS OF PERSONS UNDER THIS NOTE

If more than one person signs this Note, each person is fully and personally obligated to keep all of the promises made in this Note, including the promise to pay the full amount owed. Any person who is a guarantor, surety or endorser of this Note is also obligated to do these things. Any person who takes over these obligations, including the obligations of a guarantor, surety or endorser of this Note, is also obligated to keep all of the promises made in this Note. The Note Holder may enforce its rights under this Note against each person individually or against all of us together. This means that any one of us may be required to pay all of the amounts owed under this Note.

9. WAIVERS

I and any other person who has obligations under this Note waive the rights of presentment and notice of dishonor. "Presentment" means the right to require the Note Holder to demand payment of amounts due. "Notice of dishonor" means the right to require the Note Holder to give notice to other persons that amounts due have not been paid.

10. UNIFORM SECURED NOTE

This Note is a uniform instrument with limited variations in some jurisdictions. In addition to the protections given to the Note Holder under this Note, a Mortgage, Deed of Trust or Security Deed (the "Security Instrument"), dated the same date as this Note, protects the Note Holder from possible losses which might result if I do not keep the promises which I make in this Note. That Security Instrument describes how and under what conditions I may be required to make immediate payment in full of all amounts I owe under this Note. Some of these conditions are described as follows:

Transfer of the Property or a Beneficial Interest in Borrower.

If all or any part of the Property or any interest in it is sold or transferred (or if a beneficial interest in Borrower is sold or transferred and Borrower is not a natural person) without Lender's prior written consent, Lender may, at its option, require immediate payment in full of all sums secured by this Security Instrument. However, this option shall not be exercised by Lender if exercise is prohibited by federal law as of the date of this Security Instrument.

If Lender exercises this option, Lender shall give Borrower notice of acceleration. The notice shall provide a period of not less than 30 days from the date the notice is delivered or mailed within which Borrower must pay all sums secured by this Security Instrument. If Borrower fails to pay these sums prior to the expiration of the period, Lender may invoke any remedies permitted by this Security Instrument without further notice or demand on Borrower.

WITNESS THE HAND(S) AND SEAL(S) OF THE UNDERSIGNED.

_____(Seal)
                                                Borrower

_____(Seal)
                                                Borrower

_____(Seal)
                                                Borrower

_____(Seal)
                                                Borrower

6. Addresses the borrower's failure to repay the note as promised. A late penalty will be charged, and the lender has the right to call the note due and payable in full. It further explains that any costs and expenses incurred by the lender will be borne by the borrower.

7. Any notices given to the borrower will be sent by first class mail to the address stated or to a different address if the lender is so notified of such address.

8. Provides for all the signers (also known as makers) of the note to be jointly responsible for repayment.

9. The borrower waives any rights requiring the note holder to demand payment of the amounts due or to inform other persons that the note is past due.

10. States that the note is secured by a mortgage, deed of trust, or security instrument. The last paragraph gives the lender the right to call the note due and payable if the property is sold or transferred without permission of the note holder. In the event that the mortgagors sell the property, they are restricted from allowing the mortgage to be assumed without the mortgagee's permission.

The Mortgage

A **mortgage** is an instrument that pledges property as collateral for a debt. To pledge property without giving up possession is referred to as hypothecating the property or **hypothecation**. There are two parties to the mortgage—the **mortgagee** and the **mortgagor**. The mortgagee (the creditor) is the person or lender to whom the mortgage has been given as security. This interest can be assigned to another and occurs when the mortgage is sold to the secondary mortgage market as covered in Chapter 10.

Pledging property as security

The mortgagor (debtor) is the owner of the property put up as security. The mortgagor is also referred to as the obligor and possesses all the rights of ownership but must live up to the terms of the mortgage that has been given to the mortgagee (obligee). The note described above is backed by the mortgage that pledges the property as security for the loan. This pledge gives the lender security while permitting the mortgagor use of the property. If the borrower does not make the payments as agreed, the creditor has the right to seize and sell the property through foreclosure to satisfy the debt. Thus, the mortgagor is not paying on a mortgage but on a note (a promise to pay.) *A mortgage note is a negotiable instrument* and, as such, can be bought or sold.

Mortgagee may sell loan

The mortgage contains certain covenants that the mortgagor makes to the mortgagee, as shown in Figure 11.3:

Section 1 sets forth the borrowers' names, the amount of the loan, the lender's name, and the legal description of the property.

In *Section 2,* the mortgagors affirm that they have title to the property.

Section 3 explains that the mortgage is an open-end mortgage and that Ready Savings and Loan will loan, at its option, additional money not to exceed 110 percent of the original note. (A section on open-end mortgages appears later in this chapter.)

Defeasance clause

Section 4 is the *defeasance clause,* which states that the mortgage is defeated when the debt is paid in full; that is, when the mortgagors have abided by the terms of the mortgage and the debt has been paid, the rights that the mortgagee held to take the property if the terms were not met have been defeated. However,

Figure 11.3	A Mortgage Instrument

MORTGAGE

1 KNOW ALL MEN BY THESE PRESENTS: That <u>Kyle A. Albright and Judy A. Albright, husband and wife</u> (hereinafter called Mortgagors) in consideration of the sum of <u>One-hundred Forty-Seven thousand two hundred and no/100—dollars ($147,200.00)</u> loaned to Mortgagors, do hereby grant, bargain, sell and convey unto READY SAVINGS AND LOAN ASSOCIATION of Any City, USA (hereinafter called "Ready"), its successors and assigns, the following described real estate; situated in the County of _____ State of _____, to-wit:
Lot Eight (8) Block One (1) Confusion Hill Subdivision

2 Said Mortgagors hereby covenant with said Ready, its successors and assigns, that Mortgagors are lawfully seized of said premises, that they are free from encumbrances, and that they will forever warrant and defend the title to said premises against the lawful claims of all persons whomsoever.

3 Provided, nevertheless, these presents are upon the following conditions:
That whereas this mortgage shall secure any additional advances, with interest, which may, at the option of Ready, be made by Ready to the undersigned Mortgagors or their successors in title for any purpose, at any time before the release and cancellation of this mortgage, but PROVIDED, HOWEVER, at no time shall the aggregate principal amount secured by this mortgage, being the amount due at any time on said original note and any additional advances made, exceed an amount equal to 110 percent of the amount of the original note, but in no event shall said note exceed the maximum amount permitted by law.

4 If the said Mortgagors shall pay or cause to be paid the said sums of money when due, as set forth in said note, then this mortgage shall be null and void; otherwise, to be and remain in full force and effect;
(a)   If default should be made: in any of the payments due on said note, and any other note for additional advances made, as therein agreed to be made for three months, or
(b)   In keeping the improvements on said premises insured against loss by reason of fire, lightning, and other hazards included in extended coverage insurance in an amount not less than the unpaid balance of said mortgage loan, in a company or companies acceptable to Ready Savings & Loan, the original of such policy or policies to be held by Ready Savings & Loan, and with a mortgage clause attached to said policy or policies, in favor of Ready; or
(c)   In the payment of taxes and assessments levied upon said premises, or on this mortgage, before they are delinquent; or
(d)   If there is any change in the ownership of the real estate mortgaged herein, by sale, either outright or by land contract, or by assignment of any interest thereon or otherwise;

5 then, in any of the above set-forth events, the whole indebtedness hereby secured shall, at the option of Ready Savings & Loan, immediately become due and payable without further notice. The amount due under said note and any other note for additional advances made shall, from the date of the exercise of said option, bear interest at the maximum legal rate per annum, and this mortgage may then be foreclosed to satisfy the amount due on said note, and any other note for additional advances, together with all sums paid by Ready Savings & Loan for insurance, taxes, assessments and abstract extension charges, with interest thereon from the date of payment at the maximum legal rate.

6 PROVIDED, further that in the event that default occurs, Ready shall be entitled to the immediate possession of the premises above described, together with all rents, proceeds and issues arising out of the premises,

(continued)

Figure 11.3 continued

6   and may in its discretion use the rents so far as it deems necessary to the purpose of making repairs upon the premises and for payment of insurance premiums, taxes and assessments upon such premises, and for necessary expenses incurred in renting said premises and collecting rent therefrom, and to apply same on said note and any notes evidencing future advances hereunder until the indebtedness secured is fully paid; and for such purposes, the undersigned does hereby sell, assign, set over and transfer unto Ready all of said rents, proceeds and incomes including any land contract payments due mortgage owners or any other incomes of any type whatsoever from said property to be applied on the notes above-described, but said Ready shall in no case be liable for the failure to procure tenants, to collect rents, or to prosecute actions to recover possession of said premises.

7   The Mortgagors hereby agree that if Ready either voluntarily or involuntarily becomes or is made a party to any suit or proceeding relating to the hereinbefore described real estate, or to this mortgage or said note or notes, other than a foreclosure instituted by Ready, Mortgagors will reimburse Ready for all reasonable costs incurred in said suit or proceeding. The Mortgagors further agree that if the hereinbefore described real estate or any part thereof be condemned under the power of eminent domain, or is otherwise acquired for a public use, the damages awarded, the proceeds for the taking, and for the remaining unpaid indebtedness secured by this mortgage, be, and they hereby are, assigned to Ready and shall be paid forthwith to Ready to be applied on account of the last maturing installments of such indebtedness.

Dated this ____14th____ day of ____May____, 20 __08__ .

IN THE PRESENCE OF:

8   _____

_____   Name

_____

_____

if the mortgagors do not repay the debt as scheduled in the mortgage, they lose the property to the lender, and their opportunity to defeat the clause is lost. The section further states that the mortgagors must (a) make payments as they are due, or the lender can call the mortgage due and payable. The mortgagors also covenant that (b) they will keep insurance on the property for not less than the loan amount, with the lender co-named as beneficiary. Finally, they agree that (c) the taxes must be kept current, and (d) if the property is sold, the note is due and payable.

Section 5 reconfirms that the mortgage will be foreclosed upon if any of the items under Section 4 are violated. Known as the *alienation clause,* it allows the lender to call the balance due and payable upon the sale of the property. It is commonly referred to as the *due-on-sale clause.* This protects the lender in the event that interest rates have risen since the loan was originally placed. If the purchaser desires to assume the existing mortgage, the lender can raise the

Alienation clause

interest rate. Some states passed into law mandatory compulsion on the part of the lender to permit conventional loan assumptions. However, in July 1982 the U.S. Supreme Court ruled that federally chartered savings and loan associations can enforce the due-on-sale clause, thus superseding the state law. The news media related the ensuing pandemonium that took place in the states where sales were being consummated on the basis of the state's law.

Section 6 says that if the owner defaults in payment, the lender can immediately take possession of the premises. This clause, called the *acceleration clause,* is recited in deeds of trust, mortgages, and land contracts. It permits the lender or creditor to declare the entire sum due and payable upon certain default by the debtor. The legality of the call clause, as it is commonly known, has been upheld for loans issued by federally chartered savings and loans.

Acceleration clause

This section also provides the lender protection in the event that the mortgagor rents the property and fails to make the mortgage payment. Referred to as an *assignment of rents clause,* this provision states that the mortgagee can notify the tenants that the mortgage is in default and future rents shall be paid to the mortgagee. The lender in this case is called the *mortgagee in possession.*

Assignment of rent clause

Section 7 helps protect the lender's rights by stating that if the mortgagor is involved in a lawsuit and it results in expenses to the lender, the mortgagor will pay all costs. This section further states that the mortgagee will be first in line for payment if the property should be taken by the government. (The right of the government to take property by condemnation is called the right of eminent domain.)

Section 8 includes the date and the witness and mortgagor signatures.

Deed of Trust

A **deed of trust** is a conditional deed to secure money for the payment of a debt involving three parties to the instrument. The borrower transfers the property to a *trustee,* who holds it for the benefit of the lender until the debt is repaid in full. Upon full payment, the reconveyance clause requires the trustee to reconvey the property to the borrower. Remember, the purpose of a trust deed is to secure the loan. Widely used in some parts of the country, a trust deed is considerably easier to foreclose on than a mortgage. The lender does not hold title, only the *right* to request the trustee to hold a foreclosure sale in the event of a default in payment. If the trustee is not an authorized public trustee, the law states the foreclosure must proceed through the courts in the same manner as a routine mortgage foreclosure (see Figure 11.4). There are three parties to a deed of trust:

1. the trustor: the owner or borrower
2. the trustee: a public trustee; the disinterested third party
3. the beneficiary: the lender

Figure 11.4   Deed of Trust

F1029.LM (12/90)

_____   [Space Above This Line For Recording Data]   _____

DEED OF TRUST

THIS DEED OF TRUST ("Security Instrument") is made on _____, _____ .
The trustor is _____
_____ ("Borrower").
The trustee is _____ ("Trustee").
The beneficiary is _____ , which
is organized and existing under the laws of _____ , and whose address is
_____ ("Lender").
Borrower owes Lender the principal sum of _____
_____ Dollars (U.S.$_____). This debt is evidenced by Borrower's note
dated the same date as this Security Instrument ("Note"), which provides for monthly payments, with the full debt, if not paid earlier, due
and payable on _____
This Security Instrument secures to Lender: (a) repayment of the debt evidenced by the Note, with interest, and all renewals, extensions
and modifications; (b) the payment of all other sums, with interest, advanced under paragraph 7 to protect the security of this Security
Instrument; and (c) the performance of Borrower's covenants and agreements. For this purpose, Borrower irrevocably grants and conveys
to Trustee, in trust, with power of sale, the following described property located in _____ County, Nebraska:

which has the address of _____ , _____
Nebraska _____ ("Property Address");
            Zip Code   Street   City

TOGETHER WITH all improvements now or hereafter erected on the property, and all easements, rights, appurtenances, rents,
royalties, mineral, oil, and gas rights and profits, water rights, and stock and all fixtures now or hereafter a part of the property. All
replacements and additions shall be covered by this Security Instrument. All of the foregoing is referred to in this Security Instrument as
the "Property."

BORROWER COVENANTS that Borrower is lawfully seised of the estate hereby conveyed and has the right to grant and convey the
Property and that the Property is unencumbered, except for encumbrances of record. Borrower warrants and will defend generally the title
to the Property against all claims and demands, subject to any encumbrances of record.

THIS SECURITY INSTRUMENT combines uniform covenants for national use and non-uniform covenants with limited variations by
jurisdiction to constitute a uniform security instrument covering real property.

UNIFORM COVENANTS. Borrower and Lender covenant and agree as follows:

1. PAYMENT OF PRINCIPAL AND INTEREST; PREPAYMENT AND LATE CHARGES. Borrower shall promptly pay when due the
principal of and interest on the debt evidenced by the Note and any prepayment and late charges due under the Note.

2. FUNDS FOR TAXES AND INSURANCE. Subject to applicable law or to a written waiver by Lender, Borrower shall pay to Lender
on the day monthly payments are due under the Note, until the Note is paid in full, a sum ("Funds") equal to one-twelfth of: (a) yearly
taxes and assessments which may attain priority over this Security Instrument; (b) yearly leasehold payments or ground rents on the
Property, if any; (c) yearly hazard insurance premiums; and (d) yearly mortgage insurance premiums, if any. The items are called "escrow
items." Lender may estimate the Funds due on the basis of current data and reasonable estimates of future escrow items.

Form 3028 12/83 NEBRASKA Single Family FNMA/FHLMC UNIFORM INSTRUMENT

F1029.LM (12/90)   Page 1 of 4   _____ _____

Figure 11.4 continued

The Funds shall be held in an institution the deposits or accounts of which are insured or guaranteed by a federal or state agency (including Lender if Lender is such an institution). Lender shall apply the Funds to pay the escrow items. Lender may not charge for holding and applying the Funds, analyzing the account or verifying the escrow items, unless Lender pays Borrower interest on the Funds and applicable law permits Lender to make such a charge. A charge assessed by Lender in connection with Borrower's entering into this Security Instrument to pay the cost of an independent tax reporting service shall not be a charge for purposes of the preceding sentence. Borrower and Lender may agree in writing that interest shall be paid on the Funds. Unless an agreement is made or applicable law requires interest to be paid, Lender shall not be required to pay Borrower any interest or earnings on the Funds. Lender shall give to Borrower, without charge, an annual accounting of the Funds showing credits and debits to the Funds and the purpose for which each debit to the Funds was made. The Funds are pledged as additional security for the sums secured by this Security Instrument.

If the amount of the Funds held by Lender, together with the future monthly payments of Funds payable prior to the due dates of the escrow items, shall exceed the amount required to pay the escrow items when due, the excess shall be, at Borrower's option, either promptly repaid to Borrower or credited to Borrower on monthly payments of Funds. If the amount of the Funds held by Lender is not sufficient to pay the escrow items when due, Borrower shall pay to Lender any amount necessary to make up the deficiency in one or more payments as required by Lender.

Upon payment in full of all sums secured by this Security Instrument, Lender shall promptly refund to Borrower any Funds held by Lender. If under paragraph 19 the Property is sold or acquired by Lender, Lender shall apply, no later than immediately prior to the sale of the Property or its acquisition by Lender, any Funds held by Lender at the time of application as a credit against the sums secured by this Security Instrument.

3. APPLICATION OF PAYMENTS. Unless applicable law provides otherwise, all payments received by Lender under paragraphs 1 and 2 shall be applied: first, to late charges due under the Note; second, to prepayment charges due under the Note; third, to amounts payable under paragraph 2; fourth, to interest due; and last, to principal due.

4. CHARGES; LIENS. Borrower shall pay all taxes, assessments, charges, fines and impositions attributable to the Property which may attain priority over this Security Instrument, and leasehold payments or ground rents, if any. Borrower shall pay these obligations in the manner provided in paragraph 2, or if not paid in that manner, Borrower shall pay them on time directly to the person owed payment. Borrower shall promptly furnish to the Lender all notices of amounts to be paid under this paragraph. If Borrower makes these payments directly, Borrower shall promptly furnish to Lender receipts evidencing the payments.

Borrower shall promptly discharge any lien which has priority over this Security Instrument unless Borrower: (a) agrees in writing to the payment of the obligation secured by the lien in a manner acceptable to Lender; (b) contests in good faith the lien by, or defends against enforcement of the lien in, legal proceedings which in the Lender's opinion operate to prevent the enforcement of the lien or forfeiture of any part of the Property; or (c) secures from the holder of the lien an agreement satisfactory to Lender subordinating the lien to this Security Instrument. If Lender determines that any part of the Property is subject to a lien which may attain priority over this Security Instrument, Lender may give Borrower a notice identifying the lien. Borrower shall satisfy the lien or take one or more of the actions set forth above within 10 days of the giving of notice.

5. HAZARD INSURANCE. Borrower shall keep the improvements now existing or hereafter erected on the Property insured against loss by fire, hazards included within the term "extended coverage" and any other hazards for which Lender requires insurance. This insurance shall be maintained in the amounts and for the periods that Lender requires. The insurance carrier providing the insurance shall be chosen by Borrower subject to Lender's approval which shall not be unreasonably withheld.

All insurance policies and renewals shall be acceptable to the Lender and shall include a standard mortgage clause. Lender shall have the right to hold the policies and renewals. If Lender requires, Borrower shall promptly give to Lender all receipts of paid premiums and renewal notices. In the event of loss, Borrower shall give prompt notice to the insurance carrier and Lender. Lender may make proof of loss if not made promptly by Borrower.

Unless Lender and Borrower otherwise agree in writing, insurance proceeds shall be applied to restoration or repair of the Property damaged, if the restoration or repair is economically feasible and Lender's security is not lessened. If the restoration or repair is not economically feasible or Lender's security would be lessened, the insurance proceeds shall be applied to the sums secured by this Security Instrument, whether or not then due, with any excess paid to Borrower. If Borrower abandons the Property, or does not answer within 30 days a notice from Lender that the insurance carrier has offered to settle a claim, then Lender may collect the insurance proceeds. Lender may use the proceeds to repair or restore the Property or to pay sums secured by this Security Instrument, whether or not then due. The 30-day period will begin when the notice is given.

Unless Lender and Borrower otherwise agree in writing, any application of proceeds to principal shall not extend or postpone the due date of the monthly payments referred to in paragraph 1 and 2 or change the amount of the payments. If under paragraph 19 the Property is acquired by Lender, Borrower's right to any insurance policies and proceeds resulting from damage to the Property prior to the acquisition shall pass to Lender to the extent of the sums secured by this Security Instrument immediately prior to the acquisition.

6. PRESERVATION AND MAINTENANCE OF PROPERTY; LEASEHOLDS. Borrower shall not destroy, damage or substantially change the Property, allow the Property to deteriorate or commit waste. If this Security Instrument is on a leasehold, Borrower shall comply with the provisions of the lease, and if Borrower acquires fee title to the Property, the leasehold and fee title shall not merge unless the Lender agrees to the merger in writing.

7. PROTECTION OF LENDER'S RIGHTS IND THE PROPERTY; MORTGAGE INSURANCE. If Borrower fails to perform the covenants and agreements contained in this Security Instrument, or there is a legal proceeding that may significantly affect the Lender's right in the Property (such as a proceeding in bankruptcy, probate, for condemnation or to enforce laws or regulations), then Lender may do and pay for whatever is necessary to protect the value of the Property and Lender's rights in the Property. Lender's actions may include paying any sums secured by a lien which has priority over this Security Instrument, appearing in court, paying reasonable attorneys' fees and entering on the Property to make repairs. Although Lender may take action under paragraph 7, Lender does not have to do so.

Any amounts disbursed by Lender under paragraph 7 shall become additional debt of Borrower secured by this Security Instrument. Unless Borrower and Lender agree to other terms of payment, these amounts shall bear interest from date of disbursement at the Note rate and shall be payable, upon notice from Lender to Borrower requesting payment.

If Lender required mortgage insurance as a condition of making the loan secured by the Security Instrument, Borrower shall pay the premiums required to maintain the insurance in effect until such time as the requirement for the insurance terminates in accordance with Borrower's and Lender's written agreement or applicable law.

8. INSPECTION. Lender or its agent may make reasonable entries upon and inspections of the Property. Lender shall give Borrower notice at the time of or prior to an inspection specifying reasonable cause for the inspection.

9. CONDEMNATION. The proceeds of any award or claim for damages, direct or consequential, in connection with any condemnation or other taking of any part of the Property, or for conveyance in lieu of condemnation, are hereby assigned and shall be paid to Lender.

In the event of a total taking of the Property, the proceeds shall be applied to the sums secured by this Security Instrument, whether or not then due, with any excess paid to Borrower. In the event of a partial taking of the Property, unless Borrower and Lender otherwise agree in writing, the sums secured by this Security Instrument shall be reduced by the amount of the proceeds multiplied by the following fraction: (a) the total amount of sums secured immediately before the taking, divided by (b) the fair market value of the Property immediately before the taking. Any balance shall be paid to Borrower.

If the Property is abandoned by Borrower, or if, after notice by Lender to Borrower that the condemnor offers to make an award or

(continued)

Figure 11.4 continued

settle a claim for damages, Borrower fails to respond to Lender within 30 days after the date the notice is given, Lender is authorized to collect and apply the proceeds, at its option, either to restoration or repair of the Property or to the sums secured by this Security Instrument, whether or not then due.

Unless Lender and Borrower otherwise agree in writing, any application of proceeds to principal shall not extend or postpone the due date of the monthly payments referred to in paragraph 1 and 2 or change the amount of such payments.

10. BORROWER NOT RELEASED; FOREBEARANCE BY LENDER NOT A WAIVER. Extension of the time for payment or modification of amortization of the sums secured by this Security Instrument granted by Lender to any successor in interest of Borrower shall not operate to release the liability of the original Borrower or Borrower's successors in interest. Lender shall not be required to commence proceedings against any successor in interest or refuse to extend time for payment or otherwise modify amortization of the sums secured by this Security Instrument by reason of any demand made by the original Borrower or Borrower's successors in interest. Any forbearance by Lender in exercising any right or remedy shall not be a waiver of or preclude the exercise of any right or remedy.

11. SUCCESSORS AND ASSIGNS BOUND; JOINT AND SEVERAL LIABILITY; CO-SIGNERS. The covenants and agreements of this Security Instrument shall bind and benefit the successors and assigns of Lender and Borrower, subject to the provisions of paragraph 17. Borrower's covenants and agreements shall be joint and several. Any Borrower who co-signs this Security Instrument but does not execute the Note: (a) is co-signing this Security Instrument only to mortgage, grant, and convey that Borrower's interest in the Property under the terms of this Security Instrument; (b) is not personally obligated to pay the sums secured by this Security Instrument; and (c) agrees that Lender and any other Borrower may agree to extend, modify, forbear or make any accommodations with regard to terms of this Security Instrument or the Note without that Borrower's consent.

12. LOAN CHARGES. If the loan secured by this Security Instrument is subject to a law which sets maximum loan charges, and that law is finally interpreted so that the interest or other loan charges collected or to be collected in connection with the loan exceed the permitted limits, then; (a) any such loan charges shall be reduced by the amount necessary to reduce the charge to the permitted limit; and (b) any sums already collected from Borrower which exceeded permitted limits will be refunded to Borrower. Lender may choose to make this refund by reducing the principal owed under the Note or by making a direct payment to Borrower. If a refund reduces principal, the reduction will be treated as a partial prepayment without any prepayment charge under the Note.

13. LEGISLATION AFFECTING LENDER'S RIGHTS. If enactment or expiration of applicable law has the effect of rendering any provision of the Note or this Security Instrument unenforceable according to its terms, Lender, at its option, may require immediate payment in full of all sums secured by this Security Instrument and may invoke any remedies permitted by paragraph 19. If Lender exercises this option, Lender shall take the steps specified in the second paragraph of paragraph 17.

14. NOTICES. Any notice to Borrower provided for in this Security Instrument shall be given by delivering it or by mailing it by first class mail unless applicable law requires use of another method. The notice shall be directed to the Property Address or any other address Borrower designates by notice to Lender. Any notice to Lender shall be given by first class mail to Lender's address stated herein or any other address Lender designates by notice to Borrower. Any notice provided for in this Security Instrument shall be deemed to have been given to Borrower or Lender when given as provided in this paragraph.

15. GOVERNING LAW; SEVERABILITY. This Security Instrument shall be governed by federal law and the law of the jurisdiction in which the Property is located. In the event that any provision or clause of this Security Instrument or the Note conflicts with applicable law, such conflict shall not affect other provisions of this Security Instrument or the Note which can be given effect without the conflicting provision. To this end the provisions of this Security Instrument and the Note are declared to be severable.

16. BORROWER'S COPY. Borrower shall be given one conformed copy of the Note and of this Security Instrument.

17. TRANSFER OF THE PROPERTY OR A BENEFICIAL INTEREST IN BORROWER. If all or any part of the Property or any interest in it is sold or transferred (or if a beneficial interest in Borrower is sold or transferred and Borrower is not a natural person) without Lender's prior written consent, Lender may, at its option, require immediate payment in full of all sums secured by this Security Instrument. However, this option shall not be exercised by Lender if exercise is prohibited by federal law as of the date of this Security Instrument.

If Lender exercises this option, Lender shall give Borrower notice of acceleration. The notice shall provide a period of not less than 30 days from the date the notice is delivered or mailed within which the Borrower must pay all sums secured by this Security Instrument. If Borrower fails to pay these sums prior to the expiration of this period, Lender may invoke any remedies permitted by this Security Instrument without further notice or demand on Borrower.

18. BORROWER'S RIGHT TO REINSTATE. If Borrower meets certain conditions, Borrower shall have the right to have enforcement of this Security Instrument discontinued at any time prior to the earlier of: (a) 5 days (or such other period as applicable law may specify for reinstatement) before sale of the Property pursuant to any power of sale contained in this Security Instrument; or (b) entry of a judgment enforcing this Security Instrument. Those conditions are that Borrower: (a) pays Lender all sums which then would be due under this Security Instrument and the Note had no acceleration occurred; (b) cures any default of any other covenant or agreements; (c) pays all expenses incurred in enforcing this Security Instrument, including, but not limited to, reasonable attorneys' fees; and (d) takes such action as Lender may reasonably require to assure that the lien of this Security Instrument, Lender's rights in the Property and Borrower's obligation to pay sums secured by this Security Instrument shall continue unchanged. Upon reinstatement by Borrower, this Security Instrument and the obligations secured hereby shall remain fully effective as if no acceleration had occurred. However, this right to reinstate shall not apply in the case of acceleration under paragraph 13 or 17.

NON-UNIFORM COVENANTS. Borrower and Lender further covenant and agree as follows:

19. ACCELERATION; REMEDIES. Lender shall give notice to Borrower prior to acceleration following Borrower's breach of any covenant or agreement in this Security Instrument (but not prior to acceleration under paragraph 13 or 17 unless applicable law provides otherwise). The notice shall specify: (a) the default; (b) the action required to cure the default; (c) a date, not less than 30 days from the date the notice is given to Borrower, by which the default must be cured; and (d) that failure to cure the default on or before the date specified in the notice may result in acceleration of the sums secured by this Security Instrument and sale of the Property. The notice shall further inform Borrower of the right to reinstate after acceleration and the right to bring a court action to assert the non-existence of a default or any other defense of Borrower to acceleration and sale. If the default is not cured on or before the date specified in the notice, Lender at its option may require immediate payment in full of all sums secured by this Security Instrument without further demand and may invoke the power of sale and any other remedies permitted by applicable law. Lender shall be entitled to collect all expenses incurred in pursuing the remedies provided in this paragraph 19, including, but not limited to, reasonable attorneys' fees and costs of title evidence.

If the power of sale is invoked, Trustee shall record a notice of default in each county in which any part of the Property is located and shall mail copies of such notice in the manner prescribed by applicable law to Borrower and to the other persons prescribed by applicable law. After the time required by applicable law, Trustee shall give public notice of sale to the persons and in the manner prescribed by applicable law. Trustee, without demand on Borrower, shall sell the Property at public auction to the highest bidder at the time and place and under the terms designated in the notice of sale in one or more parcels and in any order Trustee determines. Trustee may postpone sale of all or any parcel of the Property by public announcement at the time and place of any previously scheduled sale. Lender or its designee may purchase the Property at any sale.

Figure 11.4 continued

Upon receipt of payment of the price bid, Trustee shall deliver to the purchaser Trustee's deed conveying the Property. The recitals in the Trustee's deed shall be prima facie evidence of the truth of the statements made therein. Trustee shall apply the proceeds of the sale in the following order: (a) to all expenses of the sale, including, but not limited to, Trustee's fees as permitted by applicable law and reasonable attorneys' fees; (b) to all sums secured by this Security Instrument; and (c) any excess to the person or persons legally entitled to it.

20. LENDER IN POSSESSION. Upon acceleration under paragraph 19 or abandonment of the Property, Lender (in person, by agent or by judicially appointed receiver) shall be entitled to enter upon, take possession of and manage the Property and to collect the rents of the Property including those past due. Any rents collected by Lender or the receiver shall be applied first to payment of the costs of management of the Property and collection of rents, including, but not limited to, receiver's fees, premiums on receiver's bonds and reasonable attorneys' fees, and then to the sums secured by this Security Instrument.

21. RECONVEYANCE. Upon payment of all sums secured by this Security Instrument, Lender shall request Trustee to reconvey the Property and shall surrender this Security Instrument and all notes evidencing debt secured by this Security Instrument to Trustee. Trustee shall reconvey the Property without warranty and without charge to the person or persons legally entitled to it. Such person or persons shall pay any recordation costs.

22. SUBSTITUTE TRUSTEE. Lender, at its option, may from time to time remove Trustee and appoint a successor trustee to any Trustee appointed hereunder by an instrument recorded in the county in which this Security Instrument is recorded. Without conveyance of the Property, successor trustee shall succeed to all the title, power and duties conferred upon Trustee herein and by applicable law.

23. REQUEST FOR NOTICES. Borrower requests that copies of the notices of default and sale be sent to Borrower's address which is the Property Address. Borrower further requests that copies of the notices of default and sale be sent to each person who is a party hereto at the address of such person set forth herein.

24. RIDERS TO THIS SECURITY INSTRUMENT. If one or more riders are executed by Borrower and recorded together with this Security Instrument, the covenants and agreements of each such rider shall be incorporated into and shall amend and supplement the covenants and agreements of this Security Instrument as if the rider(s) were a part of this Security Instrument.

[Check applicable box(es)]

☐ Adjustable Rate Rider   ☐ Condominium Rider   ☐ 2-4 Family Rider
☐ Graduated Payment Rider   ☐ Planned Unit Development Rider
☐ Other(s) Specify

BY SIGNING BELOW, Borrower accepts and agrees to the terms and covenants contained in this Security Instrument and in any rider(s) executed by Borrower and recorded with it.

_____ SEAL   _____ SEAL
Borrower   Borrower

_____ SEAL   _____ SEAL
Borrower   Borrower

[Space Below This Line For Acknowledgment]

STATE OF

COUNTY OF } ss:

I,_____, a Notary Public in and for said county and state, do hereby certify that

_____, personally appeared before me and is (are) known to me to be the person(s) who, being informed of the contents of the foregoing instrument, have executed same, and acknowledged said instrument to be _____ (his, her, their) free and voluntary act and deed and that _____ (he, she, they) executed said instrument for the purposes and uses therein set forth.

Witness my hand and official seal this _____ day of _____, _____.

My Commission Expires:

_____ SEAL
Notary Public

This instrument was prepared by:

Other Mortgage Clauses and Conditions

The Subordination Clause

Interest of holder
is secondary

The subordination clause states that the rights of the mortgage holder shall be secondary to subsequent encumbrances. This agreement provides that the mortgage lien will be *second in priority* to any specific existing or future liens. Since the risk involved to the lender is greater, interest rates on such mortgages are usually higher. For example, a purchaser of an $80,000 parcel of land puts down $50,000 and requests the seller to take a first mortgage of $30,000 with a subordination clause. The buyer needs a $250,000 mortgage to erect an office building. The lender of the $250,000 insists on being first in priority, even though this mortgage is technically a second mortgage. Thus, the subordination clause in the first mortgage clears the path for the buyer to obtain the $250,000 mortgage. The building loan becomes first in line and the lien on the land second.

The Prepayment Penalty Clause

The prepayment penalty clause permits the mortgagee to charge a penalty to the borrower if the loan is paid off prior to its maturity. The prepayment penalty protects the mortgagee in the event interest rates decrease; borrowers will not refinance at a lower rate if they must pay a penalty to do so. It also is a form of reimbursement to the lenders for loss of time for interest that would have been earned while they find and approve new borrowers. While FHA and VA loans never carry prepayment penalties, other mortgages may. In times of plentiful money for mortgage loans, the competition dictates that prepayment penalties not be used.

The Assumption Clause

Buyer assumes
existing mortgage

If a loan is assumed by new owners, the assumption clause in the deed says that the buyers are obligating themselves to pay off the loan. This transfers the responsibility onto the buyers. In case of default, the lender will expect the new owners to fulfill their promise. If they fail to do so, the original owners are still primarily liable since their names are on the promissory note. However, if the sellers obtain a release of liability from the lender, the sellers' obligation ends when the title is transferred. If the clause in the deed states that the buyers are purchasing the property "subject to the existing loan," the buyers acknowledge the existing loan, promise to pay, but are only secondarily liable. Assumption clauses are usually found only in VA and FHA loans.

Types of Mortgages

Open-End Mortgages

An **open-end mortgage** allows the mortgagor to extend the amount of the loan. The loan company has the option of advancing additional money to the borrower at a later date. The borrower may not have taken the full amount that could have been requested at the time the mortgage was initiated, or the loan may have been paid down enough for the mortgagor to borrow more. However, the terms of the mortgage can be changed by the lender if the borrower requests more money. For example, 10 years ago a borrower obtained a $30,000 open-end mortgage on a new home. Inflation has since added $10,000 to the original value of the home; furthermore, the mortgage is now reduced to $26,000. The lending institution agrees to loan an additional $4,000 to the borrower for remodeling. The loan is back to $30,000, the interest rate may remain the same, and the time period of the loan extended back to the original term.

Right to borrow additional money

One of the most common uses of the open-end mortgage is the construction loan. Please refer to the section on construction loans for more details. Another variation of the open-end mortgage is referred to as a home equity line of credit (HELOC). The HELOC is discussed in more detail following the section "Home Equity Loans."

Package Mortgages

The package mortgage is often used in the financing of new homes, since it expressly includes built-in appliances and any such equipment that may be offered for sale with a new home. This may include carpets, drapes, and furniture. The loan includes both real and personal property, so the purchaser is able to finance the equipment over a longer period of time and at a more favorable interest rate than if they were separately financed. This type of loan can also be used to buy a farm and tractor.

Blanket Mortgages

A single mortgage that covers more than one piece of property is referred to as a **blanket mortgage**. Developers of subdivisions often use this type of mortgage and then obtain partial releases as they sell off individual lots. A partial release clause is included in the mortgage so that specific lots can be released as they are purchased. The lender requires a specified amount to be paid on the mortgage before allowing the release of the lots.

Coverage of several properties

A real estate agent may be approached by an individual who desires to purchase a new home but currently owns another home. If the borrower's equity is sufficient, a blanket mortgage might be placed on the two properties. When either home is sold later, it would be released from the loan.

Purchase Money Mortgages

In a purchase money mortgage the seller takes back a note as all or part of the purchase price in a transaction. In some cases the buyer may not have or be able to obtain or borrow sufficient funds to purchase the property. By means of a purchase money mortgage, the transaction is consummated. The seller's agreeing

Seller holds mortgage

to hold a note may have made the difference in making the sale. Purchase money mortgages may be first or second liens. If there is an existing first lien, the purchase money mortgage the seller holds would take second lien priority. However, prompt recording of any lien is necessary to establish priority, as the first party to record a lien has priority over subsequent liens. A purchase money mortgage can be a wise investment for sellers if they do not need all their cash immediately. The interest may be greater than the interest the money would earn in a bank.

Second Mortgages (Junior Mortgages)

Second in priority

A second mortgage pledges the owner's equity in the real estate with the property as collateral. It is second in priority to the first mortgage in case of default and always subordinate (lower in priority) to any existing mortgage. Since it represents a greater risk to the lender, a higher rate of interest is required. Sometimes a seller of real estate will carry back a second mortgage to help finance the new owner. If a buyer has limited cash to invest in a home, the buyer may assume the balance of the existing mortgage, make a down payment, and obtain a second mortgage for the money needed to make up the remainder of the purchase price. The actual interest rate is in reality a combination of the old lower rate and the new second mortgage rate. The combined rate is generally lower than the current market rate on the total amount borrowed. Generally the combined loan-to-value ratio of both first and second mortgages should be less than 80 percent.

Term Mortgages

Not commonly used, term mortgages are for specified periods of time and demand full payment at the end of those periods. As stated under the mortgage payment methods earlier in this chapter, they are not amortized and are issued for only short periods of time, usually three to five years. Builders will use term mortgages since there are no monthly payments and their money is not tied up. The borrower's credit must be extremely good to obtain this type of loan.

Wraparound Mortgages

Two mortgages, only one payment

The wraparound mortgage is two or more mortgages consolidated into one payment. This mortgage may allow the buyers to purchase with a small down payment and the added benefit of a low-interest-rate first mortgage. The sellers receive all of their cash at the time of closing. The lender wraps new money around an existing assumable loan. If in the future the borrowers have the cash available, they could pay off the new money and resort to the original, low-interest mortgage. If the mortgage contains a due-on-sale clause, it cannot be wrapped.

Wrap mortgages are used when interest rates are high, allowing the buyer to take advantage of the lower rate existing mortgage without having to come up with a large down payment as in the case of a loan assumption. The following example will clarify the use of the wrap mortgage.

Assume a sale price of	$80,000	
FHA first mortgage of	50,000	6%
Seller's equity	$30,000	

The buyers do not have $30,000 to invest; their savings are only $16,000. The sellers refuse to carry back a second mortgage because they need all their equity to purchase another home. The dilemma is solved by the lender who makes wrap loans. The buyer will obtain an 80 percent loan of $64,000:

$50,000 at 6% (existing first mortgage)
14,000 at 8.5% (current rate)
$64,000 wrap mortgage

The $64,000 will be paid back over the same period as remains on the first mortgage. Assume the existing first mortgage is 5 years old, then the amortization of the wrap mortgage will be 25 years.

The buyers are pleased because they receive a less-than-market-rate loan that has only 25 years remaining instead of 30 years for a new loan; if in the future they have $14,000, they can pay off the new money and resort to the underlying first mortgage of $50,000 at 6 percent.

In today's market, a wraparound mortgage would only be used when the lender warehouses the loan and does not sell it to the secondary market.

Alternate Mortgage Plans

Most of the alternate financing available is an outgrowth of the tight money market and high interest rates of the 1980s. With the rapid rise of interest, the housing market went into a slump. Innovative and creative financing techniques were developed by lenders and real estate agents to keep homes affordable. This smorgasbord of mortgages meets a variety of needs.

Adjustable Rate Mortgages (ARMs)

In the late 1970s the variable rate mortgage became the first vehicle that allowed for interest rates to be moved up or down on home mortgages. This allowed the yield to the lender to be kept close to the market interest rates being paid to depositors. This loan was followed by the renegotiable rate mortgage in 1980, which permitted adjustments every one, three, and five years to correlate with market conditions. The Federal Home Loan Bank Board (FHLBB) sanctioned the **adjustable rate mortgage (ARM)** in 1981, and in 1988 the board set guidelines that must be conformed to in all federal transactions.

Like the variable rate mortgage, the adjustable rate offers protection to the mortgagee because it allows the mortgagee to vary the interest rate in the future.

Variable rates

Index

The interest rate may be adjusted up or down depending on the current cost of funds (called an index), usually one-year U.S. Treasury securities (referred to as T-bills). Thus, with an adjustable rate mortgage, the yield to the lender may be kept close to market interest rates. The lender adds a profit margin to the index, which varies from 2 percent to 3 percent. This margin compensates the lender for any risk involved in making the loan and allows for a reasonable profit. If the rate is increased, the monthly payments do not necessarily increase; however, negative amortization is possible. Another way to avoid increased payments is to extend the life of the loan up to a maximum of one-third of the original term. The time will not be extended, however, to a point that would reduce the payments.

Margin

Adjustment period

The adjustment period is the time during which the interest rate can be changed. Usually this is one year, although three or five years also are used. The longer time span is an advantage to the borrower if market rates are increasing and, conversely, if rates are declining, the borrower would prefer the shorter time span.

Cap rate

The amount that the interest rate may change is limited by rate caps. Federal law mandates that the lenders reveal the interest cap rate. The periodic cap rate is the amount that the rate may increase at any given time. The aggregate cap rate is the upper limit to which the rate can be raised over the full term of the loan.

Reverse Annuity Mortgages (RAMs)

Owner collects payment from lender

In the reverse annuity mortgage (RAM), homeowners 62 years or older can convert the equity they have acquired in their homes into cash. Homeowners can receive the money in a lump sum, in fixed monthly payments, as a line of credit, or in various combinations. This means that the loan increases—an exact *reversal* of the normal procedure of reducing the debt. If the owners sell the home, their equity will naturally be less. Spendable income may be more important than accumulated wealth to retirees, and the RAM can provide an income stream or lump-sum payment. The mortgage does not have to be repaid until the mortgagor moves or dies.

The RAM is available to homeowners through their local bank. HUD federally insured RAM loans have grown in recent years, from 6,600 loans in 2000 to 107,000 in 2007.

The credit crisis of 2008 resulted in all but the FHA version of Reverse Mortgage (Home Equity Conversion Mortgage of HECM) to disappear. In addition, and possibly an exciting improvement to this program for real estate agents, is that the housing and Economic Recovery Act of 2008, allowed this loan to be used for home purchase. By allowing home buyers 62 or older to purchase a home that has no monthly payments, it is expected the volume of the adverse mortgage market to increase dramatically in the coming years.

FHA will insure loans that take any of the three basic payment formulas, plus some add-on features.

1. A "tenure" loan that guarantees the homeowner will receive an agreed-upon amount for as long as the owner occupies the home as the principal residence.

2. Term loans with a definite repayment plan, such as 10 years.

3. "Line of credit" loans, which allow borrowers to take money in increments and frequency as they so choose with a fixed cap on the maximum amount.

Additionally, FHA allows lump-sum withdrawals on any of the plans. FHA will also insure fixed-rate, adjustable rate reverse mortgages, and the borrower can receive lower rates on loans in exchange for the lender receiving a percentage of future appreciation on the home, thus sharing in the equity. For example, a 75-year-old person who owns a debt-free home valued at $100,000 can qualify for an $810 monthly payment on a 5-year, fixed-term reverse mortgage at 10 percent with no appreciation sharing. If the same person extended the term to 10 years, the monthly payments would be $510. Since some of the elderly population are "house rich and cash poor," expect to hear more about reverse mortgages for this expanding group of people.

Shared Appreciation Mortgages (SAMs)

With the shared appreciation mortgage (SAM), the borrower agrees to share future benefits with the lender in exchange for a fixed, below-market interest rate. The future appreciation percentage is known as contingent interest, since the money due the lender is dependent upon the property's appreciation in value. The prearranged percentage can reach a maximum of 40 percent of the net appreciated value of the mortgaged property, payable when any one of the following occurs.

Lender shares profit

1. The property is sold.
2. The loan is paid off.
3. Ten years have passed.

If the property is not sold within the 10-year period, most SAMs require that the buyer pay the lending institution a percentage of the appreciation due. The SAM program is useful in high-growth areas where home values are likely to escalate in the future. The lender can qualify more buyers because of the lower payments and at the same time receive a potentially higher rate of return than on a fixed-rate mortgage. The lender guarantees the borrower that refinancing is available. This is not currently available to residential property buyers but may be available in some form for commercial properties.

Temporary Buydowns

The temporary buydown is a mortgage differential allowance program that permits the seller of the property to place a percentage of the sale proceeds at closing with the lender in an escrow account. This money is used to reduce the effective interest costs and monthly payments for the first two or three years of the loan. The buyer makes the offer-to-purchase contingent on the seller establishing a mortgage differential account for the purchaser, in the purchaser's name, at the time of closing. The account will have sufficient funds to effectively reduce the purchaser's monthly payment to reflect a lower interest rate for the first few

Mortgage bought down for first few years

years of the purchaser's loan. The buyer will still sign the note and mortgage at the current interest rate. In essence, the seller is prepaying interest for the buyer. The differential is established in a savings account in the purchaser's name with the lender who makes the loan.

3-2-1 Buydowns

The 3-2-1 buydown program offers the buyer 3 percent off the first year's rate, 2 percent off the second year's rate, and 1 percent off the third year's rate. These buydowns may be used with almost any type of mortgage, whether VA, FHA, or conventional. Borrowers qualify at the first-year rate if they put down 10 percent or carry a 90 percent loan-to-value (LTV) mortgage. The borrower needs to qualify at the end rate on all conventional buydowns if the LTV is greater than 90 percent. The buydown program can also be used in six-month or one-year increments. Buydowns are an appealing incentive but are meeting with disapproval from the secondary market buyers because of the high foreclosure rate.

Construction Loans

Construction loan

Construction loans are used as *short-term, interim financing* for the building of an improvement on land. The borrower must own the lot before construction begins. Plans and specifications are submitted to the lender, who has an appraisal made of the proposed structure. If approval is given for the plans, money will be advanced in installments (referred to as *draws*) as construction progresses. Before issuing any draws, the general contractor must give the lender *lien waivers* signed by the subcontractors; these state that the subcontractors have been paid and will not place liens on the property.

This type of mortgage is advantageous to the borrower because interest is paid only on the amount advanced. The lender dispenses principal only upon inspection and when the security has been improved. As a high-risk loan, a construction loan generally does not extend beyond three years, and interest is higher than conventional real estate loans.

Upon completion of construction a *"take-out"* or *permanent loan* is placed on the property. If the lender who held the construction loan does not commit to a permanent loan, the owner will need financing from another source.

Home Equity Loans

For homeowners who need extra cash but do not wish to refinance, the home equity loan may be their answer. The lender either extends a line of credit or issues a fixed loan amount. The amount available is determined by the appraised value of the real estate less the amount of the first mortgage and any other liens against the property. This amount usually will not exceed 80 percent of the value, less any outstanding loans. If a line of credit is made available, the homeowner pays interest on only the amount borrowed.

Increasingly popular in the past few years, home equity loans are in reality second mortgages without the need to refinance. As home values have risen, the owner's equity has increased, resulting in funds available to tap. Tax laws, which currently allow interest deductions only on real estate loans and not on other types of borrowing, have further enhanced the use of equity loans. Equity loans are often used to consolidate debts, finance college educations, make home improvements, or generate cash that can be used to make other real estate investments. However, if the home equity loan is used for payments other than home improvements, such as for consumer loans, the interest is not deductible unless the proceeds are used for tuition, other educational costs, or medical expenses.

Another variation of the home equity loan that gained popularity in recent years is the home equity line of credit (HELOC). The HELOC is still a home equity loan and constitutes a second mortgage on the borrower's personal residence. The difference is the HELOC is an approved line of credit (similar to a charge card) using the home equity as security. The homeowner has the option to access funds as needed and thereby only pay interest while the funds are outstanding. The traditional home equity loan pays out the entire loan amount at settlement, which causes the borrower to pay interest on the full loan amount from the first day the loan is issued. HELOCs are useful for individuals who wish to have access to their equity in the future but may not have an immediate need today. The interest on these HELOC loans is generally variable based on prime. The rate is usually subject to change monthly.

Instruments Relative to Financing

An **estoppel certificate** is an instrument executed by the mortgagor stating the validity of the full mortgage debt. In other words, it declares the exact balance of the debt to the new owner of the mortgage. It is sometimes called a *certificate of no defense* or a *declaration of no set off*. When a mortgage is assigned by the mortgagee to the new owner of the mortgage, the mortgagee must issue an assignment. The person to whom the mortgage is assigned (the assignee) acquires title and interest in the mortgage and note.

Declaring full balance of note

A *satisfaction piece* or a mortgage release is an instrument for recording and acknowledging full payment of an indebtedness that is secured by a mortgage. It means "satisfied in full." It is recorded to show the debt has been paid.

A *pledge* is money kept on deposit with the lending agency. It is held as security for a debt until the extra amount loaned to the purchaser is paid off. The pledge is an interest-bearing account but is technically a "frozen" asset that cannot be removed until the amount specified on the loan is paid. For an example of a pledge, consider a young couple wishing to purchase a home. They have the required down payment but are short in qualifying for the loan. A second party could put up the necessary amount in a pledge account with the lender. A pledge may also be used to avoid monthly payments to the lender for taxes and

Pledge held as security

homeowner insurance. The owner will pay these from personal funds, or the lender will seize the account.

An **escrow agreement** is used by the parties to a contract to carry out the terms of the agreement. The parties involved appoint a third party to act as *escrow agent*. This agent should be a disinterested party who will not benefit in any way.

For example, you have just purchased a new home but at the time of closing the carpet has not been installed. The lending institution will hold a sufficient sum back from the builder until the carpet is in place, at which time the escrow fund will be released to the builder. Another example is the loan that requires monthly payments that include not only the principal and interest payment, but one-twelfth of the annual taxes and insurance. This tax and insurance payment accumulates in an escrow account so that the lender can pay the taxes and insurance premium when they are due.

Foreclosure on a Mortgage

Nonpayment of debt

If the mortgagor fails to abide by any of the terms of the mortgage, the lending institution may bring **foreclosure** action. Usually foreclosures are the result of delinquent payments. Lenders may attempt to work out another option for payments by the debtor since they prefer not to foreclose. If the debtor sees that he cannot fulfill the commitment to meet the financial obligation, he will attempt to sell the property. Failure of the owner to obtain a sale will result in the need for the lender to foreclose. At this point the lender may pursue two courses of action: foreclosure by judicial or nonjudicial proceedings.

The Short-Sale

By late 2007 the meltdown in the mortgage market became extreme. With a rash of foreclosures due in part to subprime mortgages, many people were walking away from their debt. The rise in real estate values had induced consumer spending as homeowners refinanced mortgages and took out home equity loans. When market values drop, and if the home was bought close to peak values, the owners will likely lose if they need to sell. Foreclosures tend to drive down the market value of other homes in the neighborhood.

The **short-sale** occurs when the property owner (borrower) does not have sufficient equity to cover the mortgage and release the lien from the property. The owner must request that the lender accept a lesser amount than owed and release the lien against the property. Upon listing the property the licensee should have the seller start the process with the lender so a sale and closing are not delayed. A short-sale transaction and the adverse impact it can have on a sale requires that the seller sign the "short-sale disclosure statement." If there are two liens on the property, the first lender may accept the short-sale request, but if the second lender refuses, the sale is terminated due to the seller's inability to deliver to the buyer free and marketable title.

When accepting a short-sale many lenders will stipulate the amount of commission the licensee can charge, regardless of what the seller has agreed to in the listing contract. The lender agrees to the short-sale as it precludes going through foreclosure. The last thing a bank wants is to be a landlord, so they will modify original loan terms if a borrower runs into payment problems.

Judicial Foreclosure

A judicial foreclosure is a court action to cut out the right of redemption the debtor has in the property. In some states, after a decree of foreclosure has been entered, the mortgagor may, under certain conditions, obtain a court order postponing the foreclosure sale. The courts give the mortgagor a statutory period within which to redeem the property. Failure of the mortgagor to do so would result in losing the property. This right is known as the *right of redemption* or *equitable redemption.* If the mortgagor has considerable equity in the property, the courts may order the property sold; however, the debtor may pay the delinquent debt up until the property goes up for sale. For reinstatement, the debtor would need to make up any overdue payments and continue making subsequent payments on time. Usually constructive notice is given by filing notice that the property is in litigation. Any prospective purchaser can conduct a title search and will learn there is a notice of *lis pendens,* meaning that a lawsuit is pending.

Right of redemption

Generally, a petition is filed with the court against the debtor and anyone holding a junior lien position, stating the property involved and the amount due. A junior lien holder that is included as a defendant may take the property by redeeming the senior lien holder, and the foreclosure would be stopped. The junior lien holder would want to be certain the property value was sufficient to warrant buying out the first lien holder.

Junior lien holder rights

The other course of action for the second lien holder would be to permit the foreclosure and file a *surplus money action.* If the proceeds from the sale are sufficient, both the first lien holder and the junior lien holder will receive payment.

The sheriff auctions foreclosed property either at the site of the property or at the courthouse in an attempt to obtain market price. The lender and any prospective buyers will attend the auction. If no bids are made above the indebtedness, the mortgagee will always bid for the property at the balance due on the mortgage, less penalties and legal fees. If a bid is made by a third party for a higher amount than the mortgagee's bid, the mortgagor will receive the amount above the existing costs. A foreclosure sale does not dismiss property tax liens that may be against the property. This is one reason lenders like to escrow for taxes if they are carrying a mortgage with a large loan-to-value ratio.

Sale by auction

Once the foreclosure by judicial sale takes place, the court confirms the price to ascertain that it was fair. If the price was extremely low, the court has the power to set the sale aside.

The successful bidder will receive a sheriff's deed, which will convey whatever title the debtor held, exclusive of the debt. This deed carries no warranties, but title insurance may be purchased by the buyer.

Nonjudicial Foreclosure

In a nonjudicial foreclosure the state permits a foreclosure by *power of sale* providing the mortgage carries this clause. If the debt instrument is a deed of trust, the trustee is normally provided with the power of sale. In that situation, once the lender/beneficiary gives proper statutory notice by recording a notice of default, the right to sell the property at public auction exists. This allows for a quick recovery of the property for the lender/beneficiary. Any interest the debtor has is terminated, the property is sold, and the lender is reimbursed from the proceeds of the sale.

Deed in lieu of foreclosure

In lieu of foreclosure, the debtor may deed the property over to the mortgagee. If the lender/beneficiary accepts the deed, it would bring with it any junior liens that may be attached, which is not the case when the property is sold at auction.

The foreclosure procedure on a mortgage was originally designed to allow farmers sufficient time to harvest crops before losing the right to redeem. These same lengthy foreclosure procedures are a disadvantage to the lender on a residential property. The delayed time period of foreclosure, set by state statute of usually six months to two years, permits the debtor to stay on the property. The mortgage may provide for the appointment of a receiver who is court appointed and would be responsible to collect rents and see that the property is maintained during this period. However, the reader should keep in mind that states using the deed of trust can foreclose more quickly.

Strict Foreclosure

Upon default of the debtor, strict foreclosure permits the lender to foreclose *without a judicial sale*. The lender files a lawsuit and the court gives notice to the debtor, stating a specific time period for the debtor to exercise the right of redemption. If the debtor is unable to make the past-due payments, the title passes to the mortgagee. Regardless of the equity the debtor may have in the property, at this point the debtor loses all rights to the property. Because it puts the mortgagor at a great disadvantage, a very small percentage of states use the strict foreclosure method on defaulted mortgages.

Real Estate Mortgage Theories

Title Theory

The **title theory** evolved from the days when the rights of the mortgagee were primary. If the borrower defaulted on the loan, the mortgagee could dispossess the borrower without notice, and all the equity the borrower built up was forfeited. Today the states that adopted the title theory of real estate finance have modified the law with the defeasance clause in the mortgage pledging the property to the mortgagee, and upon payment in full the property reverts to the mortgagor. It further gives the debtor the right of redemption and a reasonable time after default to redeem the property. Title theory states use the deed of trust as the security instrument.

The Lien Theory

The **lien theory**, used by most of the states, acknowledges that borrowers retain their legal rights in the property, with the beneficiary having equitable rights. This means that borrowers keep possession and title in their property, while the lender must follow the state's legal foreclosure procedures. Lien theory states use the mortgage as the security instrument.

Intermediate Theory

Some states have a modified plan of either the title or the lien theory, referred to as an *intermediate theory,* whereby the lender does not have to wait until foreclosure to obtain possession of the property. Title is not turned over, however, until the statutory redemption period has ended.

If mortgagees do not receive the full amount due upon the foreclosure sale, they have the right to enter a *deficiency judgment* against the mortgagor. For example, if the owner has a mortgage balance due of $12,000 and the property brings only $10,000, the mortgagee may request the courts to file a deficiency judgment for the $2,000 balance due. This is an unsecured lien against the debtor.

Deficiency judgment

Liens

Ownership of real property can be lessened by the interest of another party, and while we have covered the mortgage, there are other liens that can also affect the rights of ownership.

Placing liens on property

A **lien** represents the legal monetary claim held against property that provides the lien holder security for a debt or obligation. Liens are generally enforced by court order when legal action has been commenced by the creditor and the courts authorize sale of the property to fully or partially satisfy the debt.

Liens are established as either voluntary or involuntary. A **voluntary lien** is created by the property owner, much as a mortgage is contracted by the agreement of the parties. An **involuntary lien** is created by statute, such as a **tax lien**, and is referred to as a statutory lien. The debtor is known as the *lienee* and the person who holds the lien and receives payments is the *lienor.*

Liens may be *specific (in rem)* and attach to a particular property, or the lien may be general *(in personam)* and attach to *all* the property of the debtor.

Specific Liens

Specific liens affect only the specific property they are placed against. These liens can be used to force a sale and include the following.

Liens that can force a sale

1. The *mortgage* pledges the property as collateral for the loan.
2. *Property taxes* result in a lien against the property if they are not paid. The majority of states place property **tax liens** before all other liens, even pre-existing liens. If the taxes remain delinquent for the time specified by state law, the property may be sold at a tax sale or by tax foreclosure. Notice is published and an auction held with the successful bidder receiving a tax certificate. The debtor must pay the taxes and interest accrued or permanently lose the property. After the redemption period expires, the person holding the tax certificate will be issued a tax deed or treasurer's deed.

Improvement to property

3. *Special assessments* are liens placed against real property to pay for an improvement to the property, such as sidewalks, pavement, street lights, and public utilities. If the assessment is not paid, the governing body within whose jurisdiction the property is located will place a lien on the property. For example, a street is paved, and one property has an 85-foot frontage and the other property a frontage of 95 feet. The properties will be assessed in relation to the front feet and not the value of the respective properties. If, however, a sewer line is being extended into the neighborhood, each of the properties will be equally assessed since they will benefit equally.
4. *Mechanic's liens* are placed upon property without consent of the owner. In most states a supplier of labor and materials may levy a lien against a property for nonpayment of services and material. This includes general contractors, subcontractors, laborers, and materialmen. The lien offers security to those who supply labor or furnish material in the improvement of real property. It is created by state statute and must be filed within a specified time after the work has been completed. It can only be against that one property upon which the work was performed or to which material was delivered. The mechanic must prove that an express or implied contract existed, and in some states lawsuit action must be taken by the claimant against the homeowner within a specified time or the lien is discharged.

Writ of attachment

5. *An attachment* placed against personal property by a court order is referred to as a *writ of attachment*. This prevents the property owner from leaving the state with the merchandise. Once the order is issued by the court, the sheriff of the county will seize the property in satisfaction of the debt.

General Liens

General liens are broader in scope and are capable of affecting all the property of the lienee, real and personal. General liens include the following.

1. *Federal liens* give the government the authority to place a lien on all of a debtor's personal and real property for failure to pay income taxes. The statutory period for federal tax liens is 10 years. The law permits the government to issue a tax warrant, record it in the federal tax docket in the county records, and attach a federal tax lien. Sale of the property will be made if the debt is not satisfied.

   Affect all debtor's property

2. *Judgment liens* are legally determined by the courts as to the rights of the parties involved in the dispute. The party that wins is awarded a judgment stating the amount of the claim. When the judgment (decree) is recorded, it automatically becomes a general lien upon all the real and personal property of the debtor within that particular jurisdiction. The creditor must file the lien in other counties to cover the lien in those counties.

   If the lienee does not comply with the judgment order, the general lien holder can file action to force a public sale of the real estate to satisfy the judgment. However, specific liens have priority, so mortgages, taxes, and mechanic's liens will be paid first. If the lienee decides to sell the real estate, all the liens will need to be paid in order to give clear title. A judgment lien is a lien *in personam,* since it is against all the debtor's property.

   Lien in personam

3. The *federal estate tax* is a tax imposed upon the estate of the deceased, and it must be paid, or liens can be filed against the property. A federal estate tax is levied against the decedent's estate upon transfer of the property to the devisee. The estate must file an estate tax return nine months after the date of the decedent's death. If unpaid, federal law provides for a general lien to be placed upon the property.

   Estate of deceased is taxed

   A person, referred to as a donor, may "gift" a recipient, known as a donee, and the gift tax is the obligation of the donor. No income tax is paid on the gift since it is not considered income.

4. *State inheritance tax* provides for any inherited property to be taxed at the state level. Clear title cannot be issued until payment of the tax is made. A lien will be placed against the property until the tax is paid in full. This is a state government-imposed tax upon the heirs, not the estate. If property is held in joint tenancy, the survivor inherits the deceased spouse's half-interest and, in theory, becomes obligated for payment of the inheritance tax, if any.

   Tax liens must be paid

5. *Decedents' debts* become general liens against all the deceased's assets and must be paid, or a lien will be placed against the real property. In settling the estate, all debts must be paid out of the proceeds from the sale.

6. *Child support liens* usually consist merely of paperwork to clear. The person obligated to pay the support has a lien attached to any parcel of real estate bought. If the child support has been paid, the ex-spouse will sign a voluntary release without having to go to court. If the support has not been received, the party goes to court to see that the lien is not released, thus preventing the defaulted party from selling the real estate.

7. *Corporation franchise tax* is paid by corporations in accordance with state statute. The tax is based upon capital stock that has been issued or income derived from the business. If unpaid, the tax becomes a lien upon the property owned by the corporation.

A *vendor's* (seller's) *lien* arises from the sale of property financed by a land contract when the vendee (buyer) defaults on payment. The law permits the vendor to place a lien on the unpaid balance. The vendee will forfeit the property along with all the payments made up to the time of default. Many states have a redemption period that allows the vendee to pay any overdue payments in full plus interest due within a specified time limit.

A *vendee's lien* results if the vendor fails to deliver a deed after the vendee has fulfilled his obligation. As stated in the land contract, the vendee can place a lien on the property for all the payments made to the vendor and can include the cost of any improvements made to the property.

Municipal liens can be placed against property by municipalities that supply water to property owners who fail to pay for water or other utility services.

Surety bail bond liens are the result of a bail bond being used to secure the release of a person arrested for a crime. Until the trial is held, the bail bond is surety that the person will not leave the area. The bail bond can be paid in cash or by pledging real property as surety. A bail bond lien will be filed against the property. Upon the person's release, the lien is discharged by the court.

Moratorium   A moratorium is the legal right to delay meeting a money obligation. The lending institution must agree to permit the mortgagor a legal right to delay payment.

Lis pendens means suit pending; it is public notice that a lawsuit is filed against a specific property that may affect the right to ownership of land.

Summary of Important Points

The many terms and types of mortgages and mortgage clauses relevant to the financing of real estate are covered in this chapter.

1. New creative financing programs surfaced due to the rising cost of home financing and the shortage of funds to lend. Since population growth dictates that the market for housing will not diminish, the need for making housing affordable for this generation and generations to follow is imperative.

2. Among the many creative financing techniques developed in the search for funds is the adjustable rate mortgage. This mortgage allows the lender the option of raising or lowering the interest rate after one, three, or five years.

3. There have been many changes in the mortgage market. The savings and loan industry had been the mainstay of the one- to four-family home mortgage, and its continuance could be ensured only by using renegotiable mortgages. However, with the lowering of interest rates in the early 1990s, less need for innovative mortgage plans exists.

4. Today, the mortgage banker provides most of the fixed-rate mortgages. It is not unusual for borrowers to select 15- and 20-year term mortgages instead of the traditional 30-year in an effort to save interest.

5. Since competition among lenders of money is high, new marketing ideas and techniques will continue to be presented in an effort to meet the consumer's financing needs.

6. Liens are legal claims against the property of the debtor and are either voluntary or involuntary. The mortgagor voluntarily pledges the property as security for the debt, whereas an involuntary lien is created by statute as a tax lien.

7. Liens are either specific and attach to a particular property only, or they are general and attach to all the property of a debtor.

Discussion Points

1. A borrower is applying for a loan, and while she prefers to extend the payments for 30 years, her plans include repaying the loan sooner. What type of loan should she consider?

2. Explain the difference between an amortized loan and a straight payment loan.

3. Why is a mortgage necessary if the note is the promise to repay?

4. Why would a borrower choose an adjustable rate mortgage in preference to a fixed rate conventional mortgage?

5. Explain the steps in a mortgage foreclosure for your state.

6. Why would a lender prefer a deed of trust to a note and mortgage?

7. A property carries a mortgage of $30,000; taxes of $1,760 are delinquent for two years; and a second mortgage of $7,500 was filed four years ago. Place the debts in the order of their priority.

8. Explain the difference between the title theory and the lien theory. Which does your state use?

9. Explain what a buydown mortgage is.

10. Why do mortgage lenders require property taxes and insurance to be paid in advance along with the monthly principal and interest payments? Is this requested on all types of loans?

Review Questions

Answers to these questions are found in the Answer Key section at the back of the book.

1. When monthly payments made on a loan are amortized over a period of years:
   a. the debt is liquidated all at once
   b. the payments include both principal and interest
   c. there must be a balloon payment
   d. principal is paid first

2. Discount points are charged by lending institutions:
   a. to make the loan more favorable to the lender
   b. to help the mortgagor with his down payment
   c. because the law requires they be collected
   d. to meet FDIC requirements

3. Under the terms of the mortgage, the mortgagor:
   a. has all the rights of ownership
   b. can automatically assign the mortgage to another
   c. signs a note that pledges the property as security
   d. is the primary lender

4. If the mortgagor defaults on the note:
   a. the mortgagor is given a six-month grace period
   b. the mortgage becomes due and payable
   c. upon a foreclosure sale, all the equity paid belongs to the debtor
   d. an immediate foreclosure sale ensues

5. An open-end mortgage is favorable to the mortgagor because:
   a. the loan cannot be paid off ahead of time
   b. more than one piece of property can be under a single mortgage
   c. the mortgagor may have the option of extending the amount of the loan
   d. the mortgage does not carry a prepayment clause

6. An assignment of rents allows the mortgagee to take possession:
   a. when the mortgage is assigned to another
   b. when the mortgagor defaults in meeting his payments on rental property
   c. if the mortgagor takes a second loan on the property
   d. upon a writ of execution

7. A second mortgage taken on real property:
   a. has precedence over the first mortgage
   b. is usually subordinate to any previously issued mortgage on the property
   c. has priority if it was executed earlier than the first mortgage
   d. is equal to a performance bond

8. The advantage of a deed of trust for a mortgagee is that:
   a. the title is held in trust and the foreclosure procedure is quicker
   b. no second mortgage can be made on the property
   c. there is no advantage
   d. it allows all creditors to file claims

9. Who signs the note that goes along with the mortgage?
   a. mortgagor
   b. mortgagee
   c. mortgagor and mortgagee
   d. mortgagee and assignee

10. Which lien is attached to a specific property?
    a. judgment lien
    b. general lien
    c. federal income tax lien
    d. property tax lien

11. Abigail Jones purchases a home for $90,000. She puts 20 percent down with the balance due over 20 years at 7 percent. Her monthly principal and interest payments are $558.72. What is the amount of interest paid the first month?
    a. $58.72
    b. $138.72
    c. $420.00
    d. $504.00

12. Relating to the above question, what is the approximate amount of interest Abigail Jones will have paid on the loan at its maturity?
    a. $56,984.30
    b. $62,092.80
    c. $72,000.00
    d. $134,092.80

13. The repayment of principal and interest within a specified time is characteristic of a(n):
    a. delinquent loan
    b. amortized loan
    c. accelerated loan
    d. equalized loan

14. The clause in a mortgage that allows the mortgagee to declare the entire sum due upon default by the mortgagor is:
    a. the escalator clause
    b. the acceleration clause
    c. the forfeiture clause
    d. the termination clause

15. The type of mortgage that encompasses more than one property is:
    a. a package mortgage
    b. a wraparound mortgage
    c. a blanket mortgage
    d. a net mortgage

16. This mortgage, though not commonly used, is for a specific period of time and demands full payment at the end of that period:
    a. junior mortgage
    b. direct reduction mortgage
    c. term mortgage
    d. construction loan

17. An act performed by a creditor to receive payment on a real estate loan is called:
    a. redemption
    b. escrow
    c. foreclosure
    d. assignment

18. To charge interest in excess of the amount allowable by law is:
    a. truth-in-lending
    b. discount points
    c. rent
    d. usury

19. Which mortgage allows the mortgagor to extend the amount of the loan?
    a. an open mortgage
    b. a blanket mortgage
    c. an open-end mortgage
    d. a wraparound mortgage

20. A note, as opposed to a mortgage, is a:
    a. lien
    b. personal obligation
    c. second mortgage
    d. judgment

21. On a $45,000 loan at 8 percent interest for 30 years, the interest and principal payment is $330.30. After the first payment, the loan balance would be:
    a. $44,650.00
    b. $44,750.00
    c. $43,785.00
    d. $44,969.70

22. Which permits the seller to subsidize the buyer's interest so that the first few years require lower payments from the buyer?
    a. open-end mortgage
    b. temporary buydown
    c. blanket mortgage
    d. balloon payment

23. Which clause in a mortgage allows the mortgagee to collect rents directly from a tenant when the mortgage is in default?
    a. mortgagee in possession
    b. foreclosure clause
    c. possession by law
    d. acceleration clause

24. Jane Street sold her property for $120,000. The buyer put $25,000 down, and Jane took a note back for $95,000, agreeing to transfer title when the note is paid. Jane holds a(n):
    a. land contract
    b. second mortgage
    c. interim loan
    d. purchase money mortgage

25. What do mortgages and deeds of trust have in common?
    a. number of parties
    b. redemption clause
    c. foreclosure initiation
    d. nothing

Closing Statements

KEY TERMS

abstract	origination fee
closing	prepaids
closing statement	proration
credit	reserves
credit report	settlement closing
debit	title insurance
escrow closing	title search
lien waiver	Torrens System

OVERVIEW

We have covered the listing, marketing, and financing of real property. The final step in the sale is the **closing** of the transaction. At this point, title is transferred to the purchaser.

The procedure for closing the sale varies from state to state. When a sale is handled by a real estate company, the buyer and seller rarely meet. The real estate agent writes the offer with the buyer and presents it to the seller for acceptance (Chapter 9). Once the seller signs the contract, the agent puts into motion the procedures for closing the sale. The sale may be closed through escrow and, in some states, by the real estate company. In other states, such as Illinois, the court has ruled that brokers and salespeople are authorized only to fill in blanks and/or make deletions as required on the preprinted contracts. The licensee may thus prepare the contract for signature, but it is considered unauthorized practice of law to suggest additions and/or give advice or interpretation. The sales agent is also prevented from preparing any subsequent documents, such as mortgages, deeds, a bill of sale, or notes. The law stipulates that attorneys cannot counsel sellers or buyers in which they are acting as a broker or salesperson. In those states the closing is processed by an escrow company.

This chapter explains both closing procedures by escrow, and the settlement prepared by the real estate company. The example of Kyle and Judy

Albright buying a home from Harvey and Della Wender will continue to be followed in this section. We will use the settlement procedures as handled by a real estate company.

Escrow Closing

In some states, the process of title closing is concluded by an escrow agent and is referred to as an **escrow closing**. The escrow agent is a disinterested third party who handles the closing procedure for the buyer and seller. The escrow agent's obligation commences when the buyer's earnest-money deposit is received and placed in the trust account of the escrow agent. The deed and all papers relating to the sale are delivered to the escrow agent. Escrow closings are most often handled by attorneys, title insurance companies, escrow companies, or the escrow departments of lending institutions. As disinterested third parties, these paid professionals are accountable by law to perform their duties in a timely and accurate manner. In most states the escrow agent represents both parties to the contract, there being no question of a conflict of interest, since the closing is a procedural matter and the decisions of "who pays what" have been spelled out in the purchase agreement. The escrow agent follows the exact instructions outlined in the purchase contract between the buyer and the seller, carrying out all the duties necessary to execute a uniform closing that is finalized when the escrow agent collects the balance of the funds due from the buyer, passes the deed to the buyer (or the buyer's lender), and disburses the funds to the seller. Following this chain of actions results in a paper trail of documentation that leads to a smooth closing.

Settlement by the Real Estate Firm

The **settlement closing** procedure is carried out by the real estate firm that listed the property. The real estate broker prepares closing statements, which are presented to the purchaser and seller when the sale is finalized. The **closing statement** itemizes **debits** (costs) and **credits** (assets) incurred in the purchase and sale of the property. The loan papers are prepared by the lending institution, and both the lender and the real estate agent close with the buyer, usually at the lender's office or in a conference room of the real estate firm.

Since we have followed the sale of the property at 1040 Clear Street, we will now follow the closing procedure from the time the purchase agreement was accepted by the seller to the culmination of the sale.

If the purchaser needs a loan (the cash buyer is rare), the real estate agent who sold the property sets an appointment with the lending institution and the buyer, thus facilitating the start of the loan processing. A copy of the purchase agreement is given to the lender in addition to information regarding the property.

Fees are collected from the borrower to cover the cost of the credit report and property appraisal. In compliance with RESPA, if the loan is federally related, the lender must furnish the borrower with a HUD information booklet and an estimate of the closing costs on the HUD good faith estimate. The HUD booklet is a buyer's guide to settlement costs, explaining home buyer's rights and obligations and standard closing procedures (see Chapter 10).

The lending institution follows a series of preliminary steps prior to setting the closing date.

Lender's responsibility

1. Immediately orders a **credit report**. The credit report reveals the borrower's past record in paying debts. If the borrower has been slow or delinquent in payments, the lender takes this into consideration while evaluating the risk involved in issuing a loan.

2. Orders an appraisal. The lender's appraiser inspects the property to ensure that the purchase price is not more than the property's market value.

3. Obtains verification of employment from the borrower's employer. A borrower's employment record should indicate that the borrower has been regularly employed and, preferably, possesses a marketable job skill. If the borrower's work is seasonal, difficulty may arise in meeting a monthly payment obligation. Lenders usually like to see no more than a quarter of the borrower's monthly gross income used for housing. This may vary depending on the type of financing the borrowers are requesting and their total debt ratio. The number and ages of dependents the borrower must support also are taken into consideration, and if the borrower's spouse is employed, it is credited to their ability to repay the loan.

Since the federal Equal Credit Opportunity Act (ECOA) has been in force, the lender cannot discriminate as to race, marital status, sex, or age. Today a single woman or an older person can purchase a home provided she meets the requirements of sufficient income, good credit rating, and employment stability (see ECOA in Chapter 10).

4. Obtains verification of bank deposits.
5. Obtains a survey. Surveys are often required if the lender plans to sell the mortgage (see Figure 12.1).
6. Has the underwriter review the file when all the documents are gathered, orders any additional documents that may be needed, and sets a closing date.
7. Prepares settlement statement for borrower.

If the credit report reveals no adverse information—that is, if the borrower's employment is verified as stated in the loan application; if the bank verifies the deposits as stated by the applicant; and if the appraisal is at the purchase price—the lender informs the broker they are ready to proceed with the closing.

The real estate firm that listed the property then proceeds to carry out its duties.

Real estate firm's responsibility

1. If there is an existing loan on the property, arranges for it to be paid off unless it is being assumed by the purchaser. The holder of the mortgage issues a pay-off letter (reduction certificate) stating the exact mortgage balance.
2. Obtains the sellers' signatures on the deed.

Figure 12.1 Certificate of Survey

Project No. __13130__   Location __1040 Clear St.__

Field Notes:
Found all iron pipe as shown, using SE corner, Lot 1 Old Home estates and NE corner Lot 6 Confusion Hill Subdivision. Established A12' offset line. Checked remaining distance around survey.

LAND SURVEYOR'S CERTIFICATE

I hereby certify that this plat, map, survey or report was made by me under my direct personal supervision and that I am a duly Registered Land Surveyor under the laws of the State of _____.

Legal Description:
Lot 8, Block 1 in Confusion Hill Subdivision, An Addition to Any City, Kent County, _____, as Surveyed, platted and recorded.

Plat to scale showing tract surveyed with all pertinent points.

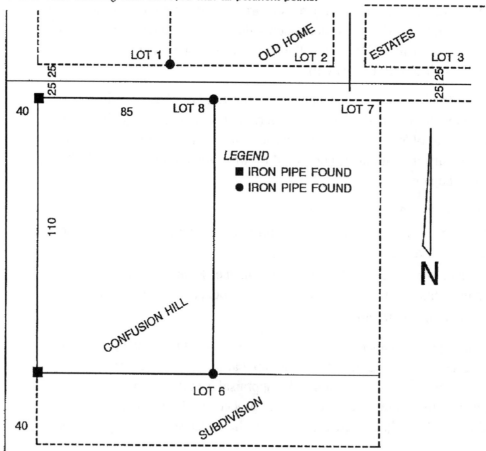

LEGEND
■ IRON PIPE FOUND
● IRON PIPE FOUND

Signature of Land Surveyor

Date Received: April 16, 2008
Official Address: Yards, Measure & Associates, Inc.
                                    11421 Goldenrod Lane, Any City, USA

Bldg. Permit No.:

3. Obtains a general lien waiver in which the sellers attest that there are no unpaid debts against the property.

4. Orders inspections, which may include (a) a wood infestation report certifying that there is no damage, (b) a structural inspection of the building if it is required in the area, and (c) any appliance and general inspections if requested in the purchase contract.

5. Orders the abstract to be extended by means of a title search or sees that title insurance is obtained. Either the abstract to the property will be brought up-to-date or title insurance will be issued. In some states this will depend on state law, and no choice will exist.

6. Completes closing statements for the buyer and seller.

Abstracts

The division of land from the time of the original land grant to the present time is explained in an **abstract** of the property. An abstract is a condensed history of the title. It reveals the "chain of title," listing all the previous owners of the land, along with any instruments affecting the title. The term instrument refers to a deed, mortgage, or any legal paper that has been acknowledged (sworn to under oath) and recorded in the office of the Registrar of Deeds.

If an abstract is used, a title search is performed by a bonded abstractor or attorney and extended (brought up-to-date). The abstractor lists any additional instruments recorded against the property since the current owner took title. The abstract does not guarantee good title; it merely lists the instruments of public record. However, the abstractor is liable if an item of record is overlooked in the search. Once the abstract is brought up-to-date, it is sent to the lender's attorney, *Searching the title* who gives an opinion as to the condition of the title, stating who the current owners are, whether their property taxes are paid, and if there are any liens against the property. This certifies the condition of the title and, in some states, is referred to as a *certificate of title*. The buyers also have their attorney check *Certificate of title* the abstract to certify the title. The attorney for the buyers examines the complete abstract beginning with the original land grant and issues an opinion on the title (see Figure 12.2).

Title Insurance

Title companies guarantee good title by having the title searched, as in the abstract method, and by issuing **title insurance**. After the title searcher sets forth the information on the property, the title insurance company's attorney renders an opinion, and the title report is written and acts as the support for a commitment (binder) to be issued. The title insurance policy states the date the **title search** was made, the owner's name, and the property address. It further states any outstanding liens, mortgages, or easements of record against the property (see

---

Figure 12.2 / **An Attorney's Abstract Opinion**

Righteous, Righteous & Caveat
Attorneys At Law
321 Legal Drive
Any City, USA

May 12, 2008

Kyle A. & Judy A. Albright
11250 Cherry Blossom Lane
Any City, USA

Dear Mr. & Mrs. Albright:

We have carefully examined Abstract of Title to the property described as:

Lot 8, Block 1, Confusion Hill Subdivision,
Any City, Kent County, USA

consisting of plat and 103 entries last certified to October 10, 1989, at 8:00 a.m. by Title Services, Inc.

We find the fee simple title to said real estate as of that date to be vested in Harvey J. Wender and Della J. Wender, husband and wife as joint tenants, subject only to the following:

1. A mortgage to Ready Savings and Loan Association dated October 13, 1991 in Book 1670 at Page 314 in the original sum of $47,500.

2. The restrictions shown in the deed at entry 163 regulating the size of any dwelling which may be erected in the addition giving the utility companies the right to install and maintain their lines along the rear lot lines.

3. The first half taxes are paid, in the sum of $1,699.98 there are no special assessments.

You are required to take notice of the rights of any persons in possession of the premises. Also, whether or not any labor has been performed or materials delivered on the premises within the last four months which might result in a lien. Also as to whether any special improvements have been planned or commenced which might later result in special taxes against the property.

Yours truly,

I. M. Righteous

IMR:rm

Figure 12.3). As with the title opinion drawn up by the attorney who examined the abstract, the title insurance policy states any possible obstacles to clear title, such as:

1. unpaid taxes or assessments not of public record
2. unrecorded liens and mortgages
3. repair work completed but not paid for

Figure 12.3 A Title Insurance Policy

SCHEDULE A
Date of Policy

Policy Number	May 14, 2008	Amount	Premium
O-121756-ram	at 2:30 P.M.	$147,200	$654.00

Ready Savings and Loan

1. Name of Insured

   Ready Savings and Loan

2. The estate or interest in the land described in this Schedule and which is encumbered by the insured Mortgage or Deed of Trust is:

   Fee Simple Title

3. The estate or interest referred to herein is at Date of Policy vested in:

   Kyle A. Albright and Judy A. Albright, husband and wife

4. The Mortgage or Deed of Trust herein referred to as the insured Mortgage or Deed of Trust, and the assignments thereof, if any, are described as follows:

   Mortgage from Kyle A. Albright and Judy A. Albright, husband and wife to Ready Savings and Loan to secure $147,200, dated May 14, 2008 and recorded May 17, 2008 in Book 2210 at Page 295, Mortgage Records.

5. The land referred to in this policy is described as follows:

   Lot 8, Block 1 in Confusion Hill Subdivision, an addition to Any City, USA, as surveyed, platted and recorded.

SCHEDULE B - PART I

This policy does not insure against loss or damage by reason of the following:

1. Rights or claims of parties in possession not shown by the public records.

2. Easements, or claims of easements, not shown by the public records.

3. Discrepancies, conflicts in boundary lines, shortage in area, encroachments, and any facts which a correct survey and inspection of the premises would disclose and which are not shown by the public records.

4. Any lien, or right to a lien, for services, labor, or material heretofore, or hereafter furnished, imposed by law and not shown by the public records.

5. General taxes paid for first 1/2 year. Special taxes or assessments now assessed or levied, but payable in future installments: None certified to the office of the County Treasurer at date hereof.

6. Protective Covenants dated March 27, 1998, filed April 3, 1998 in Book 379 at Page 709 of the Miscellaneous Records of Kent County, USA, shall run with the land for a period of twenty-five years. A five foot (5) easement across and along the rear and side boundary lines of each of said lot is hereby reserved for the construction, maintenance, operation and repair of electric and communication lines and for the erection of poles thereon, with privilege of access thereto.

SCHEDULE B - PART II

In addition to the matters set forth in Part I of this Schedule, the title to the estate or interest in the land described or referred to in Schedule A is subject to the following matters, if any be shown, but the Company insures that such matters are subordinate to the lien or charge of the insured mortgage upon said estate or interest: None.

Issued at   <u>Any City, USA</u>   Countersigned by <u>   </u>

                                                            Authorized Signatory

4. questions on exact locations of boundary lines (proclaiming that a survey should be obtained if there are any such questions)

5. any interest or claims not of public record that the purchaser could determine by inspecting the property and inquiring of the person in possession

6. any zoning restrictions that should be checked

The insurer (title company) inspects the title and validates it to the title holder; the title policy is a contract of indemnity against loss or damage arising out of matters that have occurred in the past rather than what may happen in the future. This is unlike insurance which guarantees future losses. The buyers know they are protected from defects *before* the policy is written. There are many possible causes of title defects that are not disclosed by examination. If the claim, lien, or defect has never been recorded, it will not appear on record. Such undisclosed and hidden risks include forged deeds, illegal acts of trustees, guardians, or attorneys, or false claims of ownership. Human errors in copying and recording or the loss or destruction of records also occur.

Title insurance policies are divided into four main classes. The two types most commonly issued are the owner's policy and the mortgagee's policy.

Owner's title insurance policy

1. An *owner's policy* is issued to the property owner to ensure good title, guaranteeing the owner of the real property against any title loss or damages suffered as a result of liens or defects in title that were not revealed when the examination of the title was made. Title insurance rates are not paid annually as with other types of insurance; the coverage runs indefinitely. That is, the insured will be protected against claims based upon the insured warranty of title to successors in interest. However, if the property is sold, the new owners will want to obtain a policy to cover their interest, since the owner's policy is not transferable. The owner's policy is issued for the full purchase price of the property.

Mortgagee's insurance

2. The *mortgagee's* (lender's) *policy* is issued to the holders of the mortgage because of their interest in the property created by the mortgage. The mortgagee's only concern is to provide security for the loan, so the policy is for the loan amount only. The mortgagee's policy protects the investor for the term of the mortgage. If the mortgagee assigns the loan to someone who does not see the property, the title insurance eliminates any risk problems. The policy is reassigned by the lender upon sale of the loan.

Also available are a *leasehold policy* that insures and protects the interests of a lessee under the terms and conditions of the lease as it would pertain to the property, and an *easement policy,* which is used to insure easement interests of the insured over or across a particular parcel of real estate.

The American Land Title Association (ALTA) is a group of approximately 2,000 land title companies who have banded together to promote professional standards and ethics among their members. While some members are both abstractors and title insurance agents, other members offer only one service.

The Torrens System

Robert Torrens was the originator of the **Torrens System** of title registration. Adopted in Australia in 1857, this system requires that application for title be made by the landowner. A petition requesting initial registration of the title is filed by the owner in the county where the land is located. A notice is published in the newspaper that a hearing of a suit to quiet title will be held before a court of law. All known parties having an interest in the real estate are sent copies of the publication. Once the hearing takes place, the court mandates that the owner has good and merchantable title. The Torrens Certificate of Title System requires all deeds to be registered to authenticate legal title. The certificate of title reveals the owner of record and any encumbrances against the title. Similar to the method used in car registration, this system negates the need for a title search when the property is sold. Follow-up evidence of title is comparably inexpensive as no costly examination need be made once the title is recorded. Although approximately 10 states recognize its use, lack of public acceptance has limited more active use of this system.

Registering the title

Other Prerequisites to Closing

Termite Inspection

In many states a termite and wood infestation inspection requirement is a standard part of the purchase agreement. Our purchase agreement (see Chapter 9, Figure 9.1 at Section G) states, "Purchaser, except for VA loan, agrees to pay the cost of a termite inspection of the house and attached structures, and Seller agrees to pay for any treatment or repair work found necessary. If repairs are found to be needed for issuance of termite warranty, upon completion of repairs, Purchaser agrees to accept said treated real estate."

Structural Inspection and Disclosure

In some areas of the country, structural inspections are required to be performed by qualified inspectors, with the stipulation being made a part of the offer to purchase. Questions of whether the structure is built on solid ground or properly compacted soil are of concern to sales agents and buyers of homes situated on slopes, hillsides, and newly excavated areas where the soil has been moved considerably. This was the problem faced by the Eastons in the landmark case where the California courts awarded damages to them because of structural problems that arose when the land began to buckle and slide. A standardized disclosure form is now used in California with a checklist of inspections for potential problem areas (see Chapter 9, Figure 9.3).

A growing number of states have legislated seller disclosure requiring the seller to complete a standardized form and acknowledge any faults the property may have. If an item no longer functions, such as an intercom system, this must be noted in the disclosure. This places the responsibility of revealing any defects directly upon the seller. If the questionnaire requires an answer that the seller, in good faith, is unsure of, the response should be "I don't know." If the buyer has any concerns about an item, an inspection is advisable.

Appliance and Mechanical Inspection

Across the country there are insurance plans that buyers and sellers may purchase warranting against mechanical defects. The policy may cover electrical, plumbing, heating, air conditioning, and major appliances. This provides protection to the buyer in the event that a costly defect occurs after the sale. Some insurers require that an inspection be made prior to issuing the policy.

Homeowner's Insurance

For anyone purchasing a home and obtaining a mortgage, lending institutions require the mortgagor to carry homeowner's insurance. This protects the lender's interest in the property should loss or damage to the premises occur. The borrower must give proof of fire and extended coverage by presenting an insurance binder to the mortgagee at the time the loan is closed. Some lenders will not accept a binder but insist upon a paid policy at closing. The lender is named on the policy along with the homeowner, and if damage occurs, the checks will be made out jointly to the lender and borrower.

There is a variety of coverage available to the homeowner, ranging from Homeowner 1 (HO-1) to Homeowner 5 (HO-5). The HO-5 policy is the most comprehensive plan, covering all possible types of perils, excluding only such catastrophes as earthquakes, floods, war, settling, and cracking (see the discussion in Chapter 9 on insurance and warranties).

Lien Waivers

To ensure the buyers that there are no unpaid liens against the property, the real estate firm may request that the sellers sign an affidavit attesting to the fact that there are no unpaid bills that could result in a lien against the property. This affidavit is called a **lien waiver**.

Closing Expenses

There are costs involved in the sale for both the buyer and the seller. The parties to the agreement can negotiate who will pay these expenses, and the purchase agreement will specify who is to be charged. Items that may be expenses of the closing are as follows.

1. *Transfer tax*: Most states have a tax, either referred to as a transfer fee or tax stamps, that is due upon the sale and transfer of the property. As discussed in Chapter 2, this tax is usually paid by the seller, although customs may vary.

2. *Loan fees*: Charges generally made by the lending institution include

   a. An **origination fee** (also called a service or placement fee) for issuing the loan. This fee is paid by the buyer.

   b. An *assumption fee* if the buyer is assuming an existing loan. This is a buyer expense.

   c. *Discount points,* which are paid at the time the loan is made, are based on a percentage of the loan. They can be paid by either buyer or seller, as agreed in the purchase contract. Discount points are considered prepaid interest and are tax deductible if paid by the buyer.

   d. *Prepayment penalty* on an existing loan. Some loans carry a prepayment clause that requires the seller to pay a penalty for repaying the loan before its maturity date.

   e. *Mortgage insurance premiums* are charged on some loans. An FHA loan will have an upfront mortgage insurance premium (UFMIP). This will be paid by the buyer at the time of closing or added to the loan. A conventional insured loan levies a fee of 1 percent to be prepaid at the time the loan is closed. It is paid by the borrower.

3. *Recording fees*: Charges are made to record the documents involved in the transaction. The seller pays for release of the existing mortgage and the buyer pays the cost of recording the deed and the new mortgage or deed of trust if the buyer is financing the purchase.

4. *Attorney fees*: If an attorney's services are used by the seller or buyer, they may be charged on the settlement statement.

5. *Broker's commission*: Paid by seller and negotiated between the listing broker and the principal (seller) at the time the sellers employed and listed with a broker. If the buyers employ an agent/broker, they must pay their broker or negotiate a share of the listing broker's commission (see Chapter 8).

6. *Appraisal fee*: The appraisal fee is paid by the person for whom the appraisal was ordered. The lending institution will require an appraisal, and the borrower pays the fee along with the credit report fee at the time the loan application is taken.

7. *Survey fees*: Usually paid by the buyer unless stated otherwise in the purchase agreement.

8. *Title expense*: If an abstract is being brought up to date, a title search is made, and an attorney's opinion is given. Local customs vary as to who is charged. If title insurance is being issued, the common practice in many states is to split the cost between the buyer and the seller. In other states, the buyer pays the entire cost.

9. *Escrow account*: Taxes and insurance are collected by the lender on some loans and placed in a *reserve (impound) account* so that the funds will be available to pay the insurance premium and property taxes when they are due. Added to the monthly principal and interest payment is one month's insurance and taxes. At the time of closing, the lender will collect enough to establish sufficient funds in the account to pay the taxes and insurance when they are due. For example, if the loan is closed February 15 and taxes for the first half of the year are not due until June 15, the lender will collect for the months of January, February, and March so that six months' taxes will be in the account by June 15. Since interest is paid in arrears, the buyers will not be making a payment until April.

All of the mentioned fees may not appear in the closing statement but are commonly involved in a sale.

Proration

First, let's review the total transaction to date. In Chapter 8, the property owned by Harvey J. Wender and Della Wender at 1040 Clear Street was listed by the A-1 Real Estate Company. A purchase agreement was written for $184,000 (Chapter 9), and the property was purchased by Kyle A. Albright and Judy A. Albright on April 8, 2008.

The Albrights gave A-1 Real Estate Company a $4,000 earnest-money deposit and signed for an 80 percent loan at 6 percent interest for 30 years. The taxes for the first half of the year have been paid by the Wenders. The Albrights will take possession upon closing, and all calculations regarding who owes what will be figured as of that date, based on a 30-day month. The division of expenses and credits between the buyer and seller is called **proration**.

The purchase contract in Chapter 9 indicates that certain items will be prorated at the time of settlement. Expenses such as taxes, rent, interest, and escrow deposits will be divided according to who received the benefits. If the taxes are paid in advance, as in our transaction, the sellers will receive the portion back that they did not use, and the buyers will be charged. Had the taxes been unpaid, the sellers would pay for the time the property was in their possession.

Proration requires the division of expenses between the buyer and the seller in proportion to the time each has owned or will own the property. Keep in mind that the "user" pays. In some states, the buyer is responsible for costs on the day of closing, and in other states the seller has the obligation up to and including the day of closing.

Prorations usually are computed on a 30-day month, using a 360-day year. However, some areas of the country require a 365-day year, with calculations based on the actual number of days in the month being prorated. All prorated items paid in arrears will appear as debits (charges) to the seller and credits to the buyer.

Items that are **prepaid** (paid in advance) include the following.

1. *Insurance policy*: When the buyer assumes the seller's policy, the unused portion is credited to the seller. Most parts of the country require the buyer to purchase a new policy; thus policies are seldom assumed. The buyer pays a full year's premium on a new policy.
2. *Rent*: Rent is always paid in advance, so the seller credits the buyer commencing the day after closing.
3. *Security deposits*: These deposits were required from the tenant to cover any damage made by the tenant and should be credited to the buyer.
4. *Mortgage interest*: Interest is almost always paid in arrears. Thus when a payment is made, the interest paid is for the past month.

Items that are paid *in arrears* have accrued, or accumulated, and are payable at a later date. Use has been had *before* payment is made. These items may include the following.

1. *Utilities*: They will be credited to the buyer since the buyer is the person who will receive the bill.
2. *Mortgage interest*: If the seller's mortgage is being assumed, the purchaser will be paying for the month the seller had possession (interest is paid in arrears); so a credit to the purchaser should be made.

An item that may be prepaid or paid in arrears is property taxes. The payment of taxes may vary within a state. If paid in advance, the sellers will receive credit, as they will not be using what they have prepaid for. If paid in arrears, the buyers will be paying the taxes at a later date. Since the seller had the use of the property, the taxes will be prorated and a credit given to the buyers.

EXAMPLES

1. Property taxes of $2,160 have been paid for the current year. Closing and possession is September 1. Compute the amounts debited and credited to buyer and seller.

   $2,160 ÷ 12 months = $180 a month
   4 months × $180 = $720
   A credit to the seller and a debit to the buyer.

2. Annual taxes of $1,860 are payable twice yearly, on April 15 and September 15. Closing and possession are July 15. Compute the amount debited and credited to buyer and seller.

   July 1 to July 15 are used by seller but not paid for
   $1,860 ÷ 12 months = $155 month, ½ of $155 = $77.50
   The seller is debited and the buyer is credited.

Proration is discussed again and examples are given in the math chapter, Chapter 21.

The Purchaser's Settlement Statement

Figure 12.4 shows a purchaser's settlement statement as prepared by the real estate company.

On the Debit Side

1. On the **debit** side, the first item shown is the purchase price. Since the buyers owe this amount, it appears as a cost to them.

2. Title insurance will be purchased at a cost of $654.00. In some states this cost will be equally divided between the buyer and seller, representing a $327.00 debit to the buyer. (Keep in mind that some areas of the country may charge the entire fee to either the seller or the buyer.)

3. Bleecher Insurance Company will issue a homeowner's policy for $699.96 per year, effective upon the closing date. The year's premium is payable at the time of issuance, since insurance is always payable in advance and is shown as a debit.

4. The property taxes are paid for the *first half* of the current year, so the buyer will be charged for the amount prepaid by the seller. As per our listing contract in Chapter 8, the total annual taxes are $3,399.96. This breaks down

---

Figure 12.4	A Purchaser's Settlement or Closing Statement. In Compliance with License Law, the Purchaser Receives a Copy of the Settlement Statement at the Time of Closing. A Copy Is Also Given to the Lending Institution as Required by the Real Estate Settlement Procedures Act, and the Broker Keeps a Copy in the Office Files

A-1 REAL ESTATE
1104 Homestead Avenue
Any City, USA

PURCHASER'S CLOSING STATEMENT

Name   Kyle A. and Judy A. Albright   Date 5/14/08
Address 1040 Clear Street, Any City, USA

	Debit	Credit
Purchase Price	① $184,000.00	$
Earnest Deposit		4,000.00 ⑤
First Mortgage—Ready S & L		147,200.00 ⑥
Title Insurance (1/2 cost)	327.00 ②	
Bleecher Ins. Co. (1yr. Prem.)	699.96 ③	
Prorated Taxes ($3,399.96 @ 11/2 mo. 5/14/08 to 7/1/08)	425.00 ④	
Termite Inspection	80.00	
Ready S & L Closing Costs	3,980.09	
Balance Due from Purchaser		38,312.05 ⑦
Totals	$189,512.05	$189,512.05

to $283.33 per month. Since closing and possession are set for May 15, the buyers are charged for one and one-half months of taxes, which is shown as a debit.

On the Credit Side

5. The Albrights deposited $4,000 as earnest money at the time they entered into the purchase contract. Since it was paid in advance and held in the broker's trust account, it now appears as a **credit** on the settlement statement.

6. The buyers requested an 80 percent loan on the cost of the property. Since the purchase price is $184,000 and the buyers are making a 20 percent down payment, the loan is in the amount of $147,200. *All* mortgages are a credit to the purchaser.

7. The columns must balance. By adding the credits and subtracting the total from the debit column, we find the buyer will need $38,312.05 in the form of a certified check at the time of closing.

The Lender's Settlement Statement

The lending institution will also have a settlement statement for the borrower. In compliance with RESPA, lending institutions use a standard form as shown in Figure 12.5. The costs will vary from region to region and may also vary among lenders in a given location. Since the A-1 Real Estate Company is closing the transaction, the only collection made by the loan company will be under J, number 103: $5,087.05. These costs are the lender's charges in connection with placing the loan.

The statement reveals the following:

WEB SITE

U.S. Department of Housing and Urban Development: RESPA
http://www.hud.gov/offices/hsg/sfh/res/respa_hm.cfm

1. borrowers' names
2. sellers' names
3. lending institution
4. property address
5. name of the settlement agent
6. place of settlement
7. date the sale is being closed
8. sale price (J is the borrower's summary and K is the seller's)

Proceeding Through the Borrower's Transaction (Section L)

9. This section shows the appraisal fee of $275.00 (line 803), the credit report of $21.50 (line 804), the tax servicing fee of $81.00 (line 809), the flood determination of $18 (line 813), and the commitment fee of $500.00 (line 815).

10. The lender will charge interest on the loan from the settlement date to the next month. The closing date is May 15, so interest is charged from that date to June 1. Many lenders do not request a full PITI payment until the following month (in this case, July 1) so the interest will always be one month in

Figure 12.5 The Lender's Settlement Statement

A. **Settlement Statement**	U.S. Department of Housing and Urban Development	OMB Approval No. 2502-0265

B. Type of Loan

1. ☐ FHA 2. ☐ FmHA 3. ☒ Conv. Unins. 4. ☐ VA 5. ☐ Conv. Ins.	6. File Number:	7. Loan Number: 0602EM002426	8. Mortgage Insurance Case Number:

C. Note: This form is furnished to give you a statement of actual settlement costs. Amounts paid to and by the settlement agent are shown. Items marked "(p.o.c.)" were paid outside the closing; they are shown here for informational purposes and are not included in the totals.

D. Name & Address of Borrower: Kyle A. Albright Judy A. Albright **1**	E. Name & Address of Seller: Harvey J. & Della Wender **2**	F. Name & Address of Lender: Ready Savings & Loan **3**

G. Property Location: 1040 Clear Street Any City, USA **4**	H. Settlement Agent: Ready Savings & Loan **5**	
	Place of Settlement: 8052 Alert Drive **6**	I. Settlement Date: 05/14/2008 **7**

J. Summary of Borrower's Transaction		K. Summary of Seller's Transaction	
100. Gross Amount Due From Borrower		**400. Gross Amount Due To Seller**	
101. Contract sales price	184,000.00	401. Contract sales price **8**	184,000.00
102. Personal property		402. Personal property	
103. Settlement charges to borrower (line 1400) **18**	5,087.05	403.	
104.		404.	
105.		405.	
Adjustments for items paid by seller in advance		**Adjustments for items paid by seller in advance**	
106. City/town taxes to		406. City/town taxes to	
107. County taxes to		407. County taxes to	
108. Assessments to		408. Assessments to	
109. Real Estate Taxes **19**	425.00	409.	425.00
110.		410.	
111.		411.	
112.		412.	
120. Gross Amount Due From Borrower 20	139,512.05	**420. Gross Amount Due To Seller**	184,425.00 **28**
200. Amounts Paid By Or In Behalf Of Borrower		**500. Reductions In Amount Due To Seller**	
201. Deposit or earnest money	4,000.00	501. Excess deposit (see instructions)	
202. Principal amount of new loan(s)	147,200.00	502. Settlement charges to seller (line 1400)	13,411.00 **29**
203. Existing loan(s) taken subject to		503. Existing loan(s) taken subject to	
204.		504. Payoff of first mortgage loan	
205.		505. Payoff of second mortgage loan	45,320.10 **30**
206.		506.	
207.		507.	
208.		508.	
209.		509.	
Adjustments for items unpaid by seller		**Adjustments for items unpaid by seller**	
210. City/town taxes to		510. City/town taxes to	
211. County taxes to		511. County taxes to	
212. Assessments to		512. Assessments to	
213.		513.	
214.		514.	
215.		515.	
216.		516.	
217.		517.	
218.		518.	
219.		519.	
220. Total Paid By/For Borrower 21	151,200.00	**520. Total Reduction Amount Due Seller**	58,731.10 **31**
300. Cash At Settlement From/To Borrower		**600. Cash At Settlement To/From Seller**	
301. Gross Amount due from borrower (line 120)	189,512.05	601. Gross amount due to seller (line 420)	184,425.00
302. Less amounts paid by/for borrower (line 220)	(151,200.00)	602. Less reductions in amt. due seller (line 520)	(58,731.10)
303. Cash ☒ From ☐ To Borrower **22**	38,312.05	**603. Cash** ☒ To ☐ From Seller	125,693.90 **32**

Section 5 of the Real Estate Settlement Procedures Act (RESPA) requires the following: • HUD must develop a Special Information Booklet to help persons borrowing money to finance the purchase of residential real estate to better understand the nature and costs of real estate settlement services; • Each lender must provide the booklet to all applicants from whom it receives or for whom it prepares a written application to borrow money to finance the purchase of residential real estate; • Lenders must prepare and distribute with the Booklet a Good Faith Estimate of the settlement costs that the borrower is likely to incur in connection with the settlement. These disclosures are manadatory.

Section 4(a) of RESPA mandates that HUD develop and prescribe this standard form to be used at the time of loan settlement to provide full disclosure of all charges imposed upon the borrower and seller. These are third party disclosures that are designed to provide the borrower with pertinent information during the settlement process in order to be a better shopper.

The Public Reporting Burden for this collection of information is estimated to average one hour per response, including the time for reviewing instructions, searching existing data sources, gathering and maintaining the data needed, and completing and reviewing the collection of information.

This agency may not collect this information, and you are not required to complete this form, unless it displays a currently valid OMB control number.

The information requested does not lend itself to confidentiality.

Figure 12.5 continued

L. Settlement Charges

700. Total Sales/Broker's Commission based on price $ 184,000.00	@ 7.000 % = 12,880.00	Paid From Borrowers Funds at Settlement	Paid From Seller's Funds at Settlement
Division of Commission (line 700) as follows:			
701. $ to A-1 Real Estate			
702. $ to			
703. Commission paid at Settlement			
704.			12,880.00 **23**

800. Items Payable In Connection With Loan			
801. Loan Origination Fee %			
802. Loan Discount %			
803. Appraisal Fee to Mike Powers		275.00	
804. Credit Report to Factual Data		21.50	
805. Lender's Inspection Fee			
806. Mortgage Insurance Application Fee to	**9**		
807. Assumption Fee			
808.			
809. Tax Servicing Fee to ENTERPRISE BANK, NA		81.00	
810. FLOOD DETERMINATION TO FIRST AMERICAN FLOOD DATA		18.00	
811. COMMITMENT FEE TO ENTERPRISE BANK, NA		500.00	

900. Items Required By Lender To Be Paid In Advance			
901. Interest from to @$ 24.1973 /day	**10**	362.96	
902. Mortgage Insurance Premium for months to			
903. Hazard Insurance Premium for years to			
904. years to			
905.			

1000. Reserves Deposited With Lender			
1001. Hazard insurance 3 months@$ 58.33 per month	**11**	174.99	
1002. Mortgage insurance months@$ per month			
1003. City property taxes months@$ per month			
1004. County property taxes 8 months@$ 283.33 per month	**12**	2,266.64	
1005. Annual assessments months@$ per month			
1006. months@$ per month			
1007. months@$ per month			
1008. months@$ per month			

1100. Title Charges			
1101. Settlement or closing fee to			
1102. Abstract or title search to			
1103. Title examination to			
1104. Title insurance binder to			
1105. Document preparation to Ready Savings & Loan	**13**	200.00	
1106. Notary fees to			
1107. Attorney's fees to			
(includes above items numbers:)			
1108. Title insurance to	**14**	327.00	327.00 **24**
(includes above items numbers:)			
1109. Lender's coverage $			
1110. Owner's coverage $			
1111.			
1112.			
1113.			

1200. Government Recording and Transfer Charges			
1201. Recording fees: Deed $; Mortgage $; Releases $	**15**	80.00	20.00 **25**
1202. City/county tax/stamps: Deed $; Mortgage $			
1203. State tax/stamps: Deed $; Mortgage $			184.00 **26**
1204.			
1205.			

1300. Additional Settlement Charges			
1301. Survey to			
1302. Pest inspection to	**16**	80.00	
1303.			
1304.			
1305.			

1400. Total Settlement Charges (enter on lines 103, Section J and 502, Section K)	**17**	5,087.05	13,411.00 **27**

arrears. When the borrowers make their July payment, they would then be paying the June interest. The loan of $147,200 times 6 percent interest equals $8,832 interest per year. This amount, divided by 12 months, equals $736; 15 days (1/2 month) @ $24.1973 per day = $362.96 (line 901).

11. **Reserves** will be needed if the lender is going to establish a reserve account and collect monthly taxes and insurance along with the principal and interest payment. Some lenders prefer to escrow these items to insure their payment. The annual insurance premium is $699.96. The lender will need that amount when the policy is due next May. The lender will be short two months plus one additional month as the next year's premium must be paid before May 1, thus $174.99 (line 1001).

12. The same procedure will be applied to taxes. The date when taxes are due and payable will determine the amount needed for the escrow account. Assuming the second-half taxes are due and payable August 1, the lender will require five months' escrow. Since the yearly taxes are $3,399.96, there must be $2,266.64 in the account (line 1004). In the event taxes are subsequently increased, the monthly payments will be raised accordingly. If the taxes are due and payable only once annually, another six months' escrow of taxes would have been added.

13. Ready Savings & Loan charges $200 for document preparation (line 1105).

14. The title charge will differ among lenders (and in various parts of the country), so all of the items in this section are pertinent to this particular settlement. If the settlement was handled by an attorney, title company, or escrow agency, those expenses would be noted here. Since the lender is placing a new loan on the property, it is also servicing the customer by handling the closing transaction. One-half of the title insurance costs ($327.00) are charged to the borrower (line 1108).

15. The recording fees include the buyer's deed and mortgage in the amount of $80 (line 1201). Recording fees are based on the number of pages, and trust deeds and mortgages can be very lengthy.

16. The termite and pest inspection was $80 (line 1302).

17.–18. The gross amount due from the borrower is entered on line 1400 and carried back to number 18 (line 103) under section J on page 1 of the settlement statement.

19. The buyer's tax cost is credited to the seller (line 409). In this instance, the seller had prepaid taxes, thus the buyer will reimburse the seller for the unused portion (line 109).

20. The amount due from the buyer is entered on line 120 and includes the purchase price of $184,000, the lender's charges of $5,087.05, and the prorated taxes of $425, for a total of $189,512.05.

21. The total credits in the amount of $151,200.00 to the borrower are entered on line 220. The credits include the $4,000 earnest deposit (line 201) and the $147,200 mortgage (line 202).

22. The difference between costs (line 301) and the credits (line 302) is recorded, and the total amount due from the borrower of $38,312.05 is shown on line 303.

Now let's proceed through the seller's closing costs on page 2 of the settlement statement in the right hand column under section L.

23. If two brokerage firms had been involved in the sale, one firm listing the property and another firm selling it, a division of commission might be shown. In this instance, A-1 Real Estate handled both the listing and the sale, so the sum of $12,880 is shown on line 703.

24. The sellers are charged half of the title insurance policy (line 1108).

25. The sellers are charged $20 for release of their mortgage (line 1201).

26. The state transfer tax is generally paid by the seller and will vary from state to state. In this example, it is payable on the full purchase price at $1.00 per $1,000 ($1.00 × $184,000 = $184.00 (line 1203).

27. The total charges to the seller of $13,411.00 are shown on line 1400.

28. Returning to page 1, under the K column, the selling price of $184,000 is at number 8 (line 401) of the seller's summary. This figure, added to the $425 tax credit (line 409), is brought down to number 28 (line 420) for a total of $184,425.

29. The settlement charges of $13,411 due from the seller are brought forward from number 27 (from line 1400 to line 502).

30. The amount of $45,320.10 due on the seller's mortgage, which will be paid off, is listed on line 504.

31. The costs in numbers 29 and 30 are totaled ($58,731.10) on line 520.

32. The balance due to the seller is entered on line 603. The $125,693.90 represents the difference between the debits at number 31 and the sale price of $184,000 and the tax credit of $425 totaling $184,425 at line 601. This sum must balance with the real estate firm's statement (see Figure 12.6).

The Seller's Settlement Statement

Now let's proceed to the analysis of the seller's statement as prepared by A-1 Real Estate (Figure 12.6). When the real estate broker delivers the proceeds from the sale to the seller, he also presents the closing statement, showing all disbursements. These include the following:

On the Credit Side

1. The selling price (a credit to the owner).

2. The prorated taxes of $425.00 are a credit, since the first half is paid and the buyers will reimburse the owner for the unused portion. Keep in mind that the person who has the use of the property pays the taxes.

Figure 12.6   The Seller's Closing Statement

A-1 REAL ESTATE
1104 Homestead Avenue
Any City, USA

SELLER'S CLOSING STATEMENT

Name   Harvey J. and Della Wender   Date 5/14/08

Address   1040 Clear Street, Any City, USA

	Debit	Credit
Selling Price	$	$184,000.0①
Balance of First Mortgage–		
Ready S & L	45,320.10③	
Mortgage Release	20.00④	
State Transfer Tax	184.00⑤	
Title Insurance	327.00⑥	
Prorated Taxes ($3,399.96 @ 11/2 mo. 5/15/08 to 7/1/08)		425.00②
Professional Services Fee (7%)	12,880.00⑦	
Balance Due to Seller, Proceeds	125,693.90⑧	
Totals	$184,425.00	$184,425.00

On the Debit Side

3. The mortgage balance of $45,320.10, which appears as a debit since it is owed by the seller.

4. The charge (debit) of the release of the mortgage. This is filed at the county courthouse to prove the note has been paid in full and the mortgage is no longer a lien on the property.

5. The state transfer tax, as previously explained, is based on the rate of $1.00 per $1,000 of the sale price, for a total of $184.00. This rate will vary from state to state and is generally paid for by the grantor.

6. The cost of one-half of the title insurance is $327.00.

7. The brokerage fee of 7 percent is based on the gross sales price of $184,000, so we debit the seller $12,880.00.

8. The amount of $125,693.90 is the sum due the seller as proceeds from the sale. This figure was arrived at by totaling the credit side, which shows the $184,000 sale price and the tax proration of $425, for a total of $184,425.00, and subtracting the debit column from the credits.

At the time the new loan (for the buyers) closes with the lending institution, the broker gives the lender a copy of the seller's closing statement.

Summary of Important Points

1. Real estate transactions are closed by the real estate firm or by an escrow agent (an escrow closing).

2. A closing statement itemizes the debits (costs) and credits (assets) of the buyer and seller, and each is given their statement at closing.

3. Upon approval of the buyer's credit, the lender follows a series of steps that include ordering an appraisal, a survey, and title insurance.

4. An owner's title policy guarantees the owner's investment against liens and title defects.

5. The mortgagee's (lender) title insurance policy protects the lender's loan to the borrower.

6. Prorated expenses and credits are divided between the buyer and seller, depending on who is responsible to pay or receive.

7. If a real estate firm closes a sale, along with furnishing settlement statements to the buyer and seller, the firm will complete a trust account balance sheet for their records. (See Figure 12.7.)

Figure 12.7   Trust Account Balance Sheet

A-1 REAL ESTATE COMPANY
TRUST ACCOUNT BALANCE SHEET

Wender, H.
Albright, K.

1040 Clear Street, Any City, USA

Date	Name	Ck.	Credit	Balance
1/20/08	Kyle A. Albright Judy A. Albright		$4,000.00	$4,000.00
5/14/08	Balance due from K & J Albright		38,312.05	42,312.05
5/14/08	Proceeds from Ready Savings & Loan		101,879.90*	144,191.95
5/14/08	Bleecher Insurance	441	699.96	143,491.19
5/14/08	Best Title Co.	442	654.00	142,837.19
5/14/08	Register of Deeds	444	284.00**	142,553.19
5/14/08	Ready S & L Closing Costs	445	3,980.09	138,573.10
5/14/08	Wender Proceeds	446	125,693.90	12,880.00
5/15/08	A-1 Real Estate Co.	445	12,880.00	–0–

The balance sheet from A-1 Real Estate Company Trust Account is completed as shown. This ledger sheet shows the receipts and disbursements for the sale.

*The proceeds from Ready Savings and Loan to A-1 Real Estate represent the difference between the existing loan of $45,320.10 and the new loan of $147,200.

**The $284 includes the $20 to release the old mortgage, $80 to record the new mortgage and deed, and $184 is the tax transfer cost.

The last check written will be to the real estate company for their brokerage fee. It will be placed in the firm's business account and from there will be paid to the salesperson(s) involved in the listing and sale of the property.

Discussion Points

1. Explain the difference between an escrow closing and a settlement closing.
2. Why is it necessary to have both a lender's closing statement and a statement from the closing department of the real estate firm or the escrow company?
3. Explain the three methods used in determining the condition of the title.
4. Explain the prorating of costs and why it is performed.
5. Who purchases title insurance and determines when it is essential?
6. Some of the steps involved in preparing for a closing appear below. Determine which are handled by the lender and which by the real estate firm or escrow company in your area. When applicable, indicate whether a cost is to be paid by the buyer or the seller. Since answers will vary in different states, you need to determine procedures for the state you live in.

	Responsibility of	Paid by
a. credit report	_____	_____
b. appraisal	_____	_____
c. verification of employment	_____	_____
d. bank deposit verified	_____	_____
e. property survey	_____	_____
f. order loan payoff	_____	_____
g. get deed signed	_____	_____
h. termite inspection ordered	_____	_____
i. extend abstract/title insurance	_____	_____
buyer's title insurance	_____	_____
lender's title insurance	_____	_____
j. lien waiver signed	_____	_____
k. prepare closing statements	_____	_____
l. homeowner insurance policy	_____	_____
m. broker's commission	_____	_____
n. attorney fee	_____	_____
o. loan assumption fee	_____	_____
p. discount points	_____	_____
q. origination fee	_____	_____
r. recording fees	_____	_____

Review Questions

Answers to these questions are found in the Answer Key section at the back of the book.

1. At the time of the closing, any prepaid taxes would be considered a:
   a. credit to the buyer
   b. credit to the seller
   c. debit to the seller
   d. debit to both buyer and seller

2. The mortgage release is charged to:
   a. the seller
   b. the buyer
   c. the loan company
   d. the seller's agent

3. The HUD Settlement Statement is best defined as:
   a. a means of establishing the prorations of a closing
   b. a means of regulating the real estate closing
   c. a summary of charges to be paid by the borrower and the seller at the closing of a sale
   d. a means of prohibiting the finder's fee

4. Before the closing, the lender does all of the following, EXCEPT:
   a. obtains verification of the borrower's employment
   b. orders an appraisal on the property
   c. obtains the buyers' signatures on the deed
   d. orders a credit report on the borrower

5. The cost of recording the deed is charged to:
   a. the seller
   b. the buyer
   c. the real estate firm
   d. the lending institution

6. The most accurate definition of a closing statement would be:
   a. the reconciliation of credits and debits to the buyer and seller
   b. the proration of credits due the brokerage firm
   c. the establishment of the brokerage fee due from the purchaser
   d. the establishment of all expenses due to the lender from the purchaser

7. Which of the following charges is usually the responsibility of the buyer?
   a. the insurance premium
   b. the transfer tax
   c. release of existing mortgage
   d. unpaid taxes

8. The brokerage fee is charged to:
   a. the buyer
   b. the seller
   c. the lender
   d. whoever is stipulated by agreement of all parties

9. A reserve held by the lender to pay for taxes and insurance when due is called the:
   a. closing statement
   b. proration
   c. earnest deposit
   d. escrow or impound account

10. At closing, the settlement statements do NOT show:
    a. how much the buyer pays at closing
    b. how much the seller is to receive as proceeds from the sale
    c. interest rate of loan
    d. commission proceeds

11. In the settlement statement for the sale of a house, all of the following are credited to the buyer EXCEPT:
    a. the purchase price
    b. the down payment
    c. the earnest-money deposit
    d. the purchase money mortgage

12. A copy of the buyer and seller closing cost statement should go to:
    a. buyer and seller, respectively
    b. the recorder's office where the deed is being held
    c. seller only
    d. buyer only

13. A closing takes place and the seller is delinquent $572 on his taxes. This would show on the statement as a:
    a. debit to the seller
    b. credit to the seller and debit to the buyer
    c. credit to the buyer
    d. credit to the seller

14. Mr. Smith's property tax is $948 per year and is paid in advance semiannually January 1 and July 1. He sold the property to Ms. Huff, and closing took place August 1. The settlement would show:
    a. Mr. Smith will have to pay $553
    b. Mr. Smith will be credited $79
    c. Ms. Huff will be credited $79
    d. Mr. Smith will be credited $395

15. Beverly Buyer purchases a house for $35,000. She deposits 10 percent on the contract and acquires a 75 percent loan. The lender charges her a 1 percent origination fee. How much money will Ms. Buyer need at closing?
    a. $5,250.00
    b. $5,512.50
    c. $5,750.00
    d. $9,012.50

16. When an existing mortgage is assumed by the buyer, it appears as a:
    a. credit to the seller
    b. credit to the buyer and the seller
    c. credit to the buyer, debit to the seller
    d. debit to the buyer

Answer questions 17–20 from the following information.

On May 10, 2009, Jane Sellum, a broker for A-1 Realty, listed Harry Brown's house for $82,950 for a period of 90 days. The commission is to be 7 percent of the gross sales price, with 30 percent for the listing agent. Taxes of $1,320 per year are paid, and the $302 insurance for one year was paid March 20. Agent Isaac Blake with ABC Realty sold the property July 6 for $81,000, with an August 20 closing date.

17. What commission does the listing agent earn?
    a. $1,701.00
    b. $1,741.95
    c. $4,105.50
    d. $5,806.50

18. The prorated tax amount is:
    a. $476.67
    b. $513.33
    c. $843.40
    d. $953.40

19. The taxes would appear on the closing statement as a:
    a. debit to the buyer
    b. debit to the seller
    c. credit to the buyer
    d. taxes do not appear on closing statements

20. If the buyer assumes the existing insurance policy, the prorated amount will be a:
    a. credit of $125.81 to seller
    b. credit of $176.17 to seller
    c. debit of $125.81 to seller
    d. debit of $176.17 to seller

Closing Problem

Complete the buyers' and sellers' closing statements from the following information.

On July 15 Jane and Jerry Jones listed their home at 8484 Lincoln Drive for $93,500 with A-1 Real Estate Company and agreed to pay a 7 percent commission on the sale price. June and James Jury's offer of 3 percent less than the listed price was accepted by the Joneses. Taxes of $1,320 are due in the current year and are paid in full. The title insurance policy of $430 will be paid by the buyers. Homeowner's insurance will cost the buyers $350. The mortgage release will be $7.00. Recording the deed will cost $6.00. The buyers will acquire a $72,600 loan, and the sellers have agreed to pay 1/2 of the 2 percent points charged by the lender. Closing and possession will be August 10. All prorations are based on a 30-day month. The Joneses' mortgage balance is $58,548.

BUYER			SELLER		
	Debit	Credit		Debit	Credit
Balance due			Proceeds due to seller		
Total			Total		

(continued)

OTHER ASPECTS OF REAL ESTATE

PART 3

income-producing properties. The tax aspects of real estate investment are covered.

17 The Appraisal Process

Chapter 17 discusses the appraisal of real estate and the expertise required to place a value on the property. The three approaches to value—sales comparison, cost, and income—and how they are employed in the appraisal process are explained.

18 Environmental Issues and Real Estate

Chapter 18 brings forth how the real estate licensee must be aware of the impact environmental issues have when transferring properties. The many laws enacted to protect our planet from outdoor and indoor pollution are covered in this section.

19 Fair Housing Laws

Chapter 19 covers the federal fair housing laws as they apply to the sale and rental of real property. The Fair Housing Act is explained in detail, since it is important that all people involved in the transfer of real estate abide by this decree.

20 License Law

Chapter 20 gives a general overview of the license law acts that mandate the licensing of people practicing real estate. Each state enacts its own laws and rules and regulations, so the reader should be aware that certain information may not apply to every state. The student seeking to become licensed should obtain the state license laws by contacting the department that governs and enacts the law for that state.

21 Real Estate Math

Chapter 21 covers the various mathematical problems encountered in real estate transactions. Examples in computing square footage, interest earned, profit and loss, taxes and commissions, ratio and proportion, and loan amortization are provided in this chapter.

Condominiums and Cooperatives

KEY TERMS

air lot

bylaws

common elements

condominium

cooperative

declaration

homeowners' association

Horizontal Property Act

master deed

proprietary lease

time-sharing

townhouse

unit conversions

vacation license

OVERVIEW

New lifestyles have emerged, and along with them have come new variations of homeownership. While shelter used to be limited to either homeownership or apartment rental, many new options have appeared in the housing market. The single-family home with its picket fence and rose hedge has been the traditional American dream, but it is being replaced across the country by a new mode of living. There is a growing trend toward **condominium** ownership. The word condominium is derived from the Latin words meaning "for exercising domain with others." Condominium ownership is the individual ownership of a single-family unit in a multifamily structure or group of buildings, together with joint ownership of common areas. A form of ownership, it is also a way of life, not just a type of building or living complex. A condominium can be a townhouse, a duplex, a fourplex, a high-rise structure, an office, or a commercial building. This form of group ownership provides the owners with individual and absolute title to their own living space, just as in a single-family home. Along with receiving a deed to the property, the owner has an undivided interest in the common areas of the property.

Large metropolitan cities have seen the concepts of condominium and townhouse ownership spreading. In fact, so many apartment houses were converted to condominiums that some cities placed temporary moratoriums on future conversions. In other sections of the country, the trend toward condominiums reduced rental units to a point where adequate rental housing was in jeopardy.

The history of condominiums has not been smooth. Condominium pioneers came under attack by government agencies and consumer interest groups, especially in resort and retirement areas. Unscrupulous developers took advantage of inefficient or vague laws, leaving a trail of dissatisfied buyers. Most of the misunderstanding arose over assessment fees that were far below what was necessary for proper maintenance of common areas and unit exteriors. Thus, shortly after the purchase, heavy increases in the dues were levied. Some unfortunate buyers found they had to pay extra for a garage or parking space that they had erroneously believed was part of owning a unit. Some developers also retained too much control, even to the point of retaining ownership over recreation areas and holding a long-term lease binding the association. Most of these early problems have been eliminated through enactment of stiffer laws now governing the development of condominiums.

This chapter begins by explaining the formation of a condominium regime. The townhouse, the cooperative, time-share, and vacation license will also be covered.

Creation of a Condominium Regime

Single ownership within a master deed

WEB SITE

Uniform Condominium Act: www.law .cornell.edu/uniform/ col.7.html#condo

Condominium ownership was created by a special real estate law that allows individual ownership within a larger estate. The owner of the development files a **master deed** in the land records of the county where the property is located, along with a declaration of the condominium regime. *Regime* refers to the governing system of a condominium complex. The plot and plans of the area to be developed are defined in the declaration and set forth the sponsor's intention to create the condominium. A general description of the common areas and the restrictive covenants under which the regime will operate are also included. A property that was previously a single traditional estate is thus divided into a number of units within a common area. Basically, the declaration does the following:

1. converts the property to single deed estates
2. gives a description of the units and the common areas
3. establishes the undivided interest percentages of common areas
4. through the bylaws, places authority and power with the board of directors of the **homeowners' association**

Recognized in all 50 states, the **Horizontal Property Act** provides for ownership of a specific unit of space that differs from traditional ownership of property with rights to the surface, subsurface, and air space above the property. The individual unit is not complete without an undivided interest in the whole area.

Single condominium units can be grouped together, with the owner of a unit possessing surface, subsurface, and air rights in fee simple title plus ownership as tenants in common of the common areas and recreation facilities with the

Figure 13.1 Condominium Ownership

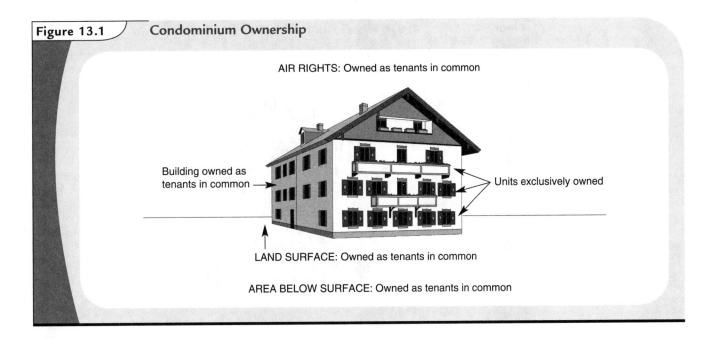

AIR RIGHTS: Owned as tenants in common

Building owned as tenants in common →

→ Units exclusively owned

↑ LAND SURFACE: Owned as tenants in common

AREA BELOW SURFACE: Owned as tenants in common

Figure 13.2 Single-family Residence

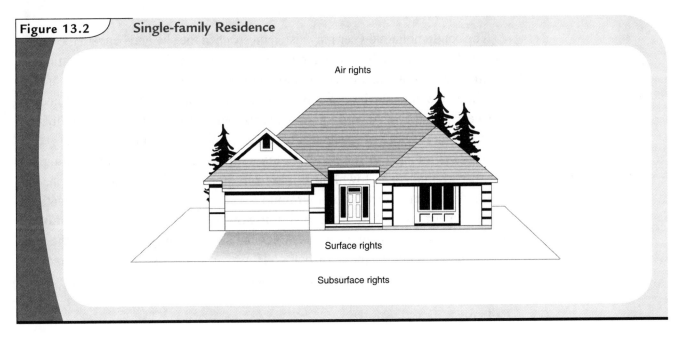

Air rights

Surface rights

Subsurface rights

other owners in the regime. If the units are in a multistoried building, the unit owners have fee simple title to their units and ownership as tenants in common in the building, air rights, surface, and subsurface rights (see Figure 13.1).

As we learned in Chapter 3 covering land descriptions, property boundaries are established by surveying a particular parcel of land. By relying on previously established reference points, the boundaries are staked out and recorded. As Figure 13.2 indicates, the boundaries are defined, and the individual has ownership of that area into the earth's surface and up into the sky above the owner's ground lot.

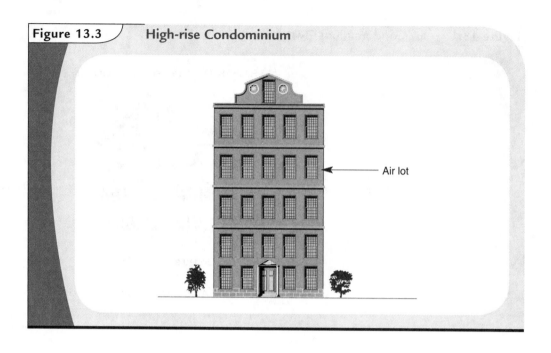

Figure 13.3 / High-rise Condominium

Air lot

Air lot in a high-rise condominium

The condominium owner may also own space in the sky and beneath the earth's surface if the unit is a duplex or a townhouse. In a high-rise type of condominium, in lieu of having title to a piece of land on the earth's surface, ownership is created that allows the individual a cubic unit of space. This space is called an apartment **air lot** (see Figure 13.3). According to this horizontal property division, the individual owners of these cubes of space also have ownership in the common areas.

There is no legal difference between a high-rise condominium building and **townhouse** units. The townhouse is a form of condominium construction. It is an individual unit joined to another unit by a common wall. The land beneath the unit is sometimes deeded to the townhouse owner and not included as part of the common area. The townhouse resembles the single-family home since the units do not have neighbors above or below. However, land costs are saved, since the units can be attached or clustered together.

Bylaws

Creation of bylaws

The condominium **declaration** states the covenants, restrictions, and conditions of the condominium regime. The **bylaws** provide for a homeowners' association to administer the affairs of the common elements and facilities and state any special rules that control the project. This gives the individual a voice in these matters and also allows the association board to levy charges against individual owners for the maintenance of the common areas. If monthly assessments are not paid by an individual, the bylaws provide for the legal enforcement of placing a lien against the delinquent owner's unit.

The developer controls the condominium from its inception through the initial stages or until the developer no longer owns the majority of the units. Later, when most of the units have been sold, control passes to resident members of the board of directors. The following articles are included in the bylaws:

1. the responsibilities of the officers and directors
2. the owner's obligations
3. a statement of the assessment to be levied and how the fees will be collected to maintain the common areas and to legally enforce payment of overdue monthly assessments
4. the establishment of an operating budget
5. any rules governing the use of recreation areas
6. provisions to maintain liability, fire, and hazard insurance on structures (this does not include unit interiors)

The Association

The homeowners' association, or the condominium council, is the governing board whose responsibilities are spelled out in the bylaws. As in corporations, the board of directors and officers are elected by members and are responsible for the control of what happens in the governing of the condominium regime. Every unit owner automatically belongs to the homeowners' association, and membership carries with it the right to voice opinions and vote at both regular and annual meetings, which are held in accordance with the bylaws. A large development may hold meetings on a regular basis, whereas a smaller regime may only hold quarterly or annual meetings. Members may vote to raise or lower monthly assessments; hire or terminate a management firm; approve, disapprove, or change the annual budget; and release or withhold payment to a contractor. The governing body is based on majority rule and will provide for:

Homeowners' association

1. an operating budget, including general operation reserve for replacement of common elements
2. collection of monthly charges and assessments
3. notice to lenders of any unpaid assessments
4. professional management, if needed
5. right of entry and rules of conduct with respect to the common areas
6. rules for use of recreational areas
7. refuse collection, water, sewer, and outside lighting

Reserve Funds

The association should maintain reserve funds for unexpected expenses. For example, a windstorm may level trees in the complex that will need to be removed. As the complex ages, new roofs and exterior painting may be needed. A buyer should ask for a financial statement from the association as a condition of the sale. The fees collected may only cover current expenses and if a deficit occurs, the new owner would be responsible for paying his unit's share.

What the Condominium Owner Receives

The owner receives an undivided interest in common in a portion of a parcel of real estate, together with fee simple title to an individual interest in his unit, which

Interest held by owner

1. has an individual deed in fee simple title
2. is separately assessed for taxes
3. can be individually mortgaged
4. is eligible for title insurance just as a separate piece of property is eligible
5. has an interest in common areas and facilities that are part of the entire building and land

Purchasers obtain a mortgage on terms agreeable to their particular needs and are not liable for default of other owners in the condominium unit. One owner may have paid cash while another may have an FHA loan or a conventional mortgage. If the loan is defaulted upon, only that unit goes into foreclosure.

Taxes and Assessments

Just as in a single-family home, all taxes and special assessments on a condominium are levied against the individual units and not against the whole condominium regime. Owners receive an individual tax assessment and are liable solely for their taxes. A lender may require that a tax escrow be included in the monthly mortgage payment, thus ensuring the other owners that taxes on all the units are paid. The maintenance and repairs of the common elements require funds, so each unit is assessed association dues according to the ratio of that unit to the total condominium units. If an owner has 1,000 square feet, that unit will be assessed for less than an owner with 1,500 square feet. Some states require that a definite formula be followed regarding this ratio which may be by value, by living area, by market price, or in equal shares. If an owner fails to pay assessments, delinquency fees may be added on to the unpaid assessment. If they continue to be unpaid, the association may place a lien on the property, which could lead to foreclosure.

Maintenance fees

Limited and Common Elements

Condominium living offers ownership both exclusively and in common. The unit is individually owned, whether an air space in a high-rise or an attached unit in a cluster arrangement.

Depending on the condominium style, the **common elements** (common areas) owned by the group may include the land and the exterior surfaces of the buildings, such as foundations, roofs, and stairways. Exterior areas will incorporate driveways, walks, parking areas, and gardens while the interior common areas will consist of corridors, lobbies, stairs, club rooms, entrances and exits,

Shared areas

storage areas, and elevators. Recreational areas may encompass swimming pools, putting greens, tennis courts, saunas, and exercise rooms. A *limited common element* refers to a common area limited to an individual unit owner, such as a balcony or parking stall. Sharing the monthly cost of maintenance and repair of the common areas with the other residents tends to reduce expenses, since the costs are divided by the group. Many of these special amenities would prove to be cost prohibitive for the single-family homeowner.

The Best of Both Worlds

Who buys condominiums? A government survey made in 1975 predicted that one in every two households will be living in some form of condominium by the year 2000. While condominiums have become increasingly popular, the aforementioned survey was a bit too optimistic. There has certainly been an increase, especially in inner cities where warehouses, vacant hotels, and old office buildings are being converted into charming lofts, utilizing old brick interiors that offer an aesthetic ambiance. Condominium living may seem unrealistic if you live in a rural area or small town, but not when you consider the highly populated urban cities such as New York, San Francisco, Boston, or Chicago. A desire for easy commuting to employment centers and scarcity of land in large metropolitan areas has resulted in the need for more living in less space.

The condominium lifestyle also carries particular appeal to people who do not want the hassle of property maintenance, including singles, divorcees, empty nesters, career-oriented couples, and retirees. Due to high land costs and growing construction costs, more living space can generally be obtained in a condominium for the same number of dollars invested. Thus, in some areas of the country it is less expensive to purchase a condominium than a single-family dwelling. Others purchase the condominium as a second home or vacation retreat. Resort areas abound with high-rise units. Owners of resort condominiums held in fee simple title may have the property manager rent the property when they are not using it, thus producing income to offset costs.

Carefree ownership

We want more for less, and the condominium can fulfill this want in terms of facilities, amenities, and creature comforts. Many condominium residents feel they have the best of both worlds: the advantages of homeownership and the benefits of apartment living. The owner has the security of living in a compound and the tax benefits of homeownership. Another attraction of condominium living is freedom from lawn care, snow removal, and exterior maintenance. This carefree lifestyle, which eliminates these outside maintenance chores for the owners and offers the availability of recreational facilities, draws many people to the condominium way of life. Investing in a condominium is also more appealing than collecting rent receipts as the owner has an opportunity to build up equity. Renting provides no deductions for income tax purposes, while the condominium owner may deduct the interest on the mortgage payments and property taxes.

The benefits of owning a condominium include:

1. amenities not often available to single-family homeowners, such as pools and tennis courts, though these amenities will vary according to cost and location.
2. freedom from exterior maintenance
3. a feeling of security provided by sophisticated security systems
4. peace of mind for the owner who is often away
5. enjoyment of the homeowners' association meetings—a camaraderie not unlike old-fashioned town hall meetings
6. social involvement for those who want to participate—some large units have organized activities for all ages and occasions
7. pride of ownership
8. more living space is often obtained for the investment since maximum use of the land is made due to rising land costs
9. minimized upkeep—limited to the unit's interior
10. choice of desirable location

The disadvantages associated with condominium living may include:

1. lack of privacy because of the close proximity to other units
2. limited private outdoor space
3. restrictions and rules that must be adhered to
4. majority rule; decisions are made jointly by the owners, so one is not in complete control of surroundings
5. parking areas may be limited

Commercial Condominiums

The rapid growth of available office space that was stimulated by tax advantages offered by the government encouraged an oversupply of commercial buildings. This phenomenon was particularly noticeable when an industry moved from the area and vacated large blocks of space. Some farsighted property owners began to offer individual space for sale. Aimed primarily at small businesses who may not have the need or resources to build their own buildings, purchasing space gives them tax benefits and the pride of ownership plus an opportunity to build equity.

One of the disadvantages of business condominiums is the inflexibility of the space. If the business needs to expand, adjoining space would probably be nonexistent. A means of avoiding this would be to purchase more space than needed and lease the extra space temporarily.

Conversions

Converting, which changes the use of real estate, began to surface widely in the late 1970s. Across the nation, 25 percent of all condominium **units** produced in

1977 were **conversions**. They became prevalent in communities that imposed rent controls, limiting the amount owners could charge tenants. With taxes and other costs rising due to inflation, owners began to view converting as the answer. For owners of apartment rentals that lent themselves easily to conversion, large profits could be made. Some concerned communities began to place moratoriums on conversions since they were reducing the amount of rentals available.

From apartment to condominium

Some convertees did only superficial "face-lifting" that consisted of a few cosmetic changes, such as fresh paint, wallpaper, and new carpeting. The buyer must realize there may be deferred maintenance, inadequate insulation and soundproofing, and that the plumbing, electrical, heating, and air conditioning should be checked. Another form of conversion is occurring in urban areas that are being revitalized. Old warehouses, offices, and school buildings are being converted to residential condominiums. The sturdy brick construction of many of these buildings lends itself to aesthetically pleasing living units close to employment centers. These buildings require more architectural and construction changes than conversion of apartment buildings already divided into living areas.

Disclosure on the resale of a unit is required in some states. A copy of the basic condominium documents and a current statement of the financial solvency of the homeowners' association and whether there are adequate reserves for any anticipated capital expenditures should be reviewed by the purchaser.

Cooperatives

In **cooperative** ownership of an apartment unit, the purchaser buys shares of stock in a nonprofit corporation, partnership, or trust that holds title to the real estate, with the shareholders owning stock. The purchaser of a cooperative apartment is thus a shareholder in a corporation whose principal asset is the building(s). Owning stock in the corporation allows the purchaser to occupy a specific unit in the building, referred to as a **proprietary lease**. The owner does not have fee simple title as the shares owned are considered personal property and as such the stock purchase must be financed by means other than a mortgage.

Owning shares of stock in real estate

The shareholder is responsible for a pro rata share of corporation expenses, which include real estate taxes, maintenance, mortgage payment, and other miscellaneous costs. The owners can deduct their portion of taxes and interest charges on the mortgage for income tax purposes only if 80 percent of the cooperative's income is derived from tenant owner rentals.

As a corporation, a cooperative is a single entity and thus if mortgaged will have a single mortgage covering the building(s). If a stockholder defaults in his or her share of assessments, the other owners are liable or risk losing their investments.

Due to this inherent hazard, a few states have passed laws to permit stock to be used as collateral and pledged to the lender, just as in purchasing a condominium. This places the burden of payment directly where it belongs, upon the debtor. Mortgaging each unit individually enables the owner to sell the property more easily. When there is a single mortgage, the seller of a unit had to either carry the financing for the purchaser or the single mortgage had to be renegotiated. These states further permit assessment of taxes on units individually, thus circumventing passing the liability on to all the shareholders.

When offering a cooperative unit for sale, the owner is offering stock and occupancy rights. A purchaser may be turned down by the vote of the cooperative board that participates in the operation of the cooperative. The shareholders may be quite selective in their decision of who they accept as purchasers. In some instances, the cooperative has the first right to buy the unit, another way of being selective.

Time-Sharing

Have you heard of "buying time"? That sounds like a ridiculous statement until you realize that we are discussing the use of a piece of real estate, known as **time-sharing**.

Joint ownership

The evolution of real estate ownership and its use began with primitive people who lived on the *first* dimension of real estate, on the land as they found it: *the length and width*. Through the ages people moved into a more permanent structure and entered the *second* dimension, house; now ownership could be measured in *length, width, and height*. We discovered a *third* dimension, owning a part or unit of a building, the condominium. Now ownership meant possessing *length, width, and height* and a specific *unit* of a building. The *fourth* dimension is buying *time* within the unit of the building.

If it can be divided, it can be sold as a time-share. Time-shares have been sold in jet airplanes, cruise ships, campsites, hotels, single-family homes, and just about any type of property that caters to people who like to travel and take vacations.

While there are many legal structures for a time-share plan, they basically can be grouped into two broad areas: (1) buying an ownership interest for an amount of time or (2) buying the right to use a living space without actually owning an interest in the real property.

Buying "right to use"

A purchaser buys an *interval ownership* and is deeded an undivided interest in a particular unit and holds title as tenants in common with other buyers of the unit. They can use, rent, give away, or will the amount of time they have purchased in the unit. Time-shares are usually sold in one- or two-week increments.

Mainly used in resort areas where full-time ownership is not practical or necessary, time-sharing allows each owner a time slot for a fixed or floating period to use the accommodations. Owners are charged an annual assessment for the costs of maintenance, upkeep of the recreational facilities, furniture replacement, and maid service.

An example of a fee title time-share follows:

Judy and Kyle Browning purchase an annual week of time in a condominium in Hawaii for the second week in January. They pay $10,000 for their share of the unit and an annual maintenance fee of $200. They receive a deed for one-fifty-second (1/52) undivided interest in the unit. The Brownings are guaranteed the exclusive use of the unit on the second week of January every year for as long as they retain their interest. They receive the same tax benefits and equity as from any other type of real estate ownership. They may sell their share for whatever the market will provide.

Let us consider the scenario of this time-share sale:

Fifty units are in the building. Each unit sells for $10,000 per week, thus each unit represents a sale of $500,000 *if* sold to *one* owner. Selling 50 weeks (2 weeks are usually reserved for refurbishing the units) at $10,000 × 50 units results in a sale price of $25,000,000. Now 2,500 people own the 50 units. The $200 annual maintenance fee paid by the 2,500 owners totals $500,000, which amply takes care of redecorating, maintenance, and staff salaries plus a management fee for the promoter-owner of the complex, who is now managing the development. While a tidy profit was made by the original owner, the purchasers have prepaid lodging for one week a year for as long as they retain their ownership.

Vacation Licenses

A **vacation license** is a form of time-sharing that offers the purchaser *the right to use* for a stated period over a given duration of time with the project developer retaining ownership. In some instances the unit will revert to the developer at the end of the specified time. Note that a vacation license gives only *the right to use, not fee simple* title as with a time-share unit.

Buying future vacations

In vacation areas that were overbuilt with condominiums, interval ownership has provided developers with a means of selling units.

One of the selling points to buyers is that they are purchasing vacation lodging for the future at today's prices. Luxury units in such exotic places as Mexico, Hawaii, the Virgin Islands, the Bahamas, and Spain offer vacations that many people could not aspire to take on an annual basis, but by prepaying "rent," these vacations are within their grasp.

Exchange Programs

One of the most evident objections to time-sharing is the idea of vacationing at the same time and same place year after year. Exchange programs are alleviating this concern: the owner swaps time with another owner at a different resort. Resorts across the country are forming exchange groups for their owners, so the owner of a time-sharing plan in California could swap for equal time in Florida. As the concept of time-sharing spreads, exchange companies are being formed

Swapping use

across the world to meet the needs of their members. For membership dues, an individual owner may join an exchange group and make application to use a unit in another resort.

Leisure time is on the increase. If the average person does not want or cannot afford a second home, a time-share program may be the answer. Potential buyers are warned that if they are thinking of buying a time-share they should make sure it is for the right reason. It should be to guarantee a vacation site every year and perhaps save money on what is charged for comparable motel or hotel accommodations. Too many people bought time-shares as an investment, and today the market is flooded with owners who want to sell, but there are few buyers.

Summary of Important Points

1. Although the traditional dream of middle-class Americans has been to own a single-family home, other types of housing have surfaced to accommodate the need for shelter, especially in areas where land is scarce, as in high-employment centers.

2. The condominium offers individual ownership of living space in a multi-unit building or group of buildings, along with an interest in the common areas and facilities. This form of ownership is appealing to people who desire to own real estate without the burden of maintenance.

3. The bylaws require that a homeowners' association is formed and officers elected to govern the association.

4. Apartment houses have been converted into condominium units. Many times the conversion units have just had "cosmetic" face-lifts, perhaps by painting and replacing carpeting. Depending on the age of the structure, the purchaser may be buying a unit that will soon need a new furnace, air conditioner, and appliances. It behooves the purchaser of a conversion unit to carefully examine these component parts.

5. Because so many condominium units are available in vacation areas such as ski resorts and beach resorts, the developers in these areas have sold units on a time-share basis. Still others have sold vacation licenses where the purchaser buys only the right to use the unit for future vacations. These licenses are sold on the premise that housing costs will continue to escalate and that the purchaser can save money by buying future vacations at today's prices.

6. When purchasing a cooperative, the buyers receive shares of stock for which they obtain the right to possession of a unit. Since the building is taxed as a single, whole unit and necessary assessments are divided proportionally among the owners, the solvency of the investment depends to a great degree upon the other shareholders. Some exclusive buildings are sold as cooperatives so that the owners can select their buyers carefully.

In essence, these owners can "tactfully" discriminate on who they wish to have as neighbors.

7. Retirement and vacation condominiums especially continue in popularity, and often the developer plays a second role in operating a management firm to oversee the rental of a vacation site project.

8. The varied choices of types of housing available today literally offer something for everyone.

Discussion Points

1. Explain the basic difference between a condominium and a cooperative.

2. Why would a purchaser decide to buy a time-share?

3. How do a time-share and a vacation license differ?

4. Explain the difference between separate, limited, and common elements.

5. Ownership of an air lot in real estate and ownership of a single-family lot differ in what respect?

6. Why is a homeowners' association necessary in a condominium regime?

Review Questions

Answers to these questions are found in the Answer Key section at the back of the book.

1. In a condominium development, decisions regarding repairs or improvements to the common areas are made by:
   a. individual tenants
   b. the homeowners' association
   c. a board of governors
   d. the real estate commission

2. What type of ownership does a condominium owner hold?
   a. fee simple
   b. estate in trust
   c. estate in rescission
   d. group ownership

3. Under the condominium type of ownership:
   a. individual units are mortgaged separately
   b. a blanket mortgage covers the regime
   c. only common areas are mortgaged
   d. none of the above

4. Individual fee ownership of a single unit in a multifamily structure is characteristic of:
   a. a cooperative
   b. a condominium
   c. a vacation license
   d. an apartment

5. Which of the following statements is true regarding condominium ownership?
   a. failure of an owner to pay taxes on his condominium creates a lien on his unit only
   b. the entire condominium regime is responsible for any tax default
   c. a tennis court in a condominium project is individually owned
   d. the condominium owner owns stock or shares in the project

6. The amenities of condominium ownership would include all of the following EXCEPT:
   a. maintenance of the common areas
   b. reduced maintenance and repair expenses in group ownership
   c. income tax deductions on mortgage interest payment
   d. shares in the project

7. The difference between a condominium and a townhouse is:
   a. only condominium owners may have fee simple title
   b. condominiums are high-rise structures
   c. townhouses have no common areas
   d. a condominium is a form of ownership, a townhouse is a form of construction

8. The time-sharing plan of ownership is best explained as:
   a. a condominium owner shares his individual unit
   b. several purchasers own a property and share in its use
   c. an easy payment plan is used in purchasing a condominium
   d. none of the above

9. The "cube of space" owned in a high-rise condominium is called:
   a. a space lot
   b. an air lot
   c. a tax lot
   d. an apartment lot

10. The owner of a condominium shares in all of the following EXCEPT:
    a. a unit deed
    b. a master deed
    c. a proprietary lease
    d. the bylaws of the owners' association

11. In a cooperative apartment complex, each unit owner usually is individually responsible for:
    a. the building insurance
    b. paying her own taxes
    c. exterior maintenance of apartment
    d. interior maintenance of apartment

12. A time-sharing estate is an example of:
    a. severalty ownership
    b. a leasehold estate
    c. a nonfreehold estate in a condominium
    d. the right to exclusive use for a specified time each year

13. Which of the following statements about a unit in a condominium building is NOT correct?
    a. it is eligible for title insurance as a separate piece of property
    b. it can be individually mortgaged
    c. there are no common areas
    d. an owner can take income tax deduction on interest paid

14. In which of the following must the owners or occupants in a building be stockholders of the corporation that owns the building?
    a. a cooperative apartment house
    b. a condominium building
    c. a townhouse
    d. time-share ownership

15. The horizontal property regime refers to:
    a. setbacks from the perimeter of a property
    b. condominium ownership
    c. homestead laws
    d. cooperatives

16. Which fee would a condominium owner be least likely expected to pay?
    a. a recreation fee
    b. a condo maintenance fee
    c. a stock transfer fee
    d. a hazard insurance fee

Leases

KEY TERMS

assignment

constructive eviction

demise

gross lease

ground lease

lease

lessee

lessor

net lease

option clause

percentage lease

periodic tenancy

reversionary interest

sale–leaseback

security deposit

sublet

surrender and acceptance

tenancy at sufferance

tenancy at will

tenancy for years

OVERVIEW

All individuals need the use of real estate as shelter or for business purposes, but many do not need or desire absolute ownership. For the segment of our population that is nomadic in nature, the desire and need for permanent ownership is not of primary concern. In fact, because many households are headed today by younger and older people, the population age distribution favors apartments. Many students living away from home, young adults working in cities, retired people, and newly married couples not certain of permanency in a locality prefer to rent until they establish definite residency. It must also be remembered that the continued trend of climbing construction costs and land costs price many people out of homeownership.

Many businesses large and small prefer leasing to ownership for a variety of strategic, cash flow, accounting, and operational reasons that are beyond the scope of this text. Leasing has several advantages for businesses: lease expirations give them the opportunity to relocate if necessary at specific future dates; they usually do not have to be concerned with property maintenance and repairs; they can expense their facilities costs each year; their lease obligations are not counted in their overall indebtedness; and they don't have to worry about getting a good price when they sell off properties they no longer need. In addition, many companies calculate that they can make more profit investing in their own business activities instead of in their own real estate. Leasing does put companies at risk of having to pay higher rents if the local market rental rates rise, but they also may be able to rent for less (or buy a building cheap) if the local market goes into decline.

The types of leases and the rights and conditions imposed by a lease for both residential and commercial uses are discussed in this chapter.

The Lease

Conveying use of real property

A **lease** is a *contract* and a *conveyance* between a **lessee** (tenant) and a **lessor** (landlord) of real property. A legal and binding agreement, it specifically documents the obligations of the lessor and the lessee. An example of a house lease is shown in Figure 14.1. A lease contract between the two parties is considered a conveyance that gives the right of possession to the tenant for which rent is paid to the landlord. This conveyance is referred to as a **demise**, or the conveyance of an estate under lease. Many leases use the phrase "to grant, demise, and let." These are the conveying terms that give the lessee the right of possession.

Upon expiration of the lease, the lessor again gains possession of the property. The lessor has a **reversionary interest** in the property while it is under lease, with the property reverting to the lessor when the lease terminates, and thus the lessor's interest includes the leased fee and the reversionary right to the property.

Leasehold Interests

As mentioned in Chapter 5, a lease is a nonfreehold estate in that it is set for a definite period of time with the rights granted by a lease constituting a leasehold interest. Leasehold estates can be classified into four main types.

Interests under lease terms

1. **Tenancy for years.** This estate is for a definite or fixed period of time as agreed to between the lessee and the lessor. The main characteristic of this lease is that it must have a *stated expiration date*. The term of a lease for years may actually be less than a year, perhaps only for a week or a month. Upon the termination of a lease for years, the tenant must vacate and surrender possession of the property. This estate is not terminated upon the death of the lessor or lessee.

2. **Periodic tenancy.** This type of estate is for a specified period to period, such as a month-to-month or year-to-year agreement. There is *no set termination date,* as the lease is automatically renewed at the end of each period. If one of the parties wishes to cancel the lease, notice to quit must be given to the other party. A tenancy from month-to-month usually requires a 30-day notice prior to the due date of the next month's rent to cancel the lease.

Figure 14.1	House Lease

THIS AGREEMENT Witnesseth: That I or we, _____
_____
have this day rented to _____
_____
in the present condition thereof, the premises known as; _____
_____
_____
_____
for the period of _____
from the _____ day of _____ , 20____ , on the following terms and
conditions, to-wit: for the use and rent thereof the said lessee, hereby promises to pay
the lessor, or to his, her or their order _____
_____ Dollars
per _____ for the whole time above stated, and to pay the same _____
_____ on the _____ of each _____ ; that lessee
will not sub-let or allow any other tenant to come in with or under him, her or them without the written consent of said lessor; that lessee will repair all injuries or damages done
the premises during his, her or their occupancy, or pay for the same; that all of his, her
or their property, whether subject to legal exemption, or not, shall be bound and subject
to the payment of rents and damages thereof; that lessee will comply with all city ordinances, will take good care of the buildings and premises, and keep them free from filth,
from danger or fire, and will keep the side-walks free from ice and snow and the house
and premises shall be kept clean. If in default of the payment of rent for a period of
_____ days after the same is due, lessee will at the request of said lessor quit and
render to lessor the peaceable possession thereof; but, for this cause, the obligation to
pay shall not cease; and finally at the end of lessees term, lessee will surrender to the
said lessor, his, her or their heirs and assigns, the peaceable possession of said demised premises with all keys, bolts, latches and repairs, if any, in as good condition as
the same was received, the usual wear and tear.

The said lessor reserves the privilege of entering and showing above property to prospective renters during the last thirty-day period of this lease or for any other reasonable purpose at any time. _____
_____
_____
_____
_____
_____

IN WITNESS WHEREOF the parties hereto have subscribed to two copies hereof, one
to be retained by each party.

Dated this _____ day of _____ , 20____ .

_____   _____
Lessor   Lessee

_____   _____
Lessor   Lessee

3. **Tenancy at will.** This nonfreehold estate at will provides for *either the lessee or the lessor to terminate* the agreement whenever they so desire. Most states require the party to give proper notice to terminate the lease. If one of the parties dies, the tenancy at will is automatically terminated.

4. **Tenancy at sufferance.** A tenant who remains in possession of the premises after the lease has expired has a tenancy at sufferance. The tenant stays in possession without the right or consent of the landlord and is referred to as a *holdover tenant.* A possessory interest in the land is held by the tenant only because the tenant stayed past the expiration date, so technically an estate in land no longer exists. The lessor may evict the lessee or may decide to accept rent from the tenant according to the terms of the previous lease. If the landlord does not evict the tenant, a periodic estate will usually be created.

Lease Contents

The following terms and conditions should be stipulated in the lease:

Provisions in a lease

1. *names* of the lessee and the lessor
2. a *description* of the leased property
3. *duration of the lease* (The commencement and termination dates of the lease should be set forth. If the lease is renewed, a new agreement should be written.)
4. the *amount of rent* to be paid should be stipulated, along with the time and the place payment is to be made
5. *possession, maintenance, improvements* and any conditions imposed upon the lessee and any exceptions to the lessee's rights
6. *liability of the parties*—the person held responsible for injuries resulting from conditions of the premises
7. *transfer by the lessee,* which is to the lessee's benefit
8. *special covenants, conditions, and provisions*

Termination of a Lease

A lease may be terminated under the following conditions.

1. *Expiration of the lease:* When the term of the lease expires, the tenancy understandably ends. Usually a written notice must be given by the party desiring to terminate the lease, especially under the terms of a tenancy at will or a periodic tenancy. A tenancy for years expires at the termination time stated in the lease, so no notice need be given. In a tenancy at sufferance, the tenant has overstayed the lease term, so it may be terminated at any time.

2. *Agreement between the parties:* By mutual agreement the landlord and tenant can sever the lease, the lessee surrendering the lease and the lessor accepting the terms. This is referred to as **surrender and acceptance**.

3. *Breach of condition:* If either the lessee or lessor breaks the terms of the lease, a breach has been committed, and the injured party may cancel the lease.

4. *Condemnation:* If a property is condemned under the right of eminent domain, the lessee must vacate the premises. In some instances compensation is given to the tenant based on the value of the remainder of the lease. The value is the difference between the *contract rent* (lease) and the *economic rent* (market value) at the time of the condemnation.

5. *Notice:* If the lessee does not give notice to quit to the lessor as required in the lease, the lessor can hold the tenant to another full term. For instance, if the lease calls for a 60-day notice if the tenant is not renewing the lease, the landlord must be notified before that 60-day time limit. Such notices to quit are usually incorporated into estates for years, periodic estates, and estates at will.

6. *Eviction of the lessee:* The lessee may be evicted through actual eviction or constructive eviction.

> Landlord's right to cancel lease

   a. *Actual eviction:* The tenant is dismissed from the premises and the lessor regains possession of the leased premises because of a contract breach. The tenant may have stayed over after the expiration of the lease (as a holdover tenant) or failed to live up to the terms of the lease (for example, failure to pay rent). A tenant's failure to move is referred to as *unlawful detainer.* Possession must be surrendered, or the lessor will take legal action to evict the lessee and have an officer of the court forcibly remove the tenant from the premises. The term distraint refers to the owner's right, pursuant to a court order, to seize the lessee's personal property if the lessee is in arrears (is behind) in the rent payment.

   b. *Constructive eviction:* A lessee may break the terms of the lease if the owner violates the covenants or terms of the lease and interferes with the quiet enjoyment of the lessee. If the owner fails to maintain the property according to the terms of the lease, the tenant may terminate the lease under **constructive eviction**. In many states, after receiving notice that repairs are needed, the landlord has 14 days to make repairs or the tenant can make them and deduct the cost from the rent payments. A tenant's withholding rent because of the landlord's failure to maintain the property in a livable condition is referred to as rent abatement. The landlord may not evict a tenant, restrict utilities, or withhold other services in retaliation against the tenant for exercising her rights.

> Tenant's right to cancel lease

Lease Provisions

Leases for one year or less do not need to be in writing. However, according to the statute of frauds in most states, if the lease is for more than one year, it must be in writing. In lieu of a written lease, the fact that the lessee takes possession is sufficient to affirm his acceptance of the lease and delivery by the lessor. A written lease provides protection for both parties and makes it easier to resolve any disputes that may arise.

Rent is customarily payable in advance, in money, chattel, labor, or provisions. The lessee has the right to enjoy the use of the property as specified in the lease, without interruption or invasion by the lessor or another.

Surrender and Acceptance

When an unexpired portion of the lease is reconveyed to and accepted by the lessor, it is termed surrender and acceptance. If the lessee abandons the demised property without the owner's acceptance, he remains liable for the lease. The landlord should endeavor to find a new tenant, but any costs of advertising or commission paid to an agent would be charged to the lessee who abandoned the lease.

Assignment and Subletting

When one **assigns** a lease, the lessee is giving the remainder of the lease over entirely. The lessees may assign their interest unless the terms of the lease expressly state otherwise. The assignee (new lessee) obtains all the rights and interests that the assignor possessed. If the assignee does not live up to the terms of the lease, the assignor will be held responsible until released by the owner. When a property is sold and there are existing leases on the premises, the leases are assigned to the new owners and are binding on them.

When a lessee **sublets** a property, he retains his interest in and responsibilities under the original lease and becomes the sublessor to a third-party subtenant. The lessee–sublessor may sublet all or part of the leasehold for a period not to exceed the term of the primary lease. Space usually cannot be subleased unless the primary lease permits it, and the proposed subtenant usually must be acceptable to the landlord.

Common Clauses in Commercial Leases

Common clauses placed in commercial leases of office, retail, and industrial space include any or all of the following:

Rental Adjustment

Rental adjustments are made to reflect the change in the purchasing power of the dollar. Such adjustments may be computed on the most recent United States Department of Labor consumer price index (CPI). The rent could thus be increased or decreased by the percentage of such increase or decrease in the CPI. This clause in a commercial lease states that the rent will not be less than the base rental stated in the lease.

Services

This statement in the lease notes that the cleaning of foyers, hallways, restrooms, and other common areas in an office building will be provided by the lessor. It may include cleaning the lessee's space.

Maintenance and Repairs

The party responsible for the maintenance and repairs of mechanical units, such as the furnace and air conditioners, is stipulated in the lease.

Exterior maintenance, such as resurfacing of the parking lot, snow removal, mowing, and tree and shrubbery trimming, are either borne by the lessor or prorated among the tenants. Because these can be expensive items, if the lessor carries these costs the lessor will consider it in the basic rent charged.

Right to Enter

The lessor reserves the right to enter the premises to make repairs and improvements. If the building needed major structural repairs, equitable compensation, not to exceed the rent amount, would be given to the tenant during the interruption.

Option Clause

An **option clause** allows the lessee the right to renew the lease upon the expiration date. The lessee may be uncertain at the time of entering into the lease agreement if he will want to remain past the initial term of the lease. For example, a real estate broker decides to open a second office and rents the branch office location with an option that will allow the broker the choice of continuing or discontinuing business at the new location.

Tenant has right to renew lease

Interruption of Business

A commercial lease will generally provide that if the building is destroyed by fire, flood, tornado, or winds and becomes unusable, the tenant is relieved from rent payment. Some businesses will carry insurance covering *interruption of business* due to damages outside of the business owner's control. Most commercial leases require the tenant to carry liability insurance in case of injury to a third party.

Change of Use by Lessee

The lease should state the use to which the tenant intends to put the property, giving the landlord the option of terminating the lease if the tenant violates the covenant. This does not imply that an infraction would be committed if the tenant leased office space for an insurance business and later decides to add a real estate firm. A problem would be created, however, if it were a shopping center and, say, a dress shop decides to open a section for shoes, and a shoe store with a similar line is leasing space and has a clause in the lease stating no competitive shoe outlet would be leased space.

Tax Adjustment

A *tax participation clause* is an agreement in a lease whereby the lessee agrees to pay all or a stated portion of any increase in real estate taxes on the leased property. If a lessor's taxes increase $1,000 over the year and the owner has five tenants leasing equal square footage, each tenant's rent would rise $200 for the year. A tax participation clause is often used on office or commercial rentals, thus offering the lessor protection against rising costs of ownership.

Improvements

Trade fixtures

The landlord is under no obligation to make improvements or alterations to the property unless it is specifically stated in the lease. If the lessee decorates and makes changes, it must be done with the agreement of the lessor, and any improvements may become the property of the lessor upon termination of the lease. Some leases specify that tenants remove improvements and return the space to its original, pre-lease condition. The exception is *trade fixtures* installed by the lessee for use in conducting business, such as display cases and shelves. These trade fixtures must be removed by the tenant by the expiration date of the lease.

Obligations of the Parties

Tenant responsibilities and rights

Landlord-tenant Law: www.law .cornell.edu/topics/ landlordtenant.html

The Uniform Residential Landlord and Tenant Act in force in many states lists the obligations of the parties to a lease. If the lease does not clearly indicate who is responsible for the conditions of the premises, this act clarifies the responsibility.

Basically, the tenant is required to keep the property clean and in good condition with the exception of the expected normal wear and tear through use. The tenant is held responsible for destroying or damaging the premises, and garbage and other wastes must be disposed of in a clean and safe manner. The tenant must not disturb other tenants or nearby neighbors and is expected to conform to the law concerning occupation of the property. The foremost responsibility of the tenant is the obligation to pay the rent in a timely manner. Rent is payable in advance; the lease will state the date that the rent is due, and if the rent is late the lease may provide for a late charge. Failure to pay as agreed in the lease is cause for the tenant's eviction.

The landlord, in turn, must comply with the minimum housing codes. He must keep the premises in good repair and in a safe, livable condition or as otherwise provided in the lease. By agreement between the landlord and tenant, the tenant may prefer to perform certain repairs in lieu of part of the rental payment.

The landlord must also see that all electrical, plumbing, and other facilities are in good repair and basically provide a habitable dwelling. It is understood the tenant will have *quiet enjoyment,* that is, the use of the property without interruption or invasion by the lessor or another.

Leases often contain a notice of intent to move clause requiring a 30- or 60-day notice. The notice may need to be in writing, or verbal notice may be acceptable.

Security Deposits

A **security deposit** is often required when the lessee takes possession of the property. This deposit is refundable upon expiration of the lease, providing the property has not been materially damaged.

In most states the landlord cannot request more than one month's rent as a security deposit. This deposit must be returned, with deductions for any repairs itemized, within a reasonable time after the tenant vacates and requests the refund. Some states provide that interest must be paid on the deposit.

Rent Control

Rent control is the action of a local governing board to place a ceiling on the rent charged by a landlord. This places a great burden on the landlord if maintenance costs, insurance, and taxes increase to any extent. In some communities where rent control is in effect, building owners are neglecting to maintain their property. Other landlords are converting apartments into condominium units. Rent control is generally mandated when apartments are scarce and rents have been greatly increased.

Types of Leases

Leases generally fall into the following categories:

The **net lease** requires the tenant to assume all or a portion of the property expenses normally paid by the owner, leaving the rent net to the lessor. Many long-term commercial and industrial leases are triple net leases. This type of lease places the responsibility of all the expenses upon the tenant, including taxes, repairs, maintenance, insurance, and generally even exterior maintenance. The triple net lease has a special appeal to the institutional lessor, such as a college or insurance company, since such a lessor would desire to avoid repairs and management concerns. Triple net leases are most common when a single tenant occupies a building. In multitenant buildings, **gross leases** are common. Under a gross lease, the single monthly rent payment includes each tenant's pro rata share of maintenance, utility, and insurance costs and real estate taxes. The landlord arranges for all services and pays taxes and makes an annual accounting to tenants.

Lessee shares building expenses

The **percentage lease** is based on a flat fee plus a percentage of the gross income received by the tenant doing business on the premises. Several factors must be considered in a percentage lease. The base rent may be low, but a percentage of the business revenue must be paid to the lessor. If the business revenue exceeds the lessee's expectations, the effective rent is subsequently increased. The percentage should be at a rate that permits the lessee to obtain a reasonable profit and provides the lessee with an incentive to generate additional volume. A percentage lease can be advantageous to both parties, allowing a lower base rent for the lessee who may be just starting in business and, as the sales volume increases, the lessor receives a percentage. A percentage lease is commonly used in leasing shopping mall space.

In the *straight, gross,* or *flat lease,* the lessee makes periodic payments of rent over a fixed period of time, with the lessee's responsibility limited to the rental payment. This lease may have a renewal option and may provide for an escalator clause to accommodate increased costs. An example of a flat lease would be an apartment lease.

Leasing bare land

The **ground lease** is used when a parcel of unimproved land is leased, usually for a long period of time. If the owner does not wish to sell the land and has no plans to build on it, a ground lease may be the answer. The tenant agrees to erect a building, so it is desirable for him to have a long-term lease. It usually is a net lease and should remain fixed for a specified period of time. Renegotiation of rent is normally based on current market value of the land. It allows the lessee to build the building without the cost of purchasing the land, and it gives the lessor a fixed, long-term return on the land.

An example of a place where ground leases might be used is on homesites in a recreational area. A provision in the lease generally stipulates the disposition of the improvements at the termination of the lease. The reversionary interest may revert to either the lessee or the lessor.

The *oil and gas lease* gives the lessee the right to explore on the land of the lessor. A flat rent is usually paid, and if oil or gas is discovered, the landowner receives royalties.

The *sandwich lease* develops when there is a sublease. The lessor is on the top layer, the lessee is in the middle, and the sublessee is on the bottom layer.

The *reappraisal lease* protects the owner by requiring periodic reappraisals of the value of the leased property. A long-term lease usually is reevaluated every five years. If the property has increased in value, the rent is increased by the percentage called for in the original lease. If the value has decreased, the rent will likewise decrease.

Seller rents back from buyer

The **sale–leaseback** of real estate provides for the property to be sold on the condition that it is leased back to the seller. The buyer becomes the lessor, and the seller is the lessee. The seller's money is released and available for inventory or reinvesting, and the seller retains possession, leasing back from the buyer. In addition, the rental payments are deductible from the seller's income tax. The sale–leaseback arrangement is desirable for the buyer also, since the investor has a guaranteed tenant and may deduct depreciation on the structure from taxable income, lessening tax liability. The new owner will also be building up equity in the investment if he finances the purchase.

The *graduated lease* is also referred to as a stepped-up lease, as it provides for a series of graded increases in the rent at stated intervals. This type of lease is advantageous to the lessee because it can start at a lower rental and increase as the business matures. It also helps keep the lessor's income up with inflation and rising market rents.

An *index lease* calls for periodic increases or decreases in rent. This change is locked into some national index, such as the cost-of-living index.

An *air lease* gives the right to occupy the space of another over a designated property. A restaurant built over a freeway and elevated walkways that connect buildings across streets are examples of property under air leases.

Summary of Important Points

1. A lease is a contract between the property owner (landlord or lessor) and the tenant (lessee) that conveys the use of the property to the tenant.

2. A lease is a nonfreehold estate and creates a binding contract between the landlord and the tenant.

3. The four major leasehold interests include the estate for years, which is for a specified time period; the periodic lease, which is for an indefinite period with no stated termination date; the tenancy at will, which allows for either the lessee or the lessor to decide the length of the lease; and the tenancy at sufferance, which occurs when the tenant has stayed past the lease term and becomes a holdover tenant.

4. The lease should define the time period, the amount of rent, the liability, possession, and responsibilities of each party.

5. If the lessee violates the terms of the lease, the lessor may institute proceedings for actual eviction of the tenant. If the lessor does not maintain the property in a livable manner, the lessee can abandon the property under the terms of constructive eviction.

6. For commercial tenants who lease space for a business, leases vary. Many owners request the tenant pay a portion of the expenses under a net lease arrangement. These expenses may include repairs, tax escalations, insurance, and maintenance.

7. Percentage leases are often imposed upon retail merchants, requiring them to pay a flat fee plus a percentage of their profits based on the volume of business they transact.

8. Assignment of a lease releases the tenant (with the landlord's approval) and passes the remainder of the lease to another tenant.

9. Subletting occurs when the tenant sublets all or a portion of the space but retains rights and obligations under the original lease.

10. There are specific leases to cover houses, apartments, farms, office buildings, retail stores, and commercial and industrial tracts. Each type of lease is designed to cover the rights and privileges of lessor and lessee of the property.

Discussion Points

1. Explain the advantages of the sale–leaseback to the seller-lessee and to the buyer-lessor.

2. Under what conditions can a lessee remove improvements made when the lease terminates?

3. If you were leasing an apartment but planned to buy a home in the near future, which type of lease would you prefer?

4. Explain the difference between an estate for years and a periodic estate.

5. What rights does the lessee have under the terms of a tenancy at sufferance?

6. Explain the difference between a sublease and the assignment of a lease.

Review Questions

Answers to these questions are found in the Answer Key section at the back of the book.

1. When the lessee assigns the lease to another:
   a. the lessee gives up the remainder of the lease
   b. a portion of the lease is retained
   c. the existing lease is terminated
   d. a portion of the space is leased for a specific time

2. When a property is sold:
   a. leases automatically expire
   b. leases are assigned to the new owner
   c. a lessee can break the terms of her lease
   d. the lessee can assign the lease to another without agreement of the purchaser

3. Demise refers to:
   a. the death of a grantor
   b. a gift by will
   c. interest by decree
   d. an estate of lease

4. One of the features of a ground lease is:
   a. it is always a net lease
   b. it is a long-term lease
   c. the term is short
   d. it is a tenancy at will

5. Which lease calls for periodic changes in the amount of the lease fee?
   a. a graduated lease
   b. a percentage lease
   c. a gross lease
   d. a net lease

6. A percentage lease refers to:
   a. a straight lease
   b. a lease with a sliding scale whereby the rent gradually increases
   c. a minimum base rent plus a percentage of the volume of sales
   d. a flat fee that diminishes over a period of years

7. Who is the final tenant on a sale–leaseback?
   a. the buyer
   b. the seller
   c. the optionor
   d. the optionee

8. A lease that requires the tenant to pay all or a stated portion of the expenses is a:
   a. gross lease
   b. flat lease
   c. percentage lease
   d. net lease

9. When the premises reach a physical condition in which the tenant is unable to occupy them for the purpose intended, the situation is legally recognized as:
   a. actual eviction
   b. constructive eviction
   c. surrender and acceptance
   d. income conversion

10. All of the following are necessary in a lease EXCEPT:
    a. the names of the parties
    b. a description of the property
    c. a renewal option
    d. the rent and terms of the lease

11. Under the terms of the estate for years, if either the lessor or lessee dies the lease is:
    a. canceled
    b. renegotiated
    c. unchanged
    d. in breach of contract

12. In a net lease arrangement, a lessee may be liable for:
    a. utilities
    b. depreciation
    c. mortgage payments
    d. special assessments

13. Cancellation of a lease by mutual consent of the lessor and lessee is referred to as:
    a. assignment of the lease
    b. renegotiation of the lease
    c. surrender and acceptance
    d. novation

14. The tenant has the least interest in a(n):
    a. estate at will
    b. periodic tenancy
    c. estate for years
    d. tenancy at sufferance

15. The reversionary interest is owned by:
    a. the mortgagor
    b. the life tenant
    c. the lessee
    d. the lessor

16. A lease may best be described as:
    a. an option and a contract
    b. consideration
    c. a contract and a conveyance
    d. an assignable contract

17. A lessee may terminate a lease by:

    a. assignment

    b. moving prior to termination date and not paying the remaining balance due

    c. constructive eviction

    d. subletting

18. A person renting an apartment would most likely have what type of lease?

    a. gross

    b. net

    c. percentage

    d. graduated

19. The lease that would be least affected by death is:

    a. tenancy at sufferance

    b. tenancy for life

    c. estate for years

    d. periodic estate

20. A landlord–tenant relationship would be which of the following?

    a. at will

    b. severalty

    c. tenancy by entireties

    d. a freehold estate

Property Management

KEY TERMS

certified property manager (CPM)

industrial parks

management budget

management contract

neighborhood shopping centers

office parks

property management

regional centers

resident manager

residential property management

strip centers

OVERVIEW

In many states a real estate license is required to manage the real estate of another person or entity. It is a natural progression for the real estate firms that specialize in the sale of investment properties to operate a management department to supervise their clients' investments. A property manager is employed to take over the management responsibility for the owner, and by applying knowledge and expertise, the manager tries to produce the greatest possible net return for the investor. The manager has a fiduciary relationship with the principal and is responsible to protect the client's investment. This chapter will cover the diversified properties that require management and the duties and obligations of the property manager.

The Need for Management

WEB SITE

Institute of Real Estate Management: www.IREM.org/index2.html

Property management has escalated in importance due to the many investors that have busy schedules allowing little time for the problems of management. These owners prefer to turn the responsibility of their investments over to capable management specialists who, because of their expertise, are able to create greater profits. Investment syndicates, composed of a number of individuals who band together to purchase investment properties, also need management firms to administer their investments. Absentee owners are becoming more prevalent and need the reliable services of management companies to care for their investments.

The owner–investor hiring a manager to oversee a large capital investment should select a management firm that has the ability to bring a profitable return to the investor. There are several professional trade organizations that train managers, offering designations and accreditation to members who complete courses in property management. The Institute of Real Estate Management (IREM), an affiliate of the National Association of REALTORS®, offers **certified property manager (CPM)** and accredited property manager (APM) designations to qualified persons. They award the accredited management organization (AMO) to qualified management firms. The Building Owners and Managers Association (BOMA) offers management courses that lead to the real property administrator (RPA) designation.

WEB SITE

National Association of Residential Property Managers: www.narpm.org

Far from being merely rent collectors, today's managers possess technical knowledge in such areas as marketing, accounting, finance, and social psychology. They must be detail oriented because they will be involved with large dollar volumes, and they must be people oriented so that they maintain a high rate of occupancy. By reviewing the manager's credentials and past performance as you would if hiring a manager to administer any other business, you can help to ensure competency that will generate high profits coupled with attention to property maintenance.

WEB SITE

American Management Association: www.amanet.org

A property manager may specialize in just one type of property and, since there are vast differences between properties, an expert in apartment management will not necessarily be as knowledgeable in managing farm properties, shopping centers, or office buildings.

Property managers also act as consultants to owners who want advice about upgrading their investment in an effort to produce a greater yield. Updating and modernizing may make a difference in profits, or converting the building to condominium units may be recommended. The building's location, economic conditions, and competition are all factors that will be analyzed in making the decision. Property management may involve specialization in any of the areas described below.

Specialization of property management

Residential Property

Duties of the residential manager

Residential property management includes the management of single-family homes, duplexes, apartment buildings, and condominium complexes. The apartment building, generally owned by one or more investors, represents the greatest opportunity for the residential manager.

WEB SITE
Building Owners and Managers Institute: www.bomi-edu.org

Among the apartment complex manager's concerns are securing and retaining tenants, collecting rents, advertising, providing cleaning and maintenance services, and keeping financial records and accounts. Investigating the prospective tenant's credit record and present employment should be standard procedure, and obtaining references from past landlords gives additional assurance of the tenant's stability. Exercising care in screening applicants results in fewer vacancies and less collection loss.

Proper maintenance and quick attention to tenant complaints means contented occupants who tend to remain longer. When vacancies do occur, a careful analysis of why is important. Effective advertising and promoting are also important. This requires a well-planned budget that includes a percentage allotted to advertising.

The federal fair housing laws must be adhered to in renting residential space. An amendment to the Fair Housing Act that became effective March 12, 1989 prohibits discrimination based on handicap or families with children. See Chapter 18 for the complete fair housing laws.

Condominium management has surfaced in the past few decades because of the increase in this residential type of ownership. Condominiums can be divided into the complexes used by permanent residents and the recreational units purchased by investors or families as vacation retreats. They require management just as do apartment buildings, except the owner-occupied units dispense with the need for interior maintenance. The need for maid services and periodic interior refurbishing exists in the leasing of furnished units. The assessments must be collected by management of both owner-occupied and rental units.

The **resident manager** is an "on-site" manager who administers the day-to-day affairs of a residential building. Living on the premises, the manager is available to consult with the tenants on any problems or concerns that arise. A pleasant, congenial resident manager is extremely helpful to the management firm in retaining good tenant relations. Resident managers collect the rent, show and lease vacancies, and see that maintenance is executed by the staff hired to perform those tasks. Any rules and regulations regarding recreational facilities, parking and storage areas, and trash removal should be presented to the tenants at the inception of the lease so that no misunderstandings develop. Resident managers are usually compensated with a living unit plus a salary that will vary depending on the size of the complex and the duties they are required to render. The security of large residential complexes in urban areas is a major factor. The safety of the residents is of primary concern. Many areas are frequented by gangs who bring crime and graffiti into urban communities. Security cameras by entrances help to secure the units.

Resident Manager
Lives on premises

Office Space

Managing leased office space is another specialty requiring careful analysis of the prospective tenants in a given building. If all the tenants create excessive traffic, the

Managing office space

available parking area may prove insufficient. While accounting firms, attorneys, and small businesses may not need an abundance of parking space, a physician or dental clinic could mean considerable traffic. The needs of the tenants must be carefully considered if the property manager expects to do justice by the owner and the tenant.

Large office buildings, especially high-rise structures, require supervision of the considerable staff needed for the operation and maintenance of the building. Trained specialists such as electricians, engineers, and purchasing agents must be supervised by trained management. The personnel needed for the accounting system alone is considerable. Cleaning, security, and maintenance usually require around-the-clock attendance to the property.

A trend toward business or **office parks** has become prevalent in some areas of the country. Usually built as one-story office buildings, this office community offers a variety of options for both the small business and the very large user. While rental cost of residential space is monthly based on the unit size, with one bedroom less than a two bedroom, commercial space is generally priced for annual use per square foot. Thus, if a 1,500-square-foot space rents for $10 a square foot, that equals $15,000 annual rent, or $1,250 per month.

Rent based on
square footage

Retail Properties

Shopping centers can be divided into three categories: neighborhood shops, strip centers, and regional centers. **Strip centers** generally consist of a single building with 4 to 12 bays that are conveniently located with easy access to and from main arteries. The larger **neighborhood shopping centers** may be made up of several buildings grouped together with 15 or more retail bays. **Regional centers** house several nationally recognized stores such as Sears and Penney's, known as anchor stores, with a broad mix of other shops. Many times these stores are all under one roof and offer covered parking, theaters, cafes, and seating facilities for the weary shopper in a central mall. Some regional centers have skating rinks to occupy youngsters while their parents shop. Any such amenities in the center enhance it in the eye of the shopper.

Periodic redecorating and refurbishing need to take place to keep competitive with new shopping malls developed in the community. Competition among retailers is keen, and with the ever-growing number of small specialty stores that are franchised, it is easier today for the entrepreneur to set up a shop and start into business with training provided by the franchisor. The commercial manager needs to understand the types of tenants best suited to the particular center. A prospective tenant may desire a clause in the lease that disallows competition from a similar store. To place several beauty salons, dress shops, or bookstores in a small neighborhood center may result in insufficient volume for any of the businesses. Many shopping bays have heating and air conditioning ducts above suspended ceilings that could conduct odors across to adjoining spaces. A restaurant specializing in fish or fried foods next door to a dress shop could create unpleasant odors in the clothing store. The rent on retail space in shopping malls is generally a flat fee plus

Managing retail stores

a percentage based on the volume of business transacted, so it is important to the owner that the merchant is successful in the business venture.

Title III of the Americans with Disabilities Act of 1992 requires that all public establishments must be accessible to persons with disabilities. Handicap signs on parking spaces close to entries, ramps built where needed, and cuts in sidewalk curbs make for easier access into public buildings.

Industrial Property

The need for industrial centers to have easy access to major traffic arteries, interstate highways, and rail transportation has led to tracts developed strictly for industrial use. The tracts are strategically located away from the core of the city. Referred to as **industrial parks,** they are built in suburban areas that will accommodate industrial needs. A listing for a warehouse will recite such items as trackage available, ceiling heights, utilities, and docks. Light industry manufacturers, bottling companies, paint distributors, and businesses in need of warehousing space are examples of merchants who locate in industrial tracts. Managers of this space will generally be the same real estate firms that sell and lease the property. Industrial use properties that are built for a special purpose usually carry long-term leases contracted on a net basis and thus require less managing.

Managing industrial parks

Hazardous waste produced by industrial sites causes environmental concern. Runoff from waste into nearby streams and lakes pollutes and endangers fish and wildlife. Toxic chemicals from manufacturers of paint, waste material from medical laboratories, and surplus waste from other industrial plants that seep into the soil and groundwater are dangerous to our health. Special sites for radioactive waste created by nuclear power plants have been established in various parts of the country.

Farmland

A farm management company provides complete services for the farm landowner. Concerned with assuring the owner maximum returns from the land, a farm management specialist analyzes the farm to evaluate its production potential.

One of the first steps is to take an inventory of the farm's soil and physical resources. The management service will also evaluate the farm's conservation practices, with the proper use of waterways and/or terrace construction, and maintenance. The farm may be adaptable to irrigation and might therefore produce a greater return for the tenant and the owner. If the soil is wet, it may be necessary to complete a tilling program to carry water away from the wet areas and thus provide more land for farming or to make the area less prone to flooding and therefore produce a higher yielding crop. The farm manager takes preventive measures to eliminate as much soil erosion as possible.

Managing agricultural property

Rotating crops prevents the exhaustion of the land's natural minerals. Crop planning also includes cost-efficient fertilizer in co-op quantities. Savings can be passed on to the owners.

The professional farm manager is responsible for the selection of the best tenant possible with lease terms on a share crop, cash rent, guaranteed bushel, or net lease basis.

By keeping abreast of the many marketing techniques available, the manager is able to offer suggestions on handling the sale of the crop to maximize profits. This may include deferred payment, price-later contracts, cash sales, or hedging.

Finally, the farm manager maintains accurate records on the farm's production to improve the returns of the farm. Complete accounting is provided for the landowner with completely audited financial statements listing expenses paid and income received from the farm. The farm management firm reviews proper insurance programs and makes recommendations to the landowner. The firm reviews and pays the real estate taxes and incorporates the data into the financial statements. The managers prepare annual summaries for the landowners for use in their income tax preparation.

With the increase of farmland being sold to corporations, the need for knowledgeable farm managers has become greater.

Special Purpose Properties

Special purpose properties include churches, resorts, theaters, clubs, schools, retirement and nursing homes, hotels and motels, and recreational sites. Each of these entities is unique to the business or activity that occurs there. Retirement communities have become more prevalent as people age. Each of these special purpose properties needs management that understands their particular needs and services.

Management Contracts

As you can see, the operations involved in such diversified real estate requires specialized training in the role of manager to properly serve the owner. Likewise, the **management contract** will differ, depending on the real estate under management.

Contents of a management contract

The contract between the principal and the manager should clearly define the responsibilities, obligations, and duties of the manager and the owner (see Figure 15.1). The contract should include the following basic items:

1. names of the parties to the contract
2. description of the property
3. the duration of the contract
4. terms of the contract
5. the management fees
6. the authority vested in the agent (owners will vary in the responsibility they relinquish to the manager)
7. a budget for operating expenses
8. a provision for monthly accounting by the manager to the owner
9. a statement as to purpose and goals

Figure 15.1   Example of a Management Contract

MANAGEMENT AGREEMENT

_____ (hereinafter called Owner), and _____
(hereinafter called Agent), agree as follows:

   A. The Owner hereby employs the Agent exclusively to rent and manage the property known as _____
upon the terms hereinafter set forth, for a period of _____ years beginning on the _____ day of _____, _____, and ending on the _____ day of _____, _____, and thereafter for yearly periods from time to time, unless on or before _____ the expiration of any such renewal period, either party hereto shall notify the other in writing that it decides to terminate this Agreement, in which case this Agreement shall be thereby terminated on said last mentioned date.

   B. The Agent Agrees:

      1. To accept the management of the above mentioned property and agrees to furnish services for the rental operation and management of the Premises.

      2. To render a monthly statement of receipts, disbursements and charges to the Owner and to remit each month the net proceeds (provided Agent is not required to make any mortgage, escrow or tax payment on the first day of the following month). Agent will remit the net proceeds or the balance thereof after making allowance for such payments to the Owner. In case the disbursements and charges shall be in excess of the receipts, the Owner agrees to pay such excess promptly, nothing herein contained shall obligate the Agent to advance its own funds on behalf of the Owner.

      3. The Agent agrees to have all employees who handle any money to be bonded.

   C. The Owner Agrees: To give the Agent the following authority and powers (all or any which may be exercised in the name of the Owner) and agrees to assume all expenses in connection therewith:

      1. To advertise the property, to display signs, and to rent said property. Agent will investigate prospective tenants and to sign leases, renew and or cancel existing leases and prepare and execute the new lease. To terminate tenancies and to sign and serve such notices as are deemed needful by the Agent; to institute and prosecute actions to remove tenants and to recover possession of the property; to sue for and recover rent: and, when expedient, to settle, compromise and release such actions or suits, or reinstate such tenancies.

      2. To collect rents due or to become due and issue receipts to deposit all funds collected hereunder in the Agent's custodial account.

      3. To refund tenants' security deposits at the expiration of leases.

      4. To hire, discharge and pay all caretakers and other employees; to make all ordinary repairs and replacements necessary to preserve the property in its present condition and for the operating efficiency thereof and all alterations and decorating required to comply with lease requirements and to enter into agreements for all necessary repairs and maintenance; to purchase supplies and pay all bills.

         a. To indemnify, defend and save the Agent harmless from all suits in connection with the Premises and from liability for damage to property and injuries to or death of any employee or other person whomsoever, and to carry at his (its) own expense public liability, and workmen's compensation insurance naming the Owner and the Agent and adequate to protect their interests.

      5. To pay any expenses incurred by the Agent, including, without limitation, attorney's fees for counsel employed to represent the Agent or the Owner.

      6. Owner agrees to pay to said agent _____ per month or _____ percent (___%) of the monthly gross receipts from the operation of the Premises during the period this Agreement remains in full force and effect, whichever is the greater amount.

      7. This Agreement may be cancelled by Owner before the termination date specified in Paragraph 1 on not less than _____ days prior written notice to the Agent, provided that such notice is accompanied by payment to the Agent of a cancellation fee in an amount equal to _____% of the management fee that would accrue over the remainder of the stated term of the Agreement. For this purpose the monthly management fee for the remainder of the stated term shall be presumed to be the same as that of the last month prior to service of the notice of cancellation.

   IN WITNESS WHEREOF, the parties hereto have affixed or caused to be affixed their respective signatures this _____ day of _____, _____.

_____   _____
Witness   Owner

_____   _____
Witness   Agent

The Management Plan

Before the contract is signed, a physical inspection of the exterior and interior of the property should be made. Deferred maintenance may need immediate attention, and minor problem areas should be prioritized. The manager must know the owner's objectives and make the owner aware of current market conditions, what the competition is, and what rents can be expected. The owner should be informed of this information on an ongoing basis. Since the owner's potential income is in direct proportion to vacancies and operating expenses, a careful plan should be formed to meet these objectives.

A typical plan used by an office building management firm would include the following:

1. assigning an experienced licensed property manager to the project
2. supervision of all services performed whether by in-house or by outside contractors with bids solicited and awarded for contractor services such as cleaning and security and supervision of contractors once bids are awarded
3. serving as a general contractor or supervising general contractors for leasehold and capital improvements
4. handling all tenant relations, including lease renewals
5. collecting rents, paying bills, and providing operating statements itemizing income and expenses on a timely basis
6. preparing an annual budget of the financial operation
7. providing maintenance personnel, as necessary, to perform repairs and maintenance of the property
8. maintaining 24-hour accessibility of the assigned property manager to immediately handle emergencies that arise at the property regardless of time or duration
9. setting up all mechanical systems not under warranty on either service contracts or in-house maintenance programs

Functions of the Manager

The manager's function is threefold:

1. secure and retain tenants, thus generating income
2. preserve the property's value by conscientious care and maintenance
3. provide financial accounting and records for the investor

Renting the Space

The primary goal of the manager is to market the client's space to yield the greatest net return. Whether the space is living accommodations, office space, or commercial space, the prospective tenant will be seeking the most advantageous location for the tenant's needs at the best price available. The manager's task is to achieve and maintain a high occupancy rate with a low turnover rate.

The manager may need to adjust the rental rate if the supply of rentals is greater than the demand. However, care must be taken not to favor any one tenant by reducing rent on a particular unit.

In leasing commercial areas it is wise to reserve space for a growing tenant to expand into by filling in with a tenant needing less space. Allowing the larger tenant an area for expansion may prevent the business from moving at a later date. It is not unusual to give a large anchor tenant concessions to induce other businesses to locate in the complex.

Collecting Rent

In an apartment complex, the tenant pays the rent when due without receiving a statement. If there is a resident manager on the premises, the rent typically is paid to that person. If business space is rented, the lease will state where the rent is to be sent. If the lessee repeatedly submits a rent payment late, the manager can determine the cause, and if it is simply thoughtlessness on the part of the lessee, a reminder a few days before would be wise. The management must have in place a collection policy that is diplomatic, yet definite. The investor relies on the management to retain tenants and collect rents so that the investment is protected.

Communications

It is imperative that management can communicate and have a good relationship with the tenants. A pleasant personality and a caring attitude is essential. Many large apartment complexes have bulletin boards to post weekly activities and any changes in the rules and regulations of the complex. Some managers print monthly newsletters that include scheduled activities, area events, or news that would be of interest to the tenants. Also, the tenants should be notified of any impending improvements that may be an inconvenience, such as repaving parking stalls or painting hallways.

The happy tenant does not move readily. The caring manager provides prompt servicing of any repairs in the tenant's unit. For the tenant who has leased the space for a long period of time, shampooing the carpet, repainting the unit, or replacing an old appliance is another means of retaining the tenant.

Advertising

An advertising program should be planned in advance and provided for in the annual budget. The vacancy factor in the area will greatly determine the type of advertising needed. For example, if the vacancy rate is high, a simple ad will not catch the consumer's attention. Apartment ads offering incentives, such as the first month's rent free or moving expense allowance, are not unusual to see. Good places to start an advertising campaign are the yellow pages of the telephone directory and the local newspaper. Some cities print apartment directories on a monthly basis; newcomers to the area often look to these for assistance in deciding where to locate. Careful attention to the type of ad placed can help ensure attracting the people the apartment complex would like to have as tenants. However, in no manner may advertising be discriminatory.

Employees

Selecting the staff

Property managers will select personnel with care, since the managers are accountable to the employer for their actions. By carefully interviewing applicants to evaluate their abilities, desires, and ambitions and following up with a good training program and adequate supervision, the manager can build a staff of conscientious employees. As word of the manager's expertise spreads, her business will expand.

Rather than having salaried staff hired to perform certain jobs, the manager may consider contracting out the work. This possibility depends on the size of the project and the labor force obtainable in the area. Managers may be able to hire certain services for less than the cost of a salaried employee. Electrical and plumbing repairs, replacing drywall, painting, and staining usually require specialized labor, so contracting for these services is often necessary.

Maintenance and Cleaning Services

To preserve the property's physical condition the manager sees that the property is kept clean and attractive. As mentioned above, prompt attention to tenant repairs will result in contented and cooperative tenants. The manager conducts routine inspections and supervises the maintenance of the complex. Manicured lawns, trimmed hedges, clean walls and floors in the corridors, and keeping all facilities in working conditions are the manager's responsibility to ensure the preservation of the client's investment.

Property maintenance falls into four categories.

1. *Preventive* maintenance of such items as mechanical equipment should be conducted on a regular basis. Changing filters on furnaces and air conditioners assures good performance and longer use of the units. Lubricating motors and working parts and repairing worn fan belts all result in better functioning and preservation of the equipment.

2. *Corrective* maintenance requires repairing any malfunctioning equipment. Plumbing problems such as leaky faucets and obstructed drains and broken furnaces, air conditioners, and water heaters are some of the items that may need repair, especially as a building ages.

3. *Ordinary* repair and cleaning involves the regular routine followed in the cleaning of entries, halls, and other common areas. Repairs that are needed, such as tacking down a torn carpet or mending a broken rail in a stair, are normal day-to-day maintenance.

4. *Construction* maintenance involves new space or renovation of existing space. It may consist of remodeling by moving walls, repainting, and

updating. Remodeling may be necessary to attract tenants and additionally adds value to the structure. Shopping malls especially need to update their facades and general appearance to lure tenants and shoppers.

Careful maintenance by the diligent manager will prevent costs at a later date that could have been avoided. This is one of the criteria of efficient management. Also, inspecting mechanical equipment each season ensures good performance and longer use.

Security and Safety

Adequate safety precautions are necessary to ensure the welfare and safety of the tenants and lessen the possibility of crime. Sufficient lighting, especially in shopping mall parking lots, will assist in deterring crime. Appropriate lighting in entries and hallways and monitoring on a regular basis for burnt-out bulbs should be standard care. Some apartment buildings and office complexes have television monitors at entries and others employ security guards.

To prevent criminal activity, locks and keys should be changed when new tenants take possession of the space. A variety of security devices are available. Older buildings may need to be updated to meet today's standards. Security arrangements to handle emergencies should be provided; these vary greatly depending on whether it is an apartment, office, or industrial building.

Resident managers should be alert to illegal drug activity or any menace that would jeopardize the safety of the tenants. They may organize periodic meetings with the tenants to discuss safety conditions and any new rules and regulations.

Smoke detectors should be located on every floor of a multilevel building so an alarm is sounded automatically in the event of a fire. Sprinkler systems that will automatically turn on if a fire occurs are another means of alerting tenants of fire danger.

The Budget

The manager prepares a financial plan that includes an annual budget for financial operation of the property. Operating statements itemizing income and expenses are presented to the owner on a timely basis. The budget outlines the expected return and expenses calculated from past years' performances, but expected trends relative to economic conditions must be considered. The budget provides the investor with a base line from which to measure the property manager's performance. Managers are often paid incentives for keeping a property at maximum capacity.

The detailed accounting of expenditures and disbursements to the owners indicates whether the manager is controlling expenses and producing the greatest net return possible for the owners without neglecting maintenance needs. He supervises the maintenance employees to ascertain that the work is skillfully accomplished with materials acquired at a reasonable rate. By insisting upon proper vouchers and receipts, the manager maintains efficient control of costs.

Operating Statement

Figure 15.2	A Typical Monthly Income and Expense Report on an Apartment Complex

INCOME & EXPENSE REPORT

Property Address: 12534 Money Lane   July 2008

Income:

18 Units @ $575	$10,350	
8 Units @ $500	4,000	
6 Units @ $475	2,850	
Total	$17,200	

Less Vacancy

1 Unit @ $500	$ 500	
Manager's Unit	475	
Total Rent		$16,225

Other Income:

Garages 20 @ $50	$ 1,000	1,000
TOTAL INCOME		$17,225

Expenses:
Salaries:

Resident Manager	$ 2,000	
Property Manager	$ 1,500	$3,500

Fixed Expenses

Insurance	305	
Taxes	580	885

Variable Expenses

Maintenance	480	
Utilities	550	1,030

Capital Expenditures

1 Refrigerator	850	
Paint	250	1,100

TOTAL EXPENSES	$6,515	
NET INCOME		$10,710
DEBT SERVICE	$2,400	
CASH FLOW		$ 8,310

A typical **management budget** for an apartment complex should contain the following items of expenses:

1. Operating expenses and maintenance service
    a. supplies
    b. painting and decorating

  c. salaries

  d. services

  e. repairs

 2. Utility expenses

  a. heating fuel

  b. electricity

  c. gas

  d. water

 3. Fixed charges

  a. real estate taxes

  b. insurance

The property manager should create a monthly written income and expense report for the owner (see Figure 15.2).

Summary of Important Points

1. Property managers are employed to tend and care for the owner's real estate investment.

2. While some investors may purchase farmland, others buy shopping centers, office buildings, or residential complexes. Since investments vary so greatly, specialization in management is required.

3. A great deal of expertise is mandatory since the property manager must try to protect the owner's investment and obtain the largest net return the property is capable of producing.

4. The manager has a detailed plan of the duties and responsibilities the property owner requires the manager to fulfill.

5. The manager's duties and responsibilities include renting the space and collecting the rent, hiring employees, maintaining the property, ensuring security, communicating with the owner and tenants, and advertising as needed.

6. The manager is the liaison between the owners and the tenants, handling the tenants' complaints and guarding the owner's interests.

7. Property maintenance includes preventive care, corrective maintenance, ordinary repair and cleaning, and constructive maintenance when necessary.

8. A budget is prepared for the financial operation of the property.

9. At the end of each month a detailed accounting of expenditures and disbursements is submitted to the owners.

Discussion Points

1. Explain why specialization in property management is important.
2. Once a commercial building is leased, why is continuous management necessary, since the leases are often long term?
3. List some of the responsibilities and obligations of the apartment manager. How do the duties of the resident manager differ from those of the property management firm?
4. What items should be incorporated into a management contract?
5. Who plans the operating budget and why is one necessary?
6. Discuss which recurring expenses are monthly costs and which are annual costs.
7. You have decided to specialize in property management. What type of property would you prefer to handle? Give reasons for your answer.
8. Why can an investor derive more net income from hiring a management firm?

Review Questions

Answers to these questions are found in the Answer Key section at the back of the book.

1. A property management contract would NOT contain:
   a. the responsibilities assigned to the manager
   b. terms of the contract
   c. the property owner's obligations
   d. renters' names

2. The manager's responsibilities include:
   a. selecting tenants on the basis of the space they require
   b. selecting and retaining tenants
   c. keeping an accurate account of his own salary
   d. advertising only when the building becomes 15 percent vacant

3. Upon signing a management contract with an owner, a broker becomes a:
   a. trustee
   b. receiver
   c. management director
   d. fiduciary

4. All of the following would be included in a typical manager's operating budget EXCEPT:
   a. the investor's profit
   b. decorating and painting
   c. the manager's salary
   d. cleaning supplies

5. Management is NOT needed by which of the following?
   a. an absentee owner
   b. an investment syndicate
   c. busy investors
   d. a resident

6. Which of the following considerations is important in selecting tenants?
   a. the compatibility of tenants
   b. the ethnic background of tenants, since this would be proof of stability
   c. the number of employees in the tenant's business and the number of customers they will serve
   d. obtaining percentage leases from tenants of office space

7. A resident manager will usually perform which of the following duties?
   a. efficient marketing of the space
   b. showing units and obtaining leases
   c. paying complex's taxes
   d. paying complex's mortgage

8. A property manager's responsibilities include all of the following EXCEPT:
   a. paying utilities
   b. investing profits
   c. renting units
   d. collecting security deposits

9. When calculating operating income, a property manager would include which of the following?
   a. income taxes
   b. allowance for vacancies and collections
   c. mortgage payments
   d. allowance for depreciation

10. All of the following statements concerning property management are true EXCEPT:
    a. a manager of commercial property would not necessarily understand farm management
    b. residential management includes the managing of condominiums
    c. managers care for the absentee owner's property
    d. the largest role of the manager is in the management of commercial property

11. This item on an income and expense report would be placed under capital expenditures:
    a. utilities
    b. insurance
    c. debt service
    d. oven and range

12. These items are always a fixed expense:
    a. maintenance and utilities
    b. insurance and taxes
    c. resident and property manager's salaries
    d. paint and repairs

13. Commercial rents are almost always based upon:
    a. the annual rate per cubic foot
    b. an annual or monthly rate per square foot
    c. a monthly rate based on the space leased
    d. a graduate scale

14. If a 3,200-square-foot commercial space rents for $9.00 a square foot, the rent per month would be:
    a. $240
    b. $2,400
    c. $2,880
    d. $28,800

15. An example of preventive maintenance is:
    a. repairing a leaky faucet
    b. changing furnace filters
    c. renovating an existing building
    d. cleaning common areas

Investment and Tax Aspects of Ownership

KEY TERMS

adjusted basis

basis

cash flow

corporations

depreciation

gain

general partnership

installment sale

joint venture

leverage

limited partnership

negative cash flow

partnership

passive income

prospectus

Real Estate Investment Trust (REIT)

S Corporation

salvage value

Securities and Exchange Commission (SEC)

straight-line depreciation

syndication

tax-free exchange

tax shelter

useful life

OVERVIEW

Since food, clothing, and shelter are essential to our very existence, most Americans decide it is more prudent to permanently own that shelter than to rent. Ownership of real estate creates the greatest portion of the estate the average person acquires. Inflation contributes to the appreciation of real estate, and most homeowners soon become cognizant of the equity building up in their homes. The sector of the country where the property is located and the local demands for housing determine appreciation of real estate. The high interest rates of the early 1980s slowed that appreciation to a standstill in many parts of the country. As interest rates began to drop in the latter part of 1982, real estate transfers again began to increase. In early 1986 interest rates dropped to 10 percent and 10.5 percent and began to stabilize, causing an increase in refinancing that kept financing institutions busy as homeowners sought the lower rates. Home sales were brisk with the backlog of consumers who felt they could now afford to purchase a home. In early 1987 interest rates had dropped to 8 percent and 8.5 percent, something not seen for many years, making homeownership even more within the realm of possibility for the average American.

The decade of the 1990s began with interest rates at 9.5 percent to 10.5 percent, and a slowing of the economy began. By 1993 the recessionary conditions brought interest rates down to 6 percent and 6.5 percent, followed by a thriving economy. As the 21st century approached, interest rates began to plummet. By 2007 they were in the 5 percent range, and once again a rush to refinance began.

This chapter is divided into two distinct areas:

1. investing in a residence
2. investing in income-producing real estate

It will explain the advantages of homeownership as an investment, illustrating the true principal and interest payments when the tax deductions are considered.

The income benefits that the investor in real estate receives will also be covered with a step-by-step analysis of an investment.

Homeownership as an Investment

Homeownership provides more than shelter; it is one of the most substantial investments that most people make. Owning a home not only enhances pride and self-worth but also provides a hedge against inflation.

The Tax Reform Act of 1986 (TRA 86) brought some sweeping changes to the nation's tax laws, some of which affect the real estate investment market, but the benefits of homeownership remain intact. Itemized deductions are retained on real estate taxes, and mortgage interest continues to be deductible for first and second homes.

Mortgage interest & tax deductible expenses

The owner of a primary residence and a second vacation home can still deduct interest paid on the mortgages and the real estate taxes. To qualify as a vacation home, the property must be occupied more than 14 days annually or 10 percent of its useful rental period. If it is used fewer than 14 days or less than 10 percent of its useful period, it is considered investment property and is eligible for depreciation in addition to deducting property taxes and mortgage insurance. An added incentive to purchase real estate is that interest is deductible from taxable income.

Home equity loans

Taxpayers can borrow on their homes (such loans are referred to as home equity loans) up to the original purchase price, plus any added improvements, and the interest on such a loan will be deductible. The Tax Reform Act of 1986 stipulates that loans backed by the appreciated value of a home, but used for purposes other than home improvements (consumer loans), are not deductible unless the proceeds are used for tuition or other educational costs or for medical expenses. Generally, it is not permissible to deduct interest paid on loans above the market value of the property.

Calculating the Benefits of Homeownership

Tax benefits of investing in real estate are reflected by an individual's gross income. For example, assume a married couple, filing jointly, will pay 28 percent income tax on their earnings. Owning a home allows the following deductions if the couple is paying on a $70,000 mortgage at 8 percent interest:

$70,000	mortgage
× .08	interest rate
$ 5,600	annual interest
× .28	tax bracket
$ 1,568	tax savings allowable

Now assume the mortgage is for 15 years. Principal and interest payments would be $9.56 for $1,000 (see amortization chart in Chapter 11), or $669.20 per month. With the tax deduction for interest that is paid, the monthly payment is effectively lowered by $130.66 to $538.54 ($1,568 interest ÷ 12 months = $130.66 per month).

In addition, the homeowner may also deduct a portion of the property taxes paid. If the taxes are $1,800 per year, 28 percent of $1,800 = $504.00 tax savings. Dividing $504 by 12 months reduces the monthly payment another $42.00, leaving an actual monthly house cost of $496.54. Add to these tax advantages the fact that equity is building and that the investment is very likely appreciating in value, and we see why people purchase rather than rent.

Appreciation and Homeownership

As construction costs and land prices rise, real estate continues to appreciate in value in many parts of the country. As discussed in Chapter 1, the supply of funds and market conditions in a given area will affect this value. More people are becoming aware that owning shelter not only brings pride of ownership but also a degree of appreciation in their investment. The demand for housing continues to grow as young adults are realizing the value of owning real estate. With people living longer, housing requirements are being constructed to meet the particular needs of each generation.

Depreciation of a Residence

A homeowner cannot depreciate property considered a residence unless a portion of that residence is used as an office; in such a case, depreciation is allowable along with deductions of business expenses. In effect, the law refrains from considering the building a residence if a portion is used for business. For example, if one room in a six-room house is used as an office, then one-sixth of the expenses of that residence may be deductible. With the advent of computers, fax machines, e-mail, and other communication technology, combined with the

Home business deductions

entrepreneurial spirit of many self-employed persons, the home office is becoming more prevalent.

How Tax Provisions Affect Sale of Principal Residence

Effective August 5, 1997, a tax bill was passed that provides substantial benefits to taxpayers who sell their principal residence. The new exclusion replaces and greatly expands the old $125,000 one-time exclusion allowed for taxpayers age 55 or over. The amount has been increased to $500,000 for married taxpayers who file a joint return; the exclusion for taxpayers who do not file a joint return is $250,000. This exclusion can be claimed every two years. Effective January 20, 2008, if one spouse dies, there is a two-year limit on the sale of property to maintain the $500,000 exclusion. It is no longer necessary to purchase a new principal residence within a 24-month period preceding or following the sale. The new exclusion does not impose any age restrictions, thus any seller is eligible. The seller must satisfy the following criteria.

1. *Ownership*: The residence must have been *owned* for a minimum of two years of the five-year period ending on the date of the sale.
2. *Use*: The property must have been *used* as the principal residence for periods aggregating at least two years of the five-year period ending on the date of the sale.
3. *Waiting period*: The *waiting* period requires that the owner must not have utilized this exclusion for any sale during the preceding two-year period.

Dates of marriage and types of ownership can have some effect on these provisions. For instance, the ownership test is satisfied if *either* you or your spouse owns the property for two of the five years ending on the date of the sale as the threshold requirement for claiming the $500,000 exclusion (as opposed to the $250,000 exclusion) is joint filing status, not joint ownership. However, there is no exception to this rule for newly married couples; they both must have used the house as their principal residence. In this scenario, the party that lived in the residence for the two-year period could claim a $250,000 exclusion.

Any losses on the sale of a principal residence remain nondeductible. If a gain is less than $250,000, the unused portion simply disappears and cannot be applied to a future sale. However, you will again be eligible for the entire exclusion two years after you sell your current residence.

If the seller qualifies for the exclusion, the first $250,000 ($500,000 for qualifying married taxpayers) of gain on the sale of the principal residence is not taxable. Any gain that exceeds this exclusion is subject to tax at capital gains rates in effect on the date of the sale. Effective May 7, 1997, the new rules reduced the capital gains tax rate from 28 percent to 20 percent (10 percent for taxpayers in the 15 percent tax bracket). There are a number of phase-in provisions affecting the rate paid.

1. To qualify for the 20 percent rate, an 18-month holding period applies to assets sold after July 28, 1997.
2. Depreciation recapture on real property is taxed at a 25 percent rate.
3. The maximum rate is scheduled to drop to 18 percent for assets acquired after December 31, 2000 and held for at least five years.

The **basis** is **adjusted**; that is, the **gain** on the old residence is subtracted from the costs of the new residence. For example:

1990 purchase price	$65,000
1992 added family room	8,500
Adjusted basis	$73,500
2008 sale price	88,000
Less selling expenses	6,330
	$81,670
Less adjusted basis	73,500
Gains from sale	8,170
New purchase	95,000
Less gain from sale	8,170
Adjusted basis	$86,830

Determining the Basis for Measuring Gain

The beginning point is calculating the purchase price of the residence. If the gain from a prior residence was rolled over, the gain that was realized and deferred must be subtracted from the cost of the present residence. If a rollover was done, a review of IRS Form 2119, entitled "Sale of Your Home," should be made. It includes a detailed worksheet to assist in determining the correct basis on your present home after the rollover of the earlier gain.

Accurate records of all improvements should be retained. Regular maintenance costs are not deductible. Only capital improvements, such as installing an air conditioner, building fences, landscaping, and adding decks and patios, are deductible items.

Costs incurred in the sale are deductible from the amount realized. These selling expenses are the actual costs involved in the sale, such as the broker's commission, legal fees, state transfer taxes, and title insurance or abstract fees.

Selling at a Loss

If a homeowner is forced to sell at a loss, the tax laws do not, regretfully, provide any assistance benefits. The *loss is not tax deductible.* The rationale is that the home was not purchased as a "for profit" investment. Gains from the sale of personal assets are taxable income, but losses are not deductible.

Real Estate as an Income-Producing Investment

Investing in real estate

American Investors in Real Estate: www.aireo.com

The investment in real estate serves many functions. With the realization that real estate is a great hedge against inflation, the number of people investing in income-producing property has grown. Leading economists have found by tracking real estate values through the years that prices keep pace with inflation.

Purchasing Real Estate vs. Fixed Income Investment

The main reasons for investing in real estate are:

1. appreciation
2. cash flow
3. equity buildup
4. tax shelter

Advantages of real estate investment

The primary purpose of the investor is to generate income (cash flow) and to achieve long-term growth of capital without substantial risk. Our most precious resource is time, and income gained other than through one's labor can be realized by limiting present spending in favor of future benefits. A person seeking a fixed return can invest in Treasury bills, certificates of deposit (CDs), corporate or municipal bonds, stocks, or savings accounts. These forms of savings are secure and produce a fixed income that is easily converted to cash, keeping in mind that early withdrawal may carry a penalty. However, inflation erodes the future purchasing power of these investment dollars. In the case of real estate, appreciation has been a big factor in attracting investors, and for many of these investors, the compelling motive is not only income but the favorable tax advantages connected with investment property.

Financial planners recommend a balanced portfolio, altering the investments to accommodate the individual's age and present and projected incomes. Investments may include buying silver, gold, coins, paintings, stamps, automobiles, and other desirable collector items. An element of risk is involved in speculative investments, and liquidating them may prove difficult with the true value unobtainable when the investor wants to cash out. Young people may look at speculative stocks while retirees will prefer investments in annuities and CDs to augment their social security payments. A well-rounded portfolio of investments may include several approaches to saving. Unfortunately, when people reach the recognized retirement age of 65, less than 10 percent have saved sufficiently to meet their retirement years with total independence. This is a startling revelation, but it is never too late to begin an investment program. For people involved in real estate, the obvious answer is to purchase what they sell.

Most people accumulate the largest portion of their estate through the equity that builds in homeownership. Thus, it only seems logical that investing in income-producing real estate would further enhance their savings.

Risk and Return

Regardless of what is used as a vehicle to increase one's wealth, the old adage "the higher the risk, the greater the return" holds true. A premium is paid for certainty and security. If we can receive 5 percent on a CD that requires no risk or management concerns, why would we invest in real estate and receive only 5 percent return? The bright side of risk is the potential of gain, and the dark side is the potential of loss. When money is lent in the anticipation of receiving the principal (money lent) back plus a return on the principal, referred to as interest, we are risking the return.

Cash Flow

Ideally, an investment property will yield a positive **cash flow**. The cash flow represents the net proceeds after all expenses are met and may be measured before or after taxes are considered. If an investor has a property that generates an annual income of $44,000 and expenses total $35,000, a net return (cash flow) of $9,000 has been earned.

Calculating net return

Income from office building		$44,000
Expenses	17,000	
Debt service (mortgage payment)	18,000	
Cash flow		$ 9,000

If the tax-deductible expenses involved in a property are greater than the income, there will be, for tax purposes, a **negative cash flow**. To some investors this negative cash flow is desirable because their main concern is to have a **tax shelter**. A tax shelter is best defined as a book loss; it is simply a phrase used to describe some of the advantages of real estate investments. Since investment property can be depreciated as an expense when figuring income tax, it provides a tax shelter for its owner. For example:

Negative cash flow

Income		$44,000
Expenses	22,000	
Interest deduction	16,000	
Depreciation deduction	8,000	
	$46,000	$44,000 = ($2,000 loss)

The owner has a book loss of $2,000. Prior to the passage of TRA 86, owning improved real estate proved to be one of the few, as well as one of the best, methods for sheltering income. The optimum situation results when the property shows a book loss but still has a positive cash flow.

With TRA 86, much of the special tax treatment that was accorded to taxpayers' investment activities was phased out. Generally, the bill considers these investments (including rental properties) **passive income**, that is, not containing the taxpayers' active involvement. Previously a taxpayer's income or loss from all sources were combined and the net amount taxed (with the exception of capital gains or losses) at the graduated rates. Today there are three classifications for income:

Income classification

1. *Active income*: earned by salaries or a business in which the taxpayer materially participates
2. *Portfolio income*: interest, annuities, dividends, royalties, and profit from the sale of portfolio assets
3. *Passive activity income*: invested funds

Losses from passive investments may no longer be used to offset ordinary income. The taxpayer may only deduct these losses from passive investments against income from passive investment; they may not be applied against active or portfolio income. The IRS has described passive investments as all rental income, interests in limited partnerships, and all other business involvements in which the taxpayer is not involved in the operation on a regular and substantial basis. Exempt are working oil and gas properties.

Losses up to $25,000 from real estate rental activities in which the taxpayer actively participates may be used to offset salaries and active business income. This $25,000 amount, however, is phased down to a 50 percent ratio for those taxpayers with income between $100,000 and $150,000. Any losses on real estate investments in excess of these amounts will be treated as passive investment losses; and the $25,000 amount is eliminated entirely.

Rate of Return

The value of an asset is determined by the stream of income it produces over the expected life of the investment. The return on the individual's cash investment can vary greatly, *depending on the ratio of cash invested to the purchase price,* and also on the *cost of financing.*

Determining
investment return

To evaluate the feasibility of an investment, the investors decide what percentage of return they want on their investment and examine the return on the actual investment. If they know they can receive a certain percentage return on CDs or Treasury bonds, they will expect more from a real estate investment because of the risks involved. However, income tax must be paid on the interest earned from savings. With a real estate investment, the earnings can be sheltered since the improvements can be depreciated.

In the income approach technique for evaluating property investments, the property's net annual income is divided by the desired rate of return. If an investor requires a 12 percent annual return and the property has a $15,000 net annual income, he should pay no more than $125,000.

$$\frac{\$15,000}{12\%} \begin{array}{l} \text{(net annual income)} \\ \text{(investor's desired} \\ \text{rate of return)} \end{array} = \begin{array}{l} \$125,000 \text{ (value of property if} \\ \text{investor is willing to accept a 12\%} \\ \text{rate of return)} \end{array}$$

The rate of investor's desired rate of return relates net operating income to the investment.

In using this capitalization method of evaluating an income-producing property, the future income is converted to present value. When the risk is greater, the capitalization rate is higher, thus the value of the income stream is lessened as the capitalization rate increases. Since a property will depreciate and lessen in value as its economic life is depleted, this must be taken into consideration when analyzing the possibility of recapturing the investment. If the remaining life of the property is 25 years, and it is depreciated on a straight-line basis, the property will depreciate at 4 percent a year. As the property depreciates, the income will likewise decline. Since the investor desires a 12 percent return on the investment, the 4 percent (recapture rate) must be added to supply the full return on the investment. Thus, in looking for a 16 percent return, the value of the property in the previous example is now reduced to $93,750.

Capitalizing income property

$$\frac{\$15,000}{16\%} \begin{array}{l} \text{(income)} \\ \text{(rate of return)} \end{array} = \$93,750 \text{ (property value to investor)}$$

Depreciation

Depreciation, as we will discuss it here, is an accounting concept used in federal tax law. It makes available to an investor in real estate a deduction from income derived from a property. For accounting and tax purposes, depreciation is based on estimates of a property's future decrease in value. Even as the investor depreciates his property, it continues to increase in value due to rising construction costs and land values. The realization of this depreciation allowance is further enhanced if the investor has used little of his resources to purchase the property. (For example, if a $60,000 property was acquired with $12,000 in cash and the balance from a loan, the investor was still able to depreciate on the *full* value of the structure.) After the value of its **useful life** (economic life) is over, the **salvage value** remains.

Property will decrease in value

The past two decades have brought dramatic changes in the depreciation methods allowed by the Internal Revenue Service. Prior to 1981, an investor chose one of four methods to depreciate any property or asset eligible for the depreciation allowance. In 1981 Congress passed the Tax Recovery Act, referred to as the Accelerated Cost Recovery System (ACRS). This act replaced the concept of "depreciating" the property with "recovering the cost," enabling the investor to use short-term write-off periods for tax purposes.

Further changes were introduced as a result of TRA 86. This act stated that residential rental property placed in service after January 1, 1987, must be depreciated on a straight-line basis over 27½ years, and that nonresidential real estate must be depreciated on a straight-line basis over 31½ years. TRA 1993 amended this to increase the depreciable lives of nonresidential properties placed in service on or after May 13, 1993. **Straight-line depreciation** is depreciation of the asset figured in equal installments over a predetermined period of time. (Automobiles and light trucks may be depreciated over five years and manufacturing equipment over a seven-year period.) Additionally, any losses resulting from depreciation cannot be used to shelter other "earned" income.

Straight-line Depreciation
Equal amounts over allowable life of the property for tax purposes

Depreciation can be taken only on the improvements and *not on the land itself,* since land does not diminish in value—literally, it does not wear out. Tax assessors separate the land and improvements when they appraise the property for tax purposes. Assuming that the market value and the cost of the property were the same as the assessed value, the following is an example of the annual depreciation cost of a single-family residential rental:

Depreciation only on improvements

Address:	7007 Mulberry Drive
Legal:	Lot 3, Block 7, Fall Rapids Subdivision
Land value:	$ 32,000
Improvements:	$ 88,000
Assessed value:	$120,000

Since the example that we have used here is a residential rental property, the amount that can be depreciated must be done over 27½ years. Continuing with our example:

Improvements:	$ 88,000 ÷ 27.5 (years)
	$ 3,200 = Annual amount available for depreciation

Leverage

The investor may borrow money to finance the greater share of an investment. By using other people's money the investor's buying power is increased. This use of borrowed funds is called **leverage**. The investor wants to put the least possible amount down and obtain the lowest available interest rate over the longest period of time. This allows the investor to accumulate the maximum amount of real estate with the minimum amount of personal funds.

Using other people's money

However, for the investor expecting a cash flow, the expenses and mortgage costs may well exceed the returns if too much leverage is used. While tax shelters, appreciation, and cash flow are all great motivators for purchasing, the investment must not be leveraged to the point that a positive cash flow is impossible. The choice the investor selects must have reasonable likelihood of satisfying the objective of increasing the purchaser's net worth. Not only does the present value need to be considered, but its future income stream should be analyzed. Mentioned earlier in this text were the forces that influence value. If the investor buys with the intention of selling or if conditions develop that necessitate a sale, economic conditions may not be conducive to a quick sale. The *lack of liquidity* is one of the biggest risk factors involved in owning real estate.

Let us take a property and analyze the difference on the rate of return when cash is paid versus leveraging with a mortgage.

1. Cash investment:

   $125,000 investment with a $15,000 net income

   $15,000 ÷ $125,000 = 12 percent return

2. Investment financed:

   $125,000 investment

   $93,750 mortgage (75%) = $31,250 equity invested subtract one year's interest at 10% ($9,375.00) from

   $15,000 = $5,625 net income.

   $5,625 (net income) ÷ $31,250 (initial investment) = 18% return annually.

Remember, the above figures on investment/financing are predicated on the rate of return on the equity invested. To many investors this is more meaningful since it considers only the amount of cash they have invested. The investment will be growing in equity and hopefully appreciating in value.

Investment Opportunities

There are various types of real estate investments from which to choose. The investor may purchase single-family homes, duplexes, fourplexes, apartments, condominiums, office buildings, strip shopping centers, farms, acreage, or bare development land. There is literally something for everyone. If the investor needs immediate income, vacant land would be a poor choice. Holding power is needed since property taxes, interest, and insurance are constant costs. The speculator gambles on the premise that the land will increase in value, a risk that all investors are not ready to assume.

Consider a typical American couple who own their own home. They have been able to accumulate $6,000 in savings, $5,000 of which they decide to use to purchase a rental house. After searching every weekend for the perfect unit, they make concessions and finally decide on an older two-story house that has been converted into two apartments and is located in a modest neighborhood. Inspections reveal newer wiring and two modern furnaces. No measurable deferred maintenance is observed. They purchase the property for $75,000 with a $70,000 loan at 8 percent interest for 20 years with monthly payments of $585.90. Insurance coverage costs $340.00 a year and annual taxes are $900. The units rent for $450 and $500 each.

Finding the right investment

Income

$450 @ 12 mos.	=	$5,400.00
$500 @ 12 mos.	=	6,000.00
Gross income	=	$11,400.00

Expenses

Insurance policy	$340.00
Supplies & materials	280.00
Taxes	900.00
Maintenance	320.00
Mortgage payments	7,030.80
	$8,870.80

$11,400.00 (income)

Net Income $ 2,027.00

This is not taking into consideration income tax deductions for interest and real estate taxes.

All physical labor such as yard care and minor repairs is done by the owners, and technically they should place a value on their time. Had the investors taken their $5,000 and invested it in a CD at 5 percent, the annual yield would have been $250, before taxes.

They realize that their profit can be wiped out if a unit remains vacant for a period of time. They have discussed with one tenant carpet replacement for his unit, with the tenant agreeing to a raise in rent from $450 to $475 a month. To recover the cost of the carpet will take two and a half years, but they are assured of a happy tenant who will not vacate the unit. The couple is pleased with their investment, and when their savings build up, they plan to search for another property.

Avoid overimproving

The principle of increasing and decreasing returns must be acknowledged. Continued improvement of a property will eventually reach a leveling-off point beyond which rents cannot be raised. To place microwaves, fireplaces, and jacuzzis in the units would not be a justifiable expense and would result in overimprovement.

The couple's upkeep and care of the property have enhanced its value, and they can use the equity in that investment to leverage buying another. They could either draw some of the equity out or use it as collateral for a blanket mortgage that could cover both properties.

Pyramiding investments

Now the *pyramiding* begins. If they were to continue the process, a portfolio of investments could be secured. The careful investor will not overleverage or the pyramid will come tumbling down. It should be built with the stability of an Egyptian pyramid and withstand all foreseeable obstacles.

The Investment Scenario

The investor now has additional taxable income; that is, the investor has spendable income plus the capital gains or equity income in the property. The investor can depreciate the real estate holdings, and the interest on the loan is deductible. The taxable income is the investment net, less interest and depreciation. The spendable income is the investment net, less principal, interest, and tax costs. The equity income is the investment net, less the income and interest, but adding the appreciation of the investment.

Income
· Taxable
· Spendable
· Builds equity

Rehabilitation Tax Credit

Congress passed an investment tax credit for investors who rehabilitate buildings that qualify as historical buildings or older buildings that can be placed back in service. The investor is saving a building and bringing it back onto the tax rolls. The allowable credit is 20 percent for certified historical buildings and 10 percent for other buildings built before 1936. A tax credit receives full value as a deduction on income tax, which is more favorable than the property tax. For example, if a taxpayer is in the 28 percent tax bracket, only that percentage of the property taxes is deductible; 28 percent of $1,500 (assumed taxes) = $420. The Rehabilitation Tax Credit would allow the full $1,500.

Refinancing vs. Selling

Equity builds up in an investment property through increased value of the property and principal reduction on the amortized loan. The owner can then refinance the property with a new loan and use the tax-free money to purchase another property. Since this is borrowed money, it is not taxable. By refinancing, taxes on gains are avoided since taxes are payable only on the sale of the property. The owner is now able to purchase additional properties with the money obtained through refinancing and thus can pyramid the holdings. By carefully choosing properties that increase in value, the owner can refinance each after holding the property for a reasonable period of time, depending on current market conditions, and use the money to purchase other properties. If the investor so chooses, taxes can be avoided forever by leaving the properties to heirs.

Freeing equity by refinancing

Tax-Deferred Exchanges and Installment Sales

To defer capital gains, an investor can make a **tax-free exchange** of the property for another like property. This simply means that *real estate must be exchanged for real estate*. A duplex could be exchanged for a sixplex, or an apartment could be traded for an office building. The quality of the property is not questioned. "Like kind" refers to the nature, class, or character of the real property. If it is not an equal exchange and additional money or goods are included, the extra money is called *boot* and, if it represents a gain, is taxed at the time of transfer. The depreciated book value of the old property will be carried to the new, and the adjustments for the additional compensation (boot) will be added to the property.

Exchanging property defers capital gains

Had the investor of the duplex at 7007 Mulberry Drive exchanged the property for another, taxes could have been deferred as follows:

| Duplex sale price | $120,000 | New fourplex | $180,000 |
| Adjusted basis | $ 41,000 | Boot needed | $ 60,000 |

The new **basis** for the fourplex is $101,000. This is the basis of the duplex, $41,000, carried over to the new purchase, plus the boot of $60,000.

When payment on the gross sale price of a property is received for a period of two or more years, the transaction qualifies as an **installment sale**. The seller is permitted to defer paying the capital gain tax on a prorated basis with receipt of the installments. A portion of the installment is treated as interest, a portion as capital gain, and a portion is nontaxable.

Capital Gains

The Taxpayer Relief Act of 1997 reestablished substantial savings in capital gains. As of May 6, 1997, the maximum capital gains tax rate is 20 percent. For individuals in the 15 percent tax bracket, tax on gains was lowered to 10 percent. Further savings were realized December 31, 2000. On any asset held for 5 or more years the taxable rate will be lowered to 18 percent, with 8 percent to individuals in the 15 percent tax bracket. The IRS Restructuring and Reform Act of 1998 lowered the retention period for real estate assets from 18 months to 12 months.

Group Business Venture

Many times business enterprises are formed by a group of individuals who have a common purpose in mind. Partnerships, corporations, syndications, and trusts hold real estate for business purposes. Investors join others in a **joint venture** since they can acquire larger properties by pooling their funds.

Pooling funds

**National Real Estate
Investors Association:
www.nationalreia.com**

Partnerships

Partnerships are formed by two or more people who join forces to carry out an idea together for profit-making reasons. The partnership may be operated in the name of the owners or in a trade name selected by the partners.

Two types of legally recognized partnerships exist: the *general partnership* and the *limited partnership.*

General Partnership

In the **general partnership** the individuals involved manage and operate the business. The partners take total responsibility for both profits and losses. Some of the disadvantages are as follows.

1. Each partner is personally liable for any debts incurred, and his personal assets may be attached.

2. One partner can obligate the others.

3. Death will terminate the partnership.

4. Consent of all partners is required for decisions.

5. Liquidity is questionable, since it may be difficult to sell a partnership interest.

The advantages include the following.

1. The partnership is not taxed (a corporation is).

2. Partners can share their money and expertise to build a business.

3. Partners are treated for tax purposes as active investors.

Limited Partnership

A **limited partnership** involves a general partner and two or more limited partners. Although the limited partners are the investors, they do not take an active role in management but are passive investors, and a general manager is paid to handle the investment. The general manager usually conceives and organizes the partnership. The agreement is so drawn that the death or withdrawal of one of the partners does not affect the partnership.

Joint investing in a limited partnership

Advantages of a limited partnership consist of these factors.

1. Limited partners are held responsible only to the amount of their investment.

2. The investor's liability is limited.

3. The investor has no management obligations.

Disadvantages of a limited partnership include the following:

1. Shares are difficult to sell or transfer since all partners usually must agree to the transfer.

2. The general manager is the responsible party and must have a good track record and be capable of operating the daily business or the investment will not be safe.

There are many combinations of limited partnerships. A typical joint venture is illustrated in Figure 16.1.

The joint purchasers of the property outlined in Figure 16.1 have an additional gross income added to the total cost:

$ 3,000,000	cost to acquire property
1,000,000	gross income
$ 4,000,000	sale price to limited partners

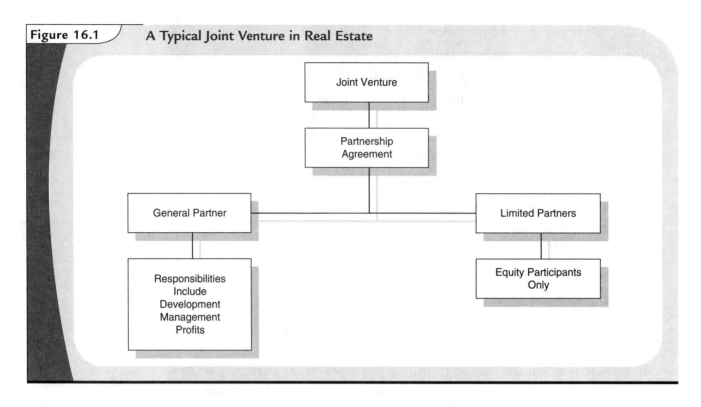

Figure 16.1 A Typical Joint Venture in Real Estate

The development and management expenses are deducted from the gross income:

$ 1,000,000	gross income
475,000	expenses
$ 525,000	net income

The limited partners will receive the full amount of their invested funds plus a percentage—say 10 percent. The balance of the profits will be evenly divided between the limited partners and the general manager.

Corporations

Corporations are legal taxable entities created by law and are considered as individual "persons." They are formed by filing articles of incorporation with the secretary of state stating the purpose for which the corporation will exist. The corporation is granted a corporate charter that permits the corporation to buy, sell, own, and function as an entity. All business will be conducted under corporate policy. The corporation should have annual meetings of the officers and board of directors, be capitalized adequately, and file annual reports with the state. A corporation, also referred to as a C Corporation, is confined to transacting business in the state in which it was incorporated and is referred to as a domestic corporation. In contrast, a foreign corporation is a corporation conducting business in another state.

A corporation is flexible, as it can consist of many shareholders or a very few. One person can run a corporation. For example, a real estate broker could form a real estate firm, incorporate, and be the sole owner and operator. In compliance with

Owning stock in a corporation

Domestic and foreign corporations

corporation rules (and real estate licensing rules), the broker must be certain not to commingle personal funds with corporate funds. Several real estate brokers can form a corporation, hire sales agents, and conduct business. The brokers could decide to invest in income-producing real estate because corporations may hold title to real property and enter into contracts under their articles of incorporation. If additional capital is needed or desired, the brokers may sell shares to the agents. Their success may be so great that they decide to go public and offer stock to the general public.

Corporations are classified as *public corporations* or *private corporations.* Public corporations are formed by the government, such as incorporated villages, towns, cities, school districts, and so on. A private corporation is established by an individual or group of people for a common purpose. A *closely held private corporation* is owned and operated by a family group or a small number of investors, whereas a publicly held private corporation will include other investors. Stock in qualifying private corporations may be sold by brokerage houses to investors. These investors elect a board of directors and this board employs management to operate the business. The investors' stock may rise or fall, depending not only on the performance of the business but also on market conditions.

The *"not for profit"* corporation includes foundations, churches, charitable groups, and organizations formed to benefit and service the public.

The corporation remains in existence until it is dissolved, referred to as a *dissolution.*

Advantages of forming a corporation are the following.

1. As an individual entity, the corporation, not the stockholders, is liable for its debt.
2. Personal injuries that occur are the responsibility of the corporation.
3. Individuals can purchase shares and receive profits without a large investment.
4. Stockholders are subject only to the loss of their investment.
5. One or a few people can manage the corporation, restricting the amount of people involved in making decisions.
6. It is relatively easy to buy and sell shares.

Disadvantages of forming a corporation include these factors.

1. The cost to incorporate and organize may be great.
2. All profits are subject to double taxation.
3. Corporations are subject to more government regulations than individuals are.

S Corporations

Originally titled Subchapter S Corporations, the rules governing these corporations were revised in 1982 and the revisions included changing their name to

Public Corporation
· Formed by government

Private Corporation
· Established by individual or group

Avoiding double taxation

S Corporations. A modified form of a corporation, S Corporations permit investors to avoid double taxation resulting from the earnings of the shareholders and the corporation. Income is not taxed at the corporate level because the shareholders are treated as partners for tax purposes. The down side of S Corporations is that they are limited to just 35 shareholders. The type of income allowed is limited and there are firm limitations on losses. Stockholders must be U.S. citizens or residents, the corporation must be domestic, and only one class of stock is issued.

Syndication

Syndication

Syndication is a term used to denote multiple participation in a real estate investment. A syndication group is composed of a general partner and two or more limited partners. Although the limited partners are the investors, they do not take an active role in management. The general partner is paid to manage the investment.

A syndication must comply with federal and state regulations. If the syndication is formed with the intent of making money on the investment, it is considered a security and must be registered with the **Securities and Exchange Commission (SEC)**.

Real Estate Investment Trusts (REITs)

Selling shares in real property

REITs make investment in real estate available to individuals by selling shares in large investment properties. By pooling the funds of many investors, the trust can purchase large properties, and the shares are easily transferable. The trustee (manager) manages the properties for the investors, and the income received is passed to the beneficiaries (investors). One of the advantages of REITs is that the revenue is not treated as corporate income, that is, it is not taxed twice.

National Association of Real Estate Investment Trusts: www.nareit.com

Real Estate Offerings as Securities

If real estate is purchased for investment, it will be considered a security and subject to jurisdiction under the Securities Act when it meets the four elements of an "investment contract" as defined by the federal Securities Act of 1933. The four elements are as follows.

1. It must be an investment of money.
2. It must be in a common enterprise.
3. It must be undertaken with the prospect of making a profit.
4. It must be one in which profit will be derived solely or substantially from the management efforts of others (whose efforts affect the success or failure of the enterprise).

A typical example of a security would be a limited partnership in which shares are sold.

The purpose of the Securities Act was to provide full and fair disclosure of securities sold in interstate commerce and through the mails and to prevent fraud in the sale of securities.

Provides disclosure

Anyone selling a security must register it with the SEC before offering the security for sale. A disclosure statement giving basic preliminary information of the enterprise must be delivered prior to or with any solicitation of an offer for the sale of the securities. This statement is referred to as a **prospectus**. A detailed accounting must be included, revealing the number of investors the partnership is seeking, all pertinent data pertaining to the property offered, and the distribution of profits and losses.

There are exceptions, as when the offering is *intrastate*—that is, offered solely in the state where the issuer resides and does business. However, the offering will need to be registered in that particular state, unless it would be exempt as a private offering. A private offering is of a limited scope and is directed to a selected type of sophisticated investor who does not need the protection offered by the SEC disclosure.

Exceptions to SEC filings

A securities license is required of anyone who offers securities for sale. The securities laws that regulate the registration and sale of securities were passed to prevent people from buying or selling a "piece of the blue sky," thus the reason for referring to the laws as *blue sky laws*.

Summary of Important Points

1. The many aspects of real estate as an investment have been covered in this chapter. The advantages include the following:
   a. the continual rise of property values as a hedge against inflation
   b. the attractive high rate of return on the investment
   c. the leverage available; since the investor borrows money to finance the purchase, his buying power is substantially increased
   d. the investor's equity buildup, since a portion of the payments apply to reducing the principal
   e. the tax shelter features
2. The major disadvantages of a real estate investment are as follows:
   a. the nonliquidity; while stocks and bonds can be sold quickly through a stockbroker, it usually takes a period of time to find a buyer for real estate
   b. the risk; an investor must be a knowledgeable buyer and understand the risks involved, which include
      1. the importance of property location
      2. the ratio of rental returns to payments
   c. the investment of a large sum of money
   d. fixity, its immobility

    e. maintenance

    f. management of the property (if the investors do not have the time, a professional management service must be hired)

3. Homeownership permits the owner to deduct from taxable income a portion of the interest and taxes they paid.

4. A tax bill, effective August 1997, allows a $500,000 exclusion for married taxpayers who file a joint return and $250,000 for taxpayers who do not file a joint return. There are no age restrictions; thus, all sellers are eligible as long as they meet the ownership, use, and waiting period requirements.

5. Depreciation of improvements on investment real estate allows the investor a deduction on taxable income. Land is not deductible.

6. Tax-deferred exchanges defer capital gains taxes.

7. Investors pool funds by investing in joint ventures.

8. Limited partners have no management concerns; the investors' liability is limited to their investment.

9. General partnerships require the partners to manage and operate the business.

10. Corporations are legal entities, formed to conduct business. They are taxed as an individual, and earnings of the shareholders are also taxed, resulting in double taxation.

11. S Corporations are limited to 35 shareholders and are not taxed.

12. The Securities and Exchange Commission monitors real estate investments that are considered securities.

Discussion Points

1. What elements should any investment possess?

2. Explain how the 1997 tax bill affects the sale of a residence.

3. Explain the philosophy of leverage.

4. Explain which of the following are depreciable for income tax purposes and give reasons for your answers: (a) personal residence, (b) office building, (c) land.

5. Why would an investor refinance a property rather than sell it?

6. According to the Tax Reform Act of 1986, when is rental income considered passive income for an office building?

7. How does a C Corporation differ from an S Corporation?

Review Questions

Answers to these questions are found in the Answer Key section at the back of the book.

1. When expenses are greater than the income produced, it is called:
   a. taxable income
   b. cash flow
   c. negative cash flow
   d. adjusted basis

2. Depreciation of real property is available to:
   a. homeowners
   b. investors
   c. renters
   d. lenders

3. The function of a real estate investment is NOT to give the investor:
   a. equity gains
   b. appreciation
   c. income
   d. a second home

4. All of the following are true EXCEPT:
   a. the primary purpose of an investment is to generate income
   b. portfolio income includes interest and royalties
   c. losses from passive income can be used to offset ordinary income
   d. the value of an asset can be determined by the stream of income it produces

5. The tax bill signed into law August 5, 1997, provides for all of the following EXCEPT:
   a. a $500,000 exclusion for taxpayers who sell their principal residence and file a joint return
   b. the new exclusion does not impose any age restrictions, thus all sellers are eligible
   c. the seller needs to have owned the property for at least five years of the ten-year period ending the date of sale
   d. a $250,000 exclusion for taxpayers who do not file a joint return

6. A disclosure statement that describes an investment opportunity is called a(n):
   a. contract
   b. shelter
   c. option to purchase
   d. prospectus

7. Leverage is best defined as:
   a. borrow the least amount of money for the shortest period of time
   b. put the least amount down, obtain the lowest interest for the longest period of time
   c. a tax-free exchange
   d. postponing capital gains

8. The following is true of a limited partnership:
   a. limited partners must assist in the management of the investment
   b. an investor's liability is limited to the amount of the investment made
   c. the partners must operate the business
   d. the investment is limited to 20 stockholders

9. The following factor has influenced people to invest in real estate:
   a. the inflation of real estate values
   b. inexpensive management
   c. the liquidity of real estate
   d. investments in real estate require little money

10. Investments that can be depreciated include:
    a. a home, when a room is used solely as an office
    b. a private residence
    c. savings deposited in a federally insured bank
    d. personal property

11. A homeowner has recorded the following expenditures: $2,300 mortgage interest, $1,250 property tax, $1,800 depreciation, $700 addition of a garage, and $1,500 sale of an easement. What would the allowable income tax deduction be?

    a. $3,550
    b. $5,350
    c. $6,050
    d. $7,550

12. After the economic life of an apartment complex has been exhausted, the owner has left:

    a. an unearned value
    b. pure profit
    c. salvage value
    d. adjusted basis

13. A retired person on a pension buys a 24-unit apartment complex. What would the buyer most likely be looking for?

    a. depreciation
    b. gross income
    c. rent income
    d. net spendable money

14. All of the following are true regarding an S Corporation EXCEPT:

    a. double taxation is avoidable
    b. it is limited to 35 shareholders
    c. shareholders are treated as partners for tax purposes
    d. there are no limitations on losses

15. Upon the sale of an investment property, any profits in excess of straight-line depreciation are considered:

    a. ordinary income
    b. earned income
    c. 30 percent tax sheltered
    d. entirely tax sheltered

16. A Real Estate Investment Trust (REIT) can best be described as:

    a. a management group that oversees investments
    b. a group of investors who pool their funds to purchase real estate
    c. a fund used to purchase vacation homes
    d. a syndication group monitored by the SEC

17. An investment is considered a security when all of the following components are present EXCEPT:

    a. it is an investment of money
    b. it is a common enterprise
    c. the investor hopes to make a profit
    d. all the investors share in managerial duties

18. The Tax Reform Act of 1986 brought forth some sweeping new changes to the tax laws. It had the greatest impact on:

    a. homeowners
    b. investment property
    c. vacation homes
    d. motor homes

19. The Wrights purchase a home for $140,000, and obtain an 80 percent loan for 15 years at 8 percent interest. Their payments are $9.56 per $1,000 of the amount borrowed. The Wrights are in the 28 percent tax bracket. What is their annual allowable tax savings for the first year on the interest paid?

    a. $1,070.00
    b. $2,508.80
    c. $2,998.00
    d. $3,384.00

20. By what amount does the Wrights' tax deduction on interest paid effectively lower their monthly payment?
    a. $209.06
    b. $349.50
    c. $550.00
    d. $1,070.72

21. The Wrights' annual property taxes are $2,400. By what amount does this reduce their effective monthly payment?
    a. $28.00
    b. $36.00
    c. $56.00
    d. $672.00

22. Considering both the interest and tax advantages, the Wrights' house payment is reduced:
    a. from $1,070.72 to $805.66
    b. from $1,120.00 to $305.87
    c. from $1,070.72 to $305.84
    d. from $1,120.00 to $764.88

23. If an investor wants a 10 percent return on property that will produce a $37,000 net annual income, the purchase price should not exceed:
    a. $85,000
    b. $300,000
    c. $370,000
    d. $3,700,000

24. For purposes of income tax, "earned" income is any income derived from:
    a. interest on investments
    b. royalties
    c. salaries
    d. annuities

The Appraisal Process

KEY TERMS

ad valorem tax

appraisal

appraisal report

capitalization rate

cost approach

depreciation

economic obsolescence

Financial Institutions Reform,
    Recovery and Enforcement Act
    (FIRREA)

functional obsolescence

gross income multiplier (GIM)

gross rent multiplier (GRM)

highest and best use

income approach

market price

market value

physical depreciation

plottage

progression

quantity survey method

regression

replacement cost

reproduction cost

sales comparison approach

tax assessment

unit-in-place cost approach method

value

OVERVIEW

Appraising is far from an exact science, but a degree of relative uniformity may be achieved by applying proven appraisal techniques along with the use of factual information. Many professional appraisers concentrate all their time on the profession and are recognized for their knowledge, skill, and experience in the field. They interpret the facts in an unbiased manner from pertinent available information. An independent fee appraiser may be called upon to support his opinions in a court of law, so diligent care is taken with each parcel appraised. Although real estate brokers and salespersons need not qualify as professional appraisers, they should be familiar with the three approaches to determining value by means of the appraisal process and should be capable of arriving at the market value of the property they intend to list and market.

This chapter will explore the many purposes for which the fee appraiser may be requested to determine valuation of a property, the steps in an appraisal, and how valuation is arrived at and shown in the written, documented appraisal report furnished to the client. Title XI of the Financial Institutions Reform, Recovery and Enforcement Act of 1989 (FIRREA) and the new regulations placed upon appraisers are addressed in this chapter.

Appraisals

An **appraisal** is an estimate of value. It is an opinion as to the worth of a particular piece of property. An appraiser must measure the value of each parcel of real estate appraised and furnish a supportable opinion.

A definite sequence of steps is followed in the appraisal process:

1. Defining the problem: identifying the parcel of real estate by the legal description and street address and stating the purpose of the appraisal
2. Collecting the data
   a. economic
   b. neighborhood
   c. property
3. Analyzing and applying the three approaches
   a. sales comparison
   b. cost
   c. income
4. Correlating the data and analyzing the results
5. Writing the appraisal report

The Purpose of an Appraisal: Defining Value

Since value means different things to different people, the purpose of the appraisal is the first question asked by the appraiser. To the owner of the property, value would be considered as market value, investment value, and value in use. The insurance agent will think in terms of insured value, while the lender is concerned with loan value. The appraiser's report will clearly state the nature of the assignment. **Value** is defined as the present worth of future benefits that accompany the ownership of real property, and for value to exist there must be benefits. Valuation may be sought to determine any of the following.

Value
Present worth of future benefits

Market value vs. market price

1. *Market value*: The most probable selling price at which a willing seller will sell and a willing buyer will buy, with neither being under abnormal pressure, is commonly referred to as **market value**. It is the price a property is expected to bring if exposed for sale on the open market, allowing a reasonable amount of time to find a purchaser who is fully aware of the uses to which the property may be put. Keep in mind that value is created by the desire of people for a commodity or a service. **Market price** is the actual

sale price of the property set through bargaining and negotiation. Market price may differ from market value if the seller needs to sell quickly.

2. *Loan value*: Prior to committing to a loan, a lending institution has an appraiser give a report on the property's value since it is the collateral for the loan. This constitutes the greatest reason for appraisals in the residential resale and refinance market.

3. *Insurance value*: The lender requires the borrower to insure the property to protect the lender's interest. The insurance policy needs to cover the amount of the loan, with the lender named as co-beneficiary. The property owner also wants to insure the investment, regardless of whether a loan is involved. In case of damage or destruction, the owner is assured of sufficient coverage to replace the structure.

4. *Estate tax value*: The value of a deceased person's real property needs to be determined for inheritance tax purposes.

5. *Lease interest*: If a commercial property carries a long-term lease, it may contain a reappraisal clause since the leasehold value may change over a period of time. Some properties, such as vacation homes or commercial buildings, are built on leased land, and the land value may vary over the length of the lease. An appraisal would be important to a buyer to determine the lease value of a property in the current market. The leases may be high, but if the leases are due to expire soon, the buyer will want to be assured the leases can be renewed at the present rate.

6. *Tax assessment*: Real property is assessed to establish its **ad valorem tax** value. The county assessor's office appraises the property, and the assessed value is provided by the law of the municipality. The city council or governing board then sets the mill levy according to the amount of money needed to meet the budget and expenses of the local government. This budget is submitted by the county auditor and approved by the council.

Determining value for taxation

To determine the amount of taxes on a property, the assessed value is multiplied by the mill levy. (A mill equals one-tenth of a cent.) Property may be taxed at its full assessed value or at a percentage of the appraised value as shown in the following example:

$270,000	appraised value
.30	percentage taxed
$ 81,000	assessed value
.070	mill levy
$ 5,670	annual taxes

Taxes are sometimes expressed in dollars, as $2.00 per $100 of appraised value. Thus, the $270,000 appraised value times $2.00 would equal $5,400 annual taxes.

7. *Eminent domain*: As discussed in Chapter 2, under the right of eminent domain the police power of a governmental body may be invoked to take the property of an individual for public use. The property is condemned, and appraisers determine its fair market value. When a fraction of an individual's property is condemned and taken (as under the right of eminent domain), the appraiser determines what the value of the property was before that portion was taken and what the remainder is now worth. This *before-and-after method* awards *just compensation* to the condemnee (property owner) for the loss of that portion of land.

8. *Financial statement*: If a person needs to borrow capital, the lender may require a current appraisal of the borrower's real estate holdings to establish the net equity the property owner has in the property.

9. *Third-party companies*: An appraisal will serve as a basis for corporations or third-party companies that purchase the homes of transferred employees.

10. *Liquidation*: In a forced sale or auction, a liquidation value is needed.

11. *Divorce cases*: An appraisal is necessary to settle disputes over distribution of assets.

At this point the difference between a competitive market analysis (CMA) as discussed in Chapter 8 and a fee appraisal should be clarified. The CMA is different in both purpose and form. The broker and salesperson need to arrive at the probable market value each time they list or sell a property. This is approached by comparing the selling price of similar properties that have recently sold in the same neighborhood or a corresponding area and by checking the listed price of expired listings. Through continuous evaluation of recent sales and expired listings, the broker and salesperson keep abreast of values and the changing market conditions that affect them. However, they are not expected to give written and certified reports such as the fee appraiser prepares. The real estate salesperson's only concern is pricing and selling the property at a realistic selling price in today's market.

Forces Affecting Value

The appraiser must consider the forces that continually affect value as property values are influenced at national, regional, and the local community levels. The four major forces that have the greatest influence on residential real estate values are as follows:

1. governmental (political) actions
2. economic (financial) forces
3. physical or environmental forces
4. sociological forces

These four forces can modify value, create value, or destroy value.

Governmental (Political) Factors

At the national level the influence of federal control over policies that affect inflation has an impact on the cost of housing. Interest rates are directly responsive to government action, thus determining the number of people who are able to buy real estate.

The political conditions in regional and local governments also affect housing purchases. Property taxes and services rendered by the local governing body affect property values. If taxes are extremely high and services, such as street maintenance and police protection, are not at acceptable standards, people may not want to move into an area or to remain there.

Local government laws and regulations that affect value include an area's master plan for structured growth, zoning laws, ordinances controlling subdivisions, building codes, environmental regulations, and fire and safety standards.

Economic (Financial) Factors

Regional and local economic conditions are important to the appraiser because they can affect value. For example, an influx of new industry will create additional employment, bringing new families and spurring retail sales. More spendable money in an area means more prosperity. Conversely, if an area loses major employers, the reverse will be true and home values are likely to plummet. A community with diversified employment provides a healthy economic outlook.

The economic prediction for the future, whether the country is booming or is in recession, and how this relates to the local economy can all affect real estate values. During inflationary times property values increase; during a recession, property values fall. Interest rates and the availability of funds for financing also all play a role in determining the value of real estate.

Physical Factors

The most important influences are conditions in the local sector. The environmental or physical conditions that affect property values include elements outside the subject property. Parks, highways, access to interstates, airports, public transportation, available utilities, and shopping centers in the region play a strong role in property values. Because real estate is immobile, it is subjected to external conditions more than any other commodity.

The topography of the land may also be a factor as it can affect construction costs. A favorable climate will draw people to a particular area, thus enhancing value.

The location of a property within a community is the primary physical factor affecting property value. Certain neighborhoods in a given area will be in greater demand and command higher prices. It may be proximity to a school for a young family or access to the interstate for another.

Sociological Factors

Understanding social elements includes evaluating the population trends of the area because, for example, the prevalent age groups determine the types of housing in demand. That is, different age groups are associated with the need for single-family homes, condominiums, apartments, or retirement complexes. Changes in family size and whether the population in the area is declining, remaining stable, or increasing also influence value.

Sociological factors include the attitudes of the people in the community. How people feel toward the local government and their opinion of the community as a desirable place to live also have an impact on value. People's attitudes concerning education and their desire for advancing the standards of the community show whether an environment is caring and stable. Cultural amenities such as theaters, arts, parks, zoos, and recreational facilities enhance the lives of the area residents.

In the final analysis, value is created when the following are present.

1. *Desire*: The commodity must be wanted.
2. *Utility*: This considers the uses to which it can be put.
3. *Scarcity*: Supply is limited.
4. *Effective purchasing power*: Money is available to buy it.

Other Factors Affecting Value

Three approaches are used in the appraisal of real property: the cost approach, the sales comparison approach, and the income approach. Before the appraiser begins to analyze each of these approaches to value, certain basic principles that affect the value must be applied. These principles are discussed below.

Highest and Best Use

Net return affects value

When we speak of the **highest and best use** of property, we are referring to the most profitable use to which it can be put. This use must be a reasonable and probable use that will result in the highest value. Briefly, the highest and best use can be defined as the use that, at the time of the appraisal, is most likely to produce the greatest net return on the land and/or building over a given period of time. *Net return* is the key phrase in this definition. It means whatever is left from gross yield after all costs are met. Sometimes net return takes a form that may not bring the greatest monetary return, for example, land for a children's zoo, a city park, or a forest preserve that will give enjoyment to thousands every year.

The appraiser must determine the property value at its *present use,* which may or may not be the highest and best use. If zoning regulations and government controls do not permit a use that conforms to present market standards, the property could not be used to its highest and best potential. If the use can be changed through rezoning, the value would be considered on that basis, less any costs involved in preparing for the rezoned use. For example, an existing building may need to be demolished.

Principle of Substitution

If the property can be substituted for another, its value is set to an extent by the cost of acquiring a like property. The knowledgeable purchaser today will "shop" and compare properties before making a selection. This is the principle of substitution, used in the sales comparison approach to appraising.

Utility Value

The utility value of a property, how it can be used, is also important in determining value. A lovely wooded lot may appear to be a perfect location for a homesite, but investigation uncovers that it has a ravine running through it, leaving no feasible spot for a building. Zoning laws and restrictive covenants can also affect the use of a property. A location that may seem ideal for a commercial building but which is zoned only for office buildings will be limited to the use designated by the zoning ordinance. Protective covenants in an area may prohibit the building of a two-story house since it would obscure the views of surrounding homeowners. When appraisers place a value on a particular property, they must carefully weigh its utility value.

Use dictates value

Functional utility refers to the usability of a building. A contractor may build one house with a highly desirable, very livable floor plan and choose a plan for another house with a poorly arranged interior. The latter may lack good window placement, have a traffic pattern that necessitates walking through the middle of one room to reach another, or lack storage area. As new innovations and more amenities are incorporated into new construction, older houses that do not have these appointments are considered less functional.

Functional utility

Principle of Contribution

The principle of contribution is the principle the appraiser applies to the *return on improvements* to the property. To improve a property may not necessarily mean that the total cost of the improvement can be added to the value of the property. While a recreation room will expand the living space of the home and make it more desirable to a buyer, the owner may not recapture the entire cost of the remodeling. Enclosing porches and updating kitchens and baths may add appeal to the property but may not return the seller's total costs.

Improvements may add value

Principle of Change

Principles of change acknowledge that the life cycle of a building dictates change, for as a neighborhood ages, new land uses may be introduced. Multifamily units may begin to emerge in once affluent neighborhoods as covenants expire and new uses develop through zoning changes. As new styles and plans are built in the suburbs, people on a higher economic scale move beyond the city's urban area. A great thrust in many cities has been to revitalize the older sectors in an effort to slow suburban sprawl and prevent the decay of the inner city areas.

Age changes value

Changes in a neighborhood may transpire slowly, but the appraiser is trained to detect the implied as well as the evident indications that result in changing conditions. As the area ages, change may occur not only in zoning regulations but also in the income level and average age of the residents. As buyers' needs and desires change, the forces of change also affect neighborhoods and cities.

New styles in home designs with the use of large expanses of well-designed windows, automated kitchens, and palatial baths appeal to still other buyers. Amenities are the extras that come with ownership. A desirable view, a wooded lot, or the privacy or location of a particular property all can be considered amenities. The amenities desired may vary with different buyers. The proximity to transportation, a shopping center, or schools may be prime considerations for one purchaser, while special energy-conserving features may be most important to another.

Scarcity

The supply will dictate the value; if property is not in demand, the value will decrease. If there is an abundant supply and the need is not there, the value will decrease. Viewing the earth from an airplane, one sees a great amount of vacant land. The problem lies in where the land is. Because of its immobility, we cannot move it closer to where the need for housing and industry is. In heavily populated areas, land is indeed scarce.

Principle of Supply and Demand

The law of supply and demand holds true in real estate as in any other commodity. If consumers have a need and a desire, the result will be value in the product. If 20 houses are built in a new subdivision, but demand is not present, the contractor will have an excess of 20 houses unless the price is lowered to encourage buyers. Conversely, if there is a demand for housing and few are available, prices will rise. The investor must determine the prospects for future growth or decline.

Transferability

Good title that can be transferred with comparable ease is important to value. While this is a legal concept and not an economic factor, value will not exist if the property cannot be transferred. Regardless of the demand, title must be capable of being transferred or its worth is diminished.

Principle of Anticipation

Future value

Value is created by anticipating the use or income that will be derived from the property in the future. The homeowner sees value in the property based on the amenities it offers, its ability to meet the buyer's needs, and consequently its present worth, while the investor will view it from the potential net income to be received from the investment. The anticipated future development of an area is always considered. Schools, highways, and shopping malls are built because of need and demand, thus indicating an increase in value.

Principle of Regression and Progression

If a property has been overimproved, the value of the overimprovement is decreased and the principle of **regression** applies. To add a $40,000 family room on a house in an area where surrounding homes are being appraised for $60,000 would not result in adding $40,000 to the market value of the overimproved property. This property will fall towards the level of surrounding homes and thus regress.

If a particular property is underimproved and in an area of more expensive homes, the principle of **progression** applies; despite the underimprovement, the value of the subject property is likely increased.

Regression
Value lowered, overimproved for neighborhood

Progression
Value increased due to neighborhood

Principle of Conformity

When a neighborhood is homogeneous, that is, the homes have a relative degree of uniformity, values tend to be higher. If the construction is architecturally compatible and an overall appearance of conformity is adhered to, values will be stabilized in the area. This is one of the reasons for covenants and restrictions in the platting of subdivisions; the property owners are assured that their investment will be secure from that standpoint.

Plottage Value

The combining of two or more parcels is called *assemblage*. The increase in the value of the new parcel is referred to as **plottage**. For example, if zoning laws permit a 6-unit building on a lot that has 15,000 square feet, the acquisition of the adjacent lot of equal size would permit the owner to build a 12-unit building. If a value of $15,000 is placed on each unit, the value has increased from a total of $90,000 ($15,000 × 6 units) to $180,000 ($15,000 × 12 units).

Plottage
Value is increased by assembling two or more properties

Collecting the Data

The appraiser maintains a database of information as a ready resource. General data on the region, the city, and the neighborhood are collected and maintained in the database. Regional and city information includes knowledge of the economic conditions of the area. The neighborhood data covers information on areas within certain street boundaries where the houses are of comparable price range and age. The average income and age of the residents and convenience to shopping, public transportation, churches, and schools are other factors considered.

After assembling the regional, city, and neighborhood data, the appraiser begins analyzing the property itself.

1. The site is evaluated; the lot size and street frontage are determined.
2. The square footage of the house is measured.
3. The condition of the house and any extra features it has are noted.
4. Any special assessments against the property are recorded in the report. A special assessment is a charge against real estate to pay for the cost of a

public improvement to the property. This assessment is made by a unit of government. Special assessments are levied for the cost of street paving, curbing, sidewalks, and sewers.

Approaches to Value

The following are three approaches to assessing property value.

1. The **sales comparison approach** compares the subject property (the property being appraised) to similar properties that have recently sold, adjusting for the differences.
2. The **cost approach** considers today's cost to rebuild and adds the land value.
3. The **income approach** capitalizes the income, converting future income to present value.

The appraiser makes the decision as to which approach best typifies the subject property. Little credence is given to the income approach when appraising single-family residences, since few are purchased for rental purposes. For these appraisals, greater reliance is placed on the cost and comparison approaches. Conversely, these approaches to value would not be given as much weight in appraising an income-producing property. When appraising a single-purpose building, such as a church, the cost approach would be most applicable since comparable properties would be difficult to locate and the church is not considered income producing.

Sales Comparison Approach

Determining value by comparison

The sales comparison approach is often referred to as the market data approach to value because the subject property (the property being appraised) is compared with properties recently sold in the same general area or in neighborhoods of similar characteristics.

The appraiser will seek comparable properties that have recently sold. Properties currently on the market for sale are not considered since no agreed-upon contract between buyer and seller exists. A minimum of three comparables provides the appraiser with the data necessary to form an opinion as to the value of the subject property. The more similar the properties, the easier it is to conclude value. Allowances and adjustments are made for any differences in the properties. The sales comparison approach to value is the most commonly used method in appraising residential property as it depends on what similar properties are actually selling for.

When locating comparables, the appraiser will first look for recently sold properties in the immediate location of the subject property. If no recent sales are available in the neighborhood, an area similar in value should be searched. It is important that the comparables have sold recently; this is especially true if the market is volatile. Depending on local conditions, adjustments for time lapsed are made either upward or down.

It is necessary to locate the same style of house; for instance, two-story houses are not compared with ranch-style houses.

Adjustments

In the preparation of a market value analysis the use of adjustments is of prime importance. Some of the adjustments appraisers look for include the following.

1. *Time*: Since market conditions change, the comparables used are kept within a short time span, usually six months to one year, depending on how volatile the current market is.

2. *Age*

3. *Location*: Understanding the differences in neighborhoods that affect lot value (location does not affect building value).

   Adjusting for differences

4. *Lot size*

5. *Quality of construction*: This should not be confused with the condition; if the quality is higher or lower than normal for the area, a reasonable adjustment should be made

6. *Porches, decks, and patios*

7. *General condition*: The cost of updating a house to bring it to the standard of other houses in the area is considered. This can include the need for exterior paint, new roofing or siding, and landscaping. Interior refurbishing would include painting, new carpeting, and wallpaper.

8. *Living area*: The appraiser uses the outside measurements in determining the square footage.

9. *Number of bedrooms*

10. *Baths*: Consideration is given to tiled baths, full, 3/4, or 1/2 baths.

11. *Basements*: Full, half, and walkout basements and whether they are finished and the quality of the finished work are considered.

12. *Garages*: Detached, single, double, or triple garages add to or detract from value.

13. *Air conditioning and heating systems*: Age, adequacy, and energy efficiency affect the value.

14. *Fireplaces*

15. *Extras*: Built-in appliances, garage door openers, and any special amenities the house may have are taken into account.

Figure 17.1 indicates the process used in comparing residential properties. Let us analyze each step. Our subject property is at 1040 Clear Street, which is the model used throughout this book.

Figure 17.1	Comparing Residential Properties

	SUBJECT	COMPARABLES		
A. Address	1040 Clear Street	1155 Clear Street	2201 Main Street	3215 Lincoln Street
B. Sale Price		$186,000	$184,000	$185,500
C. Time Adjustment		1 mo. 0	6 mos. + 1,680 add 2%	3 mos. + 850 add 1%
D. No. of rooms	6	6 0	6 0	6 0
E. No. of Bedrooms, Baths	3–2	3–2 0	3–2 0	3–2 0
F. Square Footage	1350	1300 + 2,500 50 less	1400 – 2,500 50 more	1350 0
G. Style, Const.	Ranch, frame	Ranch, fr. 0	Ranch, fr. 0	Ranch, fr. 0
H. Garage	2 car attd.	2-car attd. 0	1-car attd. + 1,500	2-car attd. 0
I. Age, Condition	7 yrs., good	2 yrs. – 2,500 excellent	7 yrs. – 1,000 excellent	10 yrs. + 1,800 good
J. Lot, Size Extras	85 × 120	85 × 120 0	85 × 110 0	90 × 110 0
K. Special Features	wood deck, fenced	wood, deck, fenced 0	patio, view 0	new carpet, fenced 0
L. Method of Sale		loan assumption – 1,000	conv. 0	VA – 2,000
M. Net Adjustments		– 1,000	+ 320	+ 650
N. Adjusted Market Price		$185,000	$184,320	$186,150
O. Indicated Value	$185,000			

Remember, *adjustments must be made to the comparable properties and not to the subject*. This is sometimes difficult to understand. Think of it in these terms: since the value of the subject property is unknown, we cannot make adjustments to it. Also important is understanding how the adjustments are made. If a property has less than the subject property it is given a plus. If it has more, it is given a minus. Thus, the appraiser must *add to the lesser property and subtract from the better property*.

A. This line lists the property addresses. All three comparables are in the same subdivision as the subject property.

B. This line states the sale price of the comparable properties.

C. Line C allows for the change in value that occurs since the date of sale. The appraiser must track carefully any economic changes that have occurred since the sale date of the properties. If property is selling for less, it will be necessary to adjust the comparables down. In the example, the area is in demand, and properties do not have a long market time even though prices have leveled off and inflation has slowed. In view of this information, comparable #1 needs no adjustment since it sold just one month ago. Comparable #2 sold six months ago, and its value has increased 2 percent, and comparable #3 sold three months ago and has a 1 percent increase.

D. and **E.** No adjustments are necessary here since there are no variations.

F. Property #1 is 50 square feet smaller, so considering that the cost per square foot is $50.00 × 50 square feet, +$2,500 is given to the property. Comparable #2 has 50 square feet more, so we give it a −$2,500.

G. Style and construction of the properties are all the same.

H. Comparable #2 has a one-car garage, so we added $1,500. This takes into consideration that it would be worth an additional $1,500 if it had an extra garage.

I. Allowance needs to be made for the differences in the age and condition of properties. Comparable #1 is only two years old and in excellent condition. Since it is five years newer than the subject and in excellent condition, a minus $2,500 is given. Comparable #2 is the same age as the subject property; however, its condition is excellent, so a minus $1,000 is credited to it. Comparable #3 is ten years old so it has developed three years of additional depreciation, and $1,800 is added to it.

J. The lot sizes vary so slightly that no allowances are made.

K. Special features can have a great effect on the sale price of a property. Wood decks and fenced yards are very fashionable in this area. While comparable #2 has neither, it does have a spectacular view that the appraiser felt "equaled out" not having the former. Properties that are treed, that offer privacy, or that are unusually well landscaped have amenities that also enhance value. Houses with professionally decorated interiors, that sparkle with cleanliness, or that have extra features such as built-in appliances, skylights, and jacuzzis have enhanced market value.

L. The financing involved in the sale can influence the price paid for the property. If a seller carries financing or an existing loan is assumed, the purchaser may pay more for favorable loan terms. The appropriate adjustments were made on comparables #1 and #3.

M. The net adjustments are totaled.

N. The adjusted market price reflects the adjustments.

O. When looking at the three comparables, no correlation is necessary since the three properties are all very similar to the subject property. We give equal value to each of the properties, and the indicated market value is $185,000. After the correlation of the properties, the appraiser states the conclusion, and the final step for the appraiser is to certify the report.

Cost Approach

The cost approach to appraising is sometimes referred to as the replacement cost method or the summation approach. The cost approach is used when appropriate or when comparable sales are not available. In implementing the cost approach, there are four methods that can be followed.

Analyzing value by cost to replace structure

1. The square foot method involves taking cost data from recent construction of a similar structure and dividing it by the square footage of the building, thus establishing the cost per square foot of that structure. If it cost $90,000 to build a 1,500-square-foot house, the cost per square foot would be $60.

The contractor figures the cost of a house by multiplying the square feet in the plan (length × width = sq ft) by the cost per square foot. Thus, 1,500 square feet (area) × $60 (cost per square foot) = $90,000.

2. The cubic-foot method requires calculations that resemble the square foot method, except that the cubic-foot method considers the volume of a building (length × width × height). This method is not used for appraising houses, but it is used for arriving at a value for warehouses and other industrial type buildings.

3. The **unit-in-place cost approach method** may be used by a contractor in determining the cost of a new building. In this approach, the cost of all component parts, including the kitchen cabinets ($18,000), the fireplace ($3,000), and so on, are computed.

4. The **quantity survey method** gives the contractor a very precise cost breakdown. This is the most detailed approach to appraising. For example, 42 kitchen cabinet hinges may cost $2.00 each or 19 drawer pulls $2.50 each. The cost of the labor is then added, and contractors can come very close to figuring the exact cost of constructing the house. They can then decide the percentage of profit they desire for their time and labor and add this to the cost of the building. The cost approach is used on special purpose buildings such as schools, police stations, or new construction. There is a difference between **replacement cost** and **reproduction cost.**

Replacement cost is constructing a building similar in design and quality to the subject property, using current costs with the materials that are available at this time. Any depreciation that has accrued on the subject property is accounted for.

Reproduction cost means recreating the structure exactly as it is. This involves estimating the actual reproduction costs at the date the appraisal is made. To actually reproduce a structure would probably not be feasible, as there would be disadvantages in addition to benefits, especially if the building is outdated. The cost of producing a duplicate does not lend itself to what a typical buyer would pay for the property. If concessions are made and changes allowed it will no longer be an exact reproduction.

The steps followed in the cost approach are as follows.

1. Estimate the value of the site as if it were vacant and used to its highest potential as governed by covenants and zoning laws. An estimate is also made on any improvements to the site.

2. Estimate the cost to replace the improvements at today's prices.

3. Deduct depreciation, physical deterioration, functional obsolescence, and exterior obsolescence.

4. Deduct all depreciation from the replacement cost to arrive at the present value of the improvement.

Figure 17.2	The Cost Approach to Appraisal, Computed by Square Footage Less Depreciation Plus Land Improvements and Land

COST APPROACH
1040 Clear Street

Replacement Cost Estimate:
  Buildings:

Residence	2000	sq. ft. at	$75.00	$150,000
Garage	2-car attd. 500	sq. ft. at	30.00	15,000
Other	(concrete) 700	sq. ft. at	4.00	2,800
Total Replacement Cost				$167,800

Less Depreciation:

Physical	(1/2%)	$8,390	
Functional	(0%)	-0-	
Economic	(0%)	-0-	
Total Depreciation			$ 8,390
Present Value of Building			$159,410
Net Value of Land Improvements (walks, fences, landscaping, etc.)			3,400
Land Value (approximately $200 per front foot in this area)			22,500
Total Value			$185,310
		Rounded:	$185,300

5. Add the land value and improvement value together for the total value of the property. Land does not depreciate.

Remember that in the cost approach the formula is: replacement cost less depreciation plus land value equals the appraisal value. Figure 17.2 indicates how the appraised value of the example property located at 1040 Clear Street was determined. The appraiser did not feel the seven-year-old residence suffered from functional or economic obsolescence. The annual physical depreciation of .5 percent was multiplied times the seven years, and the resulting 3.5 percent was then multiplied times the replacement cost (including the concrete). Most lenders now require appraisers to use the form approved by the secondary mortgage market (Freddie Mac and Fannie Mae), to facilitate the sale of the mortgage to this market (see Figure 17.3).

Depreciation

In using the cost approach method, the appraiser must determine if there is any **depreciation**. Depreciation of the property is subtracted from the replacement cost of the structure. Depreciation of real estate is defined as *loss of value from any cause.* It includes physical depreciation, functional obsolescence, and economic obsolescence.

Physical depreciation includes the normal wear and tear of a structure through use and the actions of natural elements. This form of depreciation may be curable or incurable. Curable depreciation may include the need for painting

Loss in value through wear and tear

Figure 17.3 — Uniform Residential Appraisal Report

Uniform Residential Appraisal Report   File #

The purpose of this summary appraisal report is to provide the lender/client with an accurate, and adequately supported, opinion of the market value of the subject property.

SUBJECT

Property Address		City	State	Zip Code
Borrower	Owner of Public Record		County	
Legal Description				
Assessor's Parcel #		Tax Year	R.E. Taxes $	
Neighborhood Name		Map Reference	Census Tract	

Occupant ☐ Owner ☐ Tenant ☐ Vacant   Special Assessments $ ☐ PUD   HOA $ ☐ per year ☐ per month

Property Rights Appraised ☐ Fee Simple ☐ Leasehold ☐ Other (describe)

Assignment Type ☐ Purchase Transaction ☐ Refinance Transaction ☐ Other (describe)

Lender/Client   Address

Is the subject property currently offered for sale or has it been offered for sale in the twelve months prior to the effective date of this appraisal? ☐ Yes ☐ No

Report data source(s) used, offering price(s), and date(s).

CONTRACT

I ☐ did ☐ did not analyze the contract for sale for the subject purchase transaction. Explain the results of the analysis of the contract for sale or why the analysis was not performed.

Contract Price $ Date of Contract   Is the property seller the owner of public record? ☐ Yes ☐ No   Data Source(s)

Is there any financial assistance (loan charges, sale concessions, gift or downpayment assistance, etc.) to be paid by any party on behalf of the borrower? ☐ Yes ☐ No
If Yes, report the total dollar amount and describe the items to be paid.

NEIGHBORHOOD

Note: Race and the racial composition of the neighborhood are not appraisal factors.

Neighborhood Characteristics			One-Unit Housing Trends			One-Unit Housing		Present Land Use %	
Location ☐ Urban ☐ Suburban ☐ Rural			Property Values ☐ Increasing ☐ Stable ☐ Declining			PRICE	AGE	One-Unit	%
Built-Up ☐ Over 75% ☐ 25–75% ☐ Under 25%			Demand/Supply ☐ Shortage ☐ In Balance ☐ Over Supply			$ (000)	(yrs)	2-4 Unit	%
Growth ☐ Rapid ☐ Stable ☐ Slow			Marketing Time ☐ Under 3 mths ☐ 3–6 mths ☐ Over 6 mths			Low		Multi-Family	%
						High		Commercial	%
						Pred.		Other	%

Neighborhood Boundaries

Neighborhood Description

Market Conditions (including support for the above conclusions)

SITE

Dimensions	Area	Shape	View

Specific Zoning Classification   Zoning Description

Zoning Compliance ☐ Legal ☐ Legal Nonconforming (Grandfathered Use) ☐ No Zoning ☐ Illegal (describe)

Is the highest and best use of the subject property as improved (or as proposed per plans and specifications) the present use? ☐ Yes ☐ No If No, describe

Utilities	Public	Other (describe)		Public	Other (describe)	Off-site Improvements—Type	Public	Private
Electricity	☐	☐	Water	☐	☐	Street	☐	☐
Gas	☐	☐	Sanitary Sewer	☐	☐	Alley	☐	☐

FEMA Special Flood Hazard Area ☐ Yes ☐ No   FEMA Flood Zone   FEMA Map #   FEMA Map Date

Are the utilities and off-site improvements typical for the market area? ☐ Yes ☐ No If No, describe

Are there any adverse site conditions or external factors (easements, encroachments, environmental conditions, land uses, etc.)? ☐ Yes ☐ No If Yes, describe

IMPROVEMENTS

General Description	Foundation	Exterior Description materials/condition	Interior materials/condition
Units ☐ One ☐ One with Accessory Unit	☐ Concrete Slab ☐ Crawl Space	Foundation Walls	Floors
# of Stories	☐ Full Basement ☐ Partial Basement	Exterior Walls	Walls
Type ☐ Det. ☐ Att. ☐ S-Det./End Unit	Basement Area sq. ft.	Roof Surface	Trim/Finish
☐ Existing ☐ Proposed ☐ Under Const.	Basement Finish %	Gutters & Downspouts	Bath Floor
Design (Style)	☐ Outside Entry/Exit ☐ Sump Pump	Window Type	Bath Wainscot
Year Built	Evidence of ☐ Infestation	Storm Sash/Insulated	Car Storage ☐ None
Effective Age (Yrs)	☐ Dampness ☐ Settlement	Screens	☐ Driveway # of Cars
Attic ☐ None	Heating ☐ FWA ☐ HWBB ☐ Radiant	Amenities ☐ Woodstove(s) #	Driveway Surface
☐ Drop Stair ☐ Stairs	☐ Other Fuel	☐ Fireplace(s) # ☐ Fence	☐ Garage # of Cars
☐ Floor ☐ Scuttle	Cooling ☐ Central Air Conditioning	☐ Patio/Deck ☐ Porch	☐ Carport # of Cars
☐ Finished ☐ Heated	☐ Individual ☐ Other	☐ Pool ☐ Other	☐ Att. ☐ Det. ☐ Built-in

Appliances ☐ Refrigerator ☐ Range/Oven ☐ Dishwasher ☐ Disposal ☐ Microwave ☐ Washer/Dryer ☐ Other (describe)

Finished area **above** grade contains: Rooms   Bedrooms   Bath(s)   Square Feet of Gross Living Area Above Grade

Additional features (special energy efficient items, etc.)

Describe the condition of the property (including needed repairs, deterioration, renovations, remodeling, etc.).

Are there any physical deficiencies or adverse conditions that affect the livability, soundness, or structural integrity of the property? ☐ Yes ☐ No If Yes, describe

Does the property generally conform to the neighborhood (functional utility, style, condition, use, construction, etc.)? ☐ Yes ☐ No If No, describe

Figure 17.3 continued

Uniform Residential Appraisal Report   File

| There are | comparable properties currently offered for sale in the subject neighborhood ranging in price from $ | | | to $ | |
| There are | comparable sales in the subject neighborhood within the past twelve months ranging in sale price from $ | | | to $ | |

FEATURE	SUBJECT	COMPARABLE SALE # 1		COMPARABLE SALE # 2		COMPARABLE SALE # 3	
Address							
Proximity to Subject							
Sale Price	$		$		$		$
Sale Price/Gross Liv. Area	$ sq. ft.	$ sq. ft.		$ sq. ft.		$ sq. ft.	
Data Source(s)							
Verification Source(s)							
VALUE ADJUSTMENTS	DESCRIPTION	DESCRIPTION	+(-) $ Adjustment	DESCRIPTION	+(-) $ Adjustment	DESCRIPTION	+(-) $ Adjustment
Sale or Financing Concessions							
Date of Sale/Time							
Location							
Leasehold/Fee Simple							
Site							
View							
Design (Style)							
Quality of Construction							
Actual Age							
Condition							
Above Grade	Total Bdrms. Baths	Total Bdrms. Baths		Total Bdrms. Baths		Total Bdrms. Baths	
Room Count							
Gross Living Area	sq. ft.	sq. ft.		sq. ft.		sq. ft.	
Basement & Finished Rooms Below Grade							
Functional Utility							
Heating/Cooling							
Energy Efficient Items							
Garage/Carport							
Porch/Patio/Deck							
Net Adjustment (Total)		☐ + ☐ -	$	☐ + ☐ -	$	☐ + ☐ -	$
Adjusted Sale Price of Comparables		Net Adj. % Gross Adj. %	$	Net Adj. % Gross Adj. %	$	Net Adj. % Gross Adj. %	$

I ☐ did ☐ did not research the sale or transfer history of the subject property and comparable sales. If not, explain

My research ☐ did ☐ did not reveal any prior sales or transfers of the subject property for the three years prior to the effective date of this appraisal.

Data source(s)

My research ☐ did ☐ did not reveal any prior sales or transfers of the comparable sales for the year prior to the date of sale of the comparable sale.

Data source(s)

Report the results of the research and analysis of the prior sale or transfer history of the subject property and comparable sales (report additional prior sales on page 3).

ITEM	SUBJECT	COMPARABLE SALE # 1	COMPARABLE SALE # 2	COMPARABLE SALE # 3
Date of Prior Sale/Transfer				
Price of Prior Sale/Transfer				
Data Source(s)				
Effective Date of Data Source(s)				

Analysis of prior sale or transfer history of the subject property and comparable sales

Summary of Sales Comparison Approach

Indicated Value by Sales Comparison Approach $

Indicated Value by: Sales Comparison Approach $ Cost Approach (if developed) $ Income Approach (if developed) $

This appraisal is made ☐ "as is", ☐ subject to completion per plans and specifications on the basis of a hypothetical condition that the improvements have been completed, ☐ subject to the following repairs or alterations on the basis of a hypothetical condition that the repairs or alterations have been completed, or ☐ subject to the following required inspection based on the extraordinary assumption that the condition or deficiency does not require alteration or repair:

Based on a complete visual inspection of the interior and exterior areas of the subject property, defined scope of work, statement of assumptions and limiting conditions, and appraiser's certification, my (our) opinion of the market value, as defined, of the real property that is the subject of this report is $, as of   , which is the date of inspection and the effective date of this appraisal.

and decorating or the repair of leaking faucets or malfunctioning electrical outlets. Curable depreciation covers items that have not been maintained but can be remedied at reasonable cost. Incurable depreciation occurs when an item is still serviceable but will need replacement before the economic life of the structure is depleted. Economic life refers to the period over which a building can be profitably utilized.

Functional obsolescence refers to the changes in design and construction that outdate a building. Curable functional obsolescence results from inadequate electrical wiring for today's use, outdated equipment, the need for modernizing a bathroom or installing new kitchen counters and cabinets. Incurable obsolescence is the result of a poor floor plan or a serious lack of closets. A five-bedroom house with only one bathroom and with no space to add a second bath suffers from functional obsolescence. (Undoubtedly, it also suffers from a very crowded bathroom!) As a house ages it competes with new construction and any modern amenities it may have.

Economic obsolescence is the most difficult for the property owner to control since it relates to conditions external to the property, such as the desirability of the neighborhood or changes in nearby land use. The value of a property might be diminished if the surrounding structures are not compatible. Overimprovement of a home may also result in economic obsolescence, since a $90,000 home surrounded by $50,000 homes would be less likely to attract $90,000 purchasers.

Income Approach

The **income approach** to value is based on the *net income* produced in relation to the value of the property. The appraiser determines what the anticipated future income will be and converts that to present property value. Application of the income approach is useful to the person desiring to purchase an investment property. Since risk is involved, the investor will want a greater return than a money market or savings account would bring. The income approach gains importance when the property being appraised is older, and the cost approach is less convincing because of depreciation consideration. First, we will examine the rent multiplier used in the income approach to value, a simplified version of the capitalization method.

The gross monthly rent multiplier (GMRM), or often simply stated as the **gross rent multiplier (GRM)**, is used for one- to four-family residential properties. The **gross income multiplier (GIM)** is used on commercial and industrial income property.

Gross Rent Multiplier

The indicator of value can be obtained from similar rental properties with a figure known as the *gross rent multiplier.* It is calculated by dividing the selling

Margin notes:

Depreciation may be curable or incurable

Loss caused by outdated design

Neighborhood conditions affect value

Seeking value by income derived

Using the GRM to determine value

price of comparable properties by the gross monthly income to obtain the gross rent multiplier (GRM).

A brief analysis of the steps used in the income approach for single-family residential property follows:

1. Properties recently sold and rented are used as comparables.

2. The selling price of each property is divided by its gross monthly rent to obtain the GRM.

$$\text{Selling price} \div \text{GMR} = \text{GRM} \qquad \frac{\text{Sales price}}{\text{Rent}} = \text{GRM}$$

Comparables	Date	Price	Income	GRM
1	12-07	$168,000	$900	210.00
2	1-08	171,000	850	201.18
3	2-08	173,500	900	192.78
4	3-08	174,750	950	183.95
Subject	Today	?	900	?

3. Working from the table shown, greater consideration should be given to the examples that are most similar to the subject, and the multiplier is determined from this information.

4. If the multiplier used is 190.00, we would take the monthly rent from the subject property and multiply it times the GRM; thus 190.00 × $900 = $171,000.

$$
\begin{array}{ll}
\$\ 900.00 & \text{gross rent} \\
\times\ 190.00 & \text{multiplier} \\
\hline
171,000 &
\end{array}
$$

Thus, the subject property rent × the GRM = subject's value.

This same formula can be used on commercial and industrial income-producing properties by using the gross annual income multiplier (GIM). Care must be employed by the appraiser not to use overstated income estimates or the property will have an inflated estimated value. Furthermore, gross income, whether monthly or annual, does not take into account the cost of operating the property nor are allowances for vacancies and rent collection used. The multiplier method of establishing value is a quick means of validating the authenticity of the cost and comparison approaches.

Income-Producing Properties

The income approach, based on the net income produced by a property, is used to determine present value following this simple procedure.

1. Estimate the potential gross income (PGI) the property is capable of producing. Subtract from potential gross income amounts for vacancies and rent loss. This gives you effective gross income (EGI).

Using capitalization method to determine value

2. Subtract operating expenses from the effective gross income to arrive at the net operating income (NOI). Once a history of the property is established, a pattern is set, and deriving the property's value becomes easier.

3. Determine which capitalization rate should be used. An overall capitalization rate can be extracted from the data on property recently sold by taking the net income and dividing it by the selling price.

4. Apply the capitalization formula: net income ÷ capitalization rate = value.

Capitalizing involves converting future income to present value.

Capitalization rate provides for the return of the investor's capital and a return on the capital invested (the recapture rate). See Figure 17.4 for an example of the income approach to value. Both the GRM and the GIM multipliers use gross income figures regardless of any vacancies or operating expenses; the capitalization rate uses net income.

The simplest method to determine what to pay for a property is to decide what rate of return is desirable and divide the net income by the rate of return. For example, if a building produces $15,000 net per year and the investor wants

Figure 17.4	The Income Approach to Appraisal

OPERATING STATEMENT

Potential Gross Income (PGI) (annual)		$162,000
10 units @ $600 per mo. × 12 = $72,000		
15 units @ $500 per mo. × 12 = $90,000		
Laundry Facility Income		700
Annual Gross Income		$162,700
Vacancy and Rent Loss		8,100
Effective Gross Income (EGI)		$154,600
Expenses		
FIXED EXPENSES		
Real Estate Taxes	$9,000	
Property Insurance	1,100	($10,100)
OPERATING EXPENSES		
Management (resident 6%)	9,300	
Utilities (gas, water, electricity)	4,100	
Maintenance and Repair	4,200	
Redecorating	3,000	
Replacement (appliances, equip.)	5,200	
Accounting Services	850	
Advertising	1,000	($27,650)
Total Expenses		$37,750
Net Operating Income (NOI)		$116,850

If the capitalization rate is 12 percent, the indicated value will be:

$$\frac{\$116,850}{.12} = \$973,750$$

a 10 percent return, it is feasible to spend $150,000 for the property: $15,000 ÷ 10% (or .1) = $150,000.

$$\frac{\text{Income}}{\text{Rate}} = \text{Value} \qquad \frac{\$15,000}{10\%} = \$150,000$$

Other factors that must be taken into consideration are covered in Chapter 16.

The appraiser needs to analyze the rental history, with past and present rentals serving as guides in estimating future rentals. Comparing what competitive properties are renting for in the area will be another important factor in determining value. Any change in rent anticipation will need to be documented and supported by the appraiser. Not only the quantity of rent but its durability is taken into consideration.

The appraiser will answer the following questions.

1. Is the contract rent high but of short duration?
2. Does the property have long-term, below-market-rent leases?
3. Is the property managed responsibly so that its value will be maintained?
4. What has been the past rental history of the property?
5. If the property is a regional shopping mall:
   a. Is there anchor power by a national chain, such as Penney's or Sears, that will bring customers to the site?
   b. Will the surrounding market support the mall?
   c. What is the household income of the consumers nearby?
6. Is the location premier, marginal, or off the beaten path?

Correlation of Value

Any one of the three mentioned approaches to value may be used to determine the appraisal of the subject property, but they will not necessarily yield the same value. It may be that replacing a structure would cost less than the prevailing market value if the demand were especially great.

In income-producing property, the capitalization approach is usually given the most credence. If the subject is a single-family dwelling, the income approach is generally not used. The use of the cost approach is of value if the home is comparatively new. The market value would probably come closest to the real value of our example property. If the appraisal is to be made on a property for which recent comparison sales are not obtainable, for example, a pickle factory, a library building, or a church, the cost approach will probably carry the greatest weight.

When reconciling for any spread between the three different approaches, the appraiser will weigh the average to the most applicable approach. The final step in the appraisal procedure is the written report. The purpose of the appraisal will determine the length and depth of the formal report.

The Appraisal Report

Delivery of the **appraisal report** may be by one of four methods: an oral report, a letter, a form appraisal, or a narrative report. The reports may vary in length and type depending on the request from the client. Regardless of the type of report submitted, the appraiser has gathered his information by the same process.

The minimum requirements of any report should include the following:

1. identification of the property
2. purpose of the appraisal
3. date valuation was made
4. data used to support the conclusion
5. statement of any limiting conditions and appraiser assumptions, if any
6. indication of value
7. certification by appraiser
8. signature of appraiser

Appraiser's report

The oral report is given verbally by the appraiser, either in person or by telephone, to the person who requested the appraisal. There is no documentation to substantiate the findings, so an oral report is used only when time is of the essence and a quick report is needed.

Appraiser's written report

The letter report is a formal written appraisal in letter form that identifies the property, states the purpose of the appraisal, and briefly summarizes the appraiser's findings. Usage of this simplified form is not encouraged among the professional appraisers since pertinent and crucial facts could be omitted. No data analysis or supporting information is included in the letter report. The appraiser will have made a complete appraisal and will retain this information in his permanent files as support for the report.

Form report

The form report is used extensively by appraisers who need a standardized method for their clients or employers. Mortgage lenders and mortgage insurers generally request use of the approved FNMA (Fannie Mae) and FHLMC (Freddie Mac) form, since they often anticipate selling their loans on the secondary market. All the requirements of an FHA and a VA report are on this form, eliminating any problem of missing facts (see Figure 17.3).

The form report contains the appropriate boxes to check and blanks to complete. The appraiser has the responsibility to add any additional comments pertinent to the findings. Currently this form is the most popular means of submitting appraisals.

Narrative report in summary form

The narrative report permits the appraiser to present the appraisal in summary form. A narrative report can contain a very few pages or a hundred pages. The appraiser must use good judgment in not becoming too elaborate in her writing. Many begin the report with a one- or two-page synopsis of the findings, enabling the reader to obtain a quick overview of the appraisal. The reader can then proceed through the report for verification and substantiation of the appraiser's opinion of the property's value. The narrative includes the complete steps taken in the analysis used in reaching the conclusion. Included are neighborhood data and exhibits of the comparable properties used to substantiate the appraisal. An outline of the report would include the following:

1. title page
2. letter of transmittal
3. table of contents
4. summary of the facts
5. objectives of the report
6. identification of the property
7. definition of value
8. property rights appraised
9. city data
10. neighborhood data
11. taxes, zoning, and utilities
12. description of the site and its value
13. building description and land improvements
14. analysis and interpretation
15. approaches used to determine the value
16. reconciliation
17. certification
18. conclusion of the value
19. statement of any limiting conditions or contingencies
20. appraiser's qualifications

Some professional appraisal societies require a demonstration narrative appraisal prior to acceptance in the organization, and some universities and colleges require a narrative report to be completed by students studying real estate appraisal.

The Professional Appraiser

Appraisal is the most specialized division of the real estate business, and becoming an appraiser requires comprehensive training. The farm appraiser's expertise will differ from the residential or commercial appraiser's knowledge. Just as the property manager (Chapter 15) specializes, so does the appraiser. The importance of accuracy cannot be overstated. The independent fee appraiser is a disinterested third party who follows an orderly process in determining the value of a property. The appraiser certifies that no present or future contemplated interest in the real estate being appraised exists and that the employment or fee is not contingent upon the determined value.

Specialization
by appraiser

**Appraisal Institute:
www.appraisalinstitute
.org**

In the early 1980s appraisers came under the scrutiny of the Federal Home Loan Bank because lending institutions held large numbers of defaulted loans on properties that were overvalued. If the owner of a highly leveraged property needed to sell and found the market value to be less than the loan, defaults occurred. Additionally, with the vast number of homeowners refinancing their properties in 1986, when interest rates plunged to a long-time low, lenders were concerned that, with the rush for refinancing and the resultant backlog of appraisals, carelessness could occur.

The National Association of Review Appraisers and Mortgage Underwriters has developed a form to be used in the review of narrative or residential appraisal reports. It is their intent that use of the form will substantially reduce loan loss of financial institutions by calling attention to the strengths and weaknesses of the appraisal report that lenders rely upon when making real estate loans. It is, however, the function of the autonomous reviewer to see that the valuation is based on sound judgment.

In August 1989, Congress passed the **Financial Institutions Reform, Recovery and Enforcement Act (FIRREA)**. Due to the many failed savings and loan institutions, the appraiser came "under the gun" for careless and shoddy appraisals. As a result, Title XI was attached to the FIRREA bill. Title XI provides for the regulation of appraisers in all federally related transactions. With a deadline of January 1, 1992, many states rushed to enact legislation in compliance with the federal requirements. An extension was granted to January 1993. All appraisals that are federally related must be performed by certified or licensed appraisers. As of July 1, 1991, lenders must use state-certified appraisers if they want to sell their mortgages to the secondary market. The appraisers are required to meet minimum standards, which include a written report performed in accordance with appraisal standards.

The Uniform Standards of Professional Appraisal Practice (USPAP)

WEB SITE

National Association of Master Appraisers: www.masterappraisers.org

The set of rules that regulates the preparation of appraisal reports is the Uniform Standards of Professional Appraisal Practice (USPAP). These rules spell out the ethical and technical guidelines appraisers must comply with when determining an appraisal value for use in a "federally related" transaction. One provision of the USPAP is that the appraiser, when estimating the value of a parcel of real estate, must employ all three approaches to value: comparison, cost, and income. USPAP further states that if the appraiser chooses not to consider all three approaches, the appraisal report must state which approach was not considered and why the appraiser feels it does not apply to the subject property. The criteria are as follows:

1–4 Family Residential	Commercial Property
$1 million and higher: *Must* use a *certified* appraiser	See below
$250,000–$999,999: *May* use a *licensed* appraiser; a financial institution may presume that residential property is not complex unless the institution has readily available information to the contrary	$250,000 and above: *Must* use a *certified* appraiser
$100,001–$249,999: *May* use a *licensed* appraiser *even if* the property is complex	$100,001–$249,999: *May* use a *licensed* appraiser *even if* the property is complex
$0–$100,000: No appraisal required; however, most institutions will require an appraisal	$0–$100,000: No appraisal required; however, most institutions will require an appraisal.

Even before the enactment of FIRREA, 17 states* had already required appraisers to be licensed or certified. Continuing education and minimum standards of performance are criteria sought by the appraisal institutes and societies.

Most states require licensees to fulfill the following requirements for state certification:

1. 2,000 hours of appraisal work experience
2. 60 hours of basic appraisal education
3. 15 hours of Uniform Standards of Principles and Practice (USPAP)
4. successfully pass an examination

The appraiser needs to be *state* certified to:

1. appraise federally related commercial transactions of more than $250,000
2. appraise residential properties of more than $1 million
3. appraise complex residential properties of more than $250,000
4. appraise residential properties of more than four units
5. successfully pass an examination

---

* *The 17 states are Arizona, Colorado, Delaware, Georgia, Indiana, Michigan, Minnesota, Mississippi, Nebraska, Nevada, New Mexico, Oregon, South Carolina, Tennessee, Utah, Virginia, and West Virginia.*

For *general* certification the appraiser is required to:

1. complete 1,000 hours of residential experience and 1,000 hours of commercial education
2. complete 150 hours of course work (if the state has a residential certification available, the course work is reduced to 105 hours)
3. complete 15 hours of the Uniform Standards of Principles and Practices (USPAP)
4. successfully pass an examination

In some areas of the country, lenders request that appraisers fill out environmental on-site inspection forms. While appraisers already have a responsibility to make note of any condition that could affect the property value through normal research, as they perform the appraisal there is concern over items that cannot readily be observed. Is the appraiser liable to know if there are underground storage tanks? The appraiser needs to inform the client that the appraiser is not an environmental expert and can only observe any existing problems. The appraiser also needs to take care not to report any conclusion about past, present, or future contamination. As more and more responsibility is heaped upon the appraiser, a disclaimer on such issues as environmental hazards and toxic waste should accompany the report.

As professionalism has developed among appraisers, organizations and designations have followed. Today there are many professional appraisal organizations that offer designations and certification to indicate the appraiser's qualifications and knowledge. Rigid appraisal education requirements must be met by appraisers seeking membership and designations in these associations. With local chapters across the country, techniques are taught for appraising urban, rural, and industrial properties.

WEB SITE

American Society of Farm Managers and Rural Appraisers: www.asfmra.org

The Appraisal Institute was formed in January 1991 by the merger of The American Institute of Real Estate Appraisers (AIREA), which awards the RM and MAI designations, and the Society of Real Estate Appraisers (SREA), which awards the SRA, SRPA, and SREA designations. The Appraisal Institute offers continuing education to keep appraisers abreast of industry changes.

WEB SITE

American Society of Appraisers: www .appraisers.org

While there are many more facets involved in the appraisal of real estate, the techniques and definitions presented here should be adequate to introduce you to the field of appraisal. In-depth studies of land and building residual techniques and complete detailed appraisal reports can be found in textbooks written strictly on appraisal.

Summary of Important Points

1. An appraisal is not an exact science, but an estimate of value
2. There are three main appraisal techniques: the cost approach, the sales comparison approach, and the income approach.

3. The appraisal procedure is carried out in a sequence of steps, from defining the problem and collecting the data to analyzing the subject property and applying one or more of the three approaches.

4. Depreciation is loss from any cause, affects value, and is caused by physical depreciation, economic obsolescence, and functional obsolescence.

5. The highest and best use of the property and the various principles involved in creating value are discussed in the chapter.

Discussion Points

1. How are adjustments for the differences in properties applied by the appraiser?

2. Explain the three approaches to value and describe when each is used.

3. Differentiate between market value and market price.

4. Why is it necessary for the appraiser to know the reason for an appraisal? Isn't value the same regardless of the purpose for the appraisal?

5. Explain the principle of progression and regression.

6. List the sequence of steps an appraiser follows in arriving at the value of a property.

Review Questions

Answers to these questions are found in the Answer Key section at the back of the book.

1. In preparing an appraisal report, the appraiser's first step is to:
   a. collect the data
   b. apply the cost approach
   c. write the appraisal report
   d. define the problem

2. Functional obsolescence is due to:
   a. normal wear and tear
   b. inadequate design or floor plan
   c. lack of exterior maintenance
   d. rezoning of surrounding land

3. On what type of property would the cost approach be the most accurate?
   a. a 6-month-old residence
   b. an apartment house
   c. an older property with economic obsolescence
   d. a 15-year-old residence

4. The market value of a property is commonly defined as:
   a. the highest and best use of the property
   b. the highest price at which a willing seller will sell and a willing buyer will buy
   c. the income the property is annually producing
   d. amenities attached to the property

5. The definition of depreciation is:
   a. loss in value from any cause
   b. mortgage foreclosures
   c. loss from scarcity of a product
   d. none of the above

6. Physical depreciation is brought about by:
   a. conditions outside the property
   b. functional obsolescence
   c. normal wear and tear
   d. economic conditions

7. Economic obsolescence is related to:
   a. lack of closet space
   b. poor drainage in the yard
   c. faulty heating systems
   d. conditions external to the property

8. A four-bedroom home with one bathroom suffers from:
   a. economic obsolescence
   b. functional obsolescence
   c. physical depreciation
   d. economic depreciation

9. If a property has a gross monthly income of $930 and the gross rent multiplier is 112.00, which of the following is the estimated value of the property?
   a. $83,035
   b. $104,160
   c. $1,046,000
   d. $8,303,500

10. The formula of replacement-cost-less-depreciation-plus-value-of-land is called the:
    a. income approach
    b. market data approach
    c. comparison approach
    d. cost approach

11. The summation or cost approach to value is best used on:
    a. apartment complexes
    b. service-type buildings
    c. land
    d. older homes

12. The depreciation most difficult to remedy would be:
    a. physical depreciation
    b. economic obsolescence
    c. normal wear and tear
    d. functional obsolescence

13. Which of the following is the capitalization formula used to arrive at value?
    a. net operating income ÷ cap rate = value
    b. net operating income × cap rate = value
    c. gross income × cap rate = value
    d. gross income ÷ cap rate = value

14. Utilizing a property to its greatest economic advantage is commonly referred to as:
    a. mobilization
    b. economic utility
    c. market value
    d. highest and best use

15. When applying the cost approach to value, the appraiser allows for depreciation:
    a. on land
    b. on improvements
    c. on personal property
    d. on neighboring property

16. Which of the following is not a factor to consider when using the comparison approach to value?
    a. date of sale
    b. physical features and amenities
    c. current monthly rent
    d. financing concessions

17. The square foot method used in the cost approach involves using which of the following formulas?
    a. length × width × height
    b. length × width
    c. number of drawer pulls × cost of one drawer pull
    d. 2 × length × width × height

18. A builder may use this method to estimate the price to charge for a house by using this very precise cost breakdown, such as totaling cabinet hinges and all supplies used in the construction, plus adding labor costs:
    a. replacement cost method
    b. square foot method
    c. quantity survey method
    d. cost approach

19. To calculate the present worth of future benefits of a property, which of the following is used?
    a. the capitalization formula
    b. the cost approach
    c. comparable properties
    d. the summation approach

20. Functional obsolescence would least likely include:
    a. rotting wood
    b. poor architecture
    c. an outdated kitchen
    d. bad design

21. A 25-year-old home is sound and in good condition, but has an outdated bath. The bath is suffering from:
    a. normal depreciation
    b. physical obsolescence
    c. functional obsolescence
    d. deterioration

22. The following definition defines market price:
    a. sale price
    b. replacement value
    c. the appraised value
    d. the residual value

23. What value may an appraiser NOT be employed to determine?
    a. market value
    b. loan value
    c. condemnation value
    d. past value

24. A new industry that will employ 350 people will locate in the city. This is an example of which of the following forces?
    a. physical force
    b. sociological force
    c. economic force
    d. political force

25. The best definition of an appraisal is:
    a. a means of determining depreciation
    b. a method to keep values current with reproduction costs
    c. a statement of facts that may not necessarily be true
    d. an estimate of value

26. Based on what you know about the approaches to value, which of the following would not be used to appraise land?
    a. sales comparison approach
    b. income approach
    c. market analysis approach
    d. cost approach

27. The following is a method of valuing property based on the income that it can be expected to generate.
    a. gross rent multiplier
    b. sales comparison approach
    c. summation approach
    d. cost approach

28. When two or more adjoining parcels of land are merged, the increased value is called:
    a. assemblage value
    b. plottage value
    c. salvage value
    d. conformity value

29. When using the comparison approach, the appraiser makes adjustments by:
    a. adjusting the subject property to the comparables
    b. adding value to the superior property
    c. subtracting value from the inferior property
    d. adjusting the comparables to the subject property

Environmental Issues and Real Estate

KEY TERMS

Air Quality Act of 1967

asbestos

brownfields

carbon monoxide (CO)

Clean Water Act

Coastal Zone Management Act

Comprehensive Environmental Response, Compensation, and Liability Act (CERCLA)

electromagnetic fields (EMFs)

encapsulation

Environmental Protection Agency (EPA)

Flood Control Act

formaldehyde

groundwater

landfill

lead

Lead-Based Paint Hazard Reduction Act (LBPHRA)

mold

National Environmental Policy Act (NEPA)

radon

Resource and Recovery Act (RCRA)

Safe Drinking Water Act

Superfund

Superfund Amendment and Reauthorization Act (SARA)

underground storage tanks (USTs)

wetlands

OVERVIEW

The environment has become a major concern of ecologists and scientists as the planet becomes warmer. We are beginning to realize that the pollutants in the air we breathe and the water we drink affect our health and the environment. Public awareness of these problems has brought sufficient concern that laws have been passed to protect the public health and welfare.

The real estate community and related industries are especially interested in addressing the issue because of their involvement in transferring properties in both existing neighborhoods and new developments. In Chapter 9 we learned that the seller completes a property disclosure form that will state any property defects of which the seller is aware. Buyers should schedule a home inspection to reveal any problems to the property itself; however, this examination will not cover outside issues. If the buyer raises any concerns, the licensee must invite the buyer to ask questions and seek answers.

Environmental issues touch the economic, social, and physical environment and are having an enormous impact on the way we do business. Almost daily there are reminders to save newspapers, bottles, and cans for recycling in an effort to lessen the burden on waste sites. Future pollution through population growth and development can be minimized by effective laws. Some of the acts that have been mandated in recent years to establish safeguards on the pollutants that are escaping into the atmosphere are covered in this chapter.

Outdoor Pollution Issues

The **Air Quality Act of 1967** was enacted to protect and control air pollution. It was amended in 1970 to establish air quality standards and protect the public health and welfare. The act passes responsibility to the states for control within their boundaries. Automobile fumes contributing to air pollution resulted in emission controls on all vehicles, and on some inner-city streets diesel-fueled vehicles are banned. In many cases, the effect on small industries was disastrous. It can be costly to meet requirements to curtail fumes discharged from smokestacks generated in the industrial process, but a necessary step to abate air pollution.

The National Environmental Policy Act (NEPA)

Control city smog

Passed by Congress in 1969, the **National Environmental Policy Act (NEPA)** encouraged understanding and protection of the environment to reduce future damage. It created and funded the **Environmental Protection Agency (EPA)**.

Environmental impact statements prepared by the EPA recognize and analyze the impact developments have on the economic, social, and physical environment. They cover the impact to noise, water, air quality, natural vegetation, and wildlife. In 1972 *noise control* legislation became effective due to concern that airports and the flight patterns of jet airplanes near residential subdivisions caused excessive noise. The legislation requires that noise emission standards be developed for products delivered by rail or motor carrier.

The Flood Control Act

Federal and private
insurers join to
insure flood plains

The **Flood Control Act** as amended in 1969 was passed by Congress due to the devastation of land caused by floods. Private insurance companies found that they could not issue insurance at affordable rates, so the Federal Insurance Agency (FIA) combined with independent agents to offer insurance at rates that were not excessive. To prevent a rash of development in floodplain areas, the FIA offered emergency coverage with curtailments on building in flood zones. The act requires communities to adopt plans to reduce losses in flood-prone areas by building dams and spillways. Disastrous results were experienced from the havoc wreaked by Hurricane Katrina in the New Orleans area in 2005. The levee broke and thousands of families lost their homes.

The **Coastal Zone Management Act** of 1972 offers an incentive program to coastal states that border on the Atlantic, Pacific, and Arctic Oceans, the Great Lakes, and the Gulf of Mexico. The states are required to set regulations on the methods that they will use to protect beaches from erosion, to preserve wildlife habitats, and to shelter marine life. Once the states meet federal approval, they have jurisdiction over the zones, even those occupied by federal installations. Any development in these zones must obtain a permit from a regional agency resulting in control over buildings that may damage the natural coastline and destroy wildlife habitats.

In 1972 Congress passed the Marine Protection Research and Sanctuaries Act to regulate the discharge and dumping of refuse into the offshore areas of the ocean.

The Clean Water Act

In 1972 Congress passed the **Clean Water Act** and gave the Army Corps of Engineers responsibility for issuing permits regulating the "discharge of dredged or fill material into navigable waters." The term **wetlands** was not mentioned, however, any land considered a wetland by the corps and the EPA is to remain protected waters of the United States. The EPA defines wetlands as "those areas that are inundated or saturated by surface water or ground water at a frequency and duration sufficient to support, and under normal circumstances do support, a prevalence of vegetation typically adapted for life in saturated soil conditions." This definition encompasses swamps, marshes, bogs, pine flats, prairie potholes, and even puddles with wood around them.

The clean water act protects wetlands

Some landowners found that when they prepared to develop their land it was labeled a wetland and they could not commence with the development. No compensation is provided to the property owner when land is found to contain a wetland. Although the idea of protecting wetlands is to retain the natural habitats for wildlife to survive in, many people feel wetlands should be defined based on functional value and that a statewide mapping and classification system needs to be put in place.

At one time, farmers and developers would drain and fill in wetlands in the belief it would eliminate mosquito breeding grounds. In actuality, wetlands reduce nitrogen and phosphates and remove almost 100 percent of biological oxygen demand (BOD) that kills aquatic life. The vegetation in wetlands can hold almost 90 percent of sediment from runoff.

Licensees selling and listing farms, land for development, and industrial sites need to be aware of the laws governing wetlands. They should not advise their clients, but direct them to the regulatory agencies.

The Resource and Recovery Act (RCRA)

In 1976 Congress passed the **Resource and Recovery Act (RCRA)**, which legislated the transporting, storage, treatment, and disposal of hazardous waste and required solid waste materials to be discarded in designated dump sites. The Solid Waste Disposal Act resulted in the EPA monitoring landfills and disposal sites, although most states and local governments already had the standards in place to which disposal sites must now adhere. This was a direct result of illegal disposal of toxic waste materials that have polluted the groundwater. Although millions of people depend upon septic systems for their waste disposal, FHA, Fannie Mae, and Freddie Mac require that, when available, the municipal systems be used.

EPA moniters hazardous waste disposal

Underground Storage Tanks (USTs)

An amendment to the RCRA was passed by Congress in 1984 regarding **underground storage tanks (USTs)**. The EPA is concerned that 25 percent of all underground storage tanks are leaking, contaminating the soil, and seeping into groundwater. The leaking can contribute to fires and explosions, since petroleum products are the most prevalent use for these tanks. Since December 1988, all underground storage tanks must be equipped with an EPA leak detector system. When offering property for sale, evidence of storage tanks should be checked, especially in strip shopping centers and abandoned service stations and when the presence of pumps or oil stains are obvious. Residential areas in some parts of the country use fuel oil for heating that is kept in underground tanks. If abandoned they should also be checked for leaking. Just because it is buried and not visible to the eye does not make it less of a hazard. UST owners must register their tanks and comply with the EPA regulations.

With the vast amount of properties that transfer ownership annually, our present legislation is holding both past and present owners responsible for hazardous waste removal. Lenders are concerned because of their liability when they assume title to defaulted properties.

The Comprehensive Environmental Response, Compensation, and Liability Act (CERCLA)

WEB SITE

www.epa.gov/
superfund/policy/
index.htm

Passed by Congress in 1980, the **Comprehensive Environmental Response, Compensation, and Liability Act (CERCLA)** was funded with $9 billion (commonly referred to as **Superfund**). The act provides for the organization of programs to set priorities for cleaning up the nation's worst existing hazardous waste sites. The act expired in 1985 but was reestablished and amended in 1986 as the **Superfund Amendment and Reauthorization Act (SARA)**. Former and present owners are required to pay for toxic waste cleanup regardless if they currently own the property. It defines more clearly the responsibility imposed.

However, the act included a clause that if the present owners were unaware of hazardous waste they would not be held responsible. By the end of 1989, more than 35,000 sites were listed and placed on the EPA's National Priority List (NPL). Top priority was given to 1,215 of these sites for permanent, long-term cleanup programs.

Mining Landfills

A growing number of communities are reclaiming **landfill** sites by a process called *landfill reclamation.* "Mining" landfills has provided fuel for waste-burning energy plants and recycling of materials such as glass, aluminum, and plastic that can be sold, thus creating an extra source of revenue for the community. The siting of new landfills is severely limited by economic, environmental, regulatory, and social restraints. No one seems to want to live by a landfill, a fact often cited as the NIMBY, or "not in my back yard."

Brownfields

The abandoned areas that once were industrial and commercial sites but now are vacant eyesores are referred to as **brownfields.** They not only are a blight on the landscape but often contain hazardous waste. Brownfield legislation was enacted in 2002 and funded with $250 million annually for a five-year period in an effort to clean the areas. The act does not hold owners responsible if they were not the cause of the problem. The plan is to have the property developed and back on the tax rolls in a new use. Many of these sites are in urban areas where rehabilitating old buildings or vacant plots into desirable uses has become popular.

Electromagnetic Fields (EMFs)

High-tension electric power lines and transformers produce **electromagnetic fields (EMFs).** It is a detriment when trying to sell a house with power lines that obstruct the view. It is even more difficult if people are afraid of getting cancer from the unsightly lines. There is no confirmed report substantiating the theory that they can cause cancer. However, there is a push to bury power lines, if only because they are unsightly. Every day we are in contact with electrical equipment such as cellular phone radio frequencies, television and microwaves, and other appliances. Again, studies find no correlation between illnesses caused by their use.

WEB SITE

Electromagnetic Fields: www.skepdic .com/emf.html

Indoor Pollution Issues

Indoor air pollution can be defined as chemical, physical, or biological contaminates in the air we breathe inside homes, offices, schools, and public and commercial buildings. Many cities across the nation have placed bans on indoor smoking in public facilities. Following are some other indoor air pollutants that are harmful to the public health.

The Safe Drinking Water Act

Setting safe drinking
water standards

To safeguard public drinking water, **Safe Drinking Water Act** of 1974 set minimum standards for water supply systems. It was discovered that chemical pollution had seeped into our streams and rivers, and sewage had been released into the waters. According to the EPA, as many as 40 million Americans have too much **lead** in their drinking water. Until it was banned in 1988, lead solder was widely used in plumbing. After a number of years, the lead solder inside the pipes becomes coated with minerals, and the lead stops leaching into the water.

Well water should be tested periodically since groundwater can be contaminated if nearby waste disposal systems are not properly treated. A lab certified by the EPA should test for lead content in the water.

Groundwater is water beneath the earth's surface that comprises the *water table,* the normal level at which the ground becomes inundated. In order to protect the water supply it must not be contaminated by runoff from septic systems, leaking underground storage tanks, storm drains, and the disposal of hazardous waste. Since water flows from area to area it contributes to the pollution where it travels. About 75 percent of the earth's surface is water, but a mere 1 percent is considered safe to drink. The tap water in our homes has gone through a water treatment system in an effort to supply clean water.

The Lead-Based Paint Hazard Reduction Act (LBPHRA)

WEB SITE

U.S. Environmental
Protection Agency: Lead-
Based Paint Disclosure
forms: www.epa.gov/
lead/leadbase.htm

In 1992 Congress passed the **Lead-Based Paint Hazard Reduction Act (LBPHRA)**, which requires a seller or a seller's agent to disclose any known lead hazards as part of an FHA sale or lease of a property built before 1978. HUD will insure the mortgage on a house even if it has lead-based paint. The purchaser, however, will be responsible for any removal as HUD will not remove the contamination. Lead-based paint can be hazardous to the health of children who play in an area where there are loose paint chips or dust particles.

High levels of lead can cause damage to the brain and nervous system. A simple blood test can detect excessive levels of lead. If lead-based paint is in good condition it usually does not pose a hazard. An inspection of the paint will determine how much of a hazard is present. A *risk assessment* will reveal if the paint possesses significant problems by the presence of chipped paint and dust particles.

The act requires the following.

- Landlords and sellers must disclose in writing any known lead-based paint.

- Sellers must provide purchasers with a 10-day opportunity to conduct a risk assessment or inspection for the presence of lead-based paint.

- Real estate agents must give the buyer a pamphlet issued by the EPA titled "Protect Your Family from Lead in Your Home."
- Renovators will give the pamphlet to the homeowner before starting work.
- Real estate agents must ensure compliance with these requirements.

Radon

Radon is a radioactive gas that is odorless and cannot be seen or tasted. It occurs from the breakdown of uranium in soil, rock, and water. The air pressure in the soil is usually higher than the pressure in a home. This difference in pressure acts as a vacuum and radon seeps into the home through cracks and holes in the foundation.

Radon is a gas created by natural causes

The Surgeon General warns that it is a leading cause of lung cancer, second to smoking. A purchaser may require that a home be tested to determine the range of radon in the home. Congress has set a long-term goal that the level of radon inside is no more than outside levels, about 0.4 pCi/L (liter of air). There are short-term and long-term test kits that will determine the level of radon in a home. Radon can change daily or weekly in concentration, depending on ventilation, or heating or air conditioning. Excess levels in a home can generally be reduced.

Carbon Monoxide (CO)

Carbon monoxide (CO) is a colorless, nearly odorless, and toxic gas. CO is dangerous because you cannot see, taste, or smell it. In low levels it can cause mild effects that appear to be flu-like symptoms such as headaches, nausea, and fatigue.

Carbon dioxide (CO)—a dangerous gas caused by fuel combustion

Use caution when operating gasoline-powered tools such as floor buffers, welders, compressors, and generators in buildings and semienclosed areas. The U.S. Consumer Protection Safety Commission (CPSC) recommends that every home should have a CO alarm installed. Inspections should be made of all fuel-burning appliances including furnaces, fireplaces, water heaters, space heaters, and clothes dryers for deadly CO leaks.

WEB SITE

Indoor Air Quality (carbon monoxide): www.epa.gov/ iaq/co.html

Formaldehyde

Formaldehyde is used as a raw material in the manufacturing of paint, plastic, resins, photographic materials, and building materials, including insulation. Curtains and upholstery textiles are often treated with formaldehyde resins for crease resistance. Urea-formaldehyde foam was used in the 1970s in an effort to conserve energy but has been largely discontinued. Formaldehyde creates a colorless, pungent gas. Emissions ordinarily decrease over a period of time depending upon the source. The solution to formaldehyde presence may be as simple as opening windows or as complex as utilizing experts to completely remove all insulation.

Mold

Mold is a type of fungus that can pose health hazards. Some molds produce microscopic spores that spread easily through the air. All indoor mold growth should be removed. In inspecting for mold look for water stains on walls, ceilings, woodwork, and other surfaces. Mold can grow on any substance in which moisture is present, including wood, paper, carpet, insulation, and foods. In large amounts, mold can cause serious health problems.

Because of recent lawsuits against construction firms and insurance companies, insurers are excluding mold coverage from their policies. As a result landlords, sellers, property managers, and licensees are also being named as defendants.

Licensees must be vigilant in asking for inspections if there is any doubt there may be mold in the home. A case in point illustrates the damage mold can cause:

In Southern California, Richard and Julie Licon found mold in the walls and floors of their condominium. The wood was black with mold. Their homeowners' association moved the Licons and their children to a hotel. Seven months later they moved back and again the children got seizures, nosebleeds, and other symptoms. They retested the house and found massive amounts of *Stachybotrys* in the air. A spore had grown inside the air conditioning unit. They moved out again, taking only the clothes they were wearing. They are now in litigation with the homeowners' association.

Asbestos

A mineral once used as insulation, **asbestos** is often found when remodeling existing structures. There are expensive abatement procedures involved in its removal. Most buildings with asbestos insulation present no problems as long as it is not disturbed by renovation or repairs, for only then does asbestos create a potential hazard to occupants. Current regulations restrict its use in new buildings and require strict adherence to specific guidelines when it is removed or when renovation is being performed on a building.

While once valued for its fire-resistant qualities, it is now known to be a cancer-causing material. The latency period may be years in an exposed person. Shortness of breath, a continual cough, and possible chest pains are the earliest symptoms of the disease. Asbestos fibers are generally inhaled and trapped in breathing passages and nasal hairs and, if not expelled, are then lodged in the lungs.

If a building is being remodeled, the removal of asbestos should be done only by certified and trained professionals. The area will need to be contained by plastic and high-pressure air machines used so that no particles escape outside the **encapsulated** area. This is an expensive procedure, and removal is only necessary if the area containing asbestos is being disturbed.

Going Green

We are concerned about our earth and what conditions will be like for future generations. Will we leave light footprints on our land? Are there ample resources to support our lifestyles?

New emphasis is being placed on building homes that not only conserve energy, but that are environmentally friendly. New ideas have emerged in the construction of today's buildings. Contractors are realizing that green-built homes offer quality and high-performance features that are attracting buyers. With the increased costs in heating and air conditioning and the need to conserve water, prospective home buyers are asking and demanding that homes incorporate more environmentally friendly products.

Extra insulation is being added to roofs and walls in an effort to lower heating and cooling costs. Not only is it important to have good energy performance, but the air quality inside the home is being considered for the health and welfare of the occupants. Adequate ventilation that brings outdoor air into the building to dilute indoor air pollutants is important. Air cleaners are another means of removing pollutants.

WEB SITE
www.zeroenergy.com

The items in particular that builders are addressing include:

- energy performance
- durable construction and ease of maintenance
- air quality within the structure for the occupant's health and welfare
- water conservation
- impact on the land

WEB SITE
www.housingzone
.com/forum-green/

Architectural integrity considers both the site and the region. Depending on the section of our country, placement of windows is important. In colder regions, windows should be on the east, west, and south sections of a house. In warmer areas, awnings provide shade. Planting trees not only adds to an attractive landscape, but also serves as shade. Utility companies suggest shrubs and plants that use less water.

Going green is not difficult to achieve, and both builders and consumers are taking pride in conserving our earth.

Summary of Important Points

1. Environmental controls have made people aware of the need to preserve our natural resources and aid in the preservation of our cities and the welfare of our citizens. The real estate agent must know what to look for on a property, how to clean up environmental problems, and how such problems may affect the value of real estate.

2. The Air Quality Act was enacted to protect and control air pollution.

3. The Flood Control Act authorized the Federal Insurance Agency (FIA) to join with the private insurance companies to offer flood insurance in flood zones.

4. The Clean Water Act protects wetland areas from development or drainage.

5. Underground storage tanks (USTs) must be equipped with an EPA leak detector system.

6. A fund, commonly referred to as Superfund, provides for cleaning up the nation's worst hazardous waste sites.

7. Real estate licensees must give the buyer a pamphlet issued by the EPA titled "Protect Your Family from Lead in Your Home."

8. Radon is a radioactive gas that can seep into a home through cracks and holes in the foundation.

9. Mold is a fungus caused by moisture and may cause serious health problems.

10. Asbestos is a mineral fiber once used as insulation in buildings. It must be removed if remodeling disturbs the material.

11. Carbon monoxide (CO) is a deadly gas that results from fuel-burning tools and appliances.

12. As real estate licensees, there is much that we need to be aware of when we assist buyers and sellers in the transfer of real estate. Among the concerns is being alert to hidden defects and circumstances that affect the value of real estate. Many of these concerns may be environmental issues. Being aware of how environmental problems can affect value, we must take a proactive part in the solution.

Discussion Points

1. Cite environmental issues that may affect property values in your area.

2. How does mold become a health problem?

3. If you think there may be a problem with radon in a house you have listed, what action should you take?

4. Define the term wetlands.

5. When does lead-based paint become a hazard?

Review Questions

Answers to these questions are found in the Answer Key section at the back of the book.

1. Lead ingestion occurs primarily from:
   a. drinking water and lead-based cosmetics
   b. insulation material and flaking paint
   c. hand-to-mouth activity and breathing lead dust
   d. airborne dust particles

2. All of the following are true regarding lead-based paint EXCEPT:
   a. sellers must disclose any known lead-based paint
   b. licensees must give buyers a pamphlet issued by EPA
   c. lead-based paint in good condition usually is not a hazard
   d. landlords verbally must disclose any lead-based paint

3. Which of the following pollutants has a long latency period?
   a. lead-based paint
   b. pesticides
   c. asbestos
   d. formaldehyde

4. The primary goal of underground storage tank regulation is:
   a. identify underground storage sites
   b. remove underground storage tanks
   c. protect groundwater sources
   d. line all tanks with asbestos

5. The purpose of wetlands is to:
   a. provide waste sites
   b. provide a habitat for wildlife
   c. provide an ideal place for high-rise construction
   d. protect farmland

6. The Environmental Protection Agency (EPA) was created to:
   a. deliver a model building development code
   b. enforce environmental laws
   c. provide for nontraditional zoning practices
   d. control growth by the use of building moratoriums

7. Which of the following environmental issues should the licensee be concerned with when selling or listing property?
   a. underground storage tanks
   b. lead paint
   c. the presence of radon
   d. all of the above

8. The leading cause of lung cancer, second to smoking, is:
   a. lead-based paint
   b. radon
   c. carbon monoxide
   d. mold

9. Which of the following could be eliminated as a cause of combustion pollution?
   a. unvented fireplace
   b. dirty air conditioner
   c. space heater
   d. malfunctionng furnace

10. All of the following are true regarding mold EXCEPT:
    a. it is a type of fungus that can cause health problems
    b. it can grow where moisture is present
    c. it is wise to carry insurance against mold
    d. microscopic spores can spread through the air

Fair Housing Laws

KEY TERMS

administrative law judge (ALJ)

Americans with Disabilities Act (ADA)

blockbusting

Civil Rights Act of 1866

Civil Rights Act of 1964

Department of Housing and Urban Development (HUD)

Equal Credit Opportunity Act (ECOA)

Fair Housing Act of 1968

Fair Housing Amendment Act of 1988

fair housing laws

panic peddling

redlining

restrictive covenants

steering

OVERVIEW

Every person engaged in the business of real estate should be familiar with **fair housing laws** as they relate to the sale and rental of all residential property. Federal, state, and local laws provide for equal opportunity in housing. This is the law of the land, and it is the right of every person in this country to own or rent without regard to race, color, religion, national origin, sex, handicap, or family status.

Real estate salespeople, brokers, and owners must be cognizant of and must put into practice the laws that prohibit discrimination. Individuals have a right to purchase or rent housing in any area they desire to live in, as long as they can assume the financial responsibility.

The Civil Rights Act of 1866

Equal housing opportunities

It is the policy of the United States to provide, within its constitutional limitations, for fair housing throughout the country. Fair housing law dates from the **Civil Rights Act of 1866**, which prohibited discrimination based on race. This act provided that "all citizens of the United States shall have the same right, in every state and territory, as is enjoyed by white citizens thereof to inherit, purchase, lease, sell, hold, and convey real and personal property."

The Civil Rights Act of 1964

Title VI, the **Civil Rights Act of 1964**, was passed by Congress to prohibit discrimination when a program receives federal financial assistance. The intent of Congress was to ensure that no program utilizing federal financial aid should be tainted by discriminatory acts. The **Department of Housing and Urban Development (HUD)** had set aside funds under special programs to give assistance to low-income citizens in homeownership and low-rent public housing.

The Fair Housing Act of 1968 and the Amendment Act of 1988

WEB SITE

U.S. Department of Housing and Urban Development: Fair Housing: www.hud.gov/ groups/fairhousing.cfm

In June 1968, the United States Supreme Court upheld the 1866 Civil Rights Act in the case of *Jones v. Mayer*. The original act proclaimed that all racial discrimination was illegal when selling or renting property; the court enforced it to include race, color, religion, and national origin. In the case of *Jones v. Mayer,* a black person sued for injunction and other relief with an allegation that the defendant had refused to sell him a home solely on racial grounds. The Court decision in this case upheld the 1866 law that there are no exceptions allowed because of race. In 1974 gender was added as a protected class.

The **Fair Housing Act of 1968** was changed in two respects when President Reagan signed the **Fair Housing Amendment Act of 1988** in September of that same year. Effective March 12, 1989, the amendment prohibits discrimination based on disability and familial status, that is, families with children. The act allows certain exemptions for elderly housing. The amendment further alters the procedure of enforcing Title VIII and the penalties that are imposed for a violation.

The Fair Housing Act of 1968, under Title VIII of the Civil Rights Act of 1968, prohibits the following acts:

Provisions of fair housing law

1. refusing to sell or rent to, or negotiate or deal with any person
2. quoting different terms or conditions for renting or buying housing to persons of different races, colors, religions, or national origins

3. advertising that property is available only to certain races, colors, religions, or national origins

4. not being truthful about the availability of homes for rent or sale

5. **blockbusting**, or inducing owners, for profit, to sell or rent their homes by threatening the movement of minority groups into neighborhoods

6. lenders varying terms or conditions for home loans in an effort to discriminate

7. discriminating in real estate services, multiple listing services, or broker organizations by denying membership or limiting participation

The Amendment Act of 1988 additionally prohibits the following:

Amendment Act of 1988

8. the assessment of higher security deposits to handicapped persons or to families with children

9. the segregation of such persons to particular floors or wings of a building within a complex

10. denying such persons access to all services and amenities provided in connection with the building

These laws apply to single-family housing under the following conditions:

Application of fair housing law

1. when single-family housing is privately owned and the owner employs a real estate firm (or any other person who sells or rents)

2. when single-family homes are not privately owned

3. when discriminatory advertising is used for single-family homes

4. when single-family homes are owned by private individuals who own more than three such houses and who, in any two-year period, sell more than one in which the individual was not the most recent resident

These laws apply to multifamily housing under the following conditions:

1. when multifamily dwellings containing five or more rooms or units are rented

2. when multifamily dwellings of four or fewer units or rooms are rented, if none of the units is occupied by the owner of the property

Exemptions to the Fair Housing Act

The law does not affect the sale or rental of single-family houses owned by a private individual if any of the following are true.

When exemptions are applicable

1. The person owns three or fewer houses.

2. A real estate broker is not used.

3. Discriminatory advertising is not used.

4. No more than one house in which the owner was not the most recent resident is sold during any two-year period.

5. Rooms or units in owner-occupied multifamily dwellings for two to four families are rented, and discriminatory advertising is not used.

6. The sale, rental, or occupancy of dwellings that a religious organization owns or operates for other than a commercial purpose is limited to persons of the same religion, if membership in that religion is not restricted on account of race, color, or national origin.

7. The rental or occupancy of lodging that a private club owns or operates for other than a commercial purpose is limited to the club's members. This exemption does not allow discrimination if the reason is race.

Persons with Disabilities

Housing availability to the disabled

Both the mentally and physically disabled are covered by the 1988 act. Excluded are persons currently using or who are addicted to illegal drugs and those who have been convicted of the manufacture or distribution of illegal drugs. An owner is not required by the act to provide a dwelling to any person whose tenancy poses a direct threat to the health, safety, and property of others.

Provisions of the law state that persons with disabilities (or families with children) cannot be assessed higher security deposits. Nor can they be segregated in particular sections, floors, or buildings within a development. All services and amenities provided in connection with the building must be open to them.

Accessibility for Persons with Disabilities

Reasonable modification to a unit may be made by a disabled person at the tenant's expense. However, the act permits the property owner to require the tenant to restore the unit, at the tenant's expense, to its original condition. The owner may further require that funds be placed in an escrow account to provide for the restoration.

Since March 13, 1991, all new multifamily dwellings of four or more units must be constructed to allow access and use by persons with disabilities. In buildings without elevators, only first floor units are covered by this provision.

Families with Children

Family housing

WEB SITE

U.S. Department of Housing and Urban Development: Frequently Asked Questions: www.hud.gov/offices/ theo/disabilities/ sect504fao.cfm

The 1988 amendment also extends fair housing coverage to families with children under the age of 18, though dwelling owners must abide by local ordinances governing the maximum number of persons that may occupy a unit. HUD felt that such regulations are the province of local and state governments in accordance with the preamble. If no such local ordinance exists, HUD regulations permit property owners to establish reasonable rules governing the number of persons who may occupy a unit, based on the number of sleeping areas or rooms and the overall size of the unit. The act further affords protection to any person who is pregnant or is in the process of securing legal custody of an individual not yet 18 years of age.

Elderly Exemptions

Certain exemptions were made in the 1988 amendment act for elderly housing. The act defines housing for the elderly as:

1. housing provided under any federal or state program that HUD determines as specifically designed and operated to assist elderly persons
2. housing intended for and solely occupied by persons 62 years of age or older
3. housing intended for occupancy by at least one person 55 years of age or older per unit

The act further states that 80 percent of the units must be occupied by at least one person 55 years of age or older. The policy and procedures and any publications must demonstrate the intent that it is indeed housing for the older person. Housing not 80 percent occupied by at least one person 55 years or older by September 13, 1988, may qualify for exemption if all vacancies are filled after that date by persons who meet the age requirement. In December 1995 an amendment to the federal Housing Act clarified that if a housing project qualifies for "55 and over" status it can exclude families with children, normally a violation of the Fair Housing Act. Real estate practitioners will not be liable if it is later determined that a facility is not eligible for the exemption, if (1) the facility states in writing that it complies with the requirements of the "55 and over" exemption and (2) if practitioners can show that they did not know that the facility was not eligible for the exemption. The amendment ends the provision that housing intended for and occupied by persons 55 and older must provide significant facilities and services to meet the physical and social needs of older persons.

Enforcement Procedures

The Amendment Act of 1988 provides a new enforcement system that allows all parties the choice of having the case brought before an **administrative law judge (ALJ)** or a federal district court.

Under the original Title VIII, single or isolated acts of discrimination were not subject to enforcement by the federal government. The authority invested in HUD was limited to efforts to conciliate disputes, and if these efforts proved unsuccessful the aggrieved individual could file an action in federal court. The Department of Justice's jurisdiction was limited to cases in which a continuous pattern of discrimination was evident. Complaints should be sent to the Office of Equal Opportunity (OEO) at HUD:

Filing complaints

Fair Housing
Department of Housing and Urban Development
Washington, D.C. 20410

In addition, complaints can be sent to Fair Housing in care of the nearest OEO regional office. When filing a complaint, it should be notarized, if possible, and must be sent to OEO within one year of the alleged discriminatory act. Once a complaint is filed, HUD can pursue the complaint if efforts to resolve it through the conciliation process have not been successful after 100 days. During the 100-day conciliation period, HUD can also seek temporary relief, including temporary restraining orders when such actions are necessary to carry out the intent of the act. The HUD secretary has the prerogative to file a bias complaint on his own initiative or to begin an investigation of housing practices to determine if a complaint should be filed (see Figure 19.1).

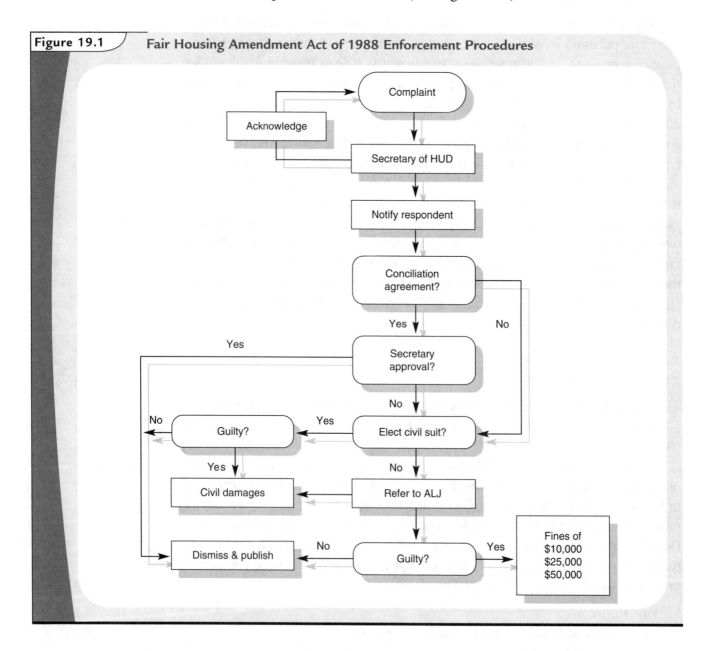

Figure 19.1 **Fair Housing Amendment Act of 1988 Enforcement Procedures**

If a charge is made by HUD following an investigation of a discrimination complaint, the involved parties have the option of having HUD file the charge in a U.S. district court, rather than referring the case to an ALJ. HUD will automatically bring the case before an ALJ if no request is made for a jury trial. The plaintiff and the respondent will both be subpoenaed. The presentation of evidence must conform to the Federal Rule of Evidence just as it would in a civil action in a U.S. district court. An ALJ may award compensatory damages, injunctive and other equitable relief, and civil monetary penalties. A penalty may be levied against the respondent up to a maximum of $10,000 if there is no prior violation; $25,000 if there has been prior violation within the preceding five-year period; and $50,000 if there have been two or more violations within the preceding seven-year period. The fines of $25,000 or $50,000 may be imposed regardless of time limits if the defendant is a single individual rather than a real estate firm engaging in more than one discriminatory housing practice. These maximum civil penalties are not automatic in every situation, and consideration is given to the nature and circumstances of the violation and past history of the violator.

Once the ALJ's order is issued, HUD must review it within 30 days or the finding becomes final. Either party has the option of obtaining a court review in a federal appeals court in the district where the violation took place. The court can stop the sale or rental of the desired housing to someone else and make it possible for the complainant to buy or rent the desired housing, or it can award damages and court costs or take other appropriate action to benefit the complainant.

It is illegal to coerce, intimidate, threaten, or interfere with a person buying, renting, or selling housing, making a complaint of discrimination, or exercising any such rights in connection with this law.

Americans with Disabilities Act

In January of 1992 the **Americans with Disabilities Act (ADA)** became law (see Figure 19.2). As stated in Chapter 10, the law protects the rights of people with disabilities. Disabilities are defined here as mental or physical impairments that substantially limit one or more of a person's major life activities.

There are four primary sections to the act. Title I says that an employer of more than 15 people cannot discriminate against a qualified person because of a disability. Title II states that all state and local government service buildings must be accessible to persons with disabilities. Title III states that all public establishments must be made accessible to persons with disabilities, and Title IV covers public communication providing for telecommunication relay services for hearing- and speech-impaired individuals.

| Figure 19.2 | Federal Fair Housing Laws |

Legislation	Civil Rights Act of 1866	Fair Housing Act of 1968 (Title VIII)	Housing and Community Development Act of 1974	Fair Housing Amendment Act of 1988	Equal Credit Opportunity Act of 1974 (lending)	Americans with Disabilities Act (1992)
Race	X	X			X	
Color		X			X	
Religion		X			X	
National Origin		X			X	
Sex			X		X	
Age					X	
Marital Status					X	
Disability			X	X		X
Family Status				X		
Public Assistance Income					X	
Enforcement Procedure				X		

Equal Credit Opportunity Act (ECOA)

Lender compliance

According to the **Equal Credit Opportunity Act (ECOA)**, enacted by Congress in 1975, lenders who make residential real estate loans must not discriminate in fixing the amount, interest, rate duration, terms, or conditions of a loan because of sex, marital status, race, color, religion, national origin, or receipt of income from public assistance. This is not to say that the lender cannot refuse a loan if the borrower is financially unable to meet the commitment.

Anyone who is legally able to enter into a contract cannot be refused credit based on age. A lender must not discriminate if a person is on social security or receives income from public assistance, such as food stamps. All applications for credit are based only on:

- credit rating
- job stability
- income basis
- net worth

Redlining

The lender must not refuse to make loans in certain neighborhoods; to do so is called **redlining**. Refusal to offer financing in a particular section of the city can lead to the decay of the area. To ensure compliance with the law, the federal government passed the Home Mortgage Disclosure Act in 1975. Large lenders with one or more offices in a particular area are required to issue annual reports on all loans so that if redlining does exist it is easily detectable.

Salesperson and Broker Obligations

Broker and agent compliance

Not only are salespersons and brokers bound by the Civil Rights Act, but if a licensee holds membership in the National Association of REALTORS®, she must also abide by Article 10 of the Code of Ethics. Article 10 requires that "the REALTOR® shall not deny equal professional service to any person for reasons of race, creed, sex, or country of national origin. The REALTOR® shall not be a party to any plan or agreement to discriminate against a person or persons on the basis of race, creed, sex, or country of national origin."

Blockbusting and Panic Peddling

A salesperson or broker must not induce nonminority homeowners to sell their properties for profit because of the introduction of minorities in or near the neighborhood. This is **blockbusting** and is prohibited by law. Great care must be taken not to solicit listings on the premise that minority groups are moving into the area, insinuating that property may lessen in value. The salesperson's conduct must be above reproach and not give the impression of **panic peddling**. Intensive door-to-door canvassing in a changing neighborhood or in a neighborhood adjacent to a changing or minority neighborhood would create suspicion.

The agent must affirmatively demonstrate full compliance with the fair housing laws and work in a like manner with all clients so that no accusation of giving less favorable treatment to a minority would occur. This involves servicing customers equally and not ignoring a minority client, submitting offers promptly, and not offering the property on less favorable terms to a minority person.

Steering

The agent must not try to avoid showing property to minority customers in certain nonintegrated areas. To take them only to minority or changing neighborhoods is **steering**. Offering a wide range of properties in all areas will alleviate any such complaint. Conversely, the salesperson should show the nonminority customer homes in all neighborhoods to avoid being accused of discouraging a buyer from seeking housing in a minority or changing neighborhood.

Equal Housing Opportunity

In 1972, the fair housing law was amended to include the requirement of equal opportunity posters. All real estate firms, model homes, and mortgage lenders must display the Equal Housing Opportunity poster, which states that housing is available equally to all people (see Figure 19.3).

WEB SITE

U.S. Department of Housing and Urban Development and Equal Opportunity: www .hud.gov/offices/thel/ progdesc/title8.cfm

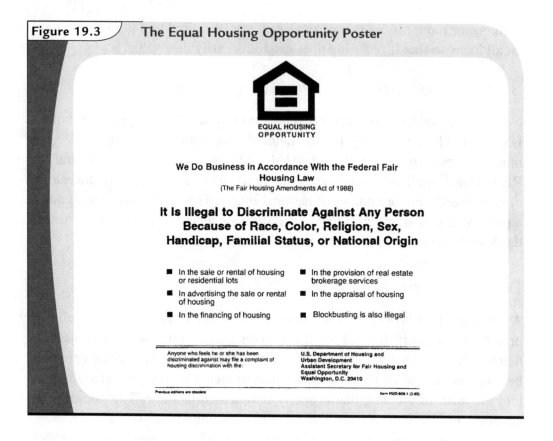

Figure 19.3   The Equal Housing Opportunity Poster

Restrictive Covenants

It is further unlawful to place racially **restrictive covenants** in the transfer, sale, or rental of housing. Many states have enacted legislation that is consistent with the federal fair housing law. Complaints are directed to the state and are handled by the appropriate state agency. If an incorporated city has enacted or adopted a resolution equivalent to the state's fair housing law, complaints will be directed to the local agency. If the complaint is not handled with reasonable promptness, the state regains jurisdiction of the complaint.

The purposes of the federal and state fair housing laws are to:

1. seek to eliminate and prevent discrimination in places of public accommodation because of race, color, sex, religion, national origin, ancestry, handicap, or family status

2. carry through the purpose of this act by conference conciliation and persuasion so that persons may be guaranteed their civil rights and so that good will be fostered

3. formulate policies to enforce the purpose of this act and make recommendations to agencies and officers of the state or local subdivisions of government in aid of such policies and purposes

4. adopt rules and regulations to carry out the powers granted by this act

5. designate one or more members of the commission or the commission staff to conduct investigations of discrimination in race, color, sex, religion, national origin, ancestry, handicap, or family status and to attempt to resolve such complaints by conference, conciliation, and persuasion, and conduct such conciliation meetings and conferences as deemed necessary to resolve a particular complaint. Such meetings shall be held in the county in which the claim arose

6. determine that probable cause exists for crediting the allegations of a complaint

7. determine that a complaint cannot be resolved by conference, conciliation, or persuasion

8. dismiss complaints when it is determined there is not probable cause to credit the allegations of a complaint

9. hold hearings, subpoena witnesses and compel their attendance, administer oaths, take the testimony of any person under oath, and in connection therewith require for examination any papers relating to any matter under investigation or in question before the commission

10. issue publications and the results of studies and research that tend to promote good will and minimize or eliminate discrimination because of race, color, sex, religion, national origin, ancestry, handicap, or family status

The NAR Code of Ethics

Members of the National Association of REALTORS® (NAR) are required to follow the NAR Code of Ethics and Standards of Practice, which was adopted in 1913. All brokers and their associated licensees are obligated to follow these guidelines and to conduct themselves in an ethical manner at all times.

WEB SITE

National Association of REALTORS®: Code of Ethics: www.realtor.org

Summary of Important Points

1. The original Civil Rights Act of 1866 was based on race only, but the spirit of fair housing experienced a breakthrough when the federal Fair Housing Act of 1968 extended the law to include race, color, religion, and national origin.

2. In 1974 an amendment included gender.

3. The amendment signed by President Reagan in September 1988 prohibits discrimination based on disability and families with children, with exclusions made for housing for the elderly.

4. In January 1992 the Americans with Disabilities Act became law. All state and local government service buildings and all public establishments must be accessible to persons with disabilities. Employers of 15 or more people

cannot discriminate against qualified persons because of a disability. Public communication systems must provide for hearing- and speech-impaired individuals.

5. Any person seeking restitution because of discrimination should file a complaint with HUD within one year after the alleged violation occurred. If it appears to be covered by the law, HUD will attempt informal, confidential conciliation in an effort to end the discriminatory practice.

6. A person may take a complaint directly to court, but again, the violation must be acted upon within one year's time.

7. The licensed salesperson and broker must take diligent care to offer all properties to any person seeking housing. The salesperson must not attempt to induce a homeowner to list a house for sale by representing to the owner that minorities are moving into the neighborhood, even when the statement is accurate.

8. Membership in the multiple listing service or in real estate organizations must not be denied to any person because of race, color, religion, national origin, or sex.

9. The affirmative marketing agreement is a commitment made by many real estate salespeople and brokers to demonstrate their compliance with fair housing laws.

10. Real estate firms are required to display the Equal Housing Opportunity poster in their offices. Anyone engaged in the real estate business must offer to all prospective purchasers equal opportunity to buy the real estate of their choice.

Discussion Points

1. If you were asked by a prospect to whom you were showing homes if there were any minority families residing in the area, how would you respond?

2. In what instances are there exceptions to the fair housing law?

3. Summarize the two methods of handling a civil complaint.

4. When can property owners be selective to whom they rent or sell their real estate?

5. List the two main provisions of the 1988 amendment to the Fair Housing Act.

Review Questions

Answers to these questions are found in the Answer Key section at the back of the book.

1. The Civil Rights Act of 1866 prohibited discrimination based on:
   a. race, color, religion, and sex
   b. race only
   c. sex only
   d. race, national origin, color, and religion

2. A complaint to the federal Fair Housing Commission must be:
   a. filed within one year after the alleged discrimination
   b. resolved within a 60-day conciliation period
   c. presented only to broker involved
   d. made by an attorney

3. The federal agency that administrates the fair housing law is:
   a. QTE
   b. HUD
   c. FFN
   d. attorney general

4. In regard to the federal Fair Housing Act, which of the following is NOT true?
   a. the complaint may be reconciled within 18 months
   b. complaints may be sent directly to HUD
   c. parties involved in a discrimination suit may request HUD to file the charge in a U.S. district court
   d. the parties may choose to have the case brought before an administrative law judge

5. The Fair Housing Act prohibits all of the following EXCEPT:
   a. discrimination in housing because of race
   b. discrimination in housing to the disabled
   c. the sale of a home in a nonintegrated neighborhood to a black family
   d. failure to rent an apartment in an adult complex to a family with children

6. Which of the following is/are NOT exempt from the Fair Housing Act?
   a. an owner of four homes
   b. a religious group that limits rentals of property it owns to members only
   c. the owner of a fourplex who resides in one unit
   d. the homeowner who sells his home without the aid of a real estate firm

7. Under the federal Fair Housing Act, which of the following is not considered a discriminatory practice?
   a. refusing to sell a house to a person of a minority race because she is unable to qualify for a loan
   b. advertising a preference to whom you will sell
   c. restricting the rental of a property by religion
   d. refusing to rent a property to a black family because the husband is disabled

8. The federal Fair Housing Act does NOT apply to which of the following?
   a. denying a person the right to buy a home because of his national origin
   b. a discriminatory restrictive provision in a deed
   c. denying lessees with pets a lease
   d. denying a person the right to buy a home because of her sex

9. Under the housing discrimination laws, which of the following is NOT an illegal act?

   a. requiring a security deposit from a disabled person

   b. refusing to show property to a person based on sex

   c. limiting a purchaser's choice by steering

   d. a lender refusing to place a loan on a property in a deteriorating neighborhood

10. Ms. Loring asked A-1 Realty to lease her home for four months while she was in Europe on vacation. She specified she preferred only white tenants. Under the Fair Housing Act, her preference is:

    a. illegal

    b. legal, since Ms. Loring is the owner-occupant

    c. legal upon acceptance of the lease agreement

    d. legal if the broker obtains the request in writing

11. Ms. Gomez and her three children went to Ace Realty to find a residence for rent. The firm assigned her to Mr. Alvarez in accordance with their policy of matching their client's race and interests as closely as possible. During the course of viewing property, Ms. Gomez asked to see an apartment in a white middle-class neighborhood that she had seen advertised in a newspaper. Mr. Alvarez said the apartment was rented, when in fact it was not. Under the Fair Housing Act:

    a. Mr. Alvarez committed illegal steering

    b. Mr. Alvarez acted in his customer's best interest

    c. it was legal, since it is approved office practice

    d. it was illegal, because Ms. Gomez is a single parent

12. The provisions covered in the Fair Housing Amendment Act of 1988 include:

    a. discrimination based on disability

    b. the assessment of higher security deposits to families with children

    c. the segregation of families with children to particular sections of an apartment complex

    d. all of the above

13. This symbol represents:

    a. HUD

    b. fair housing

    c. equal housing opportunity

    d. FHA

14. A nonprofit religious sect bought property and developed condominiums that they sold back to their church members exclusively. According to the Fair Housing Act, this was:

    a. illegal, because a religious sect cannot build condominiums

    b. illegal, because it is discriminatory

    c. legal, because a religious sect is not subject to law

    d. legal, because a religious sect is allowed to sell property exclusively to its members

15. The 1968 Fair Housing Act prohibits all of the following EXCEPT:

    a. advertising that the home is not available to a minority

    b. discrimination based on religion

    c. blockbusting

    d. discrimination based on a person's occupation

16. Which of the following is prohibited under the Amendment Act of 1988?

    a. discrimination based on sex

    b. redlining

    c. reserving one building of an apartment complex for families with children

    d. allowing a person with a disability to remodel the unit to meet the person's needs

17. The Americans with Disabilities Act provides for which of the following?

    a. the landlord must modify a unit to meet a person's disability needs

    b. families with children to be assessed a higher security deposit

    c. all services in the complex to be available to all the residents

    d. all state and public service buildings to be made accessible to persons with disabilities

18. If a lender refuses to make a loan in a neighborhood that is considered "declining" in value, it is referred to as:

    a. blockbusting

    b. redlining

    c. steering

    d. panic peddling

License Law

KEY TERMS

agent
associate broker
broker
censure
earnest money
license law
reciprocal license

revocation
rules and regulations
salesperson
subdivider
suspension
trust account

OVERVIEW

The real estate field is of great interest to everyone. Many would like to be involved. Private individuals acting in their own behalf find this very rewarding when buying, selling, and investing. In time they feel that they can offer their expertise to others and charge a fee for this service. However, this cannot be done before first obtaining a real estate license.

All 50 states have enacted legislation requiring the licensing of real estate salespeople and brokers. At this time there is no uniform **license law** covering the states, but basically their content is quite similar. The license law and the rules and regulations adopted by each state are for the express purpose of protecting the public. To further protect citizens from unscrupulous or incompetent practitioners, the law prescribes the standards and qualifications for licensing. This has elevated the standards of the real estate profession and protects licensees from unfair competition.

Mandatory education continues to be of primary concern to licensing officials in the belief that specialized knowledge will better qualify the licensee to serve the public. Most states now require completion of certified real estate courses prior to application to take the licensing examination. Many states require continuing education after becoming licensed, so licensees keep abreast of new laws and practices.

Who Needs a License?

While the laws vary from state to state, all states require that to collect a fee for the following acts a person must be licensed as a salesperson or broker. The licensee may perform the following.

- Negotiate the listing, sale, purchase, exchange, rent, lease, or option of real estate or the improvements to real estate.

- Act as a referral agent who receives a fee for providing a lead for listing, sale, purchase, exchange, rent, lease, or option of real estate.

- Manage residential, commercial, industrial, rural, or special-use properties. The licensee collects rents and performs other actions to manage the property for the owner.

- A licensee may give a broker's price opinion or comparative market analysis in the course of the real estate business.

- A licensee may sell lots or other parcels of real estate for the owner.

- Charge an advance fee to promote the sale of real estate. In this type of agreement the owner pays an "up-front" fee and the licensee promises to promote the property. A contract between the parties will state what type of promotion is to be carried out.

- Buy, sell, or deal in options. An unlicensed person may option a parcel and sell it for a profit, *however,* if this activity is a common practice, or if the person derives part of his income from such activity, the person must have a real estate license.

Exceptions

Those persons who are generally exempt from needing a license include the following:

1. an owner or lessor of real estate
2. an attorney-in-fact (someone given power of attorney by the property owner)
3. an attorney-at-law in the performance of duties performed as such attorney-at-law
4. a receiver or trustee in bankruptcy
5. the administrator or executor of a deceased estate
6. a court-appointed guardian
7. an officer or employee of a federal or state agency
8. in many states, resident managers of apartment complexes or persons employed by an owner to lease or manage the owner's property
9. a person who sells or purchases oil, gas, or mineral leases for himself or for others (called a "landman")

10. individuals who render opinions of value for real estate taxation, such as a tax assessor and his staff

11. railroad and public utilities, when the land purchased, sold, or managed is owned by the entity for their own purposes

12. employees or officers of the federal government, when working in an official capacity

Keep in mind that these exceptions do not permit a person to act in the capacity of a real estate firm without a license.

Types of Licenses

There are generally two types of licenses issued: **salesperson** and **broker**. The broker is also called the **agent**. The agent is the personal representative of the principal, usually the seller. A broker's license permits the individual to act independently, to set up a real estate office, and to hire other brokers and salespeople to work for the broker. The broker may set up her business using her own name, for example, Jane A. Smith, or may transact business under a trade name such as A-1 Real Estate Company. If the broker purchases a franchise, the broker will need to disclose the business name (whether it is Jane A. Smith or A-1 Real Estate Company) along with the franchise name. The broker may further elect to form a partnership or corporation with another broker or brokers. In most states all active members of the partnership or corporation must be licensed to conduct the business of a real estate agent.

An **associate broker** is an individual who holds a broker's license but who has elected to work for another broker in preference to owning and operating a firm.

A salesperson is a licensee who is always required to be in the employ of a broker, and all money that comes into the salesperson's possession must be given to the broker for placement into the broker's **trust account** (an account for all money belonging to others). The broker is considered by law to be legally responsible for all the actions of the salespeople.

If branch offices are opened, a broker or associate broker generally must be in charge of each branch office. Again, this is to provide adequate supervision for the sales associates. Since the broker is responsible for the actions of the salesperson, the broker will supervise and guide the salesperson's performance so that the firm is properly and lawfully represented. The salesperson will list and sell property in the name of the broker, and all advertising will be under the broker's business name.

Single License Concept

With advanced technology the agents have more control over their activities, many promoting themselves and participating in the overhead costs. The broker's responsibility and liability for independent salespeople who may

Broker and salesperson

periodically work from their home offices is causing concern since they are not subject to supervision.

Effective January 1, 1997, the state of Colorado abolished the real estate salesperson category of license, and *all* licensees are now brokers. They have three subcategories of broker licenses.

1. *Broker associate*: One who is employed and supervised by an employing broker.

2. *Independent broker*: One who is self-employed and has no employed licensees.

3. *Employing broker*: One who can employ and must supervise other licensees.

Education requirements in Colorado were increased to 168 hours of instruction, with an additional 48 hours in brokerage administration for employing brokers.

Licensing Exams

To obtain a salesperson's or broker's license, one must send proof of completion of the required courses; along with a written application and the application fee. Many states are now requiring that *all* applicants for an original salesperson or broker license undergo a criminal background check utilizing fingerprints.

Applicants must pass a written or computerized examination designed to test real estate knowledge as well as competency to perform the duties of a real estate salesperson or broker. Failure to pass the examination is grounds for denial of a license, but applicants typically are given another opportunity to take the exam. In most states an additional fee is charged to retake the exam.

In the past, individual states prepared their own exams, which placed the burden of writing, preparing, and grading the exam upon the state's real estate governing body. Now many states subscribe to exams prepared by testing services. Organizations such as Applied Measurement Professional (AMP), Assessment System Incorporated (ASI), and Psychological Services Incorporated (PSI) prepare and administer the exams for these states by providing a uniform test generally consisting of 80 to 100 questions applicable to all the states and a minimum of 30 questions relating to the individual state's licensing laws. In addition to the license law questions, the uniform test covers the fundamentals of the principles and practices of real estate. Some states permit a licensee from another state to obtain a license in a new state of residence without further examination or by taking the state portion only. Many states are now using computerized testing services, thus permitting the applicant greater flexibility in selecting a time to take the exam.

Exams differ for the salesperson and broker. A more comprehensive understanding is required from the broker. Since the broker can go into business alone, it is necessary that he understand closing procedures and the fundamentals of operating a real estate business.

Requirements of Applicants

The minimum age requirement for license applicants is generally between 18 and 21 years, with a high school diploma or its equivalent. Other prerequisites also vary. Many states require one to three years' practical experience as a salesperson prior to applying for a broker's license. Nebraska accepts 18 college credit hours or 180 classroom hours in accredited real estate courses in lieu of practical experience, while Arizona requires the equivalent of 12 classroom hours of continuing education annually. In an effort to keep agents informed of changing laws, regulations, and trends, most states have mandated continuing education. Throughout the country, education requirements are constantly increasing to better ensure the public of being represented by qualified sales representatives.

Minimum age and education

Commissions

Since the salesperson generally works as an independent contractor, the sales agent is considered self-employed and as such is responsible for social security and federal and state withholding tax payments. This requires the salesperson to file quarterly estimates of income earned. The broker does not offer fringe benefits such as accident and health insurance or retirement plans for self-employed persons. Based on IRS rulings, to do so would destroy independent contract status. The salesperson would be considered an employee of the broker.

Compensation for services

The salesperson generally earns a percentage of the commission paid to the real estate firm. Assuming the earned commission is 7 percent on a property that sells for $150,000 and further assuming that the real estate firm pays the listing salesperson 40 percent and the selling agent 40 percent, each agent would earn $4,200.

Percentages paid to sales associates on listing and sales are not uniform. The broker in this situation retained 20 percent, or $2,100, to cover the expenses of maintaining an office, paying salaries to the office staff (such as secretaries, receptionists, and bookkeepers), advertising, signs, materials, rents, management fees, and other fixed and miscellaneous expenses.

Many contract variations exist between employing brokers and sales associates. In some instances, the sales agent may receive 100 percent of the commission but will share in the office expenses, paying a percentage of the rent, utilities, secretarial costs, and so on. Under the 100 percent plan, the cost of advertising listings and purchasing signs would be the salesperson's expense. While 100 percent commission may sound alluring, sales agents must make payments on their share of the expenses even during months when they make no sales.

Commissions charged by brokerage firms vary; there is no set fee. Since the listing agreement constitutes a contract between the real estate firm and the property owner, they both determine the fee. Should a salesperson leave a company, generally the real estate firm retains the listings.

License Fees

The licensee pays a fee for the issuance of the license. The license is renewable by meeting any continuing education requirement and by paying a renewal fee. In some states the renewal fee is paid for a two- or three-year period. This license remains in force unless revoked or suspended for just cause. Since a license is a privilege, committing an infraction of the license law is cause for **revocation** or **suspension**. For states that require continuing education courses, proof of completing the required hours must be submitted before the license will be renewed.

Nonresident Licenses

Reciprocal license

The right of reciprocity is in effect among many states. A nonresident may apply for a **reciprocal license** upon showing proof of being presently licensed and engaged in business in the state of residence. A nonresident salesperson must be employed by a broker holding a nonresident license. In some states the salesperson must further sign a designation in writing that appoints the director of the real estate commission or regulatory agency to act as his licensee agent in the event that judicial or legal process is served upon the agent. This has the same effect as if it were served upon the licensee.

Fees for reciprocal licenses vary but are generally higher than for resident licenses. This license permits the recipient to go to the other state and conduct business. However, should the licensee move to that state permanently, it would be necessary to meet the requirements of that state to work as a salesperson or broker.

Reciprocity agreements between jurisdictions has broadened, with many states now recognizing and accepting other states' education requirements if they are substantially equivalent or similar. In some instances, upon moving to another state, a broker may acquire a license without further examination by simply filing the proper application and paying the required fees.

Errors and Omissions Insurance

Many states are now requiring that all licensees be covered by an errors and omissions (E & O) insurance policy. The states must make a statewide E & O policy available that meets the following guidelines.

- The policy must be available to all licensees and cannot be cancelled.
- Competitive bidding procedures must be followed.
- The governing board determines coverage, permissible deductibles, and exemptions.
- The cost cannot exceed the limit defined by the board or commission.

Licensees may choose to obtain their own coverage as long as the private policy meets minimum guidelines specified by the governing board.

Governing Bodies

The real estate commission or regulatory body enforces the license laws, which are statutes passed by the state legislature. **Rules and regulations** consistent with the law are promulgated by the state real estate commission or governing body. The licensee is further bound by rules of the local, state, and National Association of REALTORS® boards if the broker is a member. The state governing body generally consists of licensees actively engaged in the real estate industry and unlicensed people who represent the public. A director is employed to keep records of all official acts of the governing body, conduct licensing exams, issue and renew licenses, hold educational seminars for licensees, and transact any other duties the agency may require. The governing body has the full power to regulate the issuance of licenses and to revoke or suspend licenses for just cause.

The Association of Real Estate Law License Officials (ARELLO) is an organization of license law directors, regulators, officials, and commissioners who meet annually to analyze the law and rules and regulations in the various states and to keep abreast of new ideas and changes in the real estate industry. One of its concerns is the need to remove barriers that prohibit brokers from doing business across state lines. Their contention is that education requirements are similar enough among the states that brokers should be able to work in another state without taking licensing courses, passing tests, and paying the required fees to work there.

ARELLO established a computer database to help regulators locate licensees who have lost their license in one state and who may be attempting to set up business in another state. They are requesting members to send in all data on license revocations, suspensions, fines, reprimands, **censures**, or surrenders. If a license has been denied because of character objections or someone has practiced real estate without a license, their names will appear in the information. This database will permit cross-referencing among states, especially useful if more states permit licensing without examination in their state.

As mentioned earlier, today's advanced technology allows licensees to be more independent, to work out of their homes and cars using cellular phones, laptop computers, and fax machines. With an office-based environment becoming less and less the norm, this produces a burden on the broker responsible for supervising salespersons. For this reason, some states, like Colorado, have or will abolish the salesperson license and have a single license, that of broker. This makes all real estate agents responsible for their own actions.

Regulatory agencies

WEB SITE

National Association of Real Estate Brokers: www.nareb.com Association of Real Estate Licensing Law Officials: www.arello.org

Trust Accounts

Brokers must set up a trust account in a depository located in the state where they do business. Most states require that all money coming into their possession that belongs to others must be put in the designated non–interest-bearing trust account. Some states, however, require that the earnest money be placed in an interest-bearing checking account. This would include earnest-money deposits, money advanced by a buyer or seller for payment of expenses in connection with a closing, the balance received from the buyer at the time of closing, rent deposits, and other trust funds. This account is subject to inspection by the real estate governing body and, if found to be in an "unsound" condition, would be cause for revoking or suspending the broker's license. Because of the large sums of money involved, real estate commissions are extremely sensitive in the area of trust accounts and require strict adherence to balanced accounts.

A trust account is shielded from any creditors of the broker. In the event of the broker's bankruptcy or if a judgment is entered against a broker, the trust account is immune from creditor's claims because the funds are held in a fiduciary capacity by the broker. This protection makes it mandatory that the broker not mix or commingle personal funds in the account.

Earnest-Money Deposits

Upon receipt of an accepted contract, the broker puts the **earnest-money** deposit in her trust account, where it remains until the transaction is consummated or terminated. If the sale was a cooperating broker's listing, the broker issues a check to the cooperating broker's trust account since the listing company closes the sale. In states where closing of the sale is done exclusively by escrow companies, the broker transfers the earnest-money deposit and purchase agreement into the possession of the escrow agent.

Guaranty Funds (Recovery Fund)

Some states establish a special fund secured through licensing fees to compensate individuals who may incur financial losses from a licensee's negligent or illegal act. Usually this fund is tapped only after the financially insured party has pursued all legal action for recovery through the courts. If judgment liens then cannot be collected, an award from the fund may be issued for part or all of the loss. This is another effort to assure the public that the law is protective of their interests.

Advertising

Newspaper ads

All advertising by those in the real estate business must be in the name of the firm and clearly indicate that it is indeed a real estate company. This does not preclude the advertisement from carrying a salesperson's name and telephone number. No advertisement may simply give a box number or telephone number implying that the ad is being placed by a private party. This is considered a "blind ad" and is prohibited in most states.

While the broker may "puff" the goods, the ad must not intentionally misrepresent the property or the terms under which it may be purchased. "Puffing" the goods refers to using terms to attractively describe the property, such as "treed lot with lovely view." While it must have a reasonable number of trees to qualify as "treed," it would be easy for the purchasers to ascertain for themselves whether the property has a lovely view. Advertising must not be directed to or against any particular race, color, religion, national origin, sex, handicap, or families with children. When advertising property, the licensee must comply with Regulation Z of the Truth-in-Lending Act. If any mention of credit terms is made beyond the annual percentage rate (APR) and the price of the property, all of the terms must be disclosed.

Unfair Trade Practices

Licenses are granted only to persons who bear a good reputation for honesty and integrity. If a broker, associate broker, or salesperson commits an infraction of the license law, the real estate commission investigates the actions of the licensee and has the power to suspend or revoke the license or censure the licensee. The following are some of the unfair trade practices that result in such action:

Required professionalism

1. discrimination regarding the offering for sale or rent of real property because of race, color, national origin, ethnic group, sex, handicap, or families

2. the use of misleading or inaccurate advertising

3. all money coming into the possession of the licensee must be accounted for and placed in the broker's trust account unless the parties having an interest in the funds (seller and purchaser, in the case of a purchase contract) agree otherwise in writing (Placing the money directly into the broker's business or personal account is prohibited since it would constitute the commingling of funds.)

4. accepting, giving, or charging any undisclosed commission, rebate, or direct profit on expenditures made for a principal

5. attempting to represent another broker or accept a commission from another broker without the employing broker's consent

6. acting in a dual capacity as agent and principal without revealing to all parties concerned that the licensee holds a personal interest in a property

7. guaranteeing to the purchaser future profits from the resale of the real property

8. in some states, placing a "For Sale" sign on property without written consent from the owners

9. offering property for sale on terms other than those authorized by the owner or the owner's representative

10. inducing a party to break a contract for the purpose of substituting a new contract with another principal

11. failing to present all offers to purchase, including those obtained by other agents, to the owner through the listing agent when an owner has an exclusive right-to-sell listing contract

12. paying a fee or compensation to an unlicensed person

13. failing to specify a fixed expiration date in a listing contract or to leave a copy with the seller

14. failing to give a copy of the accepted purchase agreement to the seller and the purchaser

15. failing, when closing a transaction, to give a completed copy of the settlement statement showing all the receipts and disbursements to both sellers and purchasers

16. failure to reduce an offer to writing when a prospective purchaser requests the same

17. failing to present promptly all written offers to the owners for their acceptance or refusal (It is not the licensee's discretion to decide whether an offer would be acceptable to the owners. Nor can offers be held waiting for another offer to be written.)

18. giving less favorable service and treatment to minority customers and clients

Disciplinary Action

Penalties for disregarding license law

While the preceding license law violations vary from state to state, the basic necessity for ethical conduct appears in all the state license laws. When it appears to the real estate commission that a licensee is in violation of a license law, or upon receiving a sworn complaint in writing against a real estate broker or salesperson, the commission will investigate the actions of the licensee. If the investigation reveals no violation, the complaint will be dismissed. Should they determine justification for the complaint, a date will be set for a hearing. If the licensee is found guilty of an unfair trade practice, the license will be revoked or suspended or the licensee will be censured.

If a salesperson is declared guilty of a violation of the license law, the broker's license may also be in jeopardy if the broker is guilty of not properly supervising the actions of the agent. If the broker's license is suspended or revoked, all the licenses of the salespeople under the broker's supervision are suspended until they place their licenses with another broker.

Out-of-State Subdivisions

Interstate land sales

To further protect purchasers, many states have strict regulations regarding the selling of lands within their state when such land is located in another state or is of a promotional nature. Under the Interstate Land Sales Full Disclosure Act, the real estate commission requires from the applicant a full disclosure of the area of real estate being offered for sale. A recorded plat of the area, an audited financial statement, and copies of the instrument used to obtain title to the land must be submitted. The real estate commission may request a personal inspection of the property at the applicant's expense. If the purchaser has not seen the land prior to said purchase, the contract will allow the purchaser an unconditional right of refund on all payments made if the real estate is inspected within a period of not more than 4 months. The contract may be rescinded within 14 days if the purchaser has not seen the land.

The **subdivider** will need to show proof in the form of performance bonds or other security that any promised public improvements to the property can be provided.

Unlicensed Persons

When an unlicensed person acts in the capacity of a licensee and does not fall under the exceptions to the state's law, the real estate regulatory agency will bring this fact to the attention of the attorney general. Prosecution will be recommended and an injunction order to cease filed against the violator in the district court in the county where such violation occurred.

Summary of Important Points

1. Considering that the purchase of real estate is the largest investment that the average person ever makes, it is understandable that all states have laws that govern the actions of the licensed salesperson and broker.

2. Educational requirements are mandatory in most states prior to licensing, and many states also require continuing education. Since the financing of real estate has changed dramatically in the past few years, it is imperative that the salesperson keep abreast of these changes. Compulsory education is a means of giving added assurance of the licensee's competence to transact business.

3. The salesperson or broker who belongs to the National Association of REALTORS® is further bound by a code of ethics to uphold fair practices and use diligence in preparing to conduct business as a licensee.

4. Anyone who conducts the business of listing, selling, exchanging, purchasing, renting, leasing, optioning, or managing real estate for a fee, commission, or other valuable compensation must be licensed.

5. A real estate license is a privilege that can be rescinded if the licensee commits an infraction of the license law.

6. Although there are differences in the laws among various states, license law is intended to protect the consumer from unfair real estate practices.

Discussion Points

1. What is the basic purpose of license laws?
2. In what instance may a broker act for more than one party in a transaction?
3. Explain the procedure that the regulatory agency of your state follows when a licensee is accused of committing an infraction of the license law.
4. What are the requirements in your state for obtaining a salesperson's license?
5. Why is it necessary for a broker to maintain a separate trust account? Is this requirement ever waived in your state?
6. Under what circumstances may a person be refused a license?
7. Explain the differences between censure, suspension, and revocation.
8. What are the advantages of holding a broker's license as opposed to a salesperson's license?
9. Do you feel that continuing education is necessary for the licensee? Why or why not?

Review Questions

Answers to these questions are found in the Answer Key section at the back of the book.

1. By which of the following acts would a broker be in violation of real estate license laws?
   a. placing a "For Sale" sign on property with the written permission of the owner
   b. purchasing property as an undisclosed principal
   c. listing the home of a relative
   d. buying investment property

2. Which of the following is true concerning a listing contract?
   a. a copy must be left with the sellers
   b. the listing contract must not contain an expiration date
   c. buyers must be given a copy
   d. no listing can exceed 120 days

3. When a real estate broker advertises in the local newspaper, the advertisement must:
   a. always state the price of the house
   b. give the address of the house
   c. contain the broker's telephone number and business address
   d. contain the brokerage firm's name

4. If a salesperson mishandles funds:
   a. the salesperson's license may be revoked
   b. the employing broker will not be held responsible
   c. the salesperson will have 90 days to deposit funds in the trust account
   d. the local police department will fine the licensee

5. Jill Kingston has obtained a listing on a property for $89,350, and upon showing the property to a prospective buyer, she received an offer of $88,500. A salesperson from another firm shows the property and brings Jill an offer of $88,000. As Jill leaves the office to present the offers to the sellers an agent from her office hands her an offer of $89,000. How should Jill present the offers to the sellers?

   a. Jill will present her offer first and if the sellers do not accept it she will present the offer for $89,000 since it is the highest offer

   b. since Jill is the listing agent, she has the right to present her offer and if accepted, need not discuss the other offers

   c. Jill must present all of the offers

   d. only the highest offer should be presented unless one of the other offers contains more favorable terms

6. A broker may place an earnest-money deposit:

   a. in his personal account if the money is designated as to whom is purchasing the property

   b. in the company's business account

   c. in the firm's trust account

   d. with the real estate commission

7. A broker may lose her license if she fails to:

   a. give a completed copy of the closing statement to the buyer and the seller

   b. file a copy of the closing statement with the recorder's office

   c. send a facsimile of the seller's closing statement to the purchasers

   d. retain a copy of the statements in the office files for six weeks

8. A salaried employee selling tracts of land for a land developer:

   a. must be licensed

   b. must receive a commission on the sales he makes

   c. does not need a license

   d. needs a broker's license

9. A real estate salesperson can:

   a. work independently

   b. open and operate a real estate firm

   c. manage a branch office for her employing broker

   d. list, sell, and lease real property

10. Real estate law is intended to:

    a. protect the public

    b. ensure that the salesperson will be paid a commission

    c. set commission rates

    d. foster good relations between brokers and salespersons

11. Which of the following people must be licensed to transact the business of real estate?

    a. court appointed guardians

    b. real estate secretaries

    c. the executor of an estate

    d. an owner of four income-producing properties

12. A real estate licensee may NOT:

    a. work on a part-time basis

    b. lease property listed with the firm

    c. sell commercial property

    d. pay a finder's fee to a neighbor

13. A license may be revoked upon proof of:
    a. charging more than the usual rate of commission
    b. refusal to accept a listing
    c. not advertising on a weekly basis
    d. steering customers away from an urban neighborhood

14. A broker's license may be revoked under which of the following circumstances?
    a. withholding earnest money when the purchaser is rightfully entitled to return of same
    b. dividing or splitting commissions with another broker
    c. dismissing a salesperson who is not producing listings or sales
    d. sending referral fees to a licensed broker in another state

15. Which of the following is NOT an infraction of the license law?
    a. failure to submit to an owner, before her acceptance, all formal written offers received on the property
    b. quoting a price other than that stipulated by the owner because the original asking price was unrealistic
    c. informing a prospective purchaser of a latent defect in the property
    d. paying a referral fee to a neighbor

16. A salesperson in a real estate transaction may NOT accept compensation in the form of:
    a. a percentage of the listing price
    b. a percentage based on a sliding scale
    c. a flat fee
    d. a direct payment without his broker's knowledge

17. A broker fails to renew his license by the due date, but he did send it in two months later. In the interim a sale was negotiated, but the seller refused to pay the commission as agreed in the contract. Regarding this situation:
    a. the broker is not entitled to a commission
    b. the seller must pay the commission since it was agreed to in the listing contract
    c. if the broker pursues the issue and brings court action he will receive the commission
    d. the commission is due the broker since the property was listed prior to the license lapsing

18. A broker would be censured for commingling funds if she deposited earnest money in anything other than:
    a. her general real estate account
    b. her personal account, because the portion of money was due her
    c. a separate checking account designated as a trust account
    d. a separate savings account designated as a trust account

19. Which of the following is NOT a violation of license law?
    a. failure to offer property to a minority
    b. accepting an undisclosed rebate on an expenditure made for a principal
    c. quoting a price other than that stipulated by the seller
    d. showing properties to four different people in a single day

20. If a salesperson is working as an independent contractor, he is considered self-employed. Under these circumstances, the broker's responsibilities would include:
    a. withholding social security tax from the commission paid to the salesperson
    b. offering a retirement plan to the salesperson
    c. supervising the salesperson
    d. opening an IRA account for the salesperson

21. A salesperson in a real estate transaction may accept compensation from:
    a. the seller
    b. the real estate commission
    c. the buyer
    d. the employing broker

22. A license may be revoked upon proof of:
    a. charging more than the usual rate of commission
    b. refusal to accept a listing
    c. inducing a party to withdraw from a contract
    d. not advertising a property frequently

23. According to the license laws in most states, which of the following is true of a listing agreement?
    a. the listing must contain a termination date
    b. the contract must show the listing in effect until the property is sold
    c. it must be shown to any prospective purchaser
    d. all copies are retained by the real estate firm

24. A salesperson/broker ratio of commission will be determined by:
    a. the real estate commission or regulatory agency of the state
    b. the federal Fair Trade Commission
    c. statute of frauds
    d. contractual agreement

25. An agent must disclose to a potential buyer all EXCEPT:
    a. that the property is in a flood zone
    b. any existing liens
    c. that the seller is financially stressed and anxious to sell
    d. that the home has a septic system and is not on public sewer

Real Estate Math

OVERVIEW

Salespeople and brokers must have an understanding of the basic mathematical principles involved in the real estate transaction. While we covered the ad valorem tax structure on real property in Chapter 17, the amortization of a loan in Chapter 11, and the proration of costs in the settlement procedure in Chapter 12, this chapter will further elaborate on the math involved in real estate transactions.

It is necessary to correctly measure the area (square footage) of a house or a parcel of land when the sales representative lists the property. Commercial land is generally priced per square foot, so the exact amount of square footage must be determined. A contractor may price a plan by square footage. An appraiser determines value by the square footage when using the cost approach to value. Cubic footage may be important to the purchaser of a commercial building or to the contractor pouring a driveway or patio.

A general review of the approach used in percentage problems is important when fractions or percentages of a tract of land are being divided. Many of the areas of arithmetic covered in this chapter involve percentages. For example, an inflationary market results in rapidly increasing property values, so the techniques used to evaluate percentages of appreciation must be understood. If the property depreciates, the resulting loss in value must also be calculated. To an investor, the past history of the value increase on a particular piece of property is very important.

Another area of mathematics important to real estate involves taxation. Since real estate is subject to taxation, understanding the tax structure as expressed in dollars or mill levy is further explained in this chapter.

When analyzing the worth of a subdivided property, it is of value to both buyer and seller to determine the proportionate amount being sold. If a segment of a property is being taken under the right of eminent domain, the owner will want to know the proportion taken to determine the value of the land he is losing. Ratio problems concerning scales are also analyzed in this chapter since house plans are drawn to scale.

Determining the capitalization of an income-producing property is a prime concern of the investor, since the investor will want to know the rate of return on the investment.

Amortization is the liquidation of a loan by making monthly payments. This chapter explains how to determine the loan payment or to find the rate when you know the interest and principal payment. Discount problems when interest points are charged on a new loan are also included in this chapter. The differences among simple, add-on, and compound interest are explained.

When a property is sold, the financial responsibility of taxes, insurance, interest, and rents is divided (prorated) between the purchaser and seller. This is a bookkeeping procedure that the real estate agent should understand.

And last, the sales agent will be interested in computing commission problems. The split commission between real estate firms, broker–agent arrangement concerning commissions, and sliding-scale commission problems are presented in this chapter.

Measurement Problems

Let's review the following basic elements of arithmetic: The measurement of land and areas—square footage, cubic feet, acreages—are all of importance to the real estate salesperson. The following lists show the equivalents of various types of measures.

Linear Measure

12 inches = 1 foot

36 inches = 3 feet or 1 yard

Square Measure

144 square inches = 1 square foot

9 square feet = 1 square yard

Cubic Measure—Calculating Volume

1 cubic foot = 1,728 cubic inches

27 cubic feet = 1 cubic yard

Surveyor's Measure

link = 7.92 inches

chain = 66 feet or 4 rods

rod = 16½ feet or 1 perch

mile = 5,280 feet or 8 furlongs

acre = 43,560 square feet, 4,840 square yards, or 160 square rods

section = 640 acres, or 1 square mile

township = 36 sections

Circular Measure

60 seconds (") = 1 minute (')

60 minutes (') = 1 degree (°)

90 degrees (°) = 1 quadrant

360 degrees (°) = a circle

Square Footage and Yardage

To find the square footage of a square or rectangular area, multiply the lengths of the two sides together.

Area problems

area = length × width

By drawing the basic formula in a circle, the math procedure is simple to determine: just blot out the element you are looking for. Thus, if you have the total square footage and are looking for the width, divide the area by the length to obtain the width.

EXAMPLE A room measures 18 feet long and 12 feet wide. Find the area.

    A = 18' (L) × 12' (W)
    A = 216 square feet

EXAMPLE Compute the square footage of the house shown in the diagram. Square off the diagram as shown:

    A = 40' × 28' = 1,120 square feet
    B = 2' × 10' = 20 square feet
    C = 20' × 10' = 200 square feet
    Total area = 1,340 square feet

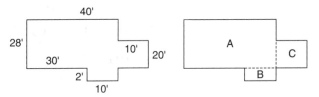

EXAMPLE To find the square yards, divide the square feet by 9 (there are 9 square feet in a square yard).

    216 square feet ÷ 9 = 24 square yards

EXAMPLE Find the *square yards* of carpet needed to cover a 15-foot × 18-foot room.

    15' × 18' = 270 square feet
    270 square feet ÷ 9 = 30 square yards

To find the *area of a triangle,* multiply the base by the height and divide by two.

area = half the base × the altitude

The altitude is the distance from the base of the triangle to its peak, as shown here by the dotted line. Line BD is the base and line AC the altitude.

EXAMPLE A triangular lot has a base of 200 feet and an altitude of 150 feet. Find the area.

A = half the base × the altitude

$A = \dfrac{200}{2} \times 150$

A = 100 × 150

A = 15,000 square feet

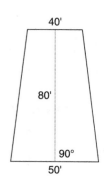

EXAMPLE To compute the square feet in the diagram, add the 2 widths:

40' + 50' = 90'.

Then divide by 2:

90' ÷ 2 = 45'.

Now multiply by the length:

45' × 80' = 3,600 square feet.

Note: An angle marked by an arc and "90°" is a right angle.

Cubic Footage and Yardage

To find the cubic footage of an area, multiply the length by the width by the height: L × W × H = cubic feet.

EXAMPLE A 20-foot × 12-foot room has a height of 8 feet. Compute the cubic footage.

L (20') × W (12') × H (8') = 1,920 cubic feet

EXAMPLE If a driveway measures 60 feet long by 8 feet wide and is 3 inches deep, what is the cubic footage (3" equals ¼ of a foot)?

60' × 8' × ¼' = 120 cubic feet

To find the *cubic yards,* divide the cubic feet by 27 (there are 27 cubic feet in a cubic yard).

EXAMPLE A driveway 54 feet long by 15 feet and 4 inches deep will be poured at a cost of $30 per cubic yard of concrete. Find the cost.

54' × 15' × ⅓' = 270 cubic feet

270 cubic feet ÷ 27 = 10 cubic yards

10 × $30 = $300

Linear Footage

Linear feet, sometimes referred to as running feet, are the measure of the distance from one point to another.

EXAMPLE A lot 100 feet wide by 150 feet deep is to be fenced on all 4 sides. How much fencing is needed?

100' + 100' + 150' + 150' = 500 feet

EXAMPLE A lot 65 feet wide by 80 feet deep will be fenced on both sides and the rear. How many linear feet of fencing is needed?

65' + 80' + 80' = 225 feet

Percentages and Fractions

Decimals and percentages

It is necessary for salespeople and brokers to understand the conversion of decimals to percentages. Remember that the whole of anything is 100 percent. Anything less than the whole is a part or percentage of the whole. For example, think of $1.00 as being the whole and 50 cents as a part—in decimal form, .50. When converting a decimal to percentage, move the decimal point two places to the right and add the percentage symbol (%). Thus, you would write .50 as 50%. Another way to think of this is $^{50}/_{100}$.

Remember, to change a percent to a decimal, move the decimal point two places to the left: 50% = .50. To change a decimal to a percent, move the decimal point two places to the right: .05 = 5%, .108 = 10.8%, 1.00 = 100%.

To change the percent to a common fraction, express it as hundredths and reduce:

$$50\% = \frac{50}{100} = \frac{1}{2} \qquad 75\% = \frac{75}{100} = \frac{3}{4}$$

To change a fraction to a percentage, express it in hundredths and then as a percentage:

$$\frac{1}{2} = \frac{50}{100} = .50 \text{ or } 50\% \qquad \frac{3}{4} = \frac{75}{100} = .75 \text{ or } 75\%$$

Fractions must have common denominators before you can add or subtract them:

$$\frac{1}{3} = \frac{4}{12}$$
$$\frac{2}{4} = \frac{6}{12}$$
$$\overline{\qquad \frac{10}{12} \text{ or } \frac{5}{6}}$$

As the example shows, $^1/_3$ and $^2/_4$ have a common denominator of 12. When they are added together, the answer is $^{10}/_{12}$, which is reduced to $^5/_6$.

In multiplying fractions, the numerators are multiplied and the denominators are multiplied. For example, when multiplying the following fractions:

$$3\frac{1}{3} \times \frac{1}{2} =$$

Change 3⅓ to an improper fraction and multiply numerators and denominators:

$$\frac{10}{3} \times \frac{1}{2} = \frac{10}{6} \quad \text{or} \quad \frac{5}{3} = \frac{12}{3}$$

To divide a fraction, the divisor is inverted and then multiplied:

$$\frac{2}{3} \div \frac{4}{5} = \frac{2}{3} \times \frac{5}{4} = \frac{10}{12} = \frac{5}{6}$$

Profit and Loss

Appreciation and depreciation

As we learned in the chapter on appraisal, depreciation is loss from any cause, whether it is physical deterioration, functional obsolescence, or economic obsolescence. If a property *depreciates* in value, it has simply lost value. If it *appreciates* in value, it has gained in value and is now worth more.

We begin with the original value of a building as 100 percent. If the useful life of a building is 50 years, it will depreciate ⅟₅₀, or 2 percent, a year. Thus, if a property depreciates 2 percent a year for 8 years, it has a 16 percent loss in value.

We subtract this loss from 100 percent:

100% − 16% = 84%

If the property is now worth, say, $16,800, this represents 84 percent of its original value. To determine its original value, we divide:

$16,800 ÷ 84% = $20,000 (original value)

When appreciation occurs, it represents a gain in value. Assuming a property at present valued at $23,000 had appreciated 3 percent a year for the last 5 years, it would have gained 15 percent in value. Its present value would thus be 115 percent of the original value.

$23,000 ÷ 115% = $20,000 (original value)

EXAMPLE If a property sold for $12,100, gaining a 10 percent profit for the owner, what was the original cost of the property?

100% (cost) + 10% (profit) = 110% (selling price)
$12,100 ÷ 110 = $11,000 (original cost of property)

Here we divided the selling price by its percentage to determine the original cost.

EXAMPLE A $40,000 house appreciates in value at the rate of 2.5 percent each succeeding year. What is the value of the house at the end of the second year?

$40,000 × 2.5% = $1,000 (appreciation the first year)
$40,000 + $1,000 = $41,000
$41,000 × 2.5% = $1,025 (appreciation the second year)
$41,000 + $1,025 = $42,025 (value after the second year)

The wording "each succeeding year" indicates *compound interest;* that is, *the interest is added to the new balance at the end of each year.*

EXAMPLE A $30,000 house appreciates 5 percent each year for 5 years. What is its present value? (In this problem we need only multiply the 5 years by 5 percent, for a total of 25 percent appreciation.)

25% × $30,000 = $7,500
$30,000 + $7,500 = $37,500 (present value)

If we know the value of a house was $20,000 ten years ago and that it depreciated 2 percent a year, we can find the present value by multiplying:

10 years × 2% = 20% (total depreciation)
The present value of the house is 80% (100% − 20% = 80%)
$20,000 × 80% = $16,000 (present value)

EXAMPLE A-1 Construction Company built a home in a new subdivision. It was sold 6 months after completion for $48,500, which represented a depreciation (loss) of 3 percent. What was the original asking price?

$48,500 ÷ 97% = $50,000 (asking price)

EXAMPLE A duplex depreciates 3 percent for 5 years. If the building originally cost $20,000, compute the present value of the duplex.

3% × 5 years = 15% (total depreciation)
$20,000 × 15% = $3,000
$20,000 − $3,000 = $17,000 (present value)

EXAMPLE Mr. Loser sells his house for $27,000, which represents a 10 percent loss over the price he originally paid for it. What did he pay for the house?

100% − 10% = 90%
$27,000 ÷ 90% = $30,000

Taxation Problems

The property tax structure is an ad valorem *(according to value)* tax. This value is determined by a tax assessor, who appraises the value of each piece of property. An assessment roll is prepared that gives a description of the property, its assessed valuation, and the owner's name.

The tax rate is referred to either as a *mill levy* or in *dollars*. In determining the taxation of a property, the assessed value is calculated by taking the percentage of the real value the taxes are based on; then the mill levy is multiplied by the assessed value. A mill represents $1/10$ of 1 cent and is written as .001. Thus, 83 mills would be written as .083, and 6.5 mills would be written as .0065.

Taxation by mill levy

EXAMPLE A property valued at $35,000 is assessed at 40 percent of its value. The mill levy is 83. Compute the annual tax.

$$\begin{array}{ccccc} \$35{,}000 & \times & 40\% & = & \$14{,}000 \\ \text{(value of property)} & & \text{(percentage taxed)} & & \text{(assessed value)} \end{array}$$

$14,000 × .083 (mill levy) = $1,162 (annual taxes)

Taxation by dollars

EXAMPLE If the assessed valuation is $20,000 and the tax rate is $4.00 per $100 of value, compute the annual tax.

The $4.00 per hundred indicates that the $20,000 assessed valuation must be divided by 100.

$20,000 ÷ 100 = $200
$200 × $4 = $800 (tax)

Ratio and Proportion

Comparing ratios

Ratio problems involve comparisons of two related numbers. A house plan or map is "scaled" so that 1 inch or a fraction of an inch equals a number of feet. *The ratios must always be equal or in proportion.*

EXAMPLE What is the scale of a house plan if a room 16 feet × 28 feet is shown on the scale as 4 inches × 7 inches?

$$\frac{4}{16} = \frac{1}{4} \qquad \frac{7}{28} = \frac{1}{4} \qquad \text{Scale is } 1/4'' = 1'$$

EXAMPLE What is the actual measurement of a property 6 inches in length by 8 inches wide if the scale is $1/8$ inch = 1 foot?

If the scale is $1/8''$ to 1', 1" = 8'
6 × 8' = 48'
8 × 8' = 64'

The measurement is 48' × 64'.

EXAMPLE In 9 months, a salesperson sells property to 1 out of every 5 prospective purchasers. How many sales would she make in 3 months if she showed property to 150 people? (Since the months involved are of no significance, we disregard the time element.)

$$\frac{5}{1} = \frac{150}{X}$$

$$\frac{150}{X} \times \frac{1}{5} = \frac{150}{5X}$$

$$\frac{150}{5} = X \qquad X = 30 \text{ sales}$$

Proportion problems

EXAMPLE How many acres are there in plot A if plot B contains 25 acres?

$$\frac{900}{X} = \frac{1,350}{25}$$

$$\frac{900}{X} \times \frac{25}{1,350} = \frac{22,500}{1,350} = 16\frac{2}{3} \text{ acres}$$

EXAMPLE If the ratio of a salesperson's commission to that of his broker is 4:6, what amount does the salesperson earn from a $3,000 commission?

4 + 6 = 10 parts

100% ÷ 10 = 10%

4 × 10% = 40% and 6 × 10% = 60%

40% of $3,000 = $1,200

Capitalization and Other Finance Problems

To solve income problems, use the formula I = R × V (income equals rate × value). This is similar to using A = L × W in finding the square footage of an area.

I = income
R = rate (interest)
V = value
Use a circle and blot out the one unknown.

EXAMPLE $140 is 3.5% of what amount?
income 4 interest rate 5 value

$$\frac{\$140 \ (I)}{.035 \ (R)} = V$$

$140 ÷ .035 = $4,000

Always divide to find the value or rate.

EXAMPLE If the quarterly interest payments are $150 on a $12,000 loan, what is the annual interest rate?

$150 × 4 (4 quarters in a year) = $600

$$\frac{\$600\ (I)}{\$12,000\ (V)} = R$$

$600 ÷ $12,000 = 5%

To determine the percentage, divide the *income* by the *investment*. (This is usually the larger number into the smaller.)

Determining value income property

EXAMPLE Compute the value of a property that has a net income of $5,480 and that returns 8 percent annually on the investment.

$$\frac{\$5,480\ (I)}{.08\ (R)} = V$$

$5,480 ÷ .08 = $68,500

Interest rate into income equals investment.

In this example, we divided the percentage rate *into* the net return to determine the value of the property.

EXAMPLE A buyer obtains a 75 percent loan on a house with a value of $28,000. What is the interest rate if the interest payments are $140 monthly?

75% × $28,000 = $21,000 loan
$140 × 12 months = $1,680 annual interest

$$\frac{\$1,680\ (I)}{\$21,000\ (V)} = R$$

$1,680 ÷ $21,000 = 8% interest rate

EXAMPLE If an investment valued at $350,000 returns 12 percent annually, what is the amount of income produced?

$350,000 (V) × 12% (R) = $42,000

EXAMPLE If the capitalization rate on a building that produces $20,000 annual income is 10 percent, find the estimated value of the structure.

$$\frac{\$20,000\ (I)}{.10\ (R)} = V$$

$20,000 ÷ .10 = $200,000

EXAMPLE Compute the value if the same building had a capitalization rate of 5 percent.

$$\frac{\$20,000\ (I)}{.05\ (R)} = V$$

$20,000 \div .05 = \$400,000$

In using the capitalization approach, remember that the *higher* the cap rate, the *lower* the appraised value.

Loan Payments

The buyer's foremost concern when purchasing a home is what the monthly loan commitment will be. The amount borrowed will be amortized over a period of years in equal payments, a portion of which will be interest, with the remainder applied toward the principal payment to gradually reduce the loan.

EXAMPLE Ms. Morley purchases a home with a $45,000 mortgage at 9¾ percent interest. If the monthly payments are $387.70, what amount is applied against the principal after the first payment?

$45,000 × .0975 = $4,387.50 annual interest
$4,387.50 ÷ 12 months = $365.63 first month's interest
$387.70 − $365.63 = $22.07 against principal

The $22.07 is deducted from the principal amount of $45,000 so that the second month begins with the remaining balance of $44,977.93.

To determine the total monthly payment if the interest is in addition to the stated principal payment, we compute the interest and add it to the principal payment.

EXAMPLE Mr. Winslow negotiates for a $30,000 loan with $200 monthly payments plus 9 percent interest.

$30,000 × .09 = $2,700 ÷ 12 months = $225 interest per month.
$200 principal payment + $225 interest payment = $425 principal and interest.

If the loan amount is unknown, but the interest payment and rate of interest are given, we compute the amount as follows:

EXAMPLE The semiannual interest payments are $400 with interest of 5 percent annually.

$400 × 2 = $800 annual interest ÷ .05 = $16,000 loan amount

Amortization problems

Loan-to-Value Ratio

Lenders loan money based on a percentage of the appraised property value. If the purchase price is more than the appraised value, the loan will be made on the *appraised value.*

EXAMPLE   If a home appraised for $93,000 and the borrower puts 20 percent down, what would the loan amount be?

$93,000 $\times$ .80 loan = $74,400

EXAMPLE   A buyer pays $115,000 for a home that appraised at 10 percent less. If the buyer pays 10 percent down, the loan amount will be:

$115,000 $\times$ .90 = $103,500 appraised value
$103,500 $\times$ .90 = $93,150.00 loan

Simple Interest

When we do not have the money to make a purchase, we borrow and pay interest, but all interest is not the same.

Simple interest is what is paid for most real estate loans. Payments are made on the unpaid balance, that is, on the amount still owed.

The formula is:

$$\text{Interest} = \text{Principal} \times \text{Rate} \times \text{Time}$$

EXAMPLE   The interest paid on a $20,000 loan at 8 percent repayable in 5 years is:

I = PRT
I = $20,000 $\times$ 0.08 $\times$ 5 years = $8,000
I = $8,000

Add-on Interest

Some lenders, especially when financing second mortgages or household items, will calculate interest on the total amount of the loan for the complete time of the loan. The interest amount is added to the principal owed for repayment over the term of the loan before calculating the monthly payments. Note how much this method increases simple interest.

EXAMPLE $20,000 $\times$ .08 $\times$ 5 years = $8,000

The $8,000 interest is added to the total principal amount owed before the payments are calculated. $20,000 + $8,000 = $28,000

The $28,000 is divided by the total number of payments (12 $\times$ 5 = 60 payments).

$28,000 $\div$ 60 = $466.67

The first payment is the same as a simple interest payment. However, the second and subsequent payments are not because the interest is still being charged on the portion of the principal that has been repaid.

Compound Interest

To calculate compound interest earned, we add interest onto interest.

EXAMPLE $500 × 10% for 1 year = $50 interest earned.

Now add the $50 to the $500, and we begin the next year with $550.

$550 × 10% = $55.00 interest earned the second year.

More Interest Problems

EXAMPLE   Mr. Jones wanted to remodel his business. He obtained a loan for $4,300 at 6 percent interest. He paid it off in 8 months. What amount of interest did he pay?

$4,300 × .06 = $258 interest for year
$258 ÷ 12 months = $21.50 per month
$21.50 × 8 months = $172 interest paid

EXAMPLE   A buyer purchases a home for $50,000. She takes out a 25-year loan for 75 percent of the purchase price. Assuming that her mortgage payments are equal and the interest payment is ¾ percent of the principal each month, what would be the amount of her first monthly payment?

$50,000 × .75 = $37,500 loan
25 years × 12 months = 300 months
$37,500 ÷ 300 months = $125 principal per month
¾% × 12 months = 9% interest per year
$37,500 × .09 = $3,375 ÷ 12 months = $281.25 interest
$125 + $281.25 = $406.25 principal and interest

EXAMPLE   Jane Jones obtains an FHA loan on a $56,000 home. The down payment scale is 3 percent of the first $25,000 and 5 percent of the balance. There is a loan fee of 2 points that the buyer is to pay. What amount should Ms. Jones bring to the closing?

3% of $25,000 = $ 750	$56,000
5% of $31,000 = $1,550	−$ 2,300 down payment
$2,300	$53,700 loan

Two points would be .02 of the loan ($53,700) = $1,074
$2,300 + $1,074 = $3,374

EXAMPLE How much less are the monthly payments on a $36,000 home than on a $40,000 home if a 75 percent loan is obtained at $8.70 a month per $1,000 of value?

$40,000 − $36,000 = $4,000 × 75% = $3,000
$3 (thousands) × $8.70 = $26.10

EXAMPLE Ms. Randall purchases a home for $58,000 and puts 10 percent down. The 20-year loan is to be repaid with a constant principal payment, and interest will be charged at the rate of ¾ percent per month. Compute the amount of the first month's payment.

$58,000 − $5,800 (10% down) = $52,200 loan
20 years × 12 months = 240 months
52,200 ÷ 240 = $217.50 principal per month
¾% × 12 months = 9% × $52,200 = $4,698 ÷ 12 = $391.50 interest per month
$217.50 + $391.50 = $609 principal and interest

Discount Problems

Discount points

A discount is an amount charged by the lender in excess of the closing costs to equalize or increase the lender's yield. In addition to the interest rate, a percentage is charged on the *amount loaned* to the borrower. The effective yield to the loan company becomes greater when these discount points are charged. A "point" is really 1 percent of the amount of the loan. If 1 point is charged on a $20,000 loan, the lender collects 1 percent of $20,000, or $200. If 2½ points are charged, the fee would be $500.

EXAMPLE Mr. Corkle purchases a $55,000 home using FHA financing. He is required to put 3 percent down on the first $25,000 loaned with 5 percent on the balance of the purchase price. The lender is charging 3.5 discount points. Compute the discount points that will be paid.

$25,000 × .97 = $24,250
$30,000 × .95 = 28,500
                 $52,750 loan amount
$52,750 × .035 = $1,846.25 discount points

Prorations

Dividing expenses by prorating

Prorating means *dividing expenses* between buyer and seller. The person who uses, must pay her share for the time used. In prorating, one must analyze the period of time involved and multiply it by the rate. Real estate prorating at the time of closing a sale may commonly include taxes, rents, insurance, and interest charges.

EXAMPLE Mr. Howard sells his home July 1, with closing and possession set for July 15. Since Ms. Stucky is assuming the loan, she has also decided to assume the insurance policy, which was paid March 1 for 1 year in the amount of $156. What amount will appear as a credit on Mr. Howard's closing statement?

March 1 to July 15 = 4½ months. (This represents the amount of insurance used by Mr. Howard, leaving 7½ months *unused*.)
$156 ÷ 12 months = $13 monthly
$13 × 7½ months = $97.50 (amount due to Mr. Howard)

EXAMPLE The mortgage being assumed by Ms. Stucky is in the amount of $15,000 at 8 percent interest. The interest has been paid to June 1. Mr. Howard is liable for the interest to the date of closing. Compute the amount he owes.

Mortgage interest proration

$15,000 × .08 = $1,200 ÷ 12 months = $100 for June, plus $50 for half of July
Total = $150

EXAMPLE I. M. Lloyd sold her home November 15 with possession set for December 5. Mr. Wiley will assume the 3-year insurance policy, which became effective July 15 of last year in the amount of $396. The annual taxes of $982.80 were paid by the owner for the first half of the year; the second half year's taxes are due and payable. What amounts are payable and by whom?

1. *Insurance*

Prorating insurance

July 15 (last year) to December 5 = 1 year, 4 months, 20 days *used* (16 months and 20 days used or 19 months and 10 days *not used*)
$396 ÷ 36 months = $11 per month × 19 months = $209
$11 ÷ 30 days = $.366 per day × 10 days = $3.67
$209 + $3.67 = $212.67 (insurance paid for and not used will be refunded to Ms. Lloyd)

2. *Taxes*

Tax proration

$982.80 ÷ 12 months = $81.90 per month
July 1 to December 5 = 5 months, 5 days taxes due
$81.90 × 5 = $409.50
$81.90 ÷ 30 days = $2.73 per day
$2.73 × 5 days = $13.65 + $409.50 = $423.15 (taxes due from seller)

2.73×25 days = \$68.25 (taxes due from buyer to complete year)

\$212.67 insurance prorate due to I. M. Lloyd

\$423.15 taxes due from Ms. Lloyd

\$68.25 taxes due from Mr. Wiley

Commissions

Earnings of real estate agents

In the real estate business a salesperson normally is paid on a commission basis. Instead of receiving a fixed salary, the salesperson is paid a percentage or proportion of the real estate he sells or lists. This straight commission earning is received only if the salesperson produces. The real estate firm, of course, must retain a portion for its fixed expenses.

EXAMPLE If a property sells for \$20,000 and a broker's commission is 6 percent, the broker's commission would be:

\$20,000 $\times$ 6% = \$1,200 commission

Split commission

EXAMPLE If a salesperson receives 35 percent of a total commission from his broker, what is the broker's share if the property sold for \$23,000 and the commission was on a 6 percent basis?

\$23,000 $\times$ .06 = \$1,380 (total commission)

100% $-$ 35%   = 65% (broker's share)

\$1,380 $\times$ 65% = \$897 (broker's portion)

"Sliding commission"

EXAMPLE Tom Lyons earns 6 percent on the first \$50,000 of a \$160,000 sale. If the total commission is \$7,400, what percentage was paid on the remainder?

\$50,000 $\times$ .06 = \$3,000

\$7,400 $-$ \$3,000 = \$4,400

\$160,000 $-$ \$50,000 = \$110,000

So: \$4,400 = what % of \$110,000?

\$4,400 (P) $\div$ \$110,000 (B) = .04 = 4% (R)

Rent commission

EXAMPLE Mr. Jones, a real estate broker, leases a property to Ms. Whitney for 5 years. Mr. Jones will receive a 5 percent commission. The rent will be \$300 per month for the first year, with a \$50-a-month increase each succeeding year. What is Mr. Jones's commission?

\$300 @ 12 months = \$ 3,600

\$350 @ 12 months = \$ 4,200

\$400 @ 12 months = \$ 4,800

\$450 @ 12 months = \$ 5,400

\$500 @ 12 months = \$ 6,000

\$24,000 $\times$ .05 = \$1,200 commission

Deductions on Income Taxes

As explained in Chapter 16, the owner of real estate has income tax deductions on the interest paid on a mortgage and on the property taxes.

EXAMPLE Jane and John Doe, who file a joint income tax return, pay 28 percent income tax on their earnings. If they have an $85,000 mortgage at 8 percent interest, their allowable tax savings would be:

Income tax deduction for interest paid

$85,000 mortgage × .08 interest = $6,800 annual interest
28% tax bracket × $6,800 interest = $1,904 savings

(For the sake of this problem we are assuming the interest on the total balance and not the unpaid balance. In reality, remember that we pay interest on the unpaid balance on most loans.)

EXAMPLE Assuming the mortgage is for 20 years, the principal and interest payments would be 8.37 per $1,000 borrowed (see amortization chart in Chapter 10) or $711.45 per month. How much will their monthly payments be effectively lowered to?

Effective monthly interest

$1,904 tax savings ÷ 12 mos. = $158.67
$711.45 monthly payment − $158.67 = $552.78

EXAMPLE The Does' yearly property taxes are $2,800. At the 28 percent tax savings, their tax savings on the property taxes will be:

$2,800 × .28 = $784 savings
$784.00 ÷ 12 mos. = $65.33

EXAMPLE Adding both the interest and property tax savings, the Does' effective monthly house payment is:

$158.67 + $65.33 = $224 total tax savings
$711.45 − $224 = $487.45

Review Questions

Answers to these questions are found in the Answer Key section at the back of the book.

1. Find the square footage of the diagram, excluding the small area indicated in the lower right hand corner:
   a. 30,000 sq. ft.
   b. 33,600 sq. ft.
   c. 33,800 sq. ft.
   d. 34,000 sq. ft.

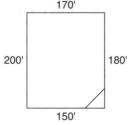

2. If a house depreciates at the rate of 2.5 percent per year for 10 years and has a present value of $112,500, what was the original value of the house?
   a. $125,000
   b. $150,000
   c. $155,000
   d. $250,000

3. A $150,000 house is assessed at 80 percent of its original cost. The property tax on the property is .03 mills. What was the approximate yearly tax (rounded off to the nearest dollar)?
   a. $460
   b. $3,600
   c. $1,440
   d. $2,800

4. A house is appraised for $25,000 and shows an assessed value of $20,000. If taxes on it are $300 yearly, what would the tax be on a house appraising at $45,000 with an assessed value of $40,000?
   a. $150
   b. $500
   c. $600
   d. $700

5. Mr. Lewis is working for Ms. Morris on a 50/50 basis. Mr. Lewis sells 360 acres at $150 an acre; another firm, ABC Realty, has the listing and splits on a 50/50 basis with Ms. Morris's firm. The commission rate is 5 percent on the first $25,000, 2.5 percent on the next $20,000, and 1 percent on the balance. How much does Mr. Lewis earn?
   a. $230
   b. $460
   c. $920
   d. $1,840

6. What portion of the whole piece of land is lot A?
   a. $\frac{1}{30}$
   b. $\frac{3}{60}$
   c. $\frac{2}{15}$
   d. $\frac{2}{9}$

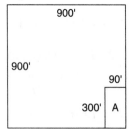

7. Find the actual measurement of a property shown as 5¾ inches long and 4½ inches wide if the scale is ⅛ inch = 1 foot:
   a. 12' × 9"
   b. 24' × 18"
   c. 36' × 32"
   d. 46' × 36"

8. A house sale is closed on July 15. The taxes of $1,746 for the calendar year have been paid. The fire insurance premium of $702 for the calendar year has also been paid. What is the total prepaid portion that the buyer will owe the seller?
   a. $1,020
   b. $1,122
   c. $1,546
   d. $2,448

9. Shelly Ford pays her taxes of $660 for the calendar year. She sells her property and closes on June 15. What is the prepaid portion due back to her?
   a. $302.50
   b. $330.00
   c. $357.50
   d. $412.50

10. An apartment house has 10 units renting at $275 a month and 12 units at $250 a month. Expenses are $6,789 annually. The vacancy factor is 15 percent annually. If you desire to make 10 percent return on your investment, approximately what should you pay for the property?
    a. $62,100
    b. $518,610
    c. $585,000
    d. $612,100

11. Carol Reed purchases a $62,000 property on which she obtains an 80 percent loan. She pays 4 discount points, and the attorney's fees and miscellaneous costs amount to $2,500. How much money should she bring to the closing?
   a. $1,984
   b. $12,400
   c. $14,900
   d. $16,884

12. What was the selling price of a property if Jerry Brown paid $350 for taxes due, has a $12,500 mortgage, paid a 6 percent broker commission, and netted $7,000 on the sale?
   a. $13,621.00
   b. $15,500.00
   c. $21,041.00
   d. $21,117.02

13. A building that cost $300,000 to construct 10 years ago has depreciated 25 percent. The land cost $51,000. Find the current appraised value:
   a. $263,250
   b. $265,000
   c. $276,000
   d. $351,000

14. Mr. Leonard owns a lot measuring 80 feet × 120 feet. The city puts in a new street in front and to the side of his house and assesses him 6 cents a square foot based on the area of this lot. His costs are:
   a. $48.00
   b. $57.60
   c. $480.00
   d. $576.00

15. If the transfer taxes are payable at the rate of 55 cents per $500 or part thereof, compute the grantor's cost on a $49,750 sale:
   a. $27.36
   b. $53.90
   c. $54.55
   d. $55.00

16. Ms. Dale buys a $20,000 property. She puts $1,000 down with the balance to be repaid over 20 years at 12 percent interest. Her monthly payments are $209.38. What is the amount of interest paid in the second month's payment?
   a. $75.44
   b. $85.79
   c. $189.06
   d. $190.00

17. What is the approximate amount of interest paid on the loan in problem 16 at its maturity?
   a. $19,000
   b. $31,500
   c. $45,400
   d. $66,100

18. The gross annual income for each of 5 apartments is $145 per month. The building is 90 percent occupied. The caretaker is paid 5 percent of the gross, and the total yearly maintenance is $1,400. Find the monthly net income of the apartments:
   a. $391.20
   b. $503.21
   c. $620.00
   d. $6,038.51

19. James Stole manages an office building with leases of $60,000 per year. His management agreement is for 7 years, with fees as follows: 7 percent the first year, 5 percent the second and third years, and 3 percent the remaining years. Find the total management fee the broker would receive:
    a. $9,000
    b. $12,000
    c. $14,400
    d. $17,400

20. Find the annual percentage rate of net return of an $88,000 investment if the weekly gross income is $225 and the monthly expenses are $370:
    a. 7%
    b. 8.25%
    c. 10%
    d. 12.5%

21. Ms. Carlson owns a 110-acre orchard that yields an average net profit of $13,000. If she sells the land and invests the money at 5 percent, what price per acre must she sell for to match her present earnings?
    a. $236.36
    b. $2,250.00
    c. $2,363.64
    d. $21,500.50

22. A building worth $430,000 rents for $1,500 a month. What is the rate of capitalization?
    a. 4%
    b. 8%
    c. 9%
    d. 23.75%

23. An office building earns $850,000 a year; expenses run 35 percent of that amount. If the property is capitalized at 12 percent, what is its approximate value?
    a. $297,500
    b. $552,500
    c. $4,604,000
    d. $6,630,000

24. Mr. Jay buys a home and obtains an $80,000 loan on which monthly payments will be $7.50 per $1,000. Annual taxes are $1,680; a 3-year fire insurance policy cost $1,800. What was the first payment, including taxes and insurance?
    a. $600
    b. $790
    c. $890
    d. $950

25. A map is drawn to scale and marked 13.5 inches × 16.5 inches. In reality that area equals 108 feet × 132 feet. What is the scale?
    a. ⅛" = 1'
    b. ¼" = 1'
    c. ⅜" = 1'
    d. 8" = 1'

26. A salesperson receives 8 percent of the first $90,000 he sells each month and 2 percent of the excess above that amount. In August, he made sales of $42,000, $48,000, $36,500, and $55,600. If he had been paid a flat 6 percent commission, how much more or less would he have made?
    a. less than $500 more
    b. less than $600 more
    c. less than $5,000 more
    d. more than $5,000 more

27. Ms. Randall's $85,000 condominium is assessed at 35 percent of value. The tax rate is $2.70 per $100 of value. If the tax increases $.35 per $100, her new tax will be:
   a. $699.13
   b. $750.00
   c. $907.38
   d. $9,073.80

28. A house is currently worth 50 percent of its original value. The land, however, has appreciated in 5 years from $60,000 to its present value of $96,000. Find the average annual rate of appreciation of the land over the 5-year period:
   a. 6.25%
   b. 12%
   c. 16%
   d. 63%

29. Now that you are entering the real estate profession, you purchase a new four-door automobile costing $19,200. Your accountant advises that you deduct $4,800 as depreciation this year. What percentage are you deducting?
   a. 4%
   b. 12%
   c. 12.5%
   d. 25%

30. The diagram contains:
   a. 5,600 sq. ft.
   b. 6,800 sq. ft.
   c. 8,000 sq. ft.
   d. 8,500 sq. ft.

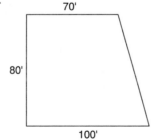

31. This type of interest is paid on the amount of principal that is still owed:
   a. simple
   b. complex
   c. compound
   d. add-on

32. Jerry and June White purchased a home for $74,500, making improvements of $5,000 for a fireplace, $1,500 for a new driveway, and $800 for painting. What is the adjusted basis of their home?
   a. $68,000
   b. $68,800
   c. $81,000
   d. $81,800

33. A home is sold for $74,500 and is appraised for $78,000. The buyer's down payment will be 20%. The loan amount will be:
   a. $14,800
   b. $59,600
   c. $62,400
   d. $74,500

34. If the Joneses are in the 30% tax bracket and their annual property taxes are $1,450 and mortgage interest is $5,200, what is their potential tax savings?
   a. $199.50
   b. $435.00
   c. $1,800.00
   d. $1,995.00

Practice Examination

This examination is to test your knowledge of the material you have studied and to prepare you for the licensing exam if you are pursuing becoming a licensed real estate salesperson or broker. Since many states adhere to a standardized multiple-choice test given by a testing service, the following 100 questions are an example of what you may expect.

Answers can be found on pages 448–449 in the Answer Key section.

PART ONE: REAL ESTATE

1. Which of the following conditions least affects our real estate markets?
   a. interest rates
   b. economic conditions of a given region
   c. supply and demand
   d. foreign market conditions

2. Which of the following conditions does NOT stimulate the purchase of homes?
   a. employment
   b. desire for a larger home
   c. rising interest rates
   d. environment

3. If property is abandoned by its owner, the state's power to claim possession of the property is known as:
   a. escheat
   b. police power
   c. eminent domain
   d. taxation

4. Which of the following is NOT considered real property?
   a. minerals
   b. firewood
   c. air rights
   d. growing trees

5. The process whereby the government takes property for the public good by the right of eminent domain is the act of:
   a. escheat
   b. reversion
   c. accretion
   d. condemnation

6. Riparian rights apply to:
   a. a reversionary interest owned in a life estate
   b. land bordering a moving body of water
   c. land under cultivation
   d. property taken by means of eminent domain

7. Possession of real property that is hostile to the true owner's title is called:
   a. tenancy at sufferance
   b. reversion
   c. adverse possession
   d. police power

8. The gradual loss of land through water and wind is called:
   a. percolation
   b. riparian
   c. alluvion
   d. erosion

9. Which of the following is a use that existed prior to current zoning regulations and is not consistent with the present zoning?
   a. a nonconforming use
   b. a variance
   c. spot zoning
   d. a special use

10. The suggestion that an individual has an ownership interest in a property when this is not the case causes a condition referred to as:
    a. reversionary interest
    b. color of title
    c. escheat
    d. eminent domain

11. Land is considered immobile because:
    a. of its fixed geographic location
    b. it is real property
    c. it is nonhomogeneous
    d. it is indestructible

12. The metes and bounds method of surveying is based primarily upon:
    a. survey lines that run east and west
    b. survey lines that run north and south
    c. a map of a subdivision
    d. a point of beginning

13. The N½ of the SW¼ of the NE¼ of a section in a government rectangular survey township contains:
    a. 160 acres
    b. 80 acres
    c. 20 acres
    d. 10 acres

14. The system of land ownership in the United States is referred to as:
    a. the feudal system
    b. the allodial system
    c. writ of passage
    d. allotment

15. The shopping center that offers a broad mix of shops, including several nationally recognized stores such as Sears and Penney's, is referred to as a(n):
    a. strip center
    b. regional center
    c. neighborhood shopping center
    d. industrial park

16. All of the following are true EXCEPT:
    a. the lot and block method of land description is employed when subdividing land into building lots
    b. the rectangular government survey uses meridians and base lines
    c. townships are divided into 48 sections
    d. a check contains 16 townships

17. Which of the following forms of a quitclaim deed is used when a property owner conveys street rights to the county or jurisdiction within which the property lies?
    a. cession
    b. warranty
    c. executor's deed
    d. gift deed

18. To give notice by recording an instrument is referred to as:
    a. constructive notice
    b. actual notice
    c. verbal notice
    d. written notice

19. Michael has a lifetime estate in 823 S. Maple. Kent will inherit the property upon Michael's death. Kent's interest is:
    a. possessory
    b. a leasehold interest
    c. a reversionary interest
    d. an easement

20. A type of deed that warrants the title against defects only during the time since the present owner has held title is called a:
    a. quitclaim deed
    b. special warranty
    c. general warranty
    d. bargain and sale

21. Which of the following statements does NOT apply to joint tenancy?
    a. all owners must acquire title at the same time
    b. all owners have equal right to possession
    c. the right of survivorship exists
    d. owners hold separate title in the same estate

22. Down zoning occurs when:
    a. a property is rezoned to a lower use
    b. a property is rezoned to a higher use
    c. spot zoning is given
    d. raw land is developed into homesites

23. A life tenant may do all of the following EXCEPT:
    a. lease the property to another individual
    b. pay taxes on the property
    c. bequeath her interest
    d. sell her interest

24. A form of ownership with the right of survivorship is known as:
    a. joint tenancy
    b. tenancy in common
    c. estate of inheritance
    d. partnerships

25. Rights of survivorship do not exist in this ownership:
    a. joint tenancy
    b. dower
    c. tenancy in common
    d. tenancy by the entirety

PART TWO: THE ORDERLY PROCESS OF A SALE

26. Which of the following elements does NOT need to be present to have a valid and enforceable contract?
    a. legality of object
    b. legal capacity of parties
    c. consideration
    d. an assignment clause

27. While viewing homes with her agent, a buyer asks if the drapes will remain in a particular house. Although the listing does not include the drapes, the agent explains that they can be written into the contract. The buyer submits an offer for the house, and it is accepted by the seller as written. Upon taking possession of the house, the buyer discovers the drapes are gone. The agent confirms that although they had discussed asking for them while viewing the property, the item had not been put into the contract. The rule that forbids the admittance of any prior oral or written evidence to vary or add to the terms of a written instrument is the:
    a. statute of frauds
    b. rule of specific performance
    c. dual contract rule
    d. parol evidence rule

28. The contracts most commonly used in real estate transactions include all of the following EXCEPT:
    a. listing contracts
    b. purchase contracts
    c. mortgages
    d. abstracts

29. Broker A has listed a property, and one of her salespersons, Agent A, is showing the property to a potential buyer. Agent A informs the prospect that the sellers are due to move out of state and are anxious to sell, and thus will be willing to lower their asking price. Which of the following is a true statement in reference to this situation?
    a. if the seller has not agreed to disclosure of this information, Agent A has breached his fiduciary obligation to the seller
    b. this is a case of dual agency
    c. since the prospective buyer is a close friend of Agent A, he may bend the rules a little without breaching his responsibilities
    d. all three are true statements

30. Owners hire real estate firms to sell their property for all of the following reasons EXCEPT:
    a. brokers financially qualify customers in advance
    b. the salesperson may purchase the property and later resell it
    c. the salesperson keeps current on available financing
    d. the salesperson is aware of market conditions and market values

31. A contract providing for payment of a commission regardless of who sells the property is a(n):
    a. net listing
    b. open listing
    c. exclusive agency
    d. exclusive right to sell

32. A listing contract must contain all of the following EXCEPT:
    a. the signatures of all parties named
    b. the agreed-upon commission
    c. nondiscrimination wording
    d. proration of closing costs

33. An agent who has the power of attorney to act for a principal in all lawful transactions concerning the principal is called:
    a. a general agent
    b. an implied agent
    c. a special agent
    d. a universal agent

34. Under what circumstances does a dual agency exist?
    a. an agent is employed by a home buyer
    b. an agent sells a property listed by the broker for whom he works
    c. an agent shows property listed by another broker
    d. a salesperson represents both buyer and seller by prior written agreement

35. A broker can accept a commission from both the buyer and the seller in some states under which of the following circumstances?
    a. upon full disclosure and consent of all parties
    b. if the broker feels he has represented both equally in the transaction
    c. providing the commission is not excessive
    d. if the listing broker is also the selling broker

36. If a buyer is concerned about the condition of the furnace in a house that she is considering purchasing, the buyer could:
    a. obtain an inspection from a qualified service
    b. purchase a buyer warranty policy
    c. have the seller purchase a buyer warranty policy
    d. any of the above

37. Fannie Mae can best be described as:
    a. a purchaser of loans in the secondary market
    b. an agency that insures private mortgages
    c. a regulatory agency that governs the interest rates charged on government loans
    d. a lender in the primary market

38. The definition that best describes the term hypothecate is:
    a. to lend money below current market rates
    b. to retain possession but pledge as security
    c. the transfer of funds from one bank to another to obtain higher interest rates
    d. to consolidate a borrower's debts

39. This act requires the lender to provide the borrower with a good faith estimate of all costs associated with closing:
    a. RESPA
    b. FNMA
    c. APR
    d. EOC

40. Which of the following loans is insured by the government?
    a. FHA
    b. VA
    c. farm loans
    d. PMI

41. A lender will make a loan on real estate based on a percentage of the property's value. This is called:
    a. the resale value
    b. the loan-to-value ratio
    c. liquidation value
    d. market value

42. *Disintermediation* defines the process whereby:
    a. depositors withdraw their funds from the savings and loans to invest them directly in corporate bonds, government securities, etc.
    b. the secondary mortgage market buys loans from the primary lender
    c. government agencies interfere in the business of making loans
    d. ceilings on loans are eliminated

43. A lien that is attached to a particular property is known as a:
    a. judgment in personam
    b. judgment in rem
    c. tort
    d. lis pendens

44. All of the following encumbrances are placed on real property by someone other than the owner EXCEPT:
    a. mechanic's lien
    b. judgment lien
    c. mortgage lien
    d. tax lien

45. The processs of amortization is best described as:
    a. reduction of debt on a payment plan
    b. mortgaging with a land contract
    c. assignment of a mortgage
    d. paying on a construction loan

46. Which of the following mortgages offers reduced payments for the first few years because a portion of the interest has been prepaid for the buyer?
    a. adjustable rate mortgage (ARM)
    b. buydown mortgage
    c. blanket mortgage
    d. land contract

47. In which of the following mortgages is the final payment substantially larger than the previous monthly payments?
    a. blanket mortgage
    b. package mortgage
    c. balloon mortgage
    d. second mortgage

48. Which of the following statements is true regarding delinquent property taxes?
    a. they become a lien against the property
    b. a lien is placed against all personal property of the debtor
    c. a federal tax lien is placed against the property
    d. they are taxed as a special assessment

49. A painting contractor paints two properties for a customer but is paid only for painting one. Which of the following is NOT true regarding a lien the contractor files?
    a. the lien will be a mechanic's lien
    b. the lien is created by statute
    c. the lien can be placed only on the one property
    d. the lien can be filed against both properties

50. Which of the following items is prorated at the time of closing?
    a. the earnest deposit
    b. proceeds from the sale
    c. the mortgage
    d. property taxes

51. Which of the following would NOT be charged to the buyer's closing statement?

    a. the purchase price

    b. the recording of the deed

    c. the new mortgage loan

    d. property taxes

52. A property owner is insured against a forged title or defects in the title by:

    a. an appraisal

    b. title insurance policy

    c. examination of the abstract

    d. homeowner's insurance

PART THREE: OTHER ASPECTS OF REAL ESTATE

53. Rules for governing the operation of a condominium development are set by:

    a. zoning laws

    b. each owner sets his own rules

    c. the development's homeowners' association

    d. local ordinance

54. Legislation governing a condominium development is referred to as:

    a. a horizontal property act

    b. a free cooperative act

    c. a vertical property act

    d. deeded restrictions

55. Disadvantages of condominium ownership could include:

    a. density

    b. limited private outdoor space

    c. limited parking area

    d. all of the above

56. Which of the following is the type of ownership that gives a proprietary lease?

    a. cooperative

    b. condominium

    c. time-share

    d. exchange program

57. All of the following statements are true EXCEPT:

    a. cooperative owners will hold shares of stock

    b. condominium owners acquire fee simple title

    c. conversion changes the use of a property

    d. a condo owner owns the common areas with other owners in joint tenancy

58. This lease provides for the payment of rent and certain costs involved in the operation and maintenance of the property:

    a. percentage lease

    b. net lease

    c. graduated lease

    d. gross lease

59. The mutual agreement between the lessee and the lessor to cancel a lease is termed:

    a. detainer

    b. notice to quit

    c. surrender and acceptance

    d. gross lease

60. Jones leases space for his bakery in a 10-year-old mall. A new shopping center is being built one mile away, so Jones decides not to renew his present lease, which expires June 10, because he feels his business will increase at the new location. The new location will be ready June 15, so Jones keeps a key so that he can remove the trade fixture at that time to the new location. Can Jones legally do this?
    a. yes, trade fixtures are property of the tenant
    b. yes, because he automatically has 30 days to remove them
    c. no, once fixtures are attached they become the property of the landlord
    d. no, trade fixtures must be removed before the lease expires

61. The instrument that transfers the right to possess property but does not convey ownership is:
    a. a lien
    b. a mortgage
    c. a lease
    d. a deed

62. A percentage lease may be used for all of the following EXCEPT:
    a. a sporting goods store
    b. a specialty shop
    c. a 10-unit apartment building
    d. a computer sales store

63. Which of the following does not have an insurable interest in the real estate?
    a. life tenant
    b. mortgagee
    c. trustee
    d. property manager

64. A property manager will generally perform which of the following functions?
    a. offer lower rental rates to preferred tenants
    b. invest the owner's profits in new buildings
    c. advertise available space
    d. make long-term decisions on capital improvements

65. A licensee may carry this type of protection insurance in the event an unintentional mistake is made when selling a house:
    a. homeowner's insurance
    b. title insurance
    c. license insurance
    d. errors and omission insurance

66. Which of the following is NOT an advantage to investing in real estate?
    a. liquidity
    b. appreciation
    c. equity build-up
    d. leverage

67. Many investors use the financial practice of leverage to:
    a. shelter their income
    b. guarantee a positive cash flow
    c. reduce their equity investment
    d. increase their equity investment

68. The Real Estate Investment Trust (REIT) offers which of the following?
    I.   real estate ownership through indirect participation
    II. shares in real property can be purchased by small investors
    III. control by all of the investors
    a. I only
    b. II only
    c. I and II
    d. I, II, and III

69. Concerns of investors include all EXCEPT:
    a. the risk involved in the project
    b. tax considerations
    c. whether inflation will erode the growth potential
    d. building equity

70. Which of the following type(s) of depreciation may be curable?
    a. physical obsolescence
    b. economic obsolescence
    c. functional obsolescence
    d. a and c

71. Functional obsolescence is primarily the result of:
    a. wearing out of the building and its components
    b. changing requirements of buyers
    c. changes in surrounding properties
    d. decreased demand

72. An appraisal report may be in the form of all EXCEPT:
    a. an oral report
    b. a letter
    c. a narrative
    d. a video report

73. The appraisal process used to establish the potential return on an investment is:
    a. the comparison approach
    b. the income approach
    c. the cost approach
    d. summation

74. The purpose of an appraisal may include all of the following EXCEPT:
    a. to determine the market value of the property
    b. for insurance purposes
    c. for loan value
    d. to determine regional value

75. The term ad valorem means:
    a. ability to repay a debt
    b. appraisal to determine value
    c. according to value
    d. insured against disaster

76. In the preparation of a market value analysis it is important that the appraiser use which of the following?
    a. the income approach
    b. adjustments for differences in the properties
    c. the quantity survey method
    d. the cost approach

77. According to the principle of conformity:
    a. value increases if a property is overimproved for the area
    b. values tend to rise if a neighborhood is homogeneous
    c. value is created by anticipation
    d. supply and demand dictate new home starts

78. In August 1989 Congress passed the Financial Institutions Reform, Recovery and Enforcement Act (FIRREA). Title XI of the bill requires:
    a. appraisers to meet minimum standards of performance
    b. that a certified appraiser be used to appraise one- to four-family residences of $1 million value and higher
    c. that all federally related appraisals be performed by a certified or licensed appraiser
    d. all of the above

79. Approximately 75% of homes discovered to have lead-based paint were built prior to:
    a. 1978
    b. 1990
    c. 1995
    d. 2002

80. Mold that is found in buildings is largely due to:
    a. asbestos insulation
    b. formaldehyde insulation
    c. lead-based paint
    d. continuous moisture problems

81. Inspections should be made on fuel-burning appliances, such as furnaces, because if defective, they can emit a toxic gas known as:
    a. radon
    b. carbon monoxide
    c. asbestos
    d. formaldehyde

82. The Superfund was established for the following reason:
    a. monitor electromagnetic fields (EMFs)
    b. clean up the worst existing hazardous waste sites
    c. safeguard public drinking water
    d. remove asbestos from public buildings

83. In 1984 an amendment to the Resource and Recovery Act (RCRA) was passed:
    a. to set minimum standards for safe drinking water
    b. to remove asbestos from buildings
    c. to regulate underground storage tanks
    d. to regulate the disposal of solid waste in designated dump sites

84. A radioactive gas that may enter a home through cracks and holes in the foundation is:
    a. carbon monoxide
    b. formaldehyde
    c. radon
    d. mold spores

85. The Rehabilitation Tax Credit was passed by Congress to:
    a. assist investors to build up an equity
    b. place old buildings back into service and onto the tax roll
    c. refinance historical buildings
    d. defer capital gains for the investor

86. Discouraging a prospective buyer from looking for housing in a particular area is considered:
    a. redlining
    b. blockbusting
    c. steering
    d. reprisal

87. A lender refuses to make a loan for a purchaser because the home is located in a certain neighborhood. This is an example of:
    a. steering
    b. redlining
    c. blockbusting
    d. legitimate procedure

88. Exemptions to the fair housing law include all of the following EXCEPT:
    a. discriminatory advertising is not used
    b. a religious group sells retirement homes in a subdivision they developed only for their members
    c. the rental of lodging that a private club owns and operates for other than commercial purposes
    d. the rental of an apartment to a family with children

89. A broker lists a home on January 5 and on January 7 learns the taxes are three years delinquent and the property is scheduled to be sold at a sheriff sale. On January 20 the house is destroyed by fire. On January 30 the owner declares bankruptcy. When was the listing voided?
    a. January 5
    b. January 7
    c. January 20
    d. January 30

90. An agent must disclose to a potential buyer all EXCEPT:
    a. that the property is in a flood zone
    b. that the home has a septic system and is not on public sewer
    c. that the seller must sell quickly
    d. that the air conditioner is not working

91. The primary reason for license law is:
    a. to protect the public
    b. to arbitrate commissions
    c. to protect the brokers
    d. to encourage continuing education programs for salespersons

92. Which of the following laws requires lenders to inform buyers and sellers of all fees and charges?
    a. the Fair Housing Act
    b. the Equal Credit Opportunity Act
    c. the Real Estate Settlement Procedures Act
    d. the Truth-in-Lending Act (Regulation Z)

93. Which of the following would NOT be an infraction of the license laws of most states?
    a. intentionally using misleading advertising
    b. acting as agent and undisclosed principal
    c. acting for more than one party without the knowledge of both parties
    d. all would be infractions

94. A house cost $77,000. Gross rents are $525 per month, with a net return to the owner of $450 per month. What is the gross rent multiplier?
    a. .07
    b. .075
    c. .08
    d. 146.7

95. Mr. Tice obtains a $65,000 loan on his home. The principal and interest payments are based on a factor of $8.54 per $1,000. The loan is for 30 years at 9 percent. How much does Mr. Tice pay in total interest over the life of the loan?
    a. $55,510
    b. $66,612
    c. $134,836
    d. $199,836

96. A broker has a four-year contract to manage a rental unit for an investor. She is to receive 50 percent of the first month's rent and 5 percent of each remaining month. The rent is $600 per month. Over the term of the contract the broker earns:
    a. $1,410
    b. $1,440
    c. $1,740
    d. $2,880

97. A two-story house measures 48' × 25' and cost $70.00 per square foot to build. What is the construction cost of the house?
    a. $84,000
    b. $96,000
    c. $168,000
    d. $230,000

98. Mrs. Charlesworth purchases a home for $90,000. She paid $4,000 as earnest deposit and is obtaining an 80 percent loan. Costs include $250 for title insurance, $360 for homeowner insurance, recording fees of $60, and a tax prorate fee of $430. Mrs. Charlesworth will need to bring a check to closing in the amount of:

a. $14,679

b. $15,100

c. $19,100

d. $22,200

99. Three members of a partnership are investing $300,000 in a $1 million venture. If partner A invests $150,000 and partner B invests $100,000, what is the equity position of the third party?

a. $\frac{1}{6}$

b. $\frac{1}{4}$

c. $\frac{1}{3}$

d. $\frac{1}{2}$

100. Susie Quinn lists her home for $170,000 with A-1 Realty. She agrees to pay a 6 percent commission on the gross sales price. The property sells for 15 percent below her asking price. The selling broker and the listing broker split the commission evenly; thus, selling broker Doe Realty receives 50 percent of the commission. He gives 20 percent to his salesperson for assisting him with the sale. Doe retains for himself:

a. $867

b. $950

c. $3,468

d. $4,335

Answer Key

CHAPTER 1

1. *b*

2. *a*

3. *b*

4. *d*

5. *c*

6. *c*

7. *b*

CHAPTER 2

1. *a*

2. *d*

3. *b*

4. *b*

5. *c*

6. *d*

7. *d*

8. *d*

9. *d*

10. *a*

11. *b*

12. *d*

13. *b*

14. *a*

15. *b*

16. *b*

17. *d*

18. *c*

19. *c*

20. *d*

CHAPTER 3

1. *d*

2. *c*

3. *d*

4. *a*

5. *d*

6. *c*

7. *c*

8. *a*

9. *c*

10. *a T10N, R2W*

    b T10N, R1E

    c T8N, R2W

    d T8N, R1E

11. *c*

12. *d*

13. *a 40 acres*

    b 10 acres

    c 20 acres

    d 80 acres

14. *b The N$\frac{1}{2}$ of the SW$\frac{1}{4}$ of the NW$\frac{1}{4}$ = 20 acres. 20 × 43,560 sq ft (area of an acre) = 871,000 sq ft. Minus 420,450 reserved = 450,750 area to build upon. 110 × 70 = 7700 sq ft for each lot. 450,750 ÷ 7,700 = 58.54 lots.*

15. *c*

16. *b*

17. *a*

18. *b*

19. *a The N$\frac{1}{2}$ of the SW$\frac{1}{4}$ = 80 acres. 80 × \$1,350 = \$10,800*

20. *c*

CHAPTER 4

1. *b*	7. *d*	13. *c*	19. *c*
2. *a*	8. *b*	14. *a*	20. *b*
3. *c*	9. *a*	15. *b*	21. *b*
4. *d*	10. *d*	16. *b*	22. *b*
5. *c*	11. *a*	17. *b*	
6. *b*	12. *c*	18. *c*	

CHAPTER 5

1. *b*	8. *a*	15. *d*	22. *c*
2. *b*	9. *b*	16. *d*	23. *b*
3. *d*	10. *c*	17. *d*	24. *d*
4. *c*	11. *c*	18. *b*	25. *c*
5. *d*	12. *b*	19. *a*	
6. *c*	13. *b*	20. *a*	
7. *b*	14. *a*	21. *c*	

CHAPTER 6

1. *d*	6. *b*	11. *d*	16. *a*
2. *c*	7. *a*	12. *a*	17. *a*
3. *a*	8. *c*	13. *b*	18. *d*
4. *a*	9. *c*	14. *d*	19. *b*
5. *c*	10. *b*	15. *c*	20. *c*

CHAPTER 7

1. *b*	5. *d*	9. *c*	13. *c*
2. *a*	6. *b*	10. *c*	14. *c*
3. *d*	7. *c*	11. *a*	15. *a*
4. *b*	8. *c*	12. *d*	

CHAPTER 8

1. *a*	**7.** *a*	**13.** *b*	**19.** *b*
2. *b*	**8.** *c*	**14.** *a*	**20.** *b*
3. *b*	**9.** *a*	**15.** *c*	**21.** *b*
4. *a*	**10.** *a*	**16.** *d*	
5. *b*	**11.** *a*	**17.** *d*	
6. *b*	**12.** *b*	**18.** *b*	

CHAPTER 9

1. *c*	**5.** *c*	**9.** *d*	**13.** *b*
2. *c*	**6.** *a*	**10.** *a*	**14.** *d*
3. *d*	**7.** *b*	**11.** *a*	**15.** *b*
4. *c*	**8.** *a*	**12.** *d*	**16.** *d*

CHAPTER 10

1. *c*	**11.** *b*	**21.** *d*	$50) \times .0225 =$ $1,824.00 *(premium amount rounded to nearest dollar amount)* $+$ $18,100.00 =$ $82,924.00 *(loan including UFMIP)*
2. *d*	**12.** *a*	**22.** *a*	
3. *b*	**13.** *b*	**23.** *d*	
4. *d*	**14.** *c*	**24.** *a*	
5. *c*	**15.** *a*	**25.** *d* $48,000 \times .9875$ $= $47,400$	
6. *c*	**16.** *d*	**26.** *d* $83,000 \times .9775$ $= $81,132.50;$ $81,100.00 *(base amount rounded down to nearest*	**27.** *c*
7. *a*	**17.** *c*		
8. *c*	**18.** *a*		
9. *d*	**19.** *b*		
10. *b*	**20.** *c*		

CHAPTER 11

1 *b*	**7.** *b*	**11.** *c* $90,000 \times .20$ *down payment =* $18,000$ $90,000 - $18,000$ $= $72,000 *loan*$ $72,000 \times 7\% =$ $5,040 *annual interest*	$5,040 \div$ *12 months =* $420.00 *interest paid*
2. *a*	**8.** *a*		
3. *a*	**9.** *a*		**12.** *b* *20 years* $\times$ *12 monthly payments = 240 payments*
4. *b*	**10.** *d*		
5. *c*			
6. *b*			

$558.72 \times 240 =$
$134,092.80$ prin-
cipal and interest
$134,092.80 -$
$72,000.00 =$
$62,092.80$ interest

13. b

14. b

15. c

16. c

17. c

18. d

19. c

20. b

21. d $45,000 \times 8\% =$
$3,600$ annual
interest
$3,600 \div$
12 months =
300 interest
$330.30 - $300 =$
30.30 against
principal reduction

$45,000 - 30.30
$= $44,969.70$

22. b

23. a

24. a

25. b

CHAPTER 12

1. b

2. a

3. c

4. c

5. b

6. a

7. a

8. d

9. d

10. c

11. a

12. a

13. a

14. d

15. b $35,000 \times 25\%$
$= $8,750$ down
payment
$35,000 - $8,750$
$= $26,250$ loan
$26,250 \times .01 =$
262.50
$8,750 + 262.50
$= $9,012.50$

$9,012.50 -$
$3,500$ (deposit) =
$5,512.50$

16. c

17. a $81,000 \times .07 =$
$5,670$ commission
30% of $5,670 =$
$1,701$

18. a August 20 – Dec 1
= 4 mos, 10 days.
$1,320 \div 12$ mos
$= 110 mo × 4
$= 440

$110 \div 30$ days =
3.67 per day ×
10 days = 36.67
$440 + $36.67 =$
476.67

19. a

20. b 302 insurance –
Aug 20 to Mar 20
unused portion.
$302 \div 12$ mos =
25.167 per
month × 7 mos =
176.17

CHAPTER 12

ANSWER TO CLOSING STATEMENT

BUYER	Debit	Credit	SELLER	Debit	Credit
Purchase price	$90,695.00		Selling price		$90,695.00
Loan		$72,600.00	Loan balance	$58,548.00	
Insurance policy	350.00		Discount point 1%	726.00	
Loan discount	726.00		Tax prorate		513.33
Tax prorate 8/10–12/31					
4 mos, 20 days	513.33		Mortgage release	7.00	
Record deed	6.00		Commission	6,348.65	
Title insurance	430.00				
Balance due		$20,120.33	Proceeds due to seller	$25,578.68	
Total	$92,720.33	$92,720.33	Total	$91,208.33	$91,208.33

CHAPTER 13

1. *b*	5. *a*	9. *b*	13. *c*
2. *a*	6. *d*	10. *c*	14. *a*
3. *a*	7. *d*	11. *d*	15. *b*
4. *b*	8. *b*	12. *d*	16. *c*

CHAPTER 14

1. *a*	6. *c*	11. *c*	16. *c*
2. *b*	7. *b*	12. *a*	17. *c*
3. *d*	8. *d*	13. *c*	18. *a*
4. *b*	9. *b*	14. *d*	19. *c*
5. *a*	10. *c*	15. *d*	20. *a*

CHAPTER 15

1. *d*	6. *c*	11. *d*	14. *b* 3,200 square feet × $9 = $28,800 ÷ 12 months = $2,400 per month
2. *b*	7. *b*	12. *b*	
3. *d*	8. *b*	13. *b*	
4. *a*	9. *b*		15. *b*
5. *d*	10. *d*		

CHAPTER 16

1. *c*	11. *a*	$112 × .08 = $8,960 annual interest $8,960 × .28 = $2,508.80 first-year tax savings	22. *a* $112,000 loan × .00956 = $1,070.72 monthly payment $1,070.72 − $209.06 and $56 = $805.66
2. *b*	12. *c*		
3. *d*	13. *d*		
4. *c*	14. *d*		
5. *c*	15. *a*		
6. *d*	16. *b*	20. *a* $2,508.80 ÷ 12 months = $209.06	23. *c* $37,000 ÷ .10 = $370,000
7. *b*	17. *d*		
8. *b*	18. *b*	21. *c* $2,400 × .28 = $672.00 savings ÷ 12 mos. = $56.00	24. *c*
9. *a*	19. *b* $140,000 × .80 = $112,000 loan		
10. *a*			

CHAPTER 17

1. *d*	9. *b*	17. *b*	25. *d*
2. *b*	10. *d*	18. *c*	26. *d*
3. *a*	11. *b*	19. *a*	27. *a*
4. *b*	12. *b*	20. *a*	28. *b*
5. *a*	13. *a*	21. *c*	29. *d*
6. *c*	14. *d*	22. *a*	
7. *d*	15. *b*	23. *d*	
8. *b*	16. *c*	24. *c*	

CHAPTER 18

1. *c*	4. *a*	7. *d*	9. *b*
2. *d*	5. *b*	8. *b*	10. *c*
3. *c*	6. *b*		

CHAPTER 19

1. *b*	6. *a*	11. *a*	16. *c*
2. *a*	7. *a*	12. *d*	17. *d*
3. *b*	8. *c*	13. *c*	18. *b*
4. *a*	9. *a*	14. *d*	
5. *c*	10. *a*	15. *d*	

CHAPTER 20

1. *b*	8. *a*	15. *c*	22. *c*
2. *a*	9. *d*	16. *d*	23. *a*
3. *d*	10. *a*	17. *a*	24. *d*
4. *a*	11. *b*	18. *c*	25. *c*
5. *c*	12. *d*	19. *d*	
6. *c*	13. *d*	20. *c*	
7. *a*	14. *a*	21. *d*	

CHAPTER 21

1. *c* $200' \times 170' = 34,000$ sq. ft.
$20 \times 20 = 400$ sq. ft. $\div 2 = 200$ sq. ft.
$34,000$ sq. ft. $- 200$ sq. ft. $= 33,800$ sq. ft.

2. *b* $2.5 \times 10 = 25\%$ depreciation
$100\% - 25\% = 75\%$
$\$112,500 \div 75\% = \$150,000$

3. *b* $\$150,000 \times .80 = \$120,000$
$\$120,000 \times .03 = \$3,600$

4. *c* $\$300 \div 20,000 = .015$ mill levy
$\$40,000 \times .015 = \$600$

5. *b* 360 acres $\times \$150 = \$54,000$
$\$25,000 \times .05 = \$1,250$
$\$20,000 \times .025 = \$500$
$9,000 \times .01 = \$90$
Total commission $= \$1,840$
Half to Morris's firm $= \$920$
Half of $\$920$ to Mr. Lewis $= \$460$

6. *a* $900' \times 900' = 810,000$ sq. ft.
$300 \times 90 = 27,000$ sq. ft.
$810,000 \div 27,000 = \frac{1}{30}$

7. *d* 1 foot $= \frac{1}{8}$ or 8 ft. $= 1$ inch
$8 \times 5\frac{3}{4} = 46$
$8 \times 4\frac{1}{2} = 36$
area $= 46' \times 36'$

8. *b* July 15 through December 31 $= 5\frac{1}{2}$ months unused
$\$1,746 + \$702 = \$2,448 \div 12$ months $= \$204$ per month $\$204 \times 5\frac{1}{2}$ months $= \$1,122$

9. *c* June 15 through December 31 $= 6\frac{1}{2}$ months unused
$\$660 \div 12 = \$55$ month $\times 6\frac{1}{2}$ months $= \$357.50$

10. *b* $\$275 \times 10 = \$2,750$ per month $\times 12$ months $= \$33,000$ annual rent
$\$250 \times 12 = \$3,000$ per month $\times 12$ months $= \$36,000$ annual rent
$\$33,000 + \$36,000 = \$69,000 \times 15\%$ vacancy $= \$10,350$
$\$69,000 - \$10,350 = \$58,650 - \$6,789$ (expenses) $= \$51,861$
$\$51,861 \div 10\% = \$518,610$

11. *d* $\$62,000 \times .80 = \$49,600$ loan $\times .04 = \$1,984.00$ (discount points)
$\$1,984.00 + \$2,500$ down payment $= \$4,484$
$\$62,000 - \$49,600 = \$12,400$ down payment plus $\$4,484 = \$16,884$ total

12. *d* $\$350 + \$12,500 + \$7,000 = \$19,850 \div .94 = \$21,117.02$

13. *c* 25% depreciation $\times \$300,000 = \$75,000$
$\$300,000 - \$75,000 = \$225,000 + \$51,000 = \$276,000$

14. *d* $120' \times 80' = 9,600$ sq. ft. $\times .06 = \$576.00$

15. *d* $\$50,000 \times 1.10 = \$55.00$

16. *c* $19,000 \times .12 = 2,280 \div 12$ mos. $= \$190.00$ interest per month
$\$209.38 - \$190 = \$19.38$ toward principal
$19,000 - 19.38 = 18,980.62 \times 12 = \$2,268.74 \div 12$ mos. $= \$189.06$

17. *b* 20 years $\times 12 = 240$ months $\times \$209.38 = \$50,251.20 - \$19,000 = \$31,251.20$

18. *b* $\$145 \times 5$ apartments $= \$725$ monthly
$\$725 \times 12$ months $= \$8,700 \times 90\% = \$7,830 \times .05 = \$391.50$
$\$1,400$ (expenses) $+ \$391.50 = \$1,791.50$ total expenses
$\$7,830$ (gross income) $- \$1,791.50 = \$6,038.50$ (yearly income)
$\$6,038.50 \div 12$ months $= \$503.21$

19. *d* 7% of $60,000 = 4,200$
5% of $60,000 = 3,000 \times 2$ years $= 6,000$
3% of $60,000 = 1,800 \times 4$ years $= 7,200$
$4,200 + 6,000 + 7,200 = \$17,400$

20. *b* $\$225 \times 52$ weeks $= \$11,700$
$\$370 \times 12$ months $= \$4,440$
$\$11,700 - \$4,440 = \$7,260$ net income
$\$7,260 \div 88,000 = .0825 = 8\frac{1}{4}\%$

21. *c* $\$13,000 = 5\%$ of what?
$\$13,000 \div 5\% = \$260,000 \div 110$ acres $= \$2,363.64$

22. *a* $\$1,500 \times 12 = 18,000 \div 430,000 = 4\%$

23. *c* $\$850,000 \times .35 = \$297,500$
$\$850,000 - \$297,500 = \$552,500$
$\$552,500 \div 12\% = \$4,604,167$

24. *b* *$80,000 × 7.50 = $600 P and I payment.*
$1,680 taxes ÷ 12 months = $140
Insurance of $1,800 ÷ 36 months =
$50. $600 + $140 + $50 = $790

25. *a* *108 ÷ 13.50 = 8*
132 ÷ 16.50 = 8
1 ÷ 8 = ⅛; therefore ⅛" = 1'

26. *c* *$42,000 + $48,000 + $36,500 + $55,600 =*
$182,100
$90,000 × 8% = $7,200
$182,100 − $90,000 = $92,100 × 2% =
$1,842
$1,842 + $7,200 = $9,042 commission
$182,100 × 6% = $10,926 − $9,042 =
$1,884 difference (less than $5,000 more)

27. *c* *$85,000 × .35 = $29,750 assessed value*
$29,750 ÷ 100 = $297.50
$297.50 × 3.05 (2.70 + .35) = $907.38

28. *b* *$96,000 − $60,000 = $36,000 ÷ 5 years =*
$7,200 per year
$7,200 ÷ $60,000 = 12%

29. *d* *$4,800 ÷ $19,200 = 25%*

30. *b* *70' × 80' = 5,600 sq. ft.*
30' × 80' = 2,400 ÷ 2 = 1,200 sq. ft.
5,600 + 1,200 = 6,800 sq. ft.

31. *a*

32. *c* *$74,500 + $5,000 + $1,500 = $81,000*
Painting is not considered a capital expense.

33. *b* *$74,500 × .80 = $59,600 (purchase price*
less 20% down payment)
Lenders base LTV on the lower of purchase
price or appraised value.

34. *d* *$1,450 + $5,200 = $6,650 × .30 = $1,995*
maximum potential benefit
There is no benefit until total itemized deduc-
tions exceed the standard deduction ($6,550
for a couple filing jointly for the 1995 tax
year). If the Joneses had no additional item-
ized deductions, their benefit would be:
$6,650 − $6,550 = $100 × .30 = $30.

PRACTICE EXAMINATION

1. *d*	**17.** *a*	**33.** *d*	**49.** *d*
2. *c*	**18.** *a*	**34.** *d*	**50.** *d*
3. *a*	**19.** *c*	**35.** *a*	**51.** *c*
4. *b*	**20.** *b*	**36.** *d*	**52.** *b*
5. *d*	**21.** *d*	**37.** *a*	**53.** *c*
6. *b*	**22.** *a*	**38.** *b*	**54.** *a*
7. *c*	**23.** *c*	**39.** *a*	**55.** *d*
8. *d*	**24.** *a*	**40.** *a*	**56.** *a*
9. *a*	**25.** *c*	**41.** *b*	**57.** *d*
10. *b*	**26.** *d*	**42.** *a*	**58.** *b*
11. *a*	**27.** *d*	**43.** *b*	**59.** *c*
12. *d*	**28.** *d*	**44.** *c*	**60.** *d*
13. *c*	**29.** *a*	**45.** *a*	**61.** *c*
14. *b*	**30.** *b*	**46.** *b*	**62.** *c*
15. *b*	**31.** *d*	**47.** *c*	**63.** *d*
16. *c*	**32.** *d*	**48.** *a*	**64.** *c*

65.	*d*	73.	*b*	81.	*b*	89.	*c*
66.	*a*	74.	*d*	82.	*b*	90.	*c*
67.	*c*	75.	*c*	83.	*c*	91.	*a*
68.	*c*	76.	*b*	84.	*c*	92.	*c*
69.	*d*	77.	*b*	85.	*b*	93.	*d*
70.	*d*	78.	*d*	86.	*c*		
71.	*b*	79.	*a*	87.	*b*		
72.	*d*	80.	*d*	88.	*d*		

94. *d $77,000 ÷ $525 = 146.67*

95. *c $65 × $8.54 = $555.10 per month payments on P & I*
$555.10 × 360 months = $199,836
$199,836 − $65,000 loan = $134,836

96. *c 12 months × 4 years = 48 months = less 1st month = 47 mos × $600 = $28,800*
$28,800 × .05 = $1,440 + $300
(half first mo. rent)
$1,740 total commission earned

97. *c 48' × 25' = 1,200 sq. ft. × 2 stories = 2,400 sq. ft.*
2,400 sq. ft. × $70 = $168,000

98. *b $90,000 × .80 = $72,000 loan, $18,000 down payment due*
$18,000 + $250 + $360 + $60 + $430 = $19,100 − $4,000 earnest deposit = $15,100

99. *a $150,000 + $100,000 = $250,000*
$50,000 = 3rd parties share
$50,000 ÷ $300,000 = ⅙

100. *c $170,000 × 85% = $144,500 sale price × .06 = $8,670*
½ of $8,670 = $4,335. 20% of $4,335 = $867
$4,335 − $867 = $3,468 for Joe Doe

Abandonment Terminating rights and title to property.

Abstract (of title) A publicly available summary of the title changes on a specific property, beginning with the original land grant.

Abstractor A title searcher and preparer of abstracts.

Acceleration clause The clause in a mortgage that allows the lender to advance the time when the entire sum owed is due and payable.

Accession An addition to real estate acquired by accretion of land through soil deposits; acquiring fixtures by a tenant.

Accretion Addition to the land through natural causes, usually by a change in water flow.

Acknowledgment The act of going before an authorized officer or notary public and declaring a legal document to be one's voluntary act and deed.

Acquisition The act of acquiring a parcel of real estate.

Acre A parcel of land that measures 43,560 square feet, or 208.71 feet square.

Actual eviction The lessee is evicted by the lessor for failure to live up to the terms of the lease.

Actual notice Notice given; knowledge of a condition.

Addendum Additions to a contract that become a part of the document; sometimes referred to as "riders" to a contract.

Adjustable Rate Mortgage (ARM) The interest rate for a mortgage will be renegotiated at set times to adjust to current interest rates.

Adjusted basis The reduction or increase of the original basis of a property caused by improvements to the property.

Administrator Person appointed by the court to settle the estate of one who died without leaving a will.

Administrator's deed A deed issued by the administrator to transfer title.

Administrative Law Judge (ALJ) Holds hearing on discrimination complaints that are filed with HUD. The ADJ has authority to award actual damages or impose monetary penalties.

Ad valorem tax An assessment on real property according to its market value.

Adverse possession Rightful owner loses land to occupant who has taken possession in a hostile, distinct, continuous, visible, and actual way for the statutory period.

Affidavit A written statement sworn to under oath.

Agency The legal relationship between principal and agent with the agent representing the principal in transactions with third parties.

Agency by estoppel Results when a principal fails to maintain due diligence over his agent and the agent exercises powers not granted to him.

Agency by ratification The express affirmation or implication whereby a principal agrees to be obligated by the acts of another who contends to act as an agent even though not employed as an agent for the principal.

Agency law Relationship in which one person has legal authority to act for another.

Agent One who is authorized to represent another; the employee of the principal, that is, the broker.

Agreement of sale A written agreement between buyer and seller for the purchase and sale of real estate. The owner retains title until the sale is consummated.

Air lot A unit of space individually owned in a multilevel condominium.

Air Quality Act of 1967 Enacted to protect and control air pollution.

Air rights The right to use or occupy air space above a designated property.

Alienation The transfer of real property from one person to another.

Alienation clause (due on sale) Permits lender to call balance of mortgage upon sale.

Allodial system The system of landownership that permits individuals to own land in fee simple title; used in the United States.

Alluvion Land gained along the shore of a waterway due to accretion.

Amenities Attractive features of a property that add to the pleasure of homeownership.

American Land Title Association (ALTA) A national association of title insurance companies, abstractors, and attorneys specializing in real estate law.

Americans with Disabilities Act (ADA) A federal law that protects the rights of the individual with mental or physical impairments.

Amortization The liquidation of a financial debt on the installment basis; equal payments are made over a period of time.

Annexation Attaching one object to another, such as a city incorporating land near its legal boundaries.

Annual Percentage Rate (APR) The effective interest rate that must be revealed under the Truth-in-Lending Act, which includes the loan origination fee and the discount points.

Annuity A series of periodic payments; for example, money received in a long-term lease.

Anticipation The principle used in appraising stating that values may change that affect the future of a property, either to its detriment or advantage.

Antitrust Act Federal and state acts to protect trade and commerce from monopolies and restrictions.

Antitrust laws Federal laws created to promote fair trade practices in the marketplace; prohibits price-fixing.

Appraisal An estimate of value made after analysis of the facts and data.

Appraisal report States the appraiser's estimate of the property value.

Appraiser Gives an unbiased estimate of value based on gathered facts.

Appreciation The increased value of property due to economic or related causes, whether temporary or permanent.

Appurtenance Rights that pass with the title to real property, such as an easement over an adjoining land.

Asbestos A mineral once used as insulation; is now banned as it is a cause of cancer and respiratory diseases.

Assemblage Gathering together two or more parcels of land to make the whole more valuable.

Assessed valuation Value placed upon real estate for taxation purposes.

Assessment A charge against real property by a unit of government, as a tax levy or a special assessment.

Assessor A public official who evaluates property for the purpose of taxation.

Assessor's map book Prepared for county records from plats the developer of the land files with the county.

Assignee The person to whom an interest has been assigned, as in the sale of a mortgage.

Assignment The transfer of interests, rights, and title, as in the assignment of a mortgage, deed, lease, or option.

Assignment of lease Lessee transfers all rights held under the terms of the lease to another.

Assignment of rent The clause in a mortgage that permits the lender to collect rents directly from a tenant upon default of mortgage payments by mortgagor.

Assignor The person who makes an assignment to the assignee.

Associate broker An individual who holds a broker license but who works for another broker.

Assumption of mortgage The obligation of a purchaser to be personally liable for payment of an existing note secured by the mortgage she assumes.

Attachment Legal seizure of property to force payment of a debt.

Attorney in fact A person who has power of attorney for another, allowing him to execute legal documents.

Attorney's opinion of title An attorney examines the abstract of title and gives an opinion certifying the condition of the title.

Auction The sale of real estate through a bidding process.

Automated underwriting Lenders' use of computer systems to speed the loan process.

Avulsion Loss of land due to sudden change in the flow of water.

Balloon payment A final payment on a note that is larger than previous payments and that repays the full debt.

Bargain-and-sale deed A deed that conveys property and in which warranties are implied by the grantor.

Base and meridian Imaginary lines used by surveyors in locating and establishing the boundaries of lands; used in the rectangular survey system.

Base rent The minimum rent paid in a percentage lease.

Base line One of the imaginary lines used in the U.S. government survey system. These lines act as points of beginning for land descriptions, running east-west and intersecting with the meridians that run north-south.

Basis The IRS determines the gain or loss and annual depreciation on an income property.

Before-and-after method An appraisal technique used when a part of the property has been condemned, as under the right of eminent domain.

Bench mark Identification symbols on a permanent marker used in measuring land elevations.

Beneficiary A person designated to receive a benefit, as in a trust deed, the lender.

Bequeath To transfer personal property by will.

Bequest A gift of personal property by will.

Biannual Semiannual; twice a year.

Biennial Taking place once every two years.

Bilateral contract A contract involving promise on the part of both parties, as in a purchase agreement.

Bill of sale A written document that transfers title to personal property.

Binder A commitment; the temporary means to insure one's interest; or an agreement that covers a down payment on the purchase of real estate.

Blanket mortgage A single mortgage that covers two or more properties.

Blockbusting Inducing an owner, for profit, to sell or rent residential property by threatening the movement of a minority group into the neighborhood.

Blue sky laws State and federal laws that regulate the registration and sale of securities.

Bond A written obligation given as security on a mortgage.

Boot Additional compensation paid in a property exchange.

Breach of contract A violation of the terms and conditions set forth in the contract.

Broker A person licensed to transact real estate negotiations for another.

Brokerage The occupation carried out by a broker; the bringing together of two parties in a real estate transaction.

Brownfields Abandoned, barren commercial and industrial sites that often contain toxic waste.

Buffer zone A corridor of land that separates two unrelated land uses, such as residential from commercial.

Building code A group of ordinances that legislate building construction within a community; the controls provide for the health and safety of the public.

Building line The distance from the perimeter of a property within which no structure may be built; a setback.

Building restrictions Limit property use and outline size of structures as set forth in the deed covenants.

Bulk transfer law *See* Uniform Commercial Code.

Bundle of rights The legal rights an owner of real estate acquires, such as the right of possession, use, enjoyment; including the right to sell, will, and mortgage.

Business cycles Shifts in the economy ranging from prosperity to recession and back again.

Buydown A cash payment to a lender that creates lower monthly mortgage payments for a period of time for the buyer.

Buyer agency A real estate agent who acts solely on behalf of the buyer and owes all fiduciary duties of agency to the buyer.

Buyer brokerage An agency relationship between a buyer and a broker.

Buyer's agent The real estate agent represents the buyer in the transaction.

Bylaws The rules and regulations of a condominium association that outline the covenants, restrictions, and conditions of the regime.

Capacity of parties All parties must be legally capable of entering into a contract.

Capitalization The process of converting future income into present capital value.

Capitalization rate The rate of interest considered a reasonable return on an investment; the sum of interest rate and recapture rate.

Carbon monoxide (CO) A colorless, odorless, toxic gas expelled from fuel-burning tools.

Cash flow The cash income or return on an investment after all expenses are met.

Caveat emptor Let the buyer beware; the buyer examines the property and buys at her own risk.

Censure To reprimand or express disapproval of the actions of a licensee.

Census report A survey taken every 10 years in the United States to determine the population.

Certificate of no defense An instrument executed by the mortgagor to the assignee upon the sale of the mortgage, revealing the amount owed. Also known as declaration of no set off and estoppel certificate.

Certificate of title A written opinion by an attorney or title company that certifies the condition of the title.

Certified Property Manager (CPM) A designation awarded to candidates who fulfill requirements as outlined by the National Institute of Real Estate Management.

Cession deed Given by a subdivider when he dedicates the streets in the subdivision to a governing body.

Chain A unit of measurement used in land surveying—66 feet.

Chain of title A record of the past owners of a property, beginning with the original land grant.

Chattel Personal property, movable in nature.

Check A measurement of land; 24 miles square containing 16 townships.

Cite To quote as authority; refer to; to summon; to notify a person of legal proceedings against her and require her appearance in court.

Civil Rights Act of 1866 A federal law that prohibits racial discrimination in the sale or rental of real estate.

Civil Rights Act of 1964 The Federal Fair Housing law that expanded upon the 1866 Civil Rights Act by prohibiting discrimination based on race, color, religion, and national origin.

Clean Water Act Enacted to protect wetlands from being disturbed.

Client Hires another to represent him; the principal in a transaction.

Closing Finalization of a sale, signing and transferring the title, and distributing the money.

Closing costs An accounting of costs and credits to buyer and seller upon finalization of a sale.

Closing statement A final settlement statement that lists the debits and credits of purchaser and seller; discloses all funds received and those necessary to close the sale.

Cloud on title A claim or interest revealed by a title search that may affect the title.

Cluster lots These lots are placed more closely together and are typically smaller than standard lots to allow room for open space in the development, referred to as "common areas."

Coastal Zone Management Act Regulates the protection of beaches from erosion, to preserve wildlife habitats, and to shelter marine life.

Codicil An addition to a will that may alter the provisions of the will.

Coinsurance The insurer and the insured share the insurance risk; calculated on the policy amount and the percent of the actual insured value.

Collateral Security given on debt.

Color of title A title that appears to be good but upon the title search is found to be defective; indicates another may have some rights of ownership.

Commingling Unauthorized mixing of personal funds with the funds of a client.

Commission The fee earned by a real estate broker for services rendered in negotiating a real estate transaction.

Common elements Land that is jointly used by all residents of an area, as in a condominium regime. Includes such items as pools, walkways, elevators, and clubhouses.

Common law An unwritten law derived from general usage and court decisions.

Community property Property acquired by either the husband or wife during their marriage.

Comparable Market Analysis (CMA) The evaluating of recent sales of properties that are comparable to the subject property in an attempt to place a market value on the subject property.

Comparison approach An appraisal method that compares the subject property to similar properties recently sold.

Complainant A person who brings a complaint against another.

Comprehensive Environmental Response, Compensation, and Liability Act (CERCLA) Sets priorities and responsibility for cleaning up the worst existing hazardous waste sites.

Compound interest Interest computed on the original sum plus accrued interest.

Concurrent ownership Property held by two or more parties, as in joint tenancy or tenancy in common.

Condemnation The legal right under eminent domain to take private property for public use with just compensation to the owner.

Condemnee The person whose property has been condemned (as by right of eminent domain).

Condominium Individual ownership of a single unit in a multiunit structure or group of buildings, with joint ownership of common elements.

Consensual dual agency The informed consent of buyer and seller that the agent is representing both their interests.

Consideration The price or substance that induces a contract, the value one party is giving another; their mutual exchange of promises.

Constant-payment mortgage A mortgage with the reduction of the loan in fixed monthly payments, a portion applying to repayment of principal and a portion to interest.

Construction loan Interim financing used during construction of the building.

Constructive eviction The breach of a covenant in a lease whereby the landlord failed to live up to terms of the lease.

Constructive notice Legal notice given.

Consummate Conclude; bring to completion, as in the finalization of a sale.

Contract An agreement between competent parties to perform a legal act.

Contribution The appraisal principle that states that the value of a component part is justified by what it adds to the overall value of the property, minus any costs.

Conventional loan A loan that is not government-insured or guaranteed. The lender generally requires a larger down payment.

Conveyance Written instrument used to transfer real estate.

Cooperative Ownership of shares or stock in a corporation for which the owner obtains a proprietary lease.

Co-ownership Two or more parties own an undivided interest in the same property.

Corporation An entity created by law that holds the rights and privileges of a natural person.

Corporeal Tangible real or personal property, as buildings and fences.

Correction deed Corrects an error that has occurred in a deed, such as the misspelling of a name.

Correction lines Placed by surveyors at 24-mile intervals to compensate for the earth's curvature in government survey systems.

Correlation of value The appraiser's final step in reconciling the value by analyzing the three approaches to arrive at an estimate of value.

Cost approach A method of appraisal based on replacement cost minus depreciation plus land value.

Counteroffer An offer made after the original offer was rejected.

Covenant Agreement or restriction found in real estate documents that regulates the use of real property.

Credit Asset; something of worth or value; an amount given to a buyer or a seller on a closing statement.

Credit report Relates the credit history of a borrower, a necessary step for the lender to verify the credit worthiness of the borrower since it reveals past performance in paying debts.

Cul de sac A road with one outlet, usually ending in a circle.

Curtesy The right of a husband to his wife's estate upon her death.

Customer Purchaser of commodity; is not represented by an agent unless expressly stated.

Datum The spot where the surveyor begins measurement of a specific parcel.

Debenture An unsecured note given as evidence of a debt, secured only by the reputation of the maker.

Debits Costs, charges against a seller or buyer in closing a sale.

Declaration The document (master deed) that establishes the condominium regime and defines the individual units within the association.

Dedication Real property given to the public by an individual, as land for a park.

Deed A written instrument that transfers ownership of real property.

Deed of reconveyance Transfers legal title from the trustee to the trustor upon payment in full of the debt.

Deed of trust Deed that secures repayment of a debt, held by a trustee until the note is paid.

Deed restriction Limits or restricts the use of real property.

Default Failure to meet an obligation, as defaulting on a mortgage.

Defeasance clause The clause in a mortgage that allows the mortgagor the right to redeem her property upon payment of her obligation.

Deficiency judgment Judgment against a debt or for the amount due the lender when the sale price is less than the funds received from a foreclosure sale.

Demise The conveyance of an estate under lease.

Department of Housing and Urban Development (HUD) *See* HUD.

Deposit Earnest money tendered in conjunction with an offer to purchase real property.

Depreciation Loss of value from any cause; an expense deduction taken when depreciating the value of an income-producing investment for income tax purposes.

Descent Property of an intestate passes to heirs by descent.

Developer An individual who adds to the value of land by erecting improvements upon the land.

Devise A gift of real estate by will.

Devisee The person to whom a gift of real estate is given by will.

Director's deed Issued when a public agency sells surplus land.

Direct reduction mortgage A set amount of the principal is paid at stated periods. Payments will vary since the interest will be less with each payment.

Disclosure statement A written statement required under the Truth-in-Lending Act that the lender issuing the loan must give to the borrower.

Discount broker Brokers who charge a lower commission than other brokers in the area.

Discount points A percentage charged by the lender to increase the yield of the loan. Each point represents 1 percent of the loan amount.

Discrimination The act of making a distinction in favor or against an individual on the basis of that individual's characteristics.

Disintermediation Funds that leave the savings and loans to go to the higher yielding markets.

Distraint Legal seizure of goods when rent is in arrears.

Doctrine of prior appropriation The first owner or user has the right to divert water for his use.

Document Formal certificate confirming facts or relaying instructions.

Dominant estate An estate that enjoys the rights of an easement through an adjoining estate known as the servient.

Dominant tenant Land benefiting from an appurtenant easement.

Donee A person who receives a gift.

Donor A person who makes a gift.

Dower The right of a wife in her husband's estate at the time of his death.

Down zoning The process of the local government reducing the allowable density for a tract of land, such as from office to apartment.

Dual agency The representation of a third party by a broker already in a principal-agent alliance, thereby creating two principals.

Dual contract Two contracts written with different terms and financing in an attempt to obtain a larger loan; a fraudulent practice.

Durability An economic characteristic of land that considers improvements made to land that are not as durable as the land.

Duress Unlawful constraint; insisting someone perform against his will.

Earnest money A deposit made by the purchaser at the time the purchase agreement is written to bind the contract.

Easement Interest in another's land, as a right of way.

Easement appurtenant An easement that runs with the land, such as a shared driveway.

Easement by prescription Rights to the land of another gained through continuous use.

Easement in gross An easement that does not run with the land and is personal in nature.

Easement of necessity Created by law when a landlocked party needs access to her property.

Economic base The stable base necessary for a community to grow and prosper; created by a diversity of resources, goods, and services supplied.

Economic life The period over which a property may be profitably utilized.

Economic obsolescence A loss in value caused by conditions external to the property and over which the owner has little or no control, such as a deteriorating neighborhood.

Economic rent The base rent justifiably payable in the open market.

Egress Exit; the right to leave a tract of land.

Electromagnetic Fields (EMFs) Produced by high-tension electric power lines and transformers.

Emblements Crops that are produced annually through labor and industry; also referred to as *fructus industriales*.

Eminent domain Right of the government to take private property for public use upon just payment to the owner.

Employee A person hired by and who takes directions from another. The employee status requires the employer to withhold social security and income taxes from the employee's salary.

Encapsulation The sealing off of an area that is being remodeled; a means of keeping asbestos fibers from escaping into the air.

Encroachment The act of trespassing or intruding upon the domain of another, such as tree branches.

Encumbrance An interest in real property that diminishes value, such as a lien or mortgage.

Environmental controls Laws passed and supervised by the Environmental Protection Agency (EPA) and other agencies for the care and protection of our environment.

Environmental Protection Agency (EPA) Created to encourage understanding and protection of the environment in an effort to reduce future damage. The EPA analyzes the impact that developments have upon economic, social, and physical environment.

Equal Credit Opportunity Act (ECOA) Prohibits lenders from discrimination on the basis of race, color, religion, national origin, sex, or marital status.

Equitable interest The difference between the value of the property and the amount owed.

Equitable title The right the purchaser has to obtain absolute title to a property as in a land contract or an accepted purchase agreement.

Equity The value of real property above the indebtedness.

Equity of redemption The right of an owner to reclaim property before it is sold in a mortgage foreclosure.

Erosion The gradual wearing away of land from natural causes.

Errors and Omissions Insurance (E&O) Insures for errors, mistakes, or liabilities in the practice of real estate.

Escalator clause The clause in a lease or mortgage allowing the holder to vary the interest rate.

Escheat Right of the sovereign state to succeed to the property of an intestate without heirs.

Escrow agreement An agreement held by a disinterested third party until terms and conditions of the instrument are met.

Escrow closing The closing of a sale by means of a third party not involved in the sale, such as a title company or an attorney.

Estate Rights in property and possessions; quantity of ownership.

Estate at sufferance A tenant who remains in possession after expiration of the lease; referred to as a holdover tenant.

Estate at will *See* tenancy at will.

Estate for years A leasehold interest extending for a definite period of time.

Estate from period to period *See* periodic tenancy.

Estate of inheritance Permits owner of real property to distribute his estate by will.

Estoppel certificate *See* certificate of no defense.

Et al. A term meaning "and others."

Et ux A term meaning "and wife."

Eviction Legal proceedings to recover possession of leased premises.

Examination of title Title opinion based on the abstract or title search.

Exclusive agency A listing that gives one brokerage firm the exclusive right to sell while the owner retains permission to sell without paying a commission.

Exclusive right to sell A listing that gives the brokerage firm the sole right to sell the property during the term of the agreement.

Executed contract The conditions of the contract have been completed.

Execution Dispossession of property; the terms of a contract have been completed.

Executor A male named in a will to carry out the terms of the will.

Executor's deed Issued by the executor of an estate; carries no warranties.

Executory contract A contract not completed, such as a purchase agreement.

Executrix A female named in a will to carry out the terms of the will.

Express contract Either oral or written, explicitly states obligations of parties and contract terms.

Ex Rel A term meaning "examination relating to."

External obsolescence Conditions that reduce the value of the property caused by forces outside of the property.

Facilitator A licensee who has no fiduciary responsibility as no agency has been formed.

Fair Credit Reporting Act Borrowers may see a summary of a report on their credit, and if errors are found, the borrower has a right to correct them.

Fair Housing Act of 1968 *See* Civil Rights Act of 1866.

Fair Housing Amendment Act of 1988 Prohibits discrimination based on handicap and familial status.

Fair housing laws Laws relating to the sale and rental of housing, ensuring equal opportunity for all people.

Federal Fair Housing Act of 1968 This law prohibits discrimination in the sale or rental of housing based on race, color, religion, national origin, or sex.

Federal Home Loan Mortgage Corporation (FHLMC) Controlled by the Federal Home Loan Bank Board, the FHLMC was created to buy conventional mortgages from savings and loan institutions.

Federal Housing Administration (FHA) A government agency that insures approved loans; created to provide homes with modest down payments.

Federal National Mortgage Association (FNMA) Created to purchase loans from qualified lenders. It is the leader in the secondary mortgage market in defining standards for underwriting loans and appraising one- to four-family residential properties; called Fannie Mae.

Federal Reserve (FED) Governing board of the nation's central bank.

Federal reserve system The central banking system that controls the money in circulation, thus determining the amount available in our economy.

Fee *See* fee simple.

Fee conditional A fee simple estate subject to the happening or nonhappening of a stated condition.

Fee determinable An estate in fee simple for a certain period of time, after which it reverts to the grantor or to his estate.

Fee simple The greatest and most complete interest in land, with absolute ownership in real property.

Fee simple absolute Gives the owner the most complete rights to real property; the highest form of ownership.

Fee simple defeasible Limits title holder to conditions as set forth by grantor.

Fee simple determinable Limits the estate holder to the terms set forth by the grantor.

Fee simple to a condition subsequent A defeasible (title), recognizable by words "but if."

Fee tail Specially named heirs are to inherit the estate. If such heirs are not available, the estate reverts to the grantor or to her heirs.

Feudal system System whereby the governing body of the land retains ownership of real property.

FHA loan A loan made by approved lenders and insured by the government.

Fiduciary Involving confidence and trust, as in the relationship between agent and principal.

Financial Institutions Reform, Recovery and Enforcement Act (FIRREA) Title IX of this act provides for the regulation of appraisers in all federally related transactions.

Finder's fee A fee paid to an individual for bringing together the parties to a transaction.

Fixture Personal property that becomes real when permanently affixed to real property, such as a light fixture, oven and range, or bookcase.

Flat fee listing The broker charges a set fee, not the usual percentage fee.

Flood Control Act The federal government combined with private insurance to provide flood insurance to homes in a floodplain.

Foreclosure The legal procedure brought by a mortgagee, after the mortgagor (borrower) defaults on the mortgage, to sell the property to satisfy the mortgage debt.

Forfeiture Giving up something of value due to failure to perform (delinquent taxes or failure to make mortgage payments both constitute forfeiture).

Formaldehyde A colorless chemical used in building materials and household products.

Fractional sections Parcel of land less than 160 acres which is usually found at the edge of a rectangular survey.

Fraud A statement made with the intention to deceive.

Free enterprise Economic system that provides an open market that allows all people to participate, creating competition and a favorable business climate.

Freehold estate An estate in real estate that conveys fee simple title, granting the maximum interests for an indefinite period.

Front foot Measurement applied to the width of a lot at the street frontage. Residential lots are often priced by the front foot.

Functional obsolescence A loss in value due to poor design or age that outmodes an improvement, such as a poor floor plan, outdated electrical wiring, or inadequate closet space.

Gain A profit received from the sale of an asset; the difference between the adjusted basis and the net selling price.

General agency Authorized by the principal to transact all affairs for the principal.

General liens Liens that can be attached to all the property of the debtor.

General partnership The partners manage and operate the business, taking responsibility for both profits and losses.

General warranty deed A deed giving fee simple title; grantors guarantee title through themselves, their heirs, and their predecessors.

Government lots Portions of land that could not be divided into equal fractional portions.

Government National Mortgage Association (GNMA) Dubbed "Ginnie Mae" and operated by HUD, this agency produces reduced interest rates for low-income purchasers and participates in the secondary mortgage market.

Government survey system *See* rectangular survey system.

Graduated lease A lease providing for a stipulated rent for an initial period, with increases or decreases at stated intervals.

Graduated Payment Plan (GPM) Monthly payments begin at a lower than normal rate with increases periodically as the borrower's income increases.

Graduate REALTORS® Institute (GRI) A professional designation earned upon completion of prescribed courses of study offered through real estate boards.

Grandfather rights A clause permitting continued use of a property that does not conform to present zoning; referred to as a nonconforming right.

Grant The transfer of title to real property.

Grant deed The grantor warrants the validity of the deed and guarantees that interest in the property has not been paid to another.

Grantee The purchaser of real estate.

Grantor The seller who conveys interest in real property.

Gross Income Multiplier (GIM) A formula used to establish value of income property. Divide the sale price by the gross annual income of comparable properties to determine the multiplier.

Gross lease A straight lease; the lessee pays only rent to the owner, as in an apartment lease.

Gross National Product (GNP) The value of all goods and services used and produced in this country.

Gross Rent Multiplier (GRM) Using comparable sales that are divided by the monthly rent and multiplying this factor by the actual rent of the subject property to arrive at a rough estimate of the property's market value.

Ground lease Rent on unimproved land.

Ground rent Earnings from unimproved land.

Groundwater The normal level at which ground becomes saturated.

Guarantor The person giving a guarantee.

Guardian The person appointed by the court to administer the affairs of a minor or other legally incapable persons.

Guardian's deed Conveys title to the estate of a minor or other persons under guardianship.

Habendum clause The "to have and to hold" clause, which defines or limits the quantity of the estate the grantor is deeding to the grantee.

Heir The person who may succeed or inherit real property even if there is no will.

Heirs and assigns The term used in deeds and wills to provide that the recipient receives a fee simple estate in lands.

Hereditament Inheritable property, real or personal.

Highest and best use As determined at the time of appraisal, the use that will produce the greatest net return over a given period of time.

Holdover tenant A lessee who remains in possession of the premises after termination of the lease.

Holographic will An entirely handwritten will that is not witnessed but is signed by the testator.

Home buyer's insurance Insurance that covers a property owner against loss due to various hazards. The coverage depends upon type of policy purchased.

Home equity loan A line of credit using the equity in a home as collateral from which the homeowner may draw capital that is taken on a prearranged basis.

Homeowners' association Composed of property owners in a condominium regime; administrates the affairs of the common elements and facilities and carries out the rules that control the project.

Homeowner's insurance policy Insurance to cover major perils to the property; required by lenders as protection for the loan placed on the property and desired by the homeowner to protect his investment.

Homestead An estate in land occupied as a residence; in some states a portion of the homestead is exempt from creditor's claims.

Home warranty insurance Offers the buyer coverage on the component parts of a house. Usually insures major appliances, electrical, plumbing, heating, and air conditioning.

Homogeneous Compatible; land use is regulated by zoning to create homogeneity and stabilize values.

Horizontal Property Act Legislation that permits the creation of condominiums.

HUD Federal Department of Housing and Urban Development. Involved in housing activities, such as rehabilitation loans, urban renewal, subsidy programs, and public housing. HUD has jurisdiction over FHA and GNMA.

Hypothecation To give as security, as when pledging a mortgage.

Immobility Incapable of being moved, fixed in location; an important physical characteristic of land.

Implied contract The act constitutes agreement to a contract.

Improvement Something that has been attached "on" the land such as a building or "to" the land such as a sidewalk or paved street, thus adding value to the land.

Inchoate Incomplete; not finished, such as a wife's right to her husband's estate under dower rights.

Income approach An appraisal method whereby the net income of an income-producing property is divided by the capitalization rate to determine the property's value.

Incorporeal rights Intangible interest in real property, such as an easement.

Indemnification Reimbursement of loss.

Indenture A binding agreement in writing, such as a deed.

Independent contractor Individual employed but paid only upon production; no salary or normal fringe benefits are paid by the employer.

Indestructible A physical characteristic of land describing that land as a permanent commodity that cannot be destroyed.

Index lease Provides for rent adjustments that conform to changes in a price index.

Industrial parks Land zoned expressly for use by manufacturing and industrial plants.

Inflation A decline in the purchasing power of money, causing the price of a commodity to rise.

Ingress The right to enter land.

Inheritance tax A tax imposed by the state on the heirs to the property of a decedent.

In lieu of Instead of; in place of.

Installment sale A means of selling real estate and postponing the capital gains tax by extending the payment over several years and paying the taxes on a pro-rata basis.

Instrument A written document capable of being recorded.

Intangible property Property that is not visible, such as the "good will" of a business.

Interest A percentage charged for the use of a principal sum.

Interim financing Temporary financing, such as a construction loan.

Interstate Land Sales Full Disclosure Act Requires disclosures to protect buyers who purchase land in their state that is located in another state.

Intestate Person who dies without leaving a will.

Involuntary alienation Loss of property for nonpayment of debts such as taxes or mortgage foreclosure.

Involuntary lien A lien placed against a property without the owner's consent, such as taxes, special assessments, mechanics' liens, or federal tax liens.

Irrevocable Unalterable; not changeable.

Joint tenancy Ownership by two or more persons with rights of survivorship.

Joint venture The operation of a single business by two or more people in an effort to raise capital and spread the risk; sometimes referred to as a general partnership.

Judgment A court decree to determine a settlement.

Judgment lien A charge upon the lands of a debtor resulting from a court decree.

Junior mortgage A mortgage subordinate to an existing or subsequent lien.

Key lot A lot that has one side adjoining the rear of another lot, usually on a corner. Key lots are valued for their locations.

Laches A delay in asserting one's legal rights, causing forfeiture of these rights.

Land The surface of the earth, the area above and below the surface, and everything attached naturally (trees, crops) thereto.

Land contract Seller finances purchaser and retains title; purchaser obtains equitable title.

Landfill Area designated for disposal of solid waste material.

Landmark A monument or marker that establishes a certain spot, such as the boundary of a property.

Land patent A document issued by the government granting fee title in public lands to miners, settlers, and war veterans.

Latent defect A material defect that is hidden from view, such as defective plumbing.

Lawful object The contract itself must be for a lawful purpose.

Lead Metal found naturally in the environment as well as in manufactured products.

Lead-based paint Used prior to 1978, it is hazardous to the health of children who play around loose paint chips or dust particles.

Lead-Based Paint Hazard Reduction Act (LBPHRA) Seller or a seller's agent must disclose any known lead hazards as part of an FHA sale or lease of a property built before 1978.

Lease A contract giving the lessee (tenant) the right to use property owned by the lessor (landlord) for a stated period of time and for a specific purpose.

Leasehold The interest a lessee has in a lease.

Lease option A clause in the option that grants the right to purchase for a specific time period at specified terms.

Lease purchase Agreement between a lessor and lessee whereby a portion of the rent applies towards the purchase price; when the agreed amount is paid, title is transferred to the lessee.

Legal description The description of property boundaries recognized by law.

Legal life estate An interest in real estate created by law such as dower, curtesy, and homestead rights.

Lessee The tenant or person given use of a property under a lease contract.

Lessor The owner of property leased to another. Holder has leasehold rights in real property.

Less than freehold estate *See* nonfreehold estate.

Leverage The use of borrowed capital to finance a purchase.

License A personal privilege or right that is nontransferable.

License law Authority given through the laws enacted by the state to regulate the actions of salespeople and brokers.

Lien A charge or claim against a debtor's property.

Lien theory Deed of trust is a security for the debt, with the trustor the title holder.

Lien waiver An affidavit signed by the sellers attesting to the fact that there are no unpaid debts against the property.

Life estate An interest in real estate limited to the lifetime of the life tenant.

Life tenant The holder of a life estate; ceases to exist upon death of the holder.

Limited agent The broker appoints a specific licensee within the firm to act for a particular buyer or seller.

Limited common area Common elements that are for the exclusive use of certain residents, such as parking stalls and storage units.

Limited partnership A group of passive investors with a sponsor or general partner who manages the investment portfolio.

Link In land measurements, a link equals 7.9 inches.

Liquidity Being able to convert a product into cash in a minimum time frame for a value close to its actual worth.

Lis pendens Notice of a suit pending that could affect ownership of land.

Listing contract The contract between the broker and the principal to negotiate the sale of the principal's property.

Littoral rights Rights of a landowner who borders a lake or other nonflowing body of water to use the water.

Livery of seizin Transfer of possession.

Loan commitment A loan approval by the lender of the loan.

Loan-to-Value ratio (LTV) The ratio of a mortgage to the appraised value or purchase price of a property.

Lot A plot of land with fixed boundaries.

Lot and block number system Location of lots within a subdivision; recorded on a subdivision plat.

Majority The age at which a person is legally entitled to handle her affairs.

Management budget A financial plan prepared by the manager that includes an annual budget for operating the property.

Management contract A contract detailing responsibilities of the owner and the manager of a property.

Marginal land Land that barely repays the cost of production.

Marketable title A title without defect.

Market price The price paid for a property.

Market value The most probable price for which the willing seller will sell and the willing buyer will buy.

Master deed The deed that is recorded and is the principal document that conveys ownership of the overall condominium regime.

Master plan A comprehensive plan to develop a community's future expansion; serves as a guideline for principal expenditures.

Mechanic's lien The right of a contractor to place a lien against property for work completed but not paid for.

Meeting of minds An agreement on specified subject matter, such as a seller accepting the offer of a buyer.

Meridian Used in the government rectangular survey system; lines that run north and south across the country.

Metes and bounds Measurements and boundaries that describe a property; using directions and distances from a point of beginning.

Mile A measurement of distance; 5,280 feet.

Mill A rate of currency used in determining property taxes.

Mill levy A tax rate expressed in one-tenth of one cent per one dollar of assessed valuation.

Minor A person not of legal age.

Misrepresentation A misstatement of a material fact that was relied upon by an innocent party.

Mold A type of fungus that poses health hazards; it grows when moisture is present.

Monument A stone or fixed object used to establish a land boundary.

Monument survey Description of a property in terms of natural and artificial boundaries.

Moratorium The legal period of delay for meeting a financial obligation.

Mortgage The pledge that secures the lender's investment and that accompanies the note.

Mortgage-Backed Security (MBS) Securities sold to investors that are "backed" by a mortgage, thus creating more funds available to lenders for loans.

Mortgage banker Originates mortgages and subsequently sells the loans to long-term investors through the secondary mortgage market; retains servicing of the loans.

Mortgage broker Person or firm acting as an intermediary between borrower and lender; does not service the loan.

Mortgage correspondent Agent for a lender who places a loan for a borrower.

Mortgagee The lender or holder of the mortgage.

Mortgagee in possession The mortgagee becomes in possession of a property when the mortgagor defaults on the note, permitting the lender to collect rents from tenant.

Mortgage Insurance Premium (MIP) An upfront charge based on the loan amount borrowed.

Mortgage lender Lending institution that makes and services mortgage loans.

Mortgagor The debtor or borrower; the owner of property that is used as security for a mortgage.

Multiple Listing Service (MLS) A group of brokers that pools listings and cooperates to sell any listing of a member firm.

National Association of Realtors® (NAR) A national trade organization that promotes fair and ethical practices among its members. All members are entitled to use the trademark REALTOR®.

National Environmental Policy Act (NEPA) Encourages understanding and protection of the environment. NEPA created and funded the Environmental Protection Act (EPA).

Negative amortization The monthly payment is less than needed to reduce the mortgage debt and thus results in an increase in the original indebtedness.

Negative cash flow Occurs when an investment yields less than the expenses, causing a negative cash return to the investor.

Negotiable instrument A promissory note that, upon meeting certain legal requirements, may be circulated freely in commerce.

Negotiate To arrange for or to transact business, such as negotiating the sale of a property.

Neighborhood shopping center Several buildings grouped together with 15 or more retail bays; easily accessible to the nearby neighborhood.

Net lease A lease whereby the lessee assumes some or all of the expenses normally paid by the owner.

Net listing Property listing at an agreed-upon net price that the seller wishes to receive with any excess going to the agent as commission.

Nonconforming use A use in violation of present zoning laws but permitted because the usage was in effect before the law. The user is said to have "grandfather rights."

Nonfreehold estate Also known as less than freehold estates, the holder has a leasehold interest under the terms of the lease.

Nonfungible Cannot substitute one parcel of real property for another; no two are alike.

Nonhomogeneous Characteristic of real property; no two parcels are alike.

Notary public Lawfully authorized official who attests to and certifies documents by his hand and official seal.

Note A written promise to pay a certain sum of money within a specified time.

Notice to quit A notice to a tenant to vacate the premises.

Novation The substitution of a new contract for an existing contract, or new parties to an obligation.

Obsolescence Lessening in value due to functional, economic, or physical conditions.

Offer and acceptance A promise by the purchaser to complete the terms of the contract upon acceptance by the seller.

Offeree A person to whom an offer is made.

Offeror A person making an offer.

Office parks Development of a parcel of land for office buildings, usually in suburban areas.

Open-end mortgage A mortgage that allows the mortgagor to borrow additional funds and extend the amount of the loan without changing the terms of the mortgage.

Open listing A nonexclusive listing, generally oral, available for sale to any number of brokers with a commission paid to the selling firm.

Open market system Allows consumers to decide what they want and the producers to compete to supply those needs.

Opinion of title A legal opinion to determine if title is clear and marketable.

Option The right to buy within a specified time.

Option clause A clause that grants the right to buy for a limited time.

Ordinance A city or county legislative enactment, such as a zoning law.

Origination fee A finance charge made by the lending institution to the borrower that covers costs of preparing the loan.

Ostensible agency An agency that occurs through the dependence of information from a third party.

Owner's association Composed of property owners who group together to administrate the affairs of the neighborhood.

Ownership The right to possess and use property to the exclusion of all others.

Ownership cycle The sequence of home purchases made by individuals to meet their evolving needs and desires.

Package mortgage A mortgage that especially designates all personal property included in the sale.

Panic peddling Creating unrest in a neighborhood by placing fear in the minds of property owners that the introduction of minorities in or near the area will lessen property values.

Parol evidence rule Oral evidence; not in writing and cannot change the terms of the written document.

Partition A court action for legal division of real estate by owners in order to sever their ownership.

Partnership Two or more parties join together in an enterprise.

Party wall A common partition between adjoining properties for use by both parties.

Passive income Income derived solely from an investment of money in an enterprise that is managed by another, such as a limited partnership.

Patent A land grant by the U.S. government to an individual.

Patent defect A material defect that can be seen upon inspection.

Percentage lease A lease whereby the lessee pays a flat sum plus a percentage of the volume of business transacted on the premises.

Percolating water Underground water that is sufficient enough to be tapped for a well.

Periodic tenancy A lease that continues from period to period with no set termination date.

Personal property Movable items not affixed to real property, such as chattels.

Personalty Chattel; personal property not permanently affixed to the real property.

Physical depreciation Caused by normal wear and tear through use and the action of the natural elements.

PITI The principal, interest, taxes, and insurance paid in monthly installments on an amortized loan.

Planned Unit Development (PUD) Community planned to allow better use of land.

Plat A map of a certain area of land.

Plat book A public record of information concerning land.

Pledge Security held by the lender until a debt is paid off.

Plottage The assembling of several parcels of land into one ownership.

Point of Beginning (POB) The starting point used in the metes and bounds description. It is marked at one corner of the property, and the description must return to this point of beginning.

Points *See* discount points.

Police power Right of the government to pass legislation protecting the safety and welfare of the public.

Positive cash flow An investment produces a net return over and above expenses.

Power of attorney A written instrument authorizing one person to act for another.

Prepaids Items paid in advance, such as taxes and insurance that are paid monthly with the principal and interest payment.

Prepayment clause A mortgage clause stating the penalty for payment of the mortgage before the actual due date.

Prescription Rights in property acquired through continuous use.

Primary mortgage market Origination of loans by lenders.

Principal The property owner who employs an agent to sell her property; also denotes money as the principal amount on a loan.

Principal meridian A survey line running due north and south, as established by the rectangular system of survey.

Prior appropriation A water use acknowledged in many western states that is based on the scarcity of water and allows the first owner to have priority over all subsequent owners.

Private Mortgage Insurance (PMI) Insurance on conventional loans that require less than a 20 percent down payment.

Probate A court of law with the authority to verify the legality of a will and carry out its instructions.

Profit a prendre The right to remove something for profit from another's land such as minerals, oil, or timber.

Progression The value of a property is enhanced if surrounding homes are of greater value.

Promissory note The note signed by the mortgagor that promises repayment of the debt.

Property Owner's interest and rights in his property to the exclusion of all others; the land and anything permanently attached, such as buildings, fences, and fixtures.

Property management A specialized branch of the real estate business that involves overseeing leasing, managing, and maintenance of another's property.

Proprietary lease The right to occupy a cooperative unit by the shareholder.

Prorations The dividing of expenses and credits between buyer and seller.

Prospectus Preliminary information on an enterprise that is required by the SEC to be given, in advance, to prospective purchasers of securities.

Public records Publicly available notice of matters concerning land.

Public trustee A disinterested third party who serves as an escrow agent under the terms of an agreement.

Purchase agreement An offer to purchase that becomes a binding contract when accepted by the owner of the property.

Purchase-money mortgage A mortgage carried by the seller to secure an unpaid balance of the purchase price.

Pyramiding Using a property to purchase another by refinancing the first property.

Qualified fee A fee simple estate with limitations set by the grantor.

Quantity survey method The totaling of all the component parts in the construction plus adding labor costs to arrive at an exact cost of the total project.

Quiet enjoyment The right to use property without disruption by the grantor or the landlord.

Quiet title action Action in court to either establish title or to remove a cloud on a title.

Quitclaim deed A deed containing no warranties, in which the grantor relinquishes any claims or rights she may have.

Quit notice Notice given to a tenant to vacate the premises.

Quorum The minimum number of members needed at any official meeting in order to conduct business (usually more than half).

Radon A radioactive gas that occurs from the breakdown of uranium in soil, rock, and water and seeps into buildings through cracks and holes in the foundation.

Range Used in the government rectangular survey system; comprises a strip of land every six miles east and west of the principal meridian.

Real estate Land and all improvements that are "on" or permanently attached and any improvements "to" the land, such as sidewalks and sewers.

Real estate commission The regulatory body that governs the actions of licensees.

Real Estate Investment Trust (REIT) Individuals pool their funds to purchase shares in large investment properties.

Real Estate Settlement Procedures Act (RESPA) An act passed by Congress in 1974 that requires lenders to provide full disclosure of closing costs to buyer and seller when the loan is federally related.

Real property The land and all improvements, plus all the rights and privileges the owner of real estate possesses; the "bundle of rights" one has.

Realtist A member of the National Association of Real Estate Brokers (NAREB), an organization of minority brokers.

Realtor® A trade name that refers to members of the National Association of REALTORS®.

Reappraisal lease A clause in a long-term lease that requires periodic appraisals to determine the economic rent.

Receiver Recipient; a person appointed under a statute to wind up a business.

Reciprocal license The ability of a licensee to obtain a license in another state, depending on that state's requirements.

Recordation The act of giving public notice by recording a legal document.

Rectangular survey system The government method of surveying land based on imaginary lines of longitude running north and south called meridians and east-west latitude lines called base lines.

Redemption The act of repurchasing real property after the mortgage is in default.

Redlining The refusal of lenders to make mortgage loans in specific neighborhoods.

Reduction certificate A document showing the balance due on a mortgage at the time the transaction is closed.

Reformation Action taken to correct a mistake in a deed or other instrument.

Regional center A large complex housing several national retail stores with a broad mix of shops that draw customers from a great distance.

Regression An overimproved property's value is affected by a lesser property.

Regulation Z Implements the truth-in-lending law through the Federal Reserve Board. Requires notice to the borrower of the true cost of the loan.

Reliction The gradual increase of land due to receding waters.

Remainder estate What is left from a life estate.

Remainderman The person who receives an estate after the termination of a life estate.

Rent The cost of using the real estate of another; the tenant pays rent to the landlord.

Replacement cost The present cost of reconstructing a new building having the same utility value as the old.

Reproduction cost The present cost of reproducing an exact replica of the old building.

Rescind Revoke, annul, or cancel (as a contract).

Rescission To revert to the original conditions.

Reserves Funds escrowed by the lender to pay for taxes and insurance when they become due.

Resident manager Person employed to manage an apartment complex and who lives on the premises.

Residential property management The business of managing the residential property of others.

Residual Remainder, as the residual value of land after the economic life of the building is over.

Resolution Trust Corporation (RTC) A federal agency formed to liquidate insolvent savings and loans and banks.

Resource and Recovery Act (RCRA) Requires that hazardous waste be placed in designated sites.

Respondent A person against whom a complaint is made.

Restrictive covenant A condition limiting the use of land, as stated in a deed.

Reverse Annuity Mortgage (RAM) The homeowner receives income from the equity in the home.

Reversion A future interest in real estate created by a grantor that provides for the property to revert to the grantor upon expiration of the interest.

Reversionary interest The future interest that reverts to a grantor or his heirs.

Revocation The rescinding of a contract; such as a buyer nullifying an offer to purchase. Also, the power of a real estate commission to take away a license for failure to conform to the license laws of that state.

Right of first refusal Gives a person first opportunity to buy or lease.

Right of redemption The period within which a debtor may redeem his property after default.

Right of survivorship The legal right to obtain ownership of the decedent's property provided for in joint tenancy and tenancy in the entirety.

Right-of-way An easement through the land of another.

Riparian rights Rights of a landowner to use waters of an adjacent stream or lake.

Rollover mortgage A renegotiable mortgage that calls for changes in interest rate at set intervals.

Rules and regulations Laws that are consistent with a state's real estate commission or governing body.

Rural Economic and Community Development Makes loans in rural areas and small communities; replaces Farmers Home Administration (FmHA).

S Corporation Investors avoid double taxation as income is not taxed on the corporate level.

Safe Drinking Water Act Governed by the EPA, it sets minimum standards for water supply systems.

Sale–leaseback The owner sells her property with the stipulation that she may lease it back from the new owner.

Sales comparison approach *See* comparison approach.

Salesperson One who is licensed by a state to render services authorized by a broker who holds a salesperson's license.

Salvage value The value that remains after the useful life is exhausted, usually 5 to 10 percent of the property's depreciable basis.

Sandwich lease A leasehold interest involving a lessor, lessee, and sublessee.

Satisfaction piece An instrument that is recorded to announce payment of the debt; a mortgage release.

Savings Association Insurance Fund (SAIF) Replaces the FSLIC fund that became insolvent due to failed thrifts. Insures savings of insured depositors' funds.

Scarcity In short supply in comparison to demand.

Sea level Zero feet in altitude; base from which altitude measurements begin.

Secondary mortgage market The sale of existing mortgages by the primary lender to the secondary mortgage market lenders, thus affording greater liquidity of mortgages.

Second mortgage A mortgage second in priority to a first mortgage; pledges the owner's equity in the property.

Section Division of land; 640 acres or one square mile.

Securities and Exchange Commission (SEC) Established to monitor the sale of securities.

Security deposit Lessor requires a deposit that is refundable at expiration of the lease if the property has not been damaged.

Seller agency Realtor has a binding agreement where the Realtor specifically represents the seller in a transaction.

Seller's agent Agent has a fiduciary relationship with the seller who is the principal in the agency agreement.

Servient estate An estate that includes an easement existing in favor of the dominant estate.

Servient tenant Land encumbered by an easement.

Setback The distance that zoning regulations require a structure to be located from the front, rear, and side property lines.

Settlement closing The broker prorates and adjusts the credits and costs for the buyer and seller upon closing the transaction.

Severable Capable of being divided.

Severalty Sole ownership by one person.

Severalty ownership Owned by one person, sole ownership.

Shared Appreciation Mortgage (SAM) The mortgagee participates in any appreciation of the property in exchange for a fixed, below-market interest rate.

Sheriff's deed Transfers property sold at a public sale; usually the result of a foreclosure.

Short-sale Borrower does not have enough equity or money to cover the mortgage and release the lien placed on the property. The owner asks the lender to accept a lesser amount than owed and release the lien.

Simple interest Interest paid on the declining balance of a loan; thus the interest payments lower as the principal amount is paid off.

Site The location of a particular parcel of land.

Situs The location or site of a real property; value is partially based on a property's situs.

Sky lease A lease with the right to occupy the space of another above the leased real estate.

Special agency Limited authority to act on behalf of the principal, such as created by a listing.

Special agent Usually limited to transacting a single business affair, such as the relationship between a brokerage firm and a principal.

Special assessment A tax levied against property for the cost of a public improvement.

Special warranty deed A deed wherein grantors guarantee title through themselves and their heirs but not their predecessors.

Specific agency Agent is given right to act for principal for one express purpose.

Specific lien Affects only the property that it is placed against.

Specific performance A remedy in a court of equity to carry out the terms of a contract.

Spot zoning Land use permitted by a zoning ordinance, although differing from current zoning of surrounding property.

Statute A law passed by the legislative body of government.

Statute of frauds State laws that require certain contracts to be in writing in order to be enforceable.

Statute of limitations The time frame within which an action may be taken to court.

Statutory law Laws created by the enactment of legislation.

Steering Limiting the choice of buyers or renters of housing by channeling them to certain neighborhoods.

Straight-line depreciation Depreciation in equal amounts each year over the life of the asset.

Straight-line method Used for tax purposes; it divides the adjusted basis of a property by the estimated remaining life of the property.

Straight loan A term loan that requires only interest to be paid with the balance due at the end of the term.

Straw man Person who purchases for another unidentified buyer; used when confidentiality is important.

Strict foreclosure No foreclosure sale is held; the lender obtains absolute title.

Strip center A building consisting of a number of units (bays) conveniently located near main arteries.

Subagency Refers to a specific client representation relationship between a property listing broker or real estate agent and another real estate broker or agent who brings the buyer to purchase the property.

Subagent An agent who may assist the appointed agent in the performance of an assignment; often created in the multiple listing services used by real estate brokers.

Subdivider A person who divides undeveloped land into smaller lots for the purpose of development.

Subdivision A parcel of land subdivided into individual lots.

Sublet Lessee retains lease but rents a portion of the premises to a sublessee.

Subordination clause Clause found in a mortgage or lease that states the rights of the holder are secondary to any existing or subsequent encumbrance.

Subpoena A legal summons requiring court appearance to give testimony.

Subrogation Substituting one person for another regarding a claim, as in a loan assumption.

Subsurface right The right to use the land beneath the surface of the earth, such as for mining or digging a well.

Summons Notification to appear in court.

Superfund Funded by the Comprehensive Environmental Response, Compensation, and Liability Act (CERCLA) it provides for the cleanup of the worst hazardous waste sites.

Superfund Amendment and Reauthorization Act (SARA) An amendment to the Comprehensive Environmental Response, Compensation, and Liability Act (CERCLA) and has the full compliance and enforcement capability as reauthorized in 1986.

Surety Legal liability for another's debt.

Surface right The right to use the surface of the land.

Surrender and acceptance The cancellation of a lease by mutual consent of the lessee and lessor.

Survey The precise measuring of the boundaries of a property from which the legal description is derived.

Suspension Placing a license on temporary retention, thus forbidding the licensee to perform the services of a salesperson or broker.

Syndication A group of people who pool their funds to invest in a common enterprise.

Tacking The legal right that permits a person to add or "tack" their time of possession on to a past claimant's adverse possession right.

Take-out loan The final permanent loan that replaces the interim construction loan.

Tax assessment A levy against property to pay for a public improvement that benefits the real estate.

Tax deed Real property sold at a public sale due to delinquent taxes.

Tax-free exchange A method of deferring capital gains taxes by exchanging one property for another.

Tax lien A charge against a property for failure to pay real estate taxes or an assessment.

Tax participation clause A lease clause whereby the tenant assumes a proportionate share of an increase in property taxes.

Tax sale The sale of property for nonpayment of taxes.

Tax shelter A phrase used to describe advantages of real estate investments, such as deductions for taxes, interest, and depreciation, resulting in the postponement, reduction, or elimination of income tax.

Temporary buydown A mortgage differential allowance program that allows the seller to place funds with the lender to reduce the borrower's payments for the first two to three years.

Tenancy at sufferance The tenant remains in possession of the leased premises after expiration of the lease.

Tenancy at will Use of the property at the will of the landlord. Either party can terminate the lease at any time since there is no set termination date.

Tenancy by the entireties Ownership by husband and wife with both spouses sharing an equal, undivided interest in the whole property.

Tenancy for years A leasehold estate that grants the lessee use for a specified period of time.

Tenancy in common An interest in real estate held by two or more persons, each having equal rights of possession but without right of survivorship.

Tenant The lessee; a person given the right to use real estate owned by another.

Tender To fulfill; to offer to perform as the terms of a contract state.

Tenements Term used to describe all types of real estate property, improvements to the land, and all rights accruing to the land.

Term mortgage Short-duration loans that are not amortized and are used for brief periods of time, such as construction loans.

Testate A person who dies leaving a will that designates the distribution of his estate.

Testator A person who leaves a will or who has died testate.

Time-sharing Joint ownership of a single unit by several purchasers that gives use for a specified time.

Title Evidence of ownership in real estate.

Title insurance Insures the holder of the policy against defects in the title.

Title search An examination of public records to establish ownership of real estate and to determine condition of the title.

Title theory Mortgagee has legal title to the property; as with a trust deed, the mortgagor acquires equitable title.

Torrens system The system of land registration whereby a certificate of title is issued.

Tort An actionable wrong, a violation of a legal right.

Townhouse A form of construction, generally in a clustered group, that is usually two stories with common walls between the units.

Township A parcel of land that contains 36 sections and that is 6 miles square.

Trade fixture Personal property that has been affixed to leased property by a tenant who uses it in his business.

Transactional agent The agent acts as an intermediary, working for the mutual interest of all parties to the transaction. *See* facilitator.

Transfer tax A charge levied by some states upon real estate when it is sold; based on the property value.

Trust account An account in which the real estate broker places all money entrusted to her by or on behalf of the principal and the customer.

Trust deed A deed held in trust by a third party until the obligation is paid; it is used to mortgage land, or to place a lien upon it.

Trustee A third party to a trust deed; the one who holds the trust deed.

Trustor The owner of the property under a trust deed.

Truth-in-lending law A federal law requiring disclosure of costs involved in obtaining a loan.

Underground Storage Tanks (USTs) Tanks that because of leaking and contaminating the soil must be equipped with an EPA leak detector system.

Underwriter The person who reviews a loan application and makes recommendation to the loan committee concerning the risk and desirability of making the loan.

Undue influence Taking unfair advantage of another by intimidating, coercion, or due to lack of understanding a contract.

Unenforceable contract A contract that may appear valid but is unenforceable in a court of law.

Uniform Commercial Code (UCC) Requires the recording of personal property that is sold for a price in excess of $500 so that the creditor may file a financial statement and reclaim the property if the debtor defaults.

Uniform Landlord/Tenant Act Regulates the landlord-tenant relationship on residential leases.

Unilateral contract A promise on the part of one party to perform a specific act according to the contract, as in an option or a listing contract.

Unit conversions The converting of apartments to condominium units.

United States Government Land Survey Also known as a rectangular land survey; a method of land description.

Unit-in-place cost approach method An appraisal technique that calculates the cost of all the component parts to be used in the construction to arrive at the value.

Universal agency Empowered to perform any act that can be lawfully authorized to an agent; usually established by power of authority.

Upfront Mortgage Insurance Premium (UFMIP) A mortgage insurance premium paid at the time an FHA loan is originated.

Useful life The economic life of an improvement; period of time over which it can be profitably utilized.

Usury The act of charging in excess of the legal interest rate.

Vacation license A right to occupy a unit in a condominium regime for a specified period of time without fee title; prepaid lodging.

Valid contract A contract that complies with the law and is legally sufficient and enforceable.

VA loans Guaranteed by the Department of Veteran Affairs and available for veterans who qualify under the law.

Valuation The process of estimating the worth of a property.

Value The current worth of all present and future benefits derived from ownership of real estate.

Variable rate mortgage Allows the lender to increase or decrease the interest rate within the parameters set down in the mortgage rate.

Variance Permission given to an individual to use land in a way that varies from current zoning laws when compliance with the zoning ordinance would create an undue hardship.

Vendee The purchaser of real property who receives equity title under the terms of a land contract.

Vendor The seller of real property who retains title in his name under terms of a land contract.

Verify To substantiate under oath.

Vested With an interest in; owned as a right in real property.

Voidable contract A contract that can be terminated even though it appears valid, such as a contract with a minor that can be rescinded by the minor.

Void contract A contract entered into for illegal purposes.

Voluntary alienation The transfer of title freely by the owner.

Voluntary lien A property lien placed with knowledge and agreement of the owner.

Waiver The voluntary surrender of rights or claims.

Warranty deed The grantor guarantees that the title is good, free, and clear of all liens and encumbrances.

Waste Property value is diminished by the neglect of a tenant, life tenant, or mortgagor.

Water rights *See* riparian rights and littoral rights.

Wetlands Areas that are saturated with ground or surface water often enough to support vegetation and are protected by the EPA.

Will The property owner (testator) transfers title by means of a written, witnessed document.

Words of conveyance Words in a deed that expressly grant the title to the grantee.

Wraparound mortgage Lenders refinance a property by lending an amount more than the existing mortgage, leaving the first mortgage in place. The complete package is considered as one loan, with the mortgagee of the wrap paying the obligation to the first mortgage.

Zero lot line The placing of a structure on the lot line without being required to have a setback from the perimeter of the property.

Zoning The regulation over the use of land within a specific municipality.

Zoning map Divides the area into districts.

Zoning ordinance Categorizes areas into the type of use permitted and sets the requirements of each zoning district.

Index